THE LIFE OF
NEVILLE CHAMBERLAIN

MARCH, 1938

THE LIFE OF
NEVILLE
CHAMBERLAIN

BY

KEITH FEILING

ARCHON BOOKS
Hamden · Connecticut
1970

First Edition 1946
Reprinted 1947
Reissued with a new Preface and Bibliography 1970

This edition first published in America by
ARCON BOOKS, 1970

10-17-74

Library of Congress catalog card No. 75 95598

Printed in Great Britain by
LOWE AND BRYDONE (PRINTERS) LTD
London

PREFACE TO 1970 REISSUE

In October 1944 Sir Winston Churchill wrote to me from Moscow. Though recovering from a high temperature, he insisted on a conference with Stalin that afternoon, yet found time to approve some extracts in this book. He added, however, that he felt the end of 1945 would be very early for its publication.

And so indeed it was, had this been conceived as the " definitive " biography, which, as my first preface shows, it emphatically was not. It rested on a different basis—that it was both provisional and independent.

It was independent because it was agreed that only the Secretary to the Cabinet should see my text before publication; and independent too because I had never known Mr. Chamberlain and must discover him as an historical figure.

How provisional it must be stands to reason. My first duty was to Mr. Chamberlain's family, who had given me their confidence and a free hand with his papers. Here I reaped sufficient reward in a letter from his sister Hilda, last survivor of Joseph Chamberlain's children, saying " I feel it is the kind of presentment of his life and work which Neville himself would have wished and valued ". For all that, from anything like final knowledge one was debarred: no archives of any government had seen the light, while at that date the Secretary to the Cabinet's veto was comprehensive and searching.

Apart, then, from the Chamberlain papers, my documents were living human beings. True, contemporary history has its compensations. The actors may interpret their parts differently, but at least they made up the cast, experienced the passion or felt the pressures from without and within, the weariness seeping down and the energies welling up. My role as I saw it, while fulfilling my task as biographer, was to be an honest *rapporteur*, to seek all possible information which could enlighten my ignorance, making plain the dire conflicts within that generation. Not that on this last one needed more illumination. Ten years earlier, Sir Winston Churchill had asked my advice on his life of Marlborough; over longer years still I often heard the views of a passionate patriot, too soon lost to us, Lord Lloyd.

But it was for posterity to give final judgement, and in these days posterity may claim to have arrived.

In my first preface my obligations were admitted to Baldwin and

v

Churchill, but not to others. Now, however, "Another race hath been, and other palms are won."

For the usefulness of this reprint two additions seem called for. The one is a select bibliography of subsequent publications, both official and private: in compiling this I am indebted to the assistance of Mr. Rohan Butler. And again, I should express my obligations more precisely, not merely to those whose names indicate their permission to print correspondence, but for the conversations, informal and unrecorded, I was allowed to hold with some who stood near to Chamberlain and the heart of the storm.

They would include the members of his family, not least Mrs. Carnegie; two Birmingham leaders, Byng Kenrick and W. A. Cadbury; Leo Amery; Lord Beaverbrook; Lord Butler of Saffron Walden; Geoffrey Dawson; J. L. Garvin; W. W. Hadley; Lord Hailsham; Lord Halifax; Lord Hankey; Sir Alec Douglas Home; Thomas Jones; Mr. Mackenzie King; and Lord Norman.

At the end of the day the decisive impress is left by the men who wielded the same power, the two between whom Chamberlain's public life was often poised, as two magnetic poles. Lord Baldwin often baffled him: "the Celt", described as the most typical of Englishmen, least definable yet most attractive of men, so passive, and yet ready on occasion to smite once and smite no more. All Chamberlains were not equally congenial to him; on the leadership crisis of 1931 he imposed silence. But for Neville's qualities he had gratitude and admiration, for loyalty under stress and for pre-eminent service to the party, while remembering almost enviously "what a debater".

My last meeting with Sir Winston was in the autumn of 1945, when the aftermath of Yalta had shattered his hopes and the electorate had deprived him of power. "The whole thing is a tragedy" was sorrowful to hear, so that any personal tragedy was half lost in this stormy sunset. But it only needed one touch, when someone spoke of his offering Chamberlain the Garter, to fire him on the master-theme of life as he saw it, on courage; the courage in this instance of a man who lived and died undoubting and undaunted, amid national disaster, mortal suffering, and the air bombardment of London.

Whatever its deficiencies this book remains a document of one historical epoch, not to be revised by anyone who belonged to that generation—to which was allotted, perhaps, rather more than its due of what Gibbon found in history, "the register of the crimes, follies and misfortunes of mankind".

1969   K. F.

PREFACE

MORE than one biography of Neville Chamberlain appeared in his lifetime, without his endorsement or assistance, and that others would be written he foresaw from the momentous events in which his last years passed. Very much earlier, too, he had quoted with approval his father's view " that a man's life should be written before he is forgotten ".

That being so, Mrs. Chamberlain and his family desired that some more authentic record should be made for his contemporaries, and for that purpose placed the whole of his papers at my disposal ; it was, moreover, their wish not to see any part of my narrative before publication. The responsibility thus laid on me (who had never known him) to select and use my material with the full freedom which is the historian's duty and desire, was a trust for which I must always be deeply grateful.

The documents for contemporary history are men, not less than the written word ; his predecessor and his successor in office, Cabinet colleagues, followers, and associates at every stage of his life, have generously allowed me not only to use their letters but to consult them in person. They will forgive the omission here of their names and even, I hope, my familiar allusion to them as figures in history. Several departments of government, and the Corporation of Birmingham, permitted me to see certain records. With special gratitude I acknowledge the gracious permission given by H.M. King George VI to print some important letters, besides the document, reproduced in facsimile at p. 205, from His Majesty's autograph collection.

This book, however, is substantially based upon private papers and can, if for that reason alone, claim only a provisional character. Of the official sources from which final history will in great part be drawn, none are yet available : neither the archives of the British government, its allies and its foes, nor the correspondence of contemporary statesmen. And again, though the generation which has endured the last twenty years has a right, I feel, to be told all possible truth, even so no contemporary history can be written like the annals of the distant dead. For that reason too it has seemed best, especially in the last controversial years, to let him speak, so far as possible, for himself. Though nine-tenths of my omissions in a great body of quotation are due to considerations of space, for the residue omitted — and for all inserted — the sole responsibility is mine.

He who writes later the definitive biography of Neville Chamberlain will find two sources of high value among his papers. There are many diaries, extending over half a century, on every subject — travel, entomology, hospitals, shooting : those on politics are rather in the nature of journals, broken as they are by many gaps, widening with the growing pressure on his time. Historically, however, the prime source is a series of letters, written weekly, and alternately, to his two surviving sisters ; four or six sheets for nearly every week from 1916 to 1940. From these every quotation in this book, not otherwise specified, is taken.

On the genesis of that long correspondence a word should be said. They had been " in politics " from their youth up ; except for comparatively short intervals, one at least of the family sat in every Cabinet from 1880 to 1940. And their father treated them on the basis of absolute confidence, with freedom of discussion of everything political. Those conversations Neville and his sisters shared till their father died : and of those conversations these letters, the full continuous record of all he did and thought, were the prolongation.

The writer of those diaries and letters was at once the most loyal of men and the most outspoken critic of unreality. Between those two attributes, each so high in his scale of values, I have attempted to hold, for our age, the balance as he would have wished.

KEITH FEILING

November 1944

CONTENTS

BOOK I. 1869–1916

BOOK II. 1917–1931

BOOK III. 1931–1937

BOOK IV. 1937–1939

BOOK V. 1939–1940

LIST OF ILLUSTRATIONS

BOOK I: 1869-1916

CHAPTER I
BACKGROUND

" It is in old age that power comes ", wrote Sir Charles Dilke, with Gladstone in his mind, but with a truth which can be extended to all the modern history of Cabinets. Pitt, whom his enemies called the angry boy, left successors more anxious than angry, and prematurely aged, with the exception of the last of his dynasty in Palmerston, still almost juvenile when he formed his first government at seventy-one. Few of those who followed were under sixty and, Palmerston and Campbell-Bannerman excepted, Neville Chamberlain was the oldest, with whom, however, it was no question of promotion lost or hope deferred, but of a late start. For though his public life was so concentrated that within twelve years of entering Parliament he had won an indisputable claim to the succession, he was fifty when he made his maiden speech, and sixty-eight when he became Prime Minister. The life we are to study is thus that of a Victorian, for whom the Queen's death was as a sunset, and the first German war like the coming of night. " The late Victorian age for me," he wrote in 1922, " before the days of motors and telephones, when new discoveries in science were thrilling the world, and the centre of Africa was still painted yellow on the map."

He was born at Birmingham, eldest child of Joseph Chamberlain by his second wife Florence Kenrick, on March 18, 1869, a year of destiny both in Birmingham and the world beyond. That year the Vatican Council met to suppress new questionings with the infallibility of St. Peter's chair. The voluptuous Queen of Spain had to flee her distressful country, so making the vacancy which Bismarck designed to be filled by a Hohenzollern, and which within twelve months he made the occasion for the downfall of France. At last de Lesseps opened the Suez Canal, which seated Britain in Egypt ; at last Lord Derby, three times Tory Prime Minister, died. Disraeli, his successor in leading the party, was writing *Lothair*, for Gladstone was in the first year of his first and greatest ministry, and just disestablishing the Irish Church. Matthew Arnold's *Rugby Chapel* lay on library tables, but so too did Karl Marx on *Capitalism* ; *The*

Ring and the Book was one year old, and Dickens had one more to live. If we stretch the epoch out to the seven years from the second Reform Bill to the fall of the Gladstone government in 1874, what new planets swim into our ken, and what sound of ideals and embattled systems in collision ! Universal education, vote by ballot, and the Civil Service opened up to such talent as competition affords ; Charity Organisation Society and Labour Representation League, both born in Neville's natal year. In Paris the Commune, in Versailles the Prussians, in Rome the Italian army. *The Dream of Gerontius* but also Froude's *Henry VIII*, Green's *Short History* but also Dilke's *Greater Britain*, Pre-Raphaelites as against Huxley's *Lay Sermons*. Walter Bagehot to summarise what politics and the City and science contributed to Victorian progress, Meredith and Hardy, Lecky and Morley, to moralise belief when this progress was reaching disillusion, Pater and Swinburne to gild decay ; while from George Eliot came the grave treatise of *Middlemarch*, the last book which Neville Chamberlain was to read on his death-bed.

In his own home 1869 was a year of beginnings. His father now became a full partner in Nettlefold and Chamberlain, the firm of screw-manufacturers which he had done most to develop since reaching Birmingham fifteen years before ; this spring he led the way in founding the National Education League, whence in due course sprang both the Birmingham Liberal caucus and the National Liberal Federation ; this autumn he first entered the city council, whence followed his mayoralty of 1873–6 which made Birmingham the pioneer of a planned society ; this year Dr. Dale, the Pope of the nonconformity to which Chamberlain was Bonaparte, was president of the Congregational Union.

On this stage a first, and what might have been a decisive, act for Neville was cut abruptly short, when in February 1875 his mother died in childbirth, on the eve of his sixth birthday. Except for dim memories of a sea holiday in Wales, or of the locket she wore, and a few of her books, he had nothing positive of hers to keep, but her death laid on her children one long-lasting deprivation. It separated them from their father. Twice widowed within twelve years before he was forty, he encased himself in outward armour, grimly finished off his mayoralty, in 1876 entered Parliament, buried himself under tides of work. " To work constantly and not to think " was what he held up, to his then dear friend John Morley, as all that a man in his place could do, while to Jesse Collings, his faithful lieutenant, he broke out, " no one has a right to be happy in this brutal world ". Though he sincerely loved his children, we hear Neville's word " for a good many years I respected and feared him more than I loved him ", with a memory, too, of the " piercing eye ", " few could face it with comfort ".

Unquestioned and inspiring as his father always was to him, other influences moulded as much his formative years. He was born a member of a new aristocracy, the character and intellect and wealth of whose leaders had made a liberal civilisation, and born in Birmingham when the Midlands' iron and coal part-ruled the world. If Manchester might think itself the Florence, the Venice of this second British renaissance was Birmingham, on the golden book of whose master class were inscribed two peculiar peoples. The one were the Quakers, from whom came Sturges, Galtons, Cadburys, and Lloyds, and the other were the Unitarians, who at Birmingham included Martineaus, Chances, Kenricks, and Chamberlains. Banned from public life for two centuries by penal codes, and from conventional society by others' prejudice and their own pride, the Unitarians kept to themselves and married apart, developed their own teaching establishments, read hugely and poured themselves out in lengthy diaries, did their best by their fellow-men. Their position made them conscious, self-conscious indeed, of their own integrity, nor were they disobedient to what Dale declared to be Birmingham's eleventh commandment, " Thou shalt keep a balance-sheet ". But their politics were more militant than the Quakers'. They saw in the nation's armed force something to beat down the powers of evil and, having suffered long from priestcraft, even in losing their Gospel zeal they retained an un-shakeable belief in the individual spirit. Nevertheless they always repressed, since they despised, emotion, generations of enforced reserve having diluted and covered their passion with an ever-exercised self-respect.

Joseph Chamberlain's biographer [1] has told sufficiently by what channels Neville's paternal heredity flowed down from the water-shed of modern England where Church and Puritan divide. Of pure Wiltshire yeoman blood, which by marriage took in rivulets from a Marian martyr and an ejected minister of 1662, their larger life began when William Chamberlain of Lacock in 1733 appren-ticed himself to a London shoemaker. Over their warehouse in Milk Street, Cheapside, three generations placidly lived, rising high in the Cordwainers' Company, worshipping with the Unitarian chapel in Carter Lane but doing their civic duty as churchwardens of St. Lawrence Jewry, taking their full-bodied port under a hos-

[1] J. L. Garvin, *The Life of Joseph Chamberlain*, vol. i.

pitable mahogany, and working for poorer neighbours round St. Paul's. Their prospects were modest, their income never over £2500 a year and usually much less, but their ideals were high. As London grew, and with it their notion of living, like Thackeray's city merchants they migrated to a purer air, so that Joseph Chamberlain, the third and the statesman, was born in 1836 at Camberwell and grew up at Highbury, Islington. From his mother, of the Sussex Harbens, came a streak of more vivacious imagination.

In 1863 the Milk Street business was wound up, the old parents making a last exodus to Birmingham, where Joseph the third had prospered. John Sutton Nettlefold, Unitarian and ironmonger of Holborn, and husband to Joseph's Aunt Martha, had taken his small screw business there in the 'forties and, having resolutely bought British rights in the American patents which were revolutionising the trade, induced his brother-in-law to sink capital in the business, together with young Joseph. By the time of Neville's birth the firm produced two-thirds of the local output and, having taken the lead in competition, were hard on the road to an almost monopoly. But for our purpose this move to Birmingham was of a deeper importance than material prosperity.

For, by the evidence of all who knew him best, Neville's strongest characteristics came from the Kenricks,[1] the family into which his father twice married. They too were migrants, though earlier ones, to Birmingham. From North Wales they came, and doubly Welsh, with small crosses of Scot and Huguenot, was his maternal descent. Kenricks of Gwersylt in Denbighshire in Charles II's days owned house property at Wrexham, where their barn made a dissenting chapel when William III stablished toleration. There John Kenrick was Presbyterian minister from the time that John Churchill won Oudenarde, preaching during the '15 in private houses when Tory mobs wrecked his chapel, and dying just before the '45 ; of whom a friend wrote that " as good Enoch, he walked with God ". Through his wife Sarah Hamilton, a daughter of the manse, he and his children's children inherited what was to be the home of their main stock, Sarah's mother having been a daughter of William Wynne, Cromwellian captain, who in 1649, the very year that the man of blood suffered, built Plas Gwern, or Wynne Hall, near Ruabon. This Sarah, long outliving her good husband, left behind her when she died not Wynne Hall only and the legacies proper to a mother in Israel, Baxter's works or White's *Power of Godliness*,

---

[1] Here the indispensable authority is Mrs. Byng Kenrick's *Annals of a Nonconformist Family*.

NEVILLE CHAMBERLAIN,
WITH HIS PARENTS, 1869

silver porringers and good linen, but a large and spreading race.

While a line of elder sons farmed at Wynne Hall, the younger set up in business as braziers at Wrexham or banker-tobacconists at Bewdley ; one grandson, Timothy, entered the ministry and was father of two other learned divines, who were veterans when Neville was young. Long they retained this intense nonconformity. The better educated went to Daventry Academy or Manchester College, York, while Unitarian book societies and preachers fill their letters. When they travelled, they marked the wretchedness of Popish countries, and so fiercely resented Pitt's war to force upon France tyranny and superstition, that they seriously discussed emigrating to America. There they would find refuge from " the vile measures of a vile court ", which had driven thither Dr. Priestley, ornament and apostle of their society in the Midlands. Even in Lord Grey's Reform Bill days their every fibre vibrated against the " Church and King " faction.

While their women-folk passed about tracts, such as *The Comforts of Arabella*, and took their many children to bathe from the new machines at Liverpool, another grandson of Mrs. John Kenrick, Archibald, advanced our subject by settling at Birmingham. He began as a buckle-maker ; but shoe buckles were going out, so that in 1791 he turned iron-founder in West Bromwich, making a name much respected for competence and character. We should mark this great-grandfather of Neville, introspective and sweet-tempered and philanthropic, whose " mind and demeanour ", said the local press when he died, "improved in amenity with advancing years " ; his interest in schools and savings societies for his workmen ; his exact knowledge of flowers and trees. For nothing could be less true than to think of this race as buried in pious seclusion. Though this first Archibald would travel far to induct some minister of his Church, he enjoyed a country dance till he was over sixty, while all the family shot partridges in Wales, loved music and painting, wished life to be full and women to be feminine.

With his two sons we reach our threshold : Archibald the second, of Berrow Court, and Timothy of Maple Bank, both in Edgbaston. These brothers each married a Paget, who were themselves first cousins, of mixed Huguenot and Unitarian descent, by whom Archibald had Harriet, Joseph Chamberlain's first wife, and Timothy had Florence, his second. Add to this that Joseph's sister Mary married Harriet's brother William, and that Florence's twin " Louie " married Joseph's brother Arthur ; that Joseph had six children, Arthur nine, and William Kenrick four ; and we have the nucleus of the compact, devoted clan within which Neville matured. It had its resulting weaknesses, but also its strength; of the sort that made Joseph's brothers vie with each other to accompany him if he were made Chief Secretary in Ireland, where murder might dog him as it had Frederick Cavendish, or which made " the clique " (or " click ", as more illiterate enemies said) a power in Birmingham, or in virtue of which sisters of a later generation helped their brothers' election expenses.

It was then a scene at Berrow Court which was the earliest in Neville's retentive memory, of his " Aunt Louie " coming to tell him he would not see his mother again.

CHAPTER II

YOUTH: 1875–1890
AGED 6-21

IF affection and comfort and good thinking make for happiness, he had a happy boyhood, of the late Victorian kind when peace and plenty seemed to be entailed upon Britain, and when science was used for their increase, not for their destruction.

His father had sold his business interests in 1874, and with the £120,000 thus realised could give his family more than his own early advantages. Two years later he entered Parliament, which kept him much of the year away from home, but though full of work and sealed in sorrow he thought the world of his children, gave them glorious presents, and was always planning their well-being. For some years two of his sisters in succession looked after them, until his eldest daughter was old enough to keep his house ; that is, until Neville was sixteen.

When his second widowhood began, the family stood thus. Of Harriet's children, Beatrice was thirteen and Austen twelve ; of Florence's, Neville was six, Ida five, Hilda three, and Ethel between one and two. One family they made, for Florence's sweet nature and their father's personality had seen to that, yet the gap was to be not unimportant in after life. A certain " deference ", Neville wrote sixty years later, entered into his habit of mind towards Austen, while as time went on their father's authority reached them through Beatrice, the most selfless of beings, blazing with intellectual ardour and public spirit.

His first home was the house which his father took on his second marriage, Southbourne in Augustus Road, Edgbaston, a suburban house looking on the still open space where Edgbaston and Harborne touched, with well-planned garden and a field for Tom Thumb, their Shetland pony. In 1880 the widower moved further out over the high ground towards Moseley, where his favourite brother, Arthur, lived at Moor Green, their father's last home, next to which he built Highbury, so-called from old memories of Islington. This, Neville's home for the next thirty years, was in the hideous roomy Victorian-Gothic style, with vast hall of arches, stained glass, and inlaid woods, out of which opened his father's sanctum ; outside there was ample space for orchid houses and roses, grounds falling to the south with views over water and common, and plenty of large trees which on summer nights Neville " treacled " for moths, with his sister Ida and Cyrus, the Persian cat, in his train. Within hail were the clan houses, the Arthur Chamberlains at Moor Green, the William Kenricks at the Grove, and Aunt Alice Kenrick (Mrs. Beale) at Maple Bank. Those were good days. Of wigwams in Moor Green's bluebell wood, feasts over a microscope in Austen's playroom, tree-climbing and tennis, and holidays in Scotland or by the sea with others of the clan.

In this circle of cousins, where twelve or thirteen girls much outnumbered their brothers, Neville — Austen being so far ahead of him — was usually the eldest boy, and their natural centre. With them he was full of humour and nicknames, mimicry, and story-telling. He was neither spoilt nor moody, and with endless botan-ising, bathing, and rounders, broken by large doses of Walter Scott and *Monte Cristo*, he was a happy and normal creature. Even in a boy's impatience ; for he was outgrowing Aunt Clara's rule, which he darkly wished might be terminated by marriage, — as in due course it was. But between Neville in his own circle, and Neville outside it, there was always some gulf fixed.

At present part of it came, no doubt, from the very number and interest of the clan. Governesses and holidays were always shared ; they had such good company in their own houses that they were prone not to trouble about company outside, and as they grew up would ride, fish, and dance with each other. So when their young stepmother a few years later would reproach them for being un-sociable, Neville may be said to have admitted it by many expressions in his later letters, which describe them as " a reticent crowd ", or deplore his " accursed shyness " as a boy. But all that side of him seems to have been driven in deeper by his schooldays.

Not that this process can be detected in his first year away from home, at a little school in the sandhills round Southport, to which he went just before his eighth birthday, and from which came the earliest letters that have been preserved. The first, weak in spelling like the rest, runs its cheerful average course as follows.

January 27th
DEAR AUNT CLARA,
I liked your letter very much. I like the schooll though I miss you all very much. Yesterday we all [? went] to the sandhills, and saw a sportsman who could not shoot anything. Please tell Ida that i was exceedingly pleased with her letter and mean to write to her next

week. My cough is nearly well, the arrangement upstairs is not the
same as I expected it [? to] be, there being six little beds (with only
one screen) and five little washingstands, besides which we have a
bath (every morning) in the bathroom.

I have spent sevenpence allready, but I do not mean to spend any
more of it just yet. Shall I send or bring the *Young Days* home [?].
Please give my love to Ida and Hilda and Ethel and Miss Drew and
Kate and Papa and yourself. Goodbye from your lov. nephew

NEVILLE.

So the others continue, sometimes with a scrap of philosophy breaking through, — " I should like to go to the daffodil fields with the
others very much indeed, but as I cannot I must be content ";
recounting hare and hounds, " something that I hate, namely
dancing ", and a visit to an uncle at Hampstead into which he
crowded some glorious life. He had a ride on the Heath, on a
pony " full of go ", a careful inspection of " General Mite " and his
fellow-midgets, " a thumscrew and a scavenger's daughter " at
the Tower, and a play " very funny indeed about asthetic people ".

But the sparkle went out of life in the next stage, a preparatory
school at Rugby where he was most unhappy, nor did it return
when in April 1882 he entered Rugby School.[1] There Austen, who
was in his last term before proceeding to Cambridge, cast some protective glory over the new boy ; he was already renowned for his
political speeches, which he exercised on his dormitory as well as on
the debating society.

Men who have enjoyed their school return to it eagerly, and look
with envy on its present inhabitants ; but not so Neville, who
never saw Rugby again except between trains, and would say he
had hated it. On the surface, his record reads as one of more than
average success. He reached the Lower Sixth before he was seventeen, ended up head of his house and top of the Modern Side, and
got his " cap ", that is, the distinction just below the School XV,
at Rugby football. But disappointing reports worried his father,
and he was not happy.

To begin with, though he did not breathe it till long after, he
was badly bullied by a boy whom Austen in his greatness had, no
doubt justly, chastised. Then his house master, the admirable
Lee-Warner, broke down in health, making room for a successor
whose nickname, " Slops ", may be taken to indicate his common
fame, perchance unmerited, among the boys. Finally, just as he was

---

[1] For this stage I am indebted to the recollections of Mr. Percival Evers and Lord
Justice Scott.

at last making some strides, his father had him transferred to the
Modern Side, then a new-fangled department, where he found himself with a ruck of smaller boys, and which left him with nothing
but dreary recollections of " Minna " or " Nathan the Wise ".
This, from the inscrutable working of a boy's pride, always remained a rankling wound.

At any rate, partly no doubt because he disliked cricket and
thought games overdone, he went his own way. We hear of him
first as " a slender dark-haired boy, rather pale, quiet and shy ",
who would sometimes " talk quickly in a low voice about things
that had caught his sense of humour ". He learned something of
the music which was to be a chief joy in his life, often accompanying
the hymn at house-prayers ; would tell others how much they missed
in not reading Dickens and Scott, instead of what then passed for
sensational fiction like Harrison Ainsworth. " Friendly, while never
asking for friendship " seems to paint him to the life, and so does
" uncompromising in his hatred of what was, and of those who were,
mean and unworthy ".

As it happens, accident has saved a tittle of direct evidence on
his character as a schoolboy, worth a good many masters' reports
or elderly reminiscence. For some years after leaving Rugby he
kept up an intermittent correspondence with a young man with
whom he had once shared a study. We may call him the prodigal
son ; he had fared ill among the husks, and was eating his heart out
in a mining state of America. Neville, then in the Bahamas, used
to pass on his picture papers, and once at least sent a very accept-
able loan. " I wonder ", answered the prodigal, " what sort of
chap you are now, whether good like you used to be ; if you are,
I expect you would be awfully shocked at me " ; asking him to go
on writing, whatever he heard to his discredit.

Naturally only a few casual memories bring back the authentic
boy of the 'eighties, with hyacinths in his study, or attesting his
religion by not turning eastward for the Creed. One comes in a
letter of his own of 1925 : " My mathematical master expressed
some surprise at my mastery of a complicated algebraical theorem,
and I replied that as it was clear that I should have to learn it sometime, I concluded I might as well do it at once. ' I perceive you
are something of a philosopher, Chamberlain ', I remember was his
comment." Once, again, a friend urged him to speak in the debating
society, of which he was a silent member. " Neville replied quite
vehemently, ' No, I don't take any interest in politics, and never
shall '. I asked his reason, and he replied, ' You don't know what

our house is like for days before my father makes one of his big speeches. Everybody has to be quiet, and even at meals conversation is subdued.' And he followed this up with this surprising statement, — 'Wretched man, he never knows what he is going to say '." None the less he went, and made his first political speech.

Several of his school friendships, as with Leslie Scott, the future Lord Justice, and Lionel Richards who married his sister Ethel, came by way of his passion for natural history. When he left, the annual report of the Natural History society deplored his loss as " a very good worker ", he was co-curator of the *vivarium* (though unhappily its goldfish died), keeper of the entomological album, and presented a list of *lepidoptera* he had noted in Rugby streets, and Frankton or Brandon woods. Summer half-holidays, when he would escape from cricket, were much his happiest times ; " he seemed to know by instinct ", wrote Lord Justice Scott, " just which bush on a woodland path we ought to beat to make a rare moth fly out ", while his own memory went back to Rugby for a parallel to the finding in 1931 of a sedge-warbler's nest with its eggs.

He left school at the new year of 1886–7, and what should be done with him ? His father's decision was a natural one, and already taken, we may think, when he had moved him to the Modern Side. Austen was being trained for politics, had helped him in the great elections of 1886, was sampling the best minds of Berlin and Paris, and within a year was to be nursing a constituency. But Neville, who in any case had shown none of that fluency and political interest, must make his living. Unitarians of Joseph Chamberlain's generation could hardly be expected to see any particular merit in the ancient universities, and if business it was to be, they believed in beginning young.

He sent Neville therefore to learn something of science, metallurgy, and engineering to the Mason College, Birmingham, where, much about the same time, the Worcestershire iron-master Alfred Baldwin sent his son Stanley for a session's lectures. Sir Josiah Mason, lately dead, was almost an incarnation of Birmingham progress and character. Before Waterloo was fought, he had hawked cakes about his native Kidderminster ; after half a century in Birmingham, at first in the split-ring business, then in creating the greatest steel pen industry of the world, and last with Elkington in electroplate, he had amassed a fortune, which at the end of his life he returned in benefactions to the city where he made it. There is a dignity about his aspirations for the college which he founded in Edmund Street, " to useful purposes for the benefit of the com-

munity . . . trusting that I, who have never been blessed with children
of my own, may yet in these students leave behind me an intelligent, earnest, industrious, truth-loving and truth-seeking progeny ".
He had in fact planted the seeds of the University of Birmingham,
of which Joseph Chamberlain already dreamed.

To Mason College Neville went daily from home for the better
part of two years, — a time for which he was never ungrateful,
since when a minister he would often speak for, or in honour of,
his old teachers and fellow-students.   It was now that he began to
steep himself in Darwin, Huxley, Wallace, and all that far-ranging
school, a world of thought in which neither his father nor Austen took
the least interest, but in which he and his sisters read widely and
argued long.   He was left a good deal to himself, for most of the
year his father was in London and his sisters at school, while few
of his contemporaries at the College were of his own sort.   As for
his work, he had learned next to nothing of science at Rugby, nor
had he the least bent to metallurgy, so faithful history must record
that, though regular in attendance, at the end of his second session
he was placed at the bottom of the list in metallurgy, mathematics,
and engineering design.   On a teacher who survived him he left
the impression of a fine character, " modest almost to shyness ".
Yet when, as they waited for some precipitation or evaporation,
talk in the laboratory strayed to Home Rule, " Neville quietly but
firmly defended his father, and ended by saying ' We hold to our
family motto, *je tiens ferme* ' ".   This was rather lofty, whereupon
the professor ventured on a rendering current in the city, " What
I get I stick to " ; " to which Neville replied, ' We do not read it
quite that way ' ".

This stage done with, the next was an apprenticeship with
Howard Smiths', chartered accountants, which involved going
about the Midlands to audit, and some experiences which he enjoyed,
staying in commercial hotels.   Here he did well, so that the firm
offered him a permanent opening, but his father had other ideas.
Really, of course, his home and family were by a long distance his
most liberal education.   Politics were its daily bread, for the study
at Highbury was the hub of Birmingham, and Birmingham the
driving-wheel of the anti-Gladstonian war.   Here came the secret-
bearers and the loyal, — Bunce of the *Post* ; Harris and Schnad-
horst, the brains of the caucus ; Jesse Collings, the faithful and
simple ; or the trade-union ally, W. J. Davis of the brass-workers.
Here were formed the immortal phrases against the Tories, who
" toil not, neither do they spin ", and here in silence matured the

speeches, which so filled the Town Hall that the benches must be taken out, and thousands would stand two hours to hear the sentences which struck like a dagger. These were the years of dear political friendship, before Dilke was broken by scandal, and before Ireland had estranged Morley ; with whom Neville's father would travel abroad in highest spirits, sometimes to confabulate with Clemenceau, sometimes to taste the good vineyards and cruder politics of Germany ; where once they dined at their ease on the high terrace of Berchtesgaden.

Small wonder that his children found other tables uninteresting, for he was one of the best talkers and best hosts in Europe, and freely admitted them to political secrets. They grew up in this reasonable, disciplined, argumentative air, where no distinction was made between sons and daughters, and where all was energised by the mind which Morley, when all was long over, described as " of all the men of action I have known, the frankest and most direct ". Life was full and good when he was fighting to keep Birmingham his own, when police watched Highbury to protect him whom the Irish styled " Judas ", and when from his bed Neville could hear his Uncle Arthur keeping the table in a roar. On spring mornings, before the leaves were too dense, he would be up in the garden at dawn to follow the birds' song-notes, enscribing on his memory what he saw and heard before the world was awake, a flock of hawfinches, a flycatcher, or red squirrels biting the young sycamores. Christmas-time, by family tradition, was the season for theatricals at one of the clan homes, sometimes *The Rose and the Ring*, and sometimes *Pickwick*, in which Neville, with no natural aptitude at all, would double the parts of Mr. Winkle and the red-nosed man.

These two fundamental years, from eighteen to twenty, when piety and old authority turn (or do not) into settled habit, passed in this way at the heart of Birmingham. His earliest memory was of being allowed to wear his father's gold mayoral chain, and since then another Chamberlain, a Martineau, and a Kenrick had passed the chair. That their position carried with it a social duty was taken for granted. " You may say ", writes one of William Kenrick's daughters, " that Neville was born a social reformer, and brought up in an atmosphere of precept and example." He had begun to follow his father's old practice of teaching the Sunday school of the Church of the Messiah in Broad Street, the spiritual descendant of Priestley's " New Meeting ". Backing on to the mean slums of Ladywood, this church organised an active mission work, having since the year of Neville's birth had for its minister the accomplished and lovable Crosskey, whose influence radiated in the city as widely, though in a different way, as Dale's from Carr Lane. That a due proportion of their money must go to charity was always their father's teaching, while Beatrice was leading the other daughters in their first steps as school managers. It was a rule of social conscience, not religious faith ; for their father had given up church attendance, and Neville developed a robust anti-clerical prejudice.

On Christmas Eve 1888 Joseph Chamberlain brought home his third wife, Mary Endicott, from New England, to whom he had written " you have made life once more a glorious and a hopeful thing ". She was very young, younger than Austen and Beatrice, but in this united family made true what her husband guaranteed to the city meeting of welcome, " She will say like Ruth of old, ' Thy people shall be my people.' " No longer only inspiring and wise, their father was happy and serene again, as the younger of his children had never seen him, — Beatrice, the self-effacing, declaring the fine truth " she brought his children closer to him ".

His stepmother, who lived to be the last person to speak to Neville, grew very fond of him, but the first impression he made, when he was twenty, was one of extreme immaturity. In large measure he was a normal, active, and cheerful young man, who thoroughly enjoyed his first horse and his first gun, and was much attached to his retriever Crusoe. In the spirit of his father's advice to them all, he had many interests, shooting and botanising, chess and Jane Austen, Darwinism and Beethoven. And about this time he formed a new bond with his father when he suddenly acquired the same passion for orchids, over which they made a habit of inspection together on Sunday mornings.

He was therefore neither unoccupied nor lonely, but yet in some ways solitary. In general conversation he would keep a disconcerting silence until he had made up his mind, and though Highbury was more full than ever of interesting visitors — in 1889, for instance, Hartington and Wolseley, Cecil Spring Rice and Selborne — he made little contact with them, and would disappear to chase moths, not men. A most lucid mind, they thought, but not fast to develop, and with nothing of his father's quick flash.

All this is common enough in many young men who stay the course best and longest, and if history were written by judging a young man's crudities, we should come away as amazed, and as deceived, as those who heard Wolfe boasting, or who listened to

Lady Mornington bemoaning Arthur, her stupid son. Yet even with this large and necessary discount in mind, Neville's first travel diaries and letters, when he was twenty, are extremely youthful ; when they bear upon matters of art, they usually become a sensible reproduction of Ruskin or other standard works, with an honest indication that he liked something more modern and downright ; when, as is more usual, they record daily movements, their matter-of-factness is hardly ever relieved, and can descend to minutest entries, such as three bad eggs at one Venetian breakfast, the specific revolutions of the ship's engines, or a pillow like a brick. From his first flying visit abroad, a fortnight in Paris at the Exposition in June 1889 with a large family party, we can extract little of significance. As he could not yet follow French, it is not surprising that he found Mounet-Sully in *Hamlet* tedious, or " soon had enough " of the Chambre des Députés.

The next expedition of the Highbury party, some from the Grove, and Jesse Collings, to Venice and Egypt in the winter of 1889–90, was a much greater experience, from which comes a stout diary (with a few sketches) and a few letters. He began to be able to express what he found beautiful in art and nature ; an " exceedingly beautiful " unfinished head by Leonardo at Milan, or Dezenzano with its " lake with the low houses round it, cypress trees growing among them, and at the back the mountains all in a blue haze ". As they steamed from Venice to Alexandria, he marked and digested. " The chief officer is an object of aversion to all of us, a creature that swaggers about and with an air of affected jollity talks nonsense to the passengers . . . have been reading *Sartor Resartus*, so hardly know whether I am standing on my head or my heels."

Arrived in Egypt, his record becomes one of a thorough sightseer, prepared by some reading, with the eye which was never to fail in exact information and in seizing effect, curiously mingled with the moods of a boy. We may take for granted his detail of the various uses for the palm tree, the mosques, carpets, and bazaars, dirt and backsheesh ; but here is a Cairo street:

6 December 1889 ; to " Aunt Lina " (Mrs. James)

Arabs in their gaudy dresses mix with the swarthy Nubians and Soudanese ; now a fat Turk trots by us on a donkey, — now a blue-gowned Arab stalks along with his huge sleepy camel, next . . . splendidly-dressed runners . . . before private carriages with long sticks, howling to the people to get out of the way.

So they proceeded in great comfort and dignity by private steamer, as far as the Second Cataract, for travelling with his father meant a good deal of officialdom ; " sheiks standing on the bank, salaaming respectfully to father ", guests at dinner " who stayed a great deal longer than was necessary ", and a review of the garrison at Wadi Halfa. Neville on the whole enjoyed almost everything, archaeology and donkey racing, sunsets and native villages. The diary, which notes " lugged round to observe every stone in the temple by Beatrice ", shows us that he was absorbing something of what he saw ; " a huge dark gulf with a forest of columns " in the temple at Esneh, " in the distance the limestone hills of a pinky colour ", or Abou Simbel where " figures of seated gods are dimly visible in the gloom ".

16 January 1890 ; to Mrs. James

there was the great Rameses, his long skinny neck and shrunken cheeks showing his great age . . . with the beautiful aquiline nose we know in the colossi of Abou Simbel . . . there was his father Seti, builder of the great hall of Karnak, nothing left now of the beauty that distinguished him in life, there was the mighty Thothemes III, the Alexander of Egyptian history, and next him his brother the weak and yielding Thothemes II.

This was written up when they had come back to Cairo, where he had dinner with the Khedive, dances, a sight of dancing dervishes (" interesting but disagreeable "), a visit to the Nile barrage with Scott-Moncrieff ; finally, dinner with the Prime Minister, sitting next Colonel Kitchener, " who is fond of flowers, so we talked a good deal about them ".

Here then was Neville at twenty, young for his years, but in substance much what he was to the end, sane and transparently sincere, sometimes grumpy, but much more often tireless and cheerful, with a touch of simplicity that makes him set down the first sight of a jackal, and that seeking for detail which reproduces every tomb, cartouche, or shade of colour. As always, he laughed easily at simple broad effects, an Arab's pidgin English or Jesse Collings on his donkey christened " Rameses the Great " ; too impatiently he wrote down as fools persons who chattered or did not interest him. " Pining for news of Highbury ", he put down, this " very shy youth " on whom he afterwards looked back.

But 1890 did not run out without a stroke which showed " there was a hard core in me " and cut away the covering of timidity, not wholly but that part he faced the world with, for good and all.

CHAPTER III

THE ISLAND: 1890–1897
AGED 21–28

In the autumn of 1890, during a visit to his wife's family, Joseph Chamberlain reached Montreal, where he came across the governor of the Bahamas, Sir Ambrose Shea. This voluble Irishman was bursting with the virtues of sisal, a plant which grew in his islands like a weed, from which he claimed that hemp of best quality could be made ; and as in an earlier business life he had dealt in hemp from Manila, he spoke with conviction. Mr. Chamberlain was in need of money, for his capital had depreciated in South American investments. Moreover, he had been four years in opposition and had always spent generously, in every sense. Having determined to investigate sisal, he asked the governor to reserve for him an option on 20,000 acres ; Austen was already with him, he would cable for Neville, and send them both to make enquiries on the spot. Late in November they duly reached Nassau, New Providence Island, the colonial capital.

There the arrival of Mr. Chamberlain's sons was a considerable event, to be hospitably celebrated over Christmas. " Austen and I are engaged in doing our duty by society ", lamented Neville, whose diary grimly notes of a farewell ball " this was if anything overdone. The programmes bore our names, and the end of the dancing room . . . was decorated with our initials in green leaves."

Betwixt and between such festivities they set out to find answers to their father's exhaustive *questionnaire*, which covered everything from costings to internal security. They inspected plantations and interviewed every imaginable person, from the coloured post-master-general (noted as " a very pleasant intelligent man ") down to squatters who, except for daily turtle soup, were paupers ; covering many hundred miles of sea to explore the out-islands. From his diary and letters we find them in a thirty-foot cutter off Abaco, in a gale ; " I tried to bring a smile to Austen's pallid countenance by reminding him of '*voilà ton Afrique ! comment la trouves-tu ?*', but he only groaned and asked for his mackintosh." On stony Inagua they speak of herons, wild horses, and clouds of mosquitoes. On Mayaguana, where the harbour was good and land promising, he was in ecstasies over the flamingoes, " swimming about like pink swans ". On Long Island, with his net he was " in hot chase after the most magnificent *papilio* I have ever seen, — after running about a mile at full speed I lost him ". And last of all to Andros, where there was much poling through swamps and dragging their launch off sandbanks. With his last comment on Nassau society, " drifting fast into a state of drivelling lunacy ", in February we find them home again with their report.

It is clear that they brought no recommendation of any one site but produced highly favourable views on sisal prospects, computing the least possible return of profit on a good investment at nearly 30 per cent. Once their plantation was firmly established, Austen believed that an annual visit from Neville would be all that was required ; " I should be very sorry ", he had written, " to think of his staying here for five years, as life is very rough in the out-islands and quite unfit for the girls, and there is no society of any kind ". Simultaneously the governor confided to the Colonial Office " the plant has singular qualities, it grows on the most arid ground, its growth is a certainty ". Fortified by such opinions, Mr. Chamberlain waived aside the unanimous advice of his brothers and decided to embark, planting as fast as he could before competitors reduced his profit. Accordingly, on May 25, 1891, Neville once more reached Nassau.

He wasted no time in making his decisions. That very day he learned from Forsyth, a surveyor who had guided him before, that Grand Bahama was unsuitable, while some other reason, perhaps the distance from Nassau, tilted the scale against Mayaguana. But he was told " of a large tract in Andros which seems worth visiting ", promptly engaged one Michael Knowles as an experienced overseer, and on the 27th, after a midday levée in evening dress (" a most terrible affair "), at midnight sailed for Andros. There after several days' prospecting he set out to walk right across the island, due west from the frontage proposed for his estate. Two days running they found no water till the evening, on the third morning " our provisions were at an end ", and a mere five miles, eastward to the sea again, was nearly the end of them. " Forsyth was very weak and ill, and Knowles quite done up, so I had to lead and force my way through dense thickets of bush and lofty fern, at this season all matted together with various vines and creepers." After three days in the bush, steering by compass and sun, he decided to be content with the land he had seen a week before, and returned to Nassau to sign an agreement.

6 June ; to Joseph Chamberlain

it is with the deepest satisfaction that I am able to inform you to-day that the first part of my business is satisfactorily concluded. I have pitched on a tract of land in Andros Island and made an agreement with the governor. . . . I find the land between lat. 25 and Keith's location to be covered with pine trees, broken by belts of good coppice . . . on the whole it is of excellent quality, very level, and unbroken by large swashies or ponds. . . . I am confident that I have secured the best site available in the Bahamas.

Neither nature nor man had blessed the islands, where Columbus had made his land-fall, and where buccaneers such as Blackbeard massed their shabby fortunes. Strung out over six hundred miles between Florida and the waters east of Cuba, they were formed and re-formed from coral debris, swollen by deposits from the Gulf Stream, and splintered by the sea, which undermined them by " ocean holes " inland and edged them with brackish lagoons. The maps counted over three thousand, ranging from some thirty inhabited islands down to minute " cays " or islets, often part-submerged, making dangerous waters of which Admiralty charts give lugubrious warning, such as " white water like shoals ", " Dead Men's Cay ", or " Hurricane Flats ". Amazing colouring of sky and ocean, peacock-blue water over a white sea-floor, humming-birds and parrots, hibiscus and orange trees, did not disperse a sense of decay. Where the long reefs and breaking surf stood guard over men's settlement, pelicans and bittern responded heavily to the pervading water, and fungi and thick maidenhair fern filled up rock fissures in the bush. There were neither rivers nor mountains to cleanse and invigorate, but all about a land of undergrowth, a languid and stunted magnificence. In winter a pleasant air ranged about 75 degrees in the shade, but in summer this rose to torrid heat, broken between April and October by heavy rains, which produced their usual abominations in mosquitoes, ants, scorpions, and centipedes.

Many adventurers had played a stake there. Settlers from Bermuda came very early for salt, sometimes staying to plant sugar or tobacco, and the Commonwealth issued a patent for Eleutheria, or " island of liberty ". Then came Charles II's proprietors, then wanderers from the Mosquito shore, and again South Carolina loyalists, bringing the mace of their Assembly with them. But in Victorian days two elements made up the great body of their people, the ubiquitous Scots and the descendants of African slaves, who between them had bred many children of the mist. They were very poor.

It was only when happier lands were impoverishing themselves by bloodshed that the islands flourished, as had Nassau by privateering during the American civil war. Since slave emancipation had hastened their decline, undergrowth and creepers covered abandoned estates and ruined walls. Their own economy must always be restricted, for neither plough nor harrow could be driven through this rocky soil, only the cutlass or machete knife, and hitherto every effort had failed to establish a substantial commerce. Sugar was really gone, cotton was a thing of shreds and patches, the pineapple trade was falling away ; the only continuous industry was sponging, and everywhere the spongers' limestone huts caught the eye. In some such stationary poverty a thin native population existed, never over twelve to the square mile, uncertainly gazing between Obi worship and Christian missionaries, shivering with fever, ravaged by leprosy and consumption.

Twenty miles of deep water separated the western point of New Providence from Andros, the largest island of the group, and the nearest to Florida and Cuba, whose flora it shared. Its name came from Sir Edmund Andros, that obstinate, unliked Channel Islander whom James II named as governor-general of all the Americas. Great Britain had betrayed little subsequent interest in its fortunes. Its present population was roughly about 3000 ; it could boast no town, no cattle, and few roads. From the limestone reef the foot sank deep in soft white marl, then to the pine barren with low thirty-foot trees, thence to the mud swamps, whose desolation was only here and there relieved by a clump of mangrove or silvery palmetto.

Neville Chamberlain's estate, some ten miles south of the island's north-eastern corner, lay on either side of its operating centre at Mastic Point, where he had a sea-frontage of two hundred yards which widened considerably as one moved inland. A quarter of a mile seawards was the reef, half-way to which vessels drawing seven foot of water could anchor in all winds. Landwards there was a gentle ascent to his "hill", a hundred and twenty feet above sea-level.

Here he landed from a sponging schooner, with everything to create from the wilderness, his inheritance being a few cocoa-nut trees and an abandoned cart-track. He must build houses for Knowles and himself, burn and clear and plant what land he could up to 10,000 acres, make roads and wharfs, engage and feed labour, import plants, foodstuffs, and every inch of building material, keep his accounts. For the first five months he lived in a three-room native hut ; his working day was twelve hours, his food sometimes ran very

short. From his long Sunday letters home a part-picture emerges
of this first continuous routine of fourteen months.

20 June

 at 5 o'clock I get up and after a cup of cocoa I go down to the field
 . . . superintend the landing of lumber or direct the men who are
 at work clearing, and sometimes I take an axe or machete myself ;
 breakfast at 9 ; return to the field, where I have my lunch sent me
 at 1. At 4 we stop . . . tea ; after which life becomes quite unbear-
 able by reason of the millions of mosquitoes, which necessitate the
 burning of " trash " on the house floor.

18 July ; diary

 suffering much from having sat on a poison-wood tree . . . black
 blisters on my leg . . . skin came off, leaving it quite raw.

11 August

 I had to measure out more land, to direct bush burning and heap
 burning, to see that the women worked, to construct a road, and to
 serve in the shop.

This store, which took many hours of labour, was indispensable
if his labour was to be kept together, and from a much longer list
compiled for Austen's amusement we find that his sales included
flour, sugar, pork and biscuits, boots and corsets ; in time, even
Christmas crackers, trimmed hats, and pink satin boots. With this
feckless childlike native labour he had endless difficulty. In his
first week there was a strike against piece-work payment. " Only
one man came to work," runs the diary, " the others having struck
for day labour. I am resolved not to give in, but to get the house
up and then import labour " ; " by slow degrees ", he told his
father, " I keep tightening the reins of discipline ".

By November he was in one room of his own house, though still
without doors or windows, but as more land was cleared, hard
walking over rocks and tree stumps increased correspondingly, till
it was six miles every day. " I have worn out 10 pairs of boots ",
he tells Beatrice that month ; " a terrible lot of fever about . . . I am
tired out." In the conditions of his life he could hardly take seriously
his father's injunction about regular meals, and warned him that if,
in his own absence, a substitute were engaged, " he must understand
that there is no society, and that food is often very scarce and very
bad". He might have added that he could only rarely bathe on
account of sharks, that every type of insect made for sleepless nights,
or that squalls and drought ruined his garden. A curt diary of

March and April 1892, during an expedition to the Grand Bahamas for plants, gives another side of his experience. A 20-ton schooner, in a heavy gale, took three days to get there ; sharing a cabin with six negroes, a broken jibstay and block, did not enhance his view of the crew, " the most contemptible, cowardly, dirty, lazy, insolent crowd I ever butted up with " ; his trading involved one day of fifteen miles' walking in soft sand, with only boiled rice and sour bread at its end.

Except in one sense he did not commiserate himself ; the pioneering months were over, his house and garden were set up, he was sailing his cutter *Beatrice*. He was ready enough for all the good side of hard work, nor need we underestimate the proportion of solid truth in what later became his settled argument, that Andros had made him. This had been instilled in him by his father.

17 September 1891 ; from Joseph Chamberlain
I feel that this experience, whatever its ultimate result on our fortunes, will have had a beneficial and formative effect on your character. At times, in spite of all the hardships and annoyances you have to bear, I am inclined to envy you the opportunity you are having to show your manhood. Remember, however, now and always that I value your health more than anything, and that you must not run any unnecessary risks either by land or sea.

To all this, however, there was another side ; that he was almost as lonely as a young man could be. His nearest neighbour, a red-bearded, kindly, but most eccentric Scot, scratched away in economic failure on his small plot, only three miles away, but in practice it meant half a day of poling and running aground in a shallow creek. His white overseer Knowles, in any case not a mental companion, was often away to other islands for plants, and when his wife joined him that too brought many troubles. Otherwise, he must depend on a chance visit from a passing sponge merchant, or the mission priest from Fresh Creek, twenty miles to the south. When his working conscience allowed him a holiday, there was always Nassau, where he made a few friends, but he loathed its unexacting social round and parochial gossip. In short — and not for his good — he was driven in upon himself, lived for his fortnightly mail, stormed if it was delayed, and delivered his soul in lengthy letters to his sisters or brief jottings in his diary.

1 July ; to Beatrice
received no less than 13 letters . . . a long and delicious morning in devouring them.

John Collier

1891, AGED 22

21 July ; diary

lucky people, all going for a European tour, while I am exiled out here alone.

9 September ; to Beatrice

almost every night I dream that I come home and in company with you all make the round of the house, the garden, the stables . . . but I am not homesick, there is too much to interest and occupy me.

By day there was work in plenty, and on Sundays letter-writing, a sail, or the garden, but nights were the testing time, and these he passed much in reading. Many novels at first, when he was hardest pressed, but a great deal of solid matter also, for very deliberate self-improvement. Now and then we get some characteristic criticism. He makes a summary of Walter Bagehot on the constitution, — " wish it contained less argument and more description " : " embarked on Prescott's *Ferdinand and Isabella* . . . edited by a horrid prig ". He delights in *Tropical Nature* . . . " curious how Wallace is carried away by his spiritualism when he treats of man " ; and again in *Middlemarch*, yet " it isn't quite such a good novel as I had thought, not so good for instance as *John Halifax*". He had another of a lonely person's best companions, having always loved a dog, as they loved him. His first on Andros was a Cuban bloodhound, " Don Juan ", who died, he thought, from poison, — " much afflicted at his painful death, for he was a very faithful dog and much attached to me ".

This summer of 1892 he had two months at home, where he became " tired of having nothing to do " in a busy family. When he came back, for a month he had the company of Austen, who reported enthusiastically on the growth of the plants, and Neville's tenacious-paternal hold over his men.

The next two years were the brief golden age of Mastic Point. His house was a delight to him. It looked on to the sea through grape trees and cocoa-nuts ; it was spacious and airy, cream-coloured with red roof, and a broad piazza running round. If in the fields he worked in cotton trousers tied with string, at home everything must be well ordered ; flowers in vases, curtains, and photographs, and drawings of orchids from Highbury ; dark Olivia to cook, and dark Eustace as houseboy. Shaded by cocoa-nuts, poincianas, and mahogany, the garden was full of Highbury seeds ; his letters report a wealth of tube-roses, linum, and oleander ; he could eat from his own fig tree. " Bliss " he called it to smoke a cigar by moonlight on the wharf, to make a rock garden round the tank, to get a snipe over the ponds. In early morning the dew streams off the red roof while the sun collects power, and in his letters we hear again the negroes' chorus as they haul to the fields :

> Dis lumbah, it very heavy to tote,
> Oh, Mr. Chimblin lumbah.

Midday, and sponging ships dip their ensigns to the flag he always kept flying ; night, and no sound but a wild dog or an owl.

To Beatrice, guide in such things, he reported on his reading ; Carlyle's *Cromwell*, Romanes on mental evolution, steady progress in German, John Richard Green and a mass of political biography. He was happier, because life was very full and incomparably more civilised. Mrs. Knowles seems to have kept an eye on his health and his food, — in spite of his first grumble " if she is going to try and take care of me, she will soon repent ". To bring him plants or hurry up the mail, he had his own white-hulled schooner, *Pride of Andros*, which he often sailed himself through the shoals. Horse and mules saved the long trudge to the fields, and replaced women's heads as the means of taking out the plants. And when he tied up his horse, another Cuban dog lay down beside it, " Chip ", " as ugly as sin, but a dog's a dog for a' that ".

By this time the " Andros Fibre Company ", with its agents in other islands, was a considerable business. He had 1500 acres cleared after a year's work, 4350 planted in December 1893, over 6000 by April 1895, while the number of labourers rose accordingly to a maximum of 800. As all of them had to get food and clothing, not to speak of crackers or corsets, the shop, which made £780 profit in 1893, became an emporium in two stories. At that date the plantation had cost nearly £13,000, a liability which was soon much increased after a fleeting visit from Joseph Chamberlain that October. " An immense crowd ", Neville told Beatrice, " yelled and waved their hats and let off guns . . . you will imagine that Father has not been here without having some ideas. His general notion is to push the tramways and machinery at once so as to get our experience, and for this I am going to Cuba . . . to look over the sugar plantations."

To Cuba he promptly went, keeping a diary of what he saw ; deep indigo mountains, light-green cane-fields, royal palms with " smooth white stems looking like stone pillars ", blue and scarlet convolvuli, and perfection in coffee and cigars. There, by train and horse, he inspected many plantations and machines ; but " the trail of the serpent Dirt is over all ". Then back again to begin collecting lumber, to blast away a hill so that he might lay his track, to order rails from England.

All this was making Mastic Point the pride of the colony. Once, to much blaring of native music, Sir Ambrose Shea came to bless and to speechify, — once, more to Neville's pleasure, Agassiz the naturalist ; together with a good many candidates for employment. Both on the plantation and its owner a good light is thrown, from his own angle naturally, by a letter from the then Rector of Andros.

28 February 1894 ; the Rev. F. B. Matthews to Archdeacon Wakefield
Mastic Point has opened its door to us at last. Webb and I went there last month and found quite a new state of things. . . . In all honesty I really think the change is due a great deal to Chamberlain. He has put down the drink and unlicensed shops with a strong hand, opened a bank for the people, and he told me that in one year over £300 had been deposited with him. Moreover the change in the demeanour of the people was most remarkable. . . . I found Chamberlain insisted on this civility being shown on his estates. . . . He seems very favourably disposed towards the Church, and made a great deal of us both. . . . But you ought to see the place, new houses springing up by the dozens everywhere, fine roads in all directions . . . railway being laid down 7 miles into the forest, and a long jetty stretching out into the deep water.

All of which bids us discount a good many forcible expressions in Neville's letters, in which grumbling always made a part of his impatient activity and blunt humours ; letters also which were usually written about midnight in a swarm of mosquitoes. Casual or inquisitive visitors tried him high ; so, " the man means fairly well, but he has no interests and he is dull, dull, dull ". Some types of missionary he could not abide, those in particular " with an unctuous speech which sets all my bristles up ", nor naturally had Matthews read " I wish all the reverends in the Bahamas were at the bottom of the sea ". All these irritabilities, now and always, were entirely irrelevant to his action. He and the missionary priests stayed in each other's houses ; he helped their good causes, while in Matthews he found a congenial friend whose gifts he admired ; " doctor, surgeon . . . a bold and experienced seaman, a boat-builder, a gardener, a magistrate and a missionary ".

What his real nature was came out in his home. When Knowles was away in the out-islands for plants, or inspecting sisal in Yucatan, Neville had to nurse his sick wife or disperse her fears, and when this " most unselfish and warm-hearted woman " died, her husband's letters are the proof of what Neville had been to them. The children, these unhappy scrawls run, are delighted with their toys, or waiting the prizes he has offered for their lessons.

As for the negroes, to this day the children of his labourers, sometimes baptized by his name, have kept his memory green, which had descended as of one who was bread-giver, adviser, and omniscience. He defeated the grog-shops, got a school opened, organised a savings bank, put broken limbs in splints, worked hard as a magistrate. On his birthday their tuneless bands processed round his piazza ; he would listen to their interminable anthems on a Sunday ; something very simple in him thoroughly enjoyed their weird English. Bold remedies from his medicine-chest, even red pepper for toothache, increased his fame ; " I have three patients now ", he tells Ethel ; " the girl with the mutilated fingers, a man with an abscess . . . and another who slashed his finger to the bone ". Some very grimy scraps of paper have preserved a few of their notes. " Mr. Lord Chimblin Dear Sir ", one offender pleads, " as the Lord Jesus is above the earth, so is you above me. Please to forgive me for the mistake of smoking " (near the engine-house). Some confess brawls, one cries " send me some operating pills ".

And though their Sabbatarianism galled him — even taking exception to his gardening on Sunday, — though they saw evil spirits in an owl's nest, and downed tools on any pretext like a wedding, the truth is that he knew them as individuals and took pride in their betterment. Let us hear a letter, forty years after, to one of them, the skipper of the *Pride*.

13 April 1933. Neville Chamberlain to John Edden
you ask me to send you a bottle of linament and some old slippers. I have got these for you, and I hope they will reach you safely, and be a help to you in getting rid of your rheumatism and in making you more comfortable. I expect your hair is white now ; mine is going grey ; but I still think of you as you were when I saw you last. Best wishes from your old boss.

We must come to the decline and fall of this society.

Having been brought home in 1894 by his father, to his own keen disappointment, he returned in the autumn to the extension on which Joseph Chamberlain had decided. After blasting and grading the track, building an engine-house, and installing a machine to clean sisal leaves for fibre, there followed some months of extreme toil. A brigantine from England brought trucks and rails ; for one feverish fortnight, almost single-handed, he was hunting up drunken

pilots, hiring lighters, transhipping in gales. " Our animals are all
out at grass ", he wrote, " . . . so we have to walk . . . 6 miles out and
6 miles back . . . three times this day have I been soaked to the skin
. . . I vary my occupations between field and engine-house . . . I
drive the engine and make the fireman feed the machine." The
negroes must be stopped joy-riding in the trucks, machinery fenced
against their self-destruction, railway curves corrected by prismatic
compass. With this primitive labour a naturally tricky business was
sometimes almost hopeless. Leaves would be cut too short, fibre
left out in a squall, oil-cans propped against the furnace. Long
bouts of neuralgia and eye strain — spectacles for reading which
he never used again till 1921 — testify to these hard days, when
he was fighting against several misfortunes and one cause of fatal
depression.

Perhaps Mrs. Knowles' death was the worst calamity, for it
broke her husband down and removed the barest semblance of a
home. " What little social life I had ", he wrote, " is gone absolutely, and I see myself condemned to a life of total solitude, mentally
if not physically." Once he broke out to Matthews, fifty miles away,
" I do indeed wish you were nearer : it is mental starvation here ".
With all their grit and vitality his letters prove it to the hilt ; " evenings are weary and long . . . hard to read from 8 to 12 " and, again,
" in my old age I have taken to higher algebra to assist in passing
away the evenings ". They dwell with more monotony on the
detail of his life, whims or failures of his subordinates, and clutch
after what may be called escapes. Besides the solace of his garden,
they breathe a growing ardour for news of the big world, which
touched him more nearly when the Salisbury government took
office, with his father as Secretary for the Colonies. " I rejoiced
greatly", he wrote in April 1895, "over Sir E. Grey's statement in
the House. I have become a Jingo of the most rampant description."
A year later he was severe on the Jameson Raid — that " a miserable adventurer should go and set everybody by the ears " — but
equally indignant against the Germans ; " how magnificent it is
to see all parties united directly there is a hint of national danger
. . . and how gloriously the Kaiser has been snubbed ".

All this time he read big books steadily, long German novels,
Trilby which is dismissed as " trash ", or Michelet in whom his relevant
zeal found " a sort of loose enthusiasm ". When work slackened —
soon we shall see why — he took up seriously what he loved ; " what
a resource the birds are for passing the time . . . I have identified
nearly half the species given in Cory's book, and in many cases have

learnt their call-notes ". Yet time hung heavily. Now he welcomed visitors, somebody " not to talk down to ", and admitted to
having enjoyed a holiday in the once-unliked Nassau hotels. In
truth, he was resisting a hopeless frustration. Exile and expenditure,
daily improvement and American machinery, all were unprofitable
against the fact that his plants did not grow.

His failure made part of those wrecked enterprises of which
imperial history is full. All over the Bahamas, but on Abaco and
Andros in particular, there were patches of sisal, with its stiff purple-
green leaves, tipped with a red cactus-like point. Once bracken,
crimson wild vine, and the shepherd's needle daisy were rooted out,
it grew freely, both on coppice land and on tracts which, like Neville's,
had to be cleared of pine and rock. In four years, it was reckoned,
the plants should be at their best.

Bald and unhappy statistics have long since proved that the
islands were never meant to grow sisal, at least on Joseph Chamberlain's scale. In 1897 the total export was a mere 400 tons, which
stood nearly stationary for the next twenty years; by 1932 the
industry was reported " almost perished ". But in Neville's day all
generally was optimism, though the surveyor-general was a marked
exception; even in 1896 Shea's successor as governor was officially
most cheerful to the Secretary of State. Obstinately hopeful, Neville
caught new ardour from every favouring rain, still buying plants on
a large scale — 600,000 in two months of 1895.

It was in January of that year that he first warned his father :
" I don't see that we shall have more than 300 acres at the outside
to cut at the end of next summer. Anxiety about this weighs on me
day and night, and takes much of the pleasure out of the work."
He induced him to abandon any idea of more clearing and, when on
his summer holiday he joined the family in the Pyrenees, convinced
him that delay must be considerable and their profits modest. Across
the diary of their movements, all along the valley at Cauterets or
in the *châteaux* of Touraine, this shadow fell.

The excitement of his new machinery evaporated in the disastrous winter of 1895-6. A fire destroyed his first output of fibre,
American buyers rejected his samples as too stiff and too short,
Knowles went crazy from sleeplessness, — " entreating me not to
shoot him ". Father and son exchanged depressing letters.

27 February 1896 ; to Joseph Chamberlain
    the plants don't grow . . . all the order and discipline that I have
    worked up will be lost, all the people will go away. . . . In spite of

all that you and Austen said before, this is *my* failure, I can't bear to think of it.

30 March ; from Joseph Chamberlain
you seem to contemplate as a possibility the entire abandonment of the undertaking in which I shall have invested altogether (with the liabilities I have accepted) about £50,000.   This would indeed be a catastrophe. . . . If the worst comes to the worst, we will all make the best of it, and remember our motto, " *Je tiens ferme* ".

Before making a final report, Neville took a holiday (" of which I feel mentally in need "), forgetting his troubles as he steered Matthews' sloop to Andros' western side.   A pencilled diary shows him threading innumerable cays, " from islands miles long to the little bare yellow rocks on which the great black cormorant sits . . . with his wings spread as though he was holding them out to dry " ; searching the swamps for duck, noting the blue heron or white egret. And once at a mission church : " it gave me quite a shock to see M. waving the incense before the altar.   He is so sensible on everyday matters."

In April his survey of yellowish stunted plants turned out " as bad as can be " ; " if we have got to give this up ", he begged his father, " I should like to get away from it as soon as possible and start on something else ".   And on the 28th of that month, " with the most bitter disappointment ", he sent his last word :

I no longer see any chance of making the investment pay. . . . I cannot blame myself too much for my want of judgement . . . no doubt a sharper man would have seen long ago what the ultimate result was likely to be.

He offered to try afresh on guaranteed land—

I should be much more than willing to spend another ten years here, if by so doing I could make a success out of the business in which I have failed.

At midsummer he was home to reach the final decisions, which he communicated to his Bahamas friends.   " No hope of saving anything from the wreck ", he told the Governor's secretary, Alfred Greenwood ; " I asked my father to allow me to begin again with better land ; but he refused, and on the whole I think he is right. It would be a waste of time for me to spend another 10 years in that hole."   To Matthews he put another side ; " there is the financial loss which is heavy, and the failure to succeed in what I have given 5 years of hard work to, and the thought that all my people will

c

relapse into what they were . . . is extremely distressing to me ".

So he went back a last time in the winter to wind things up, to find thieves breaking into the store, and to see plant and engines knocked down to a solitary bidder for £560. In March 1897 he said good-bye ; " people came and sat in my office and sobbed ", he wrote to Matthews. He kept a joint letter from thirty-three hands, thanking him for the school and the bank, and for treating them " like a true gentleman ", together with one from Thomas Bain, " I feel as if a govner is going fro us ". When he got home, through the splendours of the Diamond Jubilee " how far away ", he told Matthews in December, " the Bahamas seem already . . . yet I often think of it, and with very grateful recollections, for in spite of all the disappointments it was a great experience, and I know I am much the better and stronger for it ".

Yes, as the distance lengthened, he said the same, that Andros had made him. Initiative had become a habit, for with him alone it had rested, and confidence in his own judgement, since there had been no one else to judge. And there, no doubt, he acquired the physical resilience that stood him in good stead another half-century. Nature, says the wise man, has made nothing in vain, and when her selected gifts are suddenly tested, as it were in a furnace, they gain double strength. Sensitive and self-dependent, self-respecting and sanguine, he had gone out to Andros, and the same, doubly, he returned. How should he lose his reserve when for six years he had hardly spoken to an equal, or how not be self-dependent when for food and safety he must trust himself ? In bodily trials and mental stresses he exercised his courage and held high his religion of self-respect, the more so as he saw his white neighbours often degenerating fast. Outside his family, perhaps he had never been one who reached opinion through discussion, but for six years on Andros he could only think in silence. This experience surely drove in deeper the moralities of his temperament, of progress dependent on labour, and a duty, indistinguishable from discipline, to his neighbour ; what he did for " his people " made him happy. Yet happier still where he had always been, in filling solitude with every image of home, and finding satisfaction for his intellectual thirst in the law and beauty of nature.

Powerfully, we must conclude, Andros over-sharpened some sides of his virtue, giving him a dislike of anything untidy, over-darkening for him the incompetence of humanity *en masse*, and imparting to his energy an unreflective turn, so that a day without incessant action seemed a day wasted.

Yet here, and once for all, we have to guard against one impression, easily given but perfectly fallacious. He enjoyed, as his father had enjoyed before him, all the comforts, amenities, and amusements of most normal Englishmen of his upbringing. If this island life enhanced something of the inherited Puritan, in its entertainments it recalled the Puritan of two centuries before, who had loved horses, music, and wild nature. How every dog spontaneously attached itself to Neville, how he kept up with every horse and almost every flower at Highbury, how many negroes gave him a sort of amused but instant obedience, the pages of this immense correspondence amply show.

But to have reached the age of twenty-eight, to have had a hand in losing £50,000, to feel he had failed his father, — all this meant that youth was over. As was Andros ; except " seven thousand acres of worthless land ", which in 1921 he reports as having sold for £200, cheerfully investing most of the proceeds in a French cabinet.

CHAPTER IV

WAITING: 1897–1911

AGED 28–42

FOR the next fourteen years he lived at Highbury the average life of a young, public-spirited business man. Three events of 1906, however, made a divide : his brother's marriage, the crashing downfall of the Conservative government, and the stroke which paralysed his father and left that fighting vessel a wreck. With what courage he, and with what sacrifice his wife and daughters, endured it, Neville recorded for his own children.

Till that day Highbury was a centre of the English-speaking world, no less than Hatfield. Birmingham had followed its leader over from the one party to the other. He spoke for the nation in resisting the Chauvinists who threatened to extend French Africa from Nigeria to the Nile ; eager to test the possibility of a friendly settlement with Germany, he dragged her admirals' ambitions into the open, and the insolent opportunism of Bulow ; while the Diamond Jubilee was hardly more of a triumph for the Queen than for the Secretary of State.

Two years later, youthful as Palmerston, and in the same vein, he met the challenge of Kruger, and with the undoubted assent of the mass of the country liquidated the legacy of Gladstonianism in the South African war. Finally, he set out on a last mission, to make a beginning of imperial union through tariff reform.

In the nature of things Highbury constantly received the men who were fighting and planning for empire : Roberts, French, and Lugard, Albert Lord Grey and Selborne, Strathcona, Hewins, and Maxse. Some of them — James of Hereford and Milner, it is remembered — predicted great things for Neville, but though his life was full, in some ways it continued solitary and unrealised.

There was nothing but happiness between Joseph Chamberlain and his sons who, though they infinitely respected him, were warmed by his affection and found him the best company in the world. Yet to live in the shadow of a father who is a great man does not always bring benefit to a son, and in Neville's case some special circumstances deepened that slight, unconscious element of suppression. Freely he admitted how glad he was to be released from Andros, but public life, he felt now and long after, was not for him ;

there could hardly be room for a third Chamberlain. Austen was moving far ahead, already a junior minister ; was it not possible that in politics they might stand in each other's way ? Not that this question could yet arise : for one thing, his sense of failure did not so easily depart. Letters to his Bahamas friends show him resolutely bent on making a competence, till which time he would eschew public ambition, and after which time he believed it would be too late.

7 October 1900 ; to Alfred Greenwood
I never had any intention of standing for S. Wolverhampton or anywhere else. . . . The fact is, I was intended by nature to get through a lot of money. I should never be satisfied with a cottage, and having chucked away a competence — you know where — I am going to toil and moil till I grub it back again. Of course that doesn't prevent my taking some part in a contest like this, and I am speaking as often as my nervousness and laziness permit me (which is not much), but I haven't begun to think of politics as a career.

Such activity as he showed in politics was reflected through his father and brother, whose shadows overcast him as well as their success. He, too, was involved in the newspaper attacks during the South African war, when the whole clan were accused of profiting by armaments and he, like his Uncle Arthur, stopped the libels by an action. Moreover, though imitativeness was the last quality which could be ascribed to him, he had piety in the old Roman meaning, and closely followed in his father's steps of forty years before.

Till 1906 he was the one permanent inhabitant of Highbury, left alone there when Parliament was sitting and all rooms except his own were closed. Whenever the family came back, he spent hours with his father over the orchids and met his political guests ; still ardently practising his Darwinian studies and the love of birds, flowers, and insects. General society meant little to him. In spite of his musical ear, it was with difficulty that they taught him to waltz well enough for the Edgbaston dances, where his cousins' names usually filled his programme. He was judged to be retiring in his ways, and though he lived at the heart of politics and felt them passionately, moved round them on a wheel of his own. Circumstance and affinity drew him close to other members of the clan, whose houses were open to him when Highbury was solitary ; most of all perhaps to his mother's brother Sir George Kenrick, a mighty benefactor to Birmingham, who gave him the shooting and fishing in Scotland in which he took more and more delight.

Letters of 1902 show no enlargement of horizon, though more fixed views on public affairs :

25 January 1902 ; to F. B. Matthews

My time is divided between business and local work . . . with now and then a short holiday, and then business again. I haven't quite found *my* mission yet and feel a bit dissatisfied about it.

8 June ; to Alfred Greenwood

The strain on my father has been very great and, especially during the negotiations, even his elasticity of mind was not sufficient to keep his spirits high. But now we have got all we had been fighting for, in spite of those who, like Rosebery and C. B., have pressed us to give something away. . . . The clauses which refer to the Cape and Natal rebels seem to me masterly . . . whatever punishments are inflicted will be beyond the reach of criticism by old women at home here. . . .

A week before the date of this last letter Joseph Chamberlain spent a week-end among Sir George Holford's orchids at Weston-birt. On the last night a young man, anxious to discover the peace news from Africa, sat up late with him over his last long black cigar, — though for that particular purpose in vain. But on the future of politics at home Mr. Chamberlain was more forthcoming. Incidentally he said Austen had as good a chance as anyone of one day leading a government. If, however, it had been Neville, he would have backed him to be Prime Minister for a certainty, as he considered him the abler of the two ; but then Neville was not interested in politics.

This was five years after the end of the Bahamas venture. What Neville had been doing can only be understood when we have given its full content to his sentence that he had become a " provincial ". It is to Birmingham we must go to find the school of his politics, and in so far as he was destined to be an instrument of his epoch, a representative of many strands in our history, he came equipped from a region where they existed in profusion.

No better epitome can be found of the continuity of Britain, of its spring forward to world supremacy, the flowering of that Victorian empire, and the hard struggle to arrest its decay. The city makes the eastern outlier of the Midland plateau, which historically formed a watershed between different races and rival economic channels. Its own small river the Rea, joining the Tame, makes its way to the Trent and the North Sea, but a few miles west all the streams set off to the Severn, while south-east they flow to the Avon, and both to join the western ocean. Saxons had pushed up these southern-flowing streams, but it was the Mercians who had taken the site at Birmingham as they descended from the Trent ; each of them later making a separate Christian diocese, Lichfield for the Mercians, and the Saxons at Worcester. All round the plateau's south-eastern slopes lie the last fringes of the forest of Arden, whose pulse still beats in the city place-names, in Saltley, " the willow clearing ", or Deritend, " the deer-gate end ". Early man and early prosperity avoided this inhospitable upland, Roman roads merely skirted it, while the cities of the plain, Tamworth and Coventry, were famous before Birmingham was known. It survived and out-stripped them because it made a meeting-place, and a market, for the three shires, Warwick, Worcester, and Stafford, which converge upon it, and because its porous sandstone could give to a large population abundant water, stone for building, and sand for metal-work. By Tudor times its corn mills and leather workers had given pride of place to what Camden heard, " the sound of anvils " ; it had become the outlet for the thick-massed industries of its neighbours, the metal-smiths and nailers, iron-stone workers and charcoal burners, of Severn and her tributaries.

From this ancient history a small city had sprung, of sturdy repute when swords were ground for the Civil War, when gun barrels were needed for Marlborough, and cutlasses for the East India Company. But the streams of Birmingham were minute as com-pared with the Severn, and it could only rise to greatness when water was superseded by steam, so that its real expansion dated from the middle eighteenth century, when engines and canals cheapened its material and multiplied its energy. For what reasons, and by what great men, it ascended, is written large in national history ; very rarely, we must suppose, has one small town, since Florence and Venice, held within it such intelligence as Birmingham in the reign of George III. A whole reformed England may be predicted in the lives of Matthew Boulton and James Watt, Taylor and Murdoch, Priestley and the first Darwin.

When David Cox painted his native place, thin chimneys filled its hollows, but malt-houses and orchards dotted the hills, country stiles and trees circled Edgbaston. By Neville Chamberlain's birth a great city had engulfed them all. Its 70,000 people at the census of 1801 rose to 320,000 in 1861, and in 1911, the last date before its area was extended, to 525,000. It surmounted each succeeding phase of social revolution, from its middle position trading in almost equal proportions by the exits of the Mersey, Severn, and Thames, and a proud civic spirit conditioned this material growth. When its petty survivals of medieval government still fulminated against dogs drawing carts or pigs roaming the streets, mass meetings of its citizens extorted the grant of a municipal charter, just as they did much to storm the concession of the first Reform Bill. Eighteenth-century philanthropy had founded great traditions in medicine and music, while its education developed continuously from medieval gilds to the Edward VIth School. Joseph Chamberlain and his generation taught the city to take the common needs of its people — water, sanitation, communication, and light — into its own hand with a " sagacious audacity ", to extend those needs to libraries, museums, and things of the spirit, and to spend royally in faith. While Neville grew up and before he went on the Council, the city moved from one great undertaking to another, electric light, tramways, university, and bishopric. It spent six millions on bringing water from Wales ; it had issued seven millions of Corporation stock, and handled an income of a million and a half, of which a third came from its public trading.

Characteristics, for good or ill, of those hundred years' ferment were graved ineffaceably on Neville's outlook. Rarely, in the first place, had men triumphed more over their environment. A city on a plateau four hundred feet up, with no great river and no access to the sea, made itself an economic metropolis, carrying canals, railways, and water by locks and tunnels and aqueducts, always moving " forward ", as its motto demanded. And it had been a triumph of skilled individuals. Dependent for essential energies on its Black Country hinterland, the city craftsmen kept for themselves the final processes, which called for the skill of a multitude of home workers and small workshops. Nowhere a greater multiplicity of occupation, from the fifty stages in the gun trade down to the makers of wedding rings in garrets ; nowhere more middlemen, or varied economic links. In few great cities had " out-workers " so long survived, in none was trade unionism so weak. With wonderful elasticity Birmingham turned from one demand in its metals to another, from shoe buckles to buttons, flint-locks to bullets, tubes for cannon to tubes for gas, from nails to pens. Its leaders had been emigrants who had carved their own way, and how many times did Birmingham disdainfully resist governmental control and glory in its doctrine of self-help ! It was this tough agglomeration of workers who filled the area with their clubs and friendly societies, organised their earnings in hospitals, chapels, and voluntary institutions, and in the Town Hall drunk in the delight of politics at the feet of Bright and Chamberlain.

Those days were now passing, overcast. A long ten years' slump from 1876 onwards ended the careless supremacy of the Black Country, whose coal and iron ore was never to reach again the output of the 'seventies. Basic steel steadily superseded iron, bringing with it larger units in industry and a fierce competition from regions nearer to the sea ; mass production for a comfortable standardised democracy in itself meant an extended mechanisation. Some of the city's ancient industries were slowly dying ; yet older ones, like the home-worker nailers, whom Nettlefold and Chamberlain had helped to extinguish, at length finally fell. Already, in face of a German thrust and American tariffs, the Chamber of Commerce was asking for " fair trade ".

But while this second industrial revolution was being born, a full price had not yet been paid for the first. Much though his father's generation had done, the Birmingham to which Neville returned was full of shadows, and when Bishop Gore took leave of the city in 1911 he spoke of " a profound social discontent ". For this there were causes common to the whole country, since the Edwardian age was one of arrested progress in wages and of a conservative economic method. But Birmingham had special evils of its own. A high proportion of its people were packed in 40,000 back-to-back houses and 6000 courts, which were only now being opened to light and air, while 10 per cent of the population lived more than two to a room. Till the Welsh water reached the city in 1904, night soil had to be carted from many thousand closets, there were areas where one tap supplied thirty persons, whole streets were full of vermin, little hill-streams flooded the low-lying tenements. It was true that since the shattering reports of the 'forties the total death-rate had been halved, but infantile mortality had actually risen, in the last year of the century reaching the fearful figure of 199 in every thousand. The children who survived must play in the streets, for this half million people had barely 300 acres of open space ; even in 1911 there were 5000 recorded cases of tuberculosis.

But the tide was on the turn. A sharp contrast between the vital statistics of the old city and those of its suburbs pointed the moral, which modern transport encouraged individuals to follow. The city broke out into the country, over 60,000 persons migrating from the centre to the circumference in the first decade of the present century.

c*

When Neville Chamberlain, aged twenty-eight, set out in this changing community to make his fortune, sooner or later he was bound to enter its service. Many opportunities came as by hereditary right. Ten of his kindred filled the Mayor's office before he did so himself, and it was the family once more which helped him to begin business. A first notion that he should enter Kynochs', the great makers of explosives, was wisely vetoed by his father on political grounds, and ultimately his uncles, Arthur and Walter Chamberlain, found him two other openings. One was a directorship in Elliotts', manufacturers of copper, brass, and yellow metal at Selly Oak. This substantial limited company, of which in due course he became chairman, and which employed some 700 or 800 men, was a maker of brass-work, and in particular of " Indian squares ", which were exported to Benares to be worked up in that city of the faithful. The absorption which this company finally underwent, in Imperial Chemical Industries, it was in his time applying to its immediate rivals and, though hard hit by Japanese competition, was making a handsome profit in 1914, when he was the largest shareholder.

His second and more personal venture he described as follows :

30 October 1897 ; to Alfred Greenwood
I told you that I had become a director of some copper works, but since then I have bought another business which I am going to smash up all by myself. It is concerned with the manufacture of cabin berths, not the bedding but the metallic part, and is in Birmingham, so I shall be transformed from a colonial to a provincial.

This firm, Hoskins', in Upper Trinity Street, Bordesley, was a typical Birmingham industry with small old-fashioned shops, dating from the 1830's. It was a business for skilled men, and little over seventy were in it, strictly localised with only two rival firms, both of which were in the Birmingham area. In those days it sent men out to fit berths on Admiralty or private contract, to Glasgow or the Mersey, and on occasion to Genoa. Here also, in more sole control, he succeeded financially, though on a smaller scale.

From men in both firms, and on every rung of the ladder, it has been possible to piece together a consistent picture. As a business man, those well fitted to speak would not put him in the absolutely front rank, though recalling many good speeches to his boards, tireless energy, and administrative zeal. He was reckoned " a good seller ", knowing the value of money, ready to take a night train at any notice to clinch a contract, just as his men remember him flying up the stairs three at a time, punctual to the minute at 8.30 or 9, and away, bolt upright, on his tall bicycle at 5.30 or 6. He was a reformer, well enough equipped in science to employ chemists for the improvement of technical method, while at Hoskins' he swept away the payment of wages through foremen of the " squads " and first recognised the Wood Workers' Union. Men liked him and still praise the firmness of " a true gentleman ", who would listen to an office-boy's complaint, had learned all the detail himself, knew men by name, would instantly pick out one who looked ill, send this one to hospital or pay for another's recuperation at the sea. " Too good " — we shall hear that again — some say, for he trusted men and was sometimes taken in. On the whole, these memories always conclude, " a happy family ", with workshops closed for Christmas concert or supper, and the chairman taking part in the yearly " outing ".

In social action he was the same as ever. At Elliotts' he instituted a surgery, welfare supervisors, and, later, war benefits for injured men or their dependants ; at Hoskins' he began a 5 per cent bonus on output and a pensions scheme. In fact, from this personal spring all his social philosophy arose ; he was proud of never having a strike, and deplored the loss of the human side in big business. When he won a working man's goodwill he was openly glad, and kept it to the end, and would have been well content with a letter received after his death from a pensioner : " he was a real man in all his doings. . . . I do hope and pray I shall meet him in the next world."

Meantime he took up all sorts of public service. He continued his Sunday school work, sometimes teaching them his favourite Darwinism, was honorary secretary of the city Liberal Unionist association, active in the Chamber of Commerce, and a magistrate. When Haldane formed the Territorial Force, headquarters and ranges had to be found for new Birmingham units, and he was chairman of that committee too.

In two other local causes he took a more inherited and personal interest. So far back as 1888 his father had talked of a Midland university, which through his initiative came into existence between 1900 and 1903, with a royal charter and an annual grant from the city. As the son of its Chancellor and an original member of its Council, Neville threw himself into raising its endowments, buildings, and status. The early days of a new civic university are never easy, with business men to the right who grudge expense or demand practical usefulness, and democrats to the left who suspect a privileged class. Birmingham University therefore owed much to a middle group, who championed its claim to assistance from the rates and insisted on its dual function, as both a place of pure learning and as the concentration of the mental activity of an industrial area. In this, and in practical ways without number, he was a leader ; eminently, for example, in founding the officers' training corps, or in helping Richard Redmayne to make his chair of mining a school of research in the questions which, like ventilation underground, would directly benefit the workers.

Nearer still to his heart was the cause of the hospitals, where he at once began voluntary work for the city's ancient foundations. Of the General Dispensary, then taking 75,000 cases a year, he became honorary treasurer ; he gave much more arduous service to the General Hospital which, after a hundred years in Sumner Lane, had just been moved to a healthier site and enlarged, so that it was taking yearly 5000 in-patients and 60,000 out-patients. Here he began as a visitor, a member of the board of management, becoming chairman in 1906, and served it long after.

Such detail is less important than the spirit in which he worked. Always considerate, it is remembered, to the humblest boy clerk, he would come in straight from Hoskins' to visit the casualty ward, while in his hands the visitors' book recorded concrete suggestions ; and before he became chairman he visited London hospitals, and with his sister Ida looked into the possibility of an almoners' committee. Well in advance of what has since become common practice, he wished to make the out-patients' department primarily consultative, to create a new receiving unit, and win precious space by sending slighter cases to private practice.

A small notebook, of 1906–8, bears out other men's recollections. It sets forth what he had learnt at the London Hospital, outlines in detail the salaries, time-table, and rearranged staff which his " receiving " project would mean, carefully enumerates the balance between surgical and medical waiting cases. Nothing could be more characteristic than the pains he took in advance to ensure success, the consideration given to the views of nurses, porters, dressers, or anaesthetists, the approval of a good speech even when it rejected his plans, or his conviction despite that rejection ; " all the argument on our side ". He brought forward yet another scheme in 1908, three years before National Insurance became law, to attach a provident side to the Dispensary, whereby subscribers, choosing their own doctors, would get treatment from branch dispensaries, while friendly societies would collect subscriptions. In many conferences with all concerned, he learned that the voluntary principle could only survive by co-operation, and was feeling his way towards fusing the two big hospitals in one strong unit. His position is shown by the fact that he presided over the Midlands Hospitals conference on the Insurance Act, the general principles of which he welcomed.

Among other activities (and in 1904 he speaks of fourteen committees) two must come here, as joining this phase with that which was to come. The one flowed directly from Birmingham business, which must live by good communications. In 1906 a royal commission was appointed to consider the future of canals, an old subject of argument in this Midland city, which would form the junction of the commissioners' suggestion of " the cross ", at which a Thames–Mersey and a Humber–Severn system would intersect. When the Waterways Association was formed to promote legislation, as chairman of the executive committee he put forward the absurdity of the existing facts, in virtue of which a Birmingham barge must pass waters controlled by seven different authorities to reach Hull, or get over 160 locks to reach London. But the deputations which he led to the Board of Trade found heavy financial objection, and obstruction from the railways, rival carriers.

The second was an arena where he could meet the ablest young men in the city, the Birmingham and Edgbaston debating society, of which in due course he became president as his father had been before. There, like earlier Chamberlains, Martineaus, and Kenricks, he apprenticed himself in fortnightly debate, which covered, as such societies do, things great and small. During his term as president the society thus deplored the growing tendency towards State action as " destructive of the moral fibre of the nation ", applauded the Lords for rejecting the Budget, and on his initiative debated a congenial view, that " business men make better rulers than lawyers ".

Finally to this society (at which, all in all, his attendance was perfunctory) he gave in September 1910, as the custom for a retiring president was, an address on a serious note, taking for his subject " human development under natural selection ". Man's progress, he declared, was extinguishing species, just as drainage of the fens killed the large copper butterfly. Of the so-called positive checks, " it is natural to suppose that this disinclination to set in motion the machinery of war will grow stronger ", nor was famine any more a maker or unmaker of empire. But disease, if " stringency of selection " paused, had still to be reckoned with ; " some day, when the race has forgotten the existence of consumption or measles or smallpox, one of these diseases may reappear and, falling on a people which has laid aside its armour of immunity, bring about a catastrophe more hideous than any yet recorded ". Intellectually " we show no signs of progress " ; indeed the printing press and levelling-down might mean retrogression. Our " success-making qualities " as a nation rested, therefore, upon character, upon which natural selection still could play, on " courage, earnestness, determination, judgement, and sympathy ".

So reasoned this business man and reformer, in his forty-second year.

CHAPTER V

INNER LIFE AND THE OUTSKIRTS
OF POLITICS: 1899–1914
AGED 30–45

1911, the year after this farewell to the debating society, made the next epoch in his life, for in it he married and entered the city council. But, before passing on, there are other threads to catch, beginnings of other courses he would run.

For these years there are few letters remaining, but in compensation many diaries, and as like his father he was an ardent sightseer, though a more systematic one, they record mental habit as well as movement. In these fifteen years he was four times in France, thrice in Italy, besides Dalmatia, Algiers, Holland, Switzerland, Burma, and India ; Egypt and eastern North America he already knew, Canada and East Africa came later. On the whole he was a better-travelled man than most British ministers.

If he thought his cap knew his secret, said Henry VIII, he would throw it in the fire, and this Chamberlain would not commit introspection to paper, and when he once did so, during an unhappy time, later cut out the page. Usually his diaries stick to the prosaic business of travel and things seen, with practical notes on high prices and low, good restaurants or bad trains. Four-fifths perhaps are the comments of a man bent on seeing the best things and making the most of every day, — more than one at Pisa, he declares, would be difficult to fill — energetic always, easily and humanly exasperated, well-read in standard books of art and architecture, but not travelling far outside the British tradition. They show him more critical than receptive, considerably more intent on fact than theory. For one with a true musical ear and wide reading, he cared curiously little for rhythm in words, or perhaps put it aside as encumbering the high-road of things to be done. Colour, the soul's bridegroom, he all his life worshipped in both nature and art, though here too perhaps his appreciation passed rather through eye or intellect than the emotions, to be lodged in a separate compartment of the mind from the sympathies which he also deeply felt, pity and hope, yesterday and to-morrow. Much then of these diaries is uninteresting for wider purposes, or throws little light on his character.

But some more than usual qualities they plainly possess, — one being a clarity, a thin word for a rare combination of eye and brain, which can recreate a natural scene like a contour map. Here is part of what he sees from an Irawaddy steamer, fitted as he instantly noted with his own Hoskins' berths : " Far away on the other bank some little spots of white, pink, and yellow show where a party of Burmese are poling along by the sandbank in a long narrow dugout. Behind them is a broad patch of yellow sand crowded with cormorants, terns, fish eagles, and enormous black and white storks standing on one leg or lazily passing their wing feathers through their long black bills. Right ahead of us, beyond the pink reflections of the clouds, is a yellow streak, the further shore of the apparent lake. It is backed by a dark blue-green belt of high trees, behind which rises range after range of blue mountains, the nearest and lower ridges showing indigo in the shadows and a tinge of pink in the high lights, while the further ranges grow softer and paler, till the last cone rises out of the distant haze like a faint blue shadow capped by a dazzling pile of white cumulus."

When he first went to Italy he admits he " neither knew nor cared anything then for old pictures ", but his notes in course of time show knowledge above the average, and always, as we might expect, firm likes and dislikes. Their colouring made him love the Venetians, with Titian foremost, but colouring he put lower than expression. He could not see that Botticelli was much more than " pretty " ; Cellini's " Perseus " was " finicky " ; as for Perugino, " I cannot see any expression or sincerity in his lackadaisical saints ". Raphael was a man of genius, yet even in the " St. Cecilia " at Bologna Mary Magdalene " has a conscious air of having her portrait painted ", and many visits confirmed his belief in the superiority of Michelangelo. Here, he repeats each time he saw the Medici Chapel or the Sistine, was the supreme master.

Where he admired deeply, it was usually once for all, and he gives his reasons, as with the Venus of Milo's " calm consciousness of perfection ", or with Giotto's power that " each figure shows the man's thoughts as though they were written ". But as he stood before pictures till they took on life in his memory, and systematically compared, his comments gain substance. He contrasts Gozzoli's work at Florence with that at San Gimignano, can pick out the intarsia work at Urbino, the glass of Clermont-Ferrand, or Nelli's painting at Gubbio as the glory of frescoes in their youth ; and acquired some new favourites with more subtle flavour, Lorenzo Lotti and Andrea del Sarto.

On the whole the enterprise, energy, and enjoyment in these volumes show what he gained, and a variety of life wider than the world would have later supposed. He loved the acting of Guitry and Réjane, yet could be amused for one night at the Folies Bergères ; would bicycle forty miles in the day in Normandy, ride his horse twenty-five miles a day for a week in the Wiltshire downs, or walk fifteen or twenty, every other day, in the middle of a cure at Aix-les-Bains.

Four months in India and Burma in the winter of 1904–5 warmed his imagination and gave him an insight into lives unlike his own. Mogul architecture captivated him and he wrote, with a rare deviation into general ideas, of Akbar's mausoleum, " a fine idea, this uplifting of the tomb on high, leaving it open to the sky ". But, as with most of his race, it was the Taj that obsessed him, " there is nothing in the world to equal it ". As he went from east to west he had a week in the Central Provinces and wished he had been in the Civil Service ; toured the Punjab Sikh States with Dunlop Smith (a friend henceforward), reviewing troops and touching trays of jewels in *darbar* ; went up the Khyber with Roos-Keppel, hunted the jackal, shot a panther, rode elephants to explore Rajputana, and interviewed Scindia at Gwalior. These are his thoughts on the last days of Curzon's India :

15 January 1905 ; to Joseph Chamberlain
I have been collecting opinions about Curzon during my travels, and I am gradually coming to the conclusion that he *is* a great Viceroy. The majority of people perhaps dislike him intensely, almost always giving as their reason some childish gossip about his bad manners ; but the best men I have met have been without exception his devoted admirers. They say he is a man full of courage and strenuousness, no respecter of persons, and not to be bound by red tape, but ready to take advice if there is commonsense in it, and always bent on going to the root of every matter that comes before him.

This Indian tour turned down a page or two of his earlier life. In 1903 he thought he had found the marriage he hoped for and had his disappointment, which hit him hard, so that it was not till the Indian diary that he seems to have recaptured a sense of happiness. And it was at Patiala that he heard of the first break in this most united family, the death of his youngest sister Ethel ; " those words ", he wrote, " have been much in my mind too, that at any rate she has come into the great peace ".

Meanwhile his father's destiny steadily influenced the sense of duty in this son who did not care about politics, for in 1903 Joseph Chamberlain broke the Balfour government by the declaration for tariff reform.

31 August 1903 ; to F. B. Matthews
Don't you think it is pretty plucky of my father, after coming home in a blaze of popularity from South Africa, to risk it all by starting this great controversy . . .? I need hardly say that I am an ardent adherent — in fact I have been so for some years — and I am confident that we shall win. But whether we shall win at the next election is a much more doubtful affair.

As the Tariff Reform League developed, his father used him as an intermediary in his home region, from which he hoped again to swing over a whole party. In February 1904 Neville was still all confidence to Matthews, writing :

It is going to come. All the younger and more open-minded men are in favour of it, and they are specially attracted by what is the most important part, viz. the Colonial preference. Retaliation is very well and indeed is, I believe, right and wise, but it is not life and death as the other thing is ; that is, for the nation — I am not thinking of the individual.

While his father fought in the wilderness and too late captured the National Union, Balfour's insistence on unifying formulas completed the disunity of his party, whose prolonged twilight ended in darkness at the election of January 1906. Neville was clear that only " our splendid Birmingham " had saved anything from the wreck.

11 February 1906 ; to A. Greenwood
The majority of our party both in and out of the House are in favour of Tariff Reform, and would gladly follow if Balfour would only lead. . . . Unfortunately there are still in the House and in the machine a good many representatives of the old Tories who would never follow my father's lead even if he were willing to give it. . . . I have been doing more speechifying than usual this time, sorely against my will.

Then two events during July 1906, his father's stroke and Austen's marriage, drew him further into the open, for he was now the only Chamberlain left at Highbury who could take the field, or act as a link between Birmingham and Austen in the shadow Cabinet.

Eight feverish, and in some ways discreditable, years followed for Great Britain, on whom fell the penalty for a generation of patchwork. Intellectually the Liberal government might be deemed the strongest of modern times ; ardently it set to work to gain time against internal upheaval and foreign menace. Yet from the election of fifty-three Labour members Balfour foretold the break-up of the Liberal party, which indeed itself accelerated the destruction of its old values by measures of state socialism, its Trades Disputes Act, and intervention in industrial conflict. For while prices rose and wages lagged, production declined, at least as compared with our rivals, and the Victorian dream of progress was broken.

Other illusions, fondly cherished, were struck by mortal disease ; as, that the social contentment taught by the Church catechism would remain in a people whose intellectuals repudiated the Church's faith ; or, that peace was the consequence of free institutions ; or, that empire could easily coexist with nationality. From the great mass of the submerged unfit, the 30 per cent medically rejected for the South African war, or found on the poverty line by social investigators, there mounted a clamour for leaders of their own, redistribution of wealth, and " a good time ". The black eagle of Germany clutched with its efficient talons at the British Empire and, having over-clouded the Continent with one wing, stretched the other over the sea. Liberalism was confronted with its own logic in the national movements of India and Egypt ; while what Gladstone had magnificently promised to Ireland, and what Redmond could not restrain, was now so far exasperated by delay as to threaten the whole kingdom's security. And many thousand pages of parliamentary debate could not muffle the sound of voices prophesying war.

To find money both for imperial defence and social reform was the purpose of the Lloyd George Budget of 1909, which marked the country's descent for five years into obstinate faction, so making impossible the aspirations of Lloyd George and others for an agreed settlement of all these dangers.

Within the Unionist opposition different elements swayed to and fro, young men and old, planners and idealists, whose contentions reached a climax in 1911 over the Parliament Act, with the resulting downfall of the " die-hards ", and the die-hard revenge in expelling Balfour from the lead. As their father's name was used as a banner, the Chamberlain brothers were hotly engaged ; Austen as a candidate for the succession, which in fact fell to Bonar Law, and Neville indirectly from the cohesion of his clan. He it was who told Austen this was " the critical point of your career as well as that of the party ", and who insisted he must succeed their father in

West Birmingham if the city was to keep its political place.

Unionist leadership was incoherent, sometimes clutching at devices like the referendum, sometimes tied to indefensible positions like the Lords' right to reject money bills, and the party was caught up in the armed resistance of Ulster. The Chamberlain family believed that the Lords ought to fight to the end for what Neville, in the jargon of the day, called " the constitutional cause ". His moral from the first election of 1910 was that, if his father had been in action, they would have won ; he brought Carson to speak at Birmingham, and if not a " die-hard " himself, sympathised with their wish for strong action.

This was especially true in matters of defence, of which there is much in a letter to Greenwood of June 1908 : " Although the government has done some good things, much of their legislation appears to me crude, undigested, and very dangerous. The Old Age Pension Bill is simply a scandalous attempt to catch votes . . . a direct discouragement of thrift, to which nevertheless the general drift of thought among the working classes is tending. . . . The other point on which I am very uneasy is defence. Although Asquith has declared his intention to maintain the two-power standard in the Navy, I have no confidence that he will hold out against the fanatics and demagogues who clamour for economy at any price. . . . The understandings with France and Russia do certainly relieve us of any fears of attack from these quarters, but the real enemy is Germany, and they are worse than useless against her. It seems to me that they may very possibly drag us into war, but we'll be mighty little help if war should come."

At Christmas he took up his cue again over the Bosnian crisis : " it has opened the eyes of some of our cranks and shown them that treaties are not to be depended on for keeping the peace, and that we have got to make ourselves too strong to be attacked ". He was taking the chair for the Navy League, to demand eight new battleships, criticising this " accursed mischievous cowardly government " ; in 1910 speaking for Lord Roberts' National Service League, " our military weakness is a temptation to our enemies to attack us through our friends " ; in 1913 presiding in the Town Hall in support of Air defence.

Pulled ever closer to the middle of the storm, though still protesting it was against his will, the consequence of family tradition, or " my own incapacity to look on and see other people mismanage things ", by this time he was almost the leading citizen of Birmingham in his own right. " Shut your eyes and hear his father," veterans were beginning to say, and that in one sense he spoke like his father is clear from the echoing cries at his election speeches of " rub it in ". But he was thinking things out in his own way. He was ready for concession on the hereditary principle, and would give Ireland provincial self-government. In social questions he argued there was " no place for Liberalism as it stands to-day . . . we are in the presence of new forces trying their wings ". Low wages were the root of all evil, but no better wage standards were possible without tariff reform, which he described as " an extension of trade unionism ".

Just before the first German war he was engaged in one important task in local politics. However good were intentions at the centre, the constituencies had never suppressed the older loyalties dividing Conservative from Liberal Unionist. Wherever Joseph Chamberlain was the temperature rose higher, and a Conservative Midland Union clashed with a Midland Liberal Unionist Association, with a chance of collision in seventy-four constituencies, while from 1903 the Tariff Reform League, working from the same office as the Liberal Unionists, cut another section across the Midlands.

In 1912, when the meaning of Unionism had to be re-stated, since a younger generation were not content with a mere negative towards Ireland, a committee was set up for fusion, with Lord Dartmouth from the Midland Union as chairman and Neville leading for the Liberal Unionists ; on his initiative it was determined to overcome the first stage by duplicating the machinery, he himself to be vice-chairman. But with the outbreak of war it was laid aside.

While his public action thus expanded, his private life had also wholly changed. In 1910 he met Miss Anne Vere Cole, daughter of Major William Cole, 3rd Dragoon Guards, of West Woodhay, Wiltshire, and Mary de Vere, of Curragh Chase, County Limerick. They married in January 1911, and set up their home at Westbourne, Edgbaston, which was their home to the end ; their two children, a son and a daughter, were born within the next three years. He had waited till he was forty-two for his marriage, the perfect happiness of which influenced him all the more for that long delay. But Westbourne was hardly established before Highbury came to an end, and soon after that the peace of Europe also. The 27th June 1914 he spent with Hoskins' work-people at New Brighton ; next day Serb assassins killed the Archduke Franz Ferdinand. On July 2 he was summoned to London, not in time to see his father conscious ; he died that night, — " I looked at my watch ", says the exact diary ; " it was eight minutes past ten ". On the 6th they drove through Birmingham streets, full of enormous silent crowds, to bury him beside the two mothers of his children.

11 July 1914 ; to A. Greenwood
> I am glad to think his trials are over. But to us it means the break up of the family life. Austen cannot afford to live at Highbury, which must be pulled down and the land developed, unless it were bought as a memorial which I suppose is very unlikely. . . . I am hoping to get to Carlsbad at the end of the month with my wife.

No such memorial was achieved, nor for that matter was Carlsbad. Ardent that the chief remembrance of his father should be in his own city, Neville pleaded for Highbury to a meeting at Mr. Balfour's house, where the idea met with a cold reception. And as war came near, for Carlsbad he substituted Harrogate, where on August 2 his diary notes, " if we fail to stand by our friends, we can never hold up our heads in Europe again ". In that mood he received Austen's account, how he with Amery and George Lloyd had spurred the party leaders to put pressure on the Cabinet, and concluded with his family fervour, rather beyond the facts, that this group alone had saved the country from " eternal disgrace ". From quiet Fountains and the Brontë country he went back to deal with Birmingham at war.

CHAPTER VI

FIRST CITIZEN OF BIRMINGHAM: 1911–1916
AGED 42–47

BEFORE his marriage he had decided on a step which he had often rejected before.

5 June 1910 ; to A. Greenwood

I rather expect to go on the City Council next autumn, for we have just got a provisional order from the L.G.B. extending our boundaries so as to make us " the second city in the Empire ", and if this is confirmed by Parliament I shouldn't like to be outside the administration.

At three stages of its legislative progress he gave evidence in favour of this extension. Always economically one region, and centralised further by the University and the Education Act of 1902, the city and its suburbs formed one area for drainage, water, light, and communication. Yet this unity was splintered between two borough councils, three urban districts, one rural district, and three county councils ; five tramway systems fought for its transport, small local authorities could not provide its migrating industries with light and power. Such arguments convinced Parliament, and in June 1911 Greater Birmingham was clothed with legal existence. Its rateable value was nearly doubled, its council expanded from 72 to 120 members, population rose to 840,000, and its area to 68 square miles.

Charged with voluntary spirit and social workers, the individualist city was wrestling with late-found remedies not merely for old evils, but for new conditions that, if unchecked, must make those evils worse. For, in contrast to the core of poverty at its centre, incessant migration and experiments such as the Cadburys' at Bournville had created an outer belt of new towns, inadequately linked to the old. Meanwhile, from Westminster there came much controversy, but little positive lead. There was the poor-law commission of 1909, which divided into a Conservative majority and a collectivist minority report ; the Town Planning Act of the same year, but also the Lloyd George land taxes which threatened to make building impossible ; national insurance, yet much democratic resistance to the element of compulsion. Disputes rang in the council over new housing, more tramways, preference for British material over the foreigner. The long strikes of that hot summer left a cold ground-swell, banners and bands of the workers still filling the Bull-Ring when the enlarged council first took their chairs.

He was elected as second of three councillors from All Saints ward, one of the 79 Conservatives and Liberal Unionists who heavily outnumbered Liberals and Labour. His address dwelt on town-planning and open spaces, the need for more technical education, and a re-development of canals ; it concluded, " I am only following out the traditions in which I have been brought up, and which it is my earnest desire to maintain ". Elsewhere, pursuing an ideal to which he clung inflexibly though with ill success, he declared that in Birmingham he would know no distinction of parties : he wished to make it " the best governed city in the Empire ". True, the " golden days " of the 'seventies had left few public services to be acquired, but all still remained to do for housing and disease.

Within three years he became an alderman, and within four Lord Mayor ; a rapid promotion, even for one of his name. That he was industrious goes without saying, his bare attendances at council and its committees numbering 145, for instance, in the civic year of 1912–13. But he showed, say surviving fellow-councillors, qualities with which the world in after days did not usually credit him, of persuasiveness and conciliation ; " He should have been a Labour man," was said on those benches. For the rest, a business city respected his business powers, and a community of marked loyalties were glad to see another Chamberlain in whom they found a likeness to Joseph in independence and purpose, and one whose blows were hard.

Well he knew the ground and its human counters, and the generations linked by the habit of public service. His uncle William Kenrick was still there to represent " the golden days ", his mother's brother George Kenrick too, in whom lived the tradition of civic education ; a third uncle and a true city father in C. G. Beale ; and a young cousin, Norman Chamberlain, who was to mark his life deeply. On the opposite seats another dynasty, in Cadburys of a third generation.

By extension the city's functions had become as universal as those of Tudor magistrates. It must house, transport, and educate nearly a million people. It owned Welsh farms and Cotswold sanatoria, inspected ice-cream, and dipped sheep ; Parliament had lately directed it to administer insurance, motor cars, shop hours, tuberculosis, and feeding of children. All this was to be done by its old manner of committees with large delegated powers, unified by General Purposes and Finance committees at the centre.

The council minutes show him stalwart on behalf of the University, assertive in taking British tenders (even higher tenders) as against German, and consistently backing his cousin Norman in the provision of open spaces. With large majorities he resisted giving a minimum wage of 30s. to all the council's workmen and the implementing of Lloyd George's measures by a rate on land values ; on the other hand, several times he voted with his party opponents against deferment of an increase in teachers' salaries or a delay in extending technical schools. Very obstinately — in particular — he fought a wholesale extension of tramways in the city centre, being the first to press for powers to experiment with motor omnibuses instead.

This campaign was directly connected with his outstanding purpose, the threefold but single problem of health, housing, and town planning. Long experience in the hospitals had convinced him that health was ruled by housing, and that housing was made up of social strands which could not be separated, wage standards and employment and transportation. Naturally, then, he was put on the new-formed town-planning committee, of which he was elected chairman, and on the public health and housing committee also.

Their powers rested on a network of legislation, from Disraeli's Public Health Act to the Town Planning Act of 1909, not to speak of Birmingham local acts, with a total effect of overlapping and conflict. Of late years one of his cousins, J. S. Nettlefold, had led a militant housing policy, in a controversy which may be reduced to an old and simple element : prevention or cure ? Given that the death-rate was 24 per thousand in the central wards but only 9 in the suburbs, and population to the acre respectively 150 and 10 ; given, again, that in the centre there was a public-house for every 170 persons and the average rent such a population could afford was 5s. a week, would you cure this gathering by poultices, or prevent it spreading by the knife ? would you pull down slums or build houses ? would you concentrate on earnings, environment, or health ?

Hitherto the Birmingham policy had been one of piecemeal measures, the housing committee and an active medical officer taking the line that bad houses must be reconditioned until better houses were built. Like most reformers of that time, they set their face against municipal building, though even against their milder reconditioning method owners of property were up in revolt. But

Nettlefold and his school had also taken a larger view, visits to the Continent and contacts with other cities influencing the ideas which took shape in the Town Planning Act of 1909.

Chamberlain took town planning as the first condition of a good re-housing policy. His committee's minutes abound in proof of purpose and performance ; he had able colleagues (including George Cadbury the younger), with whom he systematically completed one task after another. This was constructive work, in which Birmingham became a model for the whole country, and valuable political training, for he had to negotiate with property owners, placate civic departments, and carry the matured schemes through a critical council.

What they accomplished was solid. Two schemes became law before the end of 1913 — 2300 acres in Harborne and the south-west, and 1500 acres in East Birmingham ; a year later, a third was well under way for Yardley and Stechford, and a fourth in its early stages, covering 8400 acres in South Birmingham. This scale of operations grew progressively greater, for the first scheme cost over £100,000, the third opened up vistas of regionalism by taking in parts of Warwickshire, and involved creating or remodelling a hundred streets.

A strong chairman and a good committee form a unit, yet if we compare his public utterances with his committee's performance, we collect the march of his thought. He hoped, he said on election as Lord Mayor, to forward " that noble and fascinating ideal, the transference of the working classes from their hideous and depressing surroundings ". Town planning must be the framework within which they could restore a natural process of building and betterment ; they must recall to life the outward migration to the suburbs, but .ensure the community's control through municipal estates, which would give the city the benefits of improvement. Yet if suburban development was the master key, they must not lose opportunities of preparing reconstruction at the centre. He had not held the chairmanship a month before his committee passed a resolution far beyond their present legal powers, " that with the view of securing a comprehensive planning of the whole area of the extended city and the adoption of a consistent policy with regard to the preservation of open spaces, ring roads, radial roads, and the division of districts into residential, business, and factory areas, the city surveyor be requested to prepare forthwith an outline town-plan for the entire city ".

Three years later, this had produced the germs of an ideal, now in part fulfilled, of a " city centre ", crowned by its most vital buildings and dearest memorials, and the heart of its main arteries. Town planning, the zoning for instance of the South Birmingham scheme to only twelve houses an acre, involved a policy for housing, and however much his temperament leaned to radical prevention, he knew something immediate must be done for the disease. In 1913 a committee was set up to enquire into housing in the poorest parts of the city and, as chairman, he drafted its interim report of October 1914.

Its point of departure was characteristic : " A large proportion of the poor in Birmingham are living under conditions of housing detrimental both to their health and morals " ; there was bad structure, but also bad human nature, owners blind to " their moral obligations ", and tenants indifferent (quoting the chief housing officer) " to the laws of God or man ". The rates must make good the first preliminary of decent sanitation. But to tear down 50,000 bad houses at the centre would be financially impossible, to destroy some only would be " playing with the subject ", to rebuild *en masse* in industrial areas would be retrograde. Only in the suburbs could life be made better with air and gardens, where town planning could prevent the making of new slums. " In the last resort, if private enterprise failed, the corporation must step in ", but their primary recommendation was not for municipal building but for municipal ownership of housing estates. Once natural migration was restored, the centre could be dealt with by planned stages. The council accepted his report, together with a town plan for the whole built-up area, but with the war all building ceased for four years, by which time Alderman Chamberlain's ideas had moved far forward.

From such activity sprang his election as Lord Mayor in 1915, an office which, like most posts in life, depends on what a man makes of it. Enough then merely to name what qualities in him were publicly commended — the conciliatory gifts which had driven through town planning, the vision of his housing report and waterways schemes, the balance evenly held between masters and men ; " a touch of the autocrat ", said the city press, but " a practical idealist ". What he himself was thinking reveals satisfaction at a path clearly marked out, in line with the family tradition.

20 November 1915 ; to Beatrice Chamberlain
    curious that you should be reminded of father by my speaking. Of course many other people say so. . . . When I began speaking, my

natural faculty for imitation led me to copy his ways, and at times I was conscious of inflections, unintentional on my part, which were a very close imitation. But gradually as my recollection became fainter and I got more practice, the differences came, and now I don't realise that there is any resemblance left. If there is any, therefore, I think it must be hereditary, and though I haven't his power of imagination or his grasp or his originality, I think I do look at things somewhat in the same way as he did.

Birmingham's normal life was in suspense. Contested elections ceased, the University was a military hospital, the Gas Department was making explosives. Recruiting and munitions extinguished its smaller industries and flooded it with new inhabitants ; rents, wages, drinking, and bereavement vexed and strained this swollen community. Belgian refugees lodged in his coach-house were a first sign of innumerable war causes in which the Lord Mayor must give a lead.

For two years his most severe private criticism was showered on the Asquith régime, which he condemned because it did not do justice to the national spirit.

Diary, 16 June 1915
the country . . . is ready for a lead, when it can get one, in the direction of compulsory service in factories coupled with limitation of employers' profits. . . . I have been appointed a member of the Central Control Board (Liquor traffic) to control liquor in munitions and transport areas. It is but one aspect of the great labour problem. The frantic competition among employers for labour has led to extravagant wages, relaxation of discipline, and bad timekeeping . . . we are starving our army for shells, and yet the great works are only putting out ¾ of their possible.

By September he was arguing both in public and private that only national service could get the best out of everyone, and determine the just principles of exemption, by co-operation between employers and trade unions.

3 June 1915 ; to Mrs. Chamberlain
The more I think over it, and the more I hear and see of the attitude of the men in the factories, the more certain I feel that National service is the only solution of the present situation, which is rapidly becoming intolerable. It must, however, be accompanied by either a surtax on, or a limitation of profits for all, because workmen will never consent to restrictions which would have the effect of putting

money into their employers' pockets. Personally I hate the idea of making profits out of the war when so many are giving their lives and limbs, and I hope and pray that the new government will have the courage and the imagination to deal with the situation promptly and properly.

War set every tone of his mayoralty. He initiated a reduction of his salary by half, took pains to give a civic welcome to men who won distinctions for valour ; his letters embrace the whole welfare of the city battalions. Declaring he could not " slobber " over recruits who came forward tardily, as chairman of the local tribunal he was thought just, but emphatic, in putting the national need foremost ; finding, for instance, no ground for exempting one petitioner who pleaded as his essential industry the export of Jews' harps to the Solomon Islands. Though he resigned from the Liquor Board because he would not be responsible for decisions taken in his often enforced absence, its problems never left his mind, and he was indignant that more was not done to stop drinking among women ; writing " I'll plague those brewers yet ", just as he left office.

On Christmas Day 1915, after spending six hours in the hospitals, he set down the chief events of his first six weeks, — a specimen of local administration that this once should be given.

I have got an arrangement for the Electric Supply committee with the M. of Munitions, by which the latter pay for an extension of the plant. Under way is a joint Coal-buying and transport committee for Gas and Electric supply. Also a joint committee on roads and bus routes between the Watch, Tram, and P.W. committees. I have averted a labour crisis by ascertaining the lowest advance that would satisfy the men's leaders, and getting the labour committee to agree to it. This carries a settlement till the end of the war, and we were in no position to fight, so I attach much importance to the settlement. I have got under way a scheme to induce the working classes to save, and I have their leaders working with me in this matter. I have made an arrangement with the coal merchants to limit prices of household coal.

Meantime he so gave the lead to heal the city's wounds, and to make it efficient or war, that through these local channels he reached national politics. With an eye on French examples, he put all his influence behind the cause of infant welfare, set up a committee to explore the price of milk and the possibility of municipal distribution, and stored coal to be sold at cost price to the poor.

But his policy never strayed far from worldly sense ; as an instance of which we take his reasons for referring wage increases for the corporation's employees to Board of Trade arbitration. " By this course we avoid any unpleasantness with manufacturers . . . we do not ourselves tear up our scrap of paper by which the men agreed that their last advance should be a settlement till the end of the war, we prevent the men coming and asking for another rise in a few months' time, and we avoid any ill feeling towards us on the part either of the men or the rate-payers."

One of his convictions must receive illustration here, to wit, that a good society must meet human beings' average desires ; the laws, he would have agreed with Burke, " go but a little way ". Of this principle of voluntary service a characteristic example in Birmingham had been the unemployment relief funds set up by his father, which were amalgamated as the City Aid Society and then, once more, with the outbreak of war, into the Citizens' Society. Late in 1916 a group of social organisations put to him one particular aspect of welfare : the influx of war workers, the dreariness and danger of their life, their moral claim on the city. He therefore inaugurated a Civic Recreation League, to link together all such bodies, youth movements especially, which would lighten the workers' leisure, and provide every activity from garden clubs to open-air music.

Music was the strongest passion of his inner life ; its function, he said once in the town hall, " had always been to purify, encourage, and comfort " ; and now his office gave him a great opportunity. The musical history of the city began in the eighteenth century with the triennial festivals, but its musicians' feuds were equally venerable, and since the 'nineties one organisation had followed another, performed its programme, exhausted both its temper and its funds. On the eve of the war Beecham was brought in to keep things together, which was hardly the rôle most congenial to his genius ; Bantock and Ernest Newman on the spot were also actively concerned, but only the Lord Mayor brought about something that would endure.

24 March 1916 ; to Beatrice

A. and I went to a concert in the town hall, and in the interval I addressed the multitude on the future of orchestral music in Birmingham. . . . I dropped a little bombshell by suggesting that we should have a first-class local orchestra, and contribute to its support out of the rates.

All through the next few years he was bidding the new organisation stabilise their finance by audacity, insisting that only by large concert halls and cheap seats could music be made at once paying and democratic, and in 1919 an annual grant from the rates made possible the city orchestra. But his hopes ranged further, — to a new school of music, an opera-house, " every club and every big works should have its own orchestra and glee society ".

In several measures essential to war he outstripped the government and created opinion. Greater Birmingham had considerable green spaces, and he set women to work on the land. On the burning question of war pensions he acted in concert with other large cities, seconding a resolution at their conference of June 1916 that pensions should be defrayed from taxation, and given as a right ; on a deputation to the Exchequer he took the lead in questioning, and was severe in comment.

30 July 1916

> held the first meeting of the Pensions committee, and suggested that they should refuse to act until McKenna produced his new scale. . . . Everyone agrees that the pensions must be adequate, — the only question is, shall they be paid for out of taxation, or voluntarily ? But as no one objects to taxation for this purpose, why on earth doesn't he tax ?

Sometimes the initiative was all his own. On the last day of January 1916 he came home by a late train, to find Birmingham having its first air raid ; " stopped by excited policemen, who told us to go home at once, which was what we were trying to do ". He found public exasperation, damaging effects on munition-making, defences chaotic. There were only four guns, " each in close proximity to a munition works. They have no proper search-lights and no inter-communicating telephones. Their observers have to signal to them with red lamps ! Their crews have never fired a shot." Three days later he submitted a scheme to the Home Secretary and other " good, wise, and eminent " men ; containing, in brief, all that are now considered the first elements of air-raid precaution, — a zone of observation, preliminary warning, simultaneous signal, and extinction of lights.

The last of these war questions left a unique memorial in the Birmingham municipal bank, which now has some £20 millions on deposit from nearly half a million citizens. To bring it to birth called out all his tenacity, nor shall we easily find a more compact example of his method and ideas. At the end of 1915 the government's discussion of war savings was incessant but undecided, high wages were being wasted, and in Birmingham the Post Office savings banks never appealed to working men. The Lord Mayor's first maxim was to keep in step with Labour ; bankers, government departments, and employers could be brought later into line.

28 November 1915

> I don't believe in McKenna's bonds . . . he is beginning at the wrong end . . . the real problem is how to make a man save who hasn't saved before. . . . My idea generally is to start a municipal savings association. The town would guarantee the interest . . . to lend the scheme the prestige and weight of the local authorities . . . you will never do any good unless you save at the source.

His native instinct to go ahead, without tarrying for any, was confirmed when the government abandoned any idea either of compulsion or of wage deductions. But one lion after another started up in his path. The Treasury vetoed his first draft, as bringing the city into competition with the Exchequer. In March he argued his case two hours with the Savings Advisory Committee, who " began by heckling me and finished up by heckling each other ". By April he had worn them down, and the Local Government Board too, and extracted a promise of legislation, but within a week Mr. Montagu retracted. Whereupon, in direct interviews and comments to the press, the Lord Mayor wielded a bigger stick ; " it would be most unfortunate if the banks could be represented in public as opposing a great patriotic movement for purely selfish reasons ", — " vexatious opposition " rang in Birmingham, " the corporation's scheme was being blocked by the corporation's bankers". But the heaviest blow came in an adverse vote from trade union secretaries, who represented the men's inveterate suspicion against employers being made aware of their savings.

14 May 1916

> I'm beat, and the Savings bank is dead. The selfishness of the banks and the apathy of the Treasury together make an impenetrable entanglement, but what makes it impossible to carry on the fighting is that I have been taken in the rear.

He refused to accept defeat ; worked through Austen, canvassed Labour leaders and friendly societies, and in June the exhausted Treasury capitulated.

Yet the Act of 1916 bore on its face the scars of conflict. Only boroughs with a population of a quarter of a million could establish

Elliott and Fry

LORD MAYOR OF BIRMINGHAM, 1915

such banks, depositors might only invest through an employer, it was to be wound up within three months of the end of the war. He resolved, however, to use this narrow front for a new advance. While he launched a campaign of 1000 meetings, he declared, " if it is really shown to meet a need, not all the bankers in Lombard St. will prevent its becoming a permanent part of the municipal undertaking ". As to this, time would show ; at present the Municipal Bank, beginning a puny life in a basement office, was pledged to pay interest of 3½ per cent on deposits which in the next three years never rose above £600,000.

On national politics his views were still full of loyalty to Austen — reflecting also a good deal of the average citizen of 1916.

3 December 1916
when you think of manpower, food production and distribution, submarine warfare, pensions, and Ireland, the list of muddles is intolerable.

And when the storm broke and Asquith disappeared, though he predicted Lloyd George would be " a very dangerous Prime Minister ", his immediate comment was " any change must be for the better ".

This year worked in him a change of outlook which, had men (himself included) been other than they were, or if others had changed in equal degree, might have altered party history. To the Church of the Messiah he spoke of the revolution in the making, " State Socialism, the sinking of the old party divisions, the new position of women " ; to the adult school, how he would support extension of a minimum wage ; again, of control of the liquor trade and closer alliance with Russia. His best ally over the Bank had been an eloquent Labour councillor, Eldred Hallas ; he was discussing relations of capital and labour with all sorts of men from General Booth to Arthur Steel Maitland, and wrote, " the Midlands are the most likely part of the country for experiments to start in, and the moment may come when there will be work for me to do in smoothing the way ".

He said this after making a speech, welcoming the Trade Union Congress to the city, which first made the country aware of him. Could they not, he asked, take into peace the unity achieved in war ? He believed tariffs indispensable but not in their miracle-working power, and victory would go to the nation which produced the largest output at the lowest cost. Employers had a right to expect harder work, stable wage conditions, and warning before

D

strikes ; workers should have a greater share of the wealth they produced, and some admission to control of management.

Human relations with Labour leaders and unaccustomed bouquets from the Radical press warmed his sense of success ; his re-election as Lord Mayor was settled.

Diary, 4 June 1916

> I think my position has been still further strengthened in the town . . .
> it is generally recognised that a new atmosphere of initiative and energy
> has been imported into the administration.

In November, on re-election, he dwelt on the power of local authorities if they stood together, the war's demonstration that Englishmen of all ranks were alike in character, the duty therefore of making equal opportunities. But in December Lloyd George formed his government, in which Austen continued as Secretary of State for India ; on the 19th, after a conference on a loan for Birmingham, Neville was ensconced in his homeward-bound train, from which he was extracted and taken to the Prime Minister, who offered him the directorship of a new department of National Service. He was given only ten minutes to decide, for the Prime Minister wished to tell Parliament that night both of the new creation and the name of its chief.

24 December

> I said several damns and thought for 2 minutes, and then I sent Austen
> to say yes. . . . I do feel so badly about all the men who have leant
> on me so much . . . it is impossible for anyone to take quite the same
> position that I had. . . . It is an appalling responsibility. If it was
> only my own career that was at stake I wouldn't care a rap, but the
> outcome of the war may depend on what I do.

Confidence, said the great Chatham, is a plant of slow growth in an aged bosom, and in Neville, at all ages, it was slow but, once grown, very assured. It was not the mind which would take easily to the adjustments, half measures, and bargainings called for by the urgencies of war.

BOOK II: 1917-1931

CHAPTER VII

MINISTER OF NATIONAL SERVICE: *1917*
AGED 47–48

I reflect that if everything was plain sailing, there would be
no credit in getting to port.

N. C., *October* 1916

This year, terrible in British history, was for Neville Chamberlain
one of bleak trial, which left enduring effects ; as must be so, when
a man is young enough to learn but too old to forget.   In a political
episode in which there is much for reflection, but little to edify, he
reached two determined conclusions, that is, to enter Parliament
but never to serve with Lloyd George again.

Men, give us more men, was the cry of the war machines, which
after two years had produced no military decision.   France, bled
white at Verdun, was believed to be incapable of another offensive.
Russia was eliminated by revolution.   Italy was gripped fast.
Roumania, entering the war late in her huckstering way, had
been swiftly destroyed.   Salonica showed no Allied enterprise,
though abundant Allied faction.   Mesopotamia seemed lost, Egypt
threatened.   As for Great Britain, since the Somme fighting had
annihilated the flower of Kitchener's armies, the forces in France
would need 100,000 men in January to maintain establishment,
and 450,000 by the end of March ; moreover, yet more men must
be found for every stage of munition-making.

Unprepared by its tradition for what earlier generations had
denounced as a " land war ", this country once more repeated, as
in 1793 or 1854, the exposure of an improvised military system.
True, Kitchener had stamped his foot and three million volunteers
sprang from the soil, Lloyd George had swept the best technical
skill and the physical flower of the remaining men into munitions.
But at the price of anomalies and injustice, which came home to
every fireside and crippled our struggle to survive.   Fearing civil
disturbance, the Asquith Cabinets gave no lead to the country's
spirit but legislated piecemeal, so that their Military Service and
Munitions Acts insinuated compulsion in an indirect and odious form.

Since they abandoned decision to a scramble between government departments, recruiting officers, and tribunals, by the autumn of 1916 one and a half million men of military age had been " badged " — protected, that is to say, from military service — mostly by the Ministry of Munitions, while another million had received temporary exemption at the hands of tribunals, which operated on varying principles and at various levels of patriotism. Evidence of the consequent demoralisation is on record in dark characters ; of " attestations " selling for £15, older married men being taken while boys of eighteen rushed into munitions, or hospitals " combed " to return wounded again to the firing line.

Cautiously the politicians explored this nettle-bed, but retreated before any clump harsh enough to sting. In September a man-power board, under Austen's chairmanship, recommended a " de-badging " of men under twenty-six, with steps to prevent the creation of new exemptions. But the Labour world, fearful of losing hard-won liberties, resented the least breath of industrial conscription, above all any compulsion to work for private employers, even though profits were now State-controlled. Serious strikes were consequently followed in November by the Trade Card agreement, which empowered selected unions to confer exemption on members enrolled as Munition volunteers. If even for industry the result was not impressive, to the problem of finding fighting men this brought nothing but a new obstruction. Yet a week before Asquith fell his Cabinet agreed that all men up to fifty-five should be liable to some form of national service, — a principle for which Chamberlain, we have seen, had long been eager.

Lloyd George's contribution to man-power in December was to create two new ministries, of Labour and National Service, and to throw overboard the late Cabinet's decision. Though declaring compulsion must be held in reserve, he made an appeal for volunteers ; a scheme for industry, in short, corresponding to the Derby Scheme for the army, which had so signally failed.

Into this chaos the Lord Mayor of Birmingham was thrown, and on personal grounds was widely welcomed. Actually the choice was due to Austen who, when Edwin Montagu not unwisely declined, pressed his brother's name on Curzon and Milner, the last of whom held a high opinion of him.

18 December 1916 ; from Milner

I have long felt a growing esteem for your strength and independence of character, and I believe we are in close sympathy, not only about

Imperial but about Home questions. Your recent speech to the Trades Unions congress confirmed me in that conviction.

So men spoke well of him ; but really it was the Bahamas quest over again, though this time with all to make from soil occupied by powerful rivals. He failed. And in 1934, in his *War Memoirs*, Lloyd George gave his version of the reasons. The task, he admitted, called for " a great breadth and boldness of conception, a remorseless energy and thoroughness of execution, and for the exercise of supreme tact ", indeed, for " a man of exceptional gifts ". But " Mr. Neville Chamberlain is a man of rigid competency ", of a type " lost in an emergency or in creative tasks at any time ", having, too, a " vein of self-sufficient obstinacy ". Only after he retired " the Ministry worked smoothly and efficiently ".

It was hardly as simple as that. Whatever his responsibility, it was shared with others, nor was the department when reorganised under Auckland Geddes free from the difficulties to which Neville succumbed. Like all the Muses, Clio is reckoned of the female sex, yet need not make the mistake of attacking persons when she should be explaining things.

After three interviews with the Prime Minister the Director-General remained ignorant of his powers. " I have never had even a scrap of paper appointing me ", was his reflection on Christmas Day, " or giving me any idea of where my duties begin and end. I don't know whether I have Ireland or Scotland as well as England. I don't know whether I have Munition volunteers. I believe I am to have a salary, but I don't know what." He was reassured, however, by Austen, — " I shall get any powers I want from the War Committee when I ask for them ".

The infant department was not made at home in the Whitehall family circle, the senior members of which refused with one accord to release some civil servants on whom he had his eye. That local stage must be brought to mind. At the War Office, Lord Derby and the Adjutant-General, Macready ; Auckland Geddes, their director of recruiting, at the National Liberal Club ; in Queen Anne's Mansions, the employment section of the Ministry of Labour, over which the titular chief was one of Lloyd George's Labour colleagues, John Hodge. Firmly entrenched, with two years' experience, stood Admiralty and Munitions. High in the firmament shone the stars of Milner and Arthur Henderson, detailed to represent the War Cabinet, while very far below glimmered the St. Ermins Hotel, from which furniture was being removed to make room for National Service. Such were the protagonists in this fight for man-power, engaged in the fog which is called trial by error.

The Prime Minister was insistent on immediate results and extreme publicity. Rightly he argued the department must have a good chief of staff, and there Chamberlain made a capital mistake in not insisting on being given a civil servant of eminence. But Lloyd George had instantly registered a bad impression, — " the wrong-shaped head ", he murmured in an aside at their first interview, — and pressed on him men of his own administrative school : a first could only temporarily be spared, a second was found unsuitable, a third did not welcome the project. Whereupon he set off with the ex-town clerk of Birmingham, who with a sprinkling of other Birmingham men made the nucleus of his growing staff. By mid-January two more serious mistakes were committed. The Director was not to have a seat in Parliament, and the Cabinet's original intention, that he should control military recruiting also, was abandoned. Already he felt that St. Ermins stood on volcanic ground.

21 January 1917

> I was convinced on Monday night that I shouldn't last much longer . . . the danger seems to have passed for the present. . . . I think I may say that at present I am on excellent terms with all the Departments.

This was a delusion. Yet we are to see that he advocated every major step in man-power policy which the course of the war proved to be vital.[1]

His first report of January 13 went direct to the point, " that the greatest and most urgent requirement is to provide for the army men who are fit for general service ". As 450,000 were needed by the end of March, he recommended cancelling all exemptions (including the Trade Card agreement) issued to men of twenty-two years or under ; though with due regard to cases reckoned indispensable by Munitions, to the army using skilled men *as* skilled men, and to exceptional hardship. But the War Cabinet, though avowedly accepting his principle, excluded munitions, mines, engineering, and every source of the best manhood.

On February 3 he returned to the charge : " I consider it my

---

[1] Side-lights from different angles on this thorny question may be found in Field-Marshal Sir William Robertson's *Soldiers and Statesmen* ; Caldwell, *Sir Henry Wilson* ; and Repington, *The First World War*.

duty to point out that if men are to be obtained in time to be trained
. . . this can only be done by prompt and drastic measures. I believe
that if these measures were universal in character they would have
a very much better chance of acceptance than any half-hearted
attempts to deal with a critical situation, and so far at any rate as
munitions works are concerned, I am convinced that the removal
of men of military age and fitness would not dislocate the output,
provided that a little time were given for adaptation to new conditions." He pressed for an Act cancelling exemptions up to the
age of thirty-one, and the progressive calling-up of groups by age.
From this first position he never budged, and the root reason of his
failure lay in the Cabinet's refusal.

22 December 1917

I cannot help speculating as to what would have been the effect on
the war if the Govt. had adopted my suggestions of January and
February last. We should have had some hundreds of thousands more
men in the field. What would Haig have done with them ? Would
he have been able to win Ostend and Zeebrugge ?

While the Prime Minister vowed he would not send more men
to be killed in more Passchendaeles, and Addison thought that
National Service should be scrapped, the basic facts did not change.
In March a Cabinet committee under Rhondda urged that 250,000
men be released from essential industries, of whom hardly 4000 were
obtained by the middle of June. Though the Trade Card agreement was cancelled, with the result of more strikes, and though
" protected occupations " were henceforth scheduled in a more
scientific order, nothing made the departments disgorge. The severe
testimony of the chief of the general staff, Sir William Robertson,
with whom Lloyd George later parted, can be reinforced by that
of the soldier on whom Lloyd George smiled, Henry Wilson, who
in July was writing : " all this is most scandalous work. The
government is afraid to comb out, and afraid of the north of
England, and terrified at Ireland, and so they are losing 1,000,000
men."

This was a conflict of policy, but the Prime Minister had also
instilled in Chamberlain an abiding sense of injury. Very quickly
declaring his disappointment that hundreds of meetings had not
been arranged to boom the industrial army, he suggested the name
of a journalist as second-in-command, Kennedy Jones, one interview with whom convinced Neville that more was at stake than
publicity. Nearly three years later he harked back to it in a con-

versation with Bonar Law : " I could not forget nor forgive L. G.'s treatment of me in deliberately concealing from me K. J.'s conditions when he tried to get me to accept him. . . . What I could not stand was the attempt to push me into a trap, an attempt actually continued in face of K. J.'s frank admission that he would only come on condition that he ran the show."

A patriotic but mystified country watched the Director-General's progress. He dashed to make speeches, with success, from Bristol to Merseyside and Falkirk. His net was flung over the professions, doctors, dentists, and clergy, which last brought conferences with the archbishops and a note, " it does make me smile when I think how I used to hate the church ". He set up a strong Labour advisory committee, hoped he had reached compromise with the Labour Exchanges, and got the Ministry of Munitions to issue a list of restricted occupations, in which future engagement of male labour would become almost impossible. But his department drew many batteries and snipers. Sections of the press visited upon him the feud of Northcliffe with Lloyd George, and the disgust of those who wished for compulsion all round. The loyalty of his parliamentary secretary Stephen Walsh did not undo the initial mistake that he himself was not in the Commons, where his powers were debated with asperity. A mingled opposition ranged over " the *ipse dixit* of this unknown man ", autocracy, industrial conscription, and the wrongs of Ireland. He felt the undergrowth choking his steps, so that by March he augured " in the long run I shall probably get pulled down ".

It is in fact now apparent that, personalities apart, he was sinking daily deeper in a slough for which he was not initially responsible. To a first fault he found himself committed in advance by the form of the Prime Minister's appeal which cried for volunteers, not for specific openings but indiscriminately, for any and every work of national importance ; all this without any survey of manpower or any guarantee of a vacuum. So with burning eloquence Lloyd George pointed this crusade of children to the holy city, but of the 400,000 who enrolled less than 20,000 male volunteers were placed, at a cost of about £10 a head. The press, teeming with cases of small businesses closing down or of men who threw up their old work but found nothing provided instead, angrily held up St. Ermins as a " palace of make-believe ".

What brought about this administrative collapse ? His instructions being to devise voluntary machinery, he depended on local authorities to popularise the appeal, on Labour Exchanges to enrol and allocate volunteers, and on government departments to release men for the army and create the vacancies. On paper his approved powers, though rather full of the blessed vagueness of " co-operation ", emphatically gave him the last word, declaring that in the event of conflict " the ultimate responsibility for the allocation . . . rests with him, and it follows that his final decision . . . must govern the action of the department ".

Alas for the rosy picture and the drab truth ! Munitions warned him off, the Admiralty kept tight hold of dockyard workers, some branches of the War Office (which rarely speaks with one voice) were reckoned hostile. But the main front of this Whitehall war lay at the Ministry of Labour.

With some qualms, but determined to do his best, he had accepted a War Cabinet decision that the Exchanges should remain under the Minister of Labour, who, however, would put them " at his disposal "

15 February 1917

The Labour Exchanges are *very* bad, and the worst of it is they don't realise it. But it would have been folly to set up new machinery to do what clearly should be their work.

Now the Exchanges were then but seven years old, and covered only seven principal trades, and to many unions and employers they were distasteful. But this was less vital than a very real administrative crux. Who was to control " substitution ", the placing of labour to replace men taken from essential industries for the army ? — the Exchanges, with their experienced local machinery, or National Service, on whom was laid the ultimate responsibility ? And this original knot was pulled tighter by urgent facts. Not only was his general appeal evaporating in disappointment, but some demands, such as that for farm labour, must be met at once. Could he hope to meet them through the Exchanges, which by the middle of March had placed less than 400 volunteers ? Many arguments made him turn to an alternative. He believed in the power of local authorities : he knew the trade union world and was on excellent terms with his Labour committee — which included Thomas, O'Grady, Tom Shaw, and David Gilmour — from whom he heard that the Exchanges' unpopularity would doom substitution. He thus proposed, with the support of the Rhondda committee, to enlist men through joint bodies of employers and employed in the non-essential trades.

For weeks over-pressed Cabinet ministers probed this adminis-

D*

trative sore. Milner described himself as "walking round the St. Ermins jungle, trying to see a way through ". Arthur Henderson produced a cloudy compromise, yet agreed that Neville's notion of trade committees seemed "the most likely to provide a solution ". In April he got his way; "substitution officers" transferred from the War Office, together with trade committees, set up his alternative machine for industrial recruitment.

But though his new staff gradually covered the country and he was able to place 100,000 workers (largely soldiers temporarily released) to get in that vital year's harvest, the fundamental obstacles remained. In June he pictured himself as "fighting and scrapping with the other departments, in the hope of gradually acquiring the powers that ought to have been handed over to me at first ". The Ministry of Labour was in the forefront of the battle, its curiously violent minutes arguing that "a packed Labour committee" was inciting trade union opinion, and that the restricted occupations order was tyrannous.

At this point two ministers appointed by Lloyd George may be called to testify. The first is Cecil Beck, whom he named, without a word to Chamberlain, as Walsh's successor as Parliamentary Secretary, and who reported that the bottle-neck was due to two prime causes : the infinitesimal release of men of military age by the departments, and the prior powers of the Labour Exchanges. In August Neville's successor, Auckland Geddes, declared " there had been no real loan of the Labour Exchanges, and that as a result there was a duplication of machinery which was proving fatal ". That, indeed, was the conclusion to which all sides were steadily but disputedly drawing nearer, that one single authority must be given control of man-power. Either National Service or Labour must relinquish direct handling of labour supply, and historically it has become clear which was bound to prevail. For no government in the midst of a desperate war would replace a running concern by a new one.

Unification, then, but around which nucleus ? Milner and the heads of the women's branch were discussing a remodelled Ministry of Labour, with " humanised " Exchanges ; his Labour committee, on the other hand, pressed on the Prime Minister that National Service had the workers' confidence. Heavy strikes and resistance to dilution weighed heavily with Lloyd George who, whatever else were decided, had now, we can hardly doubt, resolved that Chamberlain must go.

In this view he was no doubt fortified by the Director's report of June, which recalled his first recommendations of the " clean cut ", the departments' failure to release fighting men, the obstacles to his task of " controlling and regulating " man-power. To call up men by age-groups would be more difficult now, amid Labour tension and war weariness. " Nevertheless, I wish to repeat my conviction that the policy which I have twice submitted to the Cabinet is the only one which will quickly and certainly provide the men required for the army, and that, further, it is one which will commend itself to the majority of the people in this country as, on the whole, the fairest all round." It would set up a flow of substitution, directed by his local committees ; failing which, all enthusiasm would fade away. " Nor in that case can I see any justification for the continued existence of this department."

1 July

Now I am in a position that reminds me of the Bahamas when the plants didn't grow. With all the Departments against me and a chief who won't help, I see no chance of success, and if so it would be folly to let slip an opportunity of getting out on a principle.

The streams were rising now. On July 18 Derby and Rhondda, Hayes Fisher and Walter Long, signed a minute supporting his proposals ; next day he proffered his resignation, unless his report (now a month old) received an immediate reply. Lloyd George asked him to wait till the Cabinet had considered a memorandum being prepared by General Geddes, who believed " that the only rational basis for recruiting is an occupation and not an age basis ". Uneasily, with a sense he was being manœuvred into a position from which a public defensive would be impossible, he acquiesced.

On the 24th without warning, at least to Milner, the kindly figure of Derby sent up the flare which heralded a final assault. Nothing had embittered public feeling more than the War Office methods of medical examination, and a select committee of the Commons were coming to decide that it must be given to civilian hands. In giving evidence Derby suggested a more sweeping scheme for civilian control of recruiting in all its aspects. The Adjutant-General, he said, and General Geddes favoured this solution, the Prime Minister was agreed in principle.

As the public reasons given for resignations are often not the real ones, it is unnecessary to dwell on Chamberlain's letter of July 27, putting forward some compromise but asking for more Cabinet support. His Women's Section had already been trans-

ferred to Labour, while Board of Agriculture and War Office re-
occupied the field of labour for the land. On August 7 he saw
Milner, who " advised me strongly to get out of it ". Next day he
sent in his resignation. His covering letter declared that " even
if the proposals of the Director of Recruiting were adopted, they
would not produce in any reasonable time that demand for substitutes which my Trade committees have been organised to supply ".
Nor could he accept the suggestion that military recruiting should
be made over to National Service. " So huge a machine could
not be operated except by those who are intimately acquainted
with its working, and the transaction will resolve itself into nothing
more than the erection of one branch of the War Office into a
separate Department." Finally, " for the success of any scheme of
recruiting, it is essential that the head of the department should
have the full support of the Cabinet, especially in his dealings with
other labour-using or labour-supplying departments. My past
experience does not encourage me to hope that I should enjoy
this support, and accordingly I now place my resignation in your
hands."

Such public exchanges are less revealing than his contemporary
note of the parting interview :

Thursday, 9 August 1917

. . . The Cabinet then broke up and I remained behind. Ll. G. had
been reading my letter during the discussion and now enquired of
Hankey what had been the decision of the Cabinet on my Tenth
Report, to which Hankey replied that no decision had been come to,
as it had been " muddled up " by the recruiting question. Hankey
then left, and Ll. G. began saying he was sorry to receive my resignation, but as I could not accept the Cabinet's decision on recruiting, he
supposed it was no use asking me to reconsider it. He explained the
delay by saying that the Cabinet had been very busy with other
important questions, & went on to remark that my Report asked them
to reverse a decision to which they had come after long & careful
deliberation. The Report centred upon the proposal to recruit by
ages, whereas the D/R, contrary as he admitted to the whole former
policy of his department, now considered that recruiting must proceed
by occupation. I replied that the reasons for that course might or
might not be sound but that if adopted it cut the ground from under
the feet of National Service, which was based on the assumption that
the men would be taken from munitions. He made no direct answer
to this but began reverting to a remark he had made on a former
occasion, that Dr. Addison had said that it was too soon to say that the
men would not come out under the Rhondda proposals. I reminded

him that Addison himself had estimated that not more than 30,000 men would be obtained in place of the 124,000 contemplated by those proposals & that only a few of those would require substitutes. He then turned to my complaint that the Cabinet had not supported me, saying that I had had the same support as other Depts. All Depts. fought, they always had & always would. He himself had had to fight at the munitions. I remarked that the circumstances were very different. The whole *raison d'être* of my Dept. was that it was to control labour as between Depts. & that I could not do that if Depts. appealed against me to the Cabinet, & the Cabinet did not support me. I told him about the agricultural dispute which he had not heard of before, and rather warmly I protested that, although I did not wish to enter on a controversy, I could not leave him under any misapprehension as to the fact that I had a grievance. He then said that he must say what he had not intended to, viz. that all my troubles arose from my not having followed his advice in taking a Chief of the Staff. He had offered me three, Stevenson, Geddes, and Kennedy Jones, and I had refused them all. I declined to go over this old ground again, but assured him that I did not wish to embarrass the Govt. by publishing my grievances, only to make my position clear to him. He replied that he recognised the patriotism of my motives all through.

After which he gave Neville leave to publish his letter, together with his own reply. From this last we need only note a protestation against the charge of lack of support, and a statement that Chamberlain had recommended calling up age-groups " without reference to their occupations ". But this was far-fetched. From his first report to his last comment on Geddes' proposals, he contemplated putting on the military the duty of leaving indispensable men in civil occupation.

So General Geddes became a civilian and reached a concordat with the Ministry of Labour. Compared with his predecessor's, his powers were substantial. He was made judge of priorities and could set the pace in substitution, he had a seat in the Commons and the Cabinet.

Even so, the necessary logic of government harshly strained this transaction. Very soon, like Neville's echo, we hear Sir Auckland Geddes complaining that ten departments were going their own way; by the next spring the concordat was breaking down, as formulas must which try to separate the inseparable. But these rivalries are now in their tomb, the epitaph on which was engraved in 1939 " Ministry of Labour and National Service ".

There was after all a war with Germany too, and it is to the judicial pages of the official historian of man-power that we must turn for Chamberlain's vindication.[1] Geddes' long survey, he declares, " proved conclusively that for the offensive of 1918 the old individual system of exemptions would no longer serve. The solution was bulk release ". Accordingly in February 1918 his successor was given the power for which Chamberlain had asked in February 1917, of withdrawing exemptions according to age and breaking the dilatoriness of the tribunals. In March the mortal danger of the last German offensive compelled the Cabinet to meet the army's long-unheard demands. Men under twenty-three were called out of protected occupations ; munitions alone gave up 104,000 in six months.

Once only, to the Liberal Unionists of Birmingham, and with proper restraint, he broke his public silence. But his feelings were sore, his private comment acrid, the morals he drew instant, and he declined promptly the Prime Minister's offer of a knighthood (of the Order of the British Empire).

22 August ; to C. A. Vince

My recent experiences have impressed very strongly upon my mind the difficulties of attempting to carry on administration without being in the House. The Cabinet is highly sensitive to Parly. opinion, and a Minister outside the House not only cannot exert influence upon that opinion, he actually excites it against him.

29 December

Ll. G., if anyone, is personally responsible for my misfortunes, and although I should not have felt that my mouth was stopped by the acceptance of a recognition of my work, I think undoubtedly others would have said that that fact cleaned the slate.

12 January, 1918

I wonder what you thought of the Honours List. I have never ceased to congratulate myself that I did not figure among that rabble.

30 April

I see Churchill boasting about the increase of munitions output, in spite of the release of men. Precisely ! that is what I always said would happen, whereas Addison said it wouldn't and Ll. G. would not take the risk.

Such is a story of trial and error. Thirty years later it may be agreed that his substantial proposals were the right ones, without denying the imperative need for administrative unity. Nor need

---

[1] Humbert Wolfe, *Labour Supply and Regulation*, 1923.

we be blind to shortcomings in his methods or his means. In part they were those of a radical intellectual who tried to take several stages together ; in part, those of a man " not rough enough ", as some of his subordinates complained and as the Prime Minister hinted, for the governmental world of 1917, when every ministry had its snipers in Fleet Street. From many who worked with him he won lasting affection or respect ; most of all, maybe, from Walsh, Shaw, and his other Labour advisers. Yet to others again he conveyed a disconcerting formality, while he made too little allowance for different natures and entrenched interests.

He knew himself well. On the Christmas after resignation his diary says " it is hard, but I have such a power of putting disagreeable thoughts aside that doubtless it will not render me miserable for long, or sour my temperament ".

CHAPTER VIII

FIRST STEPS TO WESTMINSTER: 1917–1921
AGED 48–52

Thundering and bursting
In torrents, in waves —
Carolling and shouting
Over tombs, amid graves —
See ! on the cumber'd plain
Clearing a stage,
Scattering the past about,
Comes the new age.

M. ARNOLD.

HE had resigned on August 8 ; by the 22nd he had decided to seek a parliamentary seat, though only in Birmingham. The pressures on him were great, in part from those who loved him best, for perhaps an election might come in time to justify his policy. And in any case what else could he do ?

27 August 1917

I could not settle down to make money, much as I should like to be rich. When I think of Johnnie and Norman,[1] I feel I could not back out of public work of some kind, and although I know that half of what you say and three-quarters of what Annie says is exaggerated, yet if I didn't try people would always think I could have done something if I had tried.

But there were old men unwilling to be displaced and younger men already in the field, besides problems of the forthcoming redistribution of seats, so that not till January was agreement reached that the member for Central Birmingham should stand down in his favour ; though not before a general election. These were the months of his life which his sensitiveness perhaps found hardest to endure. Sometimes the contrast between what he had loathed in London and what he could have done in Birmingham revolted him, and what at his age could he expect to do in Parliament ? He had, we shall see, other strong reasons for depression, and as 1917 expired he was in the depths.

[1] The two cousins killed in action.

21 October 1917

Every now and then a feeling of almost irresistible nausea and revulsion comes over me at the thought of all the drudgery, the humiliation, the meanness and pettiness of that life, and of the hopeless impossibility of getting things done. And then I grind my teeth and think if it hadn't been for my d——d well-meaning brother I might still have been Lord Mayor of Birmingham, practically in control of the town and about to enter upon my third year of office.

Diary, 17 December 1917

My career is broken. How can a man of nearly 50, entering the House with this stigma upon him, hope to achieve anything? The fate I foresee is that after mooning about for a year or two I shall find myself making no progress . . . I shall perhaps be defeated in an election, or else shall retire, and that will be the end. I would not attempt to re-enter public life if it were not war-time. But I can't be satisfied with a purely selfish attention to business for the rest of my life.

Between these two dates he received a deep wound. In October he saw for the last time his cousin Norman, who in December was killed in France, though his body was only found in February. In Neville's mind that short life and glorious death were momentous. This young cousin, son of Joseph Chamberlain's brother Herbert and fifteen years his junior, was hardly known to him until they found themselves together on the city council. Between a married man of forty-two and an unmarried man of twenty-seven there is a natural gap; what causes so bridged it that the older man could write " the most intimate friend I had ", and that a rare vibration sounds in his diary when Norman's name is mentioned? In his memory he wrote his one and only book,[1] " anxious that future generations of the family should realise how greatly Norman had contributed to the family fame ".

In that book others, and especially T. E. Harvey under whom he worked at Toynbee Hall, testified to the force in this captain of Grenadiers. Belonging to a younger generation with a new social conscience, he came out of Eton and Oxford with something glowing about him. It was purpose without pretension which attracted Neville, and the same, we must think, which won response from Norman, who wrote of Neville as " one of the very few people who roused in me all the sensations of a willing and enthusiastic follower ". So in council they supported each other through thick and thin.

[1] *Norman Chamberlain, A Memoir,* by his cousin Neville Chamberlain (for private circulation). John Murray, 1923.

But his first object in writing was to show how entirely Norman's life had been given up to the boys who were victims of our urban civilisation ; how he set out to rescue them from hanging round the streets, how he insisted on playing-fields, directed their clubs and camps, at his own cost emigrated many to Canada, crossed the seas to visit them. And his enthusiasm went deeper into administration, for to him the development of after-care committees and juvenile employment exchanges was largely due. Neville loved to see things done like this ; " he had real constructive power — . . . how clear and consistent had been his purpose ", repeat his letters. All the more because he saw in Norman the qualities he regarded most, " redeemed from priggishness by a keen sense of humour, which caused him to recoil from anything approaching sloppy sentimentality or cant with positive horror ". Here was a Chamberlain indeed, too soon taken away, and working to the bitter end ; " months afterwards the first sheets of his views on education, soiled and discoloured by rain, were found upon his body in No Man's Land ".

He set about collecting material for his book at once, vainly tried to find Norman's grave in France, and for his sake took up yet another cause, the Street Boys' Union at Birmingham.

Diary, 10 February 1918
Somehow I had always associated Norman with anything I might do in the future. He was like a younger brother to me.

Diary, 27 February
Returned from W. Woodhay, where attended Memorial service for my dear friend Norman. Strange that we do not fully realise men's characters while they are alive. Only now do I begin to see the extraordinary beauty of his. His life was devoted to others, and I feel a despicable thing beside him.

13 April ; to Mrs. Chamberlain
Don't think for a moment that I should mind being called up for whatever purpose it might be. In some ways it would be a relief, because I should feel that I had done all I could.

Other troubles contributed to this depression. His wife was seriously ill in the spring, he himself had considerable spells of gouty headaches and sciatica, and all that year his weight never reached ten stone. But life must be lived, money made, and he could never rest. He reappeared in the city council and town planning committee, but rejected a sounding that he might be re-elected as Lord Mayor. He began business again at Hoskins' and Elliotts' and the Birmingham Small Arms and, as with him business always included welfare, he refused to be distracted from the city causes by large offers from outside.

All this year he was leading efforts for public health, the workers' leisure, and co-operation. He insisted on appointing welfare supervisors at the Council House, induced Elliotts' to buy land for housing, and at the Small Arms set up a labour committee to keep closer touch. His letters teem with recreation grounds, gifts in recognition of long service, concerts for the Civic Recreation League, widening frontages to push on the " city centre ". Through the Citizens' Society he brought pressure to bear on ministers for more adequate pensions for the disabled. Schemes passed through his head for a workers' settlement of house-owners at Selly Oak ; in Wales he actually experimented in sending women from the slums to the sea, though this was a failure, for his guests stayed indoors and fought with the landlady. He saw hope in proposals from the Federation of British Industries for joint committees of masters and men, to manage benefits, pensions, and policy, with majority decisions " binding on the whole trade, a favourite idea of my own ". Though he viewed with some doubt (after his own departmental experience) the suggestion to set up a separate Ministry of Health, he urged immediate concentration upon infant welfare, midwifery, and milk, and for this, as for housing, asked larger powers for local authorities ; it was " humiliating " for cities like Birmingham to be restricted to parliamentary bills.

In this summer of 1918 he seized on the nomination of Lord Robert Cecil as Chancellor of Birmingham University to do something which would make a direct appeal to the working-man, " to provide a course of general education, history, economics, local government, industrial organisation, mechanism of exchanges, English language, and a smattering of the sciences for men actually at work ". He was cheered by the enthusiasm of local labour leaders and by hearing of R. H. Tawney's approval, long continuing to believe in his experiment in the teeth of considerable disappointment.

Here we may illustrate his mind working on the war and its aftermath :

22 April 1917

This Russian revolution, which by a grim sort of irony is received everywhere with shouts of approval by our people as though it were going to win the war for us, is fermenting in all the unsteady brains of the world.

9 September 1917

. . . reading *The Town Labourer, 1760–1832* by the Hammonds. It is extraordinarily interesting and, being written avowedly from the point of view of the labourer, so excites one's sympathy that one feels rebellion would have been more than justified over and over again in the face of such gross injustice and such brutal and inhuman oppression.

16 September 1917 ; to W. A. Cadbury

There is no man in the Council whose good opinion I value more than your own. . . . I shall certainly not enter parliament as a partisan, and whatever differences may arise on new points, I shall always feel that I have much in common with the men with whom I have worked in sympathy during the last six years.

12 October 1918

A very large number of people are counting on peace before Christmas. . . . But I cannot believe that so vast a revolution could be effected in the German mind in so short a time. . . . I confess I feel nervous about the chances of our holding out for an unconditional surrender.

But his fears proved baseless and in November, hard upon the armistice, came the long-expected election, at which the government manifesto declaimed " the knell of military autocracy has sounded for ever ".

Under the Reform Act of 1918, which gave the vote to all men of twenty-one and to women over thirty, Birmingham was re-divided into twelve constituencies instead of seven, with an electorate increased thereby from 95,000 to 427,000. " As a party ", he noted, " we are utterly unready in Birmingham ", but, if so, it was no fault of his. In January he had brought to new life his achievement of 1914, the fusion of Conservative and Liberal Unionists, following on which he pressed forward a centralised organisation and finance. This decision, he wrote, " practically places the direction of Unionist politics in Birmingham in my hands. I am not quite sure whether all those present perceived this ; I did not mention it ! "

How he wished to use this power is more notable. For a year he had predicted that Arthur Henderson, having parted from Lloyd George's Cabinet in dudgeon, would drift towards Ramsay MacDonald and the I.L.P., and drew the moral " if we can secure the best Labour men to work with us by helping them to certain seats, we shall do good service ". For this reason he was in touch with the British Workers' League, which represented men whom he had grown to esteem over National Service ; he was delighted when Hallas, his Labour ally in the Bank question, received Unionist support in one of the city seats, while in another he helped a Unionist working-man to victory. Two earlier letters of this year to his wife, springing from the theme of Federalism for the Irish problem, illustrate this radical strain of his. He had long thought it, he wrote, " the only way of settling the Irish question amicably and safely. . . . It might affect my personal future very considerably. There would be decided attractions about an English as opposed to an Imperial Parliament." And, again, " it would, I suppose, destroy the Unionist party as such . . . but I should not mind that. . . . I gather from *The Times*, however, that this point of view distresses the old fogies who can't get away from the old habit of regarding the party as an end in itself, instead of an instrument for attaining ends of national importance."

This very Radical sort of Conservative found his own constituency in Ladywood, carved out of the old Central division of Birmingham, an unknown quantity of 33,000 electors who lived for the greater part in poor areas. One of his opponents, fighting on the free-trade ticket, was not in herself dangerous, but in a winter of such discontents a strong Labour candidate might have been formidable. Mr. Kneeshaw, however, was a pacifist, and the established Labour men declared against him. On a very small poll Chamberlain was consequently elected, with 9405 votes, against 2572 for the Labour man and 1552 for the Liberal.

Though he did not use the famous " coupon ", no doubt the good wishes received from Lloyd George and Bonar Law were helpful, though less perhaps than his name and his record. His address declared that reconstruction called for the setting aside of party. " I have repeatedly stated my conviction that we could best show our gratitude to those who have fought and died for England by making it a better place to live in. My sole reason for wishing to enter parliament is my desire to assist in bringing about this transformation." He went on to speak of ample pensions, a minimum wage where proved necessary, shorter hours, protection of key industries, more funds for health and welfare, and a large sum for State building of houses ; a separate appeal to women added " assistance to widows with young children, so that they may continue to have the loving care of their own mother ". To make this expenditure possible the master key must be an increase in production, to which end he would strive for co-operation between capital and labour.

At the height of the election his half-sister Beatrice died of influenza, worn out by war work and the spirit that over-strained a frail tenement. He spoke to Richard Redmayne of this " wonderfully gifted woman ", whose vivid sympathy he must miss. But neither now nor ever did his cast of mind let him dwell long on the past : " this election", he wrote, " has been a good thing for me, for it has forced me to put a sort of crust over my emotion ".

So the Coalition Parliament set out, to make the new world promised by its leader. In this enormous effort to bring back to normal the lives of many million beings, nervously exhausted but suddenly deprived of nervous exaltation, men advanced to storm by force their cities of dreams, for President Wilson and a tribe of rhetoricians foretold a new order which would guarantee brotherhood and peace. But in world wars men do not fight for the same things. While the deaf Australian leader W. M. Hughes cried loudly for a stiff peace, British Labour asked revision of the hard terms of Versailles, and while throughout 1919–21 peace conferences adjourned, without much result, from one watering-place to another, newly-created small States launched some considerable wars. Discipline was a first necessity, but demobilisation riots and police strikes proved that discipline is the lesson of war most rapidly unlearned. To restore some of the wealth blown away from the guns was a second ; but the miners asked for a six-hour day and a 30 per cent rise on wages, the Clyde wished a forty-hour week, the Labour party declared for a capital levy, over all lowered the cloud of a general strike. Sinn Fein had captured 73 seats at Westminster, which they refused to occupy. In India the slaughter at Amritsar darkened any prospect of working the Montagu-Chelmsford reforms.

Modern war, which over-tests the good in human beings while it lasts, leaves little but evil behind. So worn-out was the community for any desire but peace and comfort, so used were men to force, so high had hopes been pitched and so low was their fulfilment, so short was the world of any goods but paper money, so vast the rubble to be cleared, that unity and goodwill seemed to have left the earth. Bereaved of the best and bravest who should have bridged the gap, Britain swayed between those who would restore the old order and those who would build anew, between economy and spending, internationalism and isolation. Inflamed by the general temperature, every ancient sore of the commonwealth flared up to fever, which tore to ribbons the bandages of coalition. So till the end of 1921 Parliament and ministers laboured without ceasing, but also without principle.

Behind Lloyd George sat 526 members, nearly 400 of them Unionists, facing 63 Labour men and 33 Asquithian Liberals. This vast majority was honeycombed with communication trenches, in which the hardened troops of party bided their time. But the rôle of Neville Chamberlain was peculiar to himself. A back-bencher in the usual sense he never was, a fact from which both good and ill might flow, since his curious position as an ex-minister, his administrative record, and relationship to Austen set him apart. And this status was the more defined by his inability not to work at full stretch, as well as by the instant proof he gave of constructive power at a time when all had to be reconstructed.

By temperament, as by heredity, he leaned distinctly to his party's democratic wing, yet his dislike of unreality set up a certain sympathy with those reckoned as " die-hards ". It may indeed be found that his final criterion of political activity was always its effect on individual character, but at any rate he was never one of those who harked back to a pre-war world. Nothing shows this better than a letter on the major crisis of his first session, the Sankey report on the coal strike and the miners' considerable victory.

22 March 1919

I think they have deserved it so far as the merits of the case go. . . . Many people have been sceptical about the suggestion that there was to be a new England, and many others have never intended that it should be very different from the old, if they could help it. If they had had their way, I think we might have drifted into a revolution, but this is a real change in our industrial system . . . whether it will be nationalisation in the sense that the State owns and works the collieries, or whether, as is more likely and I think more practical, some State control will be exercised, the workmen having a voice in the direction and a share of the profits. . . . Evolution by steps is the only way in which any fundamental change can be brought about without disaster, and so I regard the future with comparative equanimity.

As to housing, though he accepted the Addison Act as an instalment but predicted ill of its finance, his own ideas were more sweeping. He would have spent a hundred millions from the Exchequer on building, — the State to own, local authorities to administer, and the individual to be given every facility to buy. It was over this that he reported Austen as " positively rude " ; adding, " I always said that if I went into the House we should differ, and we are bound to do so because our minds are differently trained. He thinks me wild, and I think him unprogressive and prejudiced."

It was, then, in general sympathy with the social objectives professed by the Coalition that he took up the spade-work, on subjects within his special knowledge. He made his maiden speech on rent restrictions, served on standing committees for the Transport and Electricity Bills, was active on tariffs in the Unionist reconstruction committee. So that the diary in August was not unsatisfied : " first session over. Have spoken 4 times in the House, but many times in standing committees on Ways and Communications and Electricity Bills. Have made no sensation, but believe I have acquired a certain position in the House as my contributions have been well received."

Two glimpses from his holidays that summer admit us into his view of war, and what he found in peace. He spent four days on the battle-fields, from Rheims to the Somme and the Ypres salient. On the Somme, we read, " nothing but weeds, shell holes, graves, and dead stumps of trees " ; in the salient, " tracts of immense thistles, the down flying in all directions " ; German prisoners " herded into their barbed wire cages in the evening . . . a humiliating spectacle for humanity, they looked like slaves, but I felt no sympathy for them " ; " it makes one savage to think that their own country is untouched ".

Not like his walks up the becks in Haweswater, with the wheatear's nest just over the water, " as if the bird liked to sit on its eggs where it could hear the tinkling of the little stream all day " ; with juniper in the cleft rocks, red deer, and ravens, and all he saw in the North in June.

By 1920 he had made his mark. He took a vigorous share in saving electricity from the Ministry of Transport, and even more in remodelling the anti-dumping bill ; characteristically refusing to support it merely because free-traders opposed, as " a rotten reason ". He was chairman of one departmental committee on slums, of another on the future of canals, and a vice-chairman of the Unionist committee on reconstruction. He made one of a deputation to remonstrate with Lloyd George on his absence from the House and extra-parliamentary pronouncements, believing " there is a real danger of our sliding into a big change in the constitution, under which the P.M. of the day . . . would deal with trade unions, employers, and interests of various kinds, direct "

In March Bonar Law, between whom and Neville there was always a mutual regard, held out to him an expectation of office, whereupon in words already quoted he spoke of National Service and the episode of Kennedy Jones. Curious indeed was Bonar Law's defence of " George " ; " if a man is not successful, he never stops to enquire the reasons but tries to get rid of him at once. He would do that with me." Still, he would be Prime Minister a long time and what, by the bye, was Neville's age ? In vain ; " I should be miserable ", ends our account, " with my head under the Goat's arm again, and am not so enamoured of office that I would sell my peace of mind for it ".

Yes, he was over fifty now ; neuralgia and gout plagued him much this year, his teeth were steadily being taken out, — as to which he reflects " fortunate elephant ! he has but one in each jaw ". He was philosophical about the near horizon, and what his father's children had done ; " although none of us has reached the very first rank, everyone of us will have left a mark, and a good clean mark too ". So he went to work in his three worlds, of Westminster, Birmingham, and business.

He enjoyed being, and meant to be, something like what his father had been in Birmingham. To keep members and editors together by a sessional dinner, to reorganise the Midland Union's funds, to watch municipal elections like a lynx, to tour Ladywood at night to see constituents in their homes, — this and much more must be done. He helped to raise another half-million for the University, and had a hand in acquiring its new site on the hills. The Bank, reinforced by his evidence, received enlarged powers under a new bill ; " I should like to get my three Lord Mayoral ideas carried through, bank, orchestra, and civic recreation ; if only I live, I fancy I shall do it ". Chairman of the Chamber of Commerce, liaison between builders and local authorities for the Midland area, new re-creation grounds, amalgamation in the air at Hoskins', staff friction to overcome at the Small Arms, no relaxation here from the full stretch.

In Parliament he added another subject to his list, in the Bastardy Bill, which in May he carried to a second reading against the government. The need was clear to a man who had worked long at infant welfare, for there were over 40,000 illegitimate children born each year, who died twice as fast as children born in wedlock. So he sponsored and redrafted the bill put up by the " Council for the unmarried mother and child ", the essence of his argument being that " the punishment of innocent children for the faults of their parents is revolting to humanity, and is contrary to the best interests of the State ". On the two points which to him seemed vital, legitimation by the parents' marriage and increased contributions from the father, he assisted during later sessions to convert opinion, and ultimately, in 1923, to change the law.

On the questions he had made his own he was learning that politics may mean taking the second best. Thus in a *Times* housing supplement he declared there was no short-cut. He would repeal the Lloyd George finance of 1909 in the hope of awaking private enterprise, and divert savings, as he claimed his bank was doing, into house-purchase ; where " every spadeful of manure dug in, every fruit tree planted ", converted a potential revolutionary into a citizen. But beyond the war arrears " there stretches away behind a vista of range upon range of slums already unfit for habitation, and daily rotting into more complete decay under the operation of the Restriction of Rents Act ".

He had more to say in an interim report on unhealthy areas, envisaging " a new authority with jurisdiction over a wide zone including London and the area lying beyond it, for purposes of town planning, transport, and finance ". For this purpose he visited Leeds and Liverpool and South Wales, seeing slums " that fairly made our hair stand on end ", staggering out of civic luncheons " more dead than alive ".

In all directions the conditions of the post-war State necessitated compromise. On tariffs, for instance, so delicate for Coalition Unionists to abandon and for Coalition Liberals to digest, they could only agree to maintain some modest preferences, and some duties to safeguard " key " industries. If it had not been for constitutional objection, he would himself have wished to pass a tariff " but hold it in suspension, with power to somebody to put it into force as and when required. This would have many advantages, cutting away the charge of profiteering, bringing in the protection only when the whole industry would be united in favour of it (I mean the labour as well as the employers), and giving manufacturers confidence in putting down capital." As for canals, finance made his old desire for State ownership out of the question, so that his committee's report was confined to one experimental area ; recommending that a public trust should reform and unify the waterways of the Trent.

Many times over, to every kind of audience, he declared himself ready for radical remedies. He would limit profits and publish trading accounts, would accept State ownership of minerals, advocated reduction of armaments, and admission of all nations to the League. While Ireland reeked with murder and the Act of 1920 proposed to set up two reluctant parliaments under a shadowy all-Ireland council, his own test was how far this prepared for the union of Ireland. If he could be sure that De Valera did not mean secession, he would not stick at Dominion status.

But what he wished, or might have done, was subjected to the ruin of Europe and to British party.

The last fireworks for peace had hardly expired before reality asked its reckoning. Prices tumbled down, reparations suffocated trade, subsidies were withdrawn, and a million unemployed signified the first post-war depression. Whether it were long or short must depend, he thought, mostly on the attitude of Labour, among whom he saw " a large number of men, and still more women, who want nothing but peace . . . if they aren't driven mad by unemployment and consequent starvation, they may keep us steady ". At the end of the year he told Alfred Greenwood that he saw a silver lining. " Speculation was going on at a reckless pace ; it has been stopped before disaster occurred. Prices were mounting every day ; this check has stopped wages demands and made employers look carefully into possible economies."

For all that, his vision of co-operation with Labour had suffered a change. It was now the official Opposition, the last fiction of its representation in the Coalition vanished, and his friend Hallas, for whom he had found a seat, joined the Labour party. They seemed to him to be living in dreams. If costs must come down, what to make of the miners' perpetual strikes and the prolongation of subsidies ? worse still, he thought, the clamour for nationalisation which, in a competitive industry, must end in industrial conscription ; worst of all, the use of industrial force for political ends. For this year a " Council of Action " threatened to down tools unless troops were withdrawn from Russia and Ireland.

To Birmingham he predicted a struggle between " privileged minorities who said they could not wait to convert the country . . . and those who believed that progress must be ordered ". He spoke of the party " that has stolen the name of Labour ", for whose spokesmen he was acquiring some intellectual contempt, privately picturing Adamson, the Fife miner who temporarily led them in the Commons, as " like an ox, heavy, stupid, pathetic, lurching about without vivacity, humour, or reason ". And as he resented Bolshevist propaganda in this country, he rejoiced in the Polish victory that saved Warsaw.

So cleavages were widening, with the future of parties, and his own, alike undecided. He hesitated whether to continue in Parliament, still had to force himself to speak, and deliberately postponed buying a London house ; not till 1922 did he cross the party rubicon by joining the Carlton Club. For what would become of party was most dubious, when once again, as had been before when the liberal-minded Canning led the Tories, the real Opposition sat on the government back benches. Some there were anxious for the purity of their principles, some felt Ulster was betrayed, some saw in General Dyer a symbol of British prestige ; on this last he reported, " I voted with the government, but not very happily, feeling strong disgust at having to endorse the censure on a man who made a bad mistake, but who perhaps saved Europeans from the most barbarous treatment ". But again, while some trusted they might yet thank God, or Lloyd George, for a reformed House of Lords, others deemed that the Prime Minister's breakfast parties and his secretariat undermined Cabinet government, that his *entourage* were unfortunate, or that honours were sold.

When a minister dislikes an element in his party, he styles it " reaction ", but from all that Lloyd George lumped together as " Mayfair ", Chamberlain was far removed. He did not profess to understand the mentality of the Tory aristocracy, only caught glimpses, he wrote, of " the strange dream life that goes on there ". And he loved to see talent at work, even when he disliked its exponent. " Hating and despising both men ", he rejoiced to hear Lloyd George demolish Northcliffe, — " an intellectual treat ", he said of another such speech, " to see art carried to such a pitch ". He declared all the debating power of the House was on the Treasury bench, Churchill being " far the most attractive speaker ". He liked Shortt's conciliatory method ; nor did Eric Geddes mean to be anything else, " but he is very like a bull, and when he puts his head down and begins to butt in play, people are apt to find that he is too clumsy an animal to be allowed off a chain ". On the other hand, he found Long " effete ", Addison incompetent, and Coalition began to jar on his strongest fibres : moral indignation, party sense, and family feeling.

With increasing force such sensations mark his first Parliament. " Have done nothing to increase my reputation with the public ", says the diary for December 1919 ; " at present I feel very little inclination to try ". Could he find no leader nearer to his heart than Lloyd George ? to whom many were fixed by interest but for whom, says a letter the same month, " there is neither personal devotion nor respect for a high character. And surely those are the things that tell in the long run." Robert Cecil perhaps ? whom " I have carefully watched and weighed ", but " terribly Cecilian " ; no, concludes the diary a year later, " impossible as a leader, he carps but makes no constructive criticism ". As 1920 went on, his papers foreshadow some party fusion. " F. E. and Winston have been hatching a plot together to capture the P.M., or to succeed him " ; in the very act of offering him office, had not Bonar Law said that fusion was inevitable and " all the Cabinet were agreed it must come soon " ?

But if so, he thinks aloud, what would become of Birmingham ? " what would be my position with the Unionist organisation here ? if I tried to get it to follow me, as it probably would, should we have to bring out candidates to oppose Austen, Amery, & Co. ? ". At the end of that year he breathes an air of labour without much hope.

Diary, 27 December 1920

> my committees have occupied all my mornings, many afternoons, and frequently part of my nights (in preparation), with the result that I have been able to put in but little time in the House. . . . This is very bad for a parliamentary career . . . and I have done nothing to increase my reputation with the public. Yet I believe I have a steadily growing position as a man of judgement among M.P.'s. . . . I have plenty of friendly acquaintances in the House, but no one whose views accord sufficiently closely with my own to tempt me into joining forces. In Birmingham my influence is probably declining. . . . But politically I have been very successful in restoring the morale of the party.

1921 splashed on its stormy way. Wages fell, benefits were cut, Dr. Addison was dropped and the housing subsidy with him, for which (last) " I am sorry ", wrote Neville. Ulster began to work its Parliament, but Sinn Fein declared war, occupying 60,000 British troops, whose organised reprisals seemed little more effective than the outbursts of the special constabulary, the " black and tans ".

Having carefully timed a holiday to avoid seeing Lloyd George receive the freedom of Birmingham, he now finished his report on slum areas, an important source of all later legislation. Its detail illustrated how cruel were the consequences of our piecemeal development ; by the 72,000 back-to-back houses of Leeds, the two-room houses of Swansea, the 13 acres of open space for South-wark's 190,000 people, or the half-million souls who must be moved if London was to expand on decent lines. Once more it repeated the necessity for bolder plans. Town planning must be extended to built-up areas. Till houses were built and finance improved, temporary remedies must be found for the slums ; moreover the character of the tenant was as important as that of the property, and some control like the Octavia Hill system was required. But no such improvement could be expected under private ownership. The report therefore recommends that local authorities be empowered to purchase and improve slum areas, on principles of compensation which would stamp bad landlords and recognise the facts of depreciation in value.

This done, he went on to an interim report on canals, and another on children " living in " on canal boats ; " lunched in the room ", he lamented on this last occasion, " on (1) a plate of cold beef and ham with plain boiled potatoes, (2) cold stewed figs and rice and (3) a bit of mouse-trap and bread ; this is the stereotyped lunch at the ministry of Health, and it has the merit of being soon over ". In May he joyfully shouted " Banbury has been caught napping, and the Bastardy Bill is through its second reading " ; for Sir Frederick Banbury, whose instinct was to resist almost all legislation, was not his type of Tory.

Meanwhile political decision had come a fraction nearer with the break-down in health of Bonar Law, which meant that Austen succeeded to the lead of the House and the party. As the year went on, Neville argued that if Austen followed Lloyd George, it would mean Unionist mutiny, while for himself Austen's promotion brought an added embarrassment. Already, for that reason, he had avoided speaking on the Budget ; in July this handicap looked him closer in the face, when he was asked to be chairman of the reconstruction committee. He could not take it, for " I could not agree to head a revolt against Austen, and a revolt might be wanted " ; for that same reason he would not be chairman of the party, though not on that ground only, for it was " a soulless job " ; adding, that for party " I care very little ".

Once only this year he seems to have made direct contact with Lloyd George, described in a letter of June with more than one shaft of light :

Breakfast at Derby House to meet the P.M. I do think breakfasting out is a barbarous practice. . . . Derby announced that the P.M. wanted to talk about licensing. So a somewhat rambling and discursive conversation followed, in the course of which the P.M. developed an interesting study of feminine psychology. They had voted for us, he said, in 1918, and we mustn't lose their vote . . . once having gone, they would not come back, for women in politics were more constant than men. I thought the little beast showed his usual astuteness in all this.

Whatever his doubts, however, he continued public support of Coalition, in face of the two transcendant questions of Labour and Ireland. When the coal industry was decontrolled, the miners struck and the " triple alliance " threatened joint action, but on " black Friday " railwaymen and transport deserted their allies. He was among the private members who listened to both masters and men, reporting that " as usual the owners made the very worst of their case " ; on the whole he thought the private members' hand in this negotiation a bad precedent. So, till the end of June, it was fought out, at a cost to the country of £250 millions, Chamberlain clear enough that fought out it must be, — " I would rather go dirty than see the government surrender ".

In the autumn, loaded with some forty topical books, he went for a month to Sicily and Rome, returning to find the party in a burning crisis. While he was on his back in the Sistine chapel, mastering the frescoes of Michelangelo, or re-reading *Garibaldi and the Thousand* on the line of their march, Irish emissaries and Cabinet ministers had met in conclave. When it became known that the treaty contemplated an Irish Parliament with wide financial powers, he found the party " distinctly mutinous ". If Bonar Law's illness had first disjointed the government, his return in recovered health threatened to destroy it ; with " intense passion " (Churchill wrote later) he signalised his new mood to Lloyd George, and in defence of Ulster meditated attacking the policy which Austen had embraced.

Loyalties, reason, and prejudice, all decided Neville on a firm support of his brother. If the party split, he wrote, allowing a Labour government to slip in, " it might bring about a financial disaster of the first magnitude ". He had come to believe that Labour leaders could not stand up to their followers, were men of froth and not of substance, while the economics of unemployment raised a wall between him and them. While they spoke of work or maintenance at full wages, while Poplar and borough councils of the same colour refused to collect rates, he kept on his predestined path of appeal to the individual virtue of the working man. In these winter months, when he was discharging thousands from the Small Arms company and paying his own taxes out of capital, he was still passionate in pursuing his scheme at the University for the civic teaching of trade unionists. In reorganising the local relief fund, and insisting on a wider appeal — for " the poor are always good to one another " — he praised the Citizens' Society's work in restoring self-respect, begging his audiences not to demoralise the people ; " let us rely a little upon our own resources, and not upon the State ".

But he positively approved of the Irish treaty, and of one certainty was convinced, that " the country would not respond to an appeal involving resort to coercive measures, which might mean 100,000 men, and one or two hundred millions of money ". So, rallying his party managers in Birmingham, he sent his stalwarts to back up Austen in the stormy party conference at Liverpool, which finally empowered their leaders to continue negotiation.

So a Chamberlain still led the party. " The real source of the trouble ", he told his business partner Platten, " has been Bonar Law, who returned with the most extraordinary ideas as to his own importance. But I think the Liverpool conference will do much to convince him . . . that the country will not now support a policy of civil war."

Yet Bonar Law might acquire a new importance from other events than Ireland, as we detect in the pages of the diary which closed 1921 and, though he knew it not, the era of Lloyd George. " A very trying year ", they note, of ruinous depression. " I have spoken more often this year than last, but my speeches have rather been solid contributions to information than debating successes, which are really what count with the House. But indeed I feel less and less inclined to take office, even if it were offered, and I certainly shall never go out of my way to get it. Sometimes I wish I were out of the House altogether, but I am not sure that I should be any happier if I were. But it is a great handicap to be the son of my father and the brother of my brother, for every success is discounted and every failure is counted double. Moreover, when one's brother is leader, all independence goes, unless one is prepared to quarrel, and I am nowhere near keen enough about politics for that. . . . A. writes that Ll. G. is thinking of a general election, and he asks me to put together some notes for the case against it. I think it would be bad tactics myself, and that the Irish settlement would never counter-balance the effects of unemployment."

MEMBER FOR LADYWOOD, 1921

CHAPTER IX

TURMOIL: 1922–1924

AGED 53–55

> The door of the Cabinet has a quality the most opposite
> to the ivory gate of Virgil : it suffers no dreams to pass
> through it.
>
> COLERIDGE

LITTLE could the diarist foresee that not one general election but three would be crowded into the next three years, nor could any contemporary have predicted that neither Lloyd George nor the Liberal party would ever hold power again. Effects so memorable call for some explanation of their causes, if we are to grasp his part and his allusions.

Many times over have recurred such years, when parties are being readjusted to fundamental change ; harsh years when followers will not change so fast as their leaders, when personality clashes with principle, and the great egoist is persuaded he acts as the pure patriot. Such storms are set up in our system by some movement on the Left, nor was his instinct at fault when he saw in Labour the one force with united conviction.

All that happened might to a great extent have been foreseen by reflecting on earlier history, which does not endorse the oversimplified view that our politics will endure two parties but not three. On the contrary, a pure two-party basis has been much the exception, for England does not object to coalitions if they avoid the name. Once more, as in 1827 or 1886, a stir on the Left divided opinion in the Left centre and the Right, and once again party combination turned on the ancient dilemma of measures or men. But the old laws of party were now subjected to new conditions, for democracy has sharpened the distinction which has always existed between the Addingtons and the Pitts, between leaders who follow opinion and leaders who create it.

In obedience to such governing factors, in 1922 we find three shades of Unionists. There were those termed " Die-hards ", who in fact often surrendered but did not die, and among whose components we must name Carson as representing the now defeated cause of Union, Salisbury as a pure type of the religious and social forces of the past century, with perhaps some hundred members

E

93

entrenched on the heights well known of old, — individualism, the white man's hard-won burden, armed nationality, and the land. But if we move towards the Left, we meet a Coalition school who, whether from long relation with Lloyd George or upbringing in industrial Britain, whether in obedience to the noble dream of a national party or from fear of Socialism, agreed in thinking that a new age had dawned in which Unionist and Liberal must be fused. For this they were prepared to pay at least a temporary price, which would include giving up all but the meekest ghost of Protection. At the moment their brain was the Chancellor, the powerful, storm-tossed, and affectionate Birkenhead. Like Canning, on whom nature, if not design, had modelled him, he believed that men of commanding talent must rule the State, a necessity to which party principle must bow. Weighty and measured in Cabinet, on his adventurous side he had found something congenial in the Irish fighting man Michael Collins, and over the Irish settlement had broken with his old leader Carson and struck up a close alliance with Austen Chamberlain.

Yet, as leader of the party, Austen must reckon with its central and largest section. These, business men and country gentlemen and lawyers, thought most of saving the party's individual life, maintained as it was in every constituency by struggles together and long-established organisation. As Ireland and India proved, their minds were not closed to the march of facts, but to persuade them that Coalition should become permanent, and Coalition under Lloyd George at that, would demand either a rare combination of events or a considerable tract of time.

Decision might, however, come from another element, the Liberal party. Asquith's return to Parliament unsettled the Coalition Liberals, who felt a new call to justify their existence, while some hoped to reunite the survivors of the great Cabinet of 1914. And though this was to underestimate both the Asquithian desire to avenge the past, and the Lloyd-Georgian determination not to lose the future, Liberalism might become one of several things to Lloyd George : a magnet, a gilded cage, or a city of refuge. There was another Liberal, Winston Churchill, for whose gifts Neville repeatedly expressed his admiration. Born heir to Tory democracy and a Conservative member before he became a Liberal minister, across the cold frontiers of party his heart warmed to Birkenhead, his chosen political comrade. In 1922 their policy was decided. Coalition must be maintained ; so squalid a thing as Bolshevism must not be allowed to divide England and France, to alienate Lloyd George from British feeling, or to install Labour in power.

That indeed might be taken as the central theme of this decade 1921–31, whether Labour could form a government or was fitted to rule, and history might record that the Coalitionists were proved right, in that two Labour governments were installed during these years, each largely to fail for any weighty national good. But in all retrospective history there is a fallacy. To deem Labour ill-fitted to rule was not to say that Labour must be refused the chance of proving the contrary, while the final Coalition of 1931 differed from that projected ten years before emphatically in this, that it included a substantial ingredient of the Labour movement. Let us return to the first stage of this considerable process.

One thing certain we find at once ; that, though Coalition might continue, it could not do so under Lloyd George. Whatever the verdict on his great service in the war, gratitude is not a common, nor always a real, political virtue, for all gifts are not suited to all seasons. For the purposes of peace, his improvisations, his apparent conviction that public money salved most wounds, his plunges from state-craft to almost racial instinct, affronted average men, and disordered government. More than any other one man, he contributed to a change in the office of Prime Minister, fundamental for our subject ; so to wield the machine as to concentrate upon himself all final decision, making his position almost presidential by his direct relations with industry, foreign States, and the press. " The personal views of one man ", Churchill wrote to Birkenhead, were jeopardising Britain by his approaches to Russia ; in defiance of Curzon and the Foreign Office his sympathy encouraged the Greeks to invade Asia Minor ; in March he dismissed Montagu for publishing the government of India's protest against this anti-Moslem policy. He had in effect broken with France, where Poincaré had come in determined to stand by every tittle of Versailles, while the Balfour declaration on inter-Allied debts equally offended France and America.

Within the Empire the Coalition policies were large, inevitable, but unfortunate. The Irish treaty had not yet resulted in a constitutional Free State ; pitched battles devastated the South ; Michael Collins who had killed so many English was slain in ambush by Irishmen ; Henry Wilson, now Ulster's military adviser, was assassinated outside his London home ; the withdrawal of British troops and flight of loyalists seared many hearts. In Egypt the Coalition conceded to Allenby what they had refused to Milner, that is, the proclamation of Egyptian independence, but murder and martial law did not cease. Dour Arab resistance to our proclamation of a Jewish home in Palestine echoed strongly in Parliament. Indian nationalism was agitated by the Khalifat movement and by the Hindus' civil disobedience ; Gandhi's arrest was painfully extracted from Lord Reading. " Anti-waste " was the last slogan of the newspapers with the largest circulation ; a committee of business men under Eric Geddes proposed to " axe " every estimate from defence to education. But the worst waste, said the government's critics, was in the honours list, which they alleged to be swollen by names of little repute or, alternatively, of too much.

Bye-election losses convinced the Coalition leaders that their tide was running out, but Lloyd George agreed with Birkenhead they might just catch it on the ebb. In January they moved for an immediate election, which was indignantly resisted by official Conservatism and extinguished by Younger, the party chairman. Having advised Austen against it, Neville told his constituents that an election would imperil trade revival, Irish confidence, and House of Lords reform, privately writing in violent terms that this " Welsh attorney and his C.L. sycophants think they can dictate a policy to the whole Unionist party ". A week's reflection induced the conclusion, " I think the mischief is done, and that the Coalition won't be the same again ".

But we must be emphatic that he was still a Coalitionist, and had nothing to do with its fall. To Birmingham he spoke of the die-hards' " reactionary Toryism ", or how it had taken thirty years for his father's following to amalgamate with Salisbury ; and indeed neither the Midlands nor the North shared the injured Conservative dignity of the home counties. He hoped always for the elimination of Lloyd George, — but if no such miracle came to pass, and if neither Europe found settlement nor Ireland an end to disorder, why then " Ll. G. will hang on, and we shall all go to blazes together ".

So upon a solid Birmingham, above all on more authority for Austen, his loyal thoughts turned. It might be that only escape from Coalition could give back life to Unionism ; but he would do nothing to hurry it, nor had he any regular contact at this date with Baldwin, Wood, and the junior ministers who, from within the fortress, were thinking of opening a gate to the besiegers. He would himself postpone an election till the party had something positive to fight on ; " to go to the country purely on economy and anti-Socialism seems bad tactics to me, and I can't imagine that

Father would have done it ". They must get ideas ; " that is where both L. G. and Winston have the pull ". He put it to Austen that a programme could be made with agriculture, something on the ballot and political levy in trade unions, poor law reform, women's legislation, and slums. But he would still only move at Austen's pace, spending as much energy in defending his seat as his own.

Besides, he was too happy, too busy, and too selfless to be absorbed in calculation for the future. Life was rarely so full or so interesting. Business was difficult, a long engineering strike crippled Midland production ; in which it was characteristic that, however much he condemned the strikers, he would help a friend amongst them, if they needed funds. At last his garden was itself again after the years which war economy had eaten ; his letters teem with the glory of his azaleas, Japanese cherries, and orchids, or the excitement of visits from a greater spotted woodpecker. His children, growing fast up to school age, brought him endless happiness, to be thought for and read to, holidays and teaching to be carefully schemed. He was becoming a better fisherman under the tuition of his friend Arthur Wood. In London, politics, flower shows, dinners, and speeches, a water-colour of Russell Flint's to buy ; not time enough, he complained, for all he wished to do and see, — " sad how I have dropped out of music again . . . life is really not long enough to follow up more than 5 or 6 interests properly ".

But as an election might come and Birmingham must be made safe, he spoke in many divisions, collected funds, instructed agents. His wife, he insisted, was " the mainspring of it all ", and should, he thought, be asked to fight the seat if he were carried off. Here one of their constituency days may stand for all the rest ; for, as his account begins, " if it bores you too much, you can skip, and anyhow I won't do it again ". Thus then, in January 1922, having done a turn of reading *Pickwick* to his daughter, he opens :

I began on Monday by receiving a deputation from a Midland constituency, who wanted my assistance in finding for them at once a candidate, who should be rich, handsome, distinguished, a brilliant speaker, and accompanied by a charming wife. I then went to the Chamber of Commerce where I spent two hours. . . . In the evening about 150 men came to Westbourne from the constituency . . . the first arrived at 7.15 and the last departed about eleven o'clock. . . . The meeting was very trying, as many, including councillors, would make tub-thumping speeches in which they denounced Labour with

terrifying violence, and adjured us to remember this " great empire
of ours on which the Sun etc." . . . Tuesday. . . . I went to one of
Annie's clubs in the afternoon and talked to them for 55 minutes, far
too long and a thoroughly rotten speech, though Annie says they
liked it.   Then I . . . set out for the pot-house in the West, where I
graciously shook hands with Austen's executive committee . . . about
22 sat down to dinner . . . soup, cold and very nasty, then an enormous piece of frozen beef, red, ragged, and calculated to blunt the
sharpest knife . . . the third course was the celebrated scrag of boiled
mutton, which the chairman devoured without winking like the
Indians in *The Dog Crusoe,* but I fainted completely away and was only
revived when they thrust beneath my nose a powerful mass of mouse-
trap cheese. . . . On Wednesday I delivered a short address to the
Y.M.C.A. after lunch, attended a meeting of the Highbury trustees,
and finished up about 7 o'clock with the Lord Mayor's boot and
clothing fund.   On Thursday I dined with the Business club and
proposed the first toast, and on Friday I went to the initiation of the
Lord Mayor and others into the Royal Antediluvian Order of Buffaloes.

This sort of thing no doubt contributed to two decisions, a short
cure at Harrogate and a swift journey to Canada, before an election
made them impossible.   To Harrogate then for early August to
improve his phosphates, where he much approved his doctor for
saying " it would be a great mistake to get up before breakfast,
and that filthy sulphur water would do me more harm than good ".
Thence with a fishing-rod to the Oykell, where he also constructed
articles for the *Birmingham Post,* advocating a transfer of unemployment benefits to the corporation so that it might set up public works.
On September 7 he sailed for Canada.   He was therefore out of
England when the victorious Turks advanced on the British line
at Chanak, which barred their way to Constantinople, when Austen
decided to fight an immediate election with Lloyd George, and
when Unionist revolt, led by Baldwin, blew Coalition away.

Though he was recalled prematurely, his six weeks in Canada
were invigorating and not without importance, for he came back
realising better the power of his father's name, with more confidence in himself, and in no mood for alliance with anyone who
did not put the cause of Empire high.

As usual, letters and diary flow on, a faithful reflection of his
purpose to listen, to help, and to learn.   There is talk in smoking-
rooms, hotels, ranches, with every condition of men, notes on the
prolific conservatism of French Canada, brands of wheat, huge
Douglas firs, on chances of Canadian–West Indian confederation,

above all on the need for more British immigrants. Two things
only he deplored in Canada as a whole : the wastage of their
natural resources, and the lack of gardens on their farms. His
pages take us from the bluffs of Labrador to Quebec and the
" immensely hospitable people " of Montreal ; along the line to
Winnipeg, all colour in the fall, gold aspens set against spruce and
pine, rivers " beautiful beyond words " as the morning mist lifted ;
so on to Banff and the Rockies, and through to Victoria, full like
England of roses. When their faces turned towards home, he delighted in the space, colour, and air round Calgary, where his diary
borrows the gleam of the Bow river ; " glimpses of the river, bright
blue and sparkling in the sun, could be seen between the trees,
and then beyond the creek more bluffs and cliffs casting dark
shadows, and behind them the yellow prairies stretching away to
the long jagged line of the Rockies ". Thence on through the
empty country north of Superior, with Laurentian rocks " like
elephants lying on their sides ", to Toronto, which he commended
equally for its Mendelssohn choir and its pure supply of milk ; to
Niagara and to New England, a last time to see the Endicott home,
where his father's replanning of the garden was religiously preserved.

Though he was waylaid for much speaking, this time he positively enjoyed it, both because he was made so welcome, and because
a responsible British voice was what Canadians most wished to
hear, when Mustapha Kemal's advance guards were unpleasantly
gesticulating across wire entanglements at Harington's minute
army. Though he found them mystified by a policy in which the
Dominion had not been consulted, on the reality of imperial sentiment he was enthusiastic. At Calgary he says : " I spoke with
a freedom and a fire that I often feel too constrained to allow
myself ; I felt I was doing good, and making them feel they must
support the Empire ". He met men with whom fate was to bring
other contacts, at Calgary Bennett, and at Ottawa Mackenzie King,
whom he set down as " a good and loyal Imperialist " and with
whom he held a conversation of weight on the Chanak crisis.

The Imperial government's dispatch, said the Premier, " merely
asked if the Dominion wished to be represented by a contingent,
should the necessity for armed resistance arise. M. K. then tele-
graphed to know if he might publish the terms but was refused
leave, which he thought unfortunate. . . . Meighen had been turned
out on the ground that he was attempting to carry on the government without any mandate . . . how then could he, having triumphed
on that very ground, take so important a step against the wishes

of his supporters and without consulting Parliament? He was a good Imperialist, he believed as I had said that British influence and power made for peace, liberty, and justice, but the democratic people of today would not suffer their policy to be dictated by Downing St., without their having a chance to say whether they approved it or not."

Two days out from New York his diary shows him already decided on the course to take through the confusion which flashed out in cables from home; the Conservative meeting at the Carlton which had voted to fight as an independent party, the resignation of Lloyd George, Bonar Law's new government, and the dissolution.

Diary, October 22

> my mind begins to clear on the political situation. I cannot imagine myself leaving the Unionist party for Ll. G., when there is no fundamental difference of policy. My only difficulty is Austen, and I have wondered whether I should go out of politics altogether. But that does not seem fair to the constituency or the party in Birmingham, which ought to be kept united. I don't want to do anything embarrassing to A., but it seems to me that he is unlikely to leave the party either, tho' he could hardly take office under Bonar Law.

In a gale off Cherbourg a letter continues the tale with his " astonishment " and " profound thanks to Providence for delivering us ". He had left England supposing that his brother would fight as leader of a separate party, but neither Austen's chivalry nor his electoral calculations had worked out that way. Offered the succession by Lloyd George, he declined it and, convinced that Labour would have at least 200 seats, held that only Coalition could save the country. The resistance he encountered spread from die-hards to under-secretaries ; Derby, the barometer of Lancashire, withdrew support ; the chairman of the party and the Chief Whip declared against coalition. Chanak then was only the last point in a long disintegration. In Middle-Eastern policy the country was used to backing the wrong horse, but not to the horse dying in its tracks ; it revolted when, turning from Irish bloodshed and drab unemployment, it found that France and Italy were behind the Turk, and that Britain would fight alone in a war brought on by indefensible diplomacy, of which half the Dominions disapproved. If this cost Lloyd George his political life, the price paid by his clients, Greek ministers and soldiers, was higher, and paid on the scaffold.

To Chamberlain October 30 meant a far-reaching decision,

for Amery brought from Bonar Law an offer of the Postmaster-
Generalship which, with some doubts (asking he might begin more
modestly with an under-secretaryship), he accepted. This led to
a difficult interview with Austen.

31 October

> I told him that in my view my acceptance would not be regarded as
> putting us in opposite camps, but rather as a link between him and
> the new government . . . facilitating his acceptance as one of the
> leaders, if not the leader, in the event of B. L. being unable to carry
> on. . . . I failed to convince him of the truth of this view, and I
> then said I should refuse, as I cared more for our personal relations
> than for politics. But I felt bound to tell him that I should consider
> my political career as ended, for one cannot go on refusing office
> when one does not differ in principles. . . . I said this in justice to
> myself, but not as an argument. However, it proved too much for
> him.

This was a hard strain, since twice now Bonar Law had stood between Austen and the hope of being Prime Minister, and however
much affection salved the wound, it was long healing, perhaps
never ceased to ache.

Hopes of reunion, however, must wait till the election was won ;
in which all that the Coalition leaders had predicted was falsified.
Labour representation, instead of being 200 or more, was only
138, but its programme was less modest, stretching out to nationalisation, " work or maintenance ", a capital levy, and revision of the
peace treaties ; " curious ", he thought, " that they should so
misunderstand the psychology of the country ". Nor did either
brand of Liberalism prosper. The Lloyd Georgians won only
57 seats, — Churchill, Addison, Montagu, and Greenwood all losing
theirs, — while Asquith's followers attained 60. So that, with a
fair margin over all others combined, the 344 Unionists might
surely hope for their full five years. In the Birmingham area they
held all twelve seats, though the Ladywood result was a shock,
for in a straight fight his majority was only 2443 against the Labour
candidate Dunstan, whose manifestos now read like fustian. Against
those glittering promises he was driven to say he had done more
for Labour as Lord Mayor than all their orators, but he found
Ladywood " desperately poor ", teeming with unemployed to whom
" no fireworks " and lower taxation made a cold appeal. Com-
forting himself with the thought that a weaker candidate would
have lost the seat, he set out to reorganise his electoral machine.

E*

This ministry lasted exactly one year, divided at May 1923 by Bonar Law's resignation and Baldwin's succession. Its composition reflected the purge which this army had made of its leaders who, a trifle too much stressing they had all the talents, marched gloomily corrective on the flank. If Bonar Law had taken up the lead where he had let it pass in 1916, his Chancellor of the Exchequer, Baldwin, brought with him the under-secretaries who had with him resisted Lloyd George, — Wood, Cunliffe Lister, Amery, and Griffith Boscawen. Salisbury, Cave, and Ronald McNeill were of the old guard ; Derby and Devonshire had lately refused office with Lloyd George. But though the ministry's direction would depend on a hundred contingencies, Neville hoped for reunion with Austen's group.

Hardly, however, had he begun to enjoy what he called the " comfortable obscurity " of the Post Office before he was uprooted. Housing was one of the sorest points before them, but Griffith Boscawen, Minister of Health, had lost his seat and was beaten in seeking another. In March 1923 the Prime Minister, who from the first took Neville into his counsel, made a bid for reunion by offering the vacant ministry to Robert Horne, who, however, declined it, being bound, we infer, by obligations to Austen and Birkenhead ; only then was it transferred to Neville, and accepted on condition of a free hand over rent restriction. In mid-March he entered the Cabinet in the office for which all his life had prepared him. " I had a wonderful reception ", he told his sisters, " from all parts of the House . . . got on good terms with the Labour members at once, and scored off Jack Jones."

Grave matters, in part inherited but some inherent in themselves, weighed on the government of 1923. In January the French, brushing aside our protestation, seized the Ruhr as their guarantee for reparations, and perhaps for even more. While at Washington Baldwin signed an exacting agreement for payment of our debt, Curzon at Lausanne was struggling with Russian and Turk, not to mention our allies. 1,300,000 unemployed and a huge shortage of houses kept up the political temperature, devastated local finance, and even poisoned foreign relations, for the Labour party could justly connect our distresses with French policy. With British feeling thus angrily swinging between the opposite poles of France and the Soviet, the process had begun which was later to imperil the State, of a penetration of domestic strife by foreign ideologies. And these wounds must be treated by a Cabinet divided between ex-Coalitionists and die-hards, a division made more fragile by the " talents " whom they had rejected, and who hardly disguised their wish not to praise their successors but to bury them.

Some of these threads we can eliminate by attending to the work of the new minister, and in particular the intertwisted matter of housing and rent restriction which, if not speedily handled, would destroy the government. Even before taking his new office he persuaded the Cabinet that housing subsidies must be renewed, though in the teeth of opposition which he notes as " the ﹐crusted old Tory ", and negotiation convinced him it was wise to be generous to the municipalities. So the core of the bill he brought forward was a substantial subsidy of £6 a house a year, for twenty years, on those completed before October 1925. In accord with Cabinet instructions, private enterprise was to have priority, though if a municipality convinced the minister, it could itself build and receive the subsidy. Subsidiary clauses would increase local authorities' power of making advances and assist house purchase, while the State would bear half the cost of slum clearance.

This, his first important speech as a minister, revealed several of his sides. It admitted the shameful spectacle of fellow-citizens, " herded together without privacy, without comfort, without almost the ordinary decencies of life " ; it took the offensive against both oppositions, — Lloyd-Georgian finance had destroyed private building, nor would " eloquent expressions of sympathy " supply houses. Though private enterprise had unassisted built 12,000 in the past six months, till time was given it for recovery a subsidy must be concentrated on the smallest houses, while the restriction of the State's liability (reversing Addison's method) would be an incentive to local economy. He asked for help in improving a bill which he commended only as " the beginning of a solution ".

Debate was critical but the bill emerged almost unchanged. That his Act would do little for rural housing, that his flat-rate subsidy would bear hardest on the poorest areas, he was well aware, but in this tangle he could only take one step at a time, concentrating, therefore, on the small urban houses from which private enterprise, unaided, could make no economic return. Actually by March 1925 schemes under this Act had been approved for nearly 200,000 houses, of which two-thirds were to be built by private enterprise.

But building was bound up in the vicious circle of rent restriction. No decontrol, cried Opposition, no increase of rents till new houses were built ; no building, responded private capital, without increased rents to meet increased costs. The bill he introduced in June came out of much controversy in Cabinet, and stabilised the existing law for two years, with one or two relaxations ; thereafter decontrol would begin, though subject to the approval of a court to hold the balance between landlord and tenant.

Since the purpose of decontrol was the reinvestment of private capital, these debates spilled over into others proceeding on the wider issue, and the longer they lasted, the further the disputants stood apart. To be born a man, the Labour logic terminated, involved a " right " to employment, a right of the unemployed to maintenance equal to the standard of those in work, a right to amenities for which his individual earnings could never pay. Such sentiment obliterated all the principles which nineteenth-century thinking had cherished, such as the duty of each locality to carry its own burden, the family as an economic unit, or the stimulus of need as a motive to work.

By midsummer both his bills were through, not before his crocuses at Westbourne had made room for rhododendrons and rock roses ; he hated to miss them while the faithful Commons deliberated whether " gargoyle " or " bourgeois " were parliamentary terms, while rude Conservatives derided Sidney Webb, and Clydesiders styled Banbury a murderer. Labour economics affronted everything in his experience and most dearly-found ideas. " Our system of local government ", runs his reply on necessitous areas, " is not based upon a system of nursing, there is too much of a tendency to rely on the government ", and although Opposition paid tribute to his reasonableness, he debated as hard as he thought. An account of the scene on June 27 when four Labour members were suspended (the parties' responsibility being about equally divided) lets in some light upon his mind :

> Though I never shout at Labour members or insult them, I cannot understand the psychology of some of our men who walked across . . . and endeavoured to reason with them . . . I think this sloppy sentimentality is quite as bad as H.'s rudeness.

He was also in charge of an agricultural rating bill, and collaborating with Amery to convince the Cabinet that the State should have a wireless chain not wholly dependent on Marconi ; altogether, much to think of in the daily walk from Knightsbridge to Whitehall.

And much at Birmingham. In February to escort the Duke of York round the Industries Fair, at which he took a first flight in an aeroplane ; " I thought as Annie wasn't there it was a good chance, and went up in a top hat ". There were funds to be raised from the rich, and a constituency of the poor to be tightened up, adequate agents placed in each division, and the achievement of a new party headquarters.

Cabinet rank brought also a first contact with foreign affairs, on which hitherto he had not trespassed outside the views of an average citizen. Like them he had been for war to a finish, detested Germans, and resented Bolsheviks ; as to the Italians at the peace congress, he gathered " they are a pretty greedy lot, but I daresay we appear the same to them, only more successful ". But by 1923 reparations and France were the stumbling-block, peace and prosperity being the twin wishes of Great Britain. While Birkenhead alleged the menacing superiority of the French Air Force, the Labour party opposed a modest advance of our own to 52 squadrons ; Snowden resisted the naval estimates ; Lansbury wished to liquidate the army.

To the accompaniment of many voices clamouring that government must do something, undefined, his letters show a growing restiveness in our rôle of neutrality. They begin with the perversity of the French ; " although France wants the money which can only be got out of a strong Germany, she always shrinks from any course which would help Germany to pay ". By June he was alarmed at the effects of the Ruhr adventure on our industry. In July he was concerned in shaping the Note which suggested that treaties did not authorise that venture, and reminded France of her debt to Britain. In September he was urging Baldwin to " strike while the iron was hot . . . because if we sit outside and look on, we cannot expect to exert any influence ". In October, after many talks with Eyre Crowe, he saw " a glimmer of hope that we may get America to take some sort of a hand ".

From these first experiences he drew other lessons. He saw the imperfections of the Lausanne peace, for " force is really the only way of obtaining justice, and the Turk knows perfectly well that whatever happens we are not going to war . . . difficult to see that the great war has had any beneficial effect whatever on the attitude of nations towards one another ". All this he felt the more in August when, in revenge for the murder of a boundary commissioner, the Italians seized Corfu, and the Council of Ambassadors, ignoring a Greek appeal to Geneva, sharply assessed the atonement which Greece should pay. Denouncing this as injustice, on the broad issue he stoutly defended the League : " it has done infinitely better than might have been expected. . . . If there had been no League, Corfu would never have been evacuated . . . the

French too would have backed Italy in order to secure Italian support in the Ruhr, if it had not been made clear that, if France did so, she would lose her position with the little Entente." Then out of policy rose matters of defence, one in particular which lasted his lifetime — the control of the Fleet Air Arm : " it appeared to me ", runs the diary, " that the Navy was right ".

On a final factor in our foreign policy his views changed, on the personality of Curzon, whose gifts he admired. Yet by June we hear : " I don't call him a great Foreign secretary, for I have never grasped what his line of policy is, and I do seem to feel that he is tempted into literary and debating scores, which cause him to lose sight for the moment of the really important end at which we are, or ought to be, aiming ". But when this was written all the government's prospects, no less than Curzon's, had been transformed.

Coalition had bisected both parties, leaving their disjointed halves wriggling towards reunion but in doubt which head to join to what tail ; indeed, of what had been the Liberal party there seemed now to be only two tails, busied in stinging one another. There might emerge, as Birkenhead and Churchill hoped, a centre group to save the country ; or, again, Austen and his friends might abandon the Welsh shepherd as incorrigible, and return to the true fold.

First decisive consequences flowed from the fact that Bonar Law's health had broken, and noting *The Times*' "recurring eulogies" of Baldwin, Neville pondered how he would get on with him, concluding it would be all right, " after all, he is a business man himself ". But when the crisis broke, his preoccupation was the future of Austen nor, though the dying Bonar Law once thought of making him his emissary to the King, had he any direct share in shaping events.

On May 23, while Austen was travelling home from France on the summons of his friends, Neville saw Baldwin.

Diary, 23 May 1923
> He said he thought this was the opportunity to heal the breach in the party. Bonar . . . also would like it, and the King had expressed his desire that he should try. . . . He did not think he ought to press for A. if it meant the resignation of some of those who had stuck by the ship in difficult times. . . .

Horne having refused to come in alone, on the 26th, in a long interview all at cross purposes, the new Prime Minister alienated Austen by an offer of the Washington embassy, and by the information that the vacant Exchequer would be offered to the Liberal McKenna.

While this was brewing at Chequers, Neville wrote thus to his sister Ida :

> I did not expect the opposition to his coming would be so strong. . . . Baldwin evidently thought at that time it could be overcome. . . . While Horne has been friendly and sociable, and has several times effectively supported the government, Austen has kept aloof . . . moreover, he is believed to have been very closely associated with Birkenhead. . . . I had rather hoped that Curzon would have been P.M., but I had not realised the extent of his unpopularity in the country. . . . The new P.M. asked me to go and see him on Wednesday . . . he is the nearest man we have to Bonar in the qualities of straightforwardness and sincerity.

Such qualities, however, he had to note, had not succeeded in conciliating Austen. These were harsh passages, but they were going to be worse, and though Neville begged his brother not to " brood ", Austen was listening to other counsels. The prospects of a Centre party indeed were waning, for Liberalism had conceived new hope for itself. But why, Birkenhead asked Austen, should they join " inferior men " like Baldwin's team ? let him study the example of the Peelites, and make his own terms when the next election had been fought, and lost. He forgot that one indispensable ingredient in a group who would be " Peelite " is the memory of a Peel.

As midsummer passed Neville felt that the government was better established, — and had not Arthur Henderson, the Carnot of Labour politics, given them ten years ? — which must lessen any hankerings after their lost leaders. In August, nearly free except for the Ruhr, he was busy getting into a permanent home at 37 Eaton Square, and so to fish again on the Oykell.

There he received a startling letter from the Prime Minister ; McKenna's candidature not having appealed to the City Unionists, the Exchequer was still begging, and he must take it. By return of post travelled back a predetermined refusal ; " what a day ! two salmon this morning, and the offer of the Exchequer this afternoon ", but " I am going to ask you not to press your offer ; I do not feel that I have any gifts for finance ". On the offer being repeated, he cut his fishing short, and capitulated after a long interview. In this, after canvassing many names, runs his letter, " B. brought forward the consideration which finally broke down my resistance. He said he had felt the need of a colleague at hand with whom he could discuss affairs as he had . . . with Bonar " ; adding that McKenna had himself suggested Neville, and that Curzon approved. The new Chancellor reflected that it revealed " a certain weakness in the government, since the P.M. feels there is no choice open to him ", and was unhappy at giving up plans for a two years' programme of Health.

This was written in the course of a Harrogate cure, with a new house in Eaton Square unfinished and now to be superseded by 11 Downing Street, with Italy defying the League and France inciting separatism in the Rhineland, Poincaré issuing smooth communiqués and receiving roughish notes from Curzon, with an Imperial Conference in the offing, and with letters from Austen suggesting that Neville's new position might end his own political life. " We are all suffering ", he wrote in October, " as every Cabinet seems to do, from the difficulty of finding time to think." But the Prime Minister had done some private thinking, to considerable purpose.

Here still was the gaping wound of unemployment on the increase and exports a bare 70 per cent of the pre-war volume, and here were Dominion ministers asking a guaranteed market. Most of all, here was the party of Disraeli split in two, his own leadership gloomily accepted by Austen and disputed by Birkenhead. Something must be found on which a reunited party could stand, and if Disraeli had called on an imperial people, was not Austen bound by his dearest memories to an imperial tariff? If such a venture led to Protection and food taxes, he must ask the electorate to free him from Bonar Law's pledge of no fundamental fiscal change.[1]

Diary, 6 October

> with regard to new duties S. B. considers that if the Board of Trade reports in favour of such things as silk, lace, tyres etc., the imposition would not conflict with the pledge, but he agreed with me that taxes on bacon, cheese, and butter, as proposed by certain of our party . . . was stirring up the fundamental question.

By the 10th he notes that Baldwin thought of an immediate dissolution ; " my own idea had been only to go in for a few extra duties in November, but to lead up by an educative campaign to a more thorough-going policy by the time we were ready for an

---

[1] The diary, under October 1927, records a view (certainly a very common one in those days) that in 1923 Lloyd George was returning from Canada with schemes for tariffs ; " if we had not gone for T.R. in 1923, Ll. G. would have done so and the Conservative party would have been out for years ".

election ", — which he would put some eighteen months ahead. Such " education " was called for not least in the Cabinet ; of its Protectionist members some wanted price stabilisation and no talk of elections, others championed a skeleton tariff, and what Chamberlain styled the " hair-trigger consciences " of their Free Trade colleagues threatened some explosive resignations. However, armed with a suitably general formula, on October 25 they outlined to a party meeting the project of a tariff to fight unemployment. He thought it served the purpose well, " it was sufficiently definite to please our people, but it was vague enough to leave the country undisturbed at the thought of an election in the very near future ".

He was wrong ; for to be both definite and vague about tariffs is given to no man, and it was not from Austen only that complaint came that no one knew what the Prime Minister meant. While Curzon and Balfour murmured " idiotic ", Austen lamented pledges that would make food taxes impossible, and when Neville embarked on an " educative " tour of speeches, a cotton magnate at Preston sounded a sadly common note, " Ye've dished the party ". But his letters made a case for the Prime Minister of some prospective importance.

November 11

> He is not so simple as he makes out. . . . Here he has sprung a protectionist policy on the country almost at a moment's notice, with a Cabinet a substantial portion of which consists of Free Traders. Not one of them has resigned, and the time when they could effectively have done so has already passed. The die-hards and Austen vie with one another in urging him to be more extreme. . . . Yet they all say that they will support him. At the same time he has anchored the thing on to unemployment. . . . He has definitely separated Ll. G. from the ex-Cabinet ministers.

But the next few days showed that Baldwin's method involved an element of living dangerously.

He was returning to his original instinct for an instant election. Both the Rothermere and Beaverbrook press declared against him, though whether for Lloyd George and free trade, or Birkenhead and tariffs, was more obscure. Churchill was courting Leicester as a Liberal ; his portrait and that of Lloyd George were retrieved from outer darkness at the National Liberal Club, to be rehung on the line. Derby was most unhappy about launching protection on Lancashire. And though a Cabinet majority had agreed on a January election, the party officials thought it had better

come at once, and on November 12 another influence reinforced them.
That day, when the Prime Minister saw Austen and Birkenhead together on the matter of reunion, he found that they too advised an instant election. But they received coldly his suggestion of an election first and office afterwards, Austen insisting they must be admitted at once, and that ultimately Birkenhead must displace Cave on the woolsack. Then the storm broke. Three junior ministers declared their intention to resign if Birkenhead were included ; on the 14th Neville found Baldwin doubtful whether he would be able to take either.

Diary, 18 November

> I told him I had always gravely doubted whether the former would not do us more harm than good. . . . But though I agreed with him in disliking intensely making any bargain with such a man, though I felt it would be almost impossible to do so if the bargain were to be at the expense of a man like Cave, yet it seemed to me too late to go back now at the dictation of under-secretaries. . . . There was a Cabinet later in the morning. . . . I asked whether he was going to tell his colleagues about the new members, but he said no, and immediately after the meeting informed me that the party chiefs (Jackson and Hall) had told him that the feeling against F. E. in the party was so strong that it was hopeless to take him in, and after talking over the situation with Derby he had resolved not to proceed. . . . F. E. with great astuteness took his rebuff with the utmost good humour, and has gone off hand-in-hand with Derby to fight for the party in Lancashire. A. is *froissé* and stiff.

So came about the immediate election, with half the front bench feeling loose in their seats and a party united· only in so far as the programme was vague. Neville must drop his planning, and the tariff advisory board he had set up under Milner, to fight for Ladywood, where Dr. Dunstan was hard at work on rent restriction and the class war. A rowdy election, which of all things he loathed, " with all the indignities and humiliations which it involves ".

Everything justified his first instinct that only a long educative campaign could have drowned the clamour of dearer food, and the Conservative loss of 86 seats left parties in chaos. Though still the strongest group, with 258 members, if the 191 Labour and 158 Liberals combined, they would be destroyed ; in any event the country had plainly rejected the heart of their programme. " The new electorate ", says the diary, " contains an immense mass of very ignorant voters of both sexes whose intelligence is low, and who have no power of weighing evidence. These voters could not grasp the idea of better employment and wages as springing from a tariff." As for Ladywood, " it seems to me almost impossible to hold that seat much longer ".

But on the first question facing all of them, what was to be done with three minority parties, his view was formed at once and never shaken. While Austen hoped the King would invite Asquith and MacDonald jointly, while powerful elements like the *Daily Mail* and Birkenhead hoped for a coalition between Asquith and Baldwin (or more preferably Derby), he was clear on all grounds that Labour should be given office. The one thing that would clinch a future Labour domination would be a merely tactical alliance between Conservatives and Liberals ; moreover, he reflected that Labour " would be too weak to do much harm but not too weak to get discredited ". Since both Asquith and Baldwin had reached the same conclusion, the end duly came on January 21, when a Labour-Liberal majority of 72 expelled the Baldwin government.

Restored by a week in the Alps, where he fell about on skis and skated again after a fifteen years' interval, he came back to clinch other questions even more searching. The party, his diary had said before Christmas, " is a nest of intrigue ", some of it directed against Baldwin's lead, but though he would agree that Baldwin did not give his Cabinet a firm guidance, he was decided there was no alternative leader. There were those who urged him to assert himself in Baldwin's counsels, but, replies the diary, " I am not and never can be a pusher, though I may act for a brief period like one by a great effort ". Besides, when " S. B." had lately asked him to go a walk, what had come of it ? " I made certain he was anxious to consult me on several difficult problems. Not a bit of it. He talked about the pelicans, and the beauty of spring at Astley, and I had the utmost difficulty in dragging in politics." Loyal but exasperated, he set to work for a party reunited under Baldwin, with as little weakening as possible on protection.

We find his energies, therefore, bent to a double task : to convince one section of his colleagues that if they wanted Austen and Horne they must take Birkenhead also, and to persuade another of the necessity of a party meeting to agree on both policy and leader. On February 5 he crowned his persistent peace-making when Baldwin and Austen dined at his house.

9 February 1924

Austen was a bit stiff at first but gradually thawed, and as soon as Annie left us I started in and called on S. B. He said what he had to say without any beating about the bush, and after one moment's hesitation A. frankly accepted the invitation. After that all went like clockwork, and very soon it was " my dear Stanley " and " my dear Austen " as if they had ne'er been parted. . . . So reunion has come at last, thanks, I think I may say, to me.

Unkindness thus buried, it remained to inter the general tariff ; yet with some hint of a *resurgam* on its tomb. For, as he had written, " education must now precede resurrection ". The wake took place at a party meeting where, almost in the exact terms of Neville's draft, Baldwin staked out the claims of imperial preference and safeguarding, with an admission that a general tariff could not be pressed without evidence that the country had changed its mind.

Something of the gloom, after the first relief, which seizes on ex-ministers, descended on him this spring, leading to renewed thoughts of exchanging politics for business, while for some months he faithfully obeyed a new doctor in eschewing meat, with no ' noticeable difference to his health. But in many ways these ten months of Opposition restored him, rousing his pugnacity and giving him new chances of construction.

To judge austerely the first Labour government, which held office on sufferance, would be unjust, but its performance was spasmodic, and flashes from its fine eyes startled the Liberals who had given it birth. As the child waxed and kicked, its poor mother waned. Soon it became clear that many Liberals, wearied of watching by the cradle of Socialism, would gladly join Conservatives in making its hearse ; all of which must affect the composition of any future Conservative government. In the instability of that summer his declared tactics were to give the enemy rope, to " make a show of doing our best to throw the government out and put the odium of keeping them in on the Liberals ", during which process he would work for a constructive programme.

Much would depend on which section of Labour dominated the MacDonald Cabinet. While Haldane stood guard over imperial defence, Thomas over the Empire, and Snowden over orthodox finance, something in the Prime Minister's ideals responded to the nation's longing for a world of peace. His active courtesies, and the replacement of Poincaré by Herriot, stilled the soreness of the Ruhr, while the drear matter of reparations moved a stage on in the acceptance of the Dawes Scheme. He was well alive to some shortcomings in his party. He compelled them to carry out the Admiralty's cruiser programme, nor did he spare their tenderest places, for a new preface to his book on Socialism spoke out against

" public doles, Poplarism, strikes for increased wages, and limitation of output ".

But both Cabinet decision and administration betrayed other influences. Preferential duties accepted at the late Imperial Conference were ignored, the McKenna duties were to end, work at Singapore was suspended. Wheatley, the militant Clydesider who had succeeded at the Ministry of Health, cancelled the order forbidding the Poplar guardians to give relief beyond an authorised scale. Restrictions on uncovenanted benefit (benefit, that is, not based on contributions) were swept away, the margins were fading between insurance and doles. There were efforts to reinstate the police strikers of 1919–20, to give control of the mines to the miners, to enfranchise Indian workers, to reduce the army to extinction. Prompt recognition of the Soviet, and Arthur Henderson's assurance that the Versailles treaties must be revised, challenged the Conservative world of Europe and America.

While this " high adventure ", as the Prime Minister liked to call it, moved swiftly towards its predestined end, Chamberlain was more active in counsel than debate. As an ex-Chancellor of the Exchequer he denounced the capital levy as a bribe, or the pedantry of Liberals who would rather jeopardise revenue than be contaminated by a whiff of protection ; for recognising there was little hope of cutting expenditure, he declared our object should be to increase income. But his chief encounters were with Wheatley. A first step was to demolish a new rent restriction bill which would, among other things, have allowed an unemployed man to live rent-free ; on which the diary records a conversation with Mac-Donald, with a sequel.

Diary, 7 April 1924
He said when he saw the bill, he was filled with consternation and told his Cabinet it would be suicide to go on with it. . . . I said he would find us ready to help in anything that would remedy real hardship. . . . A strange man, with much that is attractive about him.
    Note : Nov. 5.—But the next day he went to a meeting of Labour women and told them that the action of the Tories . . . showed that they were callously indifferent to the sufferings of the tenants ! This gave the first shock to my belief in R. M.'s sincerity. There have been a good many since.

Then came the Housing Act of 1924. It was Wheatley's contention that the Act of 1923 failed to meet the crying need, for houses to be let (for the poor could not buy) at rents which the poor could afford.   To this end, if satisfied as to conditions of letting, the new Act would extend the subsidy to £9 a year for forty years, — a rise, in capital terms, from £75 to £156, — though continuing the Act of 1923 for houses not subject to the new conditions.

Loyal, like most legislators, to his own progeny, Chamberlain believed his Act would have solved the problem by swelling the total volume ; arguing that by the process known as " filtering up ", the poor would gradually take over houses vacated by the class above them.   He protested therefore, and not he alone, since criticism from Manchester experts was as severe, that Wheatley's Act was not one to encourage building, but to subsidise the rents of a privileged class at the expense of richer and poorer alike ; moreover, that the enhanced subsidy, setting municipal and private enterprise in competition, would inevitably increase costs.   As seemingly it did, the cost of a parlour house rising by forty pounds on the average before the end of the year.

But on this subject he would not be a partisan.   On second reading, in what Wheatley's note called " a generous speech ", he declared for continuity of policy, which he admitted could only be achieved " after a certain amount of trial and error . . . we on this side will be just as much open to conviction as honourable members of the opposite side, for I believe that we are, as I give them credit for being, thoroughly desirous of seeing an end put to this age-long question, which affects the lives of so many of our fellow-citizens ".

A dry figure or two may do temporary justice to this controversy. In the year 1925-6, in round numbers, private enterprise built 66,000 houses without any State assistance and another 62,000 with a subsidy under the Chamberlain Act, while local authorities built 27,000 with the Wheatley subsidy.

But as Liberals were tired of being outraged by Labour and Labour wearied of being lectured by Liberals, the " high adventure " must soon end, and his energy demanded a policy and a leader. He was busied recasting the constitution of the Central Office, insistent also on more shadow Cabinets, " though S. B. struggles like a broncho to avoid them ".

In March he furnished Baldwin with notes for a comprehensive insurance scheme, laying down four essentials : " (1) it must be contributory, (2) it must be compulsory, (3) it must cover the 4 main needs for security ; unemployment, sickness, old age, and death leaving widows and dependents, (4) the provision for old age must offer sufficient to induce the old men to retire ".   Chairman of one committee for this matter, he set on foot another to investigate municipal reform under Hoare, " he and I are the only Socialists in the late government ". In June the party published *Aims and Principles* which he had drafted ; " it makes me laff . . . the *Herald* thinks Curzon did ". From his fishing holiday in August he wrote of what he would do, were he leader. " Every one of my colleagues who was worth anything would have some special question assigned to him. . . . I should try to be prepared with information which would enable me to formulate a policy about everything. In particular I should begin to pick out particular industries and work up the case for McKenna-dutying them, and I should try to get out a new policy for agriculture " ; on which follows detail of a wheat commission, with power to buy and store reserves, for control of prices and security in time of war.

A breeze which he and Amery had with their colleagues rose over a projected " fair trade union ", devised to push education in the protectionist cause ; and the breeze fringed a cyclone, on the cone of which rode Churchill, whose candidature for the Abbey division of Westminster, as an anti-Socialist, menaced the unity so lately created. He dreaded they might slide back into Coalition, with the advent of this renowned free-trader ; moreover, while he had promised, before Churchill clanged into the field, to speak for the official candidate, " Austen passionately declared that he should speak for Winston ". So a truce was imposed on all ex-ministers, and with Churchill's narrow defeat this cyclone receded. Yet the leadership itself might be put in jeopardy. Neville, who saw less of Baldwin of late, noted that he seemed spiritless in debate, while Austen had seldom spoken better, though he agreed with the common criticism that Austen had " a coalition mind ", nor did he like the arrangements, taking shape in the constituencies, for Conservative-Churchillian understanding. All such doubts were to fade in the glow of battle.

Parliament met in the autumn in the certainty of an upheaval, for on two questions in particular both Conservative and Liberal opinion had set hard. One was the Anglo-Soviet treaty which, after many breakdowns, had been signed through the mediation of Lansbury and others of the Left wing and which in certain contingencies would involve a British loan. The second was more ignominious. An article in the Communist *Workers' Weekly* called on the forces of the Crown to refuse to use arms against fellow-workers, whether British or foreign, and the Attorney-General laid a charge of sedition ; on second thoughts, however, — which seem

also to have been the second thoughts of Ramsay MacDonald —
he withdrew it, and the accused organ broke into paeans of triumph.
Debate at once revealed that the Liberal blood was boiling, or
perhaps frozen, in any case declining to stomach the Russian loan,
and that the Labour tactic of playing Liberal against Conservative
would work no more.　Having scientifically contrived to lose their
own vote of censure, on October 8 the Conservatives supported
a Liberal motion for a select committee which was carried by 359
to 198.　To Chamberlain's surprise, instead of resigning and throwing his enemies on the defensive, MacDonald dissolved Parliament.

A general wish for stable government, understandings between
anti-Socialists in many constituencies, and Baldwin's pledges against
protection, already pointed to a heavy defeat for Labour when,
five days before polling, the " red " Zinovieff letter was published,
in which the Third International invited British workers to plot
against the State and debauch the army.　Whatever view was
taken of its authenticity, as to which MacDonald and his colleagues
showed not a vestige of agreement, it blew sky-high the Russian
treaty and its authors.

In Birmingham every Conservative majority was reduced, one
seat was lost, meetings were rowdy, and nowhere more than in
Ladywood, whence Dr. Dunstan had moved to fight Austen in the
west, leaving Neville confronted by the more formidable Oswald
Mosley.　Often he had groaned over Ladywood, dark with poverty
and unemployment, and asking more ceaseless attention than he
had time to give.　His claim to be a good neighbour was well
justified ; week in and week out he and his wife toiled in and for
the constituency, but it was not his *milieu*.　It was already in his
mind to move to a less exacting seat, though to move before this
fight would be " desertion in face of the enemy ".

His address dwelt on MacDonald's surrender to his extremists,
pointed to an increased unemployment which the repeal of duties
had aggravated, promised that a Unionist government would reimpose them, would carry " safeguarding " further, explore mass-
production methods of housing, tackle the slums, and launch
contributory pensions ; asking help " not for a class war but for
a peaceful co-operation of all classes ".

As ever, he was confident of an increased majority, but ill reports
darkened the pouring rain of polling day, which ended with four
hours over the recount in the Town Hall after midnight ; thus
depicted by the victor : " The first count gave me a majority of 30,
then it was said to be 15, then 7, then I was out by 2, and finally

at 4.30 the Lord Mayor announced that I was returned by 77. The galleries of the Town Hall were filled with Socialists, who booed at us . . . even invaded the floor and yelled insults. . . . We hated the idea of being beaten, especially by that viper ". So much for " the peaceful co-operation of all classes ".

And now what next ? If Birmingham had been hard beset, the general Conservative triumph had been immense. Their vote had increased by two millions, they had won 413 seats as against Labour's 151, — though Labour had polled a million more than before ; Liberalism was slain, Asquith was beaten, and only 40 members would straggle after an uncomfortable trinity of leaders in Lloyd George, Simon, and Mond. This too large majority confirmed Chamberlain in his opinion that by their social reforms the new government would rise or fall. As to his own future, " I ought to be a great Minister of Health, but am not likely to be more than a second-rate Chancellor ", and though friends might be disappointed if he did not go back to the Exchequer, " that would not weigh with me one iota ". In the long run he decided for himself, telling Baldwin he would prefer Health.

But he went back to Health with notions ranging far beyond health and housing.

CHAPTER X

PERSONAL

I have kept uninfringed my nature's law ;
The inly-written chart thou gavest me
To guide me, I have steer'd by to the end.

M. ARNOLD

BEFORE we enter on the last quarter of his life, and while he takes ship for a week in Spain at the new year of 1924–5, we may endeavour to paint him as he was. For he was just on fifty-six, of an age after which time will mellow, or perchance contract character, but can hardly move its base, so that we feel free to use here evidence that sometimes comes from later years.

It is the more desirable to do so because, more than most public men, he was unknown to the public, never being one of the statesmen who expose the pageant of their heart, or reflect some image that the public has set up. " Reserve ", a " frigid " façade, " formality ", "bashfulness ", these are the common accounts even from men who professed to know him well. He perceived here a shortcoming in himself, would admit there was much in his heart that he could never express ; though while reflecting, when he began at the Ministry of Health, " I should never be a favourite with the press, like Father was or Winston is ", hoped nevertheless to win posterity's respect for his deeds.

Twenty centuries of science have left us in the dark as to the inter-relation of spirit and body. In this case the bodily frame was slight, tenacious, and late-matured ; in several years he weighed under ten stone, he was perpetually attacked by inherited gout, and never stood up well to cold. But his life was regular, simple, and strenuous, and he had the power of sleep, so that at sixty he could out-walk younger men on the hill and at seventy this energy was not abated. In the small curved head, setting of the hair, and slight build, he was Joseph's son, but the mouth was more sensitive, the eyes and expression darker and less luminous. Only rarely to the larger world a smile of well-remembered beauty threw a beam from his feelings. His voice was nothing like an orator's, though agreeable and audible without being raised, but too thin and high to carry off successfully the note of peroration, or dramatic effect.

In all life's ups and downs, in Cabinet and in private stress, he seemed to others calm, patient, a tower of strength, but in fact his composition was sensitive, high-strung, and restless. His inability to be idle, a letter of 1921 almost admits, was a danger ; if not doing something, " tho' it be only weeding the garden, an uneasy sensation creeps into my mind, and I become restless ". And when he was Prime Minister, one criticism from those well placed to speak was that he could not be prevented from filling up his day. Time was an enemy and life a combat : " a less agitated mentality ", he found by 1928, a consolation of growing age.

The firm tranquillity he shed round him was the result of discipline, for within the mood could be black, and there were depressions to be fought down. When in 1923 Protection was being shaped and fought in Cabinet, we read " it is disconcerting to find oneself so little under control ", and we remember the depth of the wound over National Service, " I often think I should like to flee away and hide myself in a South Sea Island ". Till the end he found speech-making a heavy ordeal, could not abide the necessary exhibitionism of elections, and whereas in his home, or in small companies, he could charm and delight and amuse, with numbers he often failed. He could intimidate by gruffness, and estrange by reserve.

Though discerning judges thought him too sensitive for politics, for the common use of life he had found his own armour, that dogged will which he showed in fishing by refusal to try a new place till he had tried all the flies, as well as in a hundred cases of political tenacity. Of this code, which owed nothing to dogmatic religion, he did not openly speak, though by implication always. Reading in 1939 a book on Regency England, he reflected on the distance travelled in a century, " above all in self-control ", but for his one connected piece of thought on this matter we must go to the curious source of Harmsworth's *Business Encyclopaedia*, to which, with the candid object of making a little money, he contributed in 1924 an article on " Personality and the Equipment for Success ". Wealth and honours, it begins, have no value except as a measure of effort, of an instinct rooted deep in humanity. To direct talent to success is the reward of character, given to one " whose conduct is regulated by fixed principles ". For the restoration of British industry, his immediate theme, he looked to men who will " discipline themselves ", naming as character's proper ingredients, in due order, integrity, judgement, courage, sympathy, and patience.

In himself morality owed more than in most men to heredity, or at least to a family piety of religious force. To hold up the Chamberlain standard of public service, to make known their just claims, to feel " a real thrill of exultation " in their mutual loyalty, to bring his children up to do credit to their name, this was to him all in all. His father's name was always in mind, and constantly on his lips. Year after year he pursued his project of an adequate memorial to him, for he thought the Abbey bust but moderate, and Tweed's statue " like a dreamy young parson addressing a mothers' meeting ". Others let slip his first idea of making High-bury itself that memorial, but in 1931 a new chance was offered, and now his father's study stands more or less intact as in his day, a rather lonely token of his younger son's fervour.

Whether this also derived from heredity, the Bahamas, or con-tinued circumstance, he became the most self-contained and self-reliant of men. Intimate friend, outside his family, he never apparently had, in the sense that they knew all his heart. He had plenty of friendly acquaintance, and men to whom he was drawn by affection or loyal partnership in every stage of life ; whether to Ernest Hiley, his town clerk at Birmingham, to his master in fishing, Arthur Wood, or to Halifax. But, his family always excepted, he did not depend on other human beings.

This carried its penalty with it that, though his character often brought out the best in other men, he sometimes misjudged their motives, or did not grasp what was in their mind. He had no mental antennae, no sense of anticipation, no hinterland to his mind, so one was repeatedly told. Yet in so far as this was true, and only part true it was, it very certainly did not come from lack of sympathy or consideration. A volume of letters breathe grati-tude for his own sympathy in all life's worst trials, public and private, a hundred witnesses testify to his remembered acts of kindness, to Bahama negroes, working men and journalists, sec-retaries and subordinate staff. A casual diary note on a Swiss holiday sounds his compunction that, coming in late from a long walk, " we had to keep the kitchen and the waiters attending to us alone ", and his letters, in great things and small, all bear the same witness. Curzon, he said, had been a failure " for want of a little more humanity " ; he dismisses one candidate as governess to his children for lack of " tenderness ".

In an analysis of character we have to guard against the delusion that the qualities of considerable men can be isolated, and must repeat that he was very representative of the nineteenth-century

British ruling class. He could be as insular-prejudiced as any of them ; " you cannot like him ", he says in finishing the long life of Disraeli, " he is too different, in the way that Montagu is different ". He had a strong sense of possession and, though the least luxurious of men, asked the standards to which he was used. In all spheres of life he disliked the doctrine of something for nothing, insisted on value for money, and would bargain with zest over a picture or an antique. Like his father, he was particular about dress, whether in himself or others. But with all this he was by some quality set apart, a man with his own inner light, and one nearer to his father's generation than his own in that he was predominantly a moralist, and an intellectual.

He had integrity in the full meaning of the word or, better perhaps, in what dictionaries give as its mathematical sense, " the whole sum of a series of consecutive values ". All men felt this of him. It was not just moral admiration, as voiced, to take one case, by Gilbert Barling, light of Birmingham medicine and University, " your high ideals are an inspiration to me " : it was, even more, that all men knew he would always be entirely himself. What he did not feel sincerely, he would and could not be. This explained the perpetual understatement in his speeches, which often robbed them of warmth and which was fastened on in this letter of acute perception.

7 June 1934 ; from Beaverbrook
you, like the late Bonar Law, always understate your case. That is part of your character. But you do not make headway on this understatement. You make it on the character. So do not be deceived.

It explained his loathing of emotion in public, his frequent denunciation of British sentimentality ; it explains his refusal, when Prime Minister, to listen to suggestions that he should show himself at Lords or the Derby, for if he did so he would be false. He would not be defended by a fallacious reasoning, not even borrow another man's quotation as his own. He resented being asked to achieve the common favours asked of statesmen ; on the other hand, he would come out rubbing his hands in appreciation at the ability of an attack from Stafford Cripps, and when he used the term " a thorough gentleman " of a rival, it was independent of convention, being applied alike to Donald Maclean and Stephen Walsh. He was an ill negotiator, in the sense that he would not conceal his knowledge.

Of the simplicity which must belong to integrity he had his

full share. He would blurt out his mind in homely saw or instance and, though often accused of lack of humour, had two streaks of English humour in plenty. He loved broad effects, had Dickens at his finger-tips, and enjoyed American humour a good deal more than American politics, could spend an evening alone in ecstasy at the antics of a good clown. He could also appreciate and exemplify the sardonic. He could not reduce the whisky duty, he told the House in 1935, despite " the pious origin of whisky, the addition it makes to the gaiety of nations, and the comfort it is to the aged poor ", and sent in a letter an enclosure endorsed " Autre Vexation " which runs, abbreviated, thus : " extract from a letter from a valued supporter to whom I had written to condole on the loss of his wife . . . ' my wife was ill for a very long time and, apart from this, I have during the last six months been very anxious about my thumb, which has caused me great pain ' ". In private he exercised this side, as his father had, in excellent mimicry. Yet the general soil of his being was not that in which grows the comic spirit, or of the sort that shrugs a shoulder at human weakness.

He was a moralist, very much awake to the egoisms of those whom Crashaw describes as " slippery souls with shining eyes ", and if he was partisan it was in the finer sense that he had fixed values for which he would fight. His mental definitions were black or white, he distrusted neutral greys. Our housing, he said once, must be worthy of " a proud and moral nation " : " I have searched my heart ", he told one who was questioning him about his Irish treaty, as with a moral contentment. If he thought a friend was behaving shabbily, he would let him know it, and was likely to condone poor conduct least of all in high places.

Being an intellectual, his demands for good company were earnest, and in some ways he was too much the intellectual to come down to his audiences. He could growl about " half-educated bumpkins ", — meaning, one fears, rural district councillors, — while we find him unnaturally surprised by a keeper on the Test who could not distinguish a reed bunting from a blackcap. He was thus sometimes charged with intellectual vanity, when he was, rather, only assured, resolute, or intellectually amazed.

Business habit and hunger for action made his life one of system. However late the hour, he finished his Cabinet boxes the same night and appeared with the clock next day, for like a clock he measured time so that waste of it was an affront, and precision made the pleasure of his mind. " Marvellous and beautiful " he found the instruments in a laboratory, while last thing at night he would fall heavily on a comma displaced by his department ; if he could be always master of his subject, so could others be. Training and temperament alike made him one of the class of master draftsmen, — who do not adopt easily drafts by others, — a loose argument or incoherent structure taking in his eye almost the proportion of a moral offence.

So revelling in detail and having a powerful memory, he had stored a mass of information on many things. His memory would reproduce in public the exact arguments on the organisation of music in Birmingham privately given him a year before, or casually recall that he had seen, ten years back in Algiers, cyclamen rooted in bark. The evidence of knowledge on his earliest interests, the note-books on insects and butterflies which he bequeathed to Birmingham, the botanical precision so profuse in every other letter, his many diaries with lists of favoured pictures, the number of spikes on his orchids, would give the impression of over-laboriousness if they stood alone. But with them must be set much else. There was the knowledge of nature which dumbfoundered country houses, or of china and antiquities which surprised politicians at Rome. There is Sir Hugh Allen's word for it that he knew Beethoven better than any except a very few professionals, or the detailed correspondence with Dover Wilson on Hamlet. With him such detail did not drown the constructiveness which, of all qualities, he praised in other men. He could not see the black stooks of a wet harvest without getting out a scheme for drying them by fans, or see a good picture without trying to acquire it for the Birmingham gallery.

No one could place him much below the first-class intellects, some of the best judges put him among them. Whether it came from his direct pragmatic nature or no, neither letters nor speeches do justice to the breadth of his reading, which was incessant in both French and English. Severe treatises on his old subjects, Fabre or de Vries, would accompany him abroad, and he would always return to Darwin, W. H. Hudson, or anything about Shakespeare and Beethoven. In modern history he was read above the average, while for imaginative literature he went most to those who had something of his own gifts, wherefore he never tired of Jane Austen, Samuel Butler, Henry James, and Conrad.

On the whole his mentality must, I think, be called sanguine, proud, and sensitive. Having taken infinite pains, his decision, once reached, was hard to shake, yet he respected reasoned opposition and was never found obstinate by colleagues, civil servants, or financiers ; if, on the other hand, he were attacked, as he conceived, unjustly or unreasonably resisted, his hand went to his sword. In this, as in other facets, he was much his father's son, with an instinctive preference for attack and a courage that would never go round to avoid a difficulty. That he was " a first-class fighting man " was one of the qualities which drew him to Douglas Hogg, and it will be found that he risked ease in council, popularity, even the highest office, by declining to change his chosen ground, least of all at the bidding of the market-place. There was a touch of the implacable in him, as there had been in Joseph, in particular where what he thought disloyalty was concerned, and a stout refusal to allow that good could come out of Samaria, — or Wales.

The personal feelings of public men are necessarily blended with public causes, but of vanity, for himself, as against other men, he was devoid. But, in addition to the objects nearest his heart, the family name and the party and self-respect, he was a masterful man, even a natural autocrat ; so runs the repeated word from all who had seen him at any level of authority, from the constituency up to the Cabinet. Masterful but magnanimous, dogged, but a first-class loser, a leader who fought better, and only, for causes, not for himself.

As for his inner kingdom, to reach it we should have to risk skirting emotions which in public he rigorously repressed, and from under his rejections recover the tenderness and imagination which he concealed. He had waited long, and wished ardently, for his home, and when realised he found it all-satisfying. Always loving small children, his happiness and pride in his own were exuberant ; one letter elaborates the whole plot of a Christmas play in which he is to act with them, his own part to be that of " a fool giant ". Of what he felt of his debt to his wife he often spoke in public and, as it had been at Ladywood, so he repeats in a letter of 1937 on becoming Prime Minister :

I should never have become P.M. if I hadn't had Annie to help me. . . . She has kept many who might have left me if I had been alone, but are devoted to her. But besides all this she has softened and smoothed my natural impatience and dislike of anything with a whiff of humbug about it, and I know she has saved me often from making an impression of harshness that was not intended.

Sometimes his recounting of work done, or categorical account of his flowers, is broken by a different short-lived light. This i

Bassano

MRS. CHAMBERLAIN

from an evening of March 1927, overhung by reform of the poor law : " Last night I read Conrad's *Shadow Line* and escaped from the poisonous world of politics, into that mysterious atmosphere of the Eastern seas, where he somehow contrives to hold you breathless for ages under the impending shadow of some unknown but steadily approaching disaster ". Or this, of the year before, on Beethoven : " to me a far more interesting and intriguing figure than Napoleon ". Here there was something else than his penetrating observance, which made him note, for instance, that during an eclipse the birds continue to sing, and fills many letters with a sort of etching power. " A larch which seems like a ball of golden gauze in the sun, it is so soft and so luminous, beside and around it are the birches like purple clouds " ; to picture this on the Dee, to hear the curlew " whistling indignantly " in Llanberis pass, to hear a corncrake in the heart of Birmingham, excited his mind, and went down, surely, to something superior and more old than observation. His sport meant much to him but its accompaniments even more, staghorn moss and bog plants on the moor, loosestrife and marsh-marigold by the chalk stream.

Though I do not find that he ever at length expressed it, his akinship to what was pure and harmonious in art and music seems to find a chord, without which life would be dumb, in nature's colour and rhythm. From the ugly year of National Service we hear " at last the blackcap has arrived. His song always makes a peculiar appeal to me, not only for the beauty of the notes, but because it carries a sort of pot-pourri of old associations, in which youth and Highbury and Cannes are all mixed up together." And as, like Marvell's gardener, he timed his year by flowers and trees, he drew from nature repose and refreshment for what, we may say, was intrinsically a religious mind.

The river runs through the garden, and you can follow it down some quarter mile past willows and poplars, walking through the long grass with the buttercups up to your knee, till you get to the last bend before the weir, where the stream runs dark and slow under big elms.

CHAPTER XI

THE MINISTRY OF HEALTH: 1924–1929

AGED 55–60

One person with a belief is a social power equal to ninety-nine who have only interests.

J. S. MILL

THE second Baldwin government [1] was never a coherent body, few Cabinets of twenty members can be, but as originally constituted it was outstanding in talent and true to its leader's deduction that his mandate had come from more than a party. Its measures were ample and determinate. It restored the gold standard and derated industry, slew Poplarism, and broke the general strike. Its Local Government Act was the greatest administrative reform since Gladstone's palmy days, it vastly extended social insurance, and at the Imperial Conference of 1926 laid down a new doctrine of empire. Currents of the people's new life were enclosed in the B.B.C. charter and the Central Electricity Board, asserted too in a grant of the franchise to women at the same age as men. Until its last year the deluge of the war period seemed to be ebbing and Ararat in sight ; the peace of Locarno, Germany's entry into the

[1] THE SECOND BALDWIN ADMINISTRATION, 1924–1929

PRIME MINISTER :	Baldwin.
LORD PRESIDENT :	Curzon (from April 1925, Balfour).
LORD PRIVY SEAL and Leader in the Lords :	Salisbury.
LORD CHANCELLOR :	Cave (from March 1928, Douglas Hogg, Lord Hailsham).
CHANCELLOR OF THE EXCHEQUER :	Churchill.
SECRETARIES OF STATE :	*Home :* Joynson Hicks.
	Foreign Affairs : Austen Chamberlain.
	Colonies : Amery.
	War : Worthington Evans.
	India : Birkenhead (from October 1928, Peel).
	Air : Hoare.
	Scotland : Gilmour.
BOARD OF TRADE :	Cunliffe Lister.
EDUCATION :	Eustace Percy.
ADMIRALTY :	Bridgeman.
HEALTH :	Neville Chamberlain.
AGRICULTURE :	Edward Wood (from October 1925, Guinness).
LABOUR :	Steel-Maitland.
OFFICE OF WORKS :	Peel (from October 1928, Londonderry).
DUCHY OF LANCASTER :	Lord Cecil (from October 1927, Cushendun).
ATTORNEY-GENERAL :	Douglas Hogg (from March 1928, Inskip).

League, the Disarmament Commission, the Young Plan for reparations, the Simon Commission for India, and for the world the Kellogg
Pact, all serving to encourage men to hope that the doves and
olive branches were saved from the eagles and bald-headed birds
of prey.

In this struggling for a better world Neville Chamberlain's
achievement stands out massive and unquestioned, the chapter of
his public life least controverted. Here I endeavour to disentangle
from other policies his tenure of the Ministry of Health, which
he made a vital point in the national economy in a time when
both democracy and the Conservative party were on their trial.
If the one was to make good its claim to a richer heritage without
losing the values it had inherited, or if the other was to direct it
in this path, for either purpose that ministry was an indispensable
instrument.

At its creation in 1919 it had taken over from the Local Government Board and other bodies a medley of duties. " Health " even
in its narrowest sense covered not merely hospitals and welfare,
the Nursing Council and medical education, tuberculosis and the
blind, but every cause, remote or proximate, of disease. Its officials
must watch and measure the water supply and grading of milk,
boric acid in confectionery, or phosphoric acid in raspberry cordial.
They wrote in equal volume about plague-infected rats and acti-
vated sludge, vigilantly inspected shellfish of the Menai Straits or
cockle-beds of Pegwell Bay. If such functions are deemed humdrum, other cares brought it into the central whirlpool, for it had
become the final authority for old-age pensions, poor law, housing,
and health insurance. Such powers implied ceaseless concern with
every cog of local government and every ramification between the
circumference and the centre ; in short, with every agency that
keeps everyday life in health and happiness.

However properly we may try to distinguish administration
from policy, it is not a satisfactory undertaking to apportion responsibilities between ministers of the Crown and civil servants ;
for one thing, because the very meaning of a permanent Civil
Service is to preserve continuity through political change. Yet
it will not be disputed that while civil servants thrust greatness on
some ministers, other ministers achieve it through their own powers,
nor that in this department at any rate Chamberlain belonged
to the latter class. Without diminishing the credit due to others
in a remarkable team, to his parliamentary secretary Kingsley
Wood, Arthur Robinson the permanent secretary, and the principal

medical officer, George Newman, documents attest that both initiative and strategy were much his own. His initial advantages were great, for excepting a knowledge of rural areas there was hardly a gap in his experience. His methods were exactingly laborious, designed to eliminate the word failure from his department's vocabulary. He could brief his bills better than his experts, to whom he would put every extreme possibility and demand an answer, while he explained to the Commons technicalities of rating or disease with a lucidity which the greatest advocates and medical consultants found enviable. Progress was incessant, because the minister's powers of work seemed to be boundless, in charge of one big bill in committee in the mornings, simultaneously driving another through the House, sitting on the bench into the small hours. Popularity or parliamentary psychology he was apt to ignore, or leave them to his subordinates — who, though they must brace themselves to oppose him, found he took pleasure in being convinced. " Lord, it is interesting being in office again ", that note as he got into the saddle gives the best reason for success, and was repeated when he dismounted in 1929 ; " my pleasure is in administration rather than in the game of politics . . . if I were told that I could never hold office again, I should prefer to go out now ".

Sore was the need for a resolute administration of British society, which bore many marks of a great nation in decline. The rate of increase in its population, which in multiplying had captured the world's industry and stablished an empire, had fallen so fast since 1911 that, if the process continued, the best to be hoped for in a century's time was that it would be halved.

The distribution of this dwindling nation was in many ways precarious : 50 per cent lived in towns of over 50,000 people, 10 per cent of the males were engaged in transporting the others, but only 1 per cent was serving in national defence. Its agricultural population had sharply fallen, it spent £500 millions a year on imported foodstuffs, it was saving only 10 per cent of its income for reinvestment as against 25 per cent before the war. Lavishly it had spent and wasted. From the armistice to 1926, £400 millions had gone in poor relief and unemployment benefit, £100 millions and more in subsidising rents, £1000 millions had been lost in trade disputes, local authorities' debts were rising to £1200 millions. Yet expenditure had not healed its ills. In 1929 eleven hundred thousand souls received poor relief, nearly 40 per cent of the Scots lived in two-roomed cottages, tuberculosis and venereal disease had barely diminished, in some years 50 per cent of would-be recruits for the army were medically rejected, and though unemploy-ment never sank below a million, emigration to the Empire had almost ceased. True, infantile mortality had been reduced by 50 per cent, but to what a heritage would these infants grow up ? Against this background must be set the Ministry of Health.

He was free from the elections on October 30 ; on November 7 he set his office to work on a four-year plan, and on the 19th laid before the Cabinet a list of twenty-five measures which he desired to pass.[1] Of these, twenty-one became law before he left the ministry, the remainder were incorporated in later legislation, and even this does not tell the whole story. A complete survey would take in administrative action and the ministry's powers by regula-tion ; whether to train health visitors, to stamp out adulterated foods, to keep his officers in touch with international co-operation, to set them exploring Oriental disease, or to modernise municipal by-laws.

As it is, we can only trace the more substantial legislation of his initiative, without pausing on particulars, however important or arduous their passage. Nor can this biography recount his vital measures of consolidation. " The condition of the statute law ", runs a note for the Cabinet of 1925, " governing the main activities of this ministry . . . is nothing short of scandalous ", and hence (most important but by no means all) the Public Health Act of 1926 or the Poor Law Act of 1927, dealing with over a hundred Acts of Parliament. We must address ourselves to a larger theme; to the social revolution proceeding, the administrative change for which it called, and the minister's principles.

An industrial democracy, finally enthroned by the war ending in 1918, could not be left, nor would it submit, to moulder in the ruin which that war bequeathed, nor were the remedies appropriate to the 300,000 outdoor poor of 1914 endurable to the two millions of 1926. For ten years the legislature, unable to believe in the persistence of such unemployment, prolonged temporary measures to keep the victims on relief, through which process the venerable doctrine of self-help and the old " slur " on accepting public alms were whittled away. For this result the reasons must be found in the biology of government, wherein a younger and more vigorous corpuscle will, as in the human system, expel those which are old and tired. Once the principle of health insurance and the unified services of local government had made their footing, nothing could have stopped them draining away the life left in the poor law,

[1] See Appendix.

while the scale and mobility of modern industry must bring about a revolution in local government.

From these necessities we turn back to the prepossessions which we have traced in Chamberlain's correspondence, or in his committee reports, since 1917. They embraced a conviction that for the most important services large areas must replace small, a radical readiness to use the unifying power of the State, an experienced belief in flexibility, a resolution that society should first help those who helped themselves. Had he not once said that he and Hoare were the only " Socialists " in the government of 1923 ? But the society which he envisaged would be one of securely-based, self-respecting individuals.

Inevitably other men's wishes, pressure of time, Labour opposition, must expand or deflect his programme, yet on his principles all the major legislation was built. It is to these principles, out of which in the moral descent of government must come any permanent life, that homage must first be paid. From his perpetual cogitations how best to apply them to the facts came the strongest determinants of our modern life : the supervisory State, the wider areas, the block grants, the harnessing of regulation to voluntary effort, and social insurance. With this preface we approach the two large measures of 1925.

To expand the health services into something like all-in insurance and to improve old-age pensions had both been in his mind since 1923, and we have seen how, while in Opposition, he gave his notes to Baldwin. While he privately pursued discussion with actuaries, the Labour government had also set the department to enquire, but whether Snowden could ever have converted his friends to the contributory basis was left most dubious. Such was the origin of the Widows, Orphans, and Old Age Pensions Act. It shared the compulsory and contributory basis of health insurance, with which it was interlocked, its central clause being one to give pensions, as of right, to the widows, dependent children, and orphans of those insured for health, and old-age pensions at sixty-five to insured men and their wives. As the maximum age for health and unemployment benefit was simultaneously lowered from seventy to sixty-five, the working man was only asked to contribute an additional 2d. a week.

This measure, which was not in his mind the most important but was politically the outstanding feature of the year, brought him for the first time into near relation with the Chancellor of the Exchequer.

Diary, 26 November 1924

saw Winston Churchill . . . about pensions for widows and old age. . . . I first gave him the history of the investigations . . . and he then expounded to me the picture which, as he said, he had made for himself of his next budget. He was anxious to reduce direct taxation in order to relieve industry. . . . But he would have to balance the benefits by doing something for the working classes, and for this he looked to pensions . . . it would have to be my bill, but he would have to find the money, and the question was would I start in with him, would I enter partnership and work the plan with him. . . . It seemed plain to me that he regretted that he was not Minister of Health. He spoke of the position, " you are in the van, you can raise a monument, you can leave a name in history ".

Diary, 1 May 1925

Winston's exposition of the Budget was a masterly performance, and though my office and some of my colleagues are indignant at his taking to himself the credit for a scheme which belongs to the Ministry of Health, I did not myself think that I had any reason to complain of what he said. In a sense it *is* his scheme. We were pledged to something of the kind, but I don't think we should have done it this year if he had not made it part of his Budget scheme, and in my opinion he does deserve special personal credit for his initiative and drive.

So, over the gloom of a divided Labour party, through a barrage from big industry as represented by Mond and Horne, and from the cheap press, who just now were serialising " economy ", he drove forward. There was much wrestling with the hard cases that make bad law, with hypothetical harpies who would get elderly spouses in order to qualify for widows' pensions, with the morality of payments to unmarried mothers, and most of all with an Opposition who regarded pensions not as insurance but as full maintenance. There was more than he usually exposed to the world in his speech on second reading. " The very title of this bill conjures up at once scenes of tragedy and of pathos . . . everyone of us can recall . . . the longing we had to do something to relieve sufferings that were so acute and so unnecessary." And his peroration drew the living principle of all his policy. " The power of any State to maintain its position . . . must depend always upon the character of the individuals which compose it. . . . Our policy is to use the great resources of the State, not for the distribution of an indiscriminate largesse, but to help those who have the will and desire to raise themselves to higher and better things." All this was to be found in his Housing Act of two years back, in the Rating Bill before them

which would " measure the ability of local authorities to bear their
burden ", in the poor law which he soon hoped to introduce, and
pre-eminently in the present measure, which completed " the circle
of security for the workers ". These measures, he used to say
privately, would make the ground ready for some great Act of
consolidation which in time to come would crown the purpose of
his life's work, the object of which was to set on unshakeable foundations a triple partnership between the State, the employer, and the
worker, to ensure against all the giant ills that flesh is heir to.

That summer his mind teemed with projects, for a statutory
body to control the slums or for village settlements to be attached
to sanatoria. Besides the two heavy vessels of pensions and rating,
he had others to steer before Parliament rose, one Act to continue
rent restrictions, a London valuation Act, a consolidating measure
for housing and town planning, a fourth on therapeutic substances.
Occasionally he got home to his tulips and wall-flowers, and once
to Broadlands, where he was consoled by fishing alone with a
sedge-warbler to sing to him, but when the Pensions Act passed
he had well earned the King's pleasure in " the remarkable skill,
patience, and courtesy " of his pilotage.

To his own mind, however, Rating and Valuation was more
vital as the basis for all action, though such legislation could not
be popular, must indeed be much the reverse with elements conservative, or with those superseded by reform overdue. Its chief
provisions, as he expounded them on second reading, were, first,
to transfer rating powers to " the real living bodies of to-day ", —
that is, to county, borough, and district councils ; second, to achieve
a single basis of valuation, including that for income tax, instead
of three or four ; third, to standardise assessment instead of a network of differing deductions and contradictory methods in different
districts ; and last, to keep rating up to date by quinquennial
valuation. But to convince Cabinet, House, and party would mean
a stern fight — 12,000 parish overseers would lose their powers
to 648 new rating authorities ; 600 Unions theirs to 343 new assessment areas ; all of which clearly predicted the coming end of the
guardians. So came about an unusual coalition against the bill,
of guardians, the Lansbury school of philanthropists, and Unionist
country members, not without fears from colleagues that this repul-
sive matter might take the gilt off the Budget, the widows, and
orphans.

Though the air was thick with counter-propaganda of telegrams
and sandwich-men outside the House, he held his ground, writing,

" S. B. has nobly backed me up ". But, running into heavy weather in committee, when Parliament rose he was not within sight of land.

Diary, August 9

> all through I felt that our own Whips were encouraging the Opposition. My troubles will begin again in the autumn, but I hope to surmount them, as is necessary if I am to carry out my programme of poor law and local administrative reform.

When he came back in November he found Unionist squires who dreaded Socialist councils in charge of valuation, and borough members who feared that derating of machinery would throw a heavier weight on householders and trade. He struggled on with all the legislative arts, sometimes with a considerable lightening of the ship, as by eliminating London from the bill. Two free votes balanced two important interests, the one extending to agricultural buildings the 75 per cent rate-exemption which the bill made permanent for agricultural land, and the other distinguishing the machinery to be derated. He got third reading safely over in December, with a tribute from Lansbury to " courtesy itself ". But alone he had done it ; to a meeting of 300 Unionist members he held forth, he wrote, " that to sit still and do nothing out of fear was the most contemptible and, in the long run, the most fatal policy ".

1926, the year of the general strike, coal strike, and Economy Bill, was not one conducive to fertile legislation. Before it began he put up a revised programme to the Cabinet, proposing to postpone poor law for fuller ventilation, but urging the needs of housing. " I do not know that I need argue the case for this bill further than to say that the public conscience is still deeply stirred by the comparatively slow progress in regard to slums ", and, moreover, " we are not improving housing conditions in the rural areas under the present acts as quickly as we should do in the national interest (to say nothing of the interest of our own party) ".

Yet his legislative crop was a useful one : a smoke abatement Act, a Local Government (adjustments) Act stabilising procedure for creation or extension of boroughs, a Midwives and maternity homes Act. Then came a Housing (rural workers') Act, enabling grants or loans for reconditioning of cottages, which Labour resisted as a dole to landlords (though in later years they adopted it), and, last, the Economy (miscellaneous provisions) Act covered under a long name a short, sharp controversy, turning on a reduction of the State's contribution to health insurance. Whence rose angry debates, in which the Lansbury school faithfully pursued its theme of " murdering babies ", Lloyd George leaned heavily on an alleged breach of faith with the approved societies, while the minister demonstrated that the utmost damage conceivable would be a slowing-down of " additional " benefits. But it was not a rôle which he enjoyed, and he fought stoutly against reduction of his estimates.

Diary, 28 March 1926

> . . . succeeded in getting my own way in the end. There is to be no cutting in health services or housing, and no retrospective withdrawal of grant to National Health Insurance — a proposal on which I looked with the gravest apprehension.

During the warm passages of April, when thirteen Labour members were suspended in one night for obstruction, a letter lets in some light on his inmost mind :

> One's heart is not in this d——d Economy bill, which gives one not the slightest satisfaction and has no redeeming feature from my point of view. . . . Meantime I get cursed for a thief, a cad, and a bully, because I resist organised obstruction . . . even the least sensitive among us don't like to be treated as I was treated last night by the Labour men, and though I don't believe I showed it, I did feel the strain.

His belief that no new legislation was needed for housing was borne out by the figures, which show that the total completed rose from 136,000 in the official year 1924-5 to 239,000 in 1927-8, of which some 60,000 were built without subsidy. But he was dissatisfied with building prices and used his powers to cut down subsidies ; whether, as he argued, as cause · and effect, certainly the average cost of non-parlour houses fell by £100 before 1930. He was delighted (as he always was with any of his father's special interests) with the immense growth of house purchase, under advances made easier by his own consolidation Act of 1925. As for slums, — and 11,000 Liverpool families, for example, still lived each in one room, — repair and demolition were being intensified, but the larger projects he had in mind hung fire in the financial depression, while local authorities did not smile on his plan for a central board directing regional bodies.

Before leaving housing for the question of pauperism, we shall open his note-books on the tours he made during 1925-7 — to the Bristol area, Liverpool, Manchester, and Blackburn ; Sheffield, Hull, Halifax, and Bradford ; Dundee and Newcastle, Coventry and Cardiff ; with wide sweeps over rural districts in Lancashire,

Wiltshire, Devon, Lincoln, and Norfolk. They were meant to instruct local authorities, to measure and inspire progress, most of all to teach himself, and their scope may be illustrated by one week in the West country :

> I often covered 100 miles in the day. I inspected 2 workhouses, 2 isolation hospitals, 3 tuberculosis sanatoria, a voluntary hospital, two maternity homes, a mental hospital, 2 mental deficiency centres, 2 maternity and children's welfare centres, 3 housing schemes,

with half a page more ; in 1927 his Lancashire and Yorkshire tour took in 30 institutions, 15 housing estates, and 6 slum areas. As of old he made a brief, legible, meticulous commentary. This town clerk is " deservedly popular, but too old ", this chairman " old, deaf, and feeble ", this medical officer " kind-hearted and sympathetic ", " an excellent matron here ". At Bradford " the worst slums I have come across yet ", at Halifax " rich and liberal citizens ", at Liverpool " the usual tale of nothing done by the landlord ".

He found space for humours and humanity in these concentrated notes, for there were floors and faces scrubbed to shine for the minister, eight-course luncheons which he disliked, and many an English scene.

> [*Lancashire*] sumptuous lunch at the hospital with a futile speech (mostly begging for more money) from M., and a maundering reply from me.

> [*Norfolk*, a children's hospital] the resident medical officer is a pretty young woman of about 25. . . . But though she appeared competent . . . the appointment is not a success, as the women who came wanted to know what was the good of a chit like that.

As he moved about, he tested the facts behind unemployment, the overlapping of services, and the humanity which evades the best law. Thus Grantham attributed an increase in vagrants to " greater amenities offered, better food, less work ; about half genuinely seeking work ". This comes from a new house on a Bradford municipal estate : " occupied by a drayman and his family of 12, the wife was in the maternity hospital expecting the 13th. It was a sad illustration of the fact that the housing problem is not merely a problem of housing, but of social education ".

His self-portraiture is not that of a reactionary. " Got very angry ", we hear of conversation with a Devon potentate, " on account of his attitude towards any reform " ; again, at Manchester, where housing development was opposed by " die-hard

Tories ", he advised the Labour chairman of the health committee not to hesitate in applying for compulsory powers. His general deductions were everywhere much the same. " The visit . . . has shown convincingly the need for control and supervision of health services by County Councils. The District Councils seem to be very slack in health matters, largely because their area is so small that they cannot afford improvements. . . . The number of guardians is absurdly disproportionate . . . institutions belonging to them are only ⅓ full. . . . I was impressed by the activities of the County Councils. . . . Poor Law reform is necessary, is expected, and can be passed without serious trouble, if our people will take the trouble to explain it."

Sometimes he despaired of there being enough of " our people " in local government, or feared that self-government might have to make way for bureaucracy, but a good letter on three Yorkshire cities, and their chief magistrates, redresses the balance. In one he found a triumphant Labour majority, yet " it did not appear to me that their programme contained anything that might not equally have figured in that of a progressive Conservative party " ; in a second, a mayor with " an immense stomach ", whose zeal was in visiting prisons ; the third, " a real interest in and a real understanding of the corporation's work ".

Spaced out between these renewals with his raw material were activities to improve his final product. His choice of occasions on which to take the lead — a centenary address for the Birmingham school of medicine, another to the London Hospital, the unveiling of a memorial to Patrick Manson, pioneer of tropical medicine — often reverted to his earlier interests. It fell to him to receive the reports of the voluntary hospitals commission, though he could not at the moment get them any further Exchequer assistance ; to lay the foundation stone of the London School of Hygiene and Tropical Medicine, which might train up a corps of health officers for the Empire ; he inaugurated " refresher " courses for panel doctors from country districts. In touch with the Dominions, the United States, and the League of Nations, his specialist officers were at work on all the ills of huge dispersed territories, from conferences on malaria or milk to reform of quarantine in the docks, or the health of Mecca pilgrim schooners. Out of all this we may select three matters where his own hand can be traced.

Acting on the report of the Athlone committee of 1921, he set out to explore the possibilities of post-graduate medical education in the capital of the Empire.

20 June 1926

it will be a big thing when it comes off, and should do much to raise the standard of the panel doctor, besides creating a new centre to which Dominion and Colonial M.O.'s would come instead of being forced over to Germany or Switzerland. But it *is* a job getting the doctors to agree. I have about a dozen of them on a committee of which I am chairman, and they are at present divided into at least 3 groups and several independent units.

In the sequel, his committee having recommended taking over the West London Hospital as their nucleus, his successor in office accepted their principles of a government grant and affiliation to London University, and work began in 1935.

One other hospital controversy took him back to his earliest public work. We have seen that long ago he had urged the fusion of the great Birmingham hospitals, the General and the Queen's, but in 1924 he received appeals from each for funds towards extension on their crowded sites. As Minister he explained, in a running correspondence with his former municipal colleague William Cadbury, he must walk delicately, but privately argued that extension within the city would be " a terrible and lamentable waste of money ". He therefore took his opportunities to encourage those who were working locally for a greater scheme, which would result in united administration and a move out to Edgbaston, so that clinical training could work hand in hand with the University. His influence was thus cast behind that of the Cadburys, Grant Robertson, Principal of the University, Sir Harry Vincent, Dr. Stanley Barnes, and their supporters, who in 1926 brought about the Birmingham United Hospital and agreement on a centre at Edgbaston. So, he wrote, " we might lead the country again ".

And a third arena was the replanning of London.

22 October 1926

on Thursday I received a deputation from the L.C.C. who came at my request to discuss playing fields in greater London. . . . Very shortly I am going to have a conference of L.C.C. and surrounding C.C.'s and boroughs, to try and get them to start on a greater London regional plan.

From this meeting, representing 130 local authorities, was to spring in due course all the policy of a green belt, and diversified planning for the capital area.

Looking forward to such manifold prospects, as he moved about the country he could also look back, to light on traces of his early handiwork ; the opening of a Trent canal system to bring up barges from the Humber, or a Midland musical festival where he spoke to 10,000 children, or a Labour member's bill to set up municipal banks ; bitterly he deplored the Treasury ban on their wider extension. But in the second part of his ministry he had harsher work to do.

Poor-law reform had been accepted by all parties since the commission of 1909, for the doctrines of 1834 were ill adapted to a changed world, changes much intensified by the war. It was not merely that under war conditions the old type of pauperism was in suspense, that poor-law institutions became military hospitals, or that the standards of treatment were raised ; the very existence of health insurance had entrenched an antagonistic principle which must overcome the poor law. Lastly, his experience as minister confirmed convictions to which all his earlier letters testify, that large areas and central direction must be created to reconcile economy with modern science, to get rid of overlapping authorities, and to harness voluntary effort to public institutions. Having cleared the way by his Rating Act for a single financial basis, from 1926 he was sounding all the representative associations of local bodies, notably in regard to the abolition of the guardians and the institution of Exchequer block grants, to replace the existing percentage system ; which in his view forced the State to contribute automatically to local expenditure, good or bad, and consequently, in self-defence, to intervene overmuch in detail. But from this broad road he was diverted by the effects of mass unemployment.

This problem differed in every particular from the older history of poverty, for suggestions that the workers as a body were worse off were demonstrably false. On the contrary, more people were at work than ever had been before the war ; wage rates after 1924 were rigid, especially in the sheltered industries, though the cost of living went down, and several millions had their rents part-paid from public funds. There was an uncomforting paradox about this depression. While a million unemployed jostled for work or doles, those in employment were becoming small capitalists, with investments in Post Office and trustee savings banks, friendly and building societies, rising to £750 millions, and while industrial wage rates exceeded, often by 50 per cent, those of continental Europe, a heavy overload of rates, which for steel amounted to 7s. a ton, crippled our ability to compete. This load was the price paid for a social standard ; in brief, a new democratic aristocracy did much to create the unemployment of their less fortunate brothers.

This unemployment, so unyielding but so partial, was substantially confined to two spheres, the " necessitous areas " where the basic export trades had collapsed, and the east region of London. Thus, though there were 631 poor-law Unions, one-fifth of all poor relief was packed into 15 of them when he became minister ; when he ceased, the national rate of unemployment ranged round 10 per cent, but it was 40 per cent in parts of the Durham coalfield, 60 per cent in part of the South Welsh. Again, though very distinct in origin, the two regions were in their social character identical, in that the poor law was corrupted, and local government was breaking down.

Though the general strike of 1926 increased the strain, its origin went much further back. If the story were dramatised, the figure playing opposite that of the minister must be George Lansbury, of whom he wrote " where reason reigns, he has no place ". This earnest Christian was of the type who unstring the fibre of a democratic State. Poplar under his shepherding achieved the highest percentage of pauperism in the kingdom, between 1922 and 1928 maintaining 1 in 5 or 6 of its people on outdoor relief, on which it spent more than had all London put together in 1920. By serving a term of imprisonment, politically as remunerative as that of John Wilkes, Lansbury and his brethren had wrung from the Lloyd George ministry a noted triumph, whereby the major part of the cost of its outdoor relief was debited to the Metropolitan Common Poor Fund. Automatic scales, distribution of boots and underclothing, boarding schools, went on in virtue of a doctrine candidly proclaimed, that the rates should be used not only to relieve destitution, but to change the whole standard of life. From Poplar the disease spread over a great part of East London. All pretence of keeping the old maxim of the law, that relief be given to the able-bodied only in return for some task or test-work, was abandoned. Unemployment benefit and outdoor relief were often accumulated, statistics proved that relief was often unrelated to stress of unemployment, that marriages were made, and children maintained, on the dole.

The collision long inevitable arose in West Ham, where the guardians' outstanding debt was just on £2 millions. Life there had its amenities, except for the ratepayer and the employed. Government loans enabled the guardians to carry on ; 50 per cent of their outdoor cases were receiving unemployment benefit also. But their bankers would not go on producing the golden stream, while, if he was to finance them, the Minister insisted on some modest economies, and months before the general strike had a bill drafted for taking over their powers. A part-surrender, pressure on his time, made him hold his hand ; he hoped he could wait until his big bill swept all guardians away. But after a fortnight of the general strike West Ham was relieving 1 in every 5, and the guardians came for another loan.

26 June 1926

the moderates voted with the Labour people with the deliberate object of bringing me in, as they saw no other solution. . . . I shall go in and stop in now till I get some results. . . . I am not much moved by abuse nowadays, so long as it comes from the enemy.

In this fashion came to life the Guardians' (Default) Act, which he introduced on the note " there exists in some parts open and unabashed corruption ", and which empowered him to replace elected guardians by his nominees, assigned for a year and renewable by Order. The abuse which he predicted so far developed that an attempt was made to cripple him, on the ground that Hoskins', a private company in whose affairs he had for some years taken no direct part, held Admiralty contracts. This meant a most unlovely debate, in which he did not turn the other cheek.

In the next year he superseded two more of these offenders. The Bedwelty Union, in the South Wales coalfield, and a much more pardonable bankrupt than West Ham, owed just on £1 million, or 35s. 4d. in the £. Its genuine distress was great, but its relief was indiscriminate and its system riddled by nepotism, its 57 relieving officers (Kingsley Wood reported in debate) including " 3 brothers of guardians, 3 husbands of guardians, 2 sons of guardians, 2 sons-in-law of guardians ". Chester-le-Street in the Durham mining area bore, rather, the character of a Soviet. There the large Labour majority had used their power to subsidise wages, to favour trade unionists, and to ignore family earnings ; in the general strike they constituted themselves as an emergency committee, ignoring the minority, distributed relief to almost the whole mining population, married or single and regardless of private means, and suspended officers who refused to break the law. It looked as if a trade union, masquerading as guardians, were financing an industrial dispute out of public funds.

Till the fall of this government these three appointed bodies were annually renewed with results that, so far as arithmetic goes, can be measured ; that the total numbers on outdoor relief had been reduced by two-thirds, rates cut down, and much debt extinguished. Simultaneously the Ministry inspectors were striving elsewhere to eliminate unconditional relief, and in 1927 two more blows were struck at Poplarism. In introducing the Audit (local authorities) Bill the minister described Poplar as continuing on its old course of twisting relief into a social policy ; recently the auditor had challenged the minimum wage of £4 a week which the guardians gave to all their employees, and had been upheld in the House of Lords. Surcharge and imprisonment on a distress warrant having been proved impossible, the bill provided that the amount surcharged could be recovered as a civil debt, and that guardians convicted of unreasonable, or deliberately illegal, extravagance should be disqualified from serving on any local authority for five years. A second measure restricted the extent to which Poplar and her sisters could debit their outdoor relief to the Metropolitan Common Fund.

While the forked lightnings played round his head, as the incarnation of a savage penal policy, or as leader (for this too was now coined) of a new " Fascism ", history collects the grappling of two philosophies of life, or an image of truth torn in two by her votaries. A million unemployed, say the one side, through no fault of their own ; nay, the other replies, in many thousand cases not " genuinely seeking work ", but only taking to work when relief was withdrawn. On the heart of the ministry was written " Speenhamland ", in the hand of its officers the principle of " less eligibility " for the applicant for relief than for the man at work, convinced as they were by a century of experience of the easy slope that descended to subsidising of wages and demoralisation. But democracy had shared enough in the State's benefaction to wish for more ; they saw little difference except misfortune between employed and unemployed, and would use any weapon to keep their new-won standard. " To live as God meant they should ", said a Labour member in debate, was a universal right ; though unhappily on what He had meant, men have never agreed. Yet on the issue, as presented to the minister immediately responsible, a last word may come from his best-versed opponents in those debates. " Every one in his senses ", said Susan Lawrence, " agrees that there is disgraceful administration " ; while from Sidney Webb fell a plain truth which every government must face, " Where the public purse comes to the assistance of any person . . . we have a right to ask that the facts relating to his means should be known ". And in the Webbs' history of the poor law, its pages on unconditional relief, the last epitaph of Poplarism was being composed.

So in these years was dug deeper the gulf which afterwards was to wreak so much evil. Often he felt himself alone in the breach ; " whenever ", he said on the Audit Bill, " I find inefficiency, extravagance, or illegality in local government, I am going to fight against it " ; a fight, in fact, for all his past life and treasures, of local government and self-help and independent character. Under hard abuse of his nature and intentions, his own outlook hardened. Labour, he wrote, would strive to capture local government by a policy of bribes ; would he have to " West Ham " municipalities ? A growing exasperation broke out in severe and sarcastic debate.

19 June 1927

> Stanley begged me to remember that I was addressing a meeting of gentlemen. I always gave him the impression, he said, when I spoke in the House of Commons, that I looked on the Labour party as dirt.

18 March 1928

> their gross exaggerations, their dishonesty in slurring over facts that tell against them, and their utter inability to appreciate a reasonable argument, do embitter my soul sometimes, and if I seem hard and unsympathetic to them, it is the reaction brought about by their own attitude.

Life, in fact, never taught him that neither mental nor moral integrity have the same power with democracy as an appeal to their heart. Yet when he separated suffering from disorder, he found a welcome which he prized ; as when he spoke of South Wales valleys with broken hearts and of that " precious thing ", the sense of being members of a community. The Labour men who thanked him for this, or listened with surprise to his impassioned exposition of health estimates, had before them some material for a truer judgement, even in the legislation of 1928. The National Health Insurance Act perpetuated benefits to those who had lost them by genuine unemployment, created some large new classes of insured persons, and extended additional benefits so to include specialist medical treatment. And all the energies of the " Fascist " minister were bent this year to a vast increase of local self-government. But Cabinet secrecy obscured his inmost thoughts.

In November 1927 they had under discussion proposals for dealing with the 200,000 miners whose chances of finding their own work in their own areas must be taken as dead. On December

4 (after a letter groaning over a speech to an audience of " fat stockbrokers and elderly die-hards ") his diary takes up the story :

> I called attention to the fact that no one had answered George Lane Fox's question, that the only answer that could be given was that they must be supported by the guardians, and that that was a bad answer, and I volunteered to make suggestions to the committee if one were set up. . . . I first suggested that unemployment should be assigned completely to the Employment Exchanges, that they alone should be responsible for the able-bodied unemployed, to whom they should have power to advance money on loan. This was an idea which has long been in my mind.

Since neither colleagues nor Ministry of Labour approved, he fell back upon a second parallel, which was to take shape as the Industrial Transference Board. His hopes ran high. They should attack the problem as a crusade, to drag human beings " out of these stagnant pools ". But by this date he was sunk deep in a crusade of his own.

Throughout 1925-6 he had been in negotiation with all sorts and conditions of men over poor-law reform. But before his measure reached the statute book it took on an entirely new complexion, in part derived from a long conflict in Cabinet but also from an economic necessity, that what had been begun purely as an administrative reform was caught up in emergency schemes for the amelioration of dire poverty.

On such a question he must expect to meet friction, and wear and tear. It would affect his own party. Voluntary workers like the guardians, with a hundred years of tradition behind them, could not relish condemnation and death, county councillors blenched at the prospect of redoubled responsibility, London Conservatives would make reform conditional on disfranchisement of those receiving relief, the party agricultural committee was up in arms. To all this must be added departmental warfare. For the system he contemplated of block grants, especially if they were to make a new policy for necessitous areas, he would require Exchequer assistance, and he wished to try out the new system with Health alone. In the other ministries which applied percentage grants he found no solid support ; some were hot against him, while to his dismay the Chancellor of the Exchequer wished to use block grants on an extensive scale. Such sharp differences do not commend a large measure in Cabinet, and though his first exposition left him hopeful, there soon followed a heavy reverse.

Diary, 11 February 1927

the Chief Whip appeared with a time table . . . insufficient time for Poor Law. The Prime Minister then asked whether, if a new session was begun in November, I saw any objection to postponing Poor Law till then, and dealing with block grants simultaneously. . . . I could see at once how joyfully they welcomed an excuse for putting it off, and I therefore jumped at the Prime Minister's proposal as the only chance. But of course I was desperately disappointed.

In short, the next election was writing on the wall, and while Birkenhead wrote off to Irwin in India that the bill was " far too disputable and ambitious ", its author privately growled that " the critics and the diehards and the faint hearts in chorus had frightened the Cabinet ". His gloom deepened all the spring.

5 March 1927

yesterday I succeeded at last in getting a conference with the P.M., the chief whip, and the party chairman. The P.M. has got very cold feet again, and the other two are assiduously laying ice packs to his extremities . . . harps continually on the danger of alienating our supporters in the rural districts . . . so long as we are timid and vacillating and only keep asking what they think, they will play for safety. . . . I see no advantage to any one in resignation. If Poor Law goes down, it will be a nasty snub for me, but I shall try and get Slums through, and then I think I shall have done with the Ministry of Health.

While he alternated combat and concession to the agricultural interest, he was also in collision with the Chancellor of the Exchequer, for whose gifts his letters and diary never refuse admiration, but from whom he was mentally poles apart. Of this " brilliant erratic creature " he sometimes wrote in impatient despair.

Diary, 16 June

Winston . . . is in full cry after a new and, I fear, fantastic plan for distributing 30 millions of taxation among ratepayers. . . . What we ought to do is (1) block grant health services . . . (2) add a further block grant to deal with necessitous areas ; (3) *if desired*, give some money to help to quicken the operation of my new slum improvement scheme.

So Churchill brought derating into the picture as part, but also as condition, of his alliance with Chamberlain for reform of the poor law.

18 October 1927 ; Churchill to Chamberlain

the opportunity is too good, and the safeguards are too necessary, for a purely departmental solution on my part. I see no reason why yr plans and mine shd not be interwoven. . . . You really must not expect me to produce 3 or 4 millions a year for a partial scheme of modest dimensions. That wd only hurt the Finances without helping the Govt.

No, re-echo our papers, it was impossible to work out by the next Budget, it was immoral and dangerous, " it fills me with horror as it involves some 35 millions of extra taxation and an unknown liability ".

All the spring of 1928 this battle rolled. He was insistent that industry ought still to be bound up with local government, would therefore accept a compromise for a low flat rate that all industries should pay, but drew the line at giving rate exemption to utilities like railways. Finally, when one section began to chase a new hare of total exemption, he took his ultimatum to the Prime Minister.

Diary, 28 March

I said I had had an unhappy week, facing up to resignation, and I was determined to go rather than assent to a scheme which I believed to be dangerous to the future of local government.

When they met on April 2 the fight seemed to be over ; railways were not to be derated, while industry was to pay one-quarter of local rates. He breathed relief : " I feel like a man who has been standing a siege for many months ". But the enemy, rallying, pursued him to his fishing on the Dee, for the Chancellor, reporting he felt in a robust mood, proposed to reopen the railways question. In the interests of publicity the party office felt much the same ; the Prime Minister came over to their side. He made his last stand, contriving to get it laid down that rate-aid to railways must be applied in reduction of freights and, which he valued more, to maintain the variable payment of a quarter of local rates by the industries exempted. Having saved this modicum, he sunk his objections for the sake of unity ; but not his convictions.

29 April 1928

the permanent plan, under which we pay the subsidy to the local authorities, in order that they may pass it on to the railways, in order that they may pass it on to the selected industries, is so utterly illogical, so complicated, and so completely contradictory of the opinion universally expressed a little while ago that State subsidies were economically unsound, that I could not imagine that it would not be torn to pieces at once. . . . Not a word of criticism has been heard of this most vulnerable proposal. It almost makes one long to be in opposition.

So it was that the Local Government Act had a dual origin, and a heterogeneous character.

Summer and early autumn passed in multitudinous negotiation and in pushing through a highly technical Rating and Valuation (apportionment) Bill, in which he stressed an ultimate redistribution of Exchequer grants according to need. He had to stand firm against efforts to break down the margin between what was productive and what merely distributive, and against many piteous appeals for " the small man " ; solemnly to protest, " I do not see how a fish and chip shop can possibly be regarded as a productive industry ". Whether osier-beds constituted a productive hereditament, or at what level derating should be applied, — whether, for example, on the brewer or the hop-garden — so the hours passed. But he came to the crisis cheered by his first popular triumph at the party conference at Yarmouth, whom he convinced that local government was a thing large and deserving enough to win public opinion. On November 26 he opened the second reading.

After loyal tribute to " the genius and the courage and the imagination of my right honourable friend " — *alias*, in his letters, " our stormy petrel " — he came to his own ground. Local government belonged to the people, " standing like a guardian angel between them and ill health or injustice . . . they look to it because it has ideals which they understand and which they approve, and because it is always helping and teaching them to rise to higher things ". There were indeed backward authorities which he hoped to see raised, to that standard under which he himself had the felicity to be born in Birmingham, " governed for many years by men who have been brought up in high and enlightened traditions ". But that could not be done through an obsolete machine, which held within it five serious flaws : an overlapping of poor and health services, inelastic boundaries, a local road system crushed by traffic in transit, strangulation of industry and agriculture by high rates, chaos in the relation of local and central expenditure.

If through his systematic illustration of this vast measure of 115 clauses and 12 schedules we seek the heart of his reform, it is found in a position that his father had taken before him ; that the poor law was not the code of a depressed order, but a limb of the body of social services. Therefore the necessary lines should be drawn by purpose and function, not by the harsh haphazard rule that separates rich and poor. His Act therefore abolished the boards of guardians, transferring their duties to counties and county boroughs ; it provided means whereby, when reorganisation was completed, the poor law could be broken up, its very essence being that the new authorities were empowered to treat the poor either under that law, or under the codes for health and other purposes. Each county council and county borough would submit its own administrative scheme, and with this flexibility acquired much larger controls. County Councils would take over all rural roads, together with classified roads in urban districts ; town planning must logically accompany roads ; a periodic review would investigate boundaries, including the 500 districts with a population of less than 5000.

As to finance, only rating reform could save local government from an abyss, yet derating was designed not to subsidise industry but to generalise employment. When the Exchequer made up to local authorities the £24 millions which they would lose by derating, it would simultaneously correct the present absurd basis of its grants ; whereby prosperous Oxford, for instance, received 102 pence per head as against the 44 given to hungry Merthyr Tydvil. " Necessitous areas are really only an extreme illustration of the inequalities which are to be found everywhere." Their formula in this redistribution must not be the annual percentage basis, nor given through the channel of centralised bureaucracy, but one of block grants for terms of years, based on an elastic, revisable system ; " weighted " not only with an arithmetical regard to loss of rates, or to population, but to numbers of children and the ratio of unemployment.

Even these large revisions did not exhaust this herculean Act. If he was dissuaded from cumbering it yet further with a reorganisation of London government, it provided means for reviewing the respective functions of the London County Council and the metropolitan boroughs. It reformed the registration service for births, marriages, and deaths. It provided for county schemes in the handling of infectious disease, and for whole-time medical officers of health. For the meticulous control of health services, inevitable under percentage grants, it substituted periodic broad surveys, by which government could measure the value obtained for increased expenditure.

Diary, 1 December 1928
    last Monday I moved the 2nd reading of the Local Government bill in a speech which lasted 2½ hours. . . . When I sat down, the House

cheered continuously for several minutes . . . what particularly struck and touched me was that Liberals and Labour men . . . joined with the greatest heartiness in paying their acknowledgements.

Whatever was said, in debate, in criticism of derating has little relevance to his own part in this measure on which, after fifteen most abnormal years, we can hardly pass equitable judgement. Yet it may be claimed that its flexibility, its larger regionalism, its opportunities for financial revision, the association between local government and voluntary service, were all part and parcel of convictions he long had held, and opened up broad avenues to the future. He had harnessed the ideas of the Radical reformers whence he came to the conservative, variable, self-acting groups of British society.

For the time being he felt his work here was done ; a general election was in the air, and if the government returned he was destined for another office. " I should like very much to carry through the slums and the new maternity benefit and the post-graduate school and the lunacy reform ", but these and other new things would have no end, while it was not good that either Ministry or Minister should sink into a groove.

CHAPTER XII

LAST EFFORTS IN TRANQUILLITY:
1925–1929

" You must in politics", a distinguished statesman once said
to me, " have not only a scheme before you, but a power
behind you." And this is where the Left Centre and the
Moderate Liberals fail.

BAGEHOT, " Chances for a Long Conservative
Regime in England "

THE last lights of Victorian and Edwardian politics burned low.
Rosebery, Lansdowne, Asquith, Milner, and Haldane died before
the end of this government, which was not six months old when
from its own ranks it lost Curzon.

Diary, 26 March 1925

a great figure with superhuman industry and brilliant gifts . . . but
a great failure too, when you consider his later years. Somehow he
was too much out of touch with home life and home thoughts . . .
never understood nor cared about the detailed aspirations of the working-
classes. . . . He failed to achieve the Premiership, or to keep the
Foreign Office, on account of this aloofness, but he bore his disappointment like a great gentleman.

Balfour, eleven years his senior, succeeded as Lord President, though
after the Imperial Conference of 1926 a frail and detached figure.
Nor could he ever commend himself to a son of Joseph Chamberlain.
    Two other changes affected him more nearly. Edward Wood's
departure to be Viceroy meant the loss of one whom he highly
valued, yet on whose return to office he could safely count. But
Cave's death in 1928, Hogg's acceptance of the Lord Chancellor-
ship and removal to the Lords, must change the aspect of politics,
for by that date the unavoidable question of who stood next in the
succession had become part of the groupings within this government. To him Hogg's decisiveness and fighting quality would
temperamentally appeal more than they did to Baldwin ; passing
a note in Cabinet that he was " deeply distressed ", he poured out
his feelings when his friend, already too far committed, asked advice.

Diary, 28 March 1928

I said I was quite aware that he and I were talked of as S. B.'s successor.
I was sure (on Austen's authority) that F. E. and Winston would both

serve under him. I was not sure that either would serve under me. In any case I had no wish for it ; I would not shirk it if I felt it my duty to take it, but I would not lift a finger to get it, and knew it must be fatal to my peace of mind. On the other hand I would joyfully serve under him.

Inevitable perhaps it was, for Birkenhead, the other alternative Chancellor, had exhausted his great powers and left the Cabinet in the autumn of the same year.

With these few major changes they continued over the four years, which brought him into the select, impermanent, class of *papabili*, or future prime ministers. His responsibilities and success had for one result a decision to take his release from Lady-wood. The Birmingham of his youth had almost disappeared, and in great part through his own exertions. A network of roads and bridges, thousands of municipal houses which obliterated his old landmarks, were carrying the city outwards, but in the midst Ladywood remained, poor, full of class feeling, asking attention which he had now no time to give. He was well aware that he might lose the seat ; his executive knew it also, for he was ill equipped to be hail-fellow-well-met, resented interruption, and over-used sarcasm as his counterstroke. So, after seemly correspondence, it was arranged that old Sir Francis Lowe should make room for him at the next election in the fortress of Edgbaston. Irresistibly, however strict an eye he kept on the city machine and however in-cessant his contribution to local causes, London would henceforth keep him.

For our exploration of his part in general policy we choose a text from a letter of July 1926 :

A mad lady continually sends me poems, from one of which I extract the following :
" How like a sensible umbrella,
the government of today ;
Ultroneous open or shut,
obedient to God's way."

I don't know what " ultroneous " means, but it's a nice Alice word.

In some ways those years did, indeed, make an " Alice " atmo-sphere, full of foreshortenings, telescopings, looking-glasses, of little figures trotting down short cuts, along which they travelled but rarely arrived. Like most departmental ministers he made only occasional contact with external questions, but in view of all that was to come we must show his hand when it appears, and traverse those spirals of dispute.

These were the years which are usually called those of " recovery ", though it is noticeable that recovery from war involved repudiation of substantial ingredients of the peace. The victors' unity had perished. Between Great Britain and France there were bitterly-felt differences ; Italy and Japan, each with straining pressures of population, were discontented with their lot. Of the defeated, Turkey had forced the conquerors to cede a completely new peace, while Germany had frustrated French schemes for a separate Rhineland State and half-snapped the fetters of reparations. From the outer steppes Russia had come back to politics, doubly armed. For while her soldiers broke through a debris of ramshackle republics, and her agents spun webs in Asia Minor and new Oriental nationalities, the Third International kept cells of conspiracy within every capitalist empire. The political barrier against Germany which France had erected, to replace her lost Russian alliance and the lost balance of Austro-Hungary, was the weak chain of Poland and the Little Entente, the links of which were chafing against each other, as they quivered at Russian revival or Italian penetration in the Balkans.

This infant *status quo*, which its mother France would save by force of arms, had been bequeathed by President Wilson, its other parent, a guardian in the League of Nations. But this guardian was suffering from a pernicious anaemia which only a prolonged dieting could arrest. Not merely were Russia, Germany, and the United States outside the League, but its own members freely defied it. Poland gripped half Upper Silesia, Eastern Galicia, and Vilna, one after another, by armed endeavour. Mussolini's bombardment of Corfu to intimidate Greece was matched by a French bombardment of Damascus which blew away Allied pledges to the Arabs, while the Italian example in seizing Fiume was faithfully followed by Lithuania's encroachment on the German city of Memel. Nor was membership of the League inconsistent with being a pawn. If it became necessary to restore order in Albania, the Allies admitted that this rôle should fall to Italy, while the anarchy of Abyssinia was brought into the League on the motion of France, to prevent the exploitation feared at the hands of Italy and Britain.

Even more. Not only had the United States abandoned President Wilson's offspring and repudiated all part in the peace settlement — except some indirect share in reparations — but American policy conflicted with every canon of the new order. The State Department resisted international supervision of armaments, refused to come under the Permanent Court of international justice except with the most severe reservations, and warned the League jurisdiction off from Latin America. The heavily-armed neutrality, which Americans contemplated as their future rôle, clashed absolutely with the League's very essence, of sanctions against an aggressor. And while Americans condemned the militarism of France, whose security they had once undertaken and then abandoned, they poured in loans of many hundred millions to reconstruct the Germany of which France stood in awe.

Weary of strife and ever mindful of their dead, the people of the West did not realise that collective security was a dream which each was interpreting in his own way. If Lloyd George and Curzon had declined to consider fighting to stop German encroachment on the Rhineland, Austen Chamberlain was equally emphatic that the Polish Corridor was not worth the loss of a British grenadier. British nationalism, particularly in the Dominions, was strong against indefinite commitments, and the League Assembly had implicitly accepted resolutions which left military sanctions to the volition of each several State. In this mood it was certain that Baldwin's government would never agree to the Protocol, with its tightening of sanctions, which MacDonald would have accepted ; Austen Chamberlain's work was to provide an alternative in the Treaty of Locarno, which did indeed bring Germany into the League, but which by its very emphasis on the West suggested that of Eastern Europe Great Britain must wash her hands.

Of all this only one note of a conversation with Austen survives in his brother's papers.

Diary, 22 October 1925

a great moment for him, the greatest in his life up till now, perhaps in the future. How long it will last depends on the actual results of the Pact. But if they are such as to ensure peace, as everyone believes to-day, then Locarno will be famous in history. . . . Briand he regards with feelings of real affection as well as respect. . . . Stresemann on the other hand has not a sympathetic personality. But A. expressed great admiration for his courage. . . . Mussolini always poses whenever he is in public. . . . But in private A. finds him charming, and excellent to do business with.

Emotions of Locarno soon faded in the dispute of 1926, whether Germany should be admitted singly as a permanent member of the League Council, as Britain and the Scandinavians wished, or together with Poland, even perhaps with Spain and Brazil also, to please France and the Little Entente. All of which brought upon Austen charges of being pro-French, and from his brother a criticism of the prevalent sympathy for Germany, " and the activities of that preposterous League of Nations Union, in consolidating and petrifying German public opinion ". Indeed, the ruling sentiments in this country would seem to have been three — sympathy for Germany as against France, desire to make the League the kernel of our policy, and a passion to disarm.

Since 1920 this passion had been translated into action. Government departments had been instructed to budget on the hypothesis of no major war for ten years, and our defences had been correspondingly cut down. Building of battleships was restricted by the Washington treaty of 1921–2 ; of cruisers we had less than 50 in commission. The great Air Force of 1919, of 187 squadrons, had so rapidly been dispersed that within four years there were only 18 squadrons available for home defence, and though in 1923 Hoare had initiated an increase of this home force to 52, at the end of his second term as Air Minister in 1929 it had only risen to 31. And year by year the Army Estimates had been cut to the bone.

No other country was disarming, yet both branches of Opposition heaped reproach on the government. Both criticised as provocative their recommencement of work at Singapore ; to Lansbury's school all that breathed power or Empire was odious. Once the whole Labour party united in pressing for abolition of national air forces and capital ships, while Lloyd George was combining a demand for disarmament all round with admission that the peace of Versailles ought to be revised. A clamour for economy, as well as deference to the reigning pacifism, swept the Conservative party also, and the Chancellor of the Exchequer passed much of 1925 in a battle with Bridgeman and the Admirals. For not only was our cruiser fleet wearing out, but the Sea Lords insisted that some figure like 70 was the minimum necessary for trade protection.

Two years later the same argument, on a larger scene, blew up to the same storm. Sceptical of progress by the League and disinterested in land armies, the United States initiated a naval conference, which was duly attended by Britain and Japan, but in which France and Italy refused to share. The Americans suggested a total permissible tonnage in cruiser strength and the application of the Washington parities ; our Admiralty, on the other hand, argued that the British Empire must have its own absolute minimum in smaller cruisers, but if this were made subject to a total tonnage and mathematical parity, we should be hopelessly outclassed. This issue much divided the Cabinet. Robert Cecil, having long disapproved of his colleagues' tone regarding disarmament, made it the occasion for his resignation, others would not be bound by a formula for parity ; Neville seems to have stood somewhere between the two. Though, at the year's end, his diary notes : " the Admiralty arguments seem to me unanswerable ".

In the few glimpses that remain we find, elsewhere too, the same staunch moderateness. He pressed on Birkenhead the preservation of the Indian Civil Service, on which, says the diary, " our whole fortune rested ". He was clear for decided measures to protect Shanghai against anarchy. Though he was not one of those who would have broken off terms when Russian money was sent to the miners, he shared the indignation of his party against Bolshevist propaganda in every part of the Empire. It was his wording, on " almost unendurable provocations ", which Austen adopted in 1927 to round off his final warning, to be followed up by " Jix's " police raid on the Soviet trade delegation, and the severance of diplomatic relations.

On Egypt he held strong views and would never yield on the " reservations " on which, since Milner's promise of independence, every British government stood firm. In long conversations the High Commissioner, George Lloyd, dwelt passionately on the incompatibility of that " independence " with justice, either to oppressed natives, foreign settlements, or British interests.

Diary, 15 July 1927

yesterday George Lloyd . . . came at his own request to see me . . . to talk about the position in Egypt, which he described as quite intolerable. The hearts of British officials were being broken . . . we must tell Egypt that we must know definitely that she accepted our definition of the four points. . . . I advised him not to be too modest, but to ask for a special Cabinet.

21 July

. . . I fear from what Austen told me yesterday that he is going to have trouble with G. Lloyd. . . . I begged Austen to treat him with tact and sympathy.

Two years later he had a word on the sequel, which rather by occasion than direct result followed, at the fall of Baldwin's government, when Austen's successor, Arthur Henderson, forced Lloyd's resignation and opened up yet another treaty.

11 August 1929

my own feeling is that Milner sold the pass, and to get it back was almost impossible. We have been trying what is quite impossible, viz. to steer a middle course. I hate the idea of all our good work going to the devil, as it surely will. I would hang on to the Sudan like grim death, but I rather despair of Egypt itself.

Yet, however considerable the dangers, after four years the government might cherish some hope of a world returning to normalcy. Germany was in the League, military controls over the defeated nations were being withdrawn, reparations were being duly paid, France cut down the term of her military service. If words could do duty for swords, peace was assured, for in the Kellogg Pact of 1928 sixty-three nations (most of whom were increasing their armaments) undertook to eschew war, save in self-defence. Since Lenin's death the Soviet seemed to have turned away from world revolution. In Egypt the arch-rebel Zaghlul was dead, the Simon Commission had departed to placate India, in Ireland Cosgrave was still hanging on to power. Under Poincaré France achieved the rarity of three years without a change of government, Stresemann held Germany to the path of treaty fulfilment ; British production had risen, the cost of living had gone down. But they had won these hopes at a price, for their whole administration was scarred by the process and aftermath of the general strike.

One section of Conservatives wished from the first to disarm aggressive Labour by a counter-offensive ; whence came a private member's bill aimed at the political levy which trade unions raised from their members irrespective of political opinion. For the legal right to " contract out " of this levy was, it was alleged, made impossible, either by union rules or intimidation.

On this, with many · others, he was converted by Baldwin's passionate conviction that it was not for his party to strike the first blow. He therefore volunteered his services to persuade the malcontents to accept an amendment, approving " the principle of political liberty " but declaring the question too great to be dealt with by a private member's bill. Armed with this formula, Baldwin made his famous appeal for " peace in our time ".

7 March 1925

S. B. had the parliamentary success of his career, and indeed he deserved it. Much of his speech was not directly relevant to the bill, but it . . . raised the discussion to a plane to which we do not often attain in the House of Commons.

Not that a sweetened atmosphere could bridge the gap between profits and costs : 400 collieries closed down in the first half of the year, the owners gave notice of lower wage rates, the design of A. J. Cook, the miners' secretary, for a workers' alliance took on new life.   Here, then, on the threshold stood the general strike.

Chamberlain was for peace, as were Churchill and Birkenhead, and no man welcomed more gratefully Baldwin's suggestion that a subsidy, pending an enquiry, would prevent a breakdown.

Diary, 9 August 1925

> my own view was that a stoppage of such magnitude and accompanied by such bitterness would inflict incalculable and irreparable damage on the country ; that this was not an occasion when such damage could be accepted as a necessary evil . . . that public opinion was uncertain about rights and wrongs . . . but inclined to believe that the owners at any rate were wrong. . . . The moment I heard S. B. describe this course . . . a load fell away from my heart.

Except for helping to break this decision to the owners (" not a prepossessing crowd "), he took no direct share, but he counted on this breathing space to inform the public and himself, to separate moderates from extremists, and to prepare defence against direct action.

By April 1926 the Samuel Commission reported : against prolongation of a subsidy and against nationalisation, but proposing some wage reduction on condition of acceptance of reorganisation by both sides.   Government offered to implement this report, if owners and men would accept it ; but in vain.   At the end of a month's negotiation the position was that government would not prolong the subsidy, or put pressure on the owners to withdraw their offer of a reduced wage, unless the men accepted the principle of reduction.   On May 1 the Trade Unions Congress ordered a general strike, to begin on the 3rd, if the owners' notices were not withdrawn.

To him, as to perhaps two-thirds of the country, the issue had now changed.   It had become a matter of physical power being used to force Parliament to a solution which it would not, in the absence of that menace, have taken.   This explained his insistence that the strike must be called off before negotiations were resumed, his impatience with the well-intentioned who subordinated the whole community to the miners, and his vehemence against leaders who knew the danger but dared not admit it : " constitutional government ", he wrote, " is fighting for its life ; if we failed, it would be the revolution, for the nominal leaders would be whirled away in an instant ".

From a very carefully recorded episode we need only indicate his direct activity.

Diary, 3 May. (Interview of April 30 with T.U.C. committee and miners)

> F. E. and I trying to pin them down to some statement of how they proposed to fill the gap between cost and price. . . . All that Herbert Smith would bind himself to was to discuss reductions of wages after we had put into operation the proposals for reorganisation. . . . As this would take years, it was clear that it provided no solution of the immediate difficulty. Again and again Thomas . . . declared that Smith had answered in the affirmative. . . . Each time he made this assertion there were angry and excited murmurs from Cook. . . . Time went on, 8, 9, 10 o'clock passed, and at 11 we broke off . . . having heard from Thomas one of his regular blood-curdlers, with his " My God, you don't know what this means ; if we are alive this day week, etc. etc."

On the crucial day of May 2 the Cabinet meetings were perturbed, fearing that their representatives might have been ensnared into watery and ambiguous formulas. Time was getting very short. They were responsible for the food, transport, and order of the community, and felt that some reasonable hope of a settlement must be guaranteed if they were to continue discussion. Round about the searching hour of midnight their differences were at their height. True, an ultimatum might destroy the last hope, but he at any rate thought that a less evil than burying the constitutional issue under vague speech, which might after all end in no settlement and leave them with a strike ostensibly turning on wages. It was at this moment that word came that the *Daily Mail* compositors had refused to print an article against the miners ; upon which " overt act ", together with the orders for withdrawal of labour, it was decided to break.

To separate the greater from the less, here the determinate minds of Balfour, Hogg, and himself might recall the Cabinet to first things first. But in those curious nine days, full of such good humour but also of such bad possibilities, there was an ever-present danger that those bearing the brunt would allow a fatal confusion between

G

the two parts of their business ; that is, to end this particular strike, and to make such strikes impossible for the future. The diary records his fear of the nation bleeding to death — " the best and kindest thing now is to strike quickly and hard " ; being convinced also that many strikers were forced to come out by fear of losing their union benefit. He welcomed, therefore, a proposal to shorten the strike by legislation.

But the Prime Minister snapped his fingers a great deal, Whips and private members and employers were unanimous against, thus perhaps saving the government from throwing away the very principle for which they contended, by turning a battle for the constitution into a defence of union rights. If such legislation ever had to be, this certainly was not the time. On May 12 he made one of those who accompanied Baldwin to hear from the Trades Union delegation that the strike was over. It had been proved, as Mr. Jack Jones said in one of his better interruptions, that " a general strike is general nonsense ", though to prove it had taken nine days and £30 millions.

Its effects, temporary and permanent, if we include the coal strike as its prolongation, were innumerable. On its eve unemployment had for the first time since 1921 fallen below a million, but by the December after it stood near a million and a half. Exports were down by £150 millions on the year before, the next two Budgets were thrown into confusion, swollen outdoor relief battered down the necessitous areas. Not till November did the miners return to work, substantially at the same wages as before, but now under district settlements and working under an Act making possible a 7½- or 8-hour day. That this course was right he had no doubt, nor had he patience with the view that they had been starved into submission.

13 June

if you substitute a longer working day for the wage reduction, the women and children come out of the picture altogether. The whole burden then falls on the man, and he is not going to get a lot of sympathy if he is obliged to work as long as a railwayman.

20 June

they are not within sight of starvation, hardly of under-nutrition, so well are they looked after by the guardians . . . they are living not too uncomfortably at the expense of the ratepayer, while the nation is gradually overcome by creeping paralysis.

There was yet another consequence, that this made the occasion for the last breach between the Asquithian Liberals and Lloyd George, who had voiced his pessimism and his doubts in the American press and who might build on this emergency a party of his own. Here the letter of June 13, already quoted, may be continued, as a last specimen of his now fixed bias against all moves Lloyd Georgian :

> In a situation in which he was wholly in the wrong . . . when he had attempted to collect a party of his own, first out of Unionists and then out of Labour . . . when . . . he — an ex-Prime Minister — had written down his country for the delectation of its enemies, in such a situation he contrived to divert attention from real issues.

Formally the story ended with the Trades Disputes Act upon which both Unionists and Liberals were firmly set. Periodically, with long delays that tried his temper, the Cabinet approached this thorny subject, the Prime Minister being firm that ample time be given, and the party being much divided. As the bill emerged, its principal clauses stiffened the law against intimidation, inverted the process of the political levy by laying the weight on " contracting in ", forbade local authorities to force trade unionism on their employees, and civil servants to affiliate themselves with a political party, defined and prohibited a general strike. Chamberlain was much dissatisfied. He disbelieved in the political levy clause, which he thought merely aimed at popularity, his own particular contribution being something more conciliatory and more constructive, — a proposal that no strike should be begun without a hearing by an industrial court or, if this were disliked, a statutory committee of masters and men. On this, however, he was beaten.

Diary, 16 June 1927
> Among the new clauses was one put down by Leslie Scott, backed by Mond, which was in effect the same as the one I so nearly got adopted . . . the debate showed how much we have lost by not adopting my proposal ; Lloyd George for instance complained that the bill was nothing but an attack, the government ought to have made a survey of the industrial situation, and put in some constructive proposal. This was, of course, precisely my point of view.

Yet good came out of this evil. By 1929 the Labour party had shaken off the pretensions of the Communists and their foreign fraternities. An unwonted peace, part exhaustion and part sense, reigned in industry, which was distracted by fewer stoppages in

the next decade than in any period since 1907. Trade union membership fell from the eight million peak of 1920 to little over half that
figure, and the 60 per cent who under the new Act " contracted in "
perhaps measured their real political influence. Certainly the next
election was to suggest that one result of Baldwin's Conservatism,
as perhaps it had been his purpose also, was to restore the
normal rule of British politics : that the tongue of the balance
is not the extremist but the man in the middle, moderate, or
trimmer.

For our immediate history, however, industrial trouble dogged
this government, and finally killed it. Contentment there could
not be, when both coal and cotton were working at a loss, or when
the nineteenth-century industrial North saw itself superseded by
the artificial silks and motors of the South, even though the volume
of unemployment was better than since 1920. Moreover, it is the
British habit to think in a vacuum. Ministers might justly suggest
the wider causes, point to the devaluation of the French franc, or
doubt the co-operativeness of Russia and the United States, whose
tariffs were the highest in the world, but our people refused to
admit that a million unemployed could be the fault of any government except their own. All these years various unhappy terms,
" uncovenanted ", " extended ", or " transitional " benefit, hardly
disguised the fact that mass unemployment was reducing social
insurance to a farce, and incidentally to bankruptcy. This perennial
oozing of relief soured politics. Hours of debate, pages of reports,
months of local energy passed in contest over refusal of benefit to
this or that deserving (or undeserving) person, over the hard-pressed
formula " genuinely seeking work ", or the means test as to family
earnings. Nor could government's major remedies, whether local
government reform or derating or industrial transference, enhance
their popularity, for their effects would be slow.

How then to mend the ills of this industrial revolution, and how
to staunch this running wound ? There was room for doubt,
empiricism, and gradualness, and good ground for the conflicts of
party and Cabinet. Now came into play the differences between
those whose fathers had followed Salisbury and those whose fathers
had crossed over with Chamberlain, between men who admired
Lloyd George as a second Chatham and men who detested him as
a third Jack Cade, between those whose slumber was broken by
nightmares of Socialism and those whose policy would not disdain
Socialist weapons. These tough inherited forces, which go to
make up ancient parties, had to reach predominance or parity,

revealing while they did so an acute contrast between what may
be called the Conservative and the Tory-Radical strains in the
Unionist mind.   One illustration of which may be found in the
two " free votes " of 1927-8 over the new prayer book, when a
stalwart body under Joynson Hicks and Inskip, resisting the lead
of Baldwin and the Chamberlains, coalesced with Liberals and
Labour to reject it.

Conservative annals are never intelligible unless it is recognised
that the leaders skirmish far ahead of the rank and file.   Within
the Cabinet the " die-hard " element might be reduced, after Cave's
death, to Salisbury and Ronald McNeill, who had succeeded Robert
Cecil, not forgetting, however, that, as it is a temperament rather
than a philosophy, on any particular theme it might strike some
combative chord in, let us say, Churchill or Joynson Hicks.   But
in the party there were pockets of resistance to each reorganising
measure.   Resistance to rating and valuation and local government, to Central Electricity Board and mines reorganisation ; resistance to rationalising of industry ; doubts on the cable and wireless
merger, or the racecourse betting control ; clamour against Communism, blasphemous Sunday schools and " proletarian " children ;
clamours for a cleaner break with Russia ; demands for more
assistance to Irish loyalists but for more economy in Whitehall,
for smaller service estimates but also for standing by France.   These
honourable but hardly reasoning voices might, or might not, coincide with the giant-limbed press and the watching for electoral
advantage, which are the price paid for democracy : which in
their turn may, or may not, harmonise with the legitimate, or
illegitimate, ambition of individuals.

Marching by many different roads, Cabinet ministers must for
all that reach the same assembly point.   He had none of Baldwin's
spiritual interpretation of Disraeli, a figure whom he always disliked ; yet if they did not think the least alike, they had the strongest
bond in politics, that their aversions were usually the same, and his
papers, that often criticise his leader, prove deference to his opinion
and loyalty to his service.

Diary, 9 August 1925

we have certainly suffered some loss of popularity, but not, I think,
more than any government might expect. . . . The chief points are
the trade depression, which is somehow our fault, the wanton imposition of new burdens (pensions bill), the utter failure to economise,
the foolish return to the gold standard, and just now the cowardly
surrender to the Communists over the coal crisis.

A year later such stresses were sorting out the men at the top.

10 August 1926

Austen has been almost out of sight, but remains a great figure, gradually becoming more hazy and legendary. . . . S. B. has suffered most from the strike . . . he too is worn out, and has no spirit left, but he remains the one with the greatest influence in the country. . . . Winston has decidedly improved his position and is very popular, I believe, with our side, as he is really with the whole House for the wonderful entertainment he gives them.

Inexorably political normalities reasserted themselves. The Labour party retreated rightwards, while an irresistible tendency in our system, for three parties to become two, was illustrated by Mond and Hilton Young crossing over from Liberals to Conservatives. More than half the government's voyage was done, the point at which they look back to the cargo with which they sailed, and forward to the breakers outside the haven where they would be. A new broom was found for the Central Office ; a serious fainting fit of the Prime Minister reminded his colleagues that he too was mortal ; differences over measures and men redoubled in this testing-time for all Cabinets. Faithfully Baldwin had kept to his pledge of no general tariff or food taxes, and though they had extended safeguarding, the machinery was delicate and half the applications were turned down. Neville was strongly for acting rather behind than ahead of the party, for the North was still hostile, while Churchill, and even Austen, argued that to safeguard iron and steel would violate the pledge. His own principles were unchanged, and so were Baldwin's, but they found their flock out of step, indeed butting at each other.

Diary, 1 July 1927

Last night I dined alone with the P.M. . . . He could not help feeling that if we had protected steel, we should not now be faced with the problem of 150,000 unemployable miners. But he did not know how the Chancellor would take such a proposal.

Twice that year a stiff breeze, which he was called in to lull, blew up over the Empire Marketing Board, and we find him seizing with some relief on an alternative policy in a suggested communal emigration to a national estate in Canada. He would have wished to send out a minister to clinch it at Ottawa, but laments no support from Treasury or Colonial Office.

As the election cast its shadow deeper, this pressure for Protection was intensified, and most markedly from the farmers. They showed scant gratitude for what it had been found possible to do for them within the limits of the pledge, laughing disagreeably when they were congratulated on the growing export of broccoli, or bidden to take themselves to research. This angry atmosphere reached the upper air. In the Cabinet Amery represented the teaching of Joseph Chamberlain even more ardently than his sons. He would have preferred to embark on tariffs rather than derating, complained sorely that the Exchequer ignored the economic development of Empire, and wrote to Neville Chamberlain that the Prime Minister should be urged to make a change in that key position : " it would be worth twenty or thirty seats to us if he could definitely announce that he is going to make you Chancellor of the Exchequer when we are returned ".   So illustrating Baldwin's compassionate formula of " the many-sidedness of truth ".

And since conciliation rather than control was his supreme gift, his colleagues embarrassed him with two other matters, each of them unhappily connected with an electoral pledge. In a first instance he had held out some prospect of an all-party settlement of the franchise, so that men and women might exercise it on equal terms.   But Joynson Hicks proceeded to enlarge the theme so generously in public, that they found themselves committed to votes for women at twenty-one at the very next election. Like the majority of ministers, Chamberlain deemed there was " no escape ", but some thought this suicide for the party, while Birkenhead, who admitted the pledge, protested he must have a " last kick ".

In point of fact, it was not his last. That summer the government imparted to the Lords some ideas for amendment of the Parliament Act, to include the giving to a strengthened, part-nominated, second Chamber some power of forcing a dissolution, which Birkenhead declared they would pass into law during the present Parliament. This way of ventilating the subject let in gales of criticism, for nothing is better calculated to divide a Conservative House of Commons than reform of the Lords, their inner fortress, but also, in some sense, their rival and their tomb. " We are in a nice mess now ", says a letter of June, " with our own party, who don't like the proposals, and are furious at being tied to them without having been consulted beforehand." He agreed with the decision to let opinion crystallise, himself hoping it would be content with replacing the Speaker's certificate on money bills by a joint committee.

Through four years of such vicissitude he learned to see more

than he had of old in different men, coming to feel the charm of
Birkenhead in his happy hour, and to respect Salisbury's high
character and ideal.   These years of administrative and debating
achievement made him ; for he had grown only slowly to confidence
in his own powers, or in meeting formidable attack.   His decision
and clear integrity made him a pillar ; [1] he often found himself
in the rôle of mediator, and became marked for higher things.
A note of November 1928 relates a proposal from a principal colleague that he should succeed his brother at the Foreign Office,
if Austen's health continued to decline, and under the same date
he recorded a triumphant reception at the party conference, which
marked a first recognition that he might be the future leader.

True, the succession was not open, but the opinion of the heirs
regarding their leader, and of each other, is always important ;
moreover, his relation to the Prime Minister was of capital significance in his life.   It was to be prolonged and uneven, but one
aspect of it is to be set in the forefront, in his own terms — " I
criticise him often for his lack of leadership, but I get more and more
attached to him ".

Baldwin charmed, exasperated, and perplexed him.   His letters
comment on the Prime Minister's " essential loneliness of spirit ",
his resemblance to Lincoln, even to his strange physical contortions ;
they praise the gifts of sympathy, the delight of his non-political
speeches, and his understanding of the common man.   But when
it came to positive direction, his own impatience broke upon something resiliently resistant and remote.   " I had hoped ", he noted
at Chequers in 1925, " for the disclosure of a policy . . . every time
one attempted to begin a conversation on such lines one is baffled
by a break-off, and a remark about the beauty of the scenery ".

Sometimes in Cabinet, while his leader let discussion range,
robbing his countenance of expression and meditatively stabbing
at the table with his pencil, the Minister of Health wrathfully asked
himself where was the lead.   Even a trifle could ignite that flame.

Diary, 1 November 1925

> I had noticed once or twice that S. B. didn't seem to be attending to
> me, and presently he passed an open note across the table to Winston,
> who was sitting beside me.   On the note was written

MATCHES

lent at 10.30 A.M.

Returned ?

---

[1] " How seldom one gets the plain blunt truth in the Cabinet.   Thank you, Jix "
(pencil note in Cabinet, July 1928).

This triviality, while a very grave question was being discussed under S. B.'s chairmanship, made the most deplorable impression on me.

Then there were the tardy Cabinets over trade disputes, postponement of his poor law, reversals of policy on derating. Yet deep regard and affection were there too, reinforced by a strong negative agreement that some things must not be.

Those miss a key to the history of Cabinets who forget that ministers are human, like themselves. Groups within them have, in fact, ever depended less upon identity of public conviction than on seeing life in the same way ; as may be discovered in Peel's liking for Graham, Gladstone's for Granville, or in Asquith's preference for counsel from Crewe than from more famous figures. From this angle we look a last time into this ministry, which on its formation he had hailed as a combination with no weak spot. That view he had changed. For " Cecilian consciences " he had now regard without sympathy, though Robert Cecil had to him ten years before been a leader-designate. Of those nearer to his own way of thinking, Amery was an old friend, but he felt no enduring confidence in his judgement. Hailsham was lost in the Lords, and Wood in India. For the present he stood closer to Hoare, whose imaginative shrewdness he admired and whom he would gladly have seen at the Exchequer ; nearer still, perhaps, to Cunliffe Lister. With his zeal for more safeguarding as an antidote to unemployment he much agreed ; he found his vivid relevance a rare comfort in counsel, writing, just after this government was done, " your friendship makes me feel that politics are worth while, even when things go contrariwise ". None of these, from whatever cause, were in the immediate line of succession ; neither was the Prime Minister's intimate friend Bridgeman, nor was Steel Maitland, whose work at the Labour Ministry had been most onerous but was not universally thought very successful. There was another who loomed larger in the public eye, Joynson Hicks, who launched his sporadic attacks on Communists and Russians, led Evangelical England against the new prayer book, and allowed his short and strong views to reach the world with regularity. But his health was giving way, and minor office, with a peerage, seemed the probable future.

Would power then pass to the Coalitionists, whom Baldwin had so painfully recaptured ? Their body was much depleted. Balfour was very old, Birkenhead was politically extinct, and so, it seemed, was Horne. Austen, having nearly died of pneumonia

G*

in 1928, had greatly aged, his policy of walking hand in hand with France was not liked, and though he hoped to continue at the Foreign Office if the government were returned again, larger ambitions were given up.   There remained Churchill.

Those ten talents had not, it was thought, found their best expression at the Exchequer, though the Prime Minister had conceivably placed him there because that office would keep his great powers fully stretched.   His views on this brilliant lieutenant, whom he hoped to have separated from Lloyd George, varied perhaps rather in metaphor than in substance.   For, looking from No. 10 into No. 11 Downing Street, he might well compare himself to the owner of a dark horse who might be a Derby winner, or perhaps think of a Monck among politicians, the heroic soldier impeccably loyal to those with whom he served, but with whom he might not serve always.   At intervals he revealed part of his mind on these patent political facts.

Diary, 1 July 1927
> he then discussed possibilities of leadership, if anything happened to him.   He did not want to go out, for he doubted if the party was ripe for a successor . . . thought the party would select Hogg or myself, probably myself.

A year passed, Baldwin had resolved to go on for one more Parliament ;   the date of the election was fixed for May 1929 ;   he must address himself to the crux of new blood or familiar faces.

Diary, 11 March 1929
> He enquired whether I would prefer the Colonial Office to the Exchequer.   I said I would, but that if it suited him better that I should go to the Treasury, I would not refuse to consider it.   His comment was that it would be an extraordinarily popular appointment in the party.   For one thing they liked to have the next man to the P.M. in that office. . . .   We discussed the possibility of a stalemate between Socialists and Conservatives, with L. G. holding the balance. . . . S. B. said the King's government must be carried on, but that he personally would not serve with L. G.   I said I was in the same position, and S. B. said in that case he supposed the leadership would go to Winston.

In a former generation a Churchill and a Chamberlain had stood not far apart, and to him a mere party objection would not be final, though he valued the party and, if it were divided by the prospect, on the ground that the Chancellor was in principle a free-trader, with the party no doubt he would go. But his resistance to a " Churchillian domination ", of which he had spoken uneasily when Hogg went to the Lords, lay deeper than that. To have partaken in the politics of Lloyd George, to think of regaining his alliance, here of course was one abyss, yet even this, in a last analysis, made but part of a spiritual gulf.

There was deep admiration. Of the Chancellor's last Budget speech he wrote how the House was enthralled, by " its wit, audacity, adroitness, and power ", and he knew, sometimes using the word, that he was dealing with " genius ". But mental habit and particular instance instilled discomfort in the fertility of that mind ; he instinctively reacted against anything spectacular, perhaps never grasped the sense of frustration in men who see the stage, as they deem, empty but a mighty part waiting to be played.

Indeed, parties being composite bodies, their history largely consists of such triangular relationships, as any historical analogy will suggest. What, for instance, we may reflect, was in the mind of the great Canning when for a whole decade, in part by his own doing, he found himself becalmed in a solitary inlet ? Once his man-o'-war had led the fleet, his commander had been Pitt, and his shipmates Sheridan and Dundas and Wellesley. Did he perhaps ask himself why he should give ground to the post-war claims of Peel, or ponder what on earth he was learning from Liverpool ?

Warned by such examples, we shall concede that much more than the poll as between Conservative and Labour would be at issue in the election of 1929. The omens were not promising. Labour gained much ground in the municipal councils, basic industries were black as ever, derating had fallen flat, the cheap press undermined the government's supporters. Nor did Cabinet reconstruction make any headway, though his own change from Health to Colonies was fairly settled. He, as usual, was more hopeful, counting on the budget, " constructed with both eyes on the election ", to stir the flagging gale. There were nearly six million new voters, in great part the new-enfranchised young women, but he found the Prime Minister confident : " the prospect of possibly laying out L. G., Rothermere, and Beaverbrook all at one go causes him to lick his chops lovingly ".

But if the elections were peaceful, almost passive, it was because the electors had made up their mind. Their visions of international peace and of full employment had faded, appeals to the government's record and the maxim of " safety first " left them cold. So, though higher rating valuations, or the charge of less milk for mothers, or disappointed hopes over safeguarding, may have swollen some hostile votes, substantially the majority just voted for a change. Other clear moral could hardly be deduced from the figures : 287 Labour, with 8,360,883 votes ; 261 Conservatives, with 8,664,243 ; and 59 Liberals, with 5,300,947.

In peaceful Edgbaston all had gone well, his speeches laying their stress on more safeguarding, more assistance for maternity and welfare, and a new attack on the slums. But Austen was run down to 43, and Steel Maitland lost his seat, with three others of Birmingham's twelve.

His own preferred tactics were decided at once. No alliance with the Liberals, which would stamp the capitalist parties as conspiring to cheat Labour of its due ; no tame resignation, but a ride for a fall, with an aggressive King's Speech on safeguarding, which would extinguish any unholy deal with Lloyd George. But Baldwin resigned on June 4 and MacDonald took office, numerically dependent upon the Liberals, who were demanding electoral reform. As this era ended, the diary predicted the alternatives to come.

Diary, 8 June 1929

the election has come and gone in disaster. We are out and R. Mac-Donald has formed his second Cabinet. After all, S. B. dallied so long with reconstruction that it never came. . . . I thought perhaps the general respect and affection with which he is regarded would have overborne everything else, but it was not so. . . . L. G. finishes up with less than 60 seats. His effort to revive his party has failed, thank Heaven, and we may hope that the process of disintegration will now continue until it is absorbed by others. But I am convinced that the explanation of the result of the election is to be found in the ceaseless propaganda that has been going on for years among the working classes, to the effect that things would never be right for them till a " Labour " government came in. . . . There is no conversion to Socialism. It is merely the present discontents showing themselves in a desire for change. And since L. G. is not in a position to dictate terms, and dare not yet ally himself openly with Socialists, and since the Socialists themselves have not a clear majority . . . what has happened is perhaps the best thing for the country that could have occurred. R. M.'s game is clear enough. Keep very moderate, and quiet suspicions and fears for two years. Then say to the proletariat, " if we have not been able to do all you like, that is because we have not had a majority. Here is a budget which really offers you a good taste of the millennium, and all at the expense of the rich. Give us real power, and it is yours."

I think it quite possible that he may succeed.   In that case we are out for 7 years, and if then we come back I shall be 67 if I were alive, and I daresay politics will have ceased to interest me.   On the other hand, the new government may make such blunders that, before two years are up, the country will be glad to be rid of them.

CHAPTER XIII

SLOUGH OF DESPOND: 1929-1931

AGED 60-62

Those who know most of public life are best aware how great
is the need in the case of public men for charitable construction of their motives and intent.

JOHN MORLEY

Two years it was to be, almost to a day. How the Conservative
party murmured against Baldwin in the wilderness, how he half
decided to go, and then to stay, how Churchill broke with him,
how Chamberlain became his destined successor, how a second time
its own lack of unity destroyed a Labour government, how its leader
joined hands with the Conservatives, how Lloyd George conciliated
neither Conservative nor Labour — such considerable events were
crowded into twenty-six months.

A wave of loathing for politics, gout, and physical tiredness
brought a wise decision, that he would take a long holiday, clean
out of it. He would see East Africa, then much in the public eye,
combining a sea voyage and travel with inspection of the problems
with which he must one day probably cope. But even before he
sailed the political pattern had far advanced.

Once again, as in 1923, the ship of State went hard astern. The
new government announced they would let safeguarding duties
lapse but would continue the housing subsidy which Chamberlain
had proposed to drop, replaced his appointed guardians in West
Ham by others more congenial, reopened diplomatic relations with
Russia, forced resignation on Lloyd, High Commissioner in Egypt,
and slowed down work at Singapore. Their rank and file were
pushing them to do what must invite fierce resistance, to repeal
the Trades Disputes Act, reopen the mines controversy, and extend
unemployment insurance.

MacDonald's success over the summer came in international
affairs. His conversations in America, together with Henderson's
zeal at the Foreign Office and Snowden's popular rôle over reparations as the British bulldog resisting avaricious allies, all resulted
in considerable prestige. Agreement on total evacuation of the
Rhineland, prospects of a five-power naval conference, signature
of the " optional " clause of the Permanent International Court,

hopes of a treaty with Egypt, here were grateful signs of a general appeasement. So, if their Left wing could be restrained, the Conservatives might be kept out long ; so long that he must look to his livelihood.

9 June 1929
> I have already had an offer of the chairmanship of a new company, at a salary far exceeding that of a Minister of Health. . . . I fear that so big a bribe portends a risky transaction, and I can't afford to sell my reputation.

Yet to be out some time would politically be all to the good, for the government might be counted on to hang itself, and the party situation wanted time to clear. The counters were the same as in 1923 — Baldwin, Lloyd George, and Churchill, unemployment, India, and Empire — but their respective weights had changed, and might change without limit. To say that the Liberal party was more united than for ten years past was not to say much, yet its minute strength in the Commons was not only, if united, just enough to turn the scales but much under-represented its five million electors. Lloyd George very naturally showed that he expected an early instalment of electoral reform, but as yet there was no Liberal-Labour *entente*, far less an alliance. Meanwhile unemployment, the chief plank in the Labour platform, was piercing their hand, for the figures steadily rose as the year went on. Labour itself, despite Snowden, was discussing safeguarding, while a new portent, once Bonar Law's confidant, complicated the scene, when Beaverbrook used his influence in the press on behalf of Empire free trade, with protection against the foreigner. If, then, recovery for both country and party were to be secured, if their historic garments were not to be filched by others, and if a bargain with Lloyd George, which he feared might appeal to Austen and Churchill, were to be fended off, Neville reasoned that Empire trade, freed from the crippling pledges of 1923, must be their point of departure.

On each side of this path there were lions ready to spring. Churchill wrote protesting it was " a very dangerous thing to say that we are free from all the pledges which we gave collectively to the country, and individually to our constituents at the last election ", and suggesting that such a tariff might bring about a union of thirteen million Liberal and Labour voters, while in the shadow Cabinet he found a strong majority against food taxes. So if Beaverbrook was to be made an ally, the terms would need some careful rewriting.

Diary, 26 July 1929

Beaverbrook is probably sincere in his Imperial aspirations, but mixes with them a desire to " down " S. B. His particular policy is obsolete, impracticable, and mischievous. My plan is to make tariffs or custom duties only a part of a larger Imperial trade policy.

And Baldwin, he and others thought, nay, perhaps himself thought too, did not shine in opposition ; not as Churchill had shone in this summer session. Everywhere, he wrote in October, there seemed " depression, distrust, and despair ", but if Baldwin withdrew " the succession would come either to Winston or myself, and I don't know which I should dislike most ! " Late that month a new explosive substance was embedded in their party, to whom it was revealed that their leader had conditionally agreed to the Prime Minister's and Viceroy's re-announcement of Dominion status for India. He deplored a mistake of method, but trusted Irwin, and how far beyond this single incident his conversations with Baldwin must range, comes out in a notable letter.

26 October

told him that he must give a lead and be a bit more aggressive if the party was to be held together. . . . It is all very depressing, and particularly embarrassing for me. . . . S. B. is my friend as well as my leader, and I would not on any account play L. G. to his Asquith. . . . I am thankful that for a time I am going to leave the country.

The same day, apropos of criticism he thought unjust, a letter to his wife sketched the philosophy by which he steered. " It doesn't do ", he wrote, " to look at politics from a personal point of view ; you must just go on doing what seems best and take, as it comes, its effect on yourself. The approval of one's own consciousness ought to be enough, though it isn't quite."

Labour now produced some of its promised first instalments. His Pensions Act was to be enlarged by bringing in the half-million " pre-Act " widows, a concession which meant a departure from the contributory principle at a capital cost of £100 millions, and he thought it " timorousness " not to oppose on second reading. A new unemployment insurance Act, rapidly extended under pressure from the Left, would prolong transitional benefit for a year and transfer its cost to the State, abolishing also the old test of " genuinely seeking work ". Thirdly, a coal mines bill would return to a 7½ hours' maximum working day, with provision for marketing schemes and price-fixing, and a national board on working conditions.

While these occupied the House till the eve of his departure, affording considerable space for manœuvre, he concentrated on two aspects of the purpose which he deemed essential : a new imperial policy and a reconciliation with Beaverbrook, with whom he and Hoare held a meeting with Baldwin's assent.

Diary, 4 November

he proposes to run a " Crusader " candidate at every bye-election. . . . I twice asked him what his attitude would be if we could swing our party into acceptance of a declaration that, Empire trade being our policy, we proposed to negotiate treaties for mutual advantage with Dominions and Colonies, and that for this purpose we would hold ourselves free of all limiting pledges, but would submit any treaties to ratification by Parliament. He replied . . . we should incur precisely the same difficulties as if we came all the way at once. I said I did not accept this view, as we should present our food taxes only in return for definite and specific advantages.

So far, so good. He was pleased at the reception given to a preliminary suggestive speech from Baldwin, and with Hoare began to explore detail ; enquiry with experts into possibilities both rural and industrial, and agreements between home and Dominion producers. His time was getting short, he was pressed to direct a new party research organisation, but that must wait till he returned, and three days before sailing he summarised what he left behind.

Diary, 8 December

I am very well satisfied with our beginning, both on the industrial and agricultural side. But I don't disguise from myself the difficulties. . . . Amery wants the free hand (as I do) but wants it now . . . S. B. is quite sound on the merits, but wavers backwards and forwards on the expediency. . . . Winston, of course, is dead against food taxes . . . can't see that . . . it is impossible to deal with L. G., because he couldn't deliver the goods . . . my view is, that we should at once begin educating the people to understand that our policy is Empire trade and development, and keep all the emphasis on this. . . . All we could ask would be a free hand to negotiate, with the safeguard that Parliament would have to ratify any treaty provisionally arranged. . . . I believe I could count on Sam Hoare, Austen, Leo, and possibly Steel Maitland, to back this policy. Philip would, at any rate for the present, only come part of the way. Winston, Worthy, and Salisbury would be against.

So much for tactics ; now for a new earth and sea.

His notion of a holiday was never inactivity, but change of work and scene. Two volumes of diaries fill up every crevice from Marseilles to Genoa, Port Said, Aden, Mombasa, and though he was in East Africa only from December 30 to February 16, he saw much of Kenya, spent a fortnight in Uganda, sailed on Victoria Nyanza, and went up the Nile to the Murchison Falls, thence back across Tanganyika territory to Dar-es-Salaam. His wife and daughter were with him. Sometimes he would relax, attending a fancy-dress dance as the ship entered the Indian Ocean, in domino and mask as the Grand Inquisitor; often enough a glorying in all things beautiful breaks out, whether at Stromboli under the moon, or at thousands of flamingoes on a Kenya lake " like almond blossom blowing backwards and forwards ", or the Nile " alive with birds " which he could name, black ibis and red whistling teal, white-headed fish eagles and bittern. A sort of exultation fills the page when he is veritably on Victoria Nyanza and following in Speke's steps. Too rarely, we suppose, for his own rest, he is to be found reading something other than an official report, like Renan, the *Chartreuse de Parme*, or *Peter Simple*.

More often he was seeing, learning, and interviewing, from first to last. Upon inspection of a hospital at Port Sudan follows a memorandum, to tell Arthur Henderson that the Sudan must be given a travelling dentist; six weeks later it is the tsetse fly in Uganda, with reminder that he must get their biological institute adequately financed. He recorded long talks with the governors, Donald Cameron and Grigg, with coffee planters, engineers, doctors innumerable, members of Council, European and Indian and African, handshakings with chiefs decked in ochre and pigtails. At Dar-es-Salaam an address to the legislature : " took as my text father's two lines of conduct, trusteeship for the backward races and development of undeveloped estates ; the second was easy compared with the first, in which East Africa offered the most interesting and difficult study in the world. It might be the ultimate test of our Empire worthiness."

His notes, like his health surveys of old, made the usual quick conclusions on men he met, whether on the head of a small native hospital, " a very good man, very interested in his work ", on one district officer who " seemed more like a curate than an administrator ", or on another, " extraordinarily thoughtful and considerate . . . a pleasure to see him always so perfectly groomed ". Their main content has a twofold character. Pages are covered with the problems of this diversified empire. Arab dhows which run slaves by night from Abyssinia, the future of native reserves, vaccines and soil erosion, clash and counter-claims over East African federation, and all the crops, coffee and wheat, sugar and citrus, each is noted, various views assessed, and some judgement set down. Once in Kenya he asked to be shown a sisal plantation, and looked on it, thinking of Andros, without comment. But again he could see, and reproduce in very few words, small scenes and crude detail, which sound like raw material for Kipling ; buyers and sellers in the Zanzibar clove market, who bargain by secret signs ; long-haired, nearly blind cattle perpetually mewed up in grass huts ; bands of coal tar round the coffee stems ; ear lobes so bowed down with ornaments that they must be folded back, or chiefs' widows watching a tomb screened by spears.

A wonderful, a fascinating country, he repeats, and as they steered home through the Red Sea tried to write down something for publication. But he was not in the mood, " have been in one of my fits of depression ", and at Suez found letters about home politics, " which are detestable ".

When he came out of the African sun in March 1930, heavy snow was breaking his favourite trees, while in politics he felt a chilling frost. It was to last long, and when it melted the waters were nearly to sweep our civilisation away. The giant depression had begun in America, throwing five million beings out of work, and in Great Britain the unemployed rose to sixteen hundred thousand before Easter, two millions and more by Christmas. Each few months Miss Bondfield, Minister of Labour, asked leave to borrow more for the insurance fund, the debt on which was increasing at the rate of £40 millions a year. Snowden financed a heavy deficit entirely by swelling income and surtax and death duties, a policy, Chamberlain thought, calculated " to weaken the sense of responsibility down to vanishing point, and to carry the West Ham principles through the whole country ". But how long would this Radical economist stomach a majority that had no scheme but spending ? Such a fissure in the Labour ranks might, indeed, come from other causes, for MacDonald, sickened by indiscipline, had resigned from the Independent Labour Party, and it was reported that Henderson was, as Lloyd George once wrote of another, " gunning on his own ".

Pacifism still reigned in the highest quarters. In April the London treaty settled a shipbuilding programme as between the United States, Britain, and Japan, which to the indignation of Churchill and the surviving war commanders took 50 cruisers, instead of 70, as our basic need, and accepted a numerical parity which, they contended, must leave us defenceless in many waters. Government pronounced the Air Force large enough to act as a deterrent, and withdrew grants from cadet units in schools. But the outer world seemed to be conducted on different lines. Neither France nor Italy would share in the naval treaty, an oration of Mussolini declared rifles finer than words, " finer, Blackshirts, because right unaccompanied by might is an empty word ". Though the last Rhineland zone was but lately freed, Germany was asking more concessions. Wearied of wrestling with five million workless, Brüning was ruling by arbitrary decree, a game that others could play more as to the manner born, so that when in September he dissolved the Reichstag, 107 of Hitler's followers were elected, who cried for an end of Versailles. In India Gandhi had made his march to the sea, ending in comfortable internment in an upcountry bungalow ; the Egyptian treaty had broken down again ; economic ruin plunged Latin America into several revolutions ; in Palestine bloody massacre proved that there also Britain was pursuing two irreconcilable, though high, ideals.

At home, the simple fact that MacDonald's was a minority government had most complex consequences. True, it could only carry its bills by Liberal votes, or satisfy its Left wing by defying them, but though Lloyd George often showed his teeth, it seemed increasingly doubtful whether they were all his own. In fact, the entry of Dr. Addison into the Labour Cabinet perhaps indicated a belief that Lloyd-Georgianism was dead. And even if Liberalism was not to die, its elderly child Free Trade seemed sore stricken, so that trade unionists, Manchester business, Labour economists, were all sniffing at quotas, stabilised prices, and safeguarding. For if British exports and agriculture, and American production, were all in ruins, could not salvation be found in an Empire containing a fifth of the human race ? what would happen when the Imperial Conference met in the autumn ? who would be brave enough to fight on tariffs, even on food taxes, as against an interminable vista of doles and public works ?

Such questions must be answered through the medium of democratic opinion, which included the press, this year reinforced by the Communist *Daily Worker*. Whether the press follows opinion or inspires it, and what its proper part in relation to government, these venerable dilemmas take on a new aspect when giant syndicates control the average citizens' daily reading. The power of the press barons of Lloyd George's creation, whether justly or against both justice and democratic right, might conceivably over-throw a Cabinet, or depose a leader.

As for his own party, he found it depressed and disunited. In January the chief agent reported to Davidson, chairman of the party, the crying need for a programme. Beaverbrook's " Empire crusade " was making headway, Rothermere was demanding a general tariff, and if on food taxes the barons were not agreed, neither was Conservative Britain ; North being ranged against South and Midlands, and front-bench members speaking in con-tradictory terms. He was emphatic that mere negation would not save them, nor the stock bogy of Socialist danger. The most serious effect of this report was that Baldwin adopted a device which in Balfour's day had reduced the party to confusion : four days before Chamberlain's return, he agreed that food taxes should be the subject of a second election, or a referendum.

Instantly he set to work to reconcile and reconstruct. If possible, the party must come to terms with Beaverbrook and the referendum must be suppressed, while they must find a new chairman in place of Davidson, whom he personally esteemed but whose judgement he doubted, and make out a long-range programme. So before March was out he brought about two considerable moves : the formation of a business committee, " a sort of inner shadow Cabinet ", and the chairmanship of the research department for himself.

22 March 1930

through my new department I shall have my finger on the springs of policy . . . we shall be at once an information bureau and a long-range research body. . . . I am setting up a research into unemployment and out relief . . . I shall have another committee on over-pro-duction . . . another on social and industrial problems, including thrift and co-partnership, and finally another on agriculture. I am particularly pleased with the latter, because hitherto all our investiga-tions have simply endeavoured to find some vote-catching device. . . . What we want is a survey of the whole position, which shall establish the proper proportions of the different kinds of farming. . . . My other interview was with the Beaver, whom I now call Max. . . . I confess I am getting to like the creature . . . nothing could be more frank and straightforward than his conversations with me.

His letter then proceeds with some political appraisements, of interest for illustration of his own character. Churchill he de-picted as

obsessed with a fear (studiously fostered in his mind by Ll. G.) that there will be a Lib-Lab. *bloc* in the next parliament. . . . I have no doubt that Ll. G. would make a deal with Labour if he could . . . but I do not believe that he has made, or can make, any such deal, because the Socialists simply can't afford the discredit of an alliance with him. . . . I can't help contrasting him with A. J. B.[1] Both had the chance of becoming the national statesman, beyond and above party. A. J. B. took it, and did his best work in his last years. Ll. G. was incapable of such heights and to-day, with all his gifts, no leading politician exercises less influence. . . . To me A. J. B. remained always aloof, I never got on terms with him. I admired his intellectual gifts immensely, and realised his charm, but he always seemed to me to have a heart like a stone.

Meantime he arranged for Davidson's resignation, drew up a pledge of loyalty to Baldwin, strove to keep the Central Office and Beaverbrook on the same tack. But the party seemed at sixes and sevens. In opposing the London naval treaty Churchill could count on much support, and so he could in resisting negotiation with Gandhi, though the elements that he could rally on those themes would be precisely the last to sympathise with his stand against food taxes, or any leaning towards Lloyd George. The letters that follow are sick at heart : " I am going to Briantspuddle, and perhaps on the banks of that delightful stream, in solitude, I may find some relief and repose of mind ". For the concordat of March was destroyed. The more Baldwin stressed caution and no food taxes, the faster Beaverbrook called for repudiation of the referendum which he had himself devised.

Diary, 22 June

as another crisis is now impending, I note that if only Beaverbrook had followed the advice I gave him, it would never have arisen . . . it would be a good thing if we could get rid of the referendum, but we cannot do it at B.'s dictation.

Yet, in essentials, was not the bold policy the right one ? when he spoke in free-trade Preston, how long and loud the cheering " when I mentioned father's name " ! Influential editors were telling him he should come out for the lead himself, but " I feel more and more disinclination " ; only give him the Colonial Office under someone else. And his next step was calculated to remove him from the succession, perhaps for good.

At such a moment the party chairmanship might damn, or divert, the party fortunes, and round the vacancy surged every kind of motive and loyalty. Petitions were circulating, names

---

[1] Earl Balfour had died three days before.

were being canvassed, contrasted perhaps not so much in any public view as in that deeper difference which makes one class of men demand energy, but impels others to seek the middle, or safer mind. He acquiesced in the choice of Baldwin's comrade Bridgeman, but Bridgeman refused, and then came a suggestion that he should take the post himself. For a potential leader it must be a post of danger ; clearly it must involve a temporary elimination in the House, while if he failed, or if the policy failed, he would share in his leader's ruin. Quite clearly, however, from the first he was determined to accept if he were asked ; the party might be saved " though it might ultimately break me ". As he saw it, the objective was clear, and perhaps more open to him than to any other, — to loosen Baldwin's hold on the referendum, but to make the party, not Beaverbrook, the arbiter. So he concluded the matter, " I believe it is true that I can render a service which is possible to no one else, and in the circumstances I cannot hesitate ".

Between June 1930 and March 1931 was staged the most strange act in the drama of his life, a crowded act but an act unfinished, since players and audience alike were called away to sterner business. Its main plot lay in what he called " the great policy ", but at intervals, ever getting shorter, the stage was held by other by-plots ; such questions, for instance, as whether Baldwin could continue as leader, or whether some part of Liberalism — and, if so, which part ? — could be persuaded to work with Baldwin's party. To separate such political threads is impossible, and in this case would be most misleading, for it was the web as a whole which involved Chamberlain in a position of impossible irony. The harder Baldwin was driven by Beaverbrook, the more ample the room opened for Churchill — or some other ? — while the more loyally the party chairman backed up his leader, the further removed must be that change which private desire might wish, or the party interest demand.

In a first short scene, concentrated in July, some of the actors overplayed their part. Having now a central control over seats and policy, he decided that this skirmishing must end in either peace or war, and had Beaverbrook alone been concerned, his problem would have been more simple. But in this stage Beaverbrook was closely knit with Rothermere, and Rothermere had political ambitions for his son, whose selection, it was intimated, as official candidate at a forthcoming by-election might be made the token of harmony. That, the diary sounds in forcible terms, would never do ; " our loyal supporters would say I had sold the pass ". A meeting which, with Baldwin's assent, he attended to heal the breach, he noted as " a failure ", and the same night, looking into the peace of his garden, described his ordeal. For the prospect set before him, in bald terms, was nothing less than this, that if Chamberlain took the place of Baldwin, he could count on support " 100 per cent ".

26 July

Of course, after that there was no use pursuing the subject, and we broke up. Now you see why I am gloomy. . . . The commonest loyalty makes it impossible to listen to such a suggestion, and yet the tragedy is that, most reluctantly, I have come to the conclusion that, if S. B. would go, the whole party would heave a sigh of relief.

But he would not expose either Baldwin or the Central Office to dictation ; his attempts at compromise broke down, and July ended with his putting up an official candidate at Bromley to resist the onslaught of " Empire Free Trade ". One phrase in a letter to his wife draws, from out of this hurly-burly, a notable moral : " the fact is that by temperament I am trustful, and in consequence I have been taken in more than once. But I cannot recollect having been taken in twice by the same man."

Scene one was done, the actors retired each to their several notions of how to spend an interval. He took his children to the Low Countries and the Black Forest ; armed with *Vanity Fair*, went over Waterloo ; found he could not appreciate Rubens, " his figures are coarse compared with the Italians, and in composition he cannot hold a candle to them ". Then to the Ypres salient, where peace had wrought marvels since he was last there, " what was then a blasted, derelict desert, full of tanks, barbed wire, pill-boxes, and shell-holes full of stagnant water, is now a smiling land-scape dotted with villages and bearing abundant crops ". And so on, by Baden and the Black Forest lakes and hills, enjoying cattle bells and churches and flowers, but " on the whole I loathe Ger-mans ". He was home with September, to find Bromley safely won, but the curtain ringing up for scene two ; which dragged on for nearly six inconclusive months.

Not far ahead of all parties stood a fixed date, the Imperial Conference, in mind of which some trade unionists and some ex-Liberals like Melchett were talking of tariffs. Yet his own party stood committed to a referendum, and in September the chief agent sent him a depressing memorandum. Unrest was not mended, " the referendum did much to undermine the position and authority of the leader ", and since then Beaverbrook had repudiated it.

" From that moment the suggestion that a change in the leadership was desirable has grown from a faint whisper to a loud and continuous rumbling." A constructive policy, as in 1924, might still bring the Beaverbrook vision into truer perspective ; if food taxes were to be barred, something could be done with quotas, something must be said on safeguarding and unemployment finance.

While he waited for Baldwin's return, the party chairman sent up some judicious flares, prophetic of an emergency tariff or of quotas, which his research department had worked out in detail, for he felt that, whoever the leader, the referendum must be decently buried.

Diary, 11 October

> When S. B. returned from Aix at the end of September, I saw him and advised him to make a statement of policy as soon as possible. . . . I had realised that if any party meeting was summoned . . . it would be made the occasion for a frontal attack on S. B., and I decided therefore on a letter to myself instead. I was, however, very anxious about S. B.'s position, as if his statement missed fire on account of his unpopularity, we should have fired our last shot . . . all my colleagues were equally miserable, seeing no way out. At this moment came the speeches of Bennett and other Dominion ministers at the Imperial Conference. . . . J. H. Thomas, who had led off for the government, had made no proposal whatever. . . . I realised we had an unexpected opportunity of coming out with a lead. I spent the whole day in getting a statement drafted and it was handed to the press in S. B.'s name. . . . He declared that, whatever the government might do, the Conservative party accepted the principle of Imperial preference and that, later on, guided by the views expressed at the conference, we should formulate our proposals and submit them to the electors for their definite and final assent, thus getting rid of referendum and second general election.

So the free hand was achieved, but there remained the lead. " I feel very sorry for him," runs a letter of the same day, " for I am afraid he is very unhappy . . . when the House meets at the end of the month, I fear there may be trouble."

When the shadow Cabinet came to study his draft letter, as from Baldwin to himself, which would not exclude the possibility of food taxes, unanimity was too much to expect. Churchill, he thought, might leave them, and if a break must come he would rather have it on " the great policy " than on India. But that separation was stayed for a season by protest and appeal. Meanwhile his own speeches praised his leader's decision and held up

the two futures before the country, declaring that mass unemployment had killed the doctrines of Cobden and that nothing but an
imperial policy could maintain us as a great power.

But what he had forecast did not long tarry ; a die-hard group
demanded a party meeting and, with his strenuous honesty, part
sympathetic and sardonic too, he went into action to defend his
leader. He could not be expected, he wrote, to depart when under
this cloud, he must go with his party's goodwill and respect ; " I
expect I should dream the same sort of dream if I were in his place ".
Duly he framed the necessary resolutions in a tactical order, and
duly the meeting, by 462 to 116, voted their confidence in Baldwin.
" We are now safe for a while at any rate ", says the next letter,
" from further intrigues."

This consciousness of holding a better strategic line fortified
him in dealing with further intruders, but with Beaverbrook he
was perfectly ready to work for a common objective ; that is, to
extend the " free hand " to British agriculture.

Diary, 6 December

> to feel he is pulling the wires . . . all this to him is life, and he does
> not realise himself how much more it means to him than the policy
> itself. On my side, the policy also would suit me. I have, of course,
> always wanted protection for agriculture, but it has appeared unlikely
> that we could get it until after the towns had been served. . . .
> To-day public opinion is moving so rapidly under the pressure of
> increasing unemployment, that I believe we could go the whole hog
> with safety. And my studies at the Research Department have shown
> clearly enough that the future of British farming is not in wheat, but in
> livestock, dairying, pigs, and poultry. To build up those industries, so
> vital to the general prosperity of the country, a tariff seems indispens-
> able, though it must of course be combined with other measures.

While he so meditated, forces were massing which might shatter
his hopes, or precipitate decision. Not a beam of light cheered the
dark horizon of Europe. Nazi gains in the German elections hardened
the heart of France, herself about to enjoy her fourth Cabinet of
the year. Briand's sketch for European union was ill-received, his
spacious day was over, and the ministry of 1931 was headed by
Laval, who once had been in Clemenceau's lists as a revolutionary
suspect but was now linked to forces of the Right, whose aspiration
was a gilded peace. The draft Disarmament convention remained
a skeleton that could not be clothed with flesh till the conference
met in 1932. In India the non-violent disobedience of Gandhi

had run its invariably bloody course. Meanwhile Snowden warned
the country that he foresaw a time of sacrifice, exports were down
by 20 per cent, the cotton trade was halved, wheat prices lower
than since the 'nineties. Government credit was in bad favour,
nor did an influx from a hard-run Australia recompense the flight
of gold to France.

Curious and perverse were the government's measures against
the whirlwind. It could, without controversy, subsidise grand opera
or emit a highway code for motors, but the things it put first were
not so agreeable. There would be a royal commission on unemployment insurance, a bill to tax site values in token that land belonged to " the community ", a bill for electoral reform, and another
to amend the Trades Disputes Act. The two last named were twins,
the first being the price paid to the Liberals for the assistance which,
it was hoped, they would lend to the second.

On the chairman of the Unionist party were laid immediate
tasks, besides the healing of breaches, for research on quotas and
insurance, and reorganising the Central Office. But his eyes must
be fixed on the possibility of an election. Government's existence
hung on a balance between parties, on the tip of which poised the
Welsh wizard whose mind, he told his followers, was not wedded
to economic dogma. His own party, however, was in decline.
In October Simon came out against subservience to Labour, his
Chief Whip resigned, and though government had conceded the
alternative vote, it coupled this with other clauses, much disliked.
So that by the time the Trade Unions Bill was produced in December,
it was agreed that they could make no compact and that each
Liberal must vote as his conscience decreed.

Some of Lloyd George's followers, we find, expounded this
case of conscience to Chamberlain.

Diary, 21 November
 . . . To put the government out now, and have a dissolution, would mean
 Liberal extinction, and he was not prepared to bring that about. . . .
 On the other hand, if we were prepared to work with the Liberals,
 L. G.'s terms were very moderate. He did not want office for himself
 . . . but he would like to see something done for some other members
 of his party . . . he also wanted proportional representation in the
 big towns given before a dissolution.

On this entry followed a letter, betraying interest but doubt :
" The whole argument rests on the assumption that the continued
existence of the Liberal party is a national interest, and that a

coalition between Liberals and Conservatives would be able to hold the fort for at least ten years. I doubt if either of these assumptions could be sustained."

After sundry explorations he set down his reasoning in plain terms. Simon felt that the government was a national danger, and would accept office from the Conservatives ; MacDonald might, by resigning, throw the Conservatives into confusion by forcing them to make a government ; Henderson, on the other hand, was cultivating good relations with a Liberal section ; Lloyd George's tactic was to frighten Conservatives into a treaty by working with Labour. Well, this harsh analysis continues, Beaverbrook activity might have its uses ; he would attack the Liberals at their vulnerable spot, the Trade Unions Bill. Politics, ran his Christmas thought as he planted out heaths and dwarf azaleas, were " very nauseating ".

With the first months of 1931 the crisis came visibly nearer. Gandhi and his fellows were released, and Churchill resigned from the shadow Cabinet ; Lloyd George induced most of his party to give a second reading to the Trade Unions Bill, which would repeal every essential clause of the 1927 Act. In February, however, on the trade unions' demand, the bill was withdrawn, rather than accept the definition of a general strike which the Liberals proposed. All this time unemployment insurance hobbled on its sorry way, in defiance of a Treasury warning that " borrowing on the present scale without adequate provision for repayment by the Fund would quickly call in question the stability of the British financial system ". Weighty opinions testified that the scales of relief blocked migration, impeded army recruiting, and ossified the wage structure.

Though the divisions of Liberalism were daily exposed, Liberal votes were welcome to MacDonald, whose followers at length, though with transparent distaste, agreed to the alternative vote. Yet Chamberlain remained confident that the bargain would break down. Everywhere he saw ground for hope, yet everywhere felt lack of faith, and as he listened to Beethoven in C sharp minor, so full of " tune and humour and *brio* ", he foretold an explosion. Scene two was done : the third was concentrated in the biting month of March.

If only Baldwin, he laments, would attack government instead of the press lords, and if only Beaverbrook were not " unstable as water " ; for official candidates and " Crusaders " were splitting several constituencies. And even if these were overcome, the publication of Churchill's farewell to Baldwin, the " admirable verve and dash " of his speeches, so bitter-bantering on the Liberal-Labour compact and so attractive to Conservatives who cared for India, suggested another alternative.

Diary, 23 February 1931

the question of leadership is again growing acute. . . . I am getting letters and communications from all over the country. . . . I cannot see my way out. I am the one person who might bring about S. B.'s retirement, but I cannot act when my action might put me in his place.

Derby sent gloomy prognostications of Lancashire, while great was the realm of temptation spread before him by other considerable persons. Here then we reach the crux which human relations could hardly bear, a climax which threatens but never breaks, suspended by an impish element of time.

Out of sight the orchestra struck a first chord on February 26 when he received from the principal agent yet another memorandum. He reported that, although Beaverbrook had lost ground, there were definite doubts whether the leader could carry the party to victory. And there was a more incalculable danger. Many of their supporters were worried about India : on which many, perhaps a majority, leaned rather towards Churchill than to Baldwin, but very few indeed would welcome a change of leadership springing from that particular issue. The position was so serious, he concluded, that he felt compelled to put his impression before the chairman and, if thought his duty, before the leader himself.   `

Thereupon he consulted Austen, Hoare, Cunliffe Lister, Hailsham, the Chief Whip, and Bridgeman. " Everyone without exception agreed that I was in duty bound to show the document to S. B. . . . Everyone, I think, except Willie Bridgeman, was of opinion that S. B. would have to resign." And after some hesitation it was decided to act at once.

Diary, 1 March

any remaining doubts were quite removed when I read in the evening paper that, following on . . . Sir Ernest Petter's intention of standing as an anti-Baldwinite in the bye-election in St. George's (on Worthy's death), Moore-Brabazon . . . had withdrawn on the ground that he was not prepared to champion S. B.

Eliminating some phrases he thought " too wounding ", he sent the paper to Baldwin on the morning of Sunday, March 1. After doing so, he wrote that the press barons' intervention would make for delay, " we cannot possibly sit down under that, or allow S. B. to resign at their bidding ".

That afternoon he was summoned to see Baldwin, whom he found, to his surprise, apparently resolved to retire. On this his own immediate impression is undoubted, for he added a postscript to his morning letter — " 4.30, S. B. has decided to go at once ". So near seemed the change that day that the editor of *The Times* prepared a leading article, headed " Mr. Baldwin withdraws ".

All history is there to tell us that these final dilemmas do not come from decision, or logical process. They turn, rather, on an interplay of motives, on affection and resentment, an exhaustion of mere argument, or tiltings between private scruple and public service. And historically they soon take shape in rival versions, though rising from the same bed of fact. So, inevitably, it happened now.

Late the same night Bridgeman urged his leader to stand fast, nay more, to take the offensive and fight St. George's himself ; this Chamberlain, and others, firmly discouraged, foreseeing the evil consequences of a defeat, but agreed that till this bye-election was over, resignation would be a disaster. By Tuesday, it seems, Baldwin was clear that his colleagues were against resignation at the moment, while simultaneously tidings came that Irwin had achieved a concordat with Gandhi. Perhaps what Beaverbrook had begun, Gandhi might finish, — twin instruments of fate's determination that Baldwin should not go.

Loyalty, though not shined upon, may be true as the dial, yet is not the same as faith. Though the St. George's clash and the Delhi compact strengthened Baldwin's position, the party chairman remained of opinion that nothing could rehabilitate him but a successful election. Stiffly he handed in more doubting reports from the constituencies, but loyally he threw the Central Office behind Duff Cooper's candidature against the rebel Petter, and strenuously worked upon dissentient Liberals towards an election by which Baldwin might be saved. But others were not so bound, seeing better than himself the impossibility of his rôle, while even the breath of a vacant leadership meant a partaking of counsels.

It was not, however, from his own hand but from his brother that the gesture came which made his position untenable and, we may even conjecture, tilted decision, though not in the direction meant.

Diary, 11 March

this evening Austen, without any previous communication with me, bluntly asked S. B. at the business committee when he was going to release me from the Central Office. He put it mostly on the ground that the front bench debating strength had been reduced unduly by Winston's defection and Worthy's death, but it was pretty plain what he had in mind. . . . Thinking it over since, I am inclined to the view that A. is right, though not on the ground he put forward.

So he drew up a letter of resignation, accompanied by a note asking to be relieved from a position which had " shadowed " their friendship. Then, though with his entire acquiescence in the choice of Stonehaven to succeed him, there followed several interviews from which he parted with sore feelings, disposed to see deliberateness in oversights, and thinking his hard year's service requited ill. Yet two bonds must always bring these two antithetical natures together : the public interest and a long, loyal, partnership. Almost indignantly, as he saw the enemy in confusion and the day opening for a triumphant offensive, he demanded a return of the old confidence.

Diary, 25 March

we spoke very frankly to one another. S. B. professed no grievance against me, but . . . held to his own account of Sunday [March 1] (which shows how easily a misunderstanding may arise). . . . I then told the story of my grievances. . . . He pleaded in excuse his shyness and reserve . . . and the general distress he had suffered during the last fortnight, and he declared his warm appreciation of all I had done, and his sorrow at having hurt my feelings. I went on to say that the situation with his colleagues was most serious . . . we parted shaking hands, and with the clouds removed.

As he wished, and on lines he suggested, his leader made a statement to his colleagues, who spoke out that he must take the aggressive against Labour ; to the same meeting Chamberlain produced a last achievement as chairman, which he thought must be of substantial service to Baldwin, in the shape of a peace protocol with Beaverbrook, whom he described as chastened by defeat. Not that he was under any illusion that war might not break out again, for " Max is very like Gandhi ", he wrote from the Dee ; but he was in hopeful mood, " had the day of my life and landed four salmon ", and believed that a united party could win the election.

Spring was now come, with politics still poised on the old question, whether the wanton Liberals would get themselves another crest.

Now and then some honest broker brought word that Lloyd George was ready to bargain, but his votes still seemed aimed at enhancing a nuisance value, his speeches examined between delicate-offensive thumb and finger the choice between Labour and Protection. " A masterpiece of artistry ", or " a music-hall turn with 2½ million unemployed ", our letters swing thus between technical applause and heartfelt indignation. But the world was burning.

Between March and June a Spanish revolution drove their king into exile, the French-Italian naval conversations collapsed, plans for an Austro-German customs union roused France and her client States, Chinese and Japanese clashed in Manchuria. Then fell on the world the last outcome of the depression, finding out the spots where illusion had done its worst, notably in the fragment called Austria and British social finance. Austrian credit broke, Germany was drained of foreign funds, and President Hoover proposed a year's moratorium on inter-governmental debts. But all our effort to buttress German credit failed, not merely because France seized on an economic opportunity to stamp upon Germany a political status, but because British credit was imperilled itself.

Everywhere the streams were freezing by which the wheel of life had turned. Three-fifths of the world's gold was in America and France, the wheat-producing countries were in ruins, great communities were exploring methods of barter as if they were primitive men. All the year Snowden had been preaching danger to his colleagues who, he tells us, " talked their usual clap-trap about going to the super-tax payer ", and now he was budgeting for a minimum deficit of £37 millions. Of all this Chamberlain's return to the House made him well aware.

Yet he found life very good this summer, his garden never more lovely, pages of letters flowed in praise of delphiniums and roses, while being in Opposition gave more freedom to fish the Avon, Piddle, or Char. He wrote contentedly of his new standing :

> I have, I believe, recovered the second position in the party, Winston having separated himself from his colleagues, while Hailsham has, perhaps unjustly, somewhat lost credit for his handling of the Lords, and Horne has receded into the background.

As to the outlook, sometimes he chafed impatiently at a task of Sisyphus, or pictured Lloyd George as a new Marlborough, conspiring simultaneously with Jacobites and Hanover. But bye-elections instructed him that Labour was losing ground ; and his instinct, that unemployment insurance would destroy them.

Stoutly the Trade Union Congress put recommendations to the Royal Commission, amounting to the destruction of the contributory principle, and stoutly the Minister of Labour moved that the fund's borrowing powers be raised to £115 millions. Though the Royal Commission recommended a return to solvent insurance, the government, under heavy fire from the Left, refused to touch contributions or benefits, so that their gently-named " Anomalies " Bill was not likely to save over £3 millions.

Into this combat Chamberlain threw all his energy. He dreaded a prolongation of transitional benefit, administered by some authority which would outbid the scales of public assistance, and though his own party might blench, " I would rather run the risk of losing the election than give way ". To his relief, their committee laid down two foundations, that they would not pledge themselves not to reduce benefits, and that those not in insurance must be subject to a means test.

In July, while foreign ministers discussed credits for Germany in London, and MacDonald and Henderson visited Berlin to help Germany against French pressure, thunder-clouds scattered party manœuvrings like volatile birds. Stonehaven reported what seemed like a sounding from MacDonald, a view that the dangers were too great for any one party to overcome.

Diary, 6 July

He [Ramsay MacDonald] thought a national government should be formed . . . they did not wish to be forced to vote against the two things they thought necessary, viz. reform of unemployment insurance and a tariff. . . . I subsequently saw S. B., and we agreed that our party would not stand it for a moment.

Another channel brought word that Lloyd George also foresaw a crisis too grave for one party and, putting these things together, with the stark ruin he had lately seen in Lancashire and all he heard from the City, in Chamberlain's mind took shape the pattern of what was to come. He foresaw events which would beat down Baldwin's native instinct against coalition.

Diary, 24 July

I said that would be all very well . . . where it was a question of helping Germany over her troubles, but R. M. wouldn't ask him to coalesce for that. What I foresaw the possibility of was a panic in the City, a hundred million deficit in the Budget, a flight from the £, and industry going smash. . . . It was then that R. M. would come to him, because he would not be able to count on his own people to support him. The T.U.C. would . . . say " no more sacrifices for the poor, let the rich pay ".

Circumstance did not dally, the Bank was losing gold at the rate of £2½ millions a day, and when he made that record he was aware of the main conclusions forthcoming from the May economy committee ; that the deficit on the Budget would probably be £120 millions, that the country was spending nearly a third of its income in rates and taxes, and that only austere economies could prevent depreciation of the currency. Of the £96 millions of savings which it proposed, two-thirds was to come from unemployment insurance, seeing that the fund had borrowed £60 millions since the government took office. From the Royal Commission's enquiries it had also emerged that some half of those asking for transitional benefit had paid no contribution at all, that 68 per cent of the female applicants were married, and that juvenile benefits often exceeded full-time wages.

It was in the light of this knowledge and to save the £, that on July 30, by prior arrangement, Chamberlain made his appeal to Snowden to be bold : " to be true to England is not to shut one's eyes to unpleasant facts ". He received the expected reply, that the House must unite in the task of balancing the Budget, and then, having borrowed £50 millions from New York and Paris, government adjourned Parliament. He made for Perthshire, whence he wrote from the Tummel valley how good it was to smell again the bog plants and birches.

But the drain of gold went on. £2000 millions of short-term borrowings, like wild beasts caught in a glacier, were crying out to be liquefied ; Paris and New York had lost faith in Britain. On August 11 he was called to London, where he found MacDonald and Snowden in touch with Baldwin, Samuel, and the Bank. Having ascertained that ministers were decided to balance the Budget, they separated until they could see detailed proposals : Baldwin returned to Aix, leaving the negotiation in the hands of Chamberlain who, on his return to Scotland, sketched the facts and the future, as he saw them.

15 August ; to Cunliffe Lister
the May Report confirmed the most pessimistic views circulating abroad as to the insolvency of the Budget. . . . The credits had to be encroached upon, and they began to melt away at such a pace that it was clear that it was only a matter of days before they disappeared

completely. Enquiries in Paris and New York showed that there was no chance of a loan in either quarter.

In these circumstances the Bankers, *i.e.* the Deputy Governor and Peacock, went to R. M. and told him plainly (1) that we were on the edge of the precipice and, unless the situation changed radically, we should be over it directly, (2) that the cause of the trouble was not financial but political, and lay in the complete want of confidence in H.M.G. existing among foreigners, (3) that the remedy was in the hands of the Government alone. . . .

As they were still in serious doubt as to whether any action would be taken, they asked to be allowed to put the facts before the other parties. R. M. assented, and it was in response to a message from the Deputy Governor that I went to London. . . .

At the interview R. M. was characteristically vague and woolly, but as I knew what I wanted to know, I was able to put one or two questions which elicited definite answers from him or Snowden, and the position is now pretty plain. I summarise it briefly.

The Cabinet Committee have decided that the Budget must be balanced, but there must be equality of sacrifice. The May Report contains many impossible recommendations, but the Departments are to be told to make their own proposals for reduction . . . the total reduction aimed at being in the neighbourhood of £100 millions. This will still leave a large gap to be made up out of taxation. I don't know what it is, but the Chancellor said the situation was worse than indicated by the May Committee. Their £120 m. does not of course include the Hoover £11 m. but I gathered that, in addition to that, Snowden now agrees with me that he greatly over-estimated the revenue for the year.

16 August

to secure such a measure of relief, and to do it through a Socialist government, seems to me so important in the national interest that we must give it our support, provided the proposals for equal sacrifice do not imperil British credit, or too brazenly affront ordinary rules of justice and fair play. And I don't think they will do either.

By the 20th he was back for that morning's conference, taking Hoare as his partner.

Diary, 22 August

the problem was to restore foreign confidence in British credit. This could only be done by announcing such a cut in national expenditure as would convince him (the foreigner) that we had sufficient courage to tackle the situation. I put the figure at about £100 millions, and I knew that that could not be obtained unless there was a substantial reduction in unemployment insurance benefit. I proposed therefore to concentrate on reduction, leaving all questions of taxation (including tariffs) to be dealt with hereafter.

So he and Hoare went, with the Liberals Samuel and Maclean, to Downing Street, where Snowden put forward economies of some £78 millions, at the same time telling them that the deficit would probably be nearer £170 than £120 millions. Chamberlain, his own account proceeds, declared the cuts inadequate :

> stressed two points ; first, that in view of the increased estimate of deficit, to produce economies less than the aggregate recommended by May was wrong, and second, that if unemployment benefit were left untouched, the contemplated economies . . . would certainly be jeopardised. In effect the P. M. and Snowden gave us to understand that they quite agreed, the latter saying that if you took into account both the fall in the cost of living and the rise in the benefits, the unemployed were 36% better off than in 1924.

Long Cabinets that night and next morning were offset by a meeting of the trades unions' general council, which proposed to restore foreign confidence by suspending the Sinking Fund, " mobilizing " our foreign investments, and devaluing the pound. The diary may be taken up again at three o'clock that afternoon (the 21st), when the party delegates were told the Cabinet could agree to cuts of £56 millions, only £5 millions of which would come from unemployment insurance.

> We asked whether it was proposed to announce that this was the last word, and were told " yes ". When we asked what would happen if this announcement failed to restore foreign confidence . . . Snowden replied " the deluge ".

When, after consultation and, as it were, verifying their powers, they met again that night, Conservatives found Liberals in full agreement, reinforced by a message from Lloyd George (who, it is to be feared to their relief, was on a bed of sickness) that the government proposals were derisory. At 9.30 they all faced MacDonald.

> I opened first and intimated, (1) that if these were the final proposals . . . we should turn them out immediately the House met : (2) that before then we anticipated that the financial crash must come : (3) that we considered that it was the P.M.'s bounden duty to avoid that crash : and (4) that we were ready to give him any support in our power for that purpose, either with his present, or in a reconstructed government. Samuel followed on exactly the same lines. . . . The P.M. began by drawing a touching picture of his own position (a thing

he loves to do) . . . he did not think resignation would help.   He would remain P.M. . . . invite his colleagues to support him, and tell those who would not that they might go when they liked.

As he entered on the third day of these conversations, his mind was clearing.   Given any respectable economies, the foreign bankers would give credits, " the French being anxious to get their hands on our throats as they have on the Germans " ; moreover, politically how urgent it was to get an all-party agreement and, tactically, how desirable to split the Labour party.   He would therefore urge Baldwin that, whatever the Liberals did, he should try to work with the Labour moderates, and that night, the 22nd, when he arrived from Aix, gave him a full report.

The end was now near ; a " time of great mental tension ", he wrote to his wife.   On the evening of the 23rd, with Baldwin and Samuel, he saw MacDonald, who said the credits could be raised, but that he could not keep his Cabinet.

> While a majority supported him, eight ministers had refused to accept the dole cut . . . had told the King so, recommending him to see the three party leaders. . . . For himself, he would help us to get these proposals through, though it meant his death warrant, but it would be of no use for him to join a government . . . would bring odium on us as well as himself. . . . I then intervened . . . had he considered that, tho' not commanding many votes in the House, he might command much support in the country ?   And would not a government including members of all parties hold a much stronger position ? . . . Finally, I asked him if he had considered the effect on foreign opinion.

Whether or no such arguments convinced him, next day MacDonald undertook to form a national government, time passing in what Pitt used to call the " bilious " process of allotting seats in a Cabinet of ten, constructed for the one purpose of balancing the Budget. There were many sore feelings, Austen's not least, while his brother was also disappointed that room could not be found for Hailsham, but as finally constituted the new government had four Labour men (MacDonald, Snowden, Sankey, and Thomas), four Conservatives (Baldwin, Chamberlain, Hoare, Cunliffe Lister), and two Liberals (Reading and Samuel).   For himself he returned to the Ministry of Health, but the testimony of colleagues and the instinct of opponents alike made it clear that of this great political change he was the constructive engineer.

So the first stage was accomplished, to all seeming satisfying all he had worked for. £80 millions were borrowed abroad, the Budget was balanced, — as to some £75 millions by taxation (£51 millions of this in direct taxes), and £70 millions by cuts in expenditure, from salaries of ministers down to benefits of the unemployed. But these were not done before the next stage forced itself upon them. Despite their economies they failed to save the pound, and on September 21 Britain went off gold. Demonstrations against pay reductions in the fleet at Invergordon, processions of teachers against cuts in their salaries, scuffles with the unemployed, broke down foreign confidence and strained the Cabinet, while the tariff controversy turned into a weapon of party rancour. They were therefore soon wrestling with fundamentals ; should they hold together and, if so, under what leader, and should they ask a new mandate from the electors ?

A delicate plant this co-operation was bound to be, stifled by the soil out of which it sprung, and buffeted by the oncoming future when parties must revive, with all the tangle of public interest, tactical vantage, and private ambition. Already Samuel had murmured a word about electoral reform, already important Conservatives (outside the Cabinet) were besetting Chamberlain with an offensive programme, — to eschew these unpopular economies and to dissolve on the full tariff, getting rid of Snowden and Samuel in the process. His political courage and his sense of loyalty both revolted.

Diary, 3 September

> I replied . . . we could never escape from economies at the election by shirking them beforehand . . . we should fight to greater advantage if we could say " now you know the worst, the cuts have been made, the nation has roused itself and made its sacrifice, now we come with the promise of the only remedy which can ever make it possible to bring back prosperity ". I made no comment on the cynical nature of the proposal that 4 of the Cabinet should engage in this discreditable intrigue against our colleagues.

There were indeed reasons, high, middle, and low, for a dissolution. It had been the original understanding, their present majority in the Commons was a bare sixty, the Labour ranks were in confusion, but the trouble was that a dissolution implies an agreed programme, and what were they to say about the tariff? The flow of gold was not stanched, for which there were immediate political reasons, but another of older date and deeper root, that our surplus from overseas investment, which in 1913 had stood round about £180 millions, had shrunk to less than £40 millions, and that we were facing an adverse trade balance which rose to £400 millions before the year went out.

Diary, 19 September

there is only one way of redressing it, and that is by a tariff, which Herbert Samuel refuses to consider. I should like the P.M. . . . to decide by a majority to adopt it, to accept Samuel's resignation, and . . . go to the country on a programme of the full tariff and a free hand.

But, with the pound going, the rupee threatened, and the fleet discontented, he clung to a national government, and the Conservative business committee unanimously reached far-reaching decisions.

Diary, 24 September

all were in favour of the national appeal by a national government under MacDonald, provided the programme embodied the full tariff. All agreed that the election should be at the earliest moment. All agreed that, if we went to election with R. M. as P.M., we must accept him as P.M. when we come back. . . . Truly, the Conservative party is a wonderful embodiment of good sense, patriotism, and honesty. What would have been the astonishment of the Socialist executive, if it could have overheard the Conservative executive agreeing to allow the man, who has all his life actively opposed them, now to have the credit of carrying out their own policy just when the whole country has come round to it.

But since the country was off gold, argued the Liberals, a tariff might be unnecessary; in " a very well-reasoned paper " Samuel put the case against an early election and, with Reading and Sinclair, made a pilgrimage to Lloyd George's sick bed, which the Prime Minister also attended. To the invalid it must be more urgent to postpone an election than to evade tariffs, for with time and his own recovery Liberalism might revive. But if an early election there must be, he would brandish the old flag of Free Trade. Into the sandy arena Chamberlain threw a formula, asking for a free hand and indicating that the new government would consider tariffs, but the Prime Minister refused to head an appeal unless it were unanimous, and unanimity could not be attained, for Lloyd George was urging the Liberal ministers to resign, while MacDonald, says the diary, would only make " despairing remarks ". Snowden, however, was clear that an election must be, and agreed with Chamberlain that, in some form or another, imports must be controlled.

At last, on October 5, having exhausted themselves and every other alternative, they resolved on an election with several concurrent appeals, one by MacDonald and others by the several party leaders. These, we read, were to eschew controversy, though " I do not myself see how it is going to work ".

Happily the long-accumulated British political instinct does work, with a sagacity which shears through to the ruling fact. In this case it was that the emergency was real, that Labour had proved incapable of dealing' with it, and that there was no room for Liberalism if it played a wrecking hand. This was recognised by the great bulk of the Liberal party, of whom Simon, Runciman, and Hore-Belisha were ready for the full programme, while the Reading–Samuel group so far defied Lloyd George that they accepted the need of an election, and an enquiry into tariffs as a temporary expedient. On the whole, parties worked together in response to the national mood, Chamberlain like others finding his meetings crowded, intently silent, and serious.

On October 27, by something rather over 2 to 1, or by $14\frac{1}{2}$ million votes against $6\frac{1}{2}$, democracy declared its will. Now perhaps Labour repented of having refused to hear of proportional representation, for the majority against them did much less than justice to their numerical strength. The electors returned 558 supporters of the National government, of whom 471 were Conservatives, 35 Simonite or National Liberals, and 33 Liberals of Samuel's sect. Labour had only 52 members, but in quality its downfall was even more complete, for a clean sweep was made of the ministers who had refused to follow MacDonald. Only Lansbury survived of that front bench, and within a week heavy Labour losses at the municipal elections wrote in deeper that verdict.

In Birmingham his own address was brief and decisive. Socialist ministers, " after agreeing to cuts which in several cases were considerably larger than those now in operation, ran away from their responsibilities ", though now in their election programme they promised to have no cuts at all. The country needed " permanent security ", it must restore the trade balance ; " in common with my colleagues, I recognise that no single remedy can be a complete cure, but while I am ready to examine every proposal . . . I must frankly say that I believe a tariff levied on imported foreign goods will be found to be indispensable. . . . The ultimate destiny of this country is bound up with the Empire . . . I hope to take my part in forwarding a policy which was the main subject of my father's last great political campaign."

And Birmingham surpassed itself, all twelve seats being won, and no Labour candidate returned to the city council.

Where would this great wave deposit them ? MacDonald, said one letter, had behaved justly during the election, Snowden had done much to win it ; " I hope that we may presently develop into a National Party, and get rid of that odious title of Conservative, which has kept so many from joining us in the past ".

If now we look backward to meet half-way this onward-looking gaze, we may judge that this memorable election made the end of a political age. The Radical programme of 1906–14, clinging to the older Liberal trunk, had no more fruit to give ; there might be two ways of life, two philosophies for meeting the feckless new world, but not three, and not three parties. Only three of the Lloyd George family, with two other members, represented a Liberalism in opposition, and only thirteen National Labour followed MacDonald, with whose lives, physical or political, these intermediate vitalities would crumble.

Yet parties never wholly perish, whatever happens to their frame, for from spiritual causes they spring, and the spirit which they themselves can express no longer is transmitted to, or shared among, spiritual legatees. Somehow, and in some proportions, between the Conservative and Labour parties which survived the tidal wave of 1931, must be distributed the gifts, powers, and claims of the nineteenth century.

BOOK III: 1931-1937

CHAPTER XIV
THE FIRST YEAR
AGED 62-63

> Better hard times and a continuing nation than lush, lavish
> indulgence and irrevocable decline.
>
> WINSTON CHURCHILL, *April* 15, 1929

IF in accord with custom we took as our next stage the life of a
Cabinet, it would be only because MacDonald's retirement coincided
with great historical events. In itself his exchange of office with
Baldwin signified little, the one real break of continuity having
come earlier when the Liberal ministers resigned in the autumn
of 1932.

These, later history will probably pronounce, were disastrous
years, for which all sections of the nation must shoulder some
responsibility. Older men seemed to be exhausted, or unable to
sink their differences in collaboration for the common good, while
the ability of the younger generation who had survived the holocaust inclined to flow in channels outside public life. Its old gift
of political relevance appeared to have abandoned the nation, who
were carried about by gusts of sentiment, mistook assumption for
reality, and too often confounded ends and means.

It is not, presumably, possible to separate this period of disarray
from the composition of the government which if, as Churchill
said, one of " nearly all the talents ", was irresolutely led and ill-
distributed. It suffered from one defect of Coalition, that office
must be proportioned to groups as much as to fitness. Not, of course,
that the election's major result could be evaded, whereby a Cabinet
which began with 11 Conservatives, 4 Labour, and 5 Liberals had
changed by 1935 to one of 14 Conservatives, 3 Labour, and 3
Liberals ; nor do numbers tell the whole story, for Liberals had
changed in content more than number, and Labour had lost weight.
Even so, the negative vices that look so like virtues coloured their
policy. A resolution not to be swamped in a sea of Tories would
incline the Prime Minister to go further than he otherwise might
in humouring the Liberals, while old association would tilt him in

favour of Sankey's advanced views on India, even induce more deference for Arthur Henderson's position as president of the Disarmament Conference.

Coalition involves exclusion from office of some of the party which is numerically strongest. For the moment there could be no question of taking in Churchill, whose opinion of MacDonald was low, and who was resisting the Indian settlement upon which Mac-Donald and Baldwin were set ; still less of Lloyd George, who had repudiated Simon, even reprobated Samuel, and with whom neither Baldwin nor Chamberlain would serve. But there were Conservative ex-ministers kept out for reasons which no man appreciates, whether advancing age, a doubtful verdict on the past, or no present room. Salisbury was gone, no place was found for Amery, Austen publicly waived his claim in favour of younger men. " Of course ", his brother wrote, " if he were offered the Foreign Office, he would certainly take it ", but he was not ; Locarno laurels were sere and yellowing, nothing in his French outlook corresponded to the prevailing mood.

Altogether this ministry leaves an impression of power at double remove, or metal sounding through wool, and more than one analogy takes us back to the Aberdeen coalition which invited the Crimean war ; to the Peelite quality and the Whig quantity, to Russell's exacting scruples and Palmerston's two-handed engine at the door. Yet nothing is more honourably cohesive than the loyalty which comes of working together, bringing in this instance sundry devices that kept them a working team. There was the almost congressional body to which Chamberlain refers as " the Six " ; MacDonald and Thomas, Simon and Runciman, Baldwin and himself. Behind the two last stood a committee of Conservative ministers, which he called into being, and behind that again the research department of his creation. To the Prime Minister he could never come very near. In old days he had described him as " a moral weakling ", and though he grew away — as he always did — from that asperity, he was tried, he admitted, by a mind " jobbing back on any decision ", or by that rainbow, almost somnambulist, oratory, by " my dear Mahatma " or " up and up and up ", " on and on ". From the first, and the more as MacDonald's health failed and his loneliness increased, the reality of power came back to Baldwin, whose position, we hear in 1934, " which calls upon him to supply advice and not action, exactly suits his temperament " ; advice which also embraced an admirable loyalty and self-effacement.

Now and then allusion to the " boys' brigade " in the Cabinet, or to " young Tory intellectuals ", serves to remind us that he was himself growing old, while another line cut across the Conservative majority with its two hundred new members, as across the people at large, the line dividing pre- and post-war. Yet never did elder statesmen toil more resolutely to adapt themselves to a younger age. If we ask the true meaning of those years, we may ignore the murmurings on the Right — murmurs against Ireland and India, against postponement of Lords reform, against a petroleum bill which would nationalise any oil discoveries in this island, — for the larger truth is very different. We find that the older conflict of party has been almost destroyed, that the wheel has turned back two centuries, and that under conditions far changed from the Elizabethan the main activities of the State are being nationalised, while Great Britain herself merges in a loose-knit democratic commonwealth. In such times statesmen must follow necessities, but in so far as individual agency was concerned, none was more powerful than that of the third Chamberlain, radical reformer cast in a conservative frame.

He was aware of his new position, as he was of the alternative paths before the country.

8 January 1932 ; to Sir Francis Humphrys
> altogether 1931 was a year of unhappiness and then a wonderful exhibition of determination and courage on the part of the nation. 1932 will be the year of opportunity. . . . Frankly, although the burden is heavy, I rejoice at it. To be given the chance of directing such great forces where I am convinced they should be applied, is such a privilege as one had no right to hope for ; and I intend to make the most of it.

For the Exchequer, which perhaps only the election itself decided should fall to him, could be made the key position in the State, the government having sprung out of financial ruin, and financial salvation being their immediate duty. Much must rest on his collaboration with Runciman, who took the Board of Trade, and though he never had a doubt of their personal relation, a public difference would jar a whole chain of problems, from a Liberal rebellion to a new flight from the pound. Half Europe and nearly all the Empire had followed Britain off gold ; from its old parity of 4·86 dollars the pound fell to 3·23 during December ; abnormal importations were poured in to evade an anticipated tariff, and when our exports responded to the altered exchange, France set a surtax on our goods. So far, our every effort to thaw frozen credits

in Europe was defeated.   While the French made their consent to
a monetary conference dependent on prior satisfaction over reparations, there came a dead-stop from America — " it is hereby expressly declared to be against the policy of Congress that any of
the indebtedness of foreign countries should be in any manner
cancelled or reduced ".

So although the question whether Samuel or Sinclair would
stay or resign might in itself be endured, it made one link in a
series that ended, sharp and clashing, in Berlin, where our ambassador reported Chancellor Brüning's hope that, with good fortune, he could control the peace for another six months.

6 December 1931

what I fear is a wholesale withdrawal of foreign holdings of sterling
. . . if they are realised, the holders will suffer severe losses.   If
therefore they think that the £ is likely to recover, they will hold on,
and that is why the French are so anxious to see us return to the gold
standard. . . . With what seems to me an extraordinary failure of
that logic which is supposed to be their special characteristic, they
insist on reparations before commercial credits from Germany, thus
freezing up British financial resources and threatening the stability of
the £ which they are so anxious to restore. . . . While they keep the
whole of Europe in a state of nervous anxiety and are thereby precipi-
tating the advent of Hitler to power, they are making it impossible
for Germany to pay any reparations. . . . The fact is that France and
America are both thinking of their forthcoming elections.   Any reparations settlement or adjustment must be accompanied by a corresponding settlement, or adjustment, of war debts.   Hoover knows it, but
daren't say so.   Unless he says so, France daren't move, and so we are
all locked in a suicidal embrace which will probably drown the lot
of us !   Reflect on this : (1) we remitted nearly £400 millions of
France's debt to us.   (2) if the U.S.A. had agreed to fund our debt
on the same terms as she gave to France, we should have so overpaid
that to put it right we should pay *nothing* for another 9 years !   Did
ever a country exploit her misfortunes more successfully than France ?

Wrestling with these friendly enemies in the gate, not to speak
of winding up the Indian round-table conference, he addressed
himself to his primary object, of directing the government towards
a fiscal revolution without breaking it up.   By February it was
accomplished, in three stages, each progressively more arduous
than the last.   First came proposals for preventing what older
England had called " forestalling ", — that is, a rush of imports
that would weaken the pound : hence the Abnormal Importations

Act, empowering the Board of Trade to levy duties up to 100 per cent, if necessary, on manufactured goods. Herein he was much assisted by the prior work of his research department, and notably by the report of its committee (headed by Cunliffe Lister) on an emergency tariff, which he called " a model of its kind ". But if this satisfied the orthodoxy of Snowden, Liberal discomfort much increased when the same principle was applied to agriculture.

Yet the arable problem was desperate, and Conservative pressure intense. Gilmour's first proposal probed the tender places gently with a Horticultural Imports Act, laying duties on certain vegetables, fruit, and flowers, all of which were, as Liberals must admit, " luxuries ", with which a robust people might dispense. His second was a pledge of a wheat quota before the next harvest, which raised more controversy, especially as it was to be extended to the Dominions, with whom they would meet in the summer in conference at Ottawa. On this, though Chamberlain's purpose was decided, for the present all he was concerned with was that the government should not be committed, — " to go into the Conference saying we rule out food taxes would be to kill it before it had started, and I will never consent to that ".

This sharp corner being turned and Snowden's land valuation also being successfully suspended, they rode up to their last fence of a permanent policy. In December he secured the appointment of a committee to consider the balance of trade, himself as chairman and with him Simon and Runciman, Snowden and Thomas, Gilmour and Cunliffe Lister, Hilton Young and Samuel. What arguments he put forward may be deduced from his later exposition to Parliament, — $2\frac{1}{2}$ million unemployed, a surplus of £409 millions in imports over exports, a net adverse trade balance of £113 millions. In two years our invisible exports, from shipping returns and foreign investment, were nearly £200 millions down, the very items which most depended on a recovery in world trade, of which there was no sign. How then to reverse the balance, swell the revenue, and assist employment, save by a tariff?

As he fought through his committee's discussions, conciliatory in manœuvre but unyielding in aim — " do you remember ", he wrote, " the gulf of Cattaro, how we always appeared to be in a cul-de-sac, until at the last moment a new exit appeared ? " — two facts helped him ; that Runciman was whole-hearted for a low general tariff, and that he himself would go to great lengths to keep Snowden ; for like answered to like, and these two inflexible Victorians much esteemed one another.

15 January 1932 ; to Lord Snowden

I am quite certain that you must have known all along that some sort of tariff was inevitable, with this House of Commons and this Government. You are too much of a realist to have shut your eyes to that. All the same, I hope you will recognise that I have done my best to put the tariff in the form least unpalatable ; and that, for that purpose, I have gone a very long way from the proposals on which I was occupied before the National Government was formed. What you cannot know is the amount of pains I have taken to influence my colleagues, and a large part of the press, to restrain their impatience, and to prepare themselves to take a National rather than a Party attitude. . . . Secondly, I want to point out two considerations which I think, even from the strictest Free Trade aspect, might be some mitigation of objection to the proposals which we shall have before us. The idea of a flat-rate low level tariff, subject to a number of exceptions, is in line with the policy of those countries on the Continent which are nearest to the Free Trade position. Is there not here an opportunity of beginning an association which, with the aid of a common policy on currency, may presently give the United Kingdom a preponderating influence in directing Europe as a whole back to sounder methods ? secondly, the coupling with this flat-rate tariff of additional powers . . . does provide us with such a lever as has never been possessed before by any government for inducing or, if you like, forcing industry to set its house in order. I have in my mind particularly iron and steel, and cotton ; and my belief in the advantages of protection is not so fanatical as to close my eyes to the vital importance of a thorough reorganisation of such industries as these, if they are even to keep their heads above water in the future.

Lastly, I want to say this. During the weeks that we have worked together, I have felt that, in spite of our differences on particular subjects, there was a large field in which our ideas are very nearly identical. Frankly, I do not want to see the realist element in this Cabinet weakened ; and while I could part with some of my colleagues without losing my night's rest, I should consider it a very great misfortune for the country if you found yourself unable any longer to co-operate with us.

The answer, despite some common form about " the present howling mob of Protectionists " in the Commons, was kind ; " I fully appreciate your position and difficulties, and I say with sincerity that you have appreciated ours, and have gone very far to meet them ". At last, after three stiff meetings, a temporary solution was found.

Diary, 22 January 1932

Cabinet met again this morning, and the dissentients [1] reiterated their intention to resign, although the P.M. had previously made an impressive speech dwelling first on the national danger, and then on his personal position. . . . I followed Samuel, expressing sincere regret, but not attempting to offer any compromise. I assured the P.M. that those who remained would in no way alter their relations with him. Hailsham then intervened, with a proposal which I had the day before suggested to the P.M., though I had only applied it to Snowden, as I had not expected other resignations. It was that we should agree to differ on the one point, and that dissentient ministers should be allowed to speak and vote on tariffs against the proposals of the majority.

That the tariff was his work, that what he called " the great day of my life " had come, was recognised by all men, as a note passed at the Cabinet table may show.

29 January ; from Sir Donald Maclean

I think your great father would, and mayhap may be, proud of your work today. This from an unrepentant Free Trader.

On February 4, with Joseph Chamberlain's widow and children to hear him, he put the scheme to the Commons ; a general 10 per cent duty on all goods other than those exempted by a free list — which included wheat, meat, cotton, and wool — or those already subject to duty ; an independent Tariff board, on whose recommendation the Treasury would build a superstructure of additional duties upon non-essential goods, non-essential either in the sense of luxuries, or as goods which could be produced in bulk at home ; the produce of colonies and mandated territories would enter duty-free ; the Board of Trade would be enabled to retaliate against foreign discrimination, or to lower tariffs by reciprocal treaties.

His speech was unprovocative, almost appealing. The taxpayer's " self-sacrificing and devoted patriotism ", a wonder to " less happy lands ", was reaping its reward, but world trade was ruined. Their remedy must be one so flexible that it could be adjusted to all their purposes ; to correct the trade balance, enhance the revenue, increase employment, and insure against a rise in the cost of living which, far more than by any tariff, would follow on a depreciation of the pound. This " moderate Protection " would be taken out of political pressures by being committed to an independent Board, while the Treasury would have power to protect the consumer. On Dominion goods they would impose no duties

---

[1] Snowden, Maclean, Samuel, Sinclair.

Treasury Chambers,
Whitehall S.W.

There can have been few occasions
in all our long political history when
to the son of a man who counted for
something in his day and generation
has been vouchsafed the privilege of
setting the seal on the work which the
father began but had perforce to leave
unfinished Nearly 29 years have passed
since Joseph Chamberlain entered upon
his great campaign in favour of Imperial
Reference and Tariff Reform More than
19 years have gone by since he died,
without having seen the fulfilment of his
aims and yet convinced that, if not
                                    exactly.

This extract was written in 1936 for the autograph colle

exactly in his way, yet in some modified
form his vision would eventually take
shape His work was not in vain Time
and the misfortunes of the country have
brought conviction to many who did not
feel that they could agree with him then.
I believe he would have found consolation
for the bitterness of his disappointment
if he could have foreseen that these
proposals which are the direct and
legitimate descendants of his own
conception, would be laid before the House
of Commons, which he loved, in the presence
of one and by the lips of the other of the
two immediate successors to his name and
blood   N Chamberlain

House of Commons Feb. 4ᵗʰ 1932

UARY 1932
.H. the Duke of York, later H.M. King George VI.

till after Ottawa, since they wished to enter that conference " in the true spirit of Imperial unity ". Then he expressed the feelings which he hated to make public :

Nearly twenty-nine years have passed since Joseph Chamberlain entered upon his great campaign in favour of Imperial preference and tariff reform. More than seventeen years have gone by since he died, without having seen the fulfilment of his aims and yet convinced that, if not exactly in his way, yet in some modified form his vision would eventually take shape. His work was not in vain. Time and the misfortunes of the country have brought conviction to many who did not feel that they could agree with him then. I believe he would have found consolation for the bitterness of his disappointment if he could have foreseen that these proposals, which are the direct and legitimate descendants of his own conception, would be laid before the House of Commons, which he loved, in the presence of one, and by the lips of the other, of the two immediate successors to his name and blood.

While congratulations reached him in hundreds, " from the King to my tailor ", from the bearded neighbour of Bahamas days or veterans of the Tariff Reform League, clashes and disputes signalled dangers ahead. Only Canadian remonstrance had brought about the decision of no duties on the Dominions till after Ottawa, for many counsellors had advised him to keep the preferences in hand with which to bargain. Many struggles to extend the free list, into which he put maize to the joy of Northern Ireland, and sisal for the good of East Africa, made the more important the composition of the tariff board ; for which he congratulated himself on finding a chairman in Sir George May, of the famous economy committee of 1931. And how long could the " agreement to differ " last, if all the dissentient ministers spoke out as dogmatically as Samuel ? Yet talk of broken pledges was much beside the mark, for during the election Baldwin and Chamberlain had gone out of their way to claim a free hand.

By the spring many signs predicted a revival of better times. Unprecedently heavy taxation was paid with unprecedented punctuality, bank rate was stepped down from 6 till it paused at 2 per cent, half the £80 millions borrowed the previous summer from France and America were repaid. The French removed their surtax on British coal, tariffs seemed to be bringing the foreigner to reason. But Europe was pitch dark. In February the Disarmament Conference at Geneva, in a hall new-made to hold sixty nations, met to dissect the skeleton convention which had taken ten years to make. They thrust it hurriedly back into its cupboard, and month after month passed in confabulation and debate. As they circulated through sub-committees and bureaux, the projects diminished in meaning as their dossiers grew in bulk. Anglo-Saxon resistance to French notions for an international force, German insistence that no international society could exist until Versailles were destroyed, sober British suggestions for " qualitative " disarming which would, for example, abolish air bombing — except for lesser breeds in " outlying regions " — and American propositions for a clean cut of a third all round, till at last experts were left searching for any weapon that could be accurately described as " aggressive ".   While the Lytton Commission journeyed to the Far East to enquire into facts that were already disagreeably plain, the Japanese, after overrunning Manchuria, penetrated south of the Great Wall, and landed troops at Shanghai.   In France a Herriot government succeeded to the rigid Tardieu, but Brüning fell in Germany, well before his six months were up, and was replaced by the ever-surviving von Papen.   Hindenburg had just been re-elected President, but Hitler polled 13½ million votes against him, and at the Reichstag elections in July the Nazis won 230 seats.   But though the British Service estimates were again reduced, a clerical deputation asked the Prime Minister for further disarmament:

All this would not ameliorate that part of the world's troubles which concerned the Chancellor of the Exchequer, who this year underwent his first prolonged experience of foreign affairs.   After strenuous effort, a formula had been found whereby a conference would meet at Lausanne to discuss reparations, but though his hope was ultimately to get both reparations and war debts cancelled, the eyes of the democracies were turned inward on themselves.

13 February 1932

nothing is said about a further moratorium because the French won't agree (before their election) to any total suspension of payments, and the Germans won't agree (before their election) to anything which suggests a payment at all.   And we can't mention War debts because the Americans won't agree (before their election) to consider any relaxation.

He first tried his hand on Flandin, — " a tough nut " — and then on Caillaux, — " not to be trusted " ; in April came a full-scale experience, the Danubian Conference, by which Tardieu attempted to smuggle through an economic bloc of five small States under French patronage.   But British most-favoured-nations rights seemed imperilled, it might prejudice Ottawa, moreover it was killed by opposition from Germany and Italy.

Before this he had gone, following an invariable Easter practice, to think out his Budget as he fished by the Aberdeenshire Dee, his purpose being not to allow the nation to suppose that the tide had turned. " Birches and larches make a purple mist with old gold patches in it ", but his Budget was to be like that cold sunlight. " The severe but sound and salutary finance " of Snowden, he told the House, had indeed wiped out a deficit of £74 millions, but what the blizzard meant was reflected in a drop of £20 millions in death duties and stamps alone, and income-tax and surtax would tell the same tale in the next year ; he foresaw a loss of £32 millions in inland revenue and a diminishing return from direct taxation. But this deficit would, on his estimate, be almost closed by the yield from the new tariff, while he would stop the last gap by reimposing the tea duty which Churchill had removed. Beyond revenue matters, he propounded two decisions of future importance. A committee would explore the long-drawn-out controversy on the taxation of co-operative societies ; again, he asked powers to borrow up to £150 millions in order to set up an exchange equalisation account, to arm the country against damage done by speculative capital.

He offered no relief from taxation, no gambling on the future. " Nothing could be more harmful to the ultimate material recovery of this country or to its present moral fibre . . . hard work, strict economy, firm courage, unfailing patience, these are the qualifications that are required of us, and with them we shall not fail."

Compensations came to him this month of the sort that warmed his heart, such as a letter from the governor of the Bank on almost the first honest Budget since the war, and the freedom given him of his native city, together with a Cadbury and a Lloyd, for eminent service, expecially his housing policy and " the inestimable contribution to the thrift and social life of the citizens " in the orchestra and the municipal bank. But in May, laid low by the worst gout for many years, he was contemplating a possible retirement from politics, and it was only after a cure, varied by much reading of natural history, that he set out to wrestle with *homo sapiens* at Lausanne.

Reparations had taught the world a severe lesson. 20,000 million pounds, thought the War Cabinet of 1919 ; 7000 millions, the reparations commission in 1921 ; annuities rising to 125 millions, the Dawes plan of 1924 ; totals ever dwindling, only made possible at all by American loans to Germany, which dried up in the depression, and were at last suspended by the Hoover moratorium of 1931. On this disappearing process the Lausanne conference assembled, under MacDonald's chairmanship, to set the seal. They were working perilously near Geneva, where sixty nations were at loggerheads over disarmament, while at the end of every Alpine vista they caught sight of Washington. For France certainly could not face an end of reparations, unless America remitted or relaxed her debt from the creditors of Germany. But of this the Europeans had high hopes, for had not Hoover as good as invited Europe to take the first step and spoken of further agreements during the depression?

Herriot was there with his finance minister Germain Martin, von Papen and Neurath from Germany, Hymans the Belgian, sometimes the emotional Grandi strayed in from Geneva, and representatives from all the "victor" States. MacDonald, Simon, Runciman, and Samuel were there at different times, but it appears that on Chamberlain fell the continuous brunt, in part because the Prime Minister was incapacitated by headaches and could not understand French, whereas Chamberlain understood, and by degrees ventured to speak it. But even more because he inspired a lasting affection in Herriot; "his description of you to me", wrote Sir William Tyrrell later, "is always the same, ' *Chamberlain, c'est du cristal* ' ". Such an impression he often left on individuals, though he did not, as a letter of June shows, profess to be internationally-minded.

> The foreigner [he wrote] simply can't contemplate getting down to business without long preliminary sparring. . . . They all have their different methods. The French talk at interminable length on generalities, they protest their loyalty, their frankness, and their disinterestedness. Meanwhile they send out an army of agents (they have a staff of about fifty here), who nose round and try to find out what the other fellow means to do, and where is his last ditch. The Italian affects an air of utter boredom and indifference . . . but in reality he is listening all the time, and as soon as the others seem likely to come to some conclusion, he jumps up and cries "how is it that I have not been consulted ? "

At the opening session he spoke clearly for cancellation. Italy agreed, but France stood firm, and every contact with Geneva sharpened tempers at Lausanne. And though America would be more lenient to France over debts if France were less stiff about arms, might not a total cancellation of reparations, the French suggested, rouse suspicion that Europe meant to repudiate her American debt ?

In short, while in a gout boot he explored the pleasant villages of Fribourg and Neuchâtel, political ramifications overspread their economic business. Grandi was found in tears because his Duce felt that Britain and France were dealing behind his back, the Central European clients of France were there to supplicate for loans, Neurath made disarmament a condition of any step forward, our ministers at Lausanne thought their colleagues in London were taking a perilously lofty tone towards President Hoover's scheme for a cut in armaments. Such currents underran the Beau Rivage Hôtel ; where MacDonald conducted business from the bedroom where Curzon once lost a famous pair of trousers, where Herriot slept only three hours in the night, and where Chamberlain kept off the gout with doses of colchicum.

Diary, 23 June

I then received the Austrian Chancellor, Dr. Dollfuss. . . . As I have no doubt that the visit was in consequence of an interview with the French at which they told Dollfuss that the British were holding up the loan, I explained the truth that so far as Austria was concerned there was no difficulty with us. But for purposes of their own internal politics France was asking us to undertake to join them in financial assistance to other countries, and this we could not do.

24 June

the P.M. also told me that . . . he had challenged Grandi to deny that he was making some arrangement with the Germans. . . . This reminded me of Herriot's remark . . . " *de l'Italie il y a tout à craindre, rien à espérer* ".

Cancellation being ruled out, but the British as stoutly refusing to hear of a return to annuities, they set out to investigate a German hint that they might agree to pay a lump sum. After many days it was found that, in return, they expected a settlement of disarmament on the basis of equal rights, and when he left Lausanne on June 29 Herriot was vowing he cared more for the life of France than her money.

He came home for a few days to impart to the Commons a measure hitherto kept secret, even from the Cabinet ; that is, his intention to convert £2000 millions of 5% War Loan to 3½%. Snowden, he explained, had hoped to do this and arranged the procedure ; this great mass, " hanging like a cloud over the capital market ", was preventing a general fall to easier rates. " The final and the strongest argument for immediate action is the spirit of the country " which, he declared, " is in the mood for great enterprises ". In fact, 92 per cent of the loan was converted which, with some lesser operations of the year, made an annual saving of £40 millions.

Five most disagreeable days followed on his return to Lausanne. " Warm words ", " received with jeers ", " angry and hysterical ", cover the pages of the diary.

Diary, 4 July
> Pirelli for the 3rd time raised the question of the Italian debt to us, and made it clearer that he wanted a clean sheet if the treaty were ratified, even though that meant our having to make payments to America greater than our receipts from reparations. I was very angry at his impudence.

6 July ; to Mrs. Chamberlain
> never have I seen the weakness of modern democracy so clearly demonstrated. . . . The system has produced men who have not the courage to handle the animal firmly, though if they did, it is at least possible that it would prove far more responsive than it does to weakness.

At last, by enormous British effort, a figure had been agreed of three milliards of reichsmarks in lieu of reparations, and it was now a question of finding a formula that would satisfy the Germans by mention of " equality " without alarming the French by dragging in those matters, disarmament or war guilt, which the Germans obstinately tried to insert. On July 7 when things looked desperate, Hankey suggested, says our record, " that at critical moments feeding together always helped ", and when Herriot and Germain Martin had partaken, Chamberlain pressed them, " in such French as I could muster ", for some gesture to show that " a new order was going to begin ". By one in the morning they had reached Herriot's bedroom, and after passing through " *fraternité* ", " *égalité* ", " *solidarité* ", pitched on " justice " as the blameless word. That achieved, Germain Martin made a last bid for better financial terms ; whereupon followed an honest scene.

Diary
> I made a gesture of despair, but Herriot laid his hand on my arm and turning to me he said, " my dear chancellor, I have the utmost confidence in you. I will take your own interpretation . . . if you tell me you can get no more, I shall accept that." I was greatly touched

by such a compliment ; we shook hands warmly, and our business
was at last concluded.   I got back at 3 A.M.

So next day the agreement was signed, with the bedroom phrasing
prominent, — an end of reparations, a new order, a mutual spirit
of justice.
    Two other documents were also signed at Lausanne, the first
pledging Great Britain and France to work together on disarmament and all like questions, and a second, covering Italy and
Belgium as well, to the effect that these four States would not ratify
Lausanne till they reached a settlement with their own creditors.
Was this the " line-up against America ", which critics deprecated
on both sides of the Atlantic ?   Undoubtedly here Chamberlain's
sanguine calculations played a part.   Europe, he replied in Parliament, " simply could not wait ", and having ourselves waived
every penny of future reparations we could go to Washington with
clean hands.   Having followed advice given to us by America,
we might expect that she would not " refuse to play her part in
a world settlement ".
    On July 13 the British delegation sailed for Ottawa, to which
they looked as a nucleus of hope.   Much, indeed, was accomplished.
Our currency was saved and the cost of living held, but the figures
of unemployment, soon rising to a climax of just under three millions
at the New Year, proved that world trade was destroyed.   Its total
value was one-third of that in 1929, it was reckoned that thirty
million workers were unemployed, wheat touched the lowest recorded figure for four centuries.   Whatever Europe did, or Washington denied, a prosperous and co-operative Empire would be a long
stride towards recovery.
    Our delegation was strong : Baldwin, Chamberlain, Hailsham,
Runciman, Thomas, Gilmour, and Cunliffe Lister, reinforced by
industrial advisers like Weir and civil servants like Horace Wilson,
in the background the editors of our greatest journals, not to mention
the proprietors of those with the greatest circulation.   In its composition he had early exerted himself, thinking it indispensable
that someone other than Thomas should be leader, and that Baldwin
was the right man.   If he looked forward to doing something to
complete his father's work, his hopes for the immediate future
were not pitched unduly high, being prepared for many set-backs
provided he could set the Empire on the path of preferential
trade.
    The conference was not a failure, yet neither was it a success,

failing in atmosphere rather than achievement. A large part of its shortcomings were attributed by Chamberlain to its president, Bennett, the Prime Minister of Canada, but in any case it had to get over innumerable antagonisms and conflicts of interest. These it is common to read as coming from the " sinister interests " involved in tariff-making, the vested wealth in meat or lumber or steel, ignoring the truth that a tariff in democratic societies represents many thousand human cells, all capable of making contribution to a larger union. Hard bargaining there was bound to be between half a dozen sovereign parliaments, while rival schedules must be further inflamed by the present economic discontents. For if the Dominions had long ago come out of the colonial stage of being producers of food and raw material, one fundamental result of the depression was that Great Britain had learned to value her own agriculture.

Such recognised openings for friction were by no means neglected. Representatives of British farming were there to ask for a duty on meat, Beaverbrook's inveterate hostility to Baldwin was present in full force, while attacks in the Canadian press, which it was believed the Canadian government read without displeasure, pointed angrily at Whitehall bureaucrats who were spiritually free traders, and were anyhow unsound on meat and steel. All this, disillusioning enough for a Chamberlain, might have the more serious effect of breaking up the Imperial Cabinet.

His own draft of general resolutions was brushed aside, only to emerge at the end as a mild expression of opinion, and the conference proceeded on three more humble propositions, mainly of his devising ; that preferential arrangements should aim at a gradually descending scale of duties, that the British importer should be put on the same level as the Dominion producer, and that the agricultural problem should be settled on the basis of a voluntary restriction of production. Eschewing the detail of combat in committee, we collect some illustration of his thinking on critical points.

Diary, 23 July

> we discussed with the trade commissioners the situation with regard to the various Dominions in turn. The result was very startling, as it appeared that the value of the increased trade . . . would amount to something very small. . . . But the discussion brought out a new point, at least new to me, viz. the possibility of getting a progressive decrease of duties over a period of years, so as gradually to break down the excessive protection of the home production.

24 July

Sir Atul Chatterjee came to see me. . . . India was anxious to avoid a quarrel with Russia. . . . I explained that we ourselves, while aware of the serious menace to prices of Russian action . . . had financial commitments which would be jeopardised by such drastic action as a total prohibition of Russian imports. . . . Bennett attached great importance to action against Russia, but . . . we could not agree to prohibition.

28 July

to Monetary committee, where listened for $2\frac{1}{2}$ hours to unilluminating speeches, culminating in a sort of summer school address from Henry Strakosch.

For a fortnight he wrote cheerfully. India accepted the principle of preference, Bruce for Australia agreed to restriction on meat, he found Havenga the South African most helpful, he wrestled not unsuccessfully against monetary manipulation as the sole means of raising prices, and so far carried his colleagues with him. But then the clouds thickened.

Diary, 4 August

Bennett came . . . to bring his offer. He adopted a very aggressive tone . . . declaring that we had among our official advisers persons who were interested in the import of Russian fish and lumber . . . then produced the schedule . . . his advisers reckoned that it gave British traders opportunity of getting 55 million if they were men enough to seize it. . . . Havenga to dine . . . he considered automatic extension to other Dominions of preference given to Great Britain . . . out of the question.

By this date he was reduced for his private pleasure to a little fishing with a worm — fishing in Canada, he wrote, was " a coarse unscientific affair " — while for his public edification he was advised that the Canadian offer to Great Britain would involve a positive loss. As the last hope of saving the conference, he approached Bennett direct.

Diary, 9 August

When I could get a chance to speak, I said I thought we had made a mistake . . . in attempting to value concessions in terms of money . . . even if the Dominions gave us everything we asked for, we could not get from them concessions which in their immediate effect would be comparable with what we gave them. . . . I concluded then that, if we were to carry our people with us, we must show them something that would touch their imagination. We must open up the vision of a great Imperial policy, having within itself the mainspring which would continually move us on to closer unity. . . . If that were so, the thing to which we attached importance was the declaration of policy, leading to the recognition of our right to the position of domestic competitor.

Simultaneously Runciman was threatening to sing his *nunc dimittis* over meat restriction, others felt that to propose special terms both for Canadian wheat and Australian meat would try the Cabinet and the electorate very high.   Henceforward it was one continuous fight, haggling over zinc or softwood, holding out on beef and yielding on mutton ; a little of which goes a very long way. But the issues were serious enough ; a wrecking of the conference and a break-up of the Cabinet.

Diary, 12 August

British delegation at 10 . . . the sense of disunity for the first time was oppressive. At noon Douglas (Hailsham) and I . . . joined by Bennett . . . I then came to wheat . . . we could not give our final answer till we knew where we were about meat. . . . H. and I . . . agreed that it looked like a breach.

It seemed that the Canadian Prime Minister suspected the British of concealing essential facts, the sort of charge that Chamberlain took long to forgive, which for some days brought the temperature well below freezing point ; at the same time he was fighting in the last ditch with Australia.

Diary, 15 August

another black day . . . saw Bruce and Gullett with Hailsham, and told them that we could not give them a duty.

(10.30 p.m.)

meeting in S. B.'s room . . . J. H. Thomas . . . said that his own convictions were against giving way. Walter Runciman said the same. . . . I said I was greatly embarrassed. I felt very much how loyally and helpfully W. R. and J. H. T. had behaved . . . on the other hand, if we failed to make a settlement with Bruce, the conference would be a failure, and I was in despair at the thought. . . . After the others had gone to bed, I stopped at S. B.'s request and told him that, if the conference broke down because of our refusal to put a duty on meat, I should have to fade out.

That was the darkest hour before dawn. By dint of balancing great arguments against small, by good personal bonds with each other, and by firmness, the conference was saved. Thomas gave way, considering how severe would be the effect of a breakdown upon Ireland, the Australians accepted restriction without a duty, Ramsay MacDonald gave his colleagues *carte blanche*. So the last agreement was initialled in the small hours of August 20.

Diary, 20 August

my only real disappointment was that we were not able to get a better set of general resolutions. . . . The countries of the Empire have been drifting apart pretty rapidly. We have been in time to stop the rot, and have been helped by the great prestige which has come to us over the conversion loan and the Lausanne success. . . . Most of our difficulties centred round the personality of Bennett. Full of high Imperial sentiments, he has done little to put them into practice. Instead of guiding the conference in his capacity as chairman, he has acted merely as the leader of the Canadian delegation. In that capacity he has strained our patience to the limit. . . . That in spite of all this we should have won through, has been due to our unalterable patience and firmness, coupled with our complete confidence in one another. . . . The better understanding and real liking that has sprung up among the various delegations, especially the Indians, South Africans, and Free Staters will bear fruit in future.

Yet it was a weary, disenchanted body who reached home, not cheered by hearing *en route* that the Prime Minister felt himself more than ever the prisoner of the Tories, which he might feel even more when the Liberal ministers came narrowly to examine the Ottawa agreements. To judge them fairly at once was indeed impossible. Any larger notions of permanent organisation had been rebuffed, while for monetary decisions they had merely agreed in a broad aspiration for raising prices and for exchange stability within the sterling bloc. Such grounds for hope as Chamberlain found looked therefore to the future, in an arrest to a slow decomposition of empire and in principles to which the Dominions were now pledged, that their tariff boards would put British traders on terms of reasonable competition, and should cease to protect industries with no hope of development.

But Liberal ministers could hardly be content with this fare of high hopes and plain tariffs. They had come far along the road, once renouncing a projected resignation because MacDonald declared the peace of Europe and India was at stake. They had swallowed the Wheat Act with its guaranteed prices, the tariff board had given a duty of 33 per cent to iron and steel, and though good temporary grounds could be found for these, Ottawa asked them to digest fundamentals, food taxes and the permanent frame of a mercantile empire. For Great Britain had undertaken to stabilise existing preferences for five years and to extend preference to butter, fruit, and cheese, to restrict meat production and to give Dominion producers priority over the foreigner, to place a 2s. duty on foreign wheat, to favour the tobacco and coffee of the Colonies.

Maclean having died, to Chamberlain's grief, in June, the dissentients were led by Samuel, who was stiff as himself in holding his opinion, and with whom he had at the moment another difference. This turned on the cut in pay of the police, which in the crisis it had been agreed should be carried out by two stages, the second of which was now due and must be enforced, unless unemployed and teachers and Services were to feel a rankling sense of injustice. But the Home Secretary took some objection.

Chamberlain therefore rejoiced when the inevitable break came at the end of September, in the resignation of Samuel, Snowden, and Sinclair, together with seven minor ministers, whose places were filled up without reluctance by Conservatives and National Liberals. In future, he wrote, they would be more homogeneous, on the way to " the fused party under a National name which I regard as certain to come ".

CHAPTER XV

END OF THE POST-WAR WORLD: 1932–1933
AGED 63–64

It is true ; evil must continue ; yet not this evil and that evil.

CARLYLE

TILL the end of 1932 hope still glimmered that the world might see reason, and be saved. This was the ground that MacDonald took as his justification for striving to prolong the national government ; Herriot was ready to bargain disarmament against security ; President Roosevelt's election brought promise of a new unity in American government and with it, perchance, more understanding of Europe. The same November a loss of seats by the Nazis in the Reichstag elections encouraged democracy to think that the German aberration was passing. How such hopes were shrunken by the spring, how at their last gasp by midsummer 1933, forms the background to this part of one British minister's story.

For the time we must thrust away domestic themes, however important. There was De Valera living, we hear, " in a world of his own ", weakening the 1921 treaty, and by his repudiation of the land annuity payments bringing on an Anglo-Irish tariff war. Indian reforms had emerged in a White Paper, soon to be referred to a committee of both Houses, though as between warring Indian communities Great Britain was compelled to impose a settlement, and British Conservatism asked many safeguards against damage to Imperial control. He himself had accepted the new advance with doubt, writing " we ought never to have promised responsible government at the centre till we had tried out self-government in the provinces ". But all these, together with much-controverted new Acts regarding unemployment, must be deferred to his immediate purposes.

Lausanne had shown him how inseparable were the strands of international well-being, but with foreign policy he was only occasionally concerned. When French ministers came over in November to talk disarmament and how Germany should be induced to continue at Geneva, he found Flandin desirous to link up disarmament with a settlement of the German-Polish frontiers, and insistent that France could not accept naval parity with Italy unless Great Britain guaranteed a safe connection between France and Africa. The Disarmament Conference, Chamberlain thought, made the mistake of trying too many things at once, and he sent Simon a note with proposals for disarmament by stages, of which much was heard the following year. Suffice to say here that he believed the present German government did not wish to rearm, and proceeded on the mistaken assumption that Germany could be put on probation while other States disarmed at leisure.

His own hands were full with that question without which Lausanne would end in barren leaves, a settlement of the American debt. On which, looking back in the spring of 1933, when the Far East, Disarmament Conference, American banking, and Reichstag building all roared up to heaven in explosion, he was to feel " if only we could have got a settlement with America immediately after Lausanne, I believe half these troubles would never have materialised ; but that wretched constitution made it impossible ".

In the constitutional conditions of those days, now changed, it was in fact impossible to expect brisk action either from a defeated President, a Congress part made up of representatives whose mandate had expired, or from a new President who was elected in November but would not take office till March. So Hoover, facing a half-bankrupt country, could only speak guardedly of leniency to debtors, while the same objection made it impossible to hold the World Economic Conference until Roosevelt was installed. On this unhopeful stage Chamberlain's outlook reflected the average British temper. His aim was cancellation, his method was to work for a three-year moratorium, and a final payment in a much-reduced lump sum, as at Lausanne. Whether he could " educate " America in this doctrine was another matter.

15 May 1932

Uncle Sam's view is that the scheme of total cancellation is a cynical plan for putting the whole burden on his shoulders. If you asked him *what* burden, I think he would find it difficult to give an intelligible reply. The fact is the real burden is that brought about by his own insistence on payment of debts, while refusing to allow them to be paid for in goods and services.

By the autumn, with the next instalment due before Christmas, decision was imperative, and as Washington rejected a proposal that payment be suspended pending discussion, the British government after long hesitation decided to pay.

4 December

it seemed to me that the consequences of non-payment were so serious, that though they might in the end prove inevitable, we ought to avoid them as long as there remained even a remote chance of a happy ending. If we defaulted . . . we should for ever be pointed at by Americans first and then by De Valera, and all the small States who have difficulty in meeting their obligations, as the country who sanctioned no payment of debts when it was convenient to the debtor. . . . I found that S. B. took this view very strongly, and on those very rare occasions when he expresses an opinion of his own, he is generally right.

Before payment a Note of December 1 stated the British case at full length, in classic form, the gist of which may be reduced to its one sentence, " that the payment of war debts has in their view been proved to be inconsistent with the present economic organisation of the world ". This was composed by Leith Ross, and amended by MacDonald and Chamberlain, in part to meet certain American approaches which, though soon extinguished, open for us a window into his mind. In brief, they proposed a moratorium, the very thing on which he was set, but at a price which he would not pay, a distinction by America between her treatment of Great Britain and France. The same letter, resumed, carries us forward over several stages :

Tyrrell said that Herriot wished to pay, but was alone in his Cabinet, and perhaps in the Chamber. . . . To my consternation I found a strong section who advocated that we should accept an offer so advantageous to ourselves, and let the French go hang. . . . Things got a bit warm, as I would certainly have resigned rather than accept what I should have considered a betrayal of our ally.

This being clarified, he went to Paris to give Herriot his moral support. But in vain ; the French government fell, France (not to mention Poland, Hungary, and Belgium) defaulted on their American debt, and a stiffer British Note, enclosing payment in gold, protested that annual payments could not be revived without disaster.

18 December 1932 ; from E. Herriot

MON CHER AMI,

Je suis bien touché de vostre lettre. Je ne regrette pas d'avoir prouvé la sincérité de mon attachement aux doctrines que j'ai toujours défendues ; j'en ai demandé l'application à l'Allemagne ; je veux que la France y soit fidèle. . . . Vous avez été pour moi le plus fidèle et le plus délicat des amis. Tant que durera mon existence, vous pourrez compter sur moi comme sur vous-même.

Febrile, dangerous, new activities now charged the air. In January Hitler became Chancellor of the Reich, in February the terror began. Russia moved on in her own orbit, bloody purges decimated her middle class, while an arrest of British subjects on a charge of sabotage roused the rare British capacity for indignation, which took expression in an embargo on Russian imports. In March MacDonald was at Geneva to snatch some forlorn hope out of disarmament, then at Rome to hear the Duce's ideas for treaty revision, and last, in April, at Washington to concert with the new President for the Economic Conference. But before he landed a crash drove America off gold and threw Congress into the New Deal. Within this distracted frame we set the British Budget of 1933.

He could build on some elements of recovery, for in the past year our adverse trade balance had been cut down by £120 millions, while by all normal tests the body of the people were better off. But he had to face a bleak horizon. At one end of society nearly three million unemployed, at the other a drop of 12,000 in the number of surtax payers, direct taxation and customs both far below the estimates. He took several opportunities to tell the House that Britain could not expect prosperity in a world out of joint, that we must contemplate ten years of large-scale unemployment, and he must steer between the two poles of spending and economy which variously attracted the public mind. While, then, for his own pleasure he was writing to the press of a wagtail in the Park, or modern phrasing in Shakespeare's sonnets, he was also receiving Professor Keynes and holding off many deputations, of spenders, brewers, or road transport.

In his speech, presenting a deficit of £32 millions, which was more than accounted for by the payment to America and on unemployment, his positive proposals were few. He would raise the exchange equalisation fund to £350 millions, — a decision taken well before America had gone off gold, and with no purpose of undercutting the dollar ; he remodelled the beer duty, since consumption had fallen by a third in four years, so as to cheapen the pint ; to spare the Prime Minister's feelings the land-tax valuation would be kept in being, but the undistributed profits of co-operative societies would be made liable to tax. This he commended to them

as a positive gain, for it gave a statutory pledge that their " dividend "
should be tax-free.

But he would not borrow in order to reduce taxation, nor
deliberately unbalance his Budget. Not just because it was un-
orthodox, but because they were not immune " from those grim
forces that hold the world in their grip ", a world full of instances
to prove that a deficit made no cure for falling prices. We at least
were free from the fear that there might be worse to come ; already
the fall in our trading profits was but half that of the year before ;
let them not throw away that hard-won vantage, or forfeit the
world's respect. He did not add, what he keenly felt, that remission
of our own taxation was not a good preface to a petition for remission
of our American debt.

But he suffered (he was inclined to) something of the loneliness
of a commander whose garrison were half-disposed to hoist the white
flag.

29 April 1933

I must be content to do my duty as I see it, and trust to recognition
in the future. . . . I get very weary of it sometimes . . . I wonder
whether it will seem worth while to go on after the next election. . . .
I have not got father's joy in battle . . . after all, most of what I have
worked for has been done, and now the chief task is to keep the ship
steady on the course.

But all that was ever needed to cure his depression was a new
combat, with which he was now provided in full by the Economic
Conference that was designed to restore some harmony to the
spheres. His own recommendation had been that it should meet
at Washington, as a better chance of winning over America, but
the Prime Minister was desirous to preside, and London was the
place appointed. He held hopes for some way out on the Lausanne
model, in a final settlement of European debts to the United States
for, say, £150 millions.

20 February 1933 ; to Arthur Chamberlain

although I don't think Roosevelt sees the light yet, he has leanings
that way. . . . I am not without hope that we may get our conversations with him on the basis of a general co-operation in a world policy,
resulting finally in reductions of tariffs, and all other international
barriers ; harmonisation of monetary policy ; cancellation of war
debts ; and raising of wholesale prices.

But westward the land did not look particularly bright.

I

Though cordial generalities issued from MacDonald's Washington conversations, Roosevelt was borne up by a surging public opinion, distraught by a bank panic and ruinous prices, and by a Congress more and more tempted to inflation, nor would his own courageous temper shrink from extreme remedies to find new hope for thirteen million unemployed, for which he could certainly count on support from economists with remedies cut and dried. Late in May America passed through a revolution. The President was empowered to devalue the dollar, to issue $3000 millions in paper money to redeem debt, to spend rather more in public works, to sanction great industrial codes. Bravely the new deal strode forward to the largest deficit in the world, wildly the dollar plunged downward in its relation to the pound. All of which was ill calculated to speed on the stabilisation and tariff reduction which international experts had commended, and which once the President had blessed.

Yet his international instinct was robust, and after long silence he advanced to meet the British half-way in regard to the June instalment. The Americans proposed that we should make a part payment of $10 millions ; Chamberlain recommended the offer of $5 millions as a token payment. Finally, he notes, it was " agreed to our going to $10 millions if in return we could get a satisfactory statement from Roosevelt that he did not consider we were de-faulting ". But before this payment was made, in silver, the World Conference began on June 12.

This was the final assembly of that protracted twilight, in which met face to face the figures from sixty-four nations whose paths were henceforth to part, diverge, or collide ; Schacht and Hugen-berg, Daladier and Bonnet, Cordell Hull and Maisky, Smuts and Bennett, Beneš and Dollfuss. It was killed outright in less than three weeks, yet we conjecture that it could never have lived long. Words could not reconcile the new deal and the gold bloc led by France, nor make immediate unity between producing nations overseas and the Continental peasant toiling behind tariff walls, hardly between Great Britain and her Dominions.

As leader of the British delegation he put his country's position in one of his firmest speeches. In too hopeful mood — it ran — that its old working could be restored, we had returned to gold in 1925 at the old parity, with results that still weighed us down. And since costs could not be reduced without " intolerable suffer-ing ", we could not recover equilibrium except by a raising of prices, which we must approach by many avenues. Assuredly Great Britain could not fix either the time for a return to gold, or its parity, until we had more nearly restored the proper conditions for its operation. He went on to suggest the limits of our policy. What could be done by way of public works, each country must decide for itself; there was a distinction between market quotas for assuring a remunerative price level (such as Great Britain was pursuing) and those arbitrarily protective; bilateral treaties were the easiest path to tariff reduction; with some glance at America, he denounced export and shipping subsidies. " The great concourse of nations here assembled has met to find the means of self-preservation, and it cannot afford to fail."

Yet it failed egregiously; for the causes of which we look, not to what the delegates of Estonia or San Salvador were pondering in their hearts, but to the great powers. Without stabilised exchanges the gold bloc vowed nothing could be done, to which, at first, the American delegates joined in chorus. But as June crept on Chamberlain noted that neither on exchanges nor tariffs did they speak with one voice, and then descended Professor Moley, direct from the President, with doubts whether stabilisation were not untimely. Yet he hoped the professor might be convinced.

Diary, 29 June

>we seem to have arrived at the critical stage in the Conference. Since the beginning it has been increasingly affected by the depreciation of the dollar, and by the speculative attacks which have followed on the gold countries . . . hammered out a statement which Moley felt pretty sure the President would sanction.

Next day the professor came to terms with the gold countries, of which Cordell Hull seemingly disclaimed all knowledge, but by nightfall he reported " difficulties " had come over the Atlantic telephone; Bonnet, having vainly invited Britain to ignore America, left for Paris " swearing ", says the diary, " at American perfidy "; finally, on July 1, a presidential message from the cruiser *Indianapolis* blew the Conference to smithereens. It drew a sharp contrast between the delegates, mumbling " old fetishes of so-called international bankers ", and a new America, shaking her invincible locks and making a new dollar of unchanging value, and pronounced that a nation's internal system was more vital than stability of its exchange.

Diary, 4 July

>this effusion so completely declared his intention to go his own way . . . dismissing the effect of dollar depreciation as a trifling incident of no importance, as to cause the gold countries to declare that it was useless to go on.

Indeed, while sub-committees were suitably engaged in discussing silver or most-favoured-nation clauses, all hope had gone of the larger purposes for which they had met, since each powerful State had its favourite bulwark and its destined victim. If the United States blew cold on a policy of central banks, France would not hear of lowering tariffs without currency stabilisation, while Great Britain announced they had tried, and were not prepared to reopen, public works. If anything positive was to be done, it must come through special interests like wheat or silver, or in the various regional groups, and for his own part he was busy with the British Dominions. As primary producers, as borrowers, as seed-grounds of experiment, their sympathies much inclined to Roosevelt : this he would resist, hoping to carve out of the international ruins some actual agreement for the broad space of the Empire.

Diary, 24 July

I parried this move . . . by saying I should welcome a joint declaration . . . and was ready to prepare a draft. . . . It all revolves round Ottawa . . . to serve the multiple purpose of (1) diverting the Dominions from the dangerous paths of currency depreciation and public works ; (2) putting down a joint British declaration, which may to some extent distract attention from the failure of the Conference ; and (3) furbish up the Ottawa agreements which have got a little tarnished by reason of the rather equivocal behaviour of some of the Dominions.

This manifesto reaffirmed the Ottawa resolves for a rise in the price level, deprecated inflation, and arranged for continuous Commonwealth consultation on monetary policy. But, apart from this, as he fished in Dorset, where he went " to forget the behaviour of the American President and the French delegation ", he wondered whether anything had come of it, except that they all had been forced to think. That, perhaps, might have been arranged without transporting delegates of sixty-four nations to the Geological Museum, South Kensington, whence they all came out bent on going their several ways. At the New Year America, writing the Conference's last epitaph, fixed the gold value of the dollar at 59 per cent of the old parity, westward millions of speculative gold winged their way, and the gold bloc had to watch such trade recovery as there was, flowing towards countries which had depreciated their currency.

A conversation with Bonnet may serve to wind up for ever, so far as this book is concerned, the debts which for fifteen years had plagued humanity.

Diary, 27 July

I thought it conceivable . . . that we might get an arrangement involving a 3 year moratorium, and then 20 million dollars a year for, say, 40 years. . . . What our public opinion would not stand would be that the French should treat their American creditors better than their English creditors. . . . Bonnet replied that the French felt that the Americans had let them down, by first making the Hoover moratorium apply to reparations, and then demanding payment of war debts. . . . We had never done that. Moreover, France felt that the United States had disassociated herself from Europe, while we, who were within aeroplane range, must always have an interest in Continental affairs. Both sentiment and interest therefore gave us a preference in French eyes.

The sixty-four nations having dispersed, he took in Scotland what he described as his best holiday for years, returning full of vigour and of enjoyment in his own passionate interests, some illustration of which in a single letter will lighten the gloom in which we leave 1933 :

read L. Pearsall Smith's work on Shakespeare . . . instigated by him to get Professor Stall on *Art and Artifice in Shakespeare* . . . in the meantime, reading a book on Beethoven by Turner . . . to hear a pianist this afternoon . . . Rudolf Serkin ; his technique was astonishing, but that is common nowadays. What is not so common is his artistic sense, and I thought his Beethoven and his Chopin equally good . . . to-morrow we are going to visit the Zoo, where I want particularly to see the humming birds feeding, and the birds of Paradise in their nuptial display.

The same letter reports another " token " payment to America which was to prove the last, but was not made without hearing some voices " in full cry for default ".

But his mind was not on Washington, for an even more important world conference had also collapsed, and at last our departments were released from the instruction that for ten years they need envisage no major war. From March to June the delegates at Geneva had discussed a draft put forward by Great Britain, which filled the skeleton with positive figures, of so many men, aeroplanes, or ships ; so large, or so small, the tanks or guns. And at first, as it seemed, with hopeful result. Germany itself accepted the principle of standardised armies, and a limit to " aggressive " weapons. Yet to nearly every detail nearly every nation took some exception, and though Geneva might have screwed up courage to break down the objections of Siam, during the summer such " reservations " swelled into the old dire controversy, between equality for Germany and security for France.   Under this stress Great Britain, with agreement from Italy and the United States, accepted a French demand which transformed the original convention, so that it became a proposal for disarmament by two stages of, perhaps, four years each ; Germany would not be allowed her claim to possess " samples " of the heavy weapons permitted to the victors, and only after a probationary stage to test German good faith would the heavily armed States be required to disarm at all.   It was on this ground that, in October, Germany withdrew from the conference, and declared her intention of also leaving the League.

Yet peace and disarmament were still the passion of Great Britain.   When Churchill attacked the Prime Minister's airy hopes, entreating the country rather to buttress peace through the French army, Eden came to MacDonald's defence in a remarkable speech, commended in our papers ; " that young man is coming along rapidly, not only can he make a good speech, but he has a good head, and what advice he gives is listened to by the Cabinet ". Again, though our intelligence from Berlin reported making of aeroplanes in defiance of treaty, and though our ten-year-old air programme was still ten squadrons short, it was agreed, as a pacific gesture, to leave things as they were.   Peace dominated all parties, even when Germany had expelled Jews and threatened Austria. The Unionists' party conference was anxious about defence, but its leader asked it to think again, the Labour conference pledged itself to have no hand in war, and in a memorable bye-election at East Fulham a previous Labour minority of many thousands was turned into victory, expressly on the theme of a war-mongering government.   Samuel at last led his Liberal band into formal opposition, not least on the ground of the government's bad record in disarmament, while Lloyd George was insistent that not Germany but France was the guilty party.   From these things Chamberlain drew one important deduction :

Mussolini is playing the usual double game, the Americans are chiefly anxious to convince their people that they are not going to be drawn into doing anything helpful to the rest of the world, the Germans are propaganding with a view to dividing France and England. . . . I think we must be very cautious, for it would be very easy to make a mistake.   But common prudence would seem to indicate some strengthening of our defences.

CHAPTER XVI

RECOVERY: 1933–1935
AGED 64–66

> I heaved the lead every inch of way I made. A disposition
> to expense was complained of ; to that I opposed, not mere
> retrenchment, but a system of economy, which would make
> a random expense without plan oi foresight, in future, not
> easily practicable.
>
> BURKE, *Letter to a Noble Lord*

LIKE atoms in the scheme of physics that disintegrate under " bombardment ", the world society was dissolving, each fraction disposed
to protect itself in its own small way. Their efforts, collectively
considered, were styled " recovery ", but it was recovery by dint
of friction, wherefrom we must expect to find that questions of
foreign policy loom ever larger, till they totally encompass this
biography. Yet in a world spinning so fast and so queerly the
British Commonwealth made a comparatively stable element, which
in great measure must be ascribed to the Chancellor of the Exchequer,
third apparent figure in the Cabinet but in some vital respects the
first.

In composition, after the Free Traders' departure, it remained
unchanged until Kingsley Wood was brought in on Chamberlain's
recommendation late in 1933, and Betterton, going to preside over
the Unemployment Assistance Board, made room for Oliver Stanley
in 1934. Outside the Cabinet, yet for many purposes inside, Eden
was the same year appointed Privy Seal, becoming something like
a deputy, or even an alternative, minister for foreign affairs.

This was the last phase of Ramsay MacDonald. Just as, within
the old Mahratta State, power worked outwards from a veiled
Raja to the Peishwa or mayor of the palace, who in his turn too
became a figure of legend, and at last to the fighting men with
clouds of horsemen at command, so it flowed from MacDonald via
Baldwin to Chamberlain, or more often, perhaps, in the reverse
direction. This could not under any dispensation conduce to masterful government, still less when neither Raja nor Peishwa was notable
for unbending decision. Now also were seen, clear in their operation,
some of the defects to which all British history had led, and which
its very merits facilitated ; the office of Prime Minister, so exalted

227

now that from, or at least through, him all action must derive, so trebly guarded by loyalties even when a greying shadow ; and the departmentalism of large Cabinets, whose leading ministers are so drowned in business that they cannot look ahead for port lights or compass bearings.

Commenting on the great *Life* of Joseph Chamberlain, then coming from the press, his second son contrasted the freedom taken by Gladstone's ministers to criticise each other in public with the loyalty of the present team ; to which all his own papers bring solid testimony. Yet sooner rather than later they must find a new leader. As he sat beside him on the bench he wrote with pity of MacDonald's nervous trembling, yet would complain he was only interested in problems as they affected himself, and by 1934 discovered that in Conservative opinion he was more liability than asset. MacDonald, says an acid line, reports he has converted Rothermere from opposition by a threat to resign ; " I have always heard that Rothermere was easily frightened, but I confess I find it difficult to believe that the thing was done as simply as that ".

Whatever the ratio between their merits and their good fortune, this government could point to accomplished facts. British prosperity was, it is true, on a scale much reduced from days of yore, our overseas trade amounting to a bare 60 per cent of its values before the depression. But at least the peak of 2,955,000 unemployed of January 1933 had fallen to 1,376,000 by the autumn of 1937, when the 11,000,000 in insured occupation surpassed the figure of 1929. Four million persons had been absorbed or reabsorbed into industry ; even in coal-mining the unemployment rate had been cut from 40 to 18 per cent. We had recovered a sense of security, so that Consols which had dropped to 57 rose to over 80, industrial output was up 20 per cent, iron and steel quite renewed, motor production doubled. A new policy had transformed agriculture, raising the acreage under wheat by 44 per cent ; home-produced bacon had doubled too ; the costly subsidy on sugar beet at least provided a third of our need. The cost of living, that fell till 1933 and thenceforward rose again, contributed to make an average increase of some 4 per cent in real wages, and if we look at one of the objects to which Chamberlain had given his life, to housing, in the year 1935-6, while local authorities built 52,000, private enterprise built 270,000, the moneys for half of which were advanced by building societies to wage-earning owners.

Outside the harbour bar the rollers were high, but they could

claim that their British craft was seaworthy. Assisted by America's
return to a gold standard, their device of exchange equalisation
had poured oil on the sea. If they had made a protective system,
it was a moderate one, for not a third of our imports paid a duty of
over 10 per cent, while by several commercial treaties they revised
duties downwards, or forced the withdrawal of discrimination against
our goods. Ottawa brought some considerable conflict, yet the
principles for which Chamberlain had combated were in being,
and the percentage of Imperial imports rose. Finding themselves
in transition between two different types of economy, they kept
their pitch low and their remedies lenient, preferring cheap money
to large government expenditure, and agreed regulation of imports
to tariff war. " How false is the suggestion ", he describes himself
as telling a Cambridge audience, " that this is a safety-first government destitute of new ideas, and how in fact it is continually introducing changes of a really revolutionary character." And here
there was a substantial truth, in that the agricultural legislation of
1933–4, and its sequel, reversed the whole of nineteenth-century
thought.

Of this the political source had been in his own recommendations,
devised in opposition, applied by the research department of his
making, and now set in the frame of Ottawa and tariff agreements.
If he set out from an inherited Imperial angle, he ended by planning
a new agricultural order, for he found that imports could not be
regulated for a long-term policy without controlling home production. In operation he found it meant poising many balances,
as between the Dominions and the Argentine, or between New
Zealand and Southdown mutton, or indeed between Runciman
and Walter Elliot. Nor did he cease to ask that they set out their
objective clearly, and plan accordingly.

Diary, 17 February 1934

The largest problem I see in front of us is what is to be the future of
international trade. It has shrunk to ⅓ of what it was in 1929. Is it
going to recover, or is the spirit and practice of economic nationalism
going to prevail, and each country try to live by taking in its own
washing ? On the answer to this problem depends our policy in
agriculture, in Empire relations, and in international affairs. We are
now endeavouring to increase the home production of . . . bacon,
eggs, poultry, hops, cheese, etc. How far are we to carry it ? . . .
But when we fix what we could produce if we chose, we have still to
consider whether it is wise to do all we can. . . . Behind that again
lies the question what is the proper division between Empire and

1*

foreign imports, where they compete. All these things want working out, as a basis for action.

To this we must add other measures of these years, if we are to judge aright : London Transport and Metropolitan Police Acts, modernisation of iron and steel, powers given (in accord with one of his first notions) to the cotton trade to enforce majority wage agreements ; some much against the Conservative grain, such as the Petroleum Act which vested in the State all discoveries of British oil, with others deemed necessary to save a vital interest, like the subsidy for tramp shipping. Altogether they do not seem the output of a stationary society, or a reactionary government.

On two subjects in particular, unemployment and housing, he exerted all his power, alike as Chancellor of the Exchequer and as an ex-Minister of Health, who had searched them deeply. From unemployment their origin as a government had come ; to distinguish between insurance proper and relief had been their first act, in accordance with which they had made transitional benefit a national charge. But all the fundamentals were still to be explored. On this treatment of the able-bodied unemployed every recent government had shipwrecked ; the means test was proving as two-edged a weapon as of old ; Betterton had to supersede some public assistance committees, just as Chamberlain had superseded some guardians. In October 1932 he put to his colleagues a bolder plan :

> it is nothing less than taking the whole relief of the able-bodied away from local authorities and ministers, and putting it outside party politics, by entrusting it to a statutory commission. . . . It would avoid the danger of the relief being put up to auction by the parties. Moreover, I conceive that the commissioners might be entrusted with the duty of providing some interests in life for the large numbers of men who are never likely to get work . . . they must be given organised recreation, physical exercise and, where possible, a bit of ground.

Such a reform would mark several generations, even affect the whole essence of our democracy. It was not merely that the most heavily loaded local bodies could not carry the relieving over a long term of one or two million unemployed, but that local elections were turning, more and more often, on the liberality of public assistance, and that local councillors would not face the odium of seeing their names chalked on the pavement as grinders of the faces of the poor. Labour ministers, who in 1929 had accepted the principle of a means test, now declared against it ; many Labour members were for sweeping away insurance altogether, and would allow a virile people to sink on the bed of " work or maintenance ".

Why he had become a convert to the position that unemployment must be a national charge, emerged in his recorded arguments. Provision, he reasoned, was needed to make as tolerable
as possible the lives of men and women who were likely to stay
unemployed for long, perhaps for life ; it was needed for opportunities for education, training, voluntary occupation, and recreation ; for migration overseas, and transference from place to place
at home. Local government could not withstand the financial
strain, " pressure " was undermining administration. A means
test there must be, but it could only be upheld if it could appeal
to common sense as fair and humane. Since he could find no
defensible distinction between many who were on transitional benefit
and many in receipt of poor relief, he would group them under
one authority, drawing his line rather between those receiving
outdoor relief, or training, and those cared for in institutions. Finally,
he proposed an independent authority, because a department under
a parliamentary minister would be exposed to the same party bidding
which had nearly destroyed national credit in 1931.

For another year he battled on in strong cross-currents, swirling
most fiercely round two jagged rocks, — who should be the responsible authority, and how to define the able-bodied whom it
should relieve. On the whole the final Act was rather more than
a compromise, for it embodied two-thirds of his ideas. A large
extension of unemployment insurance to new classes ; an insurance
fund whose solvency would be safeguarded by a statutory committee ;
for those outside insurance, the Minister of Labour responsible for
policy, but debarred from adjudication on individual cases ; a
statutory Unemployment Assistance Board, fortified against interference, to give relief and training to the able-bodied ; working
to a household means test, but a test humanised by paying no
regard to disability pensions, a proportion of savings, or maternity
benefit. As to finance, it would come as to 93 per cent from the
State, Chamberlain being resolute that local authorities should
not be wholly cut off from responsibility for their own unemployed.
Thus, except for medical treatment and institutions, the poor law
was at last " broken up ".

To him also was due a first initiative on behalf of the depressed
areas, which under a fire of criticism he, not too quickly, came to
see called for special remedies. This gradual process, if examined
in detail, would offer a searching study in parliamentary government.

Turning over in his mind who should be chairman of the new

Board, he thought of Trenchard, but prejudice had been worked
up against him " on account of his admirable and successful work
in cleansing the Augean stables of the Metropolitan police " ; of
Halifax, who declined and who might one day be wanted for the
Foreign Office ; finally, four commissioners were sent to investigate
the special areas, while Betterton became first chairman of the Board,
and Stanley, as Chamberlain had hoped, Minister of Labour. But
he was ill content with the commissioners' reports : " we could never
strike popular imagination by confining ourselves to these small
details ", these areas must be taken " as experimental plots or research
laboratories, in which ideas can be quickly put into operation and
tried out without reference to departments ". As he developed
the scheme to Parliament, two commissioners would cover Great
Britain, with power for compulsory acquisition of land and an
initial fund of £2 millions to use. Yet his own experience at National
Service might have suggested that individuals, functioning without
reference to departments, need not expect a bed of roses.

Again, the Housing Bill carried in 1935 owed much to him,
incorporating many of the persistent ideas in earlier letters. The
urgent needs had changed. Over two and a half million houses
had been built since the war, more than half of them without
State aid ; costs had come down, the general subsidy was withdrawn. But old slums, and the new slums made by overcrowding,
were bad as ever. On this he drew a memorandum for Hilton
Young, who called for a clearance programme from local authorities,
while a departmental committee reported in favour of his old project
of reconditioning as a temporary salve. He could have wished for
more speed.

Diary, 1 January 1934

    Last month . . . I proposed to him a programme based on a memo.
I gave him a year ago. . . . Local authorities to have statutory duty
to examine all houses unfit, or likely to become unfit. . . . In all
cases areas, not sporadic houses, to be the subject of schemes. Owners
of houses unfit to have site value ; others, to have market value less
a rebate for being in an unhealthy area, less the cost of bringing them
up to a proper standard of repair. Local authorities to retain the site
in all cases, but to have power to hand over the management to an
independent house management committee. . . . A central management commission to be appointed.

Next month he pressed for a new housing department, under
a junior minister, at the Ministry of Health, for which he had in

mind a young man with enthusiasm in Geoffrey Lloyd, his successor
in the constituency of Ladywood. Though this disappeared, the
general scheme went on, — " all the main features ", he wrote,
" come straight from me ".

From such instance we may judge his mental fertility and his
place in the Cabinet. All his days filled by exacting pressures in
foreign policy and finance, he rose and broadened under the full
stretch. Beside wider strategy he was busied with the tactics, which
must come from above, or below, if a democratic party is to live.
No man more resisted dictation from the mass press, or more resented
its assumption that the first virtue in public men is to court publicity.
But he watched the press and used its power, and with the Prime
Minister's leave regularly saw lobby correspondents. Within the party
at this date he probably initiated policy more than any other man.
He put the research department on to systematic enquiries, as into
mineral royalties, instigated the formation of a publicity bureau
which would be independent of local associations, set on foot meetings
of the Conservative ministers.

He was now, by the chronicle, well on in years, in character
not set hard but formed, each side of the shield well burnished.
Coming very late to the strife, he had put himself to learn, marked
Bonar Law well weighing each balance before giving judgement,
meditated on the art of lowering the temperature of the House,
or of extracting the last drop from a small concession. The sardonic
impatience with motives he could not respect had not diminished.
There were, he wrote on a given occasion but with extended meaning, three degrees in criticism, — " Opposition who oppose for the
sake of opposing, fellows who think they ought to have had office
and want to show the government what a mistake was made in
leaving them out, fellows who want to show how clever they are
in detecting weak points ". Or, again, the Archbishop of York
was for putting pressure on members to ensure that the first-fruits
of a Budget surplus should go to the unemployed (on which, in
fact, he had already decided). Of which we read : " in York
Minster prayers were offered for Divine guidance to be given to
the Chancellor in the disposal of his budget. But not feeling quite
certain that Providence was to be trusted in the matter, they nailed
the archbishop's letter on the door."

He went to the Dee, as usual, before this Budget of 1934, but
for the last time, for in May his friend and fishing mentor died,
Arthur Wood of Glassel, to whom he paid public tribute as " one
of those rare minds that seem to get down to the heart of any subject ",

yet with deep affection and childlike simplicity ; as indeed, his subordinates agreed, he was himself ruled by affections in the last resort.   His enthusiasms and heart's desires did not change, still Shakespeare and Samuel Butler and Conrad, still the Highbury azalea, orchids, and roses, and always Scotland : " when I walked up the hill . . . and saw the heather and the rocks and the burn again, I could have shouted for joy ".   Still finding refreshment in cool water-colours, always long pages on every aspect of his children and their fortune, still Kate the kitchen-maid of 1879 to see on her sick-bed.   One and the same long letter has a full description, with sketches, of primitive man's flint-mining in Suffolk caves, and of the new iron-works at Corby.   Never for him a world of neutral tints, but of things done, colours rejoiced in, affection deepened, and resentment unforgotten.

29 April 1933
> I too am reading the 2nd volume [of Garvin's *Joseph Chamberlain*].
> . . . I particularly admire the way Gladstone is treated.   The wickedness of the old man, his cunning and treachery, and his determination to get his own way while he has time, are plain to see.   I feel my old resentments burn up again as I read.

Perhaps he found in Charles Darwin, whose journals and letters he always came back to, the mental ideal he most admired : " the most ultra-modest of all great men . . . with his power of continually chewing over and revolving a subject, coupled with a never-ceasing speculation round and round it, till in the end he had left nothing out of consideration that could be known, and had weighed and balanced everything till every factor had its weight ".

This zeal for integrity part-explained his high regard for Snowden, the figure among his predecessors at the Exchequer whom most he resembled.   He too had been an orthodox economist who looked back to established maxims rather than to new visions, and would wish for bare lines and clean structure.   That Chamberlain was a very good Chancellor, opinion was agreed in Civil Service, Bank, and City, easy to deal with, once he had overcome suspicion of free-trade fastnesses, and rewarding to work for.   They did not find him impervious to argument, and if his approach might sometimes be on a narrow front, it always shone in clarity and logic. But what men with final financial responsibilities most appreciated was a virtue beyond finance, that in decisions involving the fortune of millions they could take his word without making a record, well assured he would stand to it through thick and thin.

In that sphere, where the Exchequer can concentrate British credit on a political purpose, he moved vigorously on, or sometimes behind, the scene.

Diary, January 1934

before the House rose in the summer I obtained the sanction . . . to a proposal that I should finance the completion of the big Cunarder, No. 534. . . . Although the press and the general public are chiefly interested in this project from the point of view of employment and British prestige, my own aim has always been to use 534 as a lever for bringing about a merger between the Cunard and White Star lines, thus establishing a strong British firm in the North Atlantic trade.

Then there was the triangular struggle over cotton goods between India, Lancashire, and Japan ; India, suffering from Japanese competition but unable, just for Lancashire's sake, to lose the Japanese market for raw cotton ; Japan, for whom trade expansion was life or death, demanding a large quota for her cotton goods and threatening recourse to America for raw material. The White Paper on Indian self-government hung in the balance, the alienation of Lancashire was not to be despised, nor in the interests of defence the antagonising of Japan, who was clamouring for naval parity and might strengthen Germany by menacing Russia. For these reasons his action was concealed.

Diary, January 1934

More was at stake than the bleached cotton market in India, since this was really the first round in a fight against Japanese competition in many other articles and in many other markets. . . . Accordingly I offered on behalf of the Treasury to stand behind the Indian government, if they would undertake to look after their own cotton crop.

With this guarantee for eight or nine millions in their pocket, that government was able to extract a reasonable bargain, but it was indeed only a first round, and within a year cotton quotas were in force in the Colonies against Japan.

It was with such decisions in mind that he meditated, as he did to his sisters, on the public view of his character. " There are some who think I am over-cautious, — timid, Amery calls it — humdrum, commonplace, and unenterprising. But I know that charge is groundless, or I should not have been the one to produce the Unemployment Assistance Board, the policy of regulation of production now generally adopted, the slum and over-crowding policy now accepted by the Minister of Health, the sending of commissioners to the derelict areas."

But in finance, he went on, confidence was his first rule ; it was the keynote and reward of the Budgets of 1934 and 1935, which here may stand together as last achievement of recovery. In the first a surplus of £31 millions, in the second of £7½ millions ; where else in the world, he asked, could this be matched ? *Bleak House*, the first speech said, was closed, and *Great Expectations* opened.

> The British people no doubt have their faults. They are slow to realise the danger, and slower still to change their habits or their methods, even when the necessity for a change stares them in the face. But they have one supreme virtue, which you will find in every class of the community. Let them once be convinced that the country is in danger, and there is no sacrifice . . . which they will not make. . . . Their truest reward is that they saved their country.

For proof he looked to Consols standing higher than before the war, to cheap money at a low record, a growth of exports by £50 millions, and an equal increase in small savings.

As ever his tone was pitched low, for the nation moved now in a humbler circle of trade, yet nothing austerely harsh or deflationary could be charged on his finance, and though his four Budgets had put £87 millions to debt redemption, he refrained from raising the fixed debt charge. He acted staunchly on the principle that those who had suffered most must be first restored. In 1934, while halving the other cuts, he restored unemployment benefit in full, and took 6d. off those income-tax payers who had found 70 per cent of the extra taxation. He had the reward which Peel and Gladstone would have applauded, an enhanced revenue from a reduced taxation and, though faced the next year by a heavy increase in estimates, boldly reduced taxation again. To restore the remaining cuts, provide a cheaper entertainment duty, to relieve that 70 per cent of income-tax payers whose taxable income fell below £135, all this asked £17 millions, which in part he recouped by a raid on the pampered darling of many in his party, the Road Fund. Eighty per cent of our prosperity, he claimed after his fourth Budget, had been won back ; " given peace abroad and a fair measure of unity at home ", he hoped to rewin the rest. But this outlook of April 1935 has taken us beyond the date when the real life of this government faded out.

" To find pasture enough for the beasts they must feed ", the dilemma as Chesterfield saw it for the old Whigs, was a question too for this huge majority. In retrospect the Right wing seems not so formidable as it was made to sound. De Valera's semi-republican moves gave them a certain gloomy satisfaction, they found too meagre the compensation for slum clearance, and then Churchill marshalled them to mass their fire against the Indian reforms. Twice over in 1933 party conferences debated these heavily, giving government roughly a two-to-one majority. At one such meeting Chamberlain, describing his audience as " exceedingly Jingo and anti-foreign " over questions of defence, informed them that they were incompetent to discuss India till the Joint Committee had reported.

He was never much moved by the sentiments, whether the deep or the superficial, which go to make a " die-hard ", coming back, for example, from speech-making in Belfast with a view that the Ulster government was an anachronism. But on Indian responsible government, we have seen, he had been a reluctant convert, while his instinct of what can be done with a party warned him that this Indian bitterness was best diverted by concession elsewhere. On one point, after two years of agitation, he helped the Conservative core of the House to its will, when the Budget of 1934 abolished Snowden's machinery for the land values tax. But this was to extinguish a flare that burned in MacDonald's lonely side-chapel of their joint temple, so that we find the Prime Minister " much upset, talked of resignation ".

Two and a half years were gone, or half their term, the time when any chance move may precipitate an avalanche, which in this instance began late in 1933 with a gesture seemingly most innocent, a bill brought forward by Salisbury to reform the Lords. For the ancient pledges of the Parliament Act stood unredeemed, and Stafford Cripps had lately made Conservative flesh creep by a programme of emergency powers for the next Labour government. Not finding themselves in agreement, they hoped to be sagely non-committal, but two National Labour ministers voted against Salisbury, Hailsham's position as leader in the Lords became irksome, there were murmurs of resignation.

By temperament Chamberlain found himself more in agreement with Hailsham than did Baldwin ; he believed also that Lords reform had something in it on merits, and might be a useful counter-irritant to India. However, though most of the Cabinet might wish for a new tribunal to replace the Speaker's certificate of what was a money bill, or would willingly see a reduced number of hereditary peers, Baldwin led a do-nothing group in regard to any change of

powers, and Thomas was full of foreboding. In due course, therefore, though 163 members signed a declaration for reform, Salisbury's motion was politely suffocated.

Meantime, violent gusts from other quarters swept over government at its exposed angles. Strongest of all over the conduct of
the Foreign Office ; " a terrible time ", we hear in late '33, and
since then more than one colleague had urged him to take that
post of danger himself. Then there was housing, for which he
was pressing a semi-separate ministry, which had been revealed
to the press with embarrassing results. He pondered a larger move.

Diary, 28 February 1934

the best solution would be to move Hilton Young and put in Kingsley
[Wood]. This could be done if Sankey would go, and Hailsham could
be moved to the woolsack, thus allowing Hilton to go to the War
Office. The attacks on Simon in the press have made it impossible
to move him, but this change might save his position.

It was thus put to the Prime Minister who, however, runs the
record, " by his inability to take swift and decisive action . . . has
missed his opportunity ".

When ministers are in this mood, it is apt to spread, and one
important colleague suggested an early election. His letter is
endorsed, " gave him reasons against, which he admitted to be
overwhelming " ; resentment at needless disturbance of confidence,
a party split over India, and the certain loss of the Prime Minister's
seat. To others he advanced an argument which perhaps weighed
no less, that Conservatives did not wish to carry the present Prime
Minister for another term of years.

But whether dissolution came late or soon, he would be ready,
and asked Baldwin to summon Conservative ministers, for whose
meeting in March he prepared an outline of subjects for discussion.
This covered nine heads. Industry in relation to international
trade, and its distribution between home, foreign, and Empire producers ; industry in relation to the State, and in particular to coal,
cotton, iron, and shipping ; agriculture ; Empire, extension of
Ottawa, redistribution of population, communications ; Lords reform, and reform of Commons procedure ; co-ordination of defence ; education ; foreign policy ; social services, notably an
improvement of the national physique. A month later he wrote
specifically of this last : " I think it would involve the periodical
inspection of the population . . . some sort of physical drill, perhaps

some sort of campaign to preach suitable diets, and maybe voluntary camps in national parks ".

Their discussions continued, housing was well under way, trade agreements approved, but there was not a clear outlook either in Europe or Cabinet, and he spent much of his summer holiday constructing memoranda on Defence.

Diary 31 July

the session ends with the party in good heart, and the government stronger than ever. But there are some ominous signs, — the murder of Dollfuss, the imminent death of Hindenburg, the slowing down of trade recovery, and the internal conditions in U.S.A., France, and Germany. I am acting Premier in Baldwin's absence abroad.

29 August ; to Alfred Greenwood

we must certainly try and get India out of the way before we embark on a general election. But we have also, before then, to decide how, on what, with whom, and above all under whom, we go. . . . Perhaps in the end some of us older ones will have to step down and make way for the young bloods (mostly in the late forties !).

He came back to the last session of the MacDonald government. Labour had captured the London County Council, and twice over had won hundreds of borough elections up and down the kingdom. The people, passionate against unemployment and war, had fixed their hope upon two formulas, collective security and economic planning, the operation of which no one could predict but which rolled richly off the tongue. But the government's tone about the first seemed coldly dubious, while they offered a paltry £2 millions for the depressed areas. Why, asked Lloyd George, did they not imitate the audacity of America ? whose deficit this year was only $3575 millions, and whose proportionate unemployment was vastly greater than our own.

In December Chamberlain was worn down by alarums from all quarters, and by a staking-out of many claims against the future. Beaverbrook was campaigning for an Empire customs union, Hailsham sore at lack of understanding of his troubles with the Lords, 75 " die-hard " votes resisted the Indian report, and all this beside the friction inherent in the Exchequer. Add to all this, he wrote, " the frightfully sudden slump in the government's stock, and the continual nagging and carping by the young Tory intellectuals." He understood that the chief whip, when asked by the Prime Minister where lay the trouble, had succinctly answered, the Betting Bill, the Incitement to Disaffection Bill, and the Foreign Secretary.

There was worse to come, for when Parliament met in January 1935 they ran into a real storm. This concerned the regulations for assisting the able-bodied unemployed, which Parliament had just approved, and which would henceforth fall to the new Board to administer ; trouble, he had long predicted, must be looked for in South Wales and other areas whose local authorities, ignoring the means test, had set up a lavish standard. But he agreed with the Minister of Labour that the Board's first proposals were too low, and worked out what seemed a golden mean. He confessed in February he had been mistaken, local variations and differences in rent often brought about too sudden a drop, so that under angry criticism the appointed day had to be postponed ; temporary funds must be found to bridge the delay, guarantees given that individuals should not suffer. One cannot but wish, he wrote mildly, " that the Board, since they had this discretion all the time, had used it more effectively to ease the transition ".

This left relations strained between the Board and the Minister of Labour, who had chivalrously shouldered all responsibility. " Resignation now ", says the diary, " would be ruinous to him and very bad for the government ", but a pacifying tea-party he gave at the Treasury went off, he lamented, only fairly well ; he concluded this ministry also must make part of that reconstruction which had become imperative. For pressure was now being exerted by the one person most concerned to save the government, and by another most anxious to destroy it, the chief whip and Lloyd George.

Captain Margesson's remonstrances had grown in volume over the Christmas season of goodwill, and suggestions were made with high authority for a general post, which would end in a smaller Cabinet and install Chamberlain at the Foreign Office. But on that particular route they made no advance.

Diary, 4 December 1934

the Foreign Office was expensive and I could not afford it, — moreover I should hate the journeys to Geneva and, above all, I should loathe and detest the social ceremonies. . . . In addition to all that, to expose myself to the suggestion that I had worked for this change, perhaps because I saw budgetary difficulties ahead and wanted to avoid them, and get a new place where I might have a chance to make myself interesting, this was too much to ask.

Asking " have you considered Eden ", for himself he refused to move, nor was he the first minister who has declined a new office because he cannot approve the successor-designate for his old one.

Moreover, the project of a small Cabinet must always be one which it is embarrassing to put before a large one, since to be relegated to the category of "without portfolio" seems to wound older men, while to be kept in the outer Cabinet injures the young, or even the middle-aged. His own views were emphatic, that room must be found for youth, and nothing done to undermine Cabinet authority. It ended, then, in a certain enlargement of " the Six " who would, as occasion called, be reinforced by others, " reconstruction " thus fading away to an intermittent co-optation.

But if they meant to persevere as a National government, might not room be made for the only begetter of Coalition? Just before the new year, and his seventy-second birthday, Lloyd George came out for a policy of youth, a new deal on broad lines for unemployment and all national purposes. His platform speeches went on to paint, in sweeping strokes, a war Cabinet, a planning council for development, a double Budget, and public control of the Bank. Instinct or information led him to point the offensive spearhead of his oratory at Chamberlain, whom he depicted as strutting about complacently in a kingdom of the blind.

So it seemed that the battle of 1929–30, not to mention that of 1921–2, was to be fought over again, fought into an election at the end of which the Welsh wizard would turn the scale. There were members of the Cabinet not averse, Baldwin himself perhaps had hesitations. This fissure might cut deep ; older influences like Austen's might coalesce with young men who dreamed of planning ; a Labour gain at Liverpool — brought about by Churchill's son splitting the Conservative vote, — Beaverbrook and his customs union, National Liberals who remembered Lloyd George as symbol of national unity, such were the flashes in an angry sky.

The Chancellor of the Exchequer stood firm. Public works, he had told the World Conference, were a panacea which Britain had tried, and had failed. In seven years ending in 1931 the State had spent on them £700 millions, yet at no one time had employment been found thereby for over 100,000 men ; to concentrate assistance on revenue-producing schemes or purposes of public import was another matter, as in the case of the great Cunarder. Moreover, when Lloyd George brought his vision down to earth, it did not seem to amount to anything new. He asked large expenditure on public utilities ; well, government had already asked Parliament to spend £34 millions on telephones, and to guarantee another £35 millions for London transport. Their Housing Bill would mass subsidies against overcrowding and for rebuilding of central urban sites they were subsidising fisheries, beef production, and tramp shipping ; a bargain for Irish cattle against British coal was making a first break in that obstruction.   Could a Lloyd George alliance improve upon these solid facts ?   His better showmanship would be hardly worth buying at the price of disintegrating the Cabinet, or another coupon election.

To Baldwin and Austen he put his sturdy decision.

6 January 1935

I have taken the opportunity of putting before him some very definite statements. . . . We have our own plans, which are less spectacular, but will probably work.   L. G. will never support the National Government except on his own terms. . . . N. C. would not refuse to accept L. G.'s support, if offered with a single mind (!) but he will in no circumstances sit in a Cabinet with him.

3 February

Austen came to tell me of his conversation with L. G. . . . describing his views on the Cabinet, — the P.M. utterly ineffective, Simon a disaster at the F.O., the C. of E. narrow, bound in red tape, and without initiative or imagination. . . . I explained that I was not prepared to sit in a Cabinet with L. G.   Austen at once interrupted me, saying " I think you are wrong ", but I continued that my motives were not personal dislike, but profound conviction that our ideas were incompatible.

By March it was agreed they would not admit Lloyd George, at any rate before the election, though they would offer an investigation of his schemes.   But a larger matter lay behind.   Hitler had announced conscription, government issued its first White Paper on defence, Europe was chaotic.   Once the India Bill was done with, someone would have to reunite the party, reconstruct the Cabinet, give a lead to the country.   MacDonald would go when the King's Jubilee was over in May, Baldwin might feel moved to go with him.

Diary, 8 March

I am more and more carrying this government on my back.   The P.M. is ill and tired, S. B. is tired and won't apply his mind to problems.   It is certainly time there was a change.

With the spring he was cheered by a good reception of his Budget, less unemployment, a feeling that Lloyd George's clarion, " an essay, not a manifesto ", had roused no echo, and by a belief that the decision to rearm and the Jubilee would both enrich the soil in which a Conservative government may thrive.   On the

Jubilee, he wrote, " my sentiments were admirably expressed by a stout flower stall-holder in Stratton Ground, who said to Mrs. A. Lyttelton . . . 'ain't it glorious to be an Englishman? this'll teach 'em ' " ; adding of the thanksgiving service in St. Paul's, " as I gazed across at the foreign ambassadors on the other side I thought, ' this'll show 'em ' ".

Sometimes, as reconstruction and the lead paused and wavered in tired minds, his notes bring back the pages of 1931, with the same impatience and the same loyalty. He learned that Baldwin would continue ; possibly, however, postponing serious Cabinet change till the autumn.

Diary, 8 April

I pointed out to Kingsley [Wood] that if this were done, there would be every opportunity for anti-Baldwin intrigues, which would be extremely embarrassing for any alternative leader.

17 May

by constant prodding I have got things moving at last, greatly aided by the general dissatisfaction with the conduct of the Air Ministry as well as the Foreign Office. . . . Our talks with L. G. drag their weary length along. . . . Nothing has emerged of any value, and I do not fear him at the elections.

On June 7 the change was made. MacDonald dropped to be Lord President, and Simon to the Home Office with, for the time being, the deputy-leadership of the House ; Londonderry handed over the Air to Cunliffe Lister ; Sankey and Gilmour disappeared, together with Hilton Young who, Chamberlain wrote to his wife, had received little gratitude for much good work " because, like me, he can't unbutton ".

25 June ; Hilton Young to N. C.

your words about me in my office are more than I deserve, but they do give me very lively pleasure. . . . I have greatly valued these four years of collaboration with you, and I have a warm sense of gratitude for the help you have given me from your citadel in housing, water, health, insurance, indeed all the main subjects on which I have been at work. Your advice and encouragement were one of my best helps, will be my best memory of the time.

With most of this he had been in accord, having himself suggested that Hoare succeed to Simon, for he believed that Eden, with whose disappointment he sympathised, would profit by holding a big departmental ministry before, as was certain, he reached the

Foreign Office. There were some misfits, perhaps an excess of personal loyalties, but so far, so good. They had finished their Lloyd George interviews and he was writing a counter-memorandum; " the impression he has left is that he is not the man he was ".

On that matter he had prevailed, but he deemed it waste of time, when he was devising the most economic means of diverting into rearmament the national savings which his four Budgets had restored, when Italian troopships were hurrying through the Suez Canal, and when German aeroplanes were coming off the line in numbers unascertained.

CHAPTER XVII

FOREIGN AFFAIRS: RETROSPECT TO 1935

> Between 1935 and 1940 we shall have reached a point that
> I should call crucial in European history.
>
> MUSSOLINI, *May* 1927
>
> The removal of the just grievances of the vanquished ought
> to precede the disarmament of the victors.
>
> WINSTON CHURCHILL, *November* 1932

IT was only from 1934 that he was directly concerned with the choice of war or peace, in the shadow of which his remaining years were to be spent. Neither his dilemma, hopes, nor failure can be appreciated without a glance backward over the space between the wars, for his inheritance was the peace of Versailles, upon which the ordeals of peace and war, not to mention its authors, have passed judgement. For which purpose it is necessary to set out some of the flaws that made it so precarious.

I. Of origin. President Wilson's " Points " suggested a peace freely negotiated between democratic governments, but the Allies imposed terms that departed from those points and enforced them by blockade.

II. Of structure. Within this severe treaty was contained its sanction, the Covenant of the League, but that Covenant itself rested on one fallacy and contained one flat contradiction. Equality of membership and responsibility was extended to great nations and small, Italy ranked with Albania, Finland could neutralise the vote of France : and while one article guaranteed the *status quo*, another more feebly enabled the Assembly to recommend revision. But in any case the beginning of real peace was poisoned by the war-guilt clause, and the exclusion of Germany from the League.

III. Of content. By the time the exhausted victors had sheathed the sword, two fateful forces had taken charge of the settlement, namely, the distant idealism of America and the desperate traditionalism of France. The New World came in to destroy the balance of the Old with the dissolvent formula of self-determination, and the Old World, France pre-eminently, so applied that formula as to suppress their enemies but favour their friends. From this compound of weariness and high intentions, ill luck and bad judgement, rose an edifice of fair proportions but fragile and rambling, to tabulate the weaker points of which is to stand amazed at seeing history so ignored.

1. Revolutionary Russia was disregarded, and in her absence territories, which she had held for a hundred or two hundred years, were assigned to others.

2. The concomitant treaty of Sèvres was proposing not merely to expel Turkey from Europe, but to partition even her homeland in Asia Minor.

3. In that belt between Baltic and Aegean, where for two thousand years conquerors have flowed and ebbed, leaving their human debris behind, all was suddenly reversed. The Habsburg Empire, together with wide provinces of Germany, Russia, and Turkey, were redistributed among thirteen little States, who between them only aggregated 104 million souls. So, but under much worse conditions, was reproduced the European scheme which France had favoured under her kings and cardinals, of a circle of vassal countries who could be brought in on the back of the Germanic Empire.

4. Lloyd George instantly protested against the cardinal danger of this régime. " I cannot conceive ", ran his famous memorandum, " any greater cause of future war than that the German people . . . should be surrounded by a mob of small States, many of them consisting of peoples who have never previously set up a stable government for themselves, but each of them containing large masses of Germans ". This vice was most apparent in four instances.

5. Six and a half million Germans were segregated in Austria, a poor fragment without hope or future. An Allied veto stopped the *anschluss* with the Reich, which our Foreign Office had recommended, and for which the Austrian assembly had declared, and this prohibition was written into the treaty.

6. The new Czecho-Slovak State was a creation of force and artifice, contradicting the principle of self-determination and submitting fragments of five races to some seven million Czechs. Both British and American warnings were buried under the strategical interests of France, and the Czechs' promise that they would make their country another Switzerland.

7. Poland, once so far-stretching a State when French queens and French agents directed her policy, had suffered terribly in the last two centuries, but out of suffering had imbibed too large ingredients of pride, violence, and revenge. The access to the sea, which Wilson promised, was found by making the German citadel of Danzig a free city under the League, and by a corridor that

divided East Prussia from the Reich ; to adjust this defiance of history and reason, said Churchill in 1933, must be " one of the greatest practical objectives of European peace-seeking diplomacy ". This was not all, for the Poles' doings during or after the peace treaties were highly aggressive. The Ruthenians of eastern Galicia, the partition of Upper Silesia, slices of White Russia and the Ukraine, the Lithuanian city of Vilna, were all taken through violence, Allied dissension, or French support.

8. Memel was another German city, which the Allies had cast for the rôle of a second Danzig, but in 1923 Lithuania occupied Memel by force.

9. Italy was left an unsatisfied power. The promises upon which she had joined the Allies were rejected in the light of President Wilson's more lofty principles, her claims to expand into Anatolia were subordinated to the Greeks. As for " equitable compensations " outside Europe, while France and the British Empire divided the German African colonies and the outlying provinces of Turkey, Italy was refused a mandate, and only in 1924 received from Britain some " light soil " in Libya and Somaliland. Nor did the Fascists' seizure of Fiume make up for all that her allies had offered at different dates in the Adriatic, which included, for example, a mandate over Albania.

10. The President's fifth " point " asked an " absolutely impartial adjustment of all colonial claims ". Was this, it might be asked, realised by the almost monopoly of France and Great Britain, the small Pacific pickings of Japan, and the vast lands that lay, temptingly outstretched, in the weakening grasp of Holland, Belgium, and Portugal ?

Explanation, and part-justification, existed for these things but, taken together, they accumulated dangers that asked for a long vigilance and guard. This standing sentinel was visualised in the League, but the League was crippled by the instant withdrawal of the United States ; by the absence of Germany till 1926 and her departure in 1933, fast following the exit of Japan ; by the absence of Russia till 1934 ; finally, by a series of aggressions or injustices in which it acquiesced. It thus fell almost at once into two armed camps, — upholders of the *status quo*, represented by France and the Little Entente, and champions of revision, Italy leading Hungary and Austria, with Russia and Turkey for certain purposes on the same side. While the League debated protocols, definitions of an aggressor, world courts or schemes for disarmament, a revival of facts marked the years of recovery. Russia and Turkey made their strength felt, Italy sturdily pushed for revision, and, as one after another of her fetters was struck off, Germany clamoured that all her great limbs be set free.

What Britain's part had been we have noticed in the course of this biography.   Her democracy were sickened of war, not exuberant about empire, and passionately believed in the possibility of lasting peace.   Nowhere had the Versailles terms been more criticised, nowhere more than in Liberal and Labour Britain was more sympathy shown for Germany ; no ministry in our history held more men who had themselves experienced war service than that of 1931, yet no power with equal responsibility had so totally disarmed.   But British ideas on the international future had never achieved coherence.   They professed, and sincerely desired, to seek collective security, yet they repudiated any conception of international forces outside British control, and from 1922 whittled away any automatic commitments.   Very especially they felt that, in the absence of America, they could not be pledged to economic sanctions, the brunt of which must fall upon the dwindling British fleet.

This incoherence grew more intense as time passed.   For though Britain could justly claim that in every measure of conciliation she had taken the lead, a foreign policy which had come to depend upon public opinion had not thereby gained in power.   Party feeling coloured our attitude to foreign States, as in the instance of Russia or of Italy, while our diplomacy was irritated, or positively cumbered, by question and answer in the House of Commons. The new atmosphere meant heavy pressure from newspapers and economic interests, with a dangerous credulity as to the strength of mere vociferation.   And it enhanced our ancient, honourable tradition of demanding relief for all the world's oppressed, Assyrians or Ukrainians, Jews or Arabs or Lebanese, which weakens national influence when it is discovered to be not the warning of an armed man, but the sentiment of an unarmed moralist.

Upon this arena of fiction alighted three savage, primitive forces : the great depression, the Japanese invasion of Manchuria, and the appointment of Hitler as Chancellor of the Reich.   Together they doomed the Disarmament Conference which, several years too late, continued during 1932-3 its attempt to square the circle.   It was soon crystal-clear that notions of international armies were far in advance of the nations' reluctance to fight for any but themselves, that France consequently would not disarm, and that Germany could only be prevented from rearming by force.   British projects for " qualitative " disarmament and MacDonald's draft convention were drowned under " reservations ", emitted by each power in turn, and it was found imperative to meet the French clamour for security. But when, to quell that fear, Britain accepted the idea of a " probationary " period, Germany threw off the dust, first of the conference, and then of the League. Security, moreover, implied political objectives, but Mussolini's notion of a Four-Power pact, which would embrace treaty revision, was killed by France and the Little Entente, while disarmament discussions were hardly kept alive by the oxygen of adjournment. Yet not all men, not perhaps the worst among them, had wholly hardened their heart.

In its daily conduct our foreign policy fell to the Prime Minister and Foreign Secretary. MacDonald's taste and high external ability for international meetings, with an honourable resolution to spend his last breath for peace, prolonged the season during which a disarmed Britain pleaded with Europe to follow her example. If this brought depression to the Service chiefs who insisted we had sunk below the margin of safety, Simon's qualities had more positive results on Cabinet, Parliament, and Europe. He was the first great lawyer to hold that office, in which supreme legal ability seems a disqualification ; for the law officer he remained, apt to split a burning political body into juristic atoms, to be over-content, perhaps, with a formula, and to leave judgement to the court. Once is enough to illustrate Chamberlain's repeated conclusion.

Diary, January 1934

Simon's weakness has given rise to much criticism. . . . He can always make an admirable speech in the House, to a brief, but . . . the fact is that his manner inspires no confidence, and that he seems temperamentally unable to make up his mind to action when a difficult situation arises.

It was this resolution, that action was imperative, which impelled him to take an active part. In the average views of his countrymen, certainly in those of his party, he shared to the full. He agreed, like Lloyd George and many more, that on disarmament Germany had some moral case, and he was no more ready than they to earmark our forces for unknown commitments. As Chancellor of the Exchequer he knew, better than any, the urgency of husbanding our resources, and feared the effects of rearmament upon industry, though less perhaps than his National Liberal colleagues. And within these very British limitations his objective was the same as that which Churchill had put to Lloyd George in memorable words during 1920 — "prudence and appeasement".[1] Four legends have, by the malignity of fortune, been fastened upon him ; that he was always hostile to collective security, that he was biassed by sympathy for Germany, that he ignored Russia, and that he impeded rearmament. It must now be shown that for the years under review, 1933-5, each is false.

This was the last expiring season of hope, between the German departure from Geneva and the Italian decision to attack Abyssinia. The first year of Hitler, far from inspiring international unity, seemed to deepen every division, its two most immediate consequences being a new activity in Russia and the disintegration of the Little Entente. For while Russia, fearful of a double thrust from Hitler and Japan, looked west for allies, a Germany that would be strong against Italy was welcome to the Jugo-Slavs, and a Germany hostile to Russia most welcome to Roumania. But to the Czechs a triumphant Germany spelled death, and Beneš firmly defied revision. While these her old satellites thus drifted apart, France was dismayed at a new attitude in Poland, whose pride was injured by Russian revival, whose fears wakened for her undue increase of territory, and whose attitude to the Czechs had never been friendly. At the lowest, the Polish-German pact of 1934 meant that Poland was preparing a counter-balance to the French-Russian system, while repudiation of her minorities treaty implied she would brook no interference with her White Russian subjects.

Much, and perchance all, would depend on Italy. True, her relations with France were as ugly as ever, over Tunis, colonies, and the Balkans. Yet a mighty Germany, unless used in very skilful doses, would do her more harm than good ; her nourishing of Dollfuss' Fascist Austria, the clientship of a revisionist Hungary, a proper humility in the Jugo-Slavs, economic outlets through Fiume and Trieste, all were menaced. So throughout 1934 Mussolini's words and actions were balanced and contradictory. As always he denounced Versailles, declaring Germany had a right to arms and that the League must be reformed ; yet he hinted that British ministers pressed France too hard, he wished to allow Germany no bombers, and demanded her return to the League. As it chanced, after four weak Cabinets in one year, after the shocking Stavisky scandal and street fighting in Paris, early in 1934 France received under Doumergue and Barthou a government with a mind

[1] *The World Crisis : The Aftermath* (1929), p. 378.

of its own. It was the aged mind of Clemenceau. They would refuse to disarm, stand on the treaties, bring Russia into the League, re-knit their Eastern alliances, and by improving relations between Italians and Jugo-Slavs open up a French-Italian front that would pin Germany down.

But the British government still held that the object of a disarmament conference was to disarm, as a preliminary to that period of appeasement which Eden defended in debate. Assuredly they were not ready to stop a part rearmament of Germany by force, being inclined to think Hitler's protestations were sincere. In February 1934 Eden reported favourably on the modest proposal for a small army and defensive air force which he had received from the Führer's lips, a year later he was arguing that a rare chance had been missed. Voices in Parliament called for revision, Lloyd George declaring outright that over disarmament the victors had broken the treaty. But that phase ended with the French Note of April, which refused to admit any German rearmament at all.

During these exchanges, and what he called very tiresome discussions with his colleagues, Chamberlain complained they were losing sight of the substance.

Diary, January 1934

my view was that we were giving too much attention to the details of disarmament, and not enough to security. . . . Hitler had proposed a series of 10 year pacts of non-aggression . . . and I desired to explore the value of this suggestion in consultation with France and Italy.

He then worked out, and carried on a long fight for, a scheme that he christened a limited liability force.

24 March

in the barest outline it consists of a mutual guarantee by, say, Germany, France, Italy, U.K., Poland, and Czecho-Slovakia, under which, on breach of the convention, each of the other signatories undertakes to put a limited specified force at the disposal of the joint body. . . . It would, in fact, be an international police force, not to replace but to aid the aggrieved party.

His diary the next day summarises his reply to a school who were arguing that Hitler's proposals be accepted, France left to make the best of it, and all European entanglements avoided.

March 25

our greatest interest was peace, in the sense of a general pacification. If to-morrow complete security reigned throughout Europe, that would be the greatest possible boon to us, with our wide trading and financial ramifications. The proposal to defy France and join up with Germany would do nothing to ensure peace. . . . Either we must play our part in pacification, or we must resign ourselves to the staggering prospect of spending 85 million £ on rearmament. . . . We should not refuse in any circumstances to consider mutual guarantees. . . . It might be that we could limit our liabilities. Let us explore, for if we refused, we must give up all hope of a peace based on security.

A week later he wrote to his wife he was " very low ", for he found in others no hope in any international force, and " if so, I see no hope for the future ". For a time, spurred by the negation of France, he persisted, but in vain, lamenting he could not expect to change long-held opinions in a few weeks, " single-handed ". But " I shall emerge again ". Critics were running, he thought, after solutions that held no " elements of workability, world pacts or economic sanctions. For the old aphorism, ' force is no remedy ', I would substitute ' the fear of force is the only remedy ' ".

He emerged again in December, when peace was jeopardized by the matter of the Saar, which under the treaty must soon vote by plebiscite whether it would return to Germany or stay under the League. German intimidation or reprisals might bring in French troops, and Simon's tentative suggestion of an Anglo-Italian force to hold the scales was meeting with much objection when he intervened.

9 December 1934

it seemed to me that we had a heaven-sent opportunity to put ourselves right with the world, take the lead, and incidentally stage an example of an international police force. . . . I strongly urged that we should ourselves propose, not an Anglo-Italian, but a truly international force . . . backed by very strong representations in the same sense from Eden in Geneva.

This was the only olive branch in a year of blood. On June 30 the blood-bath swept away Roehm's second revolution and all the circle of the suave von Papen, except himself. On July 25 Austrian Nazis murdered Dollfuss, and Italian divisions moved on the Brenner. On October 9 at Marseilles, Croat terrorists, with some Hungarian inspiration, slew King Alexander of Jugo-Slavia and M. Barthou, together with their hopes of a French-Italian-Balkan understanding.

Before, during, and after these crises Chamberlain was insistent that Germany was the enemy to watch.

1 July 1934
> in the absence of security other nations won't give up aircraft or bombing, and we shall be more likely to deter Germany from mad-dogging if we have an air force which, in case of need, could bomb the Ruhr from Belgium.

28 July
> What an ominous tragedy, with Austria once again the centre of the picture, with another murder almost on the anniversary of that of the Archduke, and with Germany once more behind, instigating, suggest-ing, encouraging bloodshed and assassination, for her own selfish aggrandisement and pride.   I felt terribly upset about poor little Dollfuss.   Like everyone who came into contact with him, I had a great admiration, and almost an affection, for him. . . . That those beasts should have got him at last, and that they should have treated him with such callous brutality, makes me hate Nazi-ism, and all its works, with a greater loathing than ever. . . . I was glad to hear of Mussolini's movements of troops.   It's the only thing Germans under-stand. . . . What does not satisfy me is that we do not shape our foreign policy accordingly.

He had indeed arrived at a conclusion that was to move him to the end ; that policy must be concentrated in proportion to power.   A note on his defence proposals, which will come in due course, makes this plain.

Diary, 6 June 1934
> this all works out as the result of the proposition that we cannot provide simultaneously for hostilities with Japan and Germany, and that the latter is the problem to which we must now address ourselves. . . . I have also been urging that we should make a unilateral declaration that the integrity of the Low Countries is a vital interest to us.

It was in that mood that he pressed the possibility of a non-aggression pact with Japan.   In any serious American assistance he disbelieved ; " we ought to know by this time ", he wrote, " that U.S.A. will give us no undertaking to resist by force any action by Japan, short of an attack on Hawaii or Honolulu ".   A memorandum, drafted but never used in Cabinet, takes us to the heart of the matter.

" At this moment, in the autumn of 1934, there is no immediate threat to our safety.   But there is a universal feeling of apprehension about the future, whether it be a matter of 2, 3, 5, or 10 years, that such a threat may materialise, and that the quarter from which it will come is Germany." If confined to Europe, they might survive it. But " if we had to contemplate the division of our forces so as to protect our Far Eastern interests, while prosecuting a war in Europe, then it must be evident that not only India, Hong-Kong, and Australasia would be in dire peril, but that we ourselves would stand in far greater danger of destruction by a fully armed and organised Germany ". He recommended, therefore, a Japanese pact, with assurances on the integrity of China and naval construction ; such a policy must, of course, be explained frankly to America, whose solid interests, he added, it could not harm.

He returned to the main point. " The *fons et origo* of all our European troubles and anxieties is Germany. If that fact be constantly present to the consciousness of our negotiators, they will not be too stiff with France, or too insistent upon her discarding weapons which she may think essential for her safety." But enquiry soon proved there was little hope forthcoming from Japan.

Meanwhile, as disarmament had failed, France concentrated on other means of security. When Barthou came to England for the last time, he warned us that a disappointed Russia might join Germany, and all the French ardour from that summer to the spring of 1935 worked for " an Eastern Locarno ", a pact of mutual assistance between Germany and her eastern neighbours. This was a dividing moment, for the alternative would be a military alliance between Russia and France. In September the Russians were ushered into the League, within whose framework this understanding must receive a suitable attire ; next month Barthou was succeeded by Laval, who was intent on closing the breach with Italy, so that thence he could bring pressure to bear on Hitler. Duly in January 1935 a French-Italian agreement was initialled, with a warning to Germany about armaments, a renewed decision to defend Austria, a settlement over the venerable friction in Tunis ; finally, making over to Italy a few more miles of Libyan desert, and a few shares in the railway that ran from French Somaliland into Abyssinia. No public mention was otherwise made of that country, where just before Christmas Italian and Abyssinian soldiers had fired on each other by the wells of Wal Wal.

In those tense months that ended with the Stresa Conference and MacDonald's resignation, the British government were resisting a drift of the world back to rival alliances, and in that broad concept Chamberlain agreed. Till Germany were proved incorrigible, he would not desist ; he would not separate from France and Italy, yet not be led blindly in their train, and would deal with Germany on a basis of reality, rearmed.

Diary, 8 March 1935

some time ago we decided to accept the German invitation to the Foreign Secretary to visit Berlin. As soon as this was made public, the Russians also asked for a visit, but said if Simon was too busy they would be very glad to receive Eden. . . . I then urged that we should announce that Simon would go to Berlin, and Eden to Moscow and Warsaw . . . got no real support and did not press it. . . . Meanwhile, the Berlin visit was fixed for yesterday (Thursday the 7th), but early this week we published a White paper in connection with a debate on Defence. . . . Hitler flew into a rage, and announced that, in consequence of a sore throat caught in the Saar, the visit must be postponed.

Though Liberal and Labour parties condemned the White Paper as one-sided and inopportune — a " deplorable document ", thought Attlee — Chamberlain, who had toned down some of its asperities, was unrepentant.

9 March

if we were not to abandon all idea of defence, we were bound to show a big increase in estimates, and bound to publish our justification. . . . That mischievous meddler Ribbentrop had, I believe, led Hitler to think that Simon was prepared to make an Anglo-German agreement of some kind. . . . It is a good thing that, when the conversations do start, they should begin on a basis of reality.

So, with armaments as their last resource, they agreed with the French to attempt " a general settlement " of all the danger points. Whether this was the best method of approach is for later history to say, but the project was unhappily encompassed with insincerity. Great Britain was thus found urging on an Eastern Locarno, for which she would certainly accept no responsibility, and declared an interest in the independence of Austria, for which she would never fight. Moreover, France and Russia had now exchanged assurances of common action, which were enough to convince Hitler he was being encircled ; grinding his heel into the unyielding floor, he would rave like an automaton that his enemies had signed a military alliance. Outward signs of these suspicions filled the first half of March ; the British White Paper, a French bill to extend their military service, and a German law, in contravention of treaty, to reimpose conscription.

Yet in the decision not to be diverted from our main purpose Chamberlain stood firm. " Hitler's Germany ", he wrote that month, " is the bully of Europe ; yet I don't despair." In the face of others' doubt, he was urgent that the projected visits should still be made, on the understanding that the Germans would discuss all points in dispute, and returned, this time successfully, to his advice that, as a riposte to Hitler, Eden should go on to Moscow. But even his optimism could not extract much from the Berlin conversations, in which Hitler incidentally remarked he had reached air parity with Britain.

30 March

> I feel one ought not to criticise the conversations when one was not there . . . but I did regret that the position was not more thoroughly explored in some respects. I never for one moment expected that Hitler would sign the Eastern Pact. He says he can't contemplate fighting alongside Communists against someone else, in consequence of events outside his control. If that be taken as genuine, I don't think it's unreasonable. But seeing that the possible antagonists in the East are Germany and Russia, and that they are divided by a band of small States, — the Baltic States, Poland, and Czecho-Slovakia, — I should have thought it was worth while to have explored the possibility of Russia and Germany mutually guaranteeing the western and eastern frontiers of those States.

This proposition, it was agreed, should be put to the forthcoming Stresa Conference, at which his own hope was that Simon would be buttressed by Baldwin and Eden. But, as Eden fell ill, in the end MacDonald and Simon were destined to confront Mussolini and Laval.

Neither considered history, as yet revealed, nor his own later verdict endorse his first cheerful view that Stresa had gone off very successfully, for the so-called " front " was a last characteristic episode of that epoch in foreign affairs. If we judge it in the light of what came before and after, from the French-Italian agreement and German conscription, the League's condemnation of that unilateral act, down to the French-Soviet and Czech-Soviet pacts of May, Hitler's speech that month, and the Anglo-German naval treaty of June, then Stresa appears not so much a " front " as a retreat *en échelon*, a scene not of action but of that " consultation " which, on the day of its assembly, Mussolini's pen described as the last resort of indecision in the face of reality.

The Duce was obsessed by Germany just now. His first interview with Hitler had perturbed him ; he gave warning that Germany at Vienna meant Germany on the Bosphorus, and that the German air force was very alarming. Indeed, neither Italy nor France were pleased with the British in the first half of 1935. Our separate protest against German conscription seemed unduly mild, we condoned Hitler's breach of faith by the visit to Berlin, Simon's zeal for an Eastern pact was reckoned cool. At Stresa itself we refused to hear of immediate sanctions against further treaty violation, or to make bilateral air pacts in advance of a general agreement. Finally, three weeks before Stresa, Simon had invited Germany to enter on naval conversations, and within six weeks of condemning the German repudiation of the Versailles military clauses we were negotiating a separate naval treaty, which carried that repudiation further still.

There were at least two other breaches in this Stresa " front ". If its main purpose was to stop the German drive to the East, it must involve some balance of French and Italian interests. But the friends of France in the Little Entente disliked the Italian theme that Austria and Hungary be permitted to rearm, while Mussolini came to think that the French-Soviet pact had shifted the equilibrium. If thus disappointed, he felt inclined to look still further east, and push on an ambition he had cherished long : to avenge the ignominy of Adowa, and to find in Abyssinia both expansion and prestige. On this the heads of mission at Stresa seem to have observed a seemly silence, though in the background their subordinates exchanged forebodings of war.

Chamberlain was, we have seen, anxious for a change in the conduct of our policy, but his letters also show that he reacted to these events in an average British way. To wit, that, if agreed disarmament were impossible, agreed armament was better than nothing ; that anything was better than rival alliances ; and that the time for forcing *diktats* on Germany had passed. Hitler's speech of May 21, in reply to the censures of Geneva, though steeped in aversion to the League, at least held out a possible return to a League of equals, a promise to keep the Locarno treaty, pledges of willingness to accept air parity, and to have a Navy limited to 35 per cent of British strength. Without, then, going so far as the *Economist*, which recorded " an overwhelming impression of sincerity ", he accepted those offers for their present worth. On the naval treaty, he wrote there was no time to be lost, taking no doubt the point of view which Eden in the dialect of that day put to

Parliament, that it was wise " to circumscribe a unilateral decision ". In fact the Admiralty pressed for it, it being understood that French sailors did not share the objection taken by their politicians.

It remains briefly to summarise his part in rearmament before the end of the MacDonald government, leaving origins and moral to be taken up again when this question swelled to a ceaseless debate.

Early in 1934 the pressure of the service chiefs at last bore fruit when government set up a Defence requirements committee of their permanent advisers, whose proposals in due course reached a Cabinet committee. Of this, by the force of his convictions as much as of his position, Chamberlain was the moving spirit, so that his individual view on the point of danger and the financial limits was reflected in the measures brought to Parliament in July.

12 May 1934

in my office the amount of work you have to do largely depends on what you make for yourself. Unhappily it is part of my nature that I cannot contemplate any problem without trying to find a solution for it. And so I have practically taken charge of the defence requirements of the country. . . . Incidentally, my investigations into this subject have led me to suggest that we should move Woolwich Arsenal from its present vulnerable position to the derelict area of South Wales.

Diary, 6 June

in accordance with my suggestion, it was decided to examine the Defence requirements committee's proposals on their merits in the first instance. . . . When the first part of this work was concluded, I suggested that I should myself undertake the revision in the light of politics and finance. . . . I have now just completed a paper making revised proposals, which bring the 5 years' expenditure down from 76 to 50 million, excluding ship-building.

Within this reduced total, however, he drastically redistributed the proportions, in accordance with his now settled opinion that Germany was the menace. He therefore largely raised the committee's figure for the Home air force but halved the additional sums for the army, and postponed the replacement of capital ships. For if air defence against Germany was the pre-eminent need, he wrote, " we certainly can't afford at the same time to rebuild our battle fleet ".

By the winter of 1934–5 the horizon was more sombre still. In November Baldwin declared that German air strength was not half of Great Britain's, but in March 1935 Hitler announced he had reached parity. Between the date of the White Paper and Hitler's speech of May 21 the Cabinet determined on a great acceleration of air power, to double the rate of expansion provided in the previous summer, and to bring the Home first-line strength to 1500 by March 1937. We can trace the mixture of motives that impelled the Chancellor of the Exchequer.

12 May 1935

Mussolini seems determined to embark on the Abyssinian adventure, which will . . . render him useless as an ally against Germany.

26 May

you ask what I thought of Hitler's speech. Well, frankly, I was intensely relieved. It has made my position much easier, for while I recognised, and indeed insisted on the necessity for such a recasting of our air programme as would show its truly formidable character . . . I have been greatly alarmed at some of the proposals, which appeared to me panicky and wasteful. . . . It is clear that Hitler laid himself out to catch British public opinion and, if possible, to drive a wedge between us and France. . . . All the same, the general effect is pacific, and to that extent good.

In this air of sceptical relief he was moving, when MacDonald handed over to his successor.

CHAPTER XVIII

ABYSSINIA AND THE RHINELAND: 1935-1936
AGED 66-67

God said, Ask what I shall give thee. And Solomon said . . .
Give therefore thy servant an understanding heart . . .
that I may discern between good and bad . . .
And Solomon awoke ; and, behold, it was a dream.

1 Kings iii, 5-15

KING GEORGE V kept his silver jubilee that May, after which Baldwin took over the trappings of power whose substance he had long controlled. In Britain's silver age he had come to the height of his influence, in his personality old civic unkindness seemed to be buried, and in the rejoicing over a good King he might find just proof that he had accomplished what he had set out to do, to root democracy in parliamentary institutions by adjusting Labour to " the old good humour " of England.

Domestically, he hoped for a respite until a good holiday had given him time to reflect on what could not be avoided, the date of the election and Cabinet reconstruction. Mercifully the Unemployment Board regulations had gone into cold storage, to emerge, it was hoped, more agreeable to the taste. Iron and steel having reached agreement with foreign cartels, their tariff protection had been made permanent. And when the India Bill became law in August, reconciliation might come about with the prodigal Churchill who, Chamberlain wrote, unlike Lloyd George never bore malice. The Lloyd George adventure was closed, for after ten meetings with him it was concluded that every ingredient for a true coalition was absent ; in this Chamberlain's tactics had been hard and unswerving for, disbelieving in his opponent's sincerity, he insisted that he be kept guessing. Since he always contended that on public works of approved merit he was devoid of prejudice, he took special pleasure in announcing a guarantee for the London Transport Board up to £35 millions, and if his intention was to force a breach, he succeeded. In June Lloyd George signed a manifesto severely critical of government policy in regard to peace and employment, and announcing the formation of a " council of action ", independent of party ; though its prime non-party activity was to cross-examine all parties' candidates. Chamberlain gave much time to the government answer, his colleagues planing away some of his sharpness of tone ; enough to say that it disputed every proposition, as either uncalled for or mistaken. But it was easier to dismiss Lloyd George than the causes for which he claimed to speak, of which the principal was Peace.

Within the next six months the country suffered a grievous disillusionment, finding that what they had idolised was no God, and the shrine empty which they had besieged. And when they made that discovery, it was human and honourable that they should refuse to recant their faith, listening rather to prophets who told them that their sins of omission had found them out. But, as Machiavelli says bitterly of another pacifier, " it was not the sins that he meant ".

The structure of 1919 was now in ruins, and part-cause, part-symptom of the collapse was a profound, though unconscious, insincerity. If the Covenant meant what it said, we were pledged to keep by force the frontier of every existing State, and to protect an indivisible peace by making every war universal ; as if the defence of a vast vulnerable empire were not enough for forty million Britons. Now it was, and always had been, certain that no British government would fulfil such commitments. Locarno itself, which the Dominions had refused to countersign, had proved it, since which time one government after another had drawn a clear line between our vital interests in western, and our unconcern with eastern, Europe. As to the use of force to enforce peace, it was not merely that, specially since the Manchurian war, the government were convinced that economic sanctions could not succeed without the help of America, or that, as Baldwin openly said, any sanction involved a danger of war. To many minds the implications of the Covenant were morally repugnant ; " I do not like the idea ", said Edward Grey, " of resorting to war to prevent war ", while a powerful school, of which Lothian was a type, protested against automatic sanctions.

While thus committed on paper to universal force, we had incontinently stripped ourselves of all arms. Since Locarno the Service estimates decreased every year down to 1934, the Navy had not been lower in personnel for forty years, we had disbanded nine cavalry regiments, sixty-one batteries, and twenty-one battalions of infantry. The Territorial Force were 40,000 below strength, the Air Force now only the fifth or sixth in Europe. Thanks to the two Labour governments the Singapore dock would not be

K*

ready till 1938, while the Navy was fast bound by their treaty of 1930, making impossible the replacement of capital ships or an increase in light craft until 1936 had expired. All this time the "no major war for ten years" rule, laid down in 1923 and only cancelled in 1932, had done its work, in the annihilation of supply, technicians, skilled craftsmen, and productive potential.

Those who most ardently championed this Covenant of force were those who also most loudly resisted rearmament. On the first expansion of the Air Force in 1934 the Labour leaders in both Houses, Ponsonby and Lansbury, were pacifists, but the official Labour amendment regretted "a policy of rearmament neither necessitated by any new commitment, nor calculated to add to the security of the nation"; the Liberals were also in opposition. On the White Paper of 1935 Attlee again moved a vote of censure; all the influence of Herbert Morrison, at the head of the London County Council, was cast on that side. Ramsay MacDonald's conversations with Chamberlain therefore reveal a fear that his government would be accused of "war-mongering", which had indeed been the Labour charge since their East Fulham victory of 1933.

How widespread and sincere was this confusion of thought was finally shown during the month of June in which Baldwin took over, in the declaration of the "Peace Ballot" organised by the League of Nations Union. "Terribly mischievous", Chamberlain had written when it was first announced, which was true in so far as anything must be mischievous that is irresponsible and evasive. The $11\frac{1}{2}$ millions who voted for an all-round reduction of armaments and abolition of aircraft voted, in the same huge majorities, that "the other nations" should enforce economic sanctions against "a State which insists on attacking another"; though a bare 2 to 1 positively declared for military sanctions also. What this would amount to if "the other nations" judged differently, or if "economic" slid into "military", was left dubious.

Such loose thinking resulted in a flabby policy. Using the exasperating voice of Palmerston and John Russell, without the striking force that had been in their aristocratic hands, British democracy vainly entreated, lectured, and hectored other countries to keep the way of peace, yet only in the end to show themselves unwilling to pay its price, and seemed to think they could keep France loyal to the League without defending French interests. Our constitutional mode had thus protested against every German measure, against an army of 300,000, aircraft, or shipbuilding, and then always accepted the accomplished fact. This process of evacuation had by 1935 brought us to the beaches. Having swallowed German conscription, at Stresa we condemned it, but then condoned it by the Naval treaty. Left-wing Britain was clear that Germany had been wronged over disarmament and still had wrongs to be righted in Danzig and the Corridor, the Archbishop of York pronounced that in his May speech Hitler's offers were " a great contribution to the secure establishment of peace ". Yet simultaneously we were insistent that no Air pact must be made unless accompanied by the Eastern pact on which Russia and France were bent, we were reiterating our guarantee of the Rhineland, our interest in Austria. But now broke a question which must test our professions : Abyssinia.

18 May 1935

   it does seem barbarous that in these days it should still be in the power of one man, for a whim or to preserve his personal influence, to throw away the lives of thousands of Italians.

   Fate could hardly have presented a worse ground for a test of principle. The Arab conquerors who had reached those precipitous highlands never achieved the civilisation of Cordova or Baghdad, descending almost to the level of the negroes whom they ruled, unredeemed by Coptic Christianity or European missions. Their empire, which had fluctuated between rival chieftains, in its present form was hardly fifty years old, representing the suppression first of Tigré, then of the desert fringes east and south, by Menelik of Shoa. By that date this relic had been forced out of isolation by the imperialism of Europe. In the year of Chamberlain's birth an Italian shipping firm, through the not unusual medium of a missionary, acquired the bay of Assab, and in 1885 the British, anxious to forestall the French, invited Italy to occupy Massowah. Thence sprang the colony of Eritrea, soon to be followed by the piecemeal taking of Italian Somaliland.

   Dreams of a protectorate, once smiled on by Menelik, were banished in 1896 in the bloody defeat of Adowa, but Menelik waxed old, and the Europeans wrote of his country, as once they had of Turkey as a sick man, and dressed up testamentary arrangements. Passing by a protocol of 1891, by which Britain acknowledged nearly all Abyssinia as in the Italian zone, our point of departure must be the tripartite treaty of 1906, which bound Britain, France, and Italy to preserve, if possible, its integrity, but to concert together for their special interests. As regards Italy, this expectancy was repeated in the treaty of 1915 which brought her to fight on the Allied side, and given a more precise definition in an agreement of 1925 ; whereby, in return for Italian support for a barrage on Lake Tsana, so vital for the water of Egypt, Britain would assist Italy to obtain a railway concession connecting her two colonies, and admit her exclusive economic influence in western Ethiopia.

Two years before this last agreement Abyssinia had been made a member of the League at the instance of France, who preferred an independent weakling to an Italian protectorate. Britain and other States had protested, for they felt that Abyssinia, in the language of the Covenant, was "inhabited by peoples not yet able to stand by themselves under the strenuous conditions of the modern world ".

For this view there was much to be said. Ras Tafari, regent since the war and crowned emperor in 1930 as Haile Selassie, could not suddenly transform a feudal vassalage and a slave civilisation by his own goodwill, his writ could not run, at least in any tolerable time, in the mountain massifs, or in the deserts where, across unmapped frontiers, nomad Somalis wandered for water and pasture. His Amharic fighting men sucked in rifles from foreign dealers, our minister or our Sudan and Kenya officials often reported murderous slave raids, and despite a "parliament" and good European advisers the country remained that precarious and provocative thing, an islet of the Dark Ages in a modern ocean. " No one ", said Churchill when war had begun, " can keep up the pretence that Abyssinia is a fit, worthy, and equal member of a league of civilised nations."

So the economic opportunities held forth to Italy by so many treaties remained unfulfilled, and as mutual suspicion grew Abyssinia turned a deaf ear. Given this half-century of disappointment, the refusal of colonies elsewhere, their lack of raw material, American restrictions on their emigration, given the sore memory of Adowa and Mussolini's concept of a new Rome, the nineteenth-century history of Africa, and the twentieth-century failure of the League either to disarm or to revise, given the silence of Stresa and the more eloquent silence of Laval, it is not surprising that the Duce's prior decision to force a settlement took effect in 1935. True to the treaty of 1906, in January he proposed to Britain a definition of their respective interests on the Red Sea.

The Chancellor of the Exchequer had derived satisfaction from the change at the Foreign Office. He had himself supported the choice of Hoare, believing that a partnership with Eden's "genius" for personal contacts would make a powerful structure. He applauded the younger minister's success in a first round at Geneva, which at least compelled Italy to accept League machinery for disposing of the original clash, writing " Eden has shown great courage and firmness, as well as remarkable skill in negotiation ". Yet Eden's direct contact with Mussolini in June failed. Deriding the sparse palm trees and sheepless desert received from France, the dictator rejected the British offer to cede their Somali port of Zeila to Abyssinia, which would then give up a part of Ogaden to Italy : speaking quietly but resignedly, he asked surrender of all the non-Amharic country conquered in the past half-century, with some sort of control over the rest, as Britain had in Egypt.

For the peace of Europe the danger was Germany, and nothing could be worse than the elimination of Italy from the anti-German camp. This immediate interest, it is often suggested, blinded our government to the yet greater evil, on a far-sighted view, of successful aggression, but of Chamberlain at least that is quite untrue.

Diary, 5 July
> it is clear after Eden's visit to Rome that Mussolini has made up his mind to eat up Abyssinia, regardless of treaties, covenants, and pacts. . . . The ideal way out is to persuade Mussolini to abandon the idea of force. The only way to do this is to convince him that he has no choice. If we and France together determined that we would take any measures necessary to stop him, we could do so, and quite easily. We could *e.g.* stop the passage of his supplies through the Suez Canal. If the French would agree to play their part, the best way would be to go privately to Mussolini and warn him of our views and intentions, at the same time assuring him of our desire to save his face and get him some compensation from the Abyssinians. If the French would not play, we have no individual (as opposed to collective) obligations, and we should not attempt to take on our shoulders the whole burden of keeping the peace. But if in the end the League were demonstrated to be incapable of effective intervention to stop this war, it would be practically impossible to maintain the fiction that its existence was justified at all.

6 July
> it seems more than ever unlikely that Laval will consent to anything that might embroil him with Mussolini. Yet if the latter goes on, he will torpedo the League, and the small States in Europe will just race one another to Berlin.

When Parliament rose in August, it was certain that an election must come soon after its return, and there were good reasons for sooner rather than later, not least the state of Europe. So the dying Arthur Henderson advised Baldwin, and so thought Hoare, though this in part for reasons domestic. For to have Ramsay MacDonald as a minister at large, critical of rearmament and the decline of civilisation, was another argument for getting a new House, which might be reckoned as Baldwin's own. The Central Office, however, not being moved, as was charitably suggested, by a wish to capture the gale of the Peace Ballot, wished to have until January to prepare, and envisaged unemployment as the chief issue.

In that field Chamberlain was digesting many plans, as for a Charing Cross bridge, hydrogenation plants, or steel-works for the distressed North, while the removal to safer areas of the Woolwich filling factory and the powder works at Waltham had been approved. But to fighting the election on unemployment he was opposed, on every ground of national interest, honesty, and tactic. He wished to fight it on Defence.

Diary, 2 August

what we want is an issue that will put them in the background and, if possible, substitute for the hope of fresh benefits a fear in the public mind,— always the strongest motive to induce people to vote. Now the Labour Party obviously intend to fasten upon our backs the accusation of being war-mongers, and they are suggesting that we have " hush-hush " plans for rearmament which we are concealing from the people. As a matter of fact, we are working on plans for rearmament at an early date, for the situation in Europe is most alarming. Germany is said to be borrowing over £1000 millions a year to get herself rearmed, and she has perfected a wonderful industrial organisation, capable of rapid expansion for the production of the materials of war. With Mussolini hopelessly tied up with Abyssinia and Great Britain disarmed, the temptation in a few years' time to demand territory etc. might be too great for Goering, Goebbels, and their like to resist. Therefore we must hurry on our own rearmament, and in the course of the next 4 or 5 years we shall probably have to spend an extra £120 millions or more in doing so. We are not yet sufficiently advanced to reveal our ideas to the public, but of course we cannot deny the general charge of rearmament, and no doubt, if we tried to keep our ideas secret till after the election, we should either fail or, if we succeed, lay ourselves open to the far more damaging accusation that we had deliberately deceived the people. In view of these considerations I have suggested that we should take the bold course of actually appealing to the country on a defence programme.

The Prime Minister reserved decision till the end of his holiday.

That came about sooner than he had bargained for, and it was the same with Chamberlain's bare fortnight at Flims, passed as he would have wished in walks over the passes, noting a yellow delphinium or a green emerald moth, or a last bloom of Alpine roses. On August 19 he was recalled. Three-power talks in Paris had framed a " reorganisation " of Abyssinia under the League, with a suggestion of territorial adjustment, but Mussolini would not look at it and bade his generals expect the signal, any day after September 10.

18 August ; from Samuel Hoare

> it is urgently necessary for the Cabinet to consider what in these circumstances our attitude should be on two assumptions : (1) that the French are completely with us, (2) that the French have backed out. It is equally urgent for the Cabinet to consider what preparations should be made to meet a possible mad dog act by the Italians. . . . Our line, I am sure, is to keep in step with the French and, whether now or at Geneva, to act with them.

But if so, it followed that the dual desire of the British people, to keep the Covenant but also to eschew war, must be passed through the mesh of the policy of Laval ; in whom we meet a chief engineer of the downfall of many things, of France and Abyssinia, the League and Sir Samuel Hoare.

Fear of Germany had impelled him to make his pact at Rome, calculating that Italian friendship could either be used to contain Germany or, at the expense perhaps of the Poles and Little Entente, as an avenue to a French-German understanding ; in any case, to uphold Austria, and to relieve France of a watch on the Alps as well as the Rhine. Was he to be asked to sacrifice this fair future for Abyssinia ? and that by Great Britain, who had always obstructed French resistance to German revival and had lately made her private bargain at the expense of the French fleet ? But much more was at stake for France. Her finances were in danger, from both Right and Left came a waft of civil war, rival ideological leagues spilled their class hatreds over into foreign affairs. The Franco-Soviet pact had been signed, but Laval delayed its ratification, it was suspected, to please his Fascist friends. Even so, a great majority of French opinion, M. Blum included, were stiff against war over Abyssinia, and long ago Laval had put to us an Italian protectorate.

Chamberlain's letters agree with his public utterances in an advance on several parallel lines. Whether sanctions could work he had clearly doubted ; " what I hope for ", so in August, " is a reconstructed League to deal with European affairs, and what I shall work for is a Britain strong enough to make it impossible for her wishes to be flouted again, as Mussolini has flouted them now ". But sanctions, he came to be convinced, must be tried out ; writing to his wife in September that they might force Italy to halt, which in turn might make Hitler waver. He was working closely with Hoare and Eden, concerting many passages, including that on a fairer distribution of raw materials, for Hoare's speech at Geneva, which nailed the British flag to collective security.

In the short two months from that utterance to the Hoare-Laval *débâcle*, his speeches pressed home the dual policy. One-sided disarmament had been " a complete, a costly, a dangerous failure " ; " if members of the League from fear of consequences were to say they would stand idly by . . . notice would have to go out to the rest of the world each is to be for himself, and the devil take the hindmost ". Yet Hoare's Geneva speech was more guarded than the sweep of its sentences, or the enthusiasm of its world audience, allowed ; Britain, so it ran, stood for the " collective " maintenance of the Covenant, " the security of the many cannot be secured by the efforts of a few ". This position must now be tested, for three decisive events compelled them : the Italian rejection of a plan put forward by the League's committee of Five, their invasion of Ethiopia, and, on October 7, the League's resolve to deliberate on sanctions.

19 October

I have always said that, when it came to a decision, Laval must come down on our side, though he would wriggle and jib up to the last moment. But the French have been as disloyal as they could . . . [some vague hopes of peace] : it may be, therefore, that the thing is not yet desperate, and that the League may still be vindicated. It would be a wonderful gain for the world, and for the resumption of progress, if it worked out so.

A date in mid-November had now been determined for the election, for which every omen seemed propitious. Sanctions had split the Labour ranks, unemployment was at last fallen below two million, while at their own party conference Churchill had eloquently buried the Indian hatchet with a tribute to the goodwill that encompassed Baldwin. On the choice of a battle standard, Chamberlain's wish to fight on Defence had not prevailed against the advice of agents and officials, but though thus officially held in reserve, Defence infiltrated his speeches over twelve constituencies.

Diary, 19 October

our party is united, Labour is torn with dissensions, Liberals have no distinctive policy, L. G. has ceased to interest. The issue has been diverted from our weakest point, unemployment and distressed areas. . . . I intend to stress support of the League as an instrument of peace, a new defence programme to enable us to perform our task of peace-preserver, the benefit of this programme to employment . . . the dangers of a Socialist administration.

He himself drew the first draft of the party manifesto, inserting sundry matters on which, without consultation, he had publicly declared, such as raising the school age and improvement of national physique. But its most carefully framed sentences related to foreign affairs ; " we shall take no action in isolation, but we shall be prepared to take our part in any collective action ".

Once more there was the complementary partnership with Baldwin, so " inscrutable " he writes, but from whom his heart desired recognition ; " as I went out ", says one line in the diary, " he said ' good-bye, old boy ', an unusually affectionate term for him ". But mutual recognition there was, and if Chamberlain gave credit to his own research department and his own activity, his whole view of politics admitted another power in Baldwin. No class programme, he believed, would ever win a modern election, which depended on the unattached voter. " If that be so," a letter runs as this election closed, " it will be the non-party men and women who will decide the nature of the governments, and the S. B.'s, if there are any, will capture them ".

But while, as politics must needs drive, he spoke of the " wreckers and runaways of 1931 ", or pointed to a million houses built and seventy million of taxes remitted, the most militant words of this election were exchanged on the theme of peace. " What we have been striving for ", he told Edgbaston, " is not the cause of a far-away country in Africa " but the League, whose first function was not to extend war but to prevent it, — adding, at Stoke, " we have never discussed military sanctions ". In a memorable speech to the Peace Society Baldwin declared, " I give you my word there will be no great armaments ", and it was in fear lest they be labelled " war-mongers " that powerful advices passed upward, to the effect they must not take in Churchill.

It was, indeed, precisely on that cry that Labour fought their campaign. When Chamberlain spoke of making up gaps, Attlee responded that he asked a blank cheque for armaments, — Attlee who had lately been asking for war against aggressors, and whom Eden had reproached with " Palmerston pales into insignificance beside the peevish truculence of the right honourable gentleman ". So Greenwood said that Chamberlain's campaign was disgraceful scare-mongering, while representations of babies in gas-masks were thought suitable election armour.

Thus, both parties protesting they stood for the Covenant but not for war, the election passed, with a measure of success unexpected for the government. Though Labour won 95 seats, even now they returned only 154 members as against 385 Unionists, while both wings of Liberals and National Labour lost more ground. He himself held Edgbaston by a 21,000 majority, Birmingham returning, for the second election running, its unbroken band of twelve.

A coalition government it remained, with 15 Unionists in a Cabinet of 22, but there was little reconstruction. Londonderry was dropped, making room for Halifax as leader in the Lords, who in turn gave way to Duff Cooper at the War Office. Cunliffe Lister had taken a peerage, and Eyres Monsell too ; " we are a weak Cabinet ", Chamberlain wrote, " particularly in the House of Commons ". Both MacDonalds having lost their seats, he did not hide his opinion that the son rather than the father, but certainly not both, should be in the Cabinet, though Baldwin preferred to wait for what time would bring. So the claims of new blood did not range beyond Duff Cooper and W. S. Morrison, the new Financial Secretary ; did not reach to a recall of Churchill.

By this third week of November not only were sanctions in force, but a League committee was to consider adding oil to the list. The Prime Minister had allowed his colleagues, and in a less degree the public also, to see his dislike of sanctions, the threat of which had united his reluctant country round the Duce. Would Mussolini, whose persuasion of British decadence was familiar to his British acquaintance, dare to attack the British Empire ? our best-versed authorities thought it possible, especially if France proved craven. In September, therefore, naval reinforcements reached Gibraltar and Alexandria, the Malta and Aden garrisons were put on a war footing ; all of which drew forth Italian movement on the borders of Egypt.

Not that anyone feared the issue of an Italian war, as such. But daily in the Cabinet room Baldwin's eye caught the sagacious face of Robert Walpole, whose vow, he remembered, had been to keep the country out of war, and whose fall had come from a war in which, against his better judgement, he was ensnared. At best, war would mean the Navy locked up in narrow Mediterranean waters, with no ships to spare for other risks, — against which who could warrant us ? If Germany seized this heaven-sent chance, or if Japan leaped on an unfinished Singapore, that danger would be on us which responsible service advisers insisted we were not ready to face, of war against three great powers. Before him lay solemn diplomatic warnings that an oil sanction meant war, that war meant Italian union with Germany at the cost of Austria's independence ; intelligence reports that the German first-line air strength was not less than 1500 machines ; reports from Berlin of Hitler's sulky mood, his boasts that he could take the Rhineland when he pleased, or Goering's full-bodied aside that all Germany asked was a plebiscite in Austria, justice for the Sudeten of Bohemia, and one colony. That was not the worst. Every Paris dispatch made it more certain that Laval would never fight, though we had extracted a pledge of resisting Italian attack ; he was bargaining that pledge against a guarantee of the Rhineland and obstructing sanctions, even refused naval facilities at Toulon and Bizerta. It might come to a war waged for " collective security ", but waged alone.

If then it was life and death to prevent this scuffle swelling to a war of Europe, not the French alliance only but, it might be claimed, the spirit of the League pointed to a double policy : to intimidate the aggressor, but to attempt conciliation. This was not concealed from the Commons or electors, and in November, with the assent of other sanctionist States, Britain and France undertook to seek a solution, in which the League committee had failed.

That committee had put forward a threefold basis : some League control of Abyssinia, some exchange of territory, and some economic opening for Italy. Nor did the prospect seem hopeless, for Mussolini had accepted the plan as regards central Abyssinia, and the Negus was believed ready to exchange territories in return for a port. Such was the situation during the election, shortly after which it was made known that the committee on the oil sanction would meet on December 12. In pursuit of our dual policy we had promised France that the application of sanctions, against Italy now or Germany hereafter, should be determined by common assent, and had informed the Duce there was no intention of enforcing sanctions that were " military " ; to which his uncomforting reply was that he would take an oil sanction as an act of war. There was one other very vital factor. A League oil sanction would be much weakened unless the United States reduced to its former proportion their exports to Italy, which had more than doubled during the present year, but whether Congress would give the President such exceptional powers, Hoare thought perfectly problematic.

Though it does not appear that Chamberlain shared the view held in some quarters that tightening the screw would break down the Fascist régime, his instincts were decidedly more combative than those of some members of his party.

Diary, 29 November

> Economic sanctions are now in force, but hitherto they have not included oil. . . . The decision really turned on the possibility of making the embargo effective. . . . U.S.A. has already gone a good deal further than usual. . . . Consequently the question is being taken seriously, Mussolini is making violent threats, and Laval once again has been wriggling.

Same date

> I replied that if anyone else would give the lead, well and good, but in the last resort, if necessary, we ought to give the lead ourselves rather than let the question go by default. . . . If we backed out now because of Mussolini's threats, we should leave the Americans in the air, and they would be unable to resist the arguments of their oil producers. . . . It was inevitable that in such circumstances U.S.A. should decline in future to help us in any way, sanctions would crumble, the League would lose its coherence, and our whole policy would be destroyed. . . . We should press Laval to tell Mussolini that, if he attacked us, France would at once come to our assistance and if he evaded this request, we should make it clear at Geneva that France, and not we, were blocking oil sanctions.

In the end the government adopted a compromise, that we should join in oil sanctions if imposed, but try to postpone their imposition pending an effort for peace.

Diary, 8 December

> the object of sanctions being to stop the war, it would obviously be absurd to proceed with them if thereby one was to prejudice an opportunity of ending the war. . . . On the other hand, we must not by showing weakness encourage Mussolini to be more intransigent. Sam, who is about to take a desperately needed holiday in Switzerland, is now in Paris discussing the latest turn of events with Laval.

Same date

by putting his great army the other side the Suez Canal, Mussolini has tied a noose round his own neck, and left the end hanging out for anyone with a Navy to pull. It would seem incredible that in such a position he should venture to attack us, and in the end I don't believe he would. . . . If only our defences were stronger, I should feel so much happier, but though we are working night and day, they aren't what I should like.

Even as he wrote, a noose was, indeed, being pulled : but by Laval, round the neck of the British Foreign Secretary.

Hoare's long strain over the India Bill had raised a doubt in Chamberlain's mind whether he was physically capable of taking the Foreign Office, and lately he had had several fainting fits. He was, moreover, representing a country unprepared and unwilling to fight, or to fight alone, and he was oppressed by a conviction of danger. France false to her word ; of American action, little sign ; Jugo-Slavia anxious to avoid war ; Malta and the fleet swamped under air attack ; warfare in areas boiling with discontent, in Egypt, Cyprus, and Palestine ; a German move on the Rhine. Heaven knows, he had toiled to bring the League into action, steadfastly denied the French wish to give Italy military control, and insisted that Abyssinia must have an adequate port. Since October his officials had been working at Paris on such lines.

On that sad evening of December Laval flourished a large dossier of proof that oil sanctions spelled war and that, if so, he could not guarantee France keeping her word, unless terms were put to Mussolini with which he might be expected to agree. And if, Hoare reflected, oil must be postponed, the League must be assured that a basis of negotiation had been found ; once more he insisted on an Abyssinian port in full sovereignty and that the terms must be an extension from those of the League committee, and reduced the territories that France wished to give. Next night, after signing with Laval a communiqué declaring they had found a basis for settlement, he departed for the Alps, and on the 9th the detail was released in the Paris press. Enough here to say that, if the terms followed Article 19 of the Covenant in revising conditions that menaced the peace of the world, they much affronted Article 16 by giving a rich reward to aggression.

That day the government agreed to accept responsibility for them, though with much dissatisfaction ; as Chamberlain later

emphasised in debate, they had not expected " final proposals ".[1]
But they sharply rejected Laval's impudent proposal that no full
detail should be given to Abyssinia, and that Britain should permanently pledge herself against an oil sanction. It was not till the
15th that Chamberlain found time to recount the growing danger,
with the clamour for Hoare's resignation, which " is of course
absurd ".

15 December

when Sam left for Paris on Saturday the 7th, we had no idea that he
would be invited to consider detailed peace proposals. I believed,
and so far as I know, my colleagues believed also, that he was going
to stop off at Paris for a few hours on his way to Switzerland, to get
the discussions with the French into such a condition that we could
say to the League, " don't prejudice the chances of a favourable issue
by thrusting in a particularly provocative extra sanction at this
moment ".   Instead of that, a set of proposals was agreed to, and
enough was allowed by the French to leak out to the press to make it
impossible for us to amend the proposals, or even to defer accepting
them, without throwing over our own Foreign Secretary. ⁄ . . Nothing
could be worse than our position.   Our whole prestige in foreign
affairs at home and abroad has tumbled to pieces like a house of
cards. If we had to fight the election over again, we should probably
be beaten. . . . You take some comfort from the thought that, if I
had been Premier, the discredit would have fallen on me instead of on
S. B.   That is true, if the same things had happened. But I affirm,
with some confidence, that they would not have happened.

Revolt spread up and outwards, especially among younger
members of the party. A loyal speech by Eden — " admirable, I
thought, in a very difficult situation " — did not check it, Hoare
was recalled from the Engadine, the Chief Whip recommended
resignation. On Chamberlain, his friend, and central figure of the
Cabinet, fell the brunt of painful speech and heavy decision. His
loyalty combined with his pragmatic mind against surrender, and
he loathed the idea of making a scapegoat, nor could his honesty
approve taking the line of putting the onus on to America. So there
was no way out, and on the 19th he wound up the debate in which
Hoare, a minister no longer, explained his burden, his fears, and the
total inaction of the League, a debate which damaged him less
than a Prime Minister who had been forced to jettison a principal
colleague, together with a policy he had himself accepted. Chamber-

[1] Cf. Halifax's speech of December 19 : " I make no secret of the fact that, when
they read the terms, they did not like them ".

lain's speech repeated they had never expected final proposals, implying, too, that France had promised no effective assistance, but his chief point was that which we have found in his letters for a year past. Despite doubts, they had decided to " try out to the last extremity the possibilities of the League ", only to find that its ultimate sanction must always be force. And how had those who now reproached them helped to arm the League ? intellectuals, sanctionists, and those who said the Tories wanted war, " all join together to say, ' above all, do not let us have any armaments ' ".

So that episode was dead, with its mischance and miscalculation.

26 December ; from Halifax

the whole affair was a thoroughly bad business. Looking back, it seems to me that the initial mistake was Sam's, in publishing his (and therefore, except at great price, *our*) assent in the Paris communiqué. And what of course explains — but doesn't justify — what we did was the habit of immense confidence we had rightly developed in him.

I am still puzzled, though, by the condemnation meted out to proposals that were not, as you said all along, so frightfully different from those put forward by the Committee of 5. But the latter were of respectable parentage ; and the Paris ones were too much like the off-the-stage arrangements of 19th century diplomacy. . . . And Sam's conclusion, from his premises of danger etc., was [illegible]. The more sure conclusion would have been to go slow with oil, etc.

That was written the week after. After several years we may extend the responsibility further, to all who, knowing their country to be half armed, commended to the electors a policy that could only be vindicated by the strong.

This heavy defeat, in the first month of a new Parliament, left a trail of troubles, great part of which weighed on one whom Churchill styled " the packhorse " of this government. Yet, as we struggle into 1936, he must never be seen as a man robbed of resilience or light. The day before the storm broke he revealed some inner thoughts, springing from the question, why not retire now before his work was shattered by rearmament ?

8 December

I suppose the answer is that I know no one that I would trust to hold the balance between rigid orthodoxy and a fatal disregard of sound principles and the rights of posterity. And, perhaps, when I come to think of it, I don't really care much what they say of me now, so long as I am satisfied myself that I am doing what is right. For it isn't as if I had ambitions which might be ruined by present unpopularity. I believe S. B. will stay on for the duration, and by next election I shall be 70 and shan't care much, I daresay, for the strenuous life of leader, even if someone else hasn't overtaken me before then.

Actually early in February Baldwin named the probability of staying on till 1938, by which time he might have got settlement with Germany and set the new King firm in the saddle. For King George V died on January 20, and Chamberlain's letter to Queen Mary held sentences of more than conventional homage :

> No one could serve his late Majesty as a Minister without feeling for him something much deeper than the loyalty due to a King, for his personal qualities inspired us all with a constantly growing devotion to him, as we realised more and more fully his complete absorption in the welfare of all his subjects, and his unfailing support and encouragement of those on whom rests the burden of responsibility for the government of the country. Hamlet's words, " Take him for all in all, I shall not look upon his like again ", come inevitably to my mind whenever I think of him.

Not " inevitably " perhaps, for he had just been reading and re-reading *What Happens in Hamlet* and was engaged in enthusiastic correspondence with its author ; for example, as follows :

15 January 1936 ; to Professor J. Dover Wilson

> . . . " dear mother " : it was not Hamlet's meaning which puzzled me, but why he should have deliberately used the phrase to Claudius. Thinking it over further, I have come to the conclusion that he says " dear mother " on purpose to draw a contradiction or comment, which will enable him once more to express in words his constant obsession about the " fleshly mansion ".

And then followed a meeting, full of talk of emendations and of Shakespeare's handwriting. All these months his letters ring the changes on what he most enjoyed : redwings in the Park, a black-bird mimicking the call of the thrush, a " glorious " Constable of Hadleigh Castle, these bore him up in a sea of troubles.

If the new King did not shoulder his responsibilities, he wrote, " he will soon pull down the throne ", but politically considered he thought Baldwin's speeches on these occasions — in which he looked on him as " the supreme master ", better than Asquith because more human — and his new rôle, as of another Melbourne to a young sovereign, would help government to recover the late disaster. Such fortification they would certainly require. Not for their legislation, which was not effectively opposed, but because the inner lines were being sapped by elements which, to him, must be peculiarly embarrassing.

Grave issues surrounded them. Eden's promotion to the Foreign Office would mean a different emphasis, but could not in itself transform the dilemma of policy. After long work in committee Chamberlain was drafting a second White Paper on rearmament and pressing for a speedy enquiry into the whole structure of Defence, which must, he felt, result in creating a new ministry. All of which we are considering here only in regard to the struggle proceeding around, and for, the Cabinet.

His brother Austen, now in his seventy-third year, was the *clou*, having lately won as a private member an influence he had never held as a minister. His intervention in the Abyssinian crisis had been weighty, his defence of Baldwin as damaging as most attacks, and he reasoned that the Cabinet were making an immense mistake in excluding Churchill. Perhaps, when Hoare went, he would have liked to return to the Foreign Office, at any rate when he received an offer of office without portfolio he did not smile on it. Meantime Hoare had returned from convalescence, sore over the past and unhappy over the future, and whether, as rumour said, he wrote a political book, or joined Churchill and Austen below the gangway, either might be disconcerting. Other ministers were restless, Baldwin told Chamberlain that, when he succeeded, he would have to make changes, and these personal questions must be handled at once, for Defence could not wait. Both were agreed that Hoare should come back, though how and when were uncertain; as to Chamberlain's proposal that Hoare should conduct the Defence enquiry or, failing him, Austen, several different quarters ruled out the first alternative, and Austen himself demolished the second.

Diary, 16 February 1936

the outstanding speech was one by Austen, in which he quoted S. B.'s speeches to show how he had been in error in estimating German advance in Air strength.

He himself circulated a note on the defects of the present system, privately writing " we have already dallied too long ", but he found Baldwin had settled on some sort of Defence ministry and was cogitating who should fill it.

Diary, 16 February (continued)

he had concluded that the best thing would be for me to take it, and for Austen to take my place until I succeeded him [S. B.], when he and I could settle what next.

His own instinct and the advice of all whom he consulted were against this move, and he declined to make it. The alternatives were full of difficulty. The party would not have an immediate return of Hoare ; if the new ministry went to Churchill, it would alarm those Liberal and central elements who had taken his exclusion as a pledge against militarism, it would be against the advice of those responsible for interpreting the party's general will, and would it not, when Baldwin disappeared, raise a disputed succession ? For a whole month these niceties and gravities were well weighed.

Diary, 1 March

I fear S. B. asks too many .opinions. They contradict one another, and then he is left in the air. . . . I feel precluded from saying anything unless directly asked, because of the shakiness of his own position. As I am thought to have a strong interest in the succession (though this has never, and shall never, affect my actions) I must not do anything which would enable enemies to say that I had deliberately induced S. B. to appoint the man whose incompetence or unpopularity was bound to wreck his own leadership. But S. B. knows my views. I still think Sam the best and, failing him, Swinton, and I would not pay any attention to public opinion if it was against either.

Medieval men submitted litigants to an ordeal by fire and the debate of March 9 was something like it ; in which Hoare was deemed to have failed, but Churchill, say our notes, " made a constructive and helpful speech ". That day, however, it was decided to appoint Inskip. Not to have a European reputation, perchance it was thought, might at this moment be an advantage, for on March 7 German troops had entered the Rhineland.

This, too, in its setting and effects, flowed from the accursed matter of Abyssinia. Britain and Italy, the two guarantors of Locarno, were at daggers drawn, sanctions had turned France sour against us, this very week they obstructed Eden's move to impose the oil sanction. Laval had fallen, their government was in the hands of the sonorous and dim Sarraut, and of Flandin, so physically significant and politically so much the reverse. During February, with a monopoly of air power and with great soldierly endurance, the Italians beat down Abyssinian resistance. Under the meagre strain of sanctions the League was disintegrating, a quarter of its members still welcomed Italian exports, Latin America was recalcitrant, Czechs and Austrians needed Italian goodwill for a Danubian bloc. When the German blow fell, the French hesitated and were lost. If a few ministers advised action, more of them feared the effect on the sacrosanct but now sickly franc, it was believed General Gamelin advised against war, while when they turned to their British allies, they found them unanimous for peace.

It was, in fact, a final example of the high-minded contradictions which had become our sustenance. Treaty bound us to resist invasion of the demilitarised zone, yet it was certain British opinion would refuse to fight against an entry of German troops into Essen or Cologne. By treaty we were guarantors, but from the first we made ourselves mediators, and though we had led in imposing sanctions on Italy, we led also in refusing to impose them on the Germans. The treaty spoke of penalties ; Eden on the contrary spoke of our motive as " the appeasement of Europe ", mainly directing his speech to show that the measures contemplated were not too severe upon Germany, or to deprecate the view of Lloyd George that we were dangerously near a military alliance with France.

This intention to repudiate a strict interpretation of Locarno was predetermined, but Hitler's bayonets also carried a bulky olive branch, in the shape of an offer to negotiate a new demilitarised zone, an Air pact, non-aggression treaties with Austria and Czecho-Slovakia, and a return to the League. We told the French that we could not continue to miss chances of reaching agreement, and Opposition insisted that such offers must be explored.

In the next stage Chamberlain became directly involved, when Eden and Halifax returned from Paris reporting that the French demanded sanctions, but when first the Locarno powers, and then the League Council, assembled in London, he and his colleagues were unanimous against any notion of war.

Diary, 12 March

talked to Flandin, emphasising that public opinion here would not support us in sanctions of any kind. His view is that, if a firm front is maintained by France and England, Germany will yield without war. We cannot accept this as a reliable estimate of a mad dictator's reactions.

To make the French " constructive ", so he saw the task, and here he found the Belgian van Zeeland " an acquisition, clear-headed, sensible, and agreeable ". When Flandin urged at least an economic boycott, he replied by suggesting an international force during negotiation, agreed to a pact for mutual assistance, and declared that, if by giving up a colony we could get lasting peace, he would consider it. On March 19 agreement was reached between the Locarno powers, with Italy glum but not dissenting. For the emergency period there were to be staff talks, a reassertion of Locarno, and the international force, while Germany would be asked not to reinforce her garrisons or fortify the zone. These accepted, they would invite her to negotiate on a new status for the Rhineland, and the pacts she had proposed. They would then put to the League a project of a conference to examine armaments, sanctions, and Germany's relation with her eastern neighbours. And last, should this " effort of conciliation fail ", Great Britain would enter into immediate consultation with France and Belgium for mutual resistance to aggression. Such was the broad outline which Eden expounded to a House suspicious in part of new commitments, and in part of French obstinacy.

28 March

> Anthony made the speech of his life, and it was not only a good speech. It showed both courage and statesmanship. . . . The success of the debate has greatly strengthened our hands in dealing with the Germans, who have been counting upon the pro-German sentiment which undoubtedly existed, and I can't help hoping that Ribbentrop will have warned Hitler that if he persists in refusing to make any contribution, he may lose the sympathy of England, and find that he has driven us into an alliance with Belgium and France.

He conceived a hostile view of the Führer's ambassador at large. Ribbentrop, he wrote, " talks without ceasing, he evades a straight question every time, and if pressed becomes very noisy and insolent. He has no intention of saying anything to Hitler that Hitler would not like to hear."

While for the next few months the Germans were prolific of assurances and totally negative in deed, London and Paris seem to have missed their opportunity of pressing home some vital matter, such as the Air pact, and this not so much owing to a bitter general election in France as to a difference of outlook between France and Britain. The French argued that conciliation had failed, the British that they had made a great concession in having staff talks, and that they could accept no wider commitment than Locarno. Their recrimination resulted in a most unsatisfactory device, a *questionnaire* addressed by Britain to Germany ; the content of which was about equally divided between the kind of insinuation which Palmerston employed to the court of Louis-Philippe and an invitation to give pledges, as on a pact with Russia, on which it was certain no pledge would ever be forthcoming.

We emerged then from this crisis, bound by a mutual bond with France and Belgium, but engaged in an effort to rebuild Locarno by diplomacy, and not, as France would have wished, by force. Other events bore, no doubt, upon our policy. On the selfsame day of May the Emperor Haile Selassie fled from his country to the coast, and a second ballot gave a majority to M. Blum and the Front Populaire ; before the month closed, a series of immense strikes paralysed the French capacity for war.

2 May

the Italian successes will encourage the French to urge that, now everything is finished, we ought to lift the sanctions, let bygones be bygones, and get Italy back to the Stresa front at once. That seems to me intolerable . . . I am sure the time has not yet come for the League to own itself beaten. All the same, it is beaten.

Certainly steps towards pacification would have to be swift, for other dark clouds lowered. In the early morning of July 13 the porter of a Madrid cemetery was roused to take in a body, with a mortal wound in the head, the body of the Right-wing leader Sotelo. A week later Herr Henlein, head of the extreme German group in Bohemia, called at the British Foreign Office, upon whom he left a favourable impression.

CHAPTER XIX

BALDWIN'S LAST YEAR: FEBRUARY 1936–MAY 1937

AGED 67–68

> For time is like a fashionable host
> That slightly shakes his parting guest by the hand,
> And with his arms outstretch'd, as he would fly,
> Grasps in the comer ; welcome ever smiles,
> And farewell goes out sighing. O, let not virtue seek
> Remuneration for the thing it was.
>
> *Troilus and Cressida*

WHILE these omens hovered on Europe's margins, the government pursued its chosen path of peace, recovery, and rearmament. Economically 1936 was a decent year. Unemployment figures kept on falling until the next summer, wages rose, industry was undisturbed by serious dispute, the number of houses built had never been exceeded. Legislation roused criticism in detail rather than over principle, for it proceeded on the empirical scheme at which modern Conservatism had arrived, of using the State's power to equalise individual opportunity, to raise the level, and equip a commonwealth. Under that broad utilitarian head we may bring the chief measures of 1936–7 : an Education bill to raise the school age to fifteen, subject to local dispensation ; a revolutionary Tithe Act promising to extinguish this immemorial charge within sixty years ; a Cotton Industry bill ; unemployment insurance for agricultural workers, with continued subsidies to air transport, the cattle trade, and the special areas.

Yet though the House of Commons' life was young, somehow government seemed old, partly perhaps because it had known no other leaders but MacDonald and Baldwin since 1923 and, again, because Baldwin's coming departure prolonged the sunset. Such Cabinet change as occurred was piecemeal. In May a matter of insurances against the Budget led to the resignation of J. H. Thomas, — not altogether to Chamberlain's surprise, though he had a warm feeling for the man, — whose place at the Colonial Office was filled by Ormsby Gore, and he in turn succeeded by Chamberlain's close friend Stanhope at the Office of Works. Next, Monsell retired, and Hoare took over the Admiralty. In October, on the death

KILDRUMMIE, ON THE DON, AUGUST 1935

From a photograph taken by Sir Francis Humphrys

of Godfrey Collins, Elliot filled the vacant Scottish secretaryship : W. S. Morrison, Chamberlain's financial secretary at the Treasury, of whom he had high hopes, was promoted to Agriculture, while to maintain the Liberal ration Hore-Belisha, Minister of Transport, was brought into the Cabinet. In fact these latter changes were made by Chamberlain as successor-designate, but he was not entirely happy, writing " we are not very fortunate in our young men ".

In his own life we meet indications of how much of his span had passed, and of his present standing. In June his grandson was born ; in July Birmingham kept the centenary of Joseph Chamberlain's birth with ceremony that moved him, for in spirit he was very near to that older Birmingham ; let not the city, ran his message, make the mistake of glorying merely in its size. Though he kept his house at Edgbaston, he rarely saw it, sold his orchids with a pang for economy's sake, and by the same token, living in No. 11 Downing Street, with No. 10 in prospect, decided to sell his London house also, letting it first as an experiment. " Did I tell you ", he wrote, " that we had let Eaton Square to Ribbentrop ? . . . amusing, considering my affection for Germans in general, and R. in particular."

He was overworked this year and, though consoled by catching a record trout in the Test, his fishing days did not stave off his worst attack of gout, which grumbled on into the winter. But his heart leaped up at the tried consolations. In the thick of the Rhineland conversations he wrote of the almond tree at No. 11, the crocuses in the Park, or the Beethoven quartets that " take me into another world ".

On the Budget of 1936, the last of the peace period, he took an opportunity to review his stewardship, making for it no claim but that it had been an " indispensable foundation ". " The two main pillars of the policy have been the introduction of the tariff and the establishment of cheap money." By the first an adverse trade balance of £104 millions had changed to a favourable balance of £37 millions, while the duties had added £34 millions to the revenue without any perceptible rise in commodity prices. Cheap money had saved interest charges of £40 millions and underpinned the building of 1¼ million houses. " Our exports of manufactured goods have increased by more than £50,000,000 a year . . . the percentage of unemployment has fallen from 22·4 to 14·4 . . . the deposits in the savings banks alone have gone up by no less than £150,000,000."

As for the future, he calculated on increases in both Customs and Inland revenue, but the White Paper confronted them with

" the largest programme of defence ever undertaken by this country in peace time ". That programme derived from " first, a gap, a legacy left from the past, which the past in its time was either unwilling or unable to bear, and secondly, the development of a new policy, the benefits of which we hope will inure to posterity, but the initial cost of which would have to be met at once ". Some part of this cost, to be carried through in five years, must in future be met by loan, but the cost of annual maintenance, which would much exceed the £158 millions originally estimated, must be found from revenue. He proposed therefore to appropriate the balance in the Road Fund, to raise income tax to 4s. 9d., and to add 2d. to the tea duty. To ask these new sacrifices was a bitter disappointment. " But no man hesitates to set his fire-fighting appliances in readiness, when already he can feel the heat of the flames on his face."

Actually another financial transaction of the year was of greater magnitude than this almost unopposed Budget, — that is, the three-power currency agreement between Great Britain, France, and the United States. Since 1931, in spite or because of exchange equalisation funds, international dealings had lost stability, the countries which nominally clung to the gold bloc desperately trying to keep their footing but one by one falling away. France was the crux. The franc had long been overvalued ; it suffered severely from the Anglo-Saxon peoples' mutual competition, and the devaluation which was inevitable was hastened by Blum's expensive social programme. But when it came, the operation of the British and American exchanges, as of late pursued, would be made impossible, and concerted action was needed to avert a period of chaos.

Diary, 25 September

> I have had a very difficult time over the sudden French decision to devalue the franc, by a method which is not at all agreeable to us. I have had to take sole responsibility in view of the secrecy necessary, — and at the moment of writing I do not yet know whether the French have succeeded in persuading the Americans to issue a declaration similar to the one on which I have agreed with Paris.

In fact, general agreement was reached that day between the three Treasuries, and a first beginning made of return to international machinery ; if not a gold standard, yet a system freed from certain dangers in managed gold.

Sole responsibility he had not outside the Exchequer, yet he was bearing the brunt of it. To his near friends he always stipulated for loyalty as the first political virtue, as indeed we know from its greatest apostle how " private friendship is the foundation of public trust ". Yet there is all party history to prove that this virtue may injure the public interest. It was, for instance, surely unnatural that he should still be in doubt whether in Baldwin's absence he or MacDonald should be left in charge, or still acquiescent in the possibility of MacDonald remaining in the Cabinet when Baldwin retired. He was experiencing too what Baldwin had felt before him, the strain of power exerted through another man, and that man ailing. Altogether they had some bad debates this summer and awkward jolts, some clash in the party on how to deal with Lords reform, and even more on how to deal with Germany. These things were symptoms of a deeper malaise, that they were suffering simultaneously from three ailments of party.

The first, hardly seen for a century before, will detain us later, an importation of foreign philosophies into politics domestic ; of which Nazi Germany Fascist Italy, and Soviet Russia were the roots, the wrangle over Jew and Arab in Palestine a side manifestation, the rival prancings and petty brutalities of Communists and Mosley's followers a local symptom.

But the second was of a type always recurrent. Not merely was the Prime Minister's position uncertain, but it was daily under critical scrutiny by powerful elements in his following, Austen, Churchill, Horne, Amery, Londonderry, Winterton, and Lloyd, ex-ministers or would-be ministers (two categories that may coincide), whose chosen ground was a subject of which several of them were masters, and concerning which the country was justly perturbed, the need of Defence. This took the two brothers back in some degree to the strains of 1923–4, and Neville strenuously opposed one of Austen's proposals, foreseeing what he called " panicky measures ", confusion in the Defence programme, and a storming of the Cabinet.

Diary, 11 July

> I saw Austen, and I believe convinced him that neither a secret session nor a conference among leaders on armaments had any prospect of producing agreement. On the other hand, I told him that a conference on policy would be a very different thing, and I should look on it sympathetically.

But this move ended more placidly in a deputation to the Prime Minister.

Finally, the smooth working of our system depends not so much on national unity in fundamentals, important though that

L

must be, as on the existence of clear-cut alternative policies. But this condition was almost absent from the two problems to which this House of Commons for ever returned. In the first, the future of the League, were confused two separate issues, how to proceed in face of an Italian victory, and how to reform the League so that such a *débâcle* might not happen again ; and how his own speech on sanctions forced the climax must be later related. More wearing to the tissue was the second, the " special " areas.

This ulcer, of localised but mass unemployment, ate into the body politic, stabbed the national conscience, roused rebellion in young Unionists, and so filled the vision of the Labour party as to blind them to all else. Not a spark of constructiveness gleamed in their votes of censure, only a multiplication or redistribution of relief, and not much larger hope came from the commissioners' suggested remedies, though Chamberlain financed one, for an investment company with £1 million guarantee. From this, from trade agreements by which coal exports should profit, and from rearmament, he foresaw some palliatives, but " when all is said and done ", we hear in November, " there must remain a large number of people for whom we can find no work in South Wales, and who must either move, or stagnate there for the rest of their lives ". But democracy prefers action to thought, to spend and not to wait, — not to wait for the raising of the school age till 1939, for tithe abolition in sixty years, for compulsion in coal reforms till 1938, or for a whole generation of middle-aged men to sink into special immobility, and at last a special grave.

This year he stood at the heart of business. It was for him to see Prince Starhemberg, " quiet, pleasant and sensible " ; King Carol of Roumania, much the reverse, " made a very unfavourable impression on me " ; or M. Blum, on whom we find this, worthy of note, in a letter of July : " He seems straightforward and sincere . . . I should say he was more of an idealist than a realist. I am sure he is honest, well-meaning and humane, but I doubt very much whether he understands the consequences of what he is doing."

Outside the Exchequer, and great activity over Defence, he was busied with the revised regulations of the Unemployment Assistance Board, which had given them such a shake a year before. The controversy was still the same, the replacement of two hundred local assistance authorities by a central body, and the objections were unchanged, the removal of individual grievances from questioning in Parliament, and the means test. Chamberlain, too, had not weakened on the system he had devised, or the evils from which he wished to escape.

4 July

there will be many more increases than decreases, and the Board will go slow except in the worst cases. But the largest cuts will naturally be in the worst places, and the Communists may try to stage some disorder in South Wales. I hear very bad accounts of the corruption, nepotism, and blackmail which is going on there.

When Parliament rose a month later, he took a cheerful view : " An unpleasant and difficult session has ended well. . . . Negotiations with Egypt look like coming to a satisfactory conclusion . . . Germany and Italy are coming to the conference, and Palestine seems to be less intractable. . . . Trade is still expanding marvellously."

Part of his holiday was spent in deputising for the Prime Minister, whose doctors had ordered him a long rest.

Diary, 7 October

On October 2 I took S. B.'s place at the mass meeting after the party conference at Margate . . . the main result . . . appears to be a general acceptance of my position as heir-apparent.

He spoke in praise of his leader, who had " raised the whole tone of our political life ", of intensified rearmament, of an Empire formed, by working together, into " a fortress of democracy ", but with most effect on a theme he had thought of four years back, the national physique. This he pursued arduously all the winter, hoping for an advisory council which would report direct to the Prime Minister and, when public opinion was ripe, would have wished to have a compulsory medical examination of the entire people.

Reading this autumn his brother's republished letters on the politics of thirty years before, he reflected on the character of the three Chamberlains. Austen's political interest, he thought, was genuine and thorough, but " he has not the eagerness of temperament and the inexhaustible vitality of Father, which kept him ever revolving some constructive idea. . . . I believe I lie somewhere between the two . . . there are very few and brief moments when I feel I can't bear to talk or think of the politics that have become my main purpose in life. Indeed, my fear is always lest this prime interest should obliterate my other interests in art or music, or books, or flowers, or natural history."

Obliterated they needs must be in the autumn of 1936. " The civil war in Spain ", says the diary, " has provoked dangerous reactions ", and together with the Abyssinian clamour at Geneva was extinguishing all hope that Germany and Italy would attend a conference. Troops must be found for the Holy Land. Defence was full of departmental friction and undetermined principles. He was in principal charge of the Three-Power currency question, Cabinet changes, and the legislative programme. An extended Factory Act, another to transfer trunk roads to the Ministry of Transport, unification of coal royalties, to these he pressed for adding another to deal with ministerial salaries which, as at present arranged, left every Prime Minister in debt, embarrassed his allotment of places, and distributed unequal salaries for equal work. He was concerned too with the memorial to King George V : " we shan't get the whole improvement I had hoped for, but we secure the new view of the Abbey and the Jewel Tower, and avoid wasting money on Parliament Square ". But the new session had hardly opened when the whole thought of ministers was taken up, not with a royal memorial but a possible ruin of royalty.

For two precious months, while the Duce's son-in-law Ciano was at Berchtesgaden, while Germany signed the anti-Comintern pact with Japan, and while Fascist soldiers entered Spain, our ministers could attend to only one thing, the determination of King Edward VIII to marry an American citizen, who was bringing divorce proceedings against her second husband. Chamberlain's austerity of standard, his impatience to make men, even kings, face reality, his instinct against procrastination, did not make him an ideal counsellor in this intertwined mass of pathos, folly, and ambition, but his papers show him anxious to avert abdication if it could be done, as well as humanly desirous of giving the King a chance of happiness. For him, however, as for all ministers, the first consideration was danger to the throne, and it was by no doing of theirs that the trouble in the end threatened a constitutional crisis.

For a month there was no advance after Baldwin's first warning in October ; the King, Chamberlain had deduced from earlier discussions on housing, was incapable of sustained purpose. In November he first declared his intention to abdicate and marry as a private citizen, but then that he wished to make a morganatic marriage. " I have no doubt ", says the diary, " that if it were possible to arrange the morganatic marriage, this would only be the prelude to the further step, of making Mrs. Simpson Queen with full rights." On December 2 the Cabinet unanimously agreed they could not be responsible for the legislation which a morganatic marriage would require. But their position was dangerous, for everything in human nature, from pure metal to base clay, was now engaged. With their curious complex of sensation, political cowardice, and thirst for power, the cheap press were taking a hand ; they must reckon with the loyalties of Churchill, and the political possibilities of a clash between sovereign and Cabinet. Many had justly seen in King Edward qualities for the making of a great sovereign ; why, it was put to democracy, should he not marry the woman of his choice ? why put a pistol to the head of this lonely man for an instant decision ? So the legend grew, and danger with it.

Chamberlain's papers are enough to convey some solid ingredients of the truth. Baldwin was the Crown's principal and, in this case, best adviser, never more Walpolean than in keeping unimpaired both the royal dignity and his own hold on the Commons, in an atmosphere where understanding of human beings was more precious than action. Strong in this sense of how large bodies move, he could afford to study others with some benevolence ; when Lloyd George was out for mischief, he might reflect, you could only see the wash of his periscope, but Churchill's hull would be half above water. Round Chamberlain, on the other hand, as the central figure of the Cabinet, flowed the necessity for constitutional precaution, anxiety that the country be kept informed or false versions corrected, and pressure for some terminus to this drawn-out trial which, he notes, was " holding up business and employment" and " paralysing our foreign policy ". Here we find wild impossibilities breaking on hard fact, veerings away from abdication, a proposal that the King broadcast to the Empire that he would morganatically marry — and that despite unanimous messages from the Dominions against it — and a willingness in the Cabinet, to the end, to accept renunciation of this marriage.

December

the public is being told that we are engaged in a fight with the King, because we have advised him to abdicate and he has refused. That is quite untrue, and we must say so. He asked us to examine the morganatic marriage proposal, we told him we could have nothing to do with it, and he has accepted that view. The public is also being told that we are trying to rush the King into a decision that he has no time to think over. That is equally untrue. He has been thinking it over for weeks, though he has been unwilling to face up to realities.

But though reminding him of the dangers to the country of protracted delay, we are not threatening him with resignation, and I do not think we shall. . . . There are only three alternatives before him : (1) marriage with Mrs. Simpson as Queen ; (2) abdication and marriage ; (3) renunciation of this marriage altogether. Now (1) is already barred, because apart from feeling in this country the Dominions have plainly said that they won't have it. The choice is therefore between (2) and (3). The general public will prefer (3), but if the King is not prepared for (3) there remains nothing but (2).

That seems plain, and on such lines, with the moral that time should be given for the natural working-out of this logic, he in fact argued. On December 9 they formally, though without hope, asked the King to reconsider his now declared purpose to abdicate ; it remained unchanged.

This had been a heavy run ; he took ten days in southern France for rest, and then back to a last session under Baldwin's lead. For dates were now fixed, the Coronation on May 12 and Baldwin's resignation on the 27th, and as these would cut across both an Imperial Conference and the Finance bill, some principal offices must be determined in advance. Like most of his predecessors, he found this his worst ordeal. For one important figure, if not given that important office, would consider retirement and writing a book, — " all ambitious politicians ", says the diary, " like to say this at such moments ". This old friend was hurt because he was not bidden to go up higher, and that old friend marvelled that the Conservative party was not more considered ; this still older friend had no doubt his inclusion would strengthen any government, so drawing the bare comment " I simply can't understand how people can be so conceited ". But before he took over, there was larger work to do and some buffets to endure.

Both Parliament and government were full of controversy, angriest perhaps over intervention or non-intervention (which earlier generations had decided came to much the same thing) in the Spanish civil war. Labour were attributing mining disasters to private enterprise, resisting Empire migration, opposing rearmament as the child of false policy or as parent of profiteering, and proffering a demand that every school child be given one free meal a day at a cost, so government estimated, of £40 millions a year. Factory Act, Livestock Industry Act, and insurance for black-coat workers, were all in their early stages. One of his particular devising, the Ministers of the Crown Bill, not merely rearranged their salaries but awarded one of £2000 to the leader of the Opposition, and

increased those of members of Parliament to £600. Moreover,
a White Paper of his drafting sketched the framework of another,
to fulfil his intentions for physical training.

But neither he nor any man could shake off the special areas,
whose unemployment still stood at twice the rate of the country
at large. On this he had pledges to redeem, which he had given
under pressure from his own party, and a first step was to increase
the Exchequer block grants by £5 millions. In March his White
Paper proposed to extend the Act of 1934 for another five years
and to enlarge the commissioners' powers in many small directions,
but though he privately admitted " the bill itself looks pretty thin ",
in debate he robustly defended the government and himself. " There
is no minister," he said, " I would even say no man, who has
worked harder or longer than I have " at this problem, breaking
out from his inner fortress with " there is one thing I do detest
in politics, and it is humbug ". For what could Lloyd George's
large loose schemes of land settlement do but destroy the arrangements painfully reached with Dominions and foreign countries, and
consequently diminish their demand for our industrial product?
With the torrent of mechanisation that displaced labour, oil replacing coal, and the effects of sanctions, it was idle to pretend
there was a speedy remedy. Let them consider that 21,000 persons
had been transferred in eight months, that Clyde shipbuilding had
doubled since 1933, that iron and steel revival must assist South
Wales, and that £35 millions of orders for rearmament had gone
to the special areas.

In February, in accord with his prediction a year before, he
announced that government would ask power to borrow £400
millions in the five-year rearmament period ; on top of which
there followed another White Paper, and on this too, he says, he
had done " most of the work ".[1] In this he asked them to expect
a Defence expenditure of not less than £1500 millions in the five
years, " a contribution indispensable to peace, and one which it is
the duty of the people of this country to make ". Defence overburdened and warped his last Budget also. Its cost for 1936-7
had risen to £186 millions, an increase of £50 millions on the
year before, but the country, he made bold to say, could stand it.
For inland revenue was still due to expand, new resources tapped
since 1932 now brought in £130 millions a year, and the savings

[1] Cf. Churchill's speech of May 31, 1937, to the Conservative party meeting : " when
the late government were at length convinced of the urgent need to rearm . . . no
one was more active than Mr. Chamberlain ".

he had made on debt charges would, alone, almost cover Defence borrowings.   They were entering the storm period under a favourable wind, because they had not weakened credit by priming the pump during the depression.

Yet for 1937–8 they must face a deficit of nearly £15 millions, and this in the main he would meet by another threepence on income tax, bringing it to 5s., and by a new scheme of his own devising.   This he styled a national Defence contribution, being a graduated tax on the profits of trades and business, the purpose of which was to find a temporary device, " capable of growth in itself ", adjustable to an expenditure that would rise to a peak and thereafter decline.   This brought a political tempest.   His announcement coincided with a new flight from the franc, British speculation in rearmament materials, and reports that America was reducing the price for gold.   His tax was complicated in detail, securities fell by many millions in a few weeks, the bubble confidence was broken. But his inner motives must be shown in his private words.

25 April 1937

I reckon it to be the bravest thing I have ever done since I have been in public life, for I have risked the Premiership. . . . It was not my successor in office, but the country in general and our successors in the next 20 years that I was thinking of. . . . Up to quite recently there was but little change in the cost of living, and I have been rather surprised that there has been little talk of profiteering.   This is partly because Labour has been doing very well. . . . But I think the general quiet may partly be ascribed to the precautions taken by us to keep down prices.   The contracts with the armament firms . . . are on very different lines from those which prevailed during the great war.

But it would be a fatal mistake to suppose that this state of things is going to last.   Prices are bounding up now . . . sub-contractors and sub-sub-contractors, who cannot be subject to the same control, are undoubtedly reaping a rich harvest.   All the elements of danger are here . . . and I can see that we might easily run in no time into a series of crippling strikes ruining our programme, a sharp steepening of costs due to wage increases, leading to the loss of our export trade, a feverish and artificial boom followed by a disastrous slump, and finally the defeat of the Government and the advent of an ignorant, unprepared, and heavily pledged Opposition, to handle a crisis as severe as that of 1931.

I don't say that N.D.C. will prevent all this, but I feel sure that it enormously diminishes the danger.

He had in fact, and in particular with his mind on the need for secrecy, embarked without taking wide counsel on an immensely difficult proposition : to tax not profits as such, but their rate of expansion. In principle he found defenders but in its application none ; Horne and the City formed a most unwonted alliance with Keynes and the economists, in resisting proposals which would bear unjustly, it seemed, on youth, enterprise, and recovery. On the day he kissed hands as Prime Minister, the finance committee of his party begged him to withdraw it ; " a bad beginning ", says the diary. He gave way, accepting the undertaking of the business world that they would find him £25 millions by some other means, which his successor duly effected in a flat rate on profits.

This spring his burdens were very heavy, in Budget and Defence, Imperial Conference, and the Coronation, which last involved speech with many important persons : Beck and the Regent of Jugo-Slavia, Marshal Blomberg and the Czech Premier Hodza, all soon to vanish like the fiction in which he was then taking delight, *Gone With the Wind*. He found them so much the harder, for his brother Austen died suddenly in March.

Diary, 19 March

went to the House yesterday and answered questions, as I wanted to get that over. The day before, I had stood behind the Speaker's chair to listen to the tributes, as I did not feel equal to sitting on the bench. . . . As I came out of the Chamber, 3 Labour members, Arthur Greenwood, William Lunn, and Neil Maclean . . : put out their hands, and said something of their respect and admiration for Austen. The House of Commons is a wonderful place. This afternoon we have been to the St. Marylebone cemetery beyond Hampstead . . . the spot chosen looks over a wide view, the birds were singing, and I felt it was a good place.

27 March ; to the Archbishop of Canterbury

from my earliest days I have looked up to Austen with perhaps much more deference, as well as affection, than is usually the case where the difference of years was so small. He was a rare good brother to me, and the only one I had.

Those deep feelings had always extinguished any divergence in politics, and though sometimes he moved uneasily at the thought of Austen watching from his angle, critical, as elder statesman and elder brother, that never dimmed their affection, or his envy of things that he too could feel but not, like Austen, well express.

L*

To others he dwelt on his brother's chivalry in the face of hard disappointments, while his mind ran much on the decree that was bringing him to the highest office in the State, which both father and brother had more reason to expect.

> I am not a superstitious man [he told his elder sister], and indeed I should not greatly care if I were never to be Prime Minister. But when I think of Father and Austen, and reflect that less than 3 months of time, and no individual, stands between me and that office, I wonder whether Fate has some dark secret in store, to carry out her ironies to the end.

Not yet. On May 28 he kissed hands, and three days after, in taking over the party, paid tribute to Baldwin, whose friendship he had found a liberal education, whose " fundamental nobility of character " and discrimination between ephemeral and lasting values set him, as he had written years ago, in the same order as Lincoln. Of his own feelings, together with that declaration, already quoted, that without his wife this had never been achieved, he wrote thus : " it has come to me without my raising a finger to obtain it, because there is no one else, and perhaps because I have not made enemies by looking after myself rather than the common cause. . . . I wish our Bee could have lived to be aware of it, for it would have meant an enormous lot to her."

And this to the friend, and kinsman by marriage, in whose Dorset home and fishing he often had great happiness :

2 June ; to Sir Ernest Debenham

> I know you will rejoice that a Chamberlain of sorts has got the position that the others ought to have had. I have been given a good start, but I am not going to boast when I am putting on my armour.

CHAPTER XX

THE INTERNATIONAL LEGACY: 1936–1937

> The efforts and frequent failures of Your Majesty's servants
> in foreign affairs must be viewed with indulgence. It is their
> destiny to be always making bricks without straw.
>
> SALISBURY to QUEEN VICTORIA, *August* 1886

THE lot had not fallen to him in a fair ground. Though all was not lost between May 1936 and May 1937, all was in solution, and of no period, knowing what even now we know, is it more difficult justly to write the unfolding, or to judge the scene as it was, not as it became. Yet let us mark well three themes : the downfall of the League, the resurrection and consequent rivalry of Germany and Russia, and the first testing of that rivalry on the blood-soaked fields of Spain. To these we must relate the mind of British statesmen, Chamberlain among them, whose diary for July 1936 affirms " we have no policy ".

In the sky of Africa hung the forsaken star of collective security :

> Like a rich jewel in an Ethiop's ear,
> Beauty too rich for use, for earth too rare ;

and it shot forth two questions ; the one immediate, how to be rid of the Abyssinian war, and the other like unto it, how to ensure that the League should not incur such disaster again.

A day or two before Churchill advocated to the Conservative foreign affairs committee the dropping of sanctions, Chamberlain recorded his general ideas.

Diary, 27 April 1936
    the League had failed to stop the war, or to protect the victim, and had thereby demonstrated the failure of collective security, as now understood. This was because collective security depended on the individual action of members of the League, whose interests and capacities alike differed widely. Our ultimate aim must be some kind of international police force, but meantime we had to find some practical way of keeping the peace. My proposal was that we should abandon the idea that the League could at present use force. . . . It should be kept in being as a moral force and focus, but for peace we should depend on a system of regional pacts, to be registered and approved by the League. . . . I thought the proposal would make it

easier for Germany to come into the League, and I was anxious that Halifax should visit Berlin and get into touch with Hitler as soon as possible.

Much against the grain he came to one firm conclusion, that it was fantastic to prolong sanctions, designed to prevent war, when the war was over, and for that matter, now that we had refused to hear of sanctions against Germany, the French were more than ever determined to end those against Italy.   On June 10 he delivered his soul to the 1900 Club :

> There are some people who do not desire to draw any conclusions at all.   I see, for instance, the other day that the President of the League of Nations Union issued a circular to its members in which he . . . urged them to commence a campaign of pressure . . . with the idea that, if we were to pursue the policy of sanctions, and even to intensify it, it is still possible to preserve the independence of Abyssinia.   That seems to me the very midsummer of madness. . . . Is it not apparent that the policy of sanctions involves, I do not say war, but a risk of war ? . . . is it not also apparent from what has happened that, in the presence of such a risk, nations cannot be relied upon to proceed to the last extremity unless their vital interests are threatened ?   That being so, does it not suggest that it might be wise to explore the possibilities of localising the danger spots of the world . . . by means of regional arrangements, which could be approved by the League, but which should be guaranteed only by those nations whose interests were vitally connected with those danger zones ?

His diary elucidates the point of these, as he put it to his audience, " provisional conclusions ".

Diary, 17 June
> I did it deliberately because I felt that the party and the country needed a lead, and an indication that the government was not wavering and drifting without a policy. . . . I did not consult Anthony Eden, because he would have been bound to beg me not to say what I proposed. . . . He himself has been as nice as possible about it, though it is of course true that to some extent he has had to suffer in the public interest. . . . At the same time as I was urging on Anthony the reform of the League, I said sanctions must come to an end, but we ought first to have from Mussolini a statement of his intentions about Abyssinia and the Eastern Mediterranean.

It was indeed high time to have done with a policy of shams, as Canada had already decided in advance of the Imperial government.   In some quarters it was the fashion to speak of a betrayal.

Yet they might have reflected that Great Britain had initiated every forward step, and borne the economic brunt, as South Wales exports alone would show. They might have pondered why it was that Russia, whose sale of oil to Italy had risen sharply, had not proposed an oil sanction ; or why thirteen States had never even banned imports from Italy. But while Labour votes resisted Eden's plea for national unity in rearmament, they shared in the general ill-informed contempt for Italian arms.

14 June 1936 ; from Lord Cavan
My fear is that the public belittle the military power of Italy. . . . I assure you the public are wrong. I know Badoglio well, and look upon him as one of the best and greatest of living soldiers.

We have to go further and to admit that no British party sincerely adopted collective security. On the contrary, they all picked and chose among the causes they would secure. No retreat from Abyssinia, cried Lloyd George, yet in the same speech vowed the people would never fight " for an Austrian quarrel " ; just as all the next year Labour allowed that they would spring to arms to prevent a German aggression on Russia, or assist a Left-wing government of Spain against rebels, but emphatically not a Nazi government of Germany.

This downfall, just and inevitable from its abuse, of a rule of law left a void which, failing a new settlement, must soon be filled either by armed alliance or popular passion. That Chamberlain already realised this race against time may be judged from a remark on Hitler's agreement of July 1936 with Mussolini, which recognised an independent but " German " Austria. " I am glad of it ; I do not take Hitler's peace professions at their face value . . . once more we are given a little longer space in which to arm."

Meantime the lesser States made helter-skelter for safety. Scandinavia and the Low Countries, Spain and the Swiss, made it clear that the only League for them was a League in which great powers did the work, without any contribution from the small. The return of Belgium to neutrality was more serious. From the German occupation of the Rhineland King Leopold and most of his subjects deduced that the wise plan was to repudiate their duties under the treaty of Locarno ; they felt, and as it proved rightly, that Britain and France, in their own interest, would continue to guarantee their defence. If this left the rôle of the Belgian army uncertain in any future war, the Dutch added as it were a footnote, that they would have no foreign forces on their soil, no, not to vindicate the Covenant.

One element in Belgium's attitude was a fear of being drawn into war by the French-Soviet pact, and wherever we look Russia casts a huge shadow. Their hatred of the Soviet surpassed the Poles' dread of Germany; in the Regent Paul of Jugo-Slavia it heavily contributed to a swing-away from the Little Entente; it predisposed Italy to suspect the Left government of M. Blum; it coloured and prolonged the civil war in Spain. In 1936-7 this mighty State was passing through another act of its revolution, the life-blood of Lenin's old guard, generals, commissars, and technicians fertilising the soil from White Russia into Asia, and what, each general staff in Europe was asking, would be the effect on a force which was believed to have two million men under arms and the greatest air strength in the world?

So Russian and German power between them demolished the post-war supremacy of France, and in the racial mosaic that history has patterned between Baltic and Black Sea were ranged disunion and blindness. Still maltreating her minorities and still bickering with the Czechs, Poland wholly ignored the interests of the League in Danzig, with the Nazi government of which she was ready to make her own transaction. In this balancing policy the Poles found a partner in the unstable King Carol of Roumania, who this autumn ejected his foreign minister Titulescu from his long-held supremacy, which had been devoted to the French system, and together with the Jugo-Slavs resisted Beneš' endeavour to pull the old alliance together. Economically the Jugo-Slavs were fast bound to the Axis chariot wheels, though at the price of some rift between dynasty and people. The Czechs were therefore isolated and, fearful lest France had lost her ability to intervene, drew nearer to Russia whose aeroplanes, bound for Spain, could find on Czech aerodromes a convenient halting-place. But, indeed, that central European pact to resist Germany, for which France had worked so long, must always have been made almost impossible, by the Czech veto on any mention of a Hapsburg, and by the refusal of the Little Entente as a whole to meet Hungary's bitter lament for her lost territories.

If resistance there was to be in this part of Europe, it must include Italy; sanctions had gone, but was Mussolini willing to act as if they had never been? It was the belief of our diplomats on the spot that the Italians, in fear that a rearmed Britain would seek revenge for Abyssinia, would gladly patch up the old relations;

it was certain that Austria would be glad to see it, and counted on Italy for her protection. But what price must be paid for making Italy a satisfied power? " Lose no time ", her ambassador Grandi broke out to the Foreign Office. But endless time was being lost in Spain, where a war threatened of a type which had not scourged the world for a century, of rival ideas and an upheaval of society.

Every decisive principle of British policy in relation to that war was laid down before Chamberlain became Prime Minister, with unanimity in Cabinet and party; proceeding from Eden's view that intervention would be " bad humanity and bad politics ", or from Churchill's, that at all costs we must keep out of " this dismal welter ". The Opposition case was, first, that here was a mere military rebellion against a normally elected democratic government, to whom it was our duty to give arms, and, second, that the Axis powers were conducting a one-sided intervention; both these premises flew in the face of notorious fact. But if, then, this was a civil war, by all precedent we should have given belligerent rights to both sides alike, which would have saved our government from much later embarrassment, and was apparently the course they would have preferred. Yet to grant these rights would have assisted General Franco with his greater command of the sea and, moreover, it was held that the free flow of arms would have multiplied the possibility of a general conflagration. For the time being we therefore accepted the French proposal of " non-intervention ", to prevent all movement of men and material, and that being so Chamberlain pressed its application in full; to protect British shipping, for instance, outside but not within Spanish territorial waters, and to make it illegal for British ships to take arms to Spain, whether from British or foreign ports.

How " non-intervention " was evaded by Germany, Italy, and Portugal on one side, and by Russia and France on the other, is well known, though Eden was emphatic that what Chamberlain called " the façade " was essential to peace. Yet the effects of the Spanish war were vital, and not least because the rivals were contesting for the soul of France, where *gardes mobiles* watched great throngs greet Blum with the clenched fist salute and cries of " *des avions pour l'Espagne* ". This clamour at last touched Great Britain. In angry debate Labour went back on " non-intervention ", asserted the government wished for a Fascist victory, and put forward plans which would, in effect, have meant intervention on the Republican side. But Eden argued throughout that our genuine neutrality would be rewarded, for even a Franco Spain would cast out foreign domination.   So far as words went, the Anglo-Italian agreement of January 1937 pledged Mussolini expressly, that no change should be made in sovereignty within the Mediterranean.

From Germany all this time came no major move, nor was Spain an arena in which their high command would stake deep. There was a final repudiation of the " servitudes " of the peace of Versailles, though Hitler's speech of the same January added that the age of surprises was over.   Yet his own tone, as that of his advisers, both in public and aside, was confident and high ; sooner or later the " German " State of Austria must be absorbed, remedy must be found both for Danzig and the Sudeten of Bohemia, Germany must have colonies.   Communism was a plague with which he would have no contact, and on that ground he cold-shouldered the now dying negotiation for a " new Locarno ", — never, while France was bound to the Soviet.   His fixed creed and his armed might had sunk shafts into the rotten places of Europe, as none had done since Napoleon, so that rival leagues in France, Iron Guards in Roumania, Arrow Cross in Hungary, and the Spanish Falange, were pioneering his next advance.

The British aim, as defined by Eden, being " settlement and appeasement", it was they who insisted on prolonging the attempt at the " new Locarno ", nor was it by any means the government alone who wished to bring Germany to the council table.   Germany wished our friendship, declared Lloyd George, after seeing their leaders : Hitlerism, said Sinclair, was a revolt against humiliation. A great mass of opinion would have considered some colonial revision, on which Chamberlain added in debate, — a courageous speech, thought Lloyd George, — that it was impossible to bind ourselves in advance never to surrender a mandate ; privately writing, " I don't believe myself that we could purchase peace and a lasting settlement by handing over Tanganyika to the Germans, but if I did, I would not hesitate for a moment ".

Towards the end of 1936, in answer to a long campaign of abuse, Eden described the purposes for which British arms might be used.   Self-defence, the defence of France and Belgium against unprovoked aggression, maintenance of our treaties with Egypt and Iraq ; and, in addition, in cases where in their judgement it would be proper under the Covenant.   Such freedom of choice he defended, for " nations cannot be expected to incur automatic military obligations save for areas where their vital interests are concerned ". This left our policy regarding eastern Europe in the air, within negative limits which were underlined by Chamberlain in a speech for which Eden sent his thanks. " We should like to see an eastern European pact . . . we should not ourselves be parties to such a pact, but that does not mean that we give a free hand to any other country to do what it likes . . . we keep, in fact, a free hand to consider the circumstances and merits of the case."

To the French and Belgian pacts, which had carried us already beyond the commitments of 1914, he was himself always anxious to add a third, a regional pact for the Pacific, and Russian rearmament pleased him to this extent, that it might give pause to the Japanese militarists. This project, however, must involve joint action with America, whence he hoped that co-operation might come with more likelihood after Roosevelt's re-election. He had underrated the force of that isolationism. A Cabinet colleague brought back word that the President was " very friendly, very afraid of war, very anxious to avoid it if it came, but likely, if we should be involved, to be in it with us in a few weeks " ; yet even this dubious optimism was shattered by the Neutrality Act of May 1937, the gist of which would be to isolate America from war by surrendering a neutral's historic rights of trade. However, an aspiration for a Pacific pact was that month written in the recommendations of the Imperial Conference.

Scattered over his papers of those six months are gleams of his ruling ideas ; that war was neither imminent nor inevitable, that we could build on some civilian elements, such as the instability of German finance, which made it less likely ; that mere wounding words were best avoided ; and, as he assured Henderson, newly appointed ambassador to Berlin, that we should persistently rearm. He was not satisfied with the attitude of the Foreign Office, would have wished, too, a more direct approach to the dictators. Baldwin, however, had not encouraged suggestions that he should make them in person, disliking the notion of negotiation through an interpreter, and affirming that a parliamentary minister could not give binding pledges.

Looking back, we seem to find government and people caught up in three rival systems — collective security, alliances, and isolation ; with much of their respective dangers, but little of their benefit. The League, we insisted, must be kept in being, though reformed ; yet the honour of the League directly threatened the peace, for we had full warning that a refusal to admit the conquest of Ethiopia would drive Italy to leave it. That would make not one League but two, one at Geneva and another of the Axis, each composed of three great powers, and in the midst a knot of small States, some with their heads in the sand, others intently watching the rising sun.

Yet though our words and deeds proved distrust of collective security, we still declared for "a general settlement", while nothing was more abhorrent to the British mind than a return to alliances. Not merely did we refuse to divide mankind into "ideological" blocs, or to sharpen the Axis by fortifying a rival camp, but we discouraged France from opening staff talks with the Soviet and declined to enlarge our commitments by mediation between German and Czech.

So their proposition was just peace ; peace, Eden told the House, " at almost any price ". But two thoughts afflict us as to the timing of their policy. After long years of following France in the last resort, with the result of blocking every German aspiration till it was realised by force, we had sharply reacted ; if they wanted to be the gendarmes of eastern Europe, we implied to the French, on their head be it. And, again, how long could we keep Europe guessing for the meaning of our "free hand", when Russia was taking deep soundings, when Mussolini was posturing as a champion of Islam, and Hitler had staked his claim to embrace all men of German blood ?

We leave a troubled scene with some interviews recorded on two days of May 1937. The Turkish Prime Minister, seeking credits for armaments ; Delbos, French foreign minister, " profoundly suspicious of the Germans " ; Marshal von Blomberg, " who repeated all the Führer's views " ; Paul of Jugo-Slavia, bitterly anti-Italian but believing Germany could be won. And last, Hodza, Prime Minister of Czecho-Slovakia, whose recommendations were three : economic co-operation in the Balkans, " an improvement in Anglo-Italian relations, and, third, no provocation to Germany which might give her the pretext for an adventure ".

CHAPTER XXI

PRIME MINISTER AND HOME POLITICS:
1937–1939
AGED 68–70

A Minister of State must have a spirit of liberal economy,
not a restrained frugality. He must enlarge his Family
Soul, and suit it to the bigger compass of a kingdom.

GEORGE SAVILE, 1st Marquess of Halifax

FATE was now to produce the last of those ironies — if that is the
word — to which his family were used ; that, being perhaps better
equipped to lead a conservative reforming ministry than any man
since Gladstone, his three years were wholly spent in the shadow,
or the utter darkness, of war. On that dire period materials for
controversy abound, but not for final truth. While the historian
of the future will scan the archives of Whitehall, Moscow, or Washington, with all the private papers which will reveal reality, the true
margins of choice, and the faults of decision, all that at present we
can do, for this climax of his life, is to survey the scene through his
eyes and let him speak for himself.[1]

As Prime Minister, he was bound to be very different from
Baldwin, for more reasons than because they were such different
men, and the contrast was sharp. Masterful, confident, and ruled
by an instinct for order, he would give a lead, and perhaps impart
an edge, on every question. His approach was arduously careful
but his mind, once made up, hard to change ; he would make
relevance a fundamental and have the future mapped out and
under control, thus asking his departmental ministers to envisage
two-year programmes. His preparation for business was, no doubt,
complete. When he fell, his files are filled with thanks from colleagues for the weight and volume of his assistance ; " you cannot
know ", wrote Ernest Brown, " what a comfort it has been to hard-
pressed departmental ministers to know that, when their subjects
have to be discussed, whoever else has not read their papers and
digested them, one man had, — the Prime Minister ".

[For footnote see following page.]

This concentration of business on himself was equally apparent as regards both Parliament and public. As leader of the House, he rarely reached out to it as a whole, though when he did so he could do it well. There was his zeal over members' pensions, when he had come across cases of ex-members of the House in poverty ; " this is an opportunity for us to show our belief in that common bond which unites us all, and to pay our tribute to the democratic system of government of which this House is the representative ". Or there was the tribute to his old opponent George Lansbury, who died six months after the war began which they had equally detested ; in which he quoted a line that was to be written later in his own memorial, " I feel sure that in the angels' books his name will be found to be written like that of Abou Ben Adhem, as one who loved his fellow men ". But, as a rule, his combative intelligence could not pretend to sentiment which he did not share, or even to conceal a dislike that he felt. He showed, therefore, little of Baldwin's long-suffering with what the historian has called erring and straying men, and when he thought them wrong he hit them hard, as he had when Minister of Health. Whether their manner of debate had any right to resent his counter-offensive is another question, but in any case he drew their fire upon himself, and ever

¹ THE CHAMBERLAIN GOVERNMENT, MAY 1937–SEPTEMBER 1939

PRIME MINISTER :   Chamberlain.
CHANCELLOR OF THE EXCHEQUER : Simon.
LORD PRESIDENT :   Halifax (February 1938, Hailsham ;   October,
                          Runciman).
CHANCELLOR :   Hailsham (March 1938, Maugham).
LORD PRIVY SEAL :   De la Warr (October 1938, Anderson).
SECRETARIES OF STATE : *Home :* Hoare.
                          Foreign : Eden (February 1938, Halifax).
                          War : Hore-Belisha.
                          Colonies : Ormsby Gore (May 1938, MacDonald).
                          Dominions : MacDonald (February 1938, Lord
                          Stanley ;   October, MacDonald ;   January
                          1939, Inskip).
                          India : Zetland.
                          Air : Swinton (May 1938, Kingsley Wood).
                          Scotland : Elliot (May 1938, Colville).
ADMIRALTY :   Duff Cooper (October 1938, Stanhope).
BOARD OF TRADE :   Oliver Stanley.
HEALTH :   Kingsley Wood (May 1938, Elliot).
EDUCATION :   Stanhope (October 1938, De la Warr).
AGRICULTURE :   Morrison (January 1939, Dorman Smith).
LABOUR :   Ernest Brown.
CO-ORDINATION OF DEFENCE : Inskip (January 1939, Chatfield).
TRANSPORT :   Burgin (April 1939, Euan Wallace).
CHANCELLOR OF DUCHY : Winterton (January 1939, Morrison).
SUPPLY :   From July 1939, Burgin.

the more as they grew more passionate over what Eden called the war of the Spanish obsession. So that question-time became full of ragged, rankling scenes between Labour, with some angels on their side but also a good deal of cloud, and a Prime Minister sensitive, maligned, and therefore severe.

In a sense it was from the first a one-man government, for much as he relied on the judgement of Halifax, he had not in the Commons, as Baldwin had, someone like himself as second-in-command, on whom he would wholly depend. Nor was the figure of his successor plain for all men to see. On that point, when pressed by others, he would not yet pronounce, and if he gave Simon the Exchequer with the second place, it was not on that ground, nor by any means principally because it would please the National Liberal group. He could not see among his colleagues the man of destiny ; Hoare had never recaptured the ground he had lost, while he would lament that the younger men showed small sign of becoming elder statesmen. Did not Churchill write this summer of " a marked and felt dearth of men of high ability " ? Enough that in Simon he found a touch-stone, a critical brain of the first order ; for positive decision he would look to himself.

In a way curiously at variance with his strong views, his Cabinet-making was cautious in the extreme, for till change was enforced by the resignation of Eden and Swinton he made none of substance, and those made thereafter opened up no new avenue. When he brought back Runciman and offered place to Samuel, there were no doubt special reasons to enlarge national unity, but the fact remained that his party, which was filled with a deep regard for himself, had little for most of the leading figures about him. And as, by the testimony of friend and foe, he stood head and shoulders above them, the result, taken with a series of hard, dividing decisions, was to intensify his solitariness as spearhead and target.

From the more " political " of his supporters rose sometimes the same complaint as we can read in profusion about Pitt or Peel, of lack of the common touch, an austerity in largesse and honours, a disposition to trust a narrow circle. But though anything like organised effort failed to break the ice, in small gatherings, in his own house or in political clubs, he won admiring devotion from younger men who had eyes to recognise virtue, and whose chief criticism was that he was too clean a man for the lower side of politics. In public life the whole party, after years of inter-mittent vision and good intent, responded to a positive lead, watching in admiration his ceaseless toil and ubiquity. He kept his hand to the end on the lever of Midland politics also, while he found and encouraged someone who could develop his creation of party research in R. A. Butler, who has described his shy gratitude for work done as one of his most endearing characteristics.

As men got close to him, which was not easy, they felt in the presence of a moral greatness, as an extract may show from letters written by two Cabinet colleagues when he died. So, from one angle, Oliver Stanley : " there were times when I differed from him in matters of policy, but what always struck me was he never resented honest differences, and indeed welcomed and encouraged expressions of opinion. The courage with which he bore the collapse of his high hopes of Munich, and later the collapse of his dreams of peace and progress, was almost unbelievable. . . . In Cabinet he was cool, decided, clear, and above all never complacent." To that courage and magnanimity Zetland bore testimony too : " he was grievously provoked by some of his colleagues, but I never knew him bear malice or say a bitter word, however grievous the provocation ".

To the people, until the days of emergency, he presented his office on a more narrow front than had Baldwin, as he himself knew and, in a measure, designed : writing that he had made it plain " I can't do all the things that S. B. did, as well as all the things he didn't do, and I consider that at present at any rate the latter are more important ". He realised it was inevitable that he should lose some of Baldwin's Liberal support, but hoped to recoup it by energising his own party.

When he won public acceptance, it was very grateful to him. From his welcome at Birmingham as its first Prime Minister, he wrote, " it reminded me of old days when the people used to run after Father's carriage . . . it does warm one's heart to feel that these people have given one their confidence so freely ", and up to or after March 1938, bye-elections and party unity in the House bore him up. That month a round-robin, collected haphazard from some 150 Conservative members who chanced to be in the House, in wishing him joy of his sixty-ninth birthday assured him of their whole-hearted confidence ; the fourth name on that list was that of Churchill.

Here, assuredly, was the most vital omission from his Cabinet, though one not to be judged in 1937 from the same angle as it might be in the Munich days and after. Party memories are long, sometimes too long, and if they all did not reach back twenty years to the Asquith government, many Conservatives would remember the

MUSIC: WITH SIR HUGH ALLEN, AT THE
UNIVERSITY OF READING

opposition to the Baldwin régime of 1931. Such considerations, necessarily conveyed to a Prime Minister, found others, some of which we met long ago, in Chamberlain's mind, though here there was not an iota of that personal feeling which severed him from Lloyd George. So that the earliest date at which " reconstruction " in that sense would have been approved was perhaps in May 1938.

With the reshuffles of 1938, however, we pass into a second phase, directly connected with new conflicts of policy, and including the loss of two nearer associates. In May Swinton resigned. If it were taken as implying censure on his administrative success, it was unjust ; substantially, he fell victim to the national anxiety as to Air progress, military and civil, and to the Commons' often demonstrated instinct that the minister directing a department, which is so deep in controversy that out of it a rival government may be born, must be on their own bench to face the fire. In October Hailsham, after two years of struggle against bad health, went also.

There were good judges who felt that, as he grew older, he was reverting to the Radical temper of his upbringing, for his choice both of measures and men implied that he sat loosely to party, and had not ceased to be a progressive reformer. But he worked in a state of siege, so that it is needless to examine measures stifled by the approach of war. His first session saw the last stages of the " black coat " Insurance Act, an immense consolidating Factory Act, and his own physical training Act. Faithful to one of his early Birmingham enthusiasms, he had a large hand in constructing the White Paper on milk, — a subject that always leads to sour parliamentary strife, — instructed his Minister of Transport to decide if he wanted a Charing Cross bridge or not, and three months before Munich was full of a vast scheme ; " a central authority to act at once as an information bureau, with special regard to the location of industry, and as a central planning body for the country as a whole. . . . It would do what nobody does now, or in fact has power to do, namely, consider the claims of agriculture, which seems to be invariably sacrificed to ' development ', of whatever character that may be." That summer, after stiff opposition in the Lords, the Coal Bill passed, nationalising royalties and permitting compulsory amalgamation. A new Housing Bill concentrated the subsidy on slum clearance and overcrowding ; Hoare moved a criminal justice bill, which voiced a whole change of public sentiment in regard to the very meaning of crime and punishment. But there were three matters, each in itself enough in ordinary days to monopolise a Cabinet, which touched him more nearly.

Though Opposition and economists, with varying shades of sorrow, predicted another depression, and though in America many millions of unemployed men, and in France many more millions of frightened money, signified a world still unordered, Great Britain on the whole held her own, till all was overcast by fear of war. But it was seen, in America and the Dominions especially, that without more restoration of international trade the practical limits had been reached of national recovery, a conclusion which must impinge upon Chamberlain's achievement at Ottawa. Though our imports from the Dominions had risen sharply, they had never ceased to jib at our quantitative restrictions, and Mackenzie King's renewed tenure of power meant a more open outlook to the United States. In this general rending of the strait-jackets in which the nations encased themselves in 1931 Chamberlain himself shared, a candid and much criticised speech at Kettering in 1938 revealing to the now stalwart agricultural interest that he put industrial recovery as high in the scale as the English farmer.

From out of such feeling and experience came the Anglo-American and Canadian-American trade treaties, which after hard bargaining were signed in November 1938. Economically they must bear considerable fruit, as between two commonwealths covering a third of world trade, as well for the reason that they reacted markedly from some of the Ottawa arrangements ; if Britain dropped the duty on American wheat, the United States lowered duties on almost a third of British exports. But in Chamberlain's mind, as in Cordell Hull's, there was a political motive also. " The reason ", he wrote a year before signature, " why I have been prepared (*pace* Amery and Page Croft) to go a long way to get this treaty, is precisely because I reckoned it would help to educate American opinion to act more and more with us, and because I felt sure it would frighten the totalitarians. Coming at this moment, it looks just like an answer to the Berlin-Rome-Tokyo axis."

There was a second question in which American opinion was almost as deeply, but less contentedly, excited. This was the mandate for Palestine, where for twenty years Great Britain had been endeavouring to reconcile two perfect incompatibles, the sonorous Balfour declaration and the earlier, equally solemn, pledge to the Arabs. For, when translated into fact, the conception of a Jewish national home clashed with the ordinary British principle, that self-government means the rule of a numerical majority. Here, as elsewhere, Hitlerism had probed the world's softest surface.

Refugees from the terror flocked to the Holy Land, in such a spate that it was reckoned the Jewish population would equal the Arab within a quarter of a century. It was not a question which Britain could afford to take lightly on any ground, political or strategic or economic, and against American goodwill must be poised the whole Muslim world. Meantime an industrial revolution swelled the original racial strife, and atrocities stained both parties, while behind barbed-wire lines such scanty British battalions as could be scraped together protected a mandate, every principle of which was in dispute, and the patrimony of the Prince of Peace.

This second Ireland heavily tested our institutions. After two enquiries, after first accepting and then rejecting a partition of Palestine, the Chamberlain government acted decisively by bringing Egypt, Iraq, and the Arab world into their consultations, and hence came about the London conference of February 1939, at which Chamberlain presided but of which Malcolm MacDonald bore the brunt. It could not find an agreed solution and therefore, in the White Paper of May, imposed one, by which the Jews would become a definite, though a protected, minority in an Arab State. On all this nothing survives in his papers, save a tribute to MacDonald's inexhaustible patience, and a stark comment on the tone of the Arab delegations.

In Palestine British failure had endured twenty years, but in Ireland for over four hundred, and since 1932 De Valera had proved that Ireland was not content with the Dominion status given her by Lloyd George. Ruling that his country was independent and indivisible, he swept away every link and symbol of British sovereignty, while in the name of his twenty-six counties he repudiated the severance of the six in the north. But there were restraining factors, even on the most austere ideal. Ireland was poor, economically dependent on Great Britain, and by temporary measures from 1935 onwards part of the trade was restored which their tariff war had destroyed. Ireland, again, was a small nation, which without Great Britain must succumb to any foreign invasion.

Before becoming Prime Minister, Chamberlain set himself to get conversations on foot, which might end the economic strains and put the two countries on some defensible basis. When in January 1938 these reached the dignified stage of a conference, it was not probable that British opinion would boggle long over land annuities, or tariffs, if measured against a satisfied Commonwealth ; though if that satisfaction involved an attack upon partition, against the will of Ulster, there was no more to be said.

Furthermore, there was the demand that the three Irish ports, which were reserved to Great Britain for security in 1921, should now be put in Irish hands. As to this, it was revealed, years later, by one of his colleagues and by one who had been chief of the naval staff, on what solid grounds of advice the government reached their decision : [1] that no forces could be spared for the protection of these ports, and that they were commanded, and even dependent for their water supply, from the land behind them.

His first impressions in the conference show how large were his hopes.

23 January 1938

I shall be grievously disappointed if we don't get an all-round agreement, on everything except partition. That is a difference that can't be bridged without the assent of Ulster, and her assent won't be given unless she has confidence in the Government of Eire, and that cannot be attained except slowly and step by step. But if De Valera will heed the good advice I gave him, I should not despair of ultimate agreement on unity, and in the meantime I am satisfied that, queer creature as he is in many ways, he is sincere, and that he is no enemy of this country.

In April agreement was reached, spurred on by the fall of Austria and Chamberlain's feeling that agreement with Ireland would be felt at Berlin ; it included a surrender of the ports, a trade agreement, and a payment by Eire of £10 millions as against much larger British claims. His conversations with De Valera encouraged him in believing that our trust would be rewarded ; he would, for instance, himself have been ready to set up munition works in Ireland, remote from danger of air warfare. Though he had his disappointment in 1940, it is only by time that his whole argument can be judged.

13 March 1938

I shall be accused of having weakly given way, when Eire was in the hollow of my hand. Only I and my colleagues (who are unanimous) can judge of this, but I am satisfied that we have only given up the small things (paper rights, and revenues which would not last) for the big things, — the ending of a long quarrel, the beginning of better relations between North and South Ireland, and the co-operation of the South with us in trade and defence. It is possible that the Austrian

[1] See the letters of Lord Chatfield (February 6, 1942) and of Lord Stanhope (February 11, 1942) to *The Times*.

incident may help me in bringing home to people here and Ulster, that this is no time for keeping open old sores.

Here, perhaps, part of a letter of sympathy, written two years after, best finds its place.

15 May 1940 ; from Eamon De Valera
I would like to testify that you did more than any former British Statesman to make a true friendship between the peoples of our two countries possible, and, if the task has not been completed, that it has not been for want of goodwill on your part.   I hope that you may still be able to work for, and that we may both be spared to see, the realisation of our dream, — to see our two peoples living side by side with a deep neighbourly sense of their value one to another, and with a friendship which will make possible whole-hearted co-operation between them in all matters of common interest.

So the heir of Joseph Chamberlain and Parnell's inheritor threw another bridge over that ancient gulf.

Of private life he had little after the new year of 1938 ; sold his London house, but found instead at Chequers an abiding joy, making himself master of its treasures, and for ever at work to plant and improve.   Concentrated work seemed to have redoubled his vigour.   He would take his Chequers policeman six-mile walks across country, in his seventieth year could shoot all day and then go on to fish by moonlight, and when that birthday passed spoke of " at least one more parliament ".

Till the end of his first year as Prime Minister he was justly assured of his hold on Cabinet, House, and people, only quarrelling with a tendency in a few of his colleagues not to think first " is this right, but how will this affect the House of Commons or my constituents ?   my method is to try and make up my own mind first as to the proper course, and then try and put others through the same course of reasoning ".

We have now to watch the application of this process to men and causes more impervious to reason.

CHAPTER XXII

REARMAMENT

A statesman who would lead his age must learn its duties. It
may be that the defence of England, the military defence,
is one of our duties. If so, we must not sit down to count
the cost. If so, it is not the age for arithmetic.

BAGEHOT

BEHIND his foreign policy lay one plain argument, which he felt
passionately but of which, till a late date, Opposition and critics
took small heed, that policy must depend on power. If that were
accepted, it followed that British policy could not embrace both
the defence of her own Empire in all seas, and a collective security
for all lands, until we had rearmed. What rearmament meant,
and his part in it, must therefore be outlined, before we discuss
the policy which by the degree of that rearmament was throughout
conditioned.

No man could feel more disgust at diverting all the national
resources to destruction, or the peril to the financial stability which
he had laboured to restore, yet on the evidence of his papers, and
by testimony of those immediately concerned, the initiative and
determinate decisions in rearmament were chiefly his. But rearmament on a large scale had been dangerously postponed.

It will be remembered how warning reached us from Berlin
in 1933 that Germany had for some years been building aeroplanes ;
how Chamberlain in 1934 initiated the first serious expansion of
the Air Force ; how in May 1935 Baldwin admitted they had much
underestimated the rate of German air progress ; and how in the
autumn of that year Chamberlain wished to fight the election,
first and foremost, on Defence. Why that was not done was first
explained by Baldwin to the Commons in a famous speech of
November 1936. To have asked a mandate for rearmament from
this pacific democracy, he said, would have made loss of the election
certain, and hence, he implied, postponed rearmament all the more,
— to which he added a little later that to re-educate democracy
involved a lag of two years, perhaps, behind a dictator.

His successor's immediate comment on that speech changes
the ground, without vastly improving it. " That was frank, and
had a good deal of truth in it, though not all the truth. S. B. had

forgotten, or did not choose to mention, the long period occupied in examining the deficiencies and drawing up a new programme, which in turn had to be reviewed and revised (mostly by me !). So far as I can remember without having looked it up, that took nearly the whole of 1934, and it was not until 1935 that we knew what we wanted to do. To the best of my recollection we then started on the programme, but we did not tell the public except in the most general terms until after the election. . . . I did not like S. B.'s 'frankness'. I thought it a terrible confession of weakness."

Certainly all this would have been different if he had had his way, and if that election of 1935 had been fought on Defence ; different, we may well think, even had they been beaten. But, things being as they were, we have again to recall the rôle of Opposition in the two first years of rearmament. Having savagely criticised "war-mongering" during the election, they went on to denounce an armaments race and to vote against the White Paper of 1936, and not till July 1937 did the more robust sections of their opinion prevail and the Labour majority cease to oppose the estimates.

Translated into terms of finance, Defence expenditure rose from its lowest point of £102 millions in 1932 to some £188 millions in 1936, £280 millions in 1937, and in 1939 at least £700 millions. How sudden was the leap in Chamberlain's diagnosis of emergency may be judged by the short space between August 1935, when his private estimate was something over £120 additional millions in the next few years, and February 1937, when the White Paper spoke of £1500 millions. Certainly he grew critical of the intelligence which they received from abroad, in particular as regards the German power of industrial expansion.

When this enlarged programme was first putting its head out of the departmental burrows and coming into the open, his papers show the ruling ideas which he put to the Defence committee of Cabinet.

The first months of 1936 passed without much progress ; " I was avoiding coming out into the open, since I was rather afraid that it would be thought I was merely advocating the cheapest way of defence, instead of the best ". But he felt his conclusion must squarely be faced, that Great Britain must limit the size of the army to be committed to a Continental war.

9 February

I have had to do most of the work on the programme, which has been materially modified as a result, and I am pretty satisfied now that, if we can keep out of war for a few years, we shall have an air force of such striking power that no one will care to run risks with it. I cannot believe that the next war, if it ever comes, will be like the last one, and I believe our resources will be more profitably employed in the air, and on the sea, than in building up great armies.

Great public servants are not immune from men's common satisfaction with their own creation, and some of those who had saved the State in the last war found no flaw in our present structure of defence. He disagreed with them, pressed on the lessons already learned in the course of expansion, impelled the decision to create a Minister for Co-ordination of Defence ; writing in that same February that rapid action was vital, " we have already dallied far too long ". He had, before this, arranged that Arthur Robinson, once his permanent secretary at the Ministry of Health, should become chairman of the Supply Board under the Committee of Imperial Defence.

Yet another year passed by before he achieved something like general acceptance of his principles, in which the interests of allies, problems of recruitment, and professional pride were all mingled, so that the first stages brought many set-backs and searchings of heart.

Diary, 25 October 1936

I must really have some decision as to the future function of the regular and territorial armies. . . . In my view, apart from any other considerations, we had not the man-power to produce the necessary munitions for ourselves and perhaps, if U.S.A. stood out, for our Allies, to man the enlarged Navy, the new Air Force, and a million-men Army. . . . We should aim at an Army of 4 divisions plus 1 mobile division, and the necessary drafts to maintain its strength, and no more for overseas work. . . . Territorials should be kept for A.A. defence.

In the letter already quoted, in regard to Baldwin's explanation of their late start, he set forth other parallel arguments :

If we were now to follow Winston's advice and sacrifice our commerce to the manufacture of arms, we should inflict a certain injury on our trade from which it would take generations to recover, we should destroy the confidence which now happily exists, and we should cripple the revenue. . . . The one criticism which has, I think, something to be said for it is that Tom [Inskip] is so occupied with supply that he has no time to attend to strategy. This is not quite true, and moreover is founded on the belief of Winston that the

Minister should himself be a strategist. . . . I consider that to be a false conception of his duties, which are rather to see that strategical problems are fairly and thoroughly worked out by the strategists. The most important of these, in my view, is the function of the Army and the Territorials in a major war or, to put it in another way, the best distribution at the outset of a major war of our man-power between the services and the supply of munitions.

The brown owl, which by token of the same letter was talking to himself in Downing Street, went on talking for more than a year before his audience got this decision which, he wrote in February 1937, gave him all he wanted. The regular Army, " armed cap-à-pie with the most modern equipment ", was to be ready " to go anywhere anytime ", while the supporting Territorial divisions, similarly equipped to go overseas, were to be limited to two. " The War Office have renounced all idea of a Continental army on the scale of 1914–18."

There was another military decision in which his part was paramount. The Board of Admiralty had never become reconciled to the control of the Fleet Air Arm by the Air Ministry ; a departmental war, he wrote, which " has been allowed to go on much too long ", showed plenty of vitality. The compromise which he brought about, and announced as Prime Minister, was based on what, to the layman, seems a defensible distinction, between shore-based aircraft and planes carried by ships of the fleet.

Here we may diverge to examine problems and progress in the light of the White Papers of 1936–8, of the first two of which he was chief architect, and for the last bore final responsibility. The pitch of armament from which they sprang was low in the extreme. Tied till the end of 1936 by the London treaty, we had 15 capital ships (3 only of post-war construction) as against 69 in 1914, and 50 cruisers as against 108. The Army was 20,000 below establishment, the Territorial Force 40,000, while the Air Force was lagging dangerously behind a German front-line strength which high authority put at 1500.

It was one merit in the programme of 1936 that it was a balanced whole, capable of variation and adjustment. Its proposals were large. A rebuilding of the battle fleet, an increase of cruisers up to 70, replacement of destroyer strength ; an increase in front-line numbers of the Home Air Force, from the 1500 planned in 1935 to 1750, exclusive of the Fleet Air Arm ; modernisation of the Army, and recruitment of four new battalions. By 1938 a good deal had been done. The tonnage building included 7 battleships,

5 aircraft carriers, 24 cruisers, and 40 destroyers. The Air programme of 1935 had been some time passed, the Air Force re-equipped with modern machines, its volunteer reserve established, in May powers were taken to raise the Home front-line strength again, to 2370, while during the year production of all types of planes was perhaps doubled. The Territorial Force recruited 45,000 men in 1937 and 77,000 in 1938. From the Air Raids Precautions Act of 1937 would develop all the detail of civil defence, the storage had begun of oil fuel, food, and raw material, food rationing was prepared, foundations were laid for a Ministry of Economic Warfare.

His papers hereafter will shed some light on that lag in rearmament which perpetually perturbed the country, and materially assisted to bring his government down, though inevitably the full facts are, more than in any branch of this study, as yet unpublished. But even on the surface of the subject a few general considerations explain a good deal.

There was, first, the fact that modern warfare lives by machines, and that machines are not created without machine tools ; here we had dissipated our old power, everything had to be imported, remodelled, or remade. Again, they were living between two mechanical ages, in the middle of a technical revolution, which applied especially to the air world, changing over as it was from wood and fabric to all-metal, or from biplane to monoplane. This revolution embraced a matter of method that touched the very shape of society ; as compared with the modern mass production of America and Germany, British mechanical industry was still individualised, highly finished in quality, but comparatively slow. Finally, they were working in obedience to financial and military advices which must in themselves limit any mass development. It was held very strongly that financial stability was our fourth, and final, military arm, that we must balance our Budgets, and avoid interference with the export trade as long as possible. It being held equally strongly that our military-political rôle must be defensive, our air experts were legislating for a force that would act principally as a deterrent against sudden aggression.

Comparatively speaking, there was little difference of opinion about the Navy, nor ever much doubt, despite some bottle-necks in production of its armament, that the programme would meet most ascertainable purposes in the event of war. The Army, on the other hand, was the Cinderella of their general views, as his diary has shown, had sat too long by a cold hearth, and suffered longest from the financial inhibitions to which, part unconsciously.

they deferred. But though, as the saying of that day went, there were to be " no more Passchendaeles ", what Army there was was to be brought up to date. He sent Hore-Belisha to the War Office on the express ground that he wished to see " drastic changes ", writing " the obstinacy of some of the Army heads in sticking to obsolete methods is incredible ". And much of substance was accomplished ; in giving authority to younger men, in bringing Army commands into closer touch with the War Office, improving the prospects before combatant officers, or cutting away some obstacles to recruitment.

But no question what was judged most vital, and in fact best realised, was that " fighting air force " on which he had been set since 1934, and in regard to which the time factor might make the difference between life and death. Two at least of its planned objectives were faithfully fulfilled. It was to be a separate arm, something more than an agency for army co-operation or the eyes of a fleet. But it was designed to fight alongside a French air force, and to operate from French air-fields, in beating off a German attack ; as it did in the end, though without either of those advantages. Nor again did the final volume of aircraft production fall, probably, very short of the standard which throughout they aimed at reaching within a year of the outbreak of war. Criticism fastens, rather, on the intermediate stages after the beginnings in 1935.

The achievement of the Air Ministry and Air Staff under Swinton was indeed of supreme merit and importance. They were not working in an atmosphere of total war ; however " air-minded " the Treasury, its maxims rather seem to have restrained the industry and sometimes left it asking for orders, till the spring of 1938 ; moreover, the very insistence upon high quality incurred risks of delay. But their performance and their decisions were equally vital. The Merlin engine and the Spitfire, the eight-gun fighter, and the first powerful bombers were their doing. They took designs from the drawing-board without waiting for test prototypes ; they faced up to, and settled, the great dilemma whether to build up huge reserves, that might become obsolete, or to frame an industrial potential that could switch over from peace to war. Yet when Swinton resigned, the gap between British and German production still existed, was thought indeed to be actually widening, and indispensable though were the " shadow " factories that his ministry devised, they represented rather an extension of a skilled craft than a total harnessing of industry to war production.

M

It was then within the limits of that earlier conception, of a rearmament not destructive to general industry, that we find Chamberlain taking vigorous action. Late in 1937, after interviewing the aircraft producers, he appointed the Bank of England's industrial adviser as their whole-time chairman, and early in 1938 set up a supply Board under the Air Council with large powers of financial anticipation. The same year he strengthened his own hand by appointing the Prime Minister's advisory panel of industrialists, who were empowered to survey progress, detect delay, and suggest remedies to himself. Missions also were sent to North America to enlarge our field of supply. But, on the whole, as might indeed have been expected, it was not till the summer of 1938, or the third year after the beginning, that the really substantial expansion began to flow.

In the second year of Inskip's tenure, and the first of Chamberlain's premiership, the departmental strains he had known of old crop up again in his papers. For if it was originally contemplated that Inskip's chief task would be to smoothe out priorities or co-ordinate strategy, in practice his time was more and more engulfed in production, a question of supply in which the Army felt a need of new machinery which the Navy and Air Force did not. The controversy that emerged, whether or no to establish a Ministry of Supply, lasted over two years. On any theory of limited military liability such a step was judged needless, and one which he at least was determined, as he was in regard to conscription, not to take till we entered a definite zone of war. Besides, his technical advisers were emphatic that the Services were much better related to supply than in 1914 ; that each Service could do better, as in Germany, by organising its own supply sections than through some omnibus ministry, the very making of which, they argued, must mean an immediate delay. He put the gist of his case in the debates of May 1938, when the air programme was under severe scrutiny. " Although in actual war a Ministry of Supply would be essential, — and indeed we have all the plans ready . . . I do not believe that a Ministry of Supply in peace-time will be effective, as the Ministry of Munitions was effective in the great war, unless you give that Ministry of Supply the same powers " ; compulsory powers, that is, over production, trade unions, and strikes ; these he doubted whether they would be given, or ought to be, in time of peace. (Yet, over a year before, German officials had been instructed to the effect that the condition of Europe was " *krieg in permanenz* ", — an undeclared but standing war.)

When in time of peace he refused to consider industrial conscription, it was not from political fears. He put it to the House that, provided we could avoid a knock-out blow, " wars are won not only now with arms and men, they are won with the reserves of resources and credit ", by staying power. That was the moral of the objectives, as he described them, in due order, of all their armament : " (1) the security of the United Kingdom . . . the resources of man-power, productive capacity, and endurance of this country, and unless these can be maintained not only in peace but in the early stages of war, our defeat is certain ; (2) trade routes ; (3) defence of British territories overseas ; not as vital as the defence of our own country, because as long as we are undefeated at home, although we sustained losses overseas, we might have an opportunity of making them good hereafter ; (4) co-operation, and the defence of the territories of any Allies ". He held this belief, not from insularity nor as a man primarily an economist, but from the convictions he had imbibed as to the nature of the next war.

This was his horizon, as to one part of the double task so long envisaged. He had written of it, privately, when first his government began : " I believe the double policy of rearmament and better relations with Germany and Italy will carry us safely through the danger period, if only the Foreign Office will play up ".

CHAPTER XXIII

FOREIGN AFFAIRS

> We had been warned that Christianity could know no
> neutrality, and history had verified the warning. It was
> incapable of co-existing permanently with a civilisation
> which it did not inspire. . . . His voice and manner, as
> these reflections developed, grew heavily oppressed, and
> his eyes — looking out upon the sunlit sea beneath him —
> seemed to be filled with a vision of gloom.
>
> LADY GWENDOLEN CECIL, *Salisbury*

THE man deceives himself who professes that in 1937 he foresaw
the decrees of Providence for 1939–41. It was not given to any
to foretell at once that the French State would crumble at a blow,
that Germany and Russia would agree to partition Poland, that
the United States would watch the disappearance of France and
the probable defeat of Britain, that Hitler would attack Russia,
that the Russian army would show itself the greatest in the world,
or that Japan would attack the United States. That lack of pre-
dictiveness cannot be the charge laid on Neville Chamberlain,
whose supreme endeavour was to prevent such things being tested,
or coming to pass.

His fundamental was an old ideal, the "appeasement of Europe"
for which all British policy had worked, with such ill success, since
the last war. Nor did his maxims differ at all from Eden's expressions in the first part of the Spanish war, as that "war settles
nothing", or "a war postponed may be a war averted". Yet
since, unlike Eden and half his Cabinet, he belonged to an older
generation who had not seen comrades fall in action at their side,
his motives bore a different emphasis, in one sense more restricted,
but in another more free from some of the post-war illusion or
disillusion.

He spoke of war with the repulsion common to Gladstone and
his father's generation, as of a barbarity outworn. War, he said,
"wins nothing, cures nothing, ends nothing" : or again, of the
last war, "when I think . . . of the 7 million of young men who
were cut off in their prime, the 13 million who were maimed and
mutilated, the misery and the sufferings of the mothers or the
fathers . . . in war there are no winners, but all are losers ". As
always, he spoke his mind most freely to a Birmingham audience.

To me [he told them in April 1938] the very idea that the hard-won savings of our people, which ought to be devoted to the alleviation of suffering, to the opening out of fresh institutions and recreations, to the care of the old, to the development of the minds and bodies of the young, — the thought that these savings should have to be dissipated upon the construction of weapons of war is hateful and damnable. Yet . . . we have no alternative but to go on with it, because it is the very breath of our British being, our freedom itself, that is at stake. . . . We pass no judgement here upon the political system of other countries, but neither Fascism nor Communism is in harmony with our temper and creed. . . . And yet . . . do not forget that we are all members of the human race, and subject to the like passions and affections, and fears and desires. There must be something in common between us if only we can find it, and perhaps by our very aloofness from the rest of Europe we may have some special part to play as conciliator and mediator. An ancient historian once wrote of the Greeks that they had made gentle the life of the world. . . . I can imagine no nobler ambition for an English statesman than to win the same tribute for his own country.

To the core of his being he felt the meaning of modern war, whose worst blows would fall on old people and children, degrading them to the burrowing life of hunted animals. No such war, he argued, must be asked of their people, " unless you feel yourself, and can make them feel, that the cause for which they are going to fight is a vital cause, — a cause that transcends all the human values, a cause to which you can point, if some day you win the victory, and say ' the cause is safe ' ". That thought never left him in his sternest endeavour. " I remember him saying," Lord Zetland wrote in a letter already quoted, " after he had flown back from Germany, that as he saw spread out like a map beneath him the mile upon mile of flimsy houses which constituted the East End of London, he could not bear to think of their inmates lying a prey to bombardment from the air." In pursuit of that purpose he would persist, though he was accused of " whining to Mussolini " ; " gibes and taunts of that kind leave me absolutely unmoved . . . let us rather ask ourselves whether what we are doing is right ".

Though he felt that the dictators had reason to ask the remedy of some grievances, and though like Canning (whose life he was carefully studying) he would not divide Europe between sheep and goats, he had no more sympathy with dictatorship than any other Englishman, and had his *ne plus ultra* lines they should not pass.

I have no bias in favour of Nazism, Fascism, or Bolshevism, because all of them seem to me inconsistent with what is all-important to me, because it is the root of my political creed, and that is individual liberty. . . . For the preservation of democracy, which means the preservation of our liberty, I myself would fight.

So he outlined his principles in public, but for this outlook we turn to two intimate documents of the early months of 1938.

This is the first entry in his diary since becoming Prime Minister nine months before :

Diary, 19 February 1938

From the first I have been trying to improve relations with the 2 storm centres, Berlin and Rome. It seemed to me that we were drifting into worse and worse positions with both, with the prospect of having ultimately to face 2 enemies at once. France, though very deeply attached to her understanding with us, has been in a terribly weak condition, being continually subject to attacks on the franc . . . together with industrial troubles and discontent which seriously affects her production of all kinds, and particularly of arms and equipment. The U.S.A. has drawn closer to us, but the isolationists there are so strong and so vocal that she cannot be depended on for help if we should get into trouble. Again, our own armament programme continued to grow, and to pile up our financial commitments to a truly alarming extent . . . the annual cost of maintenance, after we had finished rearmament, seemed likely to be more than we could find without heavily increased taxation for an indefinite period.

A month earlier he put to an American citizen, a cousin of his stepmother, some of the canons, with special reference no doubt to her country, by which he walked in this period of gaining time.

16 January 1938 ; to Mrs. Morton Prince, Boston, Massachusetts

. . . I am just now in closer relations with the American Government than has been the case within my recollection. I have made more than one attempt, while I have been Prime Minister, to draw them even closer still and I have had more than one disappointment. But I fully recognise that goodwill on the part of the U.S. Government is not wanting, the trouble is that public opinion in a good part of the States still believes it possible for America to stand outside Europe and watch it disintegrate, without being materially affected herself. I can well understand that frame of mind, and the fate of Spain and China does not invite any country to risk being involved in such miseries if she can avoid it. Indeed, we have a similar school of thought here. . . . Yet, though many people are haunted by a constantly recurring fear of war, we are too close to the danger spots for any but a few cranks to hope that we could remain safe in isolation. We are a very rich and a very vulnerable Empire, and there are plenty of poor adventurers not very far away who look on us with hungry eyes.

In spite of my disappointment, I intend to keep on doing everything I can to promote Anglo-American understanding and co-operation. Not because I want or expect America to pull our chestnuts out of the fire for us; in any co-operation we shall always do our part, and perhaps more than our share. But I believe that Americans and British want the same fundamental things in the world, peace, liberty, order, respect for international obligations, freedom for every country to devote all its resources to the improvement of the conditions of its own people, instead of being forced to pile armaments on its own back 'til it comes near to breaking. I believe that these things must be wanted too by Germans, Italians, Russians, and Japanese. But those people are in the grip of their governments, and in some cases the Governments are so constituted that they must maintain their prestige or die. They cannot afford to admit a mistake, their power is so great that they are tempted to use it to increase their prestige without regard to ultimate consequences. They pay no heed to reason, but there is one argument to which they will always give attention, and that is force. U.S.A. and U.K. in combination represent a force so overwhelming that the mere hint of the possibility of its use is sufficient to make the most powerful of dictators pause, and that is why I believe that co-operation between our two countries is the greatest instrument in the world for the preservation of peace, and the attainment of those objects of which I spoke just now.

Unhappily France keeps pulling her own house down about her ears. We are on excellent terms with her. With the Chautemps government which has just fallen we found ourselves in general agreement about all aims and objects. But France's weakness is a public danger just when she ought to be a source of strength and confidence, and as a friend she has two faults which destroy half her value. She never can keep a secret for more than half an hour, nor a government for more than nine months !

Meanwhile, as a realist, I must do what I can to make this country safe. The calm, the good sense, and the courage of the English people are amazing. They are never rattled, and they seem by some instinct to sift the situation and pick out the salient points. They are perfectly aware that, until we are fully rearmed, our position must be one of great anxiety. They realise that we are in no position to enter lightheartedly upon war with such a formidable power as Germany, much less if Germany were aided by Italian attacks on our Mediterranean possessions and communications. They know that France, though her army is strong, is desperately weak in some vital spots, and they are always alarmed lest out of loyalty to her we should be led into a quarrel over causes which are of little interest to us, and for which she could not give us decisive aid.

Therefore our people see that in the absence of any powerful ally, and until our armaments are completed, we must adjust our foreign policy to our circumstances, and even bear with patience and good humor actions which we should like to treat in very different fashion. I do not myself take too pessimistic a view of the situation. The dictators are too often regarded as though they were entirely inhuman. I believe this idea to be quite erroneous. It is indeed the human side of the dictators that makes them dangerous, but on the other hand, it is the side on which they can be approached with the greatest hope of successful issue.

I am about to enter upon a fresh attempt to reach a reasonable understanding with both Germany and Italy, and I am by no means unhopeful of getting results. I have an idea that when we have done a certain amount of spade-work here we may want help from U.S.A. It may well be that a point will be reached when we shall be within sight of agreement, and yet just unable to grasp it without a helping hand. In such an event a friendly and sympathetic President might be able to give just the fresh stimulus we required, and I feel sure that the American people would feel proud if they could be brought in to share in the final establishment of peace.

" The old trinity of faith, hope and charity ", he wrote after Munich, here was the heart of his policy. But a still more venerable trinity governed others, hatred and malice and all uncharitableness.

When first he took office, well aware that he came very late in this dangerous day, he told various gatherings of his party that he meant to stop the drift, to face facts as he found them, not as he would have wished them to be, and to shake off a collective security which this country was being asked to carry alone. He had no more patience than Eden showed with men who asked him to " call in the League " to save republican Spain ; to whom the Foreign Secretary crisply explained " there are, discreditable though honourable gentlemen opposite no doubt think it, a great many nations, members of the League, who want General Franco to win ". The League, he declared at the end of his first session, was not an end but a means ; " if the League is temporarily unable to fulfil its function to achieve that end, what is the use of repeating parrot-like that we believe in the League ? " As for the charge of betraying the cause on which they had stood at the last election, he was forth-

right about that, — " I believed it myself, I do not believe it now
. . . we must not try to delude small weak nations into thinking
that they will be protected by the League ".

But if in his revulsion from shams he discarded collective security,
so much so that cautious colleagues could hardly get him to name
it, what remained ? With an overwhelming majority of British
opinion he repudiated all idea of re-dividing the world into two
armed camps. There was, indeed, our reciprocal alliance with
France, though he had a dwindling faith in French stability, but
if he were asked to bring in Russia too, would not that be making
1914 over again, and complete the encirclement which must be
Hitler's best pretext for an early war ? For that matter, both from
our own information and from French generals he gleaned extreme
doubt whether Russia was in a condition to fight, he distrusted —
and Spain accentuated that distrust — the purity of her motives,
suspecting that she would not weep to see the Western Powers
and Germany involved in a deadly, though bourgeois, war.

There was another quarter to which he was often bidden to
look, to the great Republic which had saved us before, and shared
our staple ideals. In October 1937 President Roosevelt delivered
his Chicago speech, which denounced the epidemic of lawlessness
and spoke of a " quarantine " for infected States, but though Chamberlain gave it public welcome and trusted wholly the President's
goodwill, he was sceptical about his power. A few weeks later
the Japanese barbarous shelling of an American gunboat brought
out nothing but a stiff Note, nor did the statistics of American
trading demonstrate a passion for liberty. Three-quarters of
General Franco's oil, 65 per cent of Japan's and 90 per cent of her
scrap metal, these made a dark marginal comment on Roosevelt's
pledge to take every measure to avoid involvement in war. And
such certainly was the American rôle at the Brussels Conference
that autumn, summoned to concert means of stopping Japanese
aggression.

Consequently his private letters registered a. disbelief that we
could bring America into our calculations.

> I read Roosevelt's speech with mixed feelings . . . seeing that patients
> suffering from epidemic diseases do not usually go about fully armed
> . . . something lacking in his analogy. . . . When I asked U.S.A. to
> make a joint *démarche* at the very beginning of the dispute, they refused

Or again, and too narrowly final, " it is always best and safest to
count on nothing from the Americans but words ".

Once more we become conscious that Great Britain was entangled in the legacies of contradictory systems. In part to win American opinion we had abandoned our Japanese alliance, and behold, France was now refusing arms for China without an American guarantee of support. And in no cause of our own, but in virtue of the League and its ideals, we had antagonised three Powers armed to the teeth ; on whom, though disclaiming all notion of armed resistance, we continued to pour rebuke.

Concluding that this mingle-mangle was leading direct to war, and with his moral repugnance, tactical sense, and wish to gain time all converging, Chamberlain determined to see whether he could win a breathing space, perhaps win peace too, by a direct approach to the dictators and discussion of their grievances. Peace, he was to say later, is not obtained by " sitting still ", and on action he was all the more bent since experience showed that such approaches, if left to what is called the diplomatic channel, had a habit of running into the sand ; intercepted by sycophants and evil advisers, Ribbentrop above all, embittered by his failure as ambassador to win British liking.

A high percentage of fallacy, a proportion of malice, and a substratum of harsh truth have been written of his ingression upon foreign affairs. Whether he was too simple or too credulous, lacked the " feel " for manœuvre, or timed his moves badly, may long be disputed, or whether in fact the hour had not come for a stroke that would risk much to gain all. We shall find reason to conclude that his was not an unsuspecting nature, flattered or cajoled as to himself or another. It was on broader foundations than this that he overbuilt ; on arguments that every man has his human side, that whole peoples do not wish war, that if time is given it reason must prevail. There were, perhaps, things of which he was incapable, as of making full allowance for primitive passion, of throwing aside all the conceptions of international society, like the freedom of small States or neutrality, and, like us all, of rapidly shedding long-cherished ideas.

We have to probe more narrowly. " You cannot expect the Prime Minister ", Balfour had said, " not to interfere with Foreign Office business ", and plainly least of all when his is the final responsibility in hours of peril : so we may read in the lives of all his predecessors. But that " interference " must find its strength in concord between Prime Minister and Secretary for Foreign Affairs. Now though Chamberlain had for some years girded at the conduct of the Foreign Office, he was by no means solitary in that, while

any notion that he aimed at capturing one key position after another
is baseless.   Historically, for example, the change of permanent
Under-Secretary and the later resignation of the Foreign Secretary
himself were entirely unconnected.   Nor, again, did he ignore,
and far less was he unsupported by, diplomatic opinion, finding
in many eminent seniors of that service repeated assurance of
approval for his policy.

There was nothing, surely, predetermined about the break between Chamberlain and Eden, for we have seen how the older
man had long valued the younger's vitality and decision, while
from papers already available, which do credit to our public life,
it is clear that nothing throughout shook their mutual respect and
affection.   But between them were twenty-eight years of time, and
a wider difference of temperament.   If Eden was not sentimental,
he appealed to those, especially beyond the ranks of Conservatism,
who were possessed of a high sensibility, and he had, or so his
leader thought, " natural vibrations " on which others might play.
Among them was an intense dislike of dictators personally, in particular of Mussolini, a dislike so cordially reciprocated that it appears
positively to have influenced the relation between London and
Rome.   Yet though these two Britons looked at the world in such
different perspective, yet for the very reason that both were men
of high principle, who would not compromise a fundamental, their
relationship was always of much finer metal than some outside
could suppose.

There was another personal factor, not yet so potent as it became,
and never so potent as the outer world decided it must be, but
one that an honest history will not pass over.   This was the feeling
of the Foreign Office, that the Prime Minister preferred the amateur
advice of Sir Horace Wilson, chief industrial adviser, to their own
expert counsel.   This impeachment must, in great part, be admitted.
He had found Wilson's judgement indispensable at the Ottawa
Conference, and succeeded, as it were, to his services, since he
had been seconded, in Baldwin's time, to work under the Prime
Minister, who, for that matter, we must suppose, is entitled to
seek advice in any quarter where he thinks he will find it best.
Broadly speaking, Chamberlain was too masterful a man to look
much for policy to others, but true it is that he valued the measuring
of any nice question by an intellect the tranquillity and firmness
of which he admired, and whose precision of expression he found
congenial.   To a certain extent, I think, it reflected his own solitariness.   But, however that may be, though neither unnatural nor

unprecedented, in some phases the friction thus created did no good to the common weal.

In smaller ways he sometimes troubled not Eden only, but Eden's successor, and the Cabinet. Some thought him precipitate ; certainly he would occasionally turn the corner of a speech or impart his aspirations to the press, so that he outran or even contradicted the Foreign Office sense of what was wise. And his mind was so fixed on one great object that men felt him ruthless in waiving aside smaller stakes, or lesser values, which yet had their own reality.

In sum, he had the defect of his qualities of hopefulness and zeal for action. Had he not tried the ground, and eliminated one alternative after another ? Collective security ? let us not be tied to a corpse. Alliances ? let us not forget 1914. Isolation ? an empty dream. The Opposition policy of arms for Spain, sanctions against Japan, "standing up" to dictators ? war then, war on three fronts, and war before we were ready. He had been reading, with admiration, *The House that Hitler Built* ; "if I accepted the author's conclusions, I should despair, but I don't and won't " : never this bleak doctrine of inevitable war. In the Liberalism he heard so much of in his youth, he told Parliament, there had been confidence in the rewarding effect of trust and good faith. He would try what Edward Grey had tried, to appease the unsatisfied States by reasonable concessions in which our Allies could agree ; explore the Colonial question, as Grey had explored Morocco or Angola ; and, like Grey, refuse all prior armed commitments which would close the circle or contact the spark.

CHAPTER XXIV

JUNE 1937–MARCH 1938

The proposition is peace. Not peace through the medium
of war . . . . not peace to arise out of universal discord,
fomented from principle in all parts of the empire. . . .
It is simple peace : sought in its natural course, and in its
ordinary haunts.

BURKE, on *Conciliation with America*

" IF only we could get on terms with the Germans, I would not
care a rap for Musso ", that was his first thought ; moreover Germany, as he told some of the many who volunteered advice, was
a rising market. But his first approaches got no response. Von
Neurath, the Reich foreign minister, accepted an invitation to come
to England in June, but withdrew his acceptance on a pretext
conveniently found in Spain, while the reception of Nevile Henderson at Berlin was steely, almost fatalistic. We could not, indeed,
complain of lack of candour. We were told that Germany must
export or die, must have foreign exchange, and colonies of her
own. But it was implied that about this there was no urgency,
that colonies were rather an honourable eccentricity of their economic expert, Dr. Schacht. The German " folk " was another story.
Austria, where Germans were so misgoverned and robbed of their
manifest destiny, this could not wait long ; nor some new basis
for the Sudeten, who cried out against the Czechs ; Danzig and
the Corridor, and Memel, all in good time. The Führer had
declared his lack of interest in the West, admitted the permanent
loss of Alsace-Lorraine, had but just pledged the integrity of Belgium ; and how was he rewarded ? if he looked East, threatened
as he was by the Russian colossus, Britain warned him off, while
the British press poisoned the well of goodwill. As Henderson
absorbed the tense air of the Nuremberg party day, amid Hitler
youth marching, singing, trampling, and the skulls and cross-bones
of Himmler's police, Goering depicted the two alternatives ; of
an understanding between a British sea empire and a German
empire paramount in central Europe, or a Germany forced, by
refusal to collaborate, to prepare the destruction of Britain. Below
the mount of temptation stretched this smiling Nordic peace.

Since the highway was barred, he searched the secondary roads.

With Japan, failing American help, there was nothing to be done, not even when they machine-gunned our ambassador to China, until the scene in Europe had cleared : only memories of the past, and 700 British troops, covered our huge wealth in and round Shanghai. But could not the Axis be weakened at its Rome end ? The present atmosphere was poisonous, infected by the still unrecognised " Empire " of Ethiopia, and while Italians were inflamed by those sections of our press which rejoiced at the mediocre performance of Italian legionaries in Spain, their own press was childish and insolent. Their propaganda was inciting Arabia, they were fortifying Pantelleria and Rhodes, their first-line air strength was put at 1600 machines. Yet our representatives there, who predicted that Italy would leave the League unless it accepted the Abyssinian facts, maintained that the Duce's German connection was not his first choice. That we heard also from the Czechs ; it seemed to be proved when Italy made a first advance, reported thus :

24 July 1937

Grandi has told Eden that he wants to see me, to give me a message from Musso. I gather the effect is that he " really vas a good young man ". He has no designs in the Mediterranean, nor on Spanish territory, and only wants to be friends again. I propose to see the Count, and endeavour to find out whether there is any nigger in this woodpile.

Before he left for a rest in the Highlands, with strictest injunction against being followed by photographers, he saw Grandi twice, to whom he handed a personal letter for Mussolini, couched in general but friendly terms. That brought a corresponding reply, by air, with affectionate reminiscence of Austen, protesting that the interests of Britain and Italy did not clash in the Mediterranean or elsewhere, and welcoming an opening of conversations. But Chamberlain impressed on Grandi that Abyssinian recognition could be only one item in a comprehensive agreement, and that we should never desert our old ally France. A retrospective account defines precisely the extent of his personal action.

Diary, 19 February 1938 (continued)

I did not show my letter to the Foreign Secretary, for I had the feeling that he would object to it. Nevertheless, he made no complaint, and the Foreign Office authorised our ambassador Drummond to say that we hoped the conversations would begin in September. At that time Eden and I both recognised (and the Italians apparently agreed) that the formal recognition of their Abyssinian conquest, to which they attached great importance, must follow on some declaration by the League that Abyssinia was no longer an independent State . . . we thought then that the League might, if conversations went well, be willing to make such a declaration at their next meeting.

If that recognition must come, better give it, he reasoned, while something could be received in return. His letter had made a good impression, but in September he complains that the Foreign Office persisted in seeing a Machiavelli in the Duce ; " if we treat him like that, we shall get nowhere ". In fact, however, it was Mussolini who torpedoed any early chance of conversations by his ventures in Spain.

In that sad tenacious land a war of mutual barbarity dragged on, for if the Fascist powers had given Franco the first initiative, Russian supplies had saved Madrid. There food queues looked for arms and inspiration to the Soviet ; in fierce Catalonia women stabbed the fallen corpses ; in San Sebastian young Fascist airmen drank to the day when they would bomb Paris. With exemplary patience the British leaders in the non-intervention committee drove the rivals, Germany and Italy and Portugal on one side, and on the other Russia, through one deadlock to the next, and in July, after many naval incidents, achieved a compromise, which would have followed up a withdrawal of foreign volunteers by the grant of belligerent rights to both combatants. While each extreme disputed this, a series of attacks by nameless, but undoubtedly Italian, submarines on shipping of all nations led to the conference at Nyon, which took steps to dispose of those pirates. But this conference, under a barrage of Russian accusation, the Italians refused to attend.

We have had a great success at Nyon [Chamberlain wrote], but at the expense of Anglo-Italian relations. . . . They made the Russian note a pretext for abstention as the Russians meant they should, and now with intense chagrin they see collaboration between the British and French fleets, of a kind never known before. . . . It would be amusing, if it were not also so dangerous.

The " Machiavelli " so detestable to the Foreign Office was unworthy of that great injured name, for his lion gestures were bluster, and his fox manœuvres most transparent. Yet it must be admitted, despite his journey to Berlin and his provocative language, that this autumn his deeds were better than his words. Italy accepted the impending departure of commissions of enquiry as the first stage in the ejection of foreign fighting men from Spain, promised repeatedly no encroachment on Spanish soil or the Balearic Islands, and complained of our sloth in opening conversations. The Duce, in fact, was discovering, in Austria and the Balkans, how disagreeable it was to be the hinder end of an axis. But he was haggling, and Chamberlain deplored Eden's very natural exasperation.

> Mussolini had been more than usually insolent with his offensive remarks about bleating democracies, and his outrageous allusion to the Colonies. But Anthony should never have been provoked into a retort which throws Germany and Italy together in self defence, when our policy is so obviously to try and divide them.

Meantime, chance offered in October another possibility of sounding Berlin, when Halifax, as master of the Middleton fox-hounds, received a private invitation to a hunting exhibition which Goering had organised ; though not captivated by the prospect, thrown in, of an expedition to shoot foxes, he drew the attention of the Foreign Office to the facts. Though they were not enthusiastic, it seems they took no objection, and the Prime Minister urged it was an opening not to be missed. Nothing, certainly, could be more sterile than conditions as left by Henderson's last interview, the German evasion of Eden's questions, or Eden's pronouncement that we could not condone the use of force against Austria or the Czechs.

Between the Führer, who could hardly be dragged to an exhibition which implied the taking of animal life, and the British minister, who preferred that to the shedding of Christian blood, the natural gulf was wide, and if the conversations were of value, it was because they revealed the obstructions to any bridgehead. So there was some polite tirade against the democratic press, much protest against war between the two finest races, some emphasis from the soldier von Blomberg that the Führer's feelings for Britain were those of a scorned lover, and that an expanding population must receive more living room. On the whole, he came back with an impression that Germany, though conscious of her new strength, would do nothing catastrophic, since they felt time was on their side. On receiving this report the Prime Minister's first reaction was the need of consultation with the French ministers, before whose arrival he thus diagnosed the prospect of peaceful change :

26 November 1937

> the German visit was from my point of view a great success, because it achieved its object, that of creating an atmosphere in which it is

possible to discuss with Germany the practical questions involved in a European settlement. . . . Both Hitler and Goering said separately, and emphatically, that they had no desire or intention of making war, and I think we may take this as correct, at any rate for the present. Of course, they want to dominate Eastern Europe ; they want as close a union with Austria as they can get without incorporating her in the Reich, and they want much the same things for the Sudetendeutsche as we did for the Uitlanders in the Transvaal.

They want Togoland and Kameruns. I am not quite sure where they stand about S.W. Africa ; but they do not insist on Tanganyika, if they can be given some reasonably equivalent territory on the West Coast, possibly to be carved out of Belgian Congo and Angola. I think they would be prepared to come back to the League, if it were shorn of its compulsory powers, now clearly shown to be ineffective, and though Hitler was rather non-committal about disarmament, he did declare himself in favour of the abolition of bombing aeroplanes.

Now here, it seems to me, is a fair basis of discussion, though no doubt all these points bristle with difficulties. But I don't see why we shouldn't say to Germany, " give us satisfactory assurances that you won't use force to deal with the Austrians and Czechoslovakians, and we will give you similar assurances that we won't use force to prevent the changes you want, if you can get them by peaceful means ".

He found the French anxious for negotiation, for their country was in dire straits. The Senate had driven Blum out of office, the Communists were in opposition again and discredited by the Moscow purge, the forty-hour week had brought aircraft production down to about fifty machines a month, as against the Germans' three hundred. Fascist conspiracy and union strikes, political murder and a press debauched by foreign money, all had made a dreadful thing of the once proud and united Third Republic.

On the last days of November Chamberlain, Eden, and Halifax confronted Chautemps, his foreign minister Delbos, and his much more powerful permanent official M. Léger. The Prime Minister thought Great Britain would not refuse her contribution in the matter of colonies, though he would not admit a German " right " or allow the principle before Germany made wider concessions ; still, the French would perhaps consider an enquiry with Belgium and Portugal for a broad African scheme ? He made it clear that we should never swallow the bribe of a separate Anglo-German understanding, or meet her wishes in Eastern Europe without some satisfaction as to the League and disarmament. British opinion would not approve of maintaining Czechoslovakia, as it stood, by force, but we could not declare ourselves disinterested : we should work for a peaceful settlement, perhaps on some basis of local autonomy, and urge the Czechs to yield more liberties to their German subjects than they had up to date.

As the discussion ranged more widely, the British feared no co-operation in the Far East would be forthcoming from America, Delbos thought much the same of Russia, General Gamelin seemed to think even Roumania a better asset than the Russian army. When they came to Italy, Chamberlain refused to believe that they were naturally sympathetic to Germany, though to be sure their propaganda would continue its naïve game of attempting to separate Britain from France. The French contempt for Italy being much in evidence, they would have preferred a first approach to Berlin, but the British differed, contending that Mediterranean conversations might induce Italy to take a more stalwart line in central Europe. So that, subject to their being kept informed, the French agreed to our negotiation with Rome.

He liked Chautemps. " He was quick and witty and, as it seemed to me, quite candid and straightforward. He did not conceal his dislike for Soviet Russia. . . . He and Delbos were simply staggered when they heard what we were turning out in aeroplanes, — more than 5 times their output, I am sorry to say."

While Delbos departed, as Barthou had three years back (but oh ! how fallen, how changed !), to plumb Warsaw and the Balkans (but not Moscow), Britain and France made public their readiness to examine the Colonial problem as part and parcel of a general settlement. But they found the Germans strangely uninterested in the first, and hostile to the second. Eden, perhaps, was not disposed to think haste the path of wisdom ; we should expect some arms limitation, and no forcible change in Austria, — though that, we implied, was rather an Italian interest than a British. But nothing could be less likely than a German return to the League, seeing that Italy resigned her membership in December.

That came about, Rome reports agreed, because Italy was convinced we were evading the promised conversations. Their inspired press complained that their country was being chloroformed, and their diplomatic method was the same and as unpleasing as ever, to keep up a drum-fire of invective and intrigue to bring the dull English to their senses. Eden's interviews with Grandi in December were consequently not very progressive, and he insisted that propaganda must be silenced before conversations could begin. Properly convinced of the all-importance of carrying the French with us, he knew their reluctance to take the lead in recognising " Ethiopia ", and their threat to reopen their Pyrenean frontier to arms for Republican Spain. He probably hoped little, and perhaps cared less, about extracting any good from Rome, looking rather to discussions at Berlin, in whose fanatical racialism he detected at least one sign of grace, that they might be detached from the Japanese. Things being thus suspended, he went abroad at the New Year for a short holiday, leaving the Foreign Office in charge of the Prime Minister, whose deductions from the same set of facts were wholly different.

Diary, 19 February 1938 (continued)

In late December, before we separated for Christmas, I spoke to Anthony about the Italian situation. By that time Musso had given notice of his intention to leave the League. Our relations had steadily deteriorated. The Bari station was pouring out streams of anti-British propaganda, the press was hostile, anti-British intrigue was going on in Egypt, Palestine, and Arabia, the Berlin-Rome Axis had been greatly strengthened, Germany had signed an Anti-Comintern pact with Japan, and Italy had joined it. I told A. that I feared we were getting ourselves into a deadlock, if we stuck to it that we could not open conversations till the League had given us permission.

He found Halifax in substantial agreement that the talks ought to begin, and arguing that, when they did, the propaganda matter would solve itself ; Abyssinia must be handled through the League, though some *de facto* recognition must be given, if we were not to drift from bad to worse. The Prime Minister made it clear that in his view recognition must not be given unconditionally ; " we should approach the matter from the angle of obtaining general appeasement, to which each must make its contribution and justify *de jure* [recognition] on that ground ".

While these grave passages passed, a personal question embarrassed the Foreign Secretary. The world was free to a British citizen, but it was not the moment he would have selected for Austen Chamberlain's widow to make a long stay at Rome, though Lady Chamberlain had of course consulted him before departure. Her footing in Fascist circles differed from that of other British subjects ; she had always known Mussolini at his simplest and best, in his genuine affection for Austen and his kindness to their children. And her visit had this importance in history that, apart from the transparent Italian tactic of distinguishing between Eden and himself, the impression of her letters tended to confirm in the

Prime Minister's mind those he received from other quarters, and his previous ideas. The American and Austrian ministers at Rome were reported as urging that conversations begin at once, the Germans were highly unpopular, Ciano tried to block every channel to the Duce except his own, Italians obstinately believed that our dislike of their propaganda was a mere pretext for shelving conversations, being like ill-mannered children who make faces at their seniors without intending mortal harm. But as Hitler was due at Rome in May, it would be wise to move before him.

On January 13 what he called " a bomb " soared over the Atlantic among these Roman fires. President Roosevelt suggested that he might make a world appeal for an agreement on disarmament, keeping of treaties, and access to raw material, which, if well received, might be followed up by a meeting of American and other neutral States, as a preliminary to a world conference. This thrust in the wedge between Prime Minister and Foreign Secretary a little deeper. For while Chamberlain feared the dictators would pay no heed, or else would use this " line up of the democracies " as a pretext for a break, it was found on Eden's return that he would rather risk that calamity than the loss of American goodwill. There was a first breath of resignation. But a compromise was beaten out, America was assured we should never give *de jure* recognition in Abyssinia except as part of a wider settlement, and Chamberlain wrote that he hoped for conversations in February, — " it will be as well, for the Japs are growing more and more insolent and brutal ".

Simultaneously with the American bomb there had been an explosion in Berlin which took the British government by surprise. Marshal von Blomberg's quiet wedding to a plebeian mistress, though blessed by the Führer's presence, affronted the military caste and exposed the jealousies between Army and Nazi party, whose baser elements exploited them for a bolder game. After three weeks of uncontrollable rages, Hitler acted. He removed his friend Blomberg but also removed the protesting commander-in-chief, took on himself the supreme military command, and replaced his foreign minister von Neurath by Ribbentrop. Chamberlain's first comment was mild ; " with Ribbentrop in his place I feel all at sea again. He has always professed the strongest desire to come to an understanding with us, but his actions never appeared to be quite in keeping with his professions." At Rome, and in Berlin itself, men took a gloomier view of what these changes might import.

Europe had not long to wait.   Ribbentrop was appointed on February 4 ; on the 12th the Austrian Chancellor was summoned to the presence at Berchtesgaden and presented with an ultimatum, whereby the Austrian government would give an amnesty to all political offenders and make a Nazi Minister of the Interior, with power over the police.   For us it was not a happy moment, for the same day Eden informed Henderson of the " contributions towards appeasement " which, at the proper moment, Britain would offer and of those to be invited from Germany.   These events had a direct bearing on the Italian conversations.

Diary (*continued*)

> After a period of silence over the Blomberg affair and the retirement of generals, with the appointment of Ribbentrop as foreign minister, Schuschnigg the Austrian Chancellor was suddenly summoned to Berchtesgaden, where he was outrageously bullied by Hitler and faced with a series of demands to which he was obliged to yield, since on this occasion Mussolini gave him no support.   Very soon afterwards Ciano told Perth that he had instructed Grandi to press for an early start of the conversations in view of " possible future happenings ".

In early February he received, through his sister-in-law, a message from Mussolini that he desired an early agreement, to cover all points in dispute, and that we would not find Italy unreasonable : Grandi once more began talks with Eden, which once more ran into propaganda and Spain.   Our officials in the peninsula reported a large flow of French munitions to help the Spanish Republic ; if that flow could be arrested, Grandi intimated, Italy would not resist the British formula for the withdrawal of volunteers, to begin with 10,000 men from the side which had least, and a proportionate number from the other.

For Eden this was not enough : before conversations began, we must have some payment on account, a positive withdrawal of some volunteers.   By that, Chamberlain would have argued, we should lose what counted much more than these battered legionaries, precious time and a hope of dividing the Axis.   By February 17 he took the view that the Foreign Office wished to prevent him seeing Grandi.

Diary (*continued*)

> To intimate now that this was not the moment for conversations would be to convince Mussolini that he must consider talks with us off, and act accordingly. . . . Italian public opinion would be raised to a white heat against us.   There might indeed be some overt act of

hostility, and in any case the dictatorships would be driven closer together, the last shred of Austrian independence would be lost, the Balkan countries would feel compelled to turn towards their powerful neighbours, Czechoslovakia would be swallowed, France would either have to submit to German domination or fight, in which case we should almost certainly be drawn in. I could not face the responsibility for allowing such a series of catastrophes.

When he and Eden met Grandi on February 18, the Italian was most voluble. " He denied emphatically that any agreement concerning Austria had been made between Hitler and Mussolini, but . . . how could he move troops to the Brenner as he did before, if he felt that Great Britain was a potential enemy ? " : even at this hour conversations would encourage him to take a stronger line. Before he was dismissed, Chamberlain said he should have a final answer on Monday the 21st : " I said, however, that it would be helpful to our presentation of the case for talks, should that be our decision, if he could get his government to accept the formula [regarding volunteers] ". But already Eden had said that acceptance of the formula would not move him.

When the Cabinet met on the 19th, they were unanimous, though with a few reserves, and though much shaken by declaration of Eden's intention to resign. The Prime Minister let them see that the alternative might be his own ; " I thought it necessary to say clearly that I could not accept any decision in the opposite sense. Seeing, however, how my colleagues had been taken aback, I proposed adjournment till next day."

On Sunday he reported he had private assurances from Grandi that the formula would be accepted. But he and Eden agreed that their difference was " vital and unbridgeable ", and all efforts of mediators could not shake the Foreign Secretary, who later (" greatly to his credit, as I think ", noted the Prime Minister) made his resignation definite. And with him went Cranborne, his Under-Secretary of State.[1]

" I have won through ", Chamberlain wrote to his former colleague Rushcliffe, " but it has been only with blood and tears ", and this was one of the very rare occasions when he allowed those nearest to him to see the depth of his trouble. To the Cabinet and country it came as a heavy jolt, a challenge to their whole case, for both retiring ministers were men of high political integrity and promise, while to Eden the younger men of the Cabinet looked

[1] See the statements of those concerned in the Commons debates of February 21, 1938.

as to a nucleus and a hope. Many small touches showed his leader's feelings — a personal intervention, for instance, to re-draft the necessary press communications in a kindlier sense — while the first letter that passed between them thereafter was to be well matched by all Eden's part in the eighteen months which passed before they were reunited.

26 February 1938 ; to Anthony Eden

> After reading your speech to your constituents last night, I should like to send you a few friendly words. You had a very difficult task. You had to say enough to justify your resignation, and to vindicate your views, and the easiest, and perhaps the most popular, way would have been to emphasise differences and to call for support. I have no doubt that you have been urged to do this, perhaps by some who would not be sorry to attack the government. Anyhow, whatever the temptations, you have resisted them, and the dignity and restraint of your speech must add further to your reputation.
>
> I won't say more now than that my personal feelings towards you are unchanged, and I hope will always remain so.

But these trenches dig themselves deeper, and as time passed he came to feel that the difference was, and always had been, fundamental. For the logic of Eden's successive speeches, with appeal to the democracies, must, he felt, end in armed alliances and war.

From the crux of the Irish negotiation he had to turn to reconstructing his Cabinet and convincing the House. There were some old friends who counselled him to take the Foreign Office himself, but he was clear against the double burden, and it does not appear that he ever considered anyone but Halifax, whom the two previous prime ministers had had in mind. Opposition objection to a peer he refuted by recalling that Campbell-Bannerman had invited Cromer before asking Grey, and by undertaking to answer for the Foreign Office himself in the Commons, with the aid of R. A. Butler, successor to Cranborne. His three speeches in the two days of debate were not merely examples of his debating mastery, but charged with his deepest convictions. The conversations, he insisted, would take place within two limitations ; they must embrace a settlement in Spain, and an agreement must be approved by the League, which, again, implied that the Spanish position should not be " materially altered " by Italian reinforcements. While Opposition varied between depicting a mighty Italy which would impose on Britain and remodel Spain, or a wilting bankrupt Italy

to whom we had only to " stand up " for her to fall down, he dwelt
on the larger theme of general peace. As he saw it, peace depended
on understanding between " the four major Powers " — excluding
Russia as " half Asiatic " — and on positive effort ; on effort,
above all, to grasp the mentality of other nations. It was imperilled by
pursuing an ideological vendetta, or by asking part fulfilment of one's
own demands, not merely before agreement but before beginning
negotiation at all. And what did they gain by repeating "collective
security " ? " I believe that the policy of the party opposite, if
persisted in, this policy of holding their hands and turning their
backs, of making speeches and of doing nothing, is a policy which
must presently lead us to war."

On March 7, introducing the fourth White Paper on Defence,
he told the House that the £1500 millions he had mentioned a
year before would be much exceeded, for " we ought to make it
known that our desire for peace does not signify a willingness to
purchase peace to-day at the price of peace hereafter ". Whether
this policy of armed appeasement would succeed, only time could
tell ; meantime we passed through a stage that was hard to endure.
Yet the resignation of Eden, twice offered before Hitler's speech
of February 20, was not brought about by the dictators, in whose
capitals it was hailed with rejoicing, nor did it have any direct
bearing on the fate of Austria, which German troops entered on
March 12.

Though it is arguable that nothing could long have perpetuated
the fragmentary State set up in 1919, on the evidence before him
Chamberlain had surely little right to believe that Italy would
march to the Brenner, as she had in 1934. If he heard that the
Duce was furious, he heard also how Ciano had said Austria could
not be saved, and how Abyssinia, Spain, Libya, and armament
were straining Italian resources. But what was presumably decisive
was the inaction of France, whose disintegration and financial
collapse were fatal. When the Germans marched into Vienna
France was actually without a government, while debates in the
Chamber showed she was also without a policy. Their undertone
revealed a deplorable lack of confidence in their armaments, with
a common lament that the indispensable Italian friendship had
been lost. Some at last saw that without the closer Russian alliance
which Eden had deprecated, central Europe could not be saved ;
many realised that, though Britain would come in if France were
involved, it was for France to take the initiative in a sphere so far
from the British orbit.

As for Great Britain, Lloyd George had been perfectly right in 1936 to say they would never march in an Austrian quarrel. No British government for years had denied that in some shape or other a closer union between Germany and Austria was inevitable, and of late they had had ample warning it was not far away. Here, then, the change of Foreign Secretary did not change the issue. The last question which Eden answered in that capacity in Parliament argued it did not lie with us to initiate the " consultations " to which we were committed in the event of a threat to Austria, and when Henderson saw Hitler on March 3 it was in pursuance of instructions drafted by Eden, but continued by Halifax. We had, in short, washed our hands of Austria, except to express a wish for " reasonable solutions reasonably achieved ". Vainly Henderson, pointing to the globe in Hitler's study, spread visions of a German share in a rearranged, philanthropic Congo basin, for Goering swore they would not give up Austria for the whole of Africa, the Führer declaimed his new set piece that he would not endure interference between two German tribes, any more than Great Britain would suffer it between herself and Ireland. Many observers this spring noticed his growing isolation and passions, with the growing power of the obsequious and malignant in his court. And the speeches which began the year with lashing the German inferiority, in pride that he had healed it by the salve of armed power, developed during the Austrian plebiscite into the mystic's toneless cry, that God had raised him up to restore his native land to the Reich, and had smitten the men of little faith.

On March 11 Chamberlain had a private letter before him, repeating words with Wiedemann, Hitler's special envoy, who declared that the latest topic in his master's conversation was the imminent break-up of the British Empire. The same day he happened to be entertaining the Ribbentrops at luncheon when news came of the final ultimatum to Vienna ; that night we registered our protest against the force put on an independent State. The reply, that it was an internal matter for the German people, was in a style expected, though it was accompanied by a double pledge to the Czechs that their relations with the Reich were unaffected.

Chamberlain's contemporary letter drew more than one moral.

13 March

it is perfectly evident, surely, now that force is the only argument Germany understands, and that collective security cannot offer any prospect of preventing such events, until it can show a visible force of overwhelming strength, backed by determination to use it. And if that is so, is it not obvious that such force and determination are most effectively mobilised by alliances, which don't require meetings at Geneva, and resolutions by dozens of small nations who have no responsibilities? Heaven knows, I don't want to get back to alliances but if Germany continues to behave as she has done lately, she may drive us to it. It is tragic to think that very possibly this might have been prevented if I had had Halifax at the Foreign Office instead of Anthony at the time I wrote my letter to Mussolini. . . . For the moment we must abandon conversations with Germany, we must show our determination not to be bullied by announcing some increase or acceleration in rearmament, and we must quietly and steadily pursue our conversations with Italy. If we can avoid another violent coup in Czechoslovakia, which ought to be feasible, it may be possible for Europe to settle down again, and some day for us to start peace talks again with the Germans.

His speech next day spoke of " severest condemnation ", and of Austria as a member of the League, on the note which Hitler resented most bitterly from " the pious governesses " of Europe. What mattered more, it announced a fresh review of rearmament.

The lights were out in Vienna, and dim at Prague. Would it be possible to throw, from Rome and Paris, a beam into the darkness spreading from Berlin?

CHAPTER XXV

THE CZECH QUESTION

Hamlet. What hour now ?
Horatio. I think it lacks of twelve.
Marcellus. No, it is struck.
Hamlet, Act I, Scene iv

AT this point we must interrupt the sequence of events to summarise the elements of the Czechoslovakian problem, as presented to the Prime Minister.

The most intractable questions in Europe are the oldest, and this one went back to the thirteenth century, when German dynasties, pushing south and east, gradually overlaid Slav Bohemia with a German upper crust of landowners, merchants, learning, and religion. After three hundred years of bloody vicissitude, during which Czech armies invaded Saxony and the Rhineland and religion was exploited to cover race hatred, the Habsburgs clamped down their hold on Bohemia in the Thirty Years War, which left the Czechs one of several Slav minorities in an Empire ruled by Germans and Magyars.

By what blows all this was snapped in the nineteenth century, needs not here to be rehearsed ; enough to say that out of enlightenment and Metternich, literary revival and military defeat, Pan-German and Pan-Slav, came that wretched last state of the Habsburg empire which was torn to pieces in 1918.

The new State was set up on weak foundations : 7½ million Czechs were given authority over 3¼ million Germans, 2¼ million Slovaks, more than ½ a million of Hungarians and another ½ million of Ruthenes, besides some 80,000 Poles. Not merely were these large minorities massed, for the greater part, in blocks on the frontiers, but on frontiers which defied the principles and the pledges in virtue of which victory had been won. The Germans were refused self-determination, the Slovak argument that they had been promised a State of equal nationalities was not accepted, the economic links of the Ruthenes with Hungary were severed.

All this was dangerous, wounding to the pride of the Sudeten Germans who had filled the best regiments of the old Austrian army, and outraging the sentiment both of Poland and Hungary.

Great wisdom, good fortune, and ample time would have been needed to overcome that harsh beginning, but even before the death of the wise Masaryk too little of these was vouchsafed. No more was heard of the "sort of Switzerland", the liberal régime, which Beneš had held forth to the peace conference. The country was made a centralised State, and later, under stress and strain, in part a police State, exacerbated at every point where conflict always breaks out in a land of antagonistic races,— as to the proportion of officials, allotment of schools, or census statistics. These wrangles were still dragging their length along when the great depression cast the German areas, exactly the most industrial part of the country, into sudden poverty, a depression which had not passed when the Nazis were offering union and full employment to all Germans.

The Nazi revolution not only re-stoked the fire of race hatred, but identified that feud with the larger quarrel of Europe. In the very month of May 1935 that the Czechs made their Russian alliance, Henlein's Sudeten party captured 44 seats in the elections, polling 70 per cent of the German vote and more than any other single party in the State.

Full warnings of this volcanic condition reached London, both before and after Hitler's accession to power. The army, they ran, could not be depended on as a whole, the racial strife necessitated a system of espionage in its ranks, Germans were rarely admitted to serve in tank corps or air force. Neither Germans nor Slovaks could count on receiving justice, in their own tongue, in the law courts. Unemployment was chronic in the German region, about twice the rate of the country at large, but unemployment benefit for Germans was wholly inadequate, and much lower than for Czechs. Drastic laws of 1935-6 tightened the Czech hold on government employment, drew a wide frontier zone within which arbitrary imprisonment could be imposed, and imported a Czech police into German areas. Many local elections had been suspended for five or six years, the treaty clause in regard to Ruthenia was not observed, the Catholic Slovaks alleged offences against their religion, and breach of the understanding which would have made them equal partners. But the Germans, though not cruelly oppressed, had the harder lot. There, in any case, lay these repeated warnings, over-strained maybe in some particulars but in bulk weighty, before the British government ; that time was running short and that, if left without remedy, this problem would end in a second Thirty Years War.

As always happens in such cases, these evil humours of the

Czech State, and the grievous difficulties of Beneš, who succeeded Masaryk as President at the new year of 1935-6, were caught up in foreign relations, for the country stood at the very knot of all the twisted strands of Europe.   It was full of refugees, German Liberals and Socialists, and latterly of Austrian democrats, while a heavy press censorship showed, like a lava stream, what undying fires burned below.

Moreover, neither Beneš nor Henlein was entire master in his own house, behind them being extremer men and divided forces. This alone checked the pace of urgently necessary reform.   While Beneš and Hodza, his Slovak Premier, slowly embarked in 1937 on steps to give Germans a pinch more of office or employment, they stoutly declined to hear of anything " Swiss ", or local autonomy, let alone to have dealings with Henlein.   He, on the other hand, in his many talks to English public men, had not yet declared for separation, but he was being outpaced by some of his colleagues, who took their doubts and their hungers direct to Germany.

Nothing could conceal the international isolation of the Czechs in the first half of 1938.   All the painful effort of the French had failed to bring about decent relations between them and the Poles, who spoke of the Czechs as no gentlemen, and whose eyes were fixed on the coalfield of Teschen, of which they said the Czechs had robbed them.   Horthy, the Hungarian regent, detested them, the Jugo-Slavs were half won over to the Axis.   If they were willing to ask Russian help — which all of them were not — they doubted, considering the purges and the happenings in Spain, whether it could profit them.

While discharged Sudeten workmen half starved outside derelict factories, and their young hot-heads demonstrated in black breeches or white stockings, the fall of Austria in March 1938 threatened downfall to the Czechs.   German troops now lapped them round on three sides, their Bohemian fortifications could be turned, their trade routes were cut.   Would they advance from their position, that the Germans were only a minority in a Slav State, towards the view held by even the moderates among the Sudeten, that they must be equal partners ?   But the fall of Vienna, which made them stand fast, instantly drove the Sudeten forward.   The " Activist " parties, which hitherto had co-operated in government, now abandoned Beneš, and in April Henlein moved a long stride on in his Karlsbad speech.   To concede a full equality of status, some local autonomy, and removal of injustice, might be possible, but he proceeded to demand a change in the whole conception of

Czech foreign policy, with freedom for his people to profess German nationality and German " political philosophy ". Yet when he visited London in May he asserted that, though his party would prefer outright union with the Reich, there was still a last chance for a more limited scheme.

After six years of warning the British government, late in 1937, pressed Beneš to make serious concessions, and had induced the French to support their pressure. Zero hour was near. They were now confronted by the spectacle of the mass of the Sudeten in half-open revolt, looking to triumphant German armies which, on the jugular vein between Breslau and Vienna, could sever the narrow, ill-protected throat of Czechoslovakia in an afternoon.

CHAPTER XXVI

MARCH–AUGUST 1938

THE drift to war grew faster. In France the Blum government, formed when the Germans were entering Austria, struggled on a bare month and, while strikes again annihilated aircraft production, his foreign minister Paul Boncour, one of Geneva's fluent orators, reopened the Spanish frontier to French munitions. Franco's armies, driving for the Mediterranean, cut Republican Spain into two weak fragments. The Japanese were sweeping on in a more murderous advance, which was to push the Chinese government a thousand miles from the sea, while their southern arm clawed at the rich British interests of Hong Kong and Canton. But first things first; Chamberlain had to stop Germany attacking the Czechs, whom Hitler had included with Schuschnigg in one condemnation.

20 March

with Franco winning in Spain by the aid of German guns and Italian planes, with a French government in which one cannot have the slightest confidence and which I suspect to be in closish touch with our Opposition, with the Russians stealthily and cunningly pulling all the strings behind the scenes to get us involved in war with Germany (our Secret Service doesn't spend all its time looking out of the window), and finally with a Germany flushed with triumph, and all too conscious of her power, the prospect looked black indeed. In face of such problems, to be badgered and pressed to come out and give a clear, decided, bold, and unmistakable lead, show " ordinary courage ", and all the rest of the twaddle, is calculated to vex the man who has to take the responsibility for the consequences. As a matter of fact, the plan of the " Grand Alliance ", as Winston calls it, had occurred to me long before he mentioned it. . . . I talked about it to Halifax, and we submitted it to the chiefs of the Staff and the F.O. experts. It is a very attractive idea ; indeed, there is almost everything to be said for it until you come to examine its practicability. From that moment its attraction vanishes. You have only to look at the map to see that nothing that France or we could do could possibly save Czechoslovakia from being overrun by the Germans, if they wanted to do it. The Austrian frontier is practically open ; the great Skoda munition works are within easy bombing distance of the German aerodromes, the railways all pass through German territory, Russia is 100 miles away. Therefore we could not help Czechoslovakia — she would simply be a pretext for going to war with Germany. That we could not think of unless we had a reasonable prospect of being able to beat her to her knees in a reasonable time, and of that I see no sign. I have therefore abandoned any idea of giving guarantees to Czechoslovakia, or the French in connection with her obligations to that country.

These military considerations, he repeats later, converted him from his first impulse to give a guarantee. There were colleagues who predicted that such a refusal would break the French alliance and shake the party, but he found that Halifax had come independently to the same conclusion, which was therefore embodied in the parliamentary announcement of March 24.

After reciting Eden's Leamington speech of 1936 on British commitments, he added there were other cases in which we should fight : for " our liberty and the right to live our lives according to the standards which our national traditions and our national character have prescribed ". As for the immediate issue, under a commitment either to the Czechs direct, or to France arising out of her Czech treaty, " the decision as to whether or not this country would find itself involved in war would be automatically removed from the discretion of His Majesty's government, and the suggested guarantee would apply irrespective of the circumstances by which it was brought into operation, and over which His Majesty's government might not have been able to exercise any control ". They could not so commit themselves, expecially in an area where our vital interests were not so concerned as in France and Belgium ; that applied also to the Soviet proposal for mutual pledges against aggression, which must, furthermore, aggravate the cleavage of Europe into two camps. Holding that conflicts must be resolved peaceably, the government took note of the German pledge not to use force against the Czechs, and of the Czech undertaking to make concessions. Yet, though " force should be our last resort and not our first ", he struck two notes sharply. Obligations implied the purpose and power to fulfil them, and therefore our armament programme would be accelerated. Moreover, " legal obligations are not alone involved and, if war broke out, it would be unlikely to be confined to those who have assumed such obligations. . . . This is especially true in the case of two countries like Great Britain and France, with long associations of friendship, with interests closely inter-

woven, devoted to the same ideals of democratic liberty, and determined to uphold them."

This pronouncement had a great parliamentary success, for if
Churchill's school welcomed the implicit defence of France and
her system, others built on the central theme of carrying France
with us in armed conciliation. In the next few months he would
push forward all his parallels, — speeding up of armaments, an
agreement with Italy, and a dual endeavour at Prague and Berlin.

Appeasement stood high in those days. One after another
came the Irish settlement, the Italian treaty, trade negotiation
with America, guarantee of large credits to Turkey. In all sorts
of quarters his praises were sounded. Hertzog approved ; the
Pope applauded his courage ; Canada, wrote Tweedsmuir, after
the first shock of Eden's resignation was all with him.

2 April ; Mackenzie King to Malcolm MacDonald

I hope you will tell Mr. Chamberlain that I cannot begin to express
the admiration I feel for the manner in which he has performed a task
more difficult, I believe, than any with which any Prime Minister of
Great Britain has ever before been faced. I approve wholeheartedly
of the course he has adopted, particularly his determination to get
into touch with Italy and Germany, to seek to restore good-will between
these countries and the United Kingdom, instead of permitting ill-
will to develop to the point of another world war, and his exposure of
the unreality, and worse, of the situation at Geneva. The one mistake
that I see in British policy — and I believe it to be a very great one —
is that Great Britain has been far too slow in taking the steps which
Mr. Chamberlain himself has found it necessary to take within the
past few weeks.

His inmost thoughts were free from the complacency with which
he was charged. " I try to warn myself ", he wrote in May, " against
the dangers that beset all Prime Ministers, who are apt to be told
only the agreeable things " ; yet, again, " although I know the
danger of thinking that one is indispensable, I do not see anyone
to hand over to without undermining confidence ".

They were hard days. There were twenty-four debates on
foreign affairs before the end of July, with more than fourteen
hundred questions for him or the Under-Secretary to answer, — a
high proportion of them on Spain, largely directed to build a legend
of the Prime Minister as a Fascist, eager for a Franco victory and
truckling to any dictator. How false that was in regard to Spain is
shown by a hundred chance allusions in his letters, or by his anxiety

N

to bring about a truce ; " what suffering and misery would be saved ". Indeed, the accusation, deep sunk in America especially, that he was playing " power politics ", was the very reverse of the truth ; if there is one charge against him and Halifax which must be well weighed, it is one precisely the opposite ; that in their determination to keep the peace they too much ignored the stark requirements of power.

Yet by no means so altogether in regard to our own country. " The Germans who are bullies by nature ", proceed his May letters, " are too conscious of their strength and our weakness, and until we are as strong as they are, we shall always be kept in this state of chronic anxiety." When, he asked Arthur Robinson of the Supply Board in July, should we be ready to fight on more or less equal terms ? the reply was " in a year ".

He turned to accelerate our arms. A lag in aircraft production, part technical and part, maybe, financial, a doubt that the gap between Germany and ourselves was actually widening, a mission to buy aeroplanes in America, brewed a storm of debate in May, and the worst day, he wrote, since he had become Prime Minister. It confirmed his growing opinion that a ministry " under such continuous bombardment " must have its head in the Commons ; this, and a temporary plethora of peers in the Cabinet, led to the resignation of Swinton, whose place ultimately went to Kingsley Wood, and the replacement of Winterton, in his rôle of a deputy Air minister, by Harold Balfour. If general progress was not fast enough, it was getting faster. The 1750 first-line for the home Air Force would be ready, re-equipped with new machines, by March 1939, and that total was to be raised to 2370 by March 1940. As Japan was menacingly silent, we invoked the escalator clause of the 1936 Naval treaty to build larger capital ships. An Essential Commodities bill legalised various bulk purchases and gave the Board of Trade far-reaching powers. And though Labour voted against the new White Paper, " the provision of immense armaments to further a dangerous and unsound foreign policy ", he turned, with some satisfaction, to get the co-operation of the trades unions ; there, perhaps, lay another motive for his continued refusal to hurry on emergency measures, a Ministry of Supply or a national register.

Meanwhile, the Italian agreement was signed on April 16, preceded by an exchange of letters with Mussolini ; " you should have seen the draft put up to me by the F.O. ; it would have frozen a Polar bear ". While its formal schedules covered each point of possible collision between the two powers, each Mediterranean and each African, the sting lay in the tail of the assurances interchanged ; from Italy, a pledge to evacuate volunteers from Spain as the non-intervention committee prescribed, with an undertaking that they sought no territory or privileged position in Spain or her empire ; from Britain, an undertaking to raise at Geneva the recognition of Italian Ethiopia, with a reminder that the " settlement of the Spanish question " must be achieved before any jot of this treaty took effect.

Such was his first long step in the process he had commended, to " remove the danger spots one by one ". Its larger value would depend on the extent to which it freed Italy from a German domination, and those who negotiated it claimed this later justification, that it led to Mussolini's mediating rôle in September. Certainly the Czech government welcomed it as a necessary measure, if Italy was to be induced to take a hand in Danubian security.

We must make an end, he argued, of what Churchill had once called " blacklisted " nations ; " it is in our willingness to face realities, which we cannot change, and to make the best of them, that the difference lies between this side and the other side of the House ". Before Great Britain asked the League in May for a resolution that would leave each State free to recognise Ethiopia, or not, as it desired, half the States of Europe — including the Little Entente, Eire, and the Low Countries — had in fact given recognition. But our own recognition would still be conditioned by settlement in Spain ; a country that does not " settle " lightly.

Here, once more, he would be content with what he felt was the essence ; " if His Majesty's government think that Spain has ceased to be a menace to the peace of Europe, I think we shall regard that as a settlement of the Spanish question ". But when he said this in July, we were still refusing to put the agreement in force. As regards Great Britain herself, he contended that the Duce was keeping his word, nor did the government feel, any more than had Eden, that a rebel victory meant danger ; Franco, we were assured by the prudent and ascetic dictator of Portugal, was well disposed. For parliamentary purposes the heat and stress lay in Franco's bombardment of British ships unloading in Republican harbours, — a legitimate trade, foamed the Opposition, which we ought to protect by force of arms.

This vulnerable matter was an unhappy result of an unhappy expedient. Having rejected the ordinary rule of international law and refused belligerent rights to both sides in the name of non-intervention, Opposition expected the combatants to allow cargoes, which must prolong resistance, to reach their rivals. But would not that amount to intervention ? Chamberlain's answer at least was clear ; we would protect our merchant ships on the high seas, but not in the fighting zone, to do which would lead to intervention, and probably to war. He was invited to resist by force these attacks from the air, illegal no question in international law, if we also were entitled to refuse belligerent rights to Franco. He wrote, " I have been through every possible form of retaliation, and it is absolutely clear that none of them can be effective unless we are prepared to go to war with Franco, which might quite possibly lead to war with Italy and Germany, and in any case would cut right across my policy of general appeasement. Of course, it may come to that, if Franco were foolish enough."

Looking on that larger hope, he concentrated upon smoothing out each case as it occurred, and even more on the root of the matter, to hold Italy to a real withdrawal of volunteers. But the clue of that question was not to be found between Rome and London, but Rome and Paris.

Mussolini, he wrote, was behaving like a spoiled child, but the child was dreaming of some large new rattles, of the Jibuti railway, something nice in Tunis, and, perhaps, in Corsica and Nice. Italy and France, he said loweringly, were on opposite sides of the barricade, and till May ended a stream of French arms over the Pyrenees inflamed and excused Italian prevarication. True, the Front Populaire had vanished, Daladier and Bonnet were at the head of a " Radical " government, and large bodies of French opinion cherished hopes of a Latin bloc, which would mean recon- ciliation with Rome and a Fascist Spain. But France was not prepared to man a third frontier, stiffened by German " technicians " and " tourists ", while when it came to ceding an inch of soil to Italy, all France was solid. So the French-Italian conversations, which began in April, very soon congealed and froze.

In the last days of that month Daladier came to England, the taciturn peasant of the South on whom were pinned expectations of a French revival, and with him his foreign minister Bonnet, with his vast nose, his voracious ambition, and a political reputation slightly soiled. Most cordially they distrusted one another, and neither understood English. But understanding with Britain was imperative, and most of all about Czechoslovakia ; not merely in the light of Chamberlain's declaration, but of French shakiness since the crash of Austria, and a concerted press campaign at Paris that the Czechs were not worth the sacred blood of France.

What passed we may deduce from the continuance of British-French staff talks, the pursuance of French negotiation at Rome, a slow re-closing of the Pyrenees, and from an agreement that Britain should sound Berlin while both Allies would press the Czechs to the limit of concession.   Herein, this letter suggests, the impetus came from the British side.

1 May

fortunately the papers have had no hint of how near we came to a break over Czechoslovakia. . . . I don't find Daladier as sympathetic as Chautemps, but he seems simple and straightforward, though perhaps not so strong as his reputation.   Bonnet I have known since 1932 : he is clever, but ambitious and an intriguer.   The French are not very fortunate in their foreign secretaries.

The relevant decisions of the early summer we may reconstruct from his autumn speeches.   If a condition of appeasement was the elimination of any danger spot, we could not stand aside, for our ministers abroad agreed with the French that Hitler's intentions were serious and immediate.   On the other hand, unlike France or Russia, we were not pledged to the Czechs.   Every post-war government, from Lloyd George onwards, had refused to spread our commitments to eastern Europe ; to give such a pledge might harden the Czechs in refusing change ; nor, Chamberlain always argued, was it conceivable to ask the British electorate and Dominions to contemplate total war in order to resist a plea from a large, localised racial minority that it should enjoy self-government.   There remained then the third course, to shoulder once more the mediating rôle which had been ours so often.   At this stage we were careful not to propound any particular solution, for Hitler had spoken of autonomy in broad terms and this, we supposed, might be found within the framework of the existing State.   Our one aim, he wrote, was " a stable future for Czechoslovakia ".

Time went in this double pressure ; at Berlin, on insistence against violence, and that we might be found fighting alongside France, — at Prague, on warning that nothing could save them immediately in case of war, and that not even a victorious peace would restore their present frontiers.   Nevile Henderson's tone from Berlin was darkly fatalistic as ever, affirming that nothing but force could keep the Sudeten in the Czech State against their will.   However, though Goering thundered about cutting up this " appendix " and though they all professed belief that Beneš meant to force a break, they did not object to our initiative at Prague.

There progress was slow. A draft minorities statute, announced in March, was not made public for over two months, perhaps because the Austrian affair had set all this untempered building shaking. The Slovaks, fired by a deputation from their American brethren, and the Polish minority were also asking autonomy, and when, after some years of intermission, local elections were arranged, violent incidents filled the German region. On May 20 came the first crisis. Against heavy rumours of German troop movements the Czechs part-mobilised, the Sudeten refused to continue discussion until order was restored, and Great Britain asked Germany not to count on her standing aside. Within a week this passed, but from that date, it seems, Hitler determined on revenge for what the world's democratic press painted as a German defeat, fixing October in his mind as the last destined date. Henderson did not believe that the Germans had any immediate serious intention, but Chamberlain thought otherwise.

28 May

I cannot doubt in my own mind (1) that the German government made all preparations for a coup, (2) that in the end they decided, after getting our warnings, that the risks were too great, (3) that the general view that this was just what had happened made them conscious that they had lost prestige and (4) that they are venting their spite on us because they feel that we have got the credit for giving them a check. . . . But the incident shows how utterly untrustworthy and dishonest the German government is. . . . One thing is very clear to us, though we can say nothing about it. The *Anschluss* and the Anglo-Italian agreement together have given the Rome-Berlin axis a nasty jar.

He was being urged in these months to use our financial power to help China also, pressed by Labour to examine an embargo on oil for Japan, but concluded that in the absence of much more positive assurance from America the risk was not one to be taken alone.

29 July 1938 ; to Sir Francis Lindley

I thought long and anxiously about the proposal for a loan, and indeed one's sentiments naturally went out to the Chinese, who were fighting such a gallant battle against such overwhelming strength, but the more I think of it, the more firmly I conclude that we should commit a fatal blunder for which we should have to pay dearly in the future, if we listened to sentiment rather than reason.

Another two months rolled on of that stormy summer.   Under Rhineland sun and under arc lights hordes of workers toiled without ceasing at the Führer's West Wall.   The Labour Opposition clamoured on about arms for Republican Spain.   His own main purpose was repeated in July at the centenary of Birmingham as a city.   If British influence, as he contended, was still the most powerful in the world for good, that was because the world knew that our policy was " rooted in the conviction that there can be no peace or security or permanence of happiness for mankind except under the rule of law and order, of reason and good faith. . . . Those who endeavour to steer by these general but deep-seated principles should expect to suffer many disappointments and setbacks.   They have their motives misrepresented, and their sincerity doubted.   But men who are worthy of their salt are not going to be turned from their purpose by temporary inconvenience, or annoyances of that kind.   The government, of which I am at present the head, intends to hold on its course, which is set for the appeasement of the world."

But a course set by the stars may be turned by the waves ; speeches from Russia hailed the Czech stand in May as the proper way to deal with aggressors.   Yet M. Bonnet had his doubts.   To have a clean sweep of your generals and civil servants was not, the bourgeois world thought, perhaps wrongly, a wise preparation for war, while enquiries convinced him that Poland would never suffer the passage of Soviet troops, and that the Jugo-Slavs would not lift a finger.   So, whatever might be said of their Cabinet as a whole, the French Foreign Office agreed in bringing pressure to bear upon Prague, though as yet they jibbed at suggestions that the country might be made another Switzerland, neutralised in its international relations.

On the whole, history will probably determine that this pressure was evenly applied, with the purpose put by Churchill in the press ; " just as we demand that Germany shall not stir up strife beyond her borders, so we must make sure that the clear definitions of our attitude which have become visible shall be no encouragement to obduracy on the part of a small State, whose existence depends upon the conscience and the exertions of others ".   Although France warned the Czechs that, if they were unreasonable, she might reconsider her treaty, till September the Allies held to the integrity of Czech territory and upheld the lengthening of their military service as provoked by the violence of the German press.

Henlein having won 90 per cent of the German vote in the

communal elections, the Sudeten put out their plan for a State of co-equal national groups. The gap was wide, our endeavour was to prevent the two parties becoming set in rigid entrenchments, and we vainly begged the Czechs to publish at once those points on which they could agree. From our newly appointed " observers " word came that time was getting short, and that the younger Sudeten were fast becoming converts to union with the Reich.

That, we knew in June, was the German thesis : it was inevitable, Goering would say, why not accept it and get rid of this tension ? They grumbled that Beneš was playing for time, and in their bludgeoning way launched a press attack on Britain as encouraging Czech mobilisation. Yet their tone at headquarters was smooth. " The Germans are evidently following directions ", Chamberlain thought, " in paying me compliments, and it is difficult to be sure what the game is ", reporting a week later that Hitler was sending an important agent for private conversations.

This was Captain Wiedemann, once the Führer's superior officer in the last war, who interviewed Halifax in mid-July. Declaring he came without the knowledge of Ribbentrop, the captain spread the salt, its savour now rather stale, very thick in Eaton Square ; the Führer still wished good relations with England, was still hurt that his offers and his Naval treaty had not been more handsomely rewarded. How should we relish a visit from Goering for a full discussion ? Very much, we replied, in principle, but Czecho-slovakia lay between, and the atmosphere would be cleared by a promise not to use force. The captain said he was authorised to promise that no force was intended at present ; they might even pledge themselves for a year, but he would not answer for the consequences if any Sudeten were " massacred ".

A few days later Chamberlain took up this familiar loophole with the German ambassador. It was not a pretext that we should accept ; we too had been accused of weakness in not retaliating in Spain, but in the end had got our way without violence. However if, as was only too likely, Czech-Sudeten conversations reached a deadlock, we understood that Hitler would agree to any method of setting them on foot again.

We had already, in fact, proposed to the Czechs to send an investigator, and though they were not pleased, since it seemed to place their government on an equality with its discontented subjects, they accepted. The Germans were grumpy, for it was published before they were told, and they were not mellowed by the visit of the King and Queen to Paris. Under such auspices began the sojourn of Lord Runciman in Czechoslovakia, from August 3 till September 16 ; who went, Chamberlain told the Commons, not as an arbitrator but as investigator and mediator, independent of governments. Yet how could we disown interest in an agent on whose appointment we had insisted ?

Our ambassador in Berlin disbelieved in this experiment, nor did Runciman himself leave in a confident mood. Yet he set negotiation going again and, together with the French, pressed Beneš to draft what was called the 4th Plan, which accepted the gist of Henlein's Karlsbad basis. But to be given all they asked was the last thing which the Sudeten extremists wanted, and once more they manufactured an incident to break off. In this episode the British method was perhaps too tardy, for if we were to go to the extent, as Runciman ultimately did, of pressing one particular solution, the responsibility became ours and it was mistaken to lose the initiative. Bonnet and Henderson urged a speedy pronouncement, but it was not till September 2 that Runciman sent word to Hitler that, if the parties disagreed, he could have a plan ready by about the 15th ; that was late, for the Nazi party meeting was to open at Nuremberg on the 5th, and to be closed by Hitler's speech on the 12th, and while it sat, blood began to flow. German troop movements had not ceased all through August, and though it was believed the generals were against war, the Führer's silence and Ribbentrop's impertinence were not wholesome signs. Could nothing but force bring them to reason ?

By August 30, after a visit to Balmoral, the Prime Minister had in mind a last expedient, hinted at in nothing but vague terms to his family correspondents.

3 September

is it not positively horrible to think that the fate of hundreds of millions depends on one man, and he is half mad ? I keep racking my brains to try and devise some means of averting a catastrophe, if it should seem to be upon us. I thought of one so unconventional and daring that it rather took Halifax's breath away. But since Henderson thought it might save the situation at the 11th hour, I haven't abandoned it, though I hope all the time that it won't be necessary to try it.

If all else failed, he would see Hitler face to face.

N*

CHAPTER XXVII

BACKGROUND OF MUNICH

TWENTY years divided them in age, and though men come to fourscore years they do not outgrow their first twenty, while revolution and war had graved deeper that original difference. To the one, sensitive and high-minded product of the Victorian peace, fell a broad road of prosperity and honour, the inherited assumptions and the proved victory of British ideals, the morality of an island which identified its triumph with peace, and its policy with fair dealing. He was now old, brought to power by the chances of politics, though even more by his disciplined efficiency, but brought very late, so that half of life and more had passed, arduous and honourable and confined, before he was concerned with the decisions by which nations rise and fall. He shared all the cherished convictions of nineteenth-century England, though he had made for them a channel of his own. Without Gladstone's vision of a divine scheme of liberty which would penetrate the world's gross mind, and having none of Salisbury's theology which transcended earthly politics and left them inferior, he had found his religion of peace in nature and the service of men. " Every leader in every country," he said after Munich, " whatever may be his political creed, must surely put as the first of his aims the improvement of the lot of his fellow-creatures." Years, he added, had taught him " the futility of ambition, if ambition leads to the desire for domination ". Happiness was dependent on " freedom from apprehension, upon the possession of that peace of mind without which no material comforts can bring satisfaction ". A world without fear, because it had peace of mind.

The man he was going to see had enjoyed no comforts till he had taken them by storm, and had never known peace of mind. Born and bred in resentment against squalid circumstance, a corrupt society, and a weak State, with an inferiority ten times multiplied by the defeat of his race in war, in war alone he had found some appeasement for his hatreds. There he had assembled his vision, and there heard the blind voice, which had carried him upwards through such ugly avenues as pedlar and regimental runner and police spy ; the voice which he must strain and debase, and never allow to be hushed, in beer taverns, noisy heated halls, or at street corners. He had gone under, suffered imprisonment and contempt, and in endurance hardened his shallow reading of history and deep scorn for men ; debauched, easily corruptible, and influenced creatures, whom only master natures could direct, and over whom only master races should prevail. This hatred and contempt had given him the faith which had borne down parliaments and routine-minded soldiers ; he would rid himself, and then all his race, of fear. Peace of mind he could never have, he must have fast motors and films and throbbing Wagnerian music, lightning building, and all things which would hasten action and deaden thought. No, not peace, but a satisfaction ; that the fear he had mastered should henceforth be both weapon and slave.

Yet though his intensity of will and the exaggeration of his distorted mirror grew upon him, in the working hours of contemptuous calculation he worked to his old rules, — the loathsomeness of Jewry, the terrifying weight of Bolshevist Russia, the decadence of France. As for Great Britain, how many times had he not put to these obstinate islanders the only reasonable and Nordic scheme, that they keep the sea and leave to him the land mass of Europe ? And now, with Austria won and the West Wall rising, they could not expect him not to take the Germans of Bohemia, which would bend that Russian spear-head back against Russia, bring him Ukrainian wheat and Roumania's oil, and empower him to tear out the last puny pages of Versailles in Memel and Danzig.

Many have spoken, and written, as if Chamberlain's first object at Munich was to gain time to arm against an inevitable war. He would, indeed, have been unfit for his position if that had not been in his mind ; as, we know from letters already quoted, it long had been. But it was never his first motive, which was plain enough, simply the rightness of peace and the wrongness of war. " It can't be right ", he was heard to repeat to himself, walking up and down the Downing Street garden in the last emergency, on the passing of which he took the stand never abandoned till his last breath ; " even if it were to fail, I should still say that it was right to attempt it. For the only alternative was war, and I would never take that awful responsibility upon my shoulders unless it were forced upon me by the madness of others."

Moreover, that notion of a Machiavellian subtlety which, very characteristically, many Germans have since adopted, that he out-manœuvred Hitler by gaining time, is untrue in another sense, that it over-isolates the Munich episode. To him it was a part, forced on him at the sword's point it is true, but still a part, of a policy pursued before and after, to settle the danger spots by an agreed solution, and so to create an atmosphere of confidence wherein lasting peace might grow. If he could see readjustment of the peace of Versailles by peaceful conference and by a return to the principles which that peace had professed, he cared little — it may be, too little — for strategical loss and gain.

From this fiery passion for peace came both his great strength in those days, and his weakness thereafter. He made himself the champion of common humanity ; in his mind, as innumerable phrases in his letters tell us, was the picture of a world at peace, of children growing, young men marrying, old men scything, all that nature gave, all hope, all delight, — all, alternatively, to be plunged into hatred, sorrow, and death, a darkness over the earth. Believing that all men in all nations must desire peace, he took too large comfort from every token that reached him, and failed by a noble infirmity, of hoping too much from human nature.

We return to the practical limits within which he must act, as he described them at the time.

11 September

I fully realise that, if eventually things go wrong and the aggression takes place, there will be many, including Winston, who will say that the British government must bear the responsibility, and that if only they had had the courage to tell Hitler now that, if he used force, we should at once declare war, that would have stopped him. By that time it will be impossible to prove the contrary, but I am satisfied that we should be wrong to allow the most vital decision that any country could take, the decision as to peace or war, to pass out of our hands into those of the ruler of another country, and a lunatic at that. I have been fortified in this view by reading a very interesting book on the foreign policy of Canning.[1] . . . Over and over again Canning lays it down that you should never menace unless you are in a position to carry out your threats, and although, if we have to fight I should hope we should be able to give a good account of ourselves, we are certainly not in a position in which our military advisers would feel happy in undertaking to begin hostilities if we were not forced to do so.

There is another consideration which, of course, our critics cannot have in mind, and that is the plan, the nature of which I think you have guessed correctly. The time for this has not yet arrived, and it is always possible that Hitler might act so unexpectedly as to forestall it. That is a risk which we have to take, but in the meantime I do

[1] Professor Harold Temperley's *Foreign Policy of Canning*.

not want to do anything which would destroy its chance of success because, if it came off, it would go far beyond the present crisis, and might prove the opportunity for bringing about a complete change in the international situation.

When he wrote thus, our government's public attitude was unchanged, if a fraction stiffer. Simon's Lanark speech of August 27 was followed up by the warning which Henderson took back to Germany, that if France were attacked Great Britain might be involved. Our urgency with Beneš to produce the 4th Plan before Hitler committed himself was coupled with a declaration to Germany which assumed the integrity of Czech territory, and that France would stand by her bond ; on September 9 we called up mine-layers and mine-sweepers, on the 11th Chamberlain announced the probability that we should go to the help of France.

But the Germans had one weapon of insidious power, the Anglo-Saxon formula of self-determination. If Czechs and Germans could not live together, why not revise the frontiers ? so murmured more than one organ of the press, and notably *The Times* leading article of September 7, which the Foreign Office disavowed. On the 12th, at Nuremberg, Hitler furiously demanded it for " these tortured creatures ", though naming no time limit ; the bloodshed and rioting in the Sudeten country, which preceded his speech, was much enlarged, especially in that Eger district which our Foreign Office, twenty years before, had recommended should be ceded to Germany. On the 13th the Czechs proclaimed martial law and Henlein broke off negotiation, two days after fleeing to Germany ; Runciman's misgivings were realised, that the 4th Plan could not long hold the ground, and when he left for London on the 16th, he advised that self-determination should be given. Our information was that German troops, panzer divisions included, might strike at any minute on the pretext of some new incident, to anticipate the Czech mobilisation.

Fairly to assess Chamberlain's motives, let us suppose that France did not come into it, and piece together his utterances on a single point, whether it was our duty, or to our interest, to intervene if Czechoslovakia were invaded. Apart from the practical obstacles we have seen in his mind, the certainty that the country would be overrun, or the probability that a prior declaration of our intention would have hardened the Czechs, it was, as he said in his blunt way, " a far-away country " to whom we had no treaty obligation, apart from the Covenant of the League. He believed also that the country "would not have followed us if we had tried to lead it into war to prevent a minority from obtaining autonomy, or even from choosing to pass under some other government". We could not always undertake to protect every small State against the bullying of a great one, — "if we have to fight, it must be on larger issues than that"; it must be on something "irresistible", on such a cause as would arise if he were "convinced that any nation had made up its mind to dominate the world by fear of its force". There were also the Dominions to think of. What he said to Parliament was simply this, that "it would have been difficult to convince them that we should have been justified in giving such an assurance"; in fact, he could have said much more. South Africa was decided to remain neutral in such a quarrel; the Australian Labour party were against intervention; it was most doubtful whether, in such a cause, Mackenzie King could rally Canadian opinion as a whole. He did not live to read a final testimony on this matter from a quarter better equipped, perhaps, than any other to pronounce.

8 November 1940; from the Editor of "The Times"
   No one who sat in this place, as I did during the autumn of '38, with almost daily visitations from eminent Canadians and Australians, could fail to realise that war with Germany at that time would have been misunderstood and resented from end to end of the Empire.

If the issue, then, could be so simplified, we reach a question of degree; Chamberlain would have fought, but only to resist a domination of the world by force.
   In a sense it was so simplified, for before he first visited Hitler, enquiries at Paris convinced him that France had no intention of fighting. Even the tone in the mass of the French press must have delighted the German heart, but he had before him also the utterances of French ministers. If Daladier spoke bitterly of Beneš' procrastination, Bonnet was much more forthcoming: let Great Britain arbitrate, and if the Czechs refused a fair offer, it was their funeral. His instinct had always been to water down the French-Soviet pact, — better a deal with Germany, thought French business men, than to be ruled by the Front Populaire, — and after seeing Litvinov in early September he declared his instinct was confirmed. Russia, he seems to have said, would speak loud but not act, nor would Roumania allow Russian planes to cross her territory. This pacifism ran diagonally across all French parties, for if there was

a Left-wing contingent for war, Blum himself would not commit the Socialists.

Hitler spoke on September 12, and next day the French Cabinet took their decision.   They had before them Chamberlain's communiqué of the 11th, to the effect that Britain would not stand aside if " the integrity of France " was menaced, together with Bonnet's view on Russia and the last reports on their own forces. Our own belief was that their Air Force only possessed some 700 modern machines, of which a high proportion were in Africa, production of aircraft was not thought to be more than 40 a month, tanks and anti-tank guns were negligible.   The French Cabinet's practical decisions on this Tuesday the 13th amounted to little more than this : not to mobilise, but to ban public meetings on international questions, and to seek a conference.   Bonnet apparently urged that any solution was better than war, even a Sudeten plebiscite ;   France would not sacrifice ten million men to stop three million Germans joining the Reich.   Strong hints were passed to Prague that France was reconsidering, and at night Daladier seems to have suggested to Chamberlain that together they should approach Hitler.   But Chamberlain had already taken his measures alone.

13 September ; to Adolf Hitler

In view of increasing critical situation, I propose to come over at once to see you, with a view to trying to find peaceful solution. I propose to come across by air, and am ready to start to-morrow. Please indicate earliest time at which you can see me, and suggest place of meeting. Should be grateful for very early reply.

A letter to his elder sister takes up the story :

19 September

in my last letter I wondered what might happen before I wrote again, for I knew the hour must be near, if it was to come at all.   Two things were essential, first, that the plan should be tried just when things looked blackest, and second that it should be a complete surprise . . . on Tuesday night I saw that the moment had come and must be taken, if I was not to be too late.   So I sent the fateful telegram and told the Cabinet next morning what I had done. . . . At last during the afternoon my anxiety was relieved.   Hitler was entirely at my disposal, and would not Mrs. Chamberlain come too !   Afterwards I heard from Hitler himself, and it was confirmed by others who were with him, that he was struck all of a heap, and exclaimed " I can't possibly let a man of his age come all this way ; I must go to London ". Of course, when he considered it further, he saw that wouldn't do, and indeed it would not have suited me, for it would have deprived my coup of much of its dramatic force. But it shows a side of Hitler that would surprise many people in this country.

When he left England on September 15 on his first long flight, he carried various alternatives which had been under discussion, but he knew the weakness of his weapons. Looking back later, he compared himself to a man called on to play poker with a gangster, with no cards in his hand, and, above all, he was depressed by a total want of confidence in France. Apart from, and far beyond, these heavy thoughts, he was impelled by his zeal to stop men returning to the killing of each other ; had war come, he was to say, " the people of this country would have lost their spiritual faith altogether ". To win that respite, he told friends both before and after, and much more to win lasting peace, he would pay a price, in the prestige of his country and his own good fame.

He was speeded by many messages of acclamation, as from Baldwin, and the governments of Canada and Australia, which were echoed by those who spoke for other nations with whom he had tried to build peace.

15 September ; from Eamon De Valera

you will have succeeded or failed when you receive this. I merely write to tell you that one person at least is completely satisfied that you are doing the right thing — no matter what the result. I believe you will be successful. Should you not be so, you will be blamed for having gone at all. To stop half way, — to stop short of taking any action which held out even the slightest chance of success, in view of what is involved, would be wrong. Should you fail, you need have no qualms. What a business man would do, you, who have at this moment the fate of millions, who cannot help themselves, depending on you, are certainly entitled to do and should do.

May God bless your efforts.

16 September ; from Count Grandi

you have been human, while unfortunately traditional diplomacy sometimes loses touch with humanity. I wish you every success in the task you have undertaken. Difficulties ahead are still so great, but you have broken the evil spell, and millions of mothers in Europe, and in the world over, are blessing you to-day.

The aeroplane passed through a storm as it reached Munich ; soon after noon, he stepped out to be met by Ribbentrop's mechanical smile, and the rolling of drums.

CHAPTER XXVIII

BERCHTESGADEN AND GODESBERG

As Priam to Achilles for his son,
So you, into the night, divinely led,
To ask that young men's bodies, not yet dead,
Be given from the battle not begun.
JOHN MASEFIELD

PART of the price he was to pay that very day, the price which not he alone but a whole generation had incurred, and in due course, since he stood foremost in the breach, was to pay more. Whether it was necessary to pay it, let not our still uninformed judgement undertake boldly to say, but whether he was a man armed to do battle with Hitler is fit for discussion here. Simple he was, as his letters show, and obstinately sanguine in that he was bent on finding decency even in dictators, and on counting his blessings. Believing in reason, he judged a time must come, or perhaps had come, when even Hitler would conclude that it would pay him to stop aggression. But was he bamboozled, just taken in, wholly deceived, into a conviction he had won a lasting peace? That was not so. He came back saying that Hitler was abnormal, incalculable, surrounded by evil advisers ; thought, incidentally, that he could not be long-lived in this state of hysteria ; and he said, to one who saw him off on his second flight, that he was going to fight with a wild beast. His whole policy was an act of faith, a policy which clearly cannot exist if doubts are always being cast upon it in public, yet it was not a roseate picture that he painted to his colleagues, on whom he impressed that, however difficult, they must push along two parallel roads of conciliation and re-armament.

Through the mist of the Bavarian afternoon vibrated the last news of Europe. Meetings in Poland and Hungary to stake out their claims against the Czechs ; action at Prague of Polish, Magyar, and Slovak minorities ; Mussolini's " open letter " to Runciman, which declared for plebiscites for all the races, and that Hitler was not arming in order to rule over Czechs ; in Paris Blum praising Chamberlain's " noble audacity " ; Right-wing papers calling for the clean cut ; Bonnet's press and Flandin's press and half the Labour press all against war. In the Sudeten country the blinds were pulled down, on either side the Bohemian mountains a noise of trains and convoys rolling up with engines of battle. All these things are in mind as his familiar account takes us from the Munich aerodrome.

19 September (continued)

I felt quite fresh and was delighted with the enthusiastic welcome of the crowds who were waiting in the rain, and who gave me the Nazi salute and shouted " heil " at the tops of their voices all the way to the station. There we entered Hitler's special train for the 3 hours journey to Berchtesgaden. . . . All the way up there were people at the crossings, the stations, and at the windows of the houses, all heiling and saluting. . . . We drove to the Brown House a good deal higher up the mountain. The entrance of the house is on one side opening on to a sort of terrace, from which a flight of steps descends to the road. Half way down these steps stood the Fuehrer, bareheaded and dressed in a khaki-coloured coat of broadcloth with a red armlet and a swastika on it, and the military cross on his breast. He wore black trousers, such as we wear in the evening, and black patent-leather lace-up shoes. His hair is brown, not black, his eyes blue, his expression rather disagreeable, especially in repose, and altogether he looks entirely undistinguished. You would never notice him in a crowd, and would take him for the house painter he once was. After saying some words of welcome, he took me up the steps and introduced me to a number of people, among whom I only distinguished General Keitel, a youngish pleasant-faced smart-looking soldier. We then entered the house, and passed along a very bare passage through a smaller room to the celebrated chamber, or rather hall, one end of which is entirely occupied by a vast window. The view, towards Salzburg, must be magnificent, but this day there were only the valley and the bottoms of the mountains to be seen.

At the opposite end is a raised dais, on which a large round table was laid for tea. . . . On the walls were a number of pictures by old German and Italian masters. Just behind me was a large Italian nude.

We sat down, I next to Hitler, with the interpreter on his other side. He seemed very shy, and his features did not relax while I endeavoured to find small talk.

I. " I have often heard of this room, but it's much larger than I expected."

H. " It is you who have the big rooms in England."

I. " You must come and see them sometime."

H. " I should be received with demonstrations of disapproval."

I. " Well, perhaps, it would be wise to choose the moment."

At this H. permitted himself the shadow of a smile.

After we had finished tea, H. asked abruptly what procedure I proposed. Would I like to have two or three present at our talk ? I replied that, if convenient to him, I would prefer a *tête à tête*. Thereupon he rose, and he and I and the interpreter . . . walked upstairs, and through a long room with more pictures (and more nudes), till we arrived at his own room. This was completely bare of ornament. There wasn't even a clock, only a stove, a small table with 2 bottles of mineral water (which he didn't offer me), 3 chairs, and a sofa. Here we sat and talked for 3 hours.

For the most part H. spoke quietly and in low tones. I did not see any trace of insanity, but occasionally he became very excited and poured out his indignation against the Czechs in a torrent of words, so that several times I had to stop him and ask that I might have a chance to hear what he was talking about. I soon saw that the situation was much more critical than I had anticipated. I knew that his troops and tanks and guns and planes were ready to pounce, and only awaiting his word, and it was clear that rapid decisions must be taken if the situation was to be saved. At one point he seemed to be saying that he was going in at once, so I became indignant, saying that I did not see why he had allowed me to come all this way, and that I was wasting my time. He quieted down then, said if I could assure him that the British Government accepted the principle of self-determination (which he had not invented), he was prepared to discuss ways and means. I said I could give no assurance without consultation. My personal opinion was that on principle I didn't care two hoots whether the Sudetens were in the Reich, or out of it, according to their own wishes, but I saw immense practical difficulties in a plebiscite. I could, however, break off our talk now, go back and hold my consultations, and meet him again. That is a possible procedure, he said, but I am very sorry that you should have to make two journeys. However, next time I shall come to meet you somewhere near Cologne. Then I asked him how the situation was to be held in the meantime, and he promised not to give the order to march unless some outrageous incident forced his hand.

On the way downstairs he was much more cordial than on going up. He asked what time I had to leave, with a view to my seeing his scenic beauties in the morning, and when I said I must go early, since lives were being lost, he said "Oh well, when all this is over you must come back, and I will take you to my tea house at the top of the mountain ". . . . I had established a certain confidence, which was my aim, and on my side, in spite of the hardness and ruthlessness I thought I saw in his face, I got the impression that here was a man who could be relied upon when he had given his word. . . . I have

been at it hard ever since. I saw Runciman on Friday on my return.
. . . Yesterday I got up early to meet the French ministers, and we
had an exhausting day with them, which didn't finish till after midnight. That also resulted in unanimity, and we have sent our proposals
to the Czechs. . . . I have still many anxious days before me, but
the most gnawing anxiety is gone, for I feel that I have nothing to
reproach myself with, and that on the contrary up to now things are
going the way I want.

Great was the responsibility he had taken on himself. He
disliked the impact of Hitler, his abrupt turns from shouting to
courtesy, and called him (as some men styled himself) a blinkered
mind. But he never believed, any more than Henderson or the
Americans in Berlin believed, that Hitler was bluffing. On the
contrary, he told the House " my visit alone prevented an invasion ".
Evidence came to support that conviction in Polish troop movements, and in Italian staff preparations in case it proved more
than a localised war.

There were some among his colleagues who felt this journey
detrimental to a British minister's prestige, but that, as he told
Parliament, he reckoned as nothing when millions of lives were
at stake ; it was a larger matter that he had accepted the principle
of self-determination, under threat of an ultimatum. They now
had Runciman present with them, who declared that only prompt
cession of districts where the Sudeten made " an important majority "
could avert an upheaval ; Henderson's report, much impressed
by Goering, that it alone could stop a general war ; the French
press, and the Italian demonstrations. What more argument Chamberlain brought may be conjectured from his speeches, — that
Hitler vowed this redemption of Germans was his last territorial
claim, that the surgeon who deals with disease long neglected must
cut deep, that the alternative was a war which might well bring
in both Italy and Japan. He spoke, no doubt, of his opinion, which
our ambassadors had helped to shape, as to the moral disunity
of France, and her total unpreparedness to fight.

That impression was confirmed when on September 18 Daladier
and Bonnet came to London ; the most that could be said was
that they were blowing hot and cold, and seemed, implicitly, to
be asking Great Britain to find them a way out. The agreement
reached in this conference accepted self-determination, ruled out
a plebiscite as leading to dangerous claims from the other minorities,
indicated that a transfer of areas with over 50 per cent of Germans
would best fit the case, suggested that an international body, with

Czech representation, should adjust frontiers and exchange of populations, and promised an international guarantee to replace the Czech alliances with France and Russia.

During the next two days the Labour party discovered a fatal flaw in the proposition that, with France and Russia, we should make a stand. We could not depend on France, the Prime Minister told their deputation, in part for the very reason that France disbelieved in Russia taking any action ; while when they invited French workers' representatives to join in their counsels, they found them unwilling, or divided. They were also made aware, as indeed they had been in March, of our own unpreparedness in some essential armaments.

On September 20 the Czech government rejected the Anglo-French proposals ; in the early morning of the 21st a British Note was presented, declaring that only those proposals could arrest an immediate attack, and an even stronger French Note, which in effect warned them that, if they continued obdurate, France would stand aside. Yielding, they said, to unheard-of pressure, the Czechs gave way, and early on the 22nd Chamberlain flew to Godesberg on the Rhine, to determine ways and means of carrying out what seemed a settled conclusion. Polish detachments were closing in on Teschen, the Hungarian ministers had visited Berchtesgaden.

From the Petersburg Hotel he drove down to the ferry, crossing the Rhine under many thousand eyes, to meet Hitler at that Dreesen hostelry from which, four years back, he had issued to open the blood-bath of 1934. In that ill-omened place Dr. Jekyll had disappeared, and in his stead were the craft and ferocity of Hyde. Making play at first with the Polish and Hungarian claims, Hitler demanded immediate occupation of German-speaking areas by German troops ; three hours thus passed in recrimination, ending in agreement to meet at 11.30 next day and a renewed promise from Hitler not to move his army during negotiation.

Next morning, however, Friday, September 23, Chamberlain sent a letter over the river early.

> I do not think you have realised the impossibility of my agreeing to put forward any plan unless I have reason to suppose that it will be considered by public opinion in my country, in France, and indeed in the world generally, as carrying out the principles already agreed upon in an orderly fashion, and free from the threat of force. . . .
> In the event of German troops moving into the areas as you propose, there is no doubt that the Czech government would have no option but to order their forces to resist.

All the morning he paced the balcony with Henderson, and when well on in the afternoon an answer came, it only proved that Hitler meant to have his display of armed might and to ruin the Czechs in panic if he could not in blood. The Sudeten, he declared, were not coming back to the Reich in virtue of other nations' benevolence, but by the Reich's irrevocable decision to implement their will for self-determination : the Czechs were only playing for time.

Chamberlain's answer was brief ; as intermediary, he would put the German proposal to Prague, and asked that it be embodied in a memorandum ; " it has become necessary that I should at once report the present situation to my colleagues and to the French government. I propose therefore to return to England."

It was arranged that Hitler's memorandum should be delivered at a final meeting, which began that night at 10.30 and went on into the small hours. Though the Führer's tone was more con- ciliatory, his memorandum was even worse than it had sounded in words ; military occupation should begin in two days' time, up to a line drawn by the German staff, and not so much as a cow should be moved from the Sudetenland. This, Chamberlain said, was a *diktat* imposed on an undefeated country. " I declared that the language and the manner of the document, which I described as an ultimatum rather than a memorandum, would profoundly shock public opinion in neutral countries, and I bitterly reproached the Chancellor for his failure to respond in any way to the efforts which I had made to secure peace." Hitler then, yielding an inch, moved forward his time-table for total occupation to October 1, adding, " you are the only man to whom I have ever made a con- cession ". Before parting, the two had some .words alone. Once more Hitler, with great earnestness, declared this was the last of his ambitions in Europe, and once more he spread out the old vision " you take the sea and we the land " ; colonies remained, but they were no matter for war.

Recrossing the river in the early morning of September 24, Chamberlain must have learned that British opinion was hardening ; he had heard also, while with Hitler, that the Czechs had mobilised, both Britain and France having told them they could no longer take the responsibility of advising them in the opposite sense. A few hours of sleep, and he was flying back to London.

On Sunday the 25th he held three Cabinets, and it was deter- mined to refuse the Godesberg ultimatum, the Czechs already having done so. On the 26th Daladier and Bonnet were present and agreed, not very convincingly, to the formula of action that,

if the Czechs were attacked, France would march ; a British communiqué (issued without consultation with Russia) added that
Britain and Russia would stand by France ; on the 27th, orders
issued to mobilise the fleet ; a broadcast was drafted to be used
in the event of war.   After weeks of restraint under the foulest
abuse, the Czechs were showing signs of a desperate resolve, — to
repudiate the Anglo-French proposal as cancelled by Godesberg,
to buy off Poland and Hungary, and to manœuvre for time, in the
belief perhaps that the Chamberlain and Daladier governments
might fall, and that the first clash would sweep the Western powers
to their side.

War might be unavoidable, but from the British ministers'
point of view nothing had occurred to make its conditions less
perilous.   All the French had done was to call up two categories
of their reserves, or not much above half a million men, and in
the London conversations Gamelin left an unhappy impression.
As to Russia, Chamberlain remained sceptical ; from the con-
fabulations with Litvinov at Geneva nothing in his view seemed
to emerge on which he could build ; for that matter, whatever
their reasoning, the Czechs themselves refrained from asking Russian
assistance.   If the world's moral opinion weighed at all, great
importance must indeed be given, — and prompt was our acknowledgement, — to President Roosevelt's appeals, but moral opinion
was not marketable in central Europe, and these very statements
made it explicit that the United States assumed no obligation.

All through the 26th and 27th hope seemed to be gone.   On
the afternoon of the first day Horace Wilson presented to Hitler
a letter from Chamberlain, reminding him of the ill consequences
he had predicted at Godesberg, and asking for a German-Czech
conference, in which Britain was ready to take part.   But Mr. Hyde
was at his worst ; gesticulating and shouting that he would have
the territory by October 1, come what may, — on second thoughts,
he must have the Czech acceptance by Wednesday the 28th
at 2 P.M.   That night he spoke to the masses in Berlin : he
was grateful to Mr. Chamberlain ; once the Sudeten were saved
he had no further interest in the Czechs, but Beneš was playing
with them all.   Early next day, Tuesday the 27th, Chamberlain
issued another statement — " it seems to me incredible that the
peoples of Europe, who do not want war with one another, should
be plunged in a bloody struggle over a question on which agreement
has already been largely obtained " ; the British government regarded themselves as morally responsible for seeing that the Czechs

fulfilled the Anglo-French terms. At noon Wilson interviewed Hitler again ; no response, save that if the Czechs rejected his memorandum, he would "smash" them. Yet his last word was to express hope that we would do our best for a settlement, and in a letter to Chamberlain he, for the first time, deigned to defend his memorandum by something that might be called reasoning. But Henderson seems to have given up hope ; a scheme and time-table which he submitted that night, on Halifax's instructions, for an orderly occupation by stages, was ill received.

That Tuesday night Chamberlain broadcast to the British peoples. "How horrible, fantastic, incredible, it is that we should be digging trenches and trying on gas-masks here because of a quarrel in a far-away country between people of whom we know nothing. . . . I would not hesitate to pay even a third visit to Germany, if I thought it would do any good. . . . I am myself a man of peace to the depths of my soul. Armed conflict between nations is a nightmare to me ; but if I were convinced that any nation had made up its mind to dominate the world by fear of its force, I should feel that it must be resisted. Under such a domination, life for people who believe in liberty would not be worth living : but war is a fearful thing, and we must be very clear, before we embark on it, that it is really the great issues that are at stake."

Later, about 10.30, he received Hitler's letter which, unlike the Godesberg memorandum, declared his willingness to join in a guarantee of the new frontiers, and gave more assurances about the plebiscite. The gap seemed to be narrowing. He therefore personally drafted this reply :

> After reading your letter I feel certain that you can get all essentials without war, and without delay. I am ready to come to Berlin myself at once to discuss arrangements for transfer with you and representa-tives of the Czech government, together with representatives of France and Italy if you desire. I feel convinced that we could reach agree-ment in a week. However much you distrust the Prague government's intentions, you cannot doubt the power of the British and French governments to see that the promises are carried out fairly and fully and forthwith. As you know, I have stated publicly that we are prepared to undertake that they shall be so carried out. I cannot believe that you will take the responsibility of starting a world war, which may end civilization, for the sake of a few days' delay in settling this long-standing problem.

Simultaneously he wrote a personal message for Mussolini, telling him of this last appeal : "I trust your Excellency will inform the

German Chancellor that you are willing to be represented and urge him to agree to my proposal, which will keep our peoples out of war ".

That done, he sat up till after two o'clock, preparing the speech he must make to Parliament this day, now the 28th ; the German ultimatum would expire at 2 P.M.

He reaped some benefit now from the Mediterranean pacification. Franco issued a declaration of neutrality in a war which he hoped might be avoided. The Italians had only partially mobilised ; the Duce's desire, it may be guessed, was not to assist a German military triumph, but rather some diplomatic outcome from which Hungary and Poland would benefit, and some nucleus be formed of resistance to Germany in the Balkans. Between ten and eleven on the 28th he received both an appeal from Roosevelt and Chamberlain's message, and took action at once. His ambassador in Berlin, whose zeal for peace was ceaseless, was ordered to advise Hitler to postpone mobilisation for twenty-four hours.

At that hour in Berlin the elements were boiling to effervescence, out of which might step either Jekyll or Hyde ; Goering and some of the soldiers were disputing furiously against Ribbentrop in the presence of that double creature whom they all knew as master. This was raging when Henderson got his instructions to present Chamberlain's message. But an earlier initiative had been taken by France.

In the past three days the bent of the French Foreign Office had become very visible. Their inspired press even implied that the firm British communiqué, naming Russia, was a forgery, while the organs of the Right were bitter against Mandel, Reynaud, and other ministers who wished to stand fast. On the night of the 27th, when Chamberlain took his independent steps, the French ordered their ambassador at London to urge an approach to Mussolini, and told François-Poncet at Berlin to give Hitler a detailed scheme. This it was which he was waiting to do all the early morning of the 28th ; it went considerably further than any British proposal as to the territory it would make over for immediate German occupation.

In the middle of François-Poncet audience, about 11.45, Hitler received Mussolini's first advice ; when he was seeing Henderson, there came the second, that Chamberlain's scheme of a conference should be accepted, and that Italy would participate. Soon after three o'clock, by which time he was assured of Mussolini's presence in person, Hitler asked Chamberlain and Daladier to meet him the following day at Munich.

At that hour the House of Commons were assembled to hear the Prime Minister's account of his long endeavour. He looked worn and haggard as, almost discarding his notes, he rehearsed the facts and arguments we have seen ; though not the one now sunk deep in his mind, that France could not be depended on. Slowly he brought the story down to the last few hours ; he was coming to its end, with Hitler's postponement of mobilisation on Mussolini's advice, when he received from Halifax, who was sitting in the peers' gallery, the invitation to Munich, — how unexpectedly, his next letter will show. He went on :

> Signor Mussolini has accepted, and I have no doubt M. Daladier will also accept. I need not say what my answer will be. Mr. Speaker, I cannot say any more. I am sure that the House will be ready to release me now, to go and see what I can make of this last effort.

There had been no such scene since Edward Grey's speech of August 1914 which united the nation in making war. Both leaders of Opposition supported the adjournment, well aware that the Czechs' acceptance of the Anglo-French proposal must make the basis of peace ; a peace, Attlee hoped, without sacrifice of principle, — a peace, said Sinclair, giving Czechoslovakia an independent life in its new frontiers. Early next morning he began his third flight, hoping, he told the crowd, he might soon say " out of this nettle, danger, we pluck this flower, safety ".

CHAPTER XXIX

MUNICH

FEW historic documents are more banal, even more unimportant, than the terms drawn up at Munich, but nothing in recent history could be more decisive of life and death for men and nations than the spirit which Munich roused, or the question how long that spirit could live. No one disliked more intensely some aspects of the terms, and even more the conditions of signature, than Chamberlain, though he felt that the Czechs and the League had, by their resistance or delay, part drawn the tragedy on themselves. He justified it as a means to an infinitely greater end.

2 October 1938 ; to the Archbishop of Canterbury

You will, I know, realise that I am almost overwhelmed with what I have to do, and will excuse a brief reply to your moving letter. The knowledge of all the heartfelt prayers that were going up for the success of my efforts has helped to sustain me in the terrible hours through which I have passed. I am sure that some day the Czechs will see that what we did was to save them for a happier future. And I sincerely believe that we have at last opened the way to that general appeasement which alone can save the world from chaos.

All, then, that he felt of the scene, and of all it might hold, as he put it to those nearest his heart, shall precede its detail.

2 October

the letters which you and Ida sent me on Friday, the day of my return, were what I wanted, for in such moments one's heart goes out instinctively to one's nearest and dearest, and the consciousness of their touch gives the strength one needs.

In these strenuous days I have lost all sense of time and recollection of days, and I hardly know, and certainly have now no wish to recall, where I was a week ago. I only know that, as the hours went by, events seemed to be closing in, and driving us to the edge of the abyss with a horrifying certainty and rapidity. Only Annie knows what I went through in those agonising hours, when hope seemed almost extinguished, and only I know how heroically she maintained her courage and her confidence. . . . For me, I confess that it seemed only too possible that all the prayers of all the peoples of the world, including Germany herself, might break against the fanatical obstinacy of one man. I daresay Annie has told you, or will tell you, of the birth of the last desperate snatch at the last tuft of grass on the very verge of the precipice. That the news of the deliverance should come to me in the very act of closing my speech in the House, was a piece of drama that no work of fiction ever surpassed.

The events of the next 48 hours entailed terrific physical and mental exertions. I was up the night before till after 2 A.M. preparing my speech. Then came the early rising, the scenes at the aerodrome, and the long flight to Munich. The rest of that day, till after 2 o'clock next morning, was one prolonged nightmare, and I have only gradually been able since then to sort out my impressions.

Hitler's appearance and manner when I saw him appeared to show that the storm signals were up, though he gave me the double hand-shake that he reserves for specially friendly demonstration. Yet these appearances were deceptive. His opening sentences, when we gathered round for our conference, were so moderate and reasonable, that I felt instant relief.

Mussolini's attitude all through was extremely quiet and reserved. He seemed to be cowed by Hitler, but undoubtedly he was most anxious for a peaceful settlement, and he played an indispensable part in attaining it. . . . His manner to me was more than friendly ; he listened with the utmost attention to all I said, and expressed the strong hope that I would visit him early in Italy, where I should receive a very warm welcome.

I found an opportunity of talking to him about Spain, and suggesting that the Four-Power Conference should call on the 2 sides to observe a truce, while we helped them to find terms of settlement. He promised to think over this suggestion, which I afterwards made also to Hitler, but he told me that he was " fed up " with Spain, where he had lost 50,000 men in dead and wounded, that he was sick of Franco, who continually threw away all chances of victory, that he had no territorial claims there whatever, that he was satisfied that there was now no chance of Bolshevism getting the upper hand, and that he was very shortly going to withdraw 10,000 men.

I asked Hitler about 1 in the morning, while we were waiting for the draftsmen, whether he would care to see me for another talk. He jumped at the idea, and asked me to come to his private flat, in a tenement house where the other floors are occupied by ordinary citizens. I had a very friendly and pleasant talk : on Spain (where he too said he had never had any territorial ambitions), economic relations with S.E. Europe, and disarmament. I did not mention colonies, nor did he. At the end I pulled out the declaration, which I had prepared beforehand, and asked if he would sign it. As the interpreter translated the words into German, Hitler frequently ejaculated "*ja, ja*", and at the end he said "yes, I will certainly sign it; when shall we do it?" I said "now", and we went at once to the writing-table, and put our signatures to the two copies which I had brought with me.

Even the descriptions of the papers give no idea of the scenes in the streets as I drove from Heston to the Palace. They were lined from one end to the other with people of every class, shouting themselves hoarse, leaping on the running board, banging on the windows, and thrusting their hands into the car to be shaken. The scenes culminated in Downing St., when I spoke to the multitudes below from the same window, I believe, as that from which Dizzy announced peace with honour 60 years ago.

We came here yesterday immediately after lunch, and walked up through Crow's Close to the Chequers church way. I came nearer there to a nervous breakdown than I have ever been in my life. I have pulled myself together, for there is a fresh ordeal to go through in the House. After that I *must* make an effort to get away, if only for a week.

We must return to the Führer House at Munich, at 12.30 on September 29, where the four leaders met in conference that extended over the next thirteen hours. Speed was the essence, for the guns were still trained in Bohemia, and speed too was subsequently given by French and British alike as the reason why it was impossible to bring Russia into their consultations; Chamberlain raised the question of Czech representatives being present, but it was decided that the four powers who had the responsibility must make the settlement. Mussolini's contribution, which in preventing German mobilisation had been decisive, was useful for mediation in conference too, in part because he alone understood English, French, and German, and it was an Italian draft, immediately accepted by Daladier, which made the basis for discussion. Except for two short anti-Czech tirades, Hitler was calm, and the British were agreeably — perhaps too easily — surprised by the broad scope that the Germans would give to the international commission. Ribbentrop was, as usual, sulky and unhelpful, childishly displeased at the popular acclamation of Chamberlain, even doing his best to see that the British should be taken by more obscure streets, and never allowed to move alone. As for the French, whatever Chamberlain duly said in Parliament, their rôle at Munich was passive, and deepened his uneasiness at dependence on an ally whose domestic politics seemed so demoralised. He could work with Daladier, but felt he had no confidence in his own position.

Every amendment which he secured was designed to emphasise that this was a peaceful diplomatic procedure ; words to show they were working on a basis already agreed, others to avoid admission that the Polish and Hungarian claims could be settled by force, or the clause giving to individuals a right of option. What he was most unhappy about was the guarantee for the future Czech State, refusing to accept it in a form which would have bound Great Britain to act individually. But, Mussolini being warm in favour, the principle was accepted, subject to determination in detail.

What then were the differences between Godesberg and Munich, so that on one the British and French were ready to fight, but on the other to make peace ? " On the difference between those two documents ", he told the Commons, " will depend the judgement whether we were successful in what we set out to do, namely to find an orderly instead of a violent method of carrying out an agreed decision." He put them thus : the operation of that decision under international supervision ; military occupation, not on the single day of October 1, but by five stages ; occupation to a line, not fixed by the Germans but by an international commission ; definition of plebiscite areas also by the same body, and their provisional occupation by an international force ; omission of those brutal clauses which would have forbidden the refugees to take a stick of furniture, or a bite of food ; the right to opt, within six months, to pass into Czech territory. Even so, these amendments, made under stress of arms in the background, depended wholly for their worth on how they were fulfilled.

So it was not really the difference between two documents which massed an almost unanimous Empire behind him, or made up the true significance of " Munich ", nor even his claim to have saved " Czechoslovakia from destruction, and Europe from Armageddon ". We can search for it and find it in many places ; in the public utterances of the Empire's leaders, in an almost unbroken press, and in the small selection he chose to keep of the 40,000 letters which he received. This chorus of gratitude for what he had attempted was led by his sovereign.

30 September ; from H.M. King George VI

I am sending this letter by my Lord Chamberlain, to ask you if you will come straight to Buckingham Palace, so that I can express to you personally my most heartfelt congratulations on the success of your visit to Munich.

In the meantime, this letter brings the warmest of welcomes to one who, by his patience and determination, has earned the lasting gratitude of his fellow-countrymen throughout the Empire.

When the letters and speeches are read again, from veterans of war, from old colleagues like Baldwin or old rivals like Lansbury, from public men of every party and every hue, from bishops, painters, or unemployed, all British folk of every class and realm, the motives moving them are found to be various. In many the ruling feeling was that this had not been a stake, as one notable fighting man said, " that Britons should be asked to die for ". In some, especially those who knew war best, appeared that argument which in due course was to swallow up most other arguments, that precious time had been won in which to rearm. In others, well fitted to judge, admiration of his courage and resource ; as Hankey wrote for instance, " at every point your touch was unerring, your vision prophetic, your patience and energy inexhaustible ". A deeper tribute came from men who, versed in the waging of the last war, or the making of the last peace, felt that a fatal current might have been reversed, and the edge of the axe turned away.

30 September ; from Lord Weir

Since 1919 world leadership has led mainly in harmful and dangerous directions. You are the first leader to bring about a definite and abrupt deflection of the harmful stream. . . . After this week no one, and no nation, will be quite the same in thought or action. The possibilities for good are tremendous in the light of the new faith you have given the world.

Smuts too spoke in that strain :

a great champion has appeared in the lists, God bless him. The path of the peacemaker was difficult and dangerous, but he gave no thought for himself, or his future. He risked all, and I trust he has won all.

By such gradations we come to the thought which Maxton put in debate, that he had done " something that the mass of the common people in the world wanted done ". This was the thought which filled the letters from the poor and the parents of young sons, which accompanied the flowers and poems and umbrellas and fishing rods which rained in on Downing Street, filled the crowds which saw him on the Palace balcony with the King, which all the next year would troop after him at Highland railway stations, or in once hostile South Wales. Their thought was a deep and simple one, that total war was an abomination, and that in it they would

not see their children killed, crippled, blinded, made imbecile, as
their fathers or their contemporaries had been. Among those
letters from the common folk he kept one from his old friend Kate,
kitchen-maid in his father's house sixty years before.

October ; from Kate Bird

I have felt so terribly thrilled and proud with what you were trying
to do. . . . And you must feel terribly glad, my dear Mr. Neville,
that it fell to you to face that German, and talk as you must have
done. . . . All I can say further is that this old woman, friend of
your boyhood, wishes for you and your loved ones a happy contented
old age. You will never be forgotten.

That was the serious historical fact of this week, that round
this " flying messenger of peace " (as Mussolini called him) were
wrapped the last hopes of the mass of mankind, that the world
might learn some better way of deciding its differences than the
killing of its best young men. Kings wrote to him ; peasants from
all countries in huddled illiterate scrawls. " I express to you ",
came from the King of the Belgians, " the heartiest thanks of one
to whom destiny has entrusted the sacred responsibility of many
human beings." " Mister Chamberlain," follows on the same file,
from Rome, " God may bless your white head. I am an Italian
mother." In Brussels they struck a medal to the " apostle of peace " ;
Dutchmen sent their tulips ; he received a request for a piece of
his umbrella to make a relic in a Greek icon ; streets were named
after him as they had been for Gladstone. But it was the testimony
of the general repugnance to war in Germany which stayed longest
in his mind.

That did not depend merely on what he had himself seen, in
the cheering crowds that broke the police cordons, even the Brown
Shirts cheering, but on all that came from British reporters, French
diplomats, and experienced travellers. Their general impression
was the same ; the glum silence in Berlin, the growing criticism
of the régime, and the concentration upon his person of their aspiration for peace. Some dared to write to him direct, others indirectly.

October 1938 ; from a German ex-naval officer

I feel like one having been condemned to death, and set free in the last
minute. . . . It is my fervent wish to let Mr. Chamberlain know that
we will thank him and bless him, all our life long.

2 October ; from a Göttingen professor

Never again ! that is the main idea, not only among the professors,
but also among the students . . . that is even what the army thinks.

. . . We know how much the British Prime Minister has done to prepare the settlement. The crowds cheering him during his three days' trip through Germany really expressed the general feeling of admiration, even of love, which he has won.

Above all such, or the like from the great Hugo Stinnes, we shall prefer one received, the March following, when this hope seemed perished, from a German woman : " we feel as long as you are there, the masses in Germany cannot be talked into the belief of English aggression ".

Had he then done something greater than to prevent immediate war, and reached the heart of Germany ? even found a heart in Hitler ? On the way home in the aeroplane, and again later, he said he thought that in the last conversation at Hitler's flat he had for a moment discovered a human being. He had asked him, if the Czechs still resisted, to spare Prague attack from the air, asked him to think over getting a truce in Spain, spoken of a world disarmament conference, and relaxation in international trade. That done, he had asked him to sign this declaration :

We, the German Fuehrer and Chancellor, and the British Prime Minister, have had a further meeting to-day, and are agreed in recognising that the question of Anglo-German relations is of the first importance for the two countries and for Europe.

We regard the agreement signed last night, and the Anglo-German Naval agreement, as symbolic of the desire of our two peoples never to go to war with one another again.

We are resolved that the method of consultation shall be the method adopted to deal with any other questions that may concern our two countries, and we are determined to continue our efforts to remove possible sources of difference, and thus to contribute to assure the peace of Europe.

That night he spoke from the window at Downing Street, not of design but for the purpose of dispersing the huge multitude below :

This is the second time in our history that there has come back from Germany to Downing Street peace with honour. I believe it is peace for our time.

Yet two days before, on setting out, when someone suggested that very phrase from Disraeli, he rejected it with impatience, and within a week asked the House not to read overmuch into words " used in a moment of some emotion, after a long and exhausting day, after I had driven through miles of excited, enthusiastic,

o

cheering people ". No, he was not deceived, neither by Hitler's moods nor by the exultant relief of London ; " all this will be over in three months ", he said to Halifax as their car struggled through the crowd, and he had prepared his statement for Hitler to sign, in hope but also in calculation. For if it were honoured, well and good ; if repudiated, it would brand the guilty party before all mankind. This also he spoke of on the journey home.

The middle path which he stressed would be arduous, easy to misrepresent, and easy to miss. He must exploit a hope as though he believed it to the hilt, deny surrender without boasting of victory, entrench a firm position by rearming and yet give no cause for war, and submit to provocation for a greater end, till time were on his side. Yet the hope was so great, the vision of the masses in all countries, who for a short season hung on his name, so moved him, that sometimes he reckoned too little of the other side. Till hope was visibly dead at his feet, he would follow its gleam.

30 September ; from Lord Baldwin

> you have everything in your own hands now, — for a time — and you can do anything you like. Use that time well, for it won't last.

CHAPTER XXX

STRAIN AND STRESS, SEPTEMBER 1938– MARCH 1939

> If New and Old, disastrous feud,
> Must ever shock, like armed foes,
> And this be true, till Time shall close,
> That Principles are rain'd in blood :
>
> Not yet the wise of heart would cease
> To hold his hope thro' shame and guilt,
> But with his hand against the hilt,
> Would pace the troubled land, like Peace.
>
> TENNYSON

RELIEVED from a war which they had not feared, but on the merits of which they were divided and the prospect of which they abhorred, the British peoples began to weigh up loss and gain. The logic of the four days' debate in the Commons in October was, indeed, not strong, for all parties had speeded the Prime Minister with blessings on his way to Munich where, as they well knew, the Sudetenland would be taken from the Czechs. But these debates and the discussions which he met with immense patience were full of sentiment that felt outraged, and of fears for our good name and strategic interest.

Munich was, as the sense of the House and the press recognised, a marginal case ; it was peace but not justice, it was full of things which, as he himself admitted, could not be liked. On the central fact, of giving up the Sudeten, the Cabinet had been unanimous, but facts never explain history. What was found most unlovely was the circumference of Munich, and what was loathed rather the German jackboot than their racial claim. Moreover, they were all dealing in uncomfortable imponderable matter, in balancings whether trust or force answered best with Germans, or whether the future would be better now that we were rid of a disputable, barely defensible, past. Although, therefore, the debate cut across parties — the Clydesiders' passion for peace, for example, rather outweighing the normal Labour view of how " collective security " had been betrayed — and though very large majorities approved Munich, he parted depressed from House and Cabinet when at last he contrived to reach the Tweed whence — among dark woods and Cheviot sheep — he wrote to Rushcliffe that he was " trying to forget Europe ".

Even for a week, however, one question could not be forgotten, that his party were deeply divided in motive, even when accepting the facts and even though Duff Cooper's had been the only actual resignation. Nor were such feelings confined only to younger men, for Hailsham, though convinced of the wisdom of making the agreement, was entirely sceptical about Hitler's undertakings. Numerically the party cave was small, for only some thirty normal supporters abstained from voting, but their little company was highly officered, by Churchill, Eden, Cranborne, Amery, besides Duff Cooper, and had in its ranks some who had stood very near to Chamberlain of old.

Amery's speech, for example, had voiced many " sombre and disquieting considerations " ; not, he added, with any desire to blame the Prime Minister, " who knows far better than any of us those weaknesses in our defence for which we might have been paying to-day a dreadful price. The blame rests upon all of us."

6 October ; from L. C. S. Amery

your speech moved me very deeply, and very, very nearly persuaded both myself and Anthony Eden to vote. I only hope, most sincerely, that the misgivings which even you could not dispel to-day, will be disproved by the events of the near future.

6 October ; from Lord Lloyd

I want to send you this line to tell you how very deeply I have felt differing from you over this crisis. I never particularly minded differing with S. B., for our ways of thought and outlook were entirely different. But with you it has always been different. I have always looked forward to your being P.M., admired your courage — as I do to-day — applauded your Italian policy, and felt for the first time for years entirely happy about Conservative leadership. But on this tremendous issue I have felt deeply, and thought it my duty to speak as I have done. I hope it will not affect our personal relations, for I should mind that still more.

He felt these differences, and the vituperation about " betrayal ", sometimes dipping for an antidote into the pile of thousands of humble letters and embarrassing gifts, the tide of which still flowed. Streams of advice came in too, both from colleagues and advisers unasked. Hoare and Hore-Belisha, it seems, wished for a Ministry of Supply ; some would seize the golden moment and dissolve, some begged him to reconstruct his government, and among them the one on whose counsel he most leaned.

Halifax found himself in growing agreement with the position which Eden's speeches reiterated this winter, that there was urgent need of a greater national unity in foreign affairs. It was true, he wrote on October 11, that if he took in some of the Opposition they might soon disagree " with the policy that you are trying to pursue of getting on terms with dictators " — " however much you may feel, as we were saying to each other the other day, that while hoping for the best it is also necessary to prepare for the worst ". But in some practical measures they might well be convinced, and such an offer would have real value. His conclusion was weighty.

> My instinct, therefore, does on the whole lead me to feel that this is the psychological moment for endeavouring to get national unity, and that, if for any reason it is not taken, it may be a long time before another recurs. The advantages from a Parliamentary point of view would obviously be very great, and from the international point of view I think my mind is clear that on balance the advantages would also be considerable. . . . I should not myself rate too high the annoyance caused to dictators by the inclusion of some of those whom they dislike, because I think your own position is great enough in their eyes to carry it, and to make it plain that you had attracted those who might join you to your policy rather than abandoned your policy to attract them.

Halifax seldom wrote at such length, and Chamberlain's private comments were equally long, but adverse. Not that he felt in the least happy, or content, with the tributes laid at his feet in letters and verse, Rhine wine or horseshoes.

16 October
> Perhaps if I were differently constituted, I might just sit back and bask in this popularity while it lasted. But I am already a little impatient with it, because it seems to assume so much. We have avoided the greatest catastrophe, it is true, but we are very little nearer to the time when we can put all thoughts of war out of our minds, and settle down to make the world a better place.

He must go back to reconstruct, with two places to fill, for Lord Stanley died only a fortnight after Duff Cooper resigned. Was he then to make offers to Labour and to Eden, as Halifax advised ? He feared the difference went deeper than Eden's speeches suggested. " What makes him think it possible to get unity is my insistence on the necessity for rearmament, and the news that

I didn't like Hitler personally. He leaves out, or chooses not to see for the moment, that the conciliatory part of the policy is just as important as the rearming." No, he did not want a long running fight of doubt in Cabinet, but more power for his policy. An election he would not have now, yet sooner or later he must ask for a mandate that would give confidence abroad, and assurance at home, of a government with a continuous aim.

Nor, though he at once set on foot a review of the defence deficiencies revealed by the days of Munich, would he have a Ministry of Supply, which must begin by slowing the pace and might in the end be redundant : " a lot of people ", he wrote at the end of October, " seem to me to be losing their heads, and talking and thinking as though Munich had made war more, instead of less, imminent ".

Consequently his first measures of reconstruction did not meet the common demand, either in their scope or in his choice of men. His close friend Stanhope took Duff Cooper's place at the Admiralty ; he thought Hailsham's health too frail to go on, and asked him to resign the Lord Presidency, to make room for Runciman ; he offered a place to Herbert Samuel, though unsuccessfully ; John Anderson. became Privy Seal, in special charge of civil defence. If these appointments enhanced, on balance, the Cabinet's distinction, they were not pleasing either to youth or to party. Several junior ministers, up in arms against the lag in rearmament, were asking for a large head on a charger. Agriculture was bickering and grumbling as usual. The Milk Bill had to be thrown overboard to pacify back-benchers, even doubling the barley subsidy left the farmers discontented. By December Chamberlain was wondering whether he could ever shake down with this " uneasy and disgruntled House " without an election.

Nothing is more difficult than to convince a Conservative Prime Minister that his Cabinet requires change, against which many honourable motives join in revolt. He was not a man to be moved by the quick-change commands of the popular press, but now he was being told by private members of high character that they feared some senior colleagues wanted courage, and some junior ministers lacked loyalty. He found this trust in himself exasperating, when so combined with a reflection on his choice, and whether his choice was right or wrong, it has to be said that it was deliberate. He was perfectly alive to, even to a point shared in, the criticism of the higher command, and admitted doubt as to the judgement of some younger ministers, but " survey the back

benches ? ", he said to one whose opinion he much respected,
" I am continually doing it " ; the result of which survey duly
went elsewhere thus, " the material available is meagre in the
extreme, and I don't remember any time when there was so little
promise among the younger men in the Government and on the
back benches ".

The further changes of January did not reflect either youth
or party, though strengthening two of the angles most exposed.
Chatfield replaced Inskip in co-ordination of Defence, with W. S.
Morrison as his deputy in the Commons ; Inskip took the Dominions
office left vacant by Lord Stanley's death ; Dorman Smith, once
president of the Farmer's Union, would now survey Agriculture
with a new bias, as Minister.

Foreign policy, which had divided the party into groups, dictated also the lines of business, so that in proportion as men thought
they were moving nearer to war or to peace, so they spoke and
voted. Whether the national register of service should be voluntary,
as he insisted to a party meeting, or compulsory, the gaps in air-raid
precautions, export guarantees to under-cut Germany's political
method of trading, so their time passed. On a free vote he exerted
himself in favour of a contributory pensions scheme for ex-members
of Parliament in need, which became law on the eve of war.

6 February 1939 ; from H. B. Lees Smith
> may I express my sincere appreciation of the steady support that you
> have given to the proposal for pensions for M.P.'s, without which it
> would certainly not have been passed. Your help is fully recognised
> by our side of the House, although this may not be expressed to you
> personally.

One-half of his policy, rearmament, did not pause, was indeed
at last getting into a steady flow, and was telling on the unemployment figures which, after a bad spell, fell all the first half of 1939,
until in August they touched the lowest level for ten years. His
post-Munich speeches were careful to underline our defensive purpose, and that agreed disarmament must be our final aim, but were
equally positive on acceleration of effort, and candid in the reason
for it. " Disarmament on the part of this country can never be
unilateral again. We have tried that once, and we very nearly
brought ourselves to disaster." And again, " if there has been a
mistake, it is not the mistake of not having a ministry of Supply ;
it has been the mistake of not realising soon enough the necessity
for some of these armaments ",

It was, in fact, in the year after Munich that his toils of 1936 bore fruit. The Air programme of May 1938 for a first-line strength of 2370 at home would, Kingsley Wood now announced, once more be speeded up, and whereas less than 3000 aircraft were forthcoming in 1938, 1939 produced 8000. In February the borrowing powers for the five-year programme were doubled, from £400 to £800 millions. In March the defence estimates for the coming year reached nearly £600 millions, or well over twice the total of 1937. The tonnage building for the Navy would much exceed the great days of 1912–14, gun production potential had risen fivefold in four years, its fuel reserves were complete. Hore-Belisha's plans contemplated 6 Regular divisions, of which 2 would be armoured, and 13 Territorial divisions, available for service overseas, — with 2 more in Palestine — and in April this figure of 19 was raised to 32.

If in all this he never relaxed, still it was but a means to his end ; " the goal is not only peace, but confidence that peace can be maintained ". That confidence seemed to be planted only in his own bosom, for with the passage of autumn to winter the confusion of Europe was deplorable. France was a mass of faction ; Daladier finally broke the Front Populaire by ostracising the Communists, while large sections of the Right and business world hoped for a compact with Germany, which would spare France some of the exhortations to resist of which, coming from England, the French were getting tired. But one indispensable condition for his purpose must be the bettering of relations between France and Italy, and this he could not achieve. Far from it ; the winter saw organised cries in the Italian Chamber of " Nice, Tunis, Corsica ", and elderly ministers singing the Fascist hymn ; an Italian denunciation of Laval's Rome pact of 1935 ; a military tour by Daladier in Corsica and Tunis. Meantime he himself experienced the swollen-headed, blackmailing diplomacy of Rome.

Just after Munich, where Mussolini had mentioned the forthcoming withdrawal of his infantry from Spain, we received a request that the agreement so long suspended should be put in force as soon as those troops reached Naples, — as they did, in fact, late in October. On the merits, Chamberlain wrote, both Halifax and himself were agreeable, since they thought that the Spanish question had ceased to threaten peace. But the message was accompanied by dark hints of a German military alliance, the country was not in the mood for more pressure, and the House just rising. It was therefore not until November that he asked the Commons to approve the agreement, which would of course carry with it recognition *de jure* of Italian Ethiopia. He rehearsed the urgency from Australia, the approval of South Africa and, once again, Mussolini's pledges, together with Franco's declaration of neutrality during the crisis. He asked them to put an end here and now to the notion " that it is our desire to keep any State at arm's length ", and to make peace in the Mediterranean as a long step to peace in general. But in December Franco began the advance on Catalonia which was to carry him to victory — a sore moment for the fears and the pride of France. For other reasons he felt that more contact with France was needed, and hence initiated the visit which he and Halifax paid to Paris on November 23.

6 November

I felt it to be the right thing for many reasons,— to give French people an opportunity of pouring out their pent-up feelings of gratitude and affection, to strengthen Daladier and encourage him to *do* something at last to put his country's defences in order, and to pull his people into greater unity, to show France, and Europe too, that if we were anxious to make friends with Germany and Italy, we were not on that account going to forget our old Allies, and finally to make it possible for me to go to Rome in January, which is what I am trying to arrange. I feel that Rome at the moment is the end of the Axis on which it is easiest to make an impression. I don't believe that Spain is a menace to European peace any longer,— all the same I should immensely like to stop the conflict there, and although Musso wasn't very forthcoming on the subject at Munich, I got the idea that it would be worth while to take it up with him again, after our own Agreement had come into force. But of course I want a lot more than that. An hour or two *tête à tête* with Musso might be extraordinarily valuable in making plans for talks with Germany, and if I had explored the subject first with France, we might see some way of getting a move on. In the past, I have often felt a sense of helpless exasperation at the way things have been allowed to drift in foreign affairs, but now I am in a position to keep them on the move, and while I am P.M. I don't mean to go to sleep.

Though the " pent-up feelings " of the French involved a few cries of *à bas Munich*, the Paris visit was useful, not least because it brought some joint planning for air defence ; he pronounced the conversations most satisfactory and, though disliking a bullet-proof closed car, derived much pleasure from the cheering crowds. If the French agreed without enthusiasm to the Rome visit, the British welcomed the news that Ribbentrop would soon follow them to

Paris, to sign a declaration on the same lines as Chamberlain had with Hitler. But their conversations cannot have been cheerful about Germany, from which issued not a sparkle of good tidings.

Hitler was disgusted with his people and his moderates, whose clamour for peace had made him retreat, and discontented with himself for giving way : he visited his resentment on others, Schacht and Wiedemann for instance sinking well into the background. And this Chamberlain myth displeased him. Humble folk in Munich, who had sent flowers to the British minister in those great days, now received warning that pacifism of that sort was objectionable, and that not Chamberlain but their own Führer had saved the peace ; yes, Dr. Goebbels and his press went off at full tilt — they had won peace by force, by showing they were not afraid of war. But more particularly was he infuriated by Chamberlain's exhortation to rearmament, and by the critical tone in the British Opposition and press. To the French ambassador he dwelt upon British selfishness and their rooted antagonism, while his every speech betrayed his ambitions and his fears. They enlarged upon his only true friend, the Duce ; on the war-mongers, Churchill and Eden, who might any day replace this good Chamberlain ; indeed, was not Chamberlain himself glanced at when he gloried in the heroic ideal of a Nazi leader, as contrasted with the " umbrella-carrying types " of the bourgeois world ? Let the British " governesses ", went on this dreary sarcasm, drop the airs of the Versailles epoch ; let them look to their own failure in Palestine, and not to central Europe, of which they knew nothing. Germany was not going to walk with a palm branch in this armed world, and her régime was a domestic affair of the German people. But the world did not think so in November when, taking as pretext the murder of an attaché in Paris, the most brutal of pogroms attacked the German Jews.

Was he for this, or for the Roman cries of " Nice and Corsica ", to give up the struggle ? He thought not ; though letters show his indignation at these " barbarities ", and one other incident marked his private feeling. This winter he was approached with an enquiry whether, as a gesture to those Germans who looked on him as the hope of peace, he would accept the honorary presidency of the Deutsche-Shakespeare-Genossenschaft, which no Briton had held since King Edward VII. He declined on the ground of pressure on his time, but told his intermediary that he did so, in fact, because that learned society had expelled their Jewish members.

Another matter, later to be vital, was already in dispute, and that was the fulfilment of the Munich decisions. There, it will be remembered, it had been agreed to leave frontiers and plebiscites to a commission consisting of the German secretary of State, a Czech delegate, and the ambassadors of France, Great Britain, and Italy, at Berlin. Since the Saar proceedings were the model, the basis was a return to the population status as in 1918, — before, that is, it had been affected by deliberate Czech colonisation. But the last census and map available before that date turned out to be the Austrian census of 1910. Finding both France and Italy ready to accept the German contention on this point, Henderson also agreed, and has given us his reasons ; that " rigged " plebiscites would thereby be avoided, and the Germans tied to a line from which they could not swerve. The rough effect was that the line proposed at Munich was extended to something much more like that of Godesberg ; indeed, by direct " negotiation " with the Czechs the Germans later squeezed out more population and more villages.

This was bad, but the issue of the international guarantee was worse still. He had accepted it with foreboding, but much had been made of it by some of his colleagues in debate, as giving to the Czechs some compensation for the security they had lost, by putting them in the position of another Switzerland. Germany and Italy had promised to join in it, once the Poles and Hungarians were satisfied.

But Munich had broken the central vault which carried the stresses in that ill-balanced fabric. The moment that the State was in peril, Slovaks and Ruthenians extracted their own autonomy, while Hungarians and Poles marched to make a common frontier in the Carpathians. After a month of anarchy the Germans in November, much to the discontent of their good allies, enforced an award, which preserved the mass of Slovakia and Ruthenia to the Czech State. When Chamberlain visited Paris, it would seem that the British were desirous to water down this guarantee, arguing it should only take effect if three of the four great powers concerned were in agreement, and that Germany would never accept the participation of Russia. But when at last in February the two Allies raised the question, they found the Germans suggesting that it had better be forgotten. Odd things were going on in Eastern Europe. Hitler was spreading before the Poles a notion of joint action against Russia, and of securing colonies : on the other hand, maps were being prepared for him which cheerfully painted Danzig and Memel as restored to the Reich.

In December Chamberlain was in his lowest mood, torn between resentful democracy and incalculable dictators, " forced by circumstances to walk continually through dark and perilous ways ", as he put it to the Foreign Press Association. He spoke at that banquet to some empty chairs, for the German pressmen absented themselves, on reading in his advance script a protest at their vituperation against Baldwin, who had appealed for the Jews, and perhaps on reading his hint that the forms of government were not eternal. It was bad enough to have Munich criticised as a defeat for the democracies, to be warned that an election would be unsafe, and to have half revolt against his Cabinet.

11 December

> worse than that is the continual venomous attacks by the German press, and the failure of Hitler to make the slightest gesture of friendliness. At the same time Musso takes the opportunity of writing offensive articles about " Dialogues on the Thames " which, though most directly pointed at the unhappy Negus and Benes, take the democracies in general to task and hold them up to ridicule.

He protests " at my age and in my position there can be nothing more for me to want " ; nothing but to carry the policy he believed to be right, the kernel of which he thus stated in the last debate of the year. The past treatment of Germany, he said, had been " neither generous nor wise " ; " unless this strong and virile people can be induced, in partnership with others, to improve the general lot, there will be neither peace nor progress in Europe in the things that make life worth living ". But he was wearying of one-sided effort. " It takes two to make an agreement . . . I am still waiting for a sign from those who speak for the German people . . . it would be a tragic blunder to mistake our love of peace, and our faculty for compromise, for weakness."

There were other signs of this hardening mood, as dire 1938 at last ended ; the emphasis on rearmament, a stiff Note to Japan, export guarantees for China, a refusal to hear of belligerent rights for Franco until foreign troops had gone, a firm declaration that cession of colonies was not being considered, and another that an attack on Tunis would be taken as a breach of the Italian agreement. On January 4, 1939, Roosevelt's message to Congress, though still emphasising " methods short of war ", called for defence against aggression, and Chamberlain issued words to approve this conception of freedom and " ordered human progress ". But as he walked, with his dog Spot for company, in the Chequers plantations, he often thought his time there would be short, and when he left for Rome on January 10 felt how heavily loaded were the dice.

Some of those with him found Mussolini curt, even discourteous at times, but there was no question as to the success of the primary British object, to reach the Italian people. He wrote and spoke, privately, of the crowds who thronged streets and country level-crossings to see him, of his audience at the Vatican and Cardinal Pacelli's admiration of the struggle for peace, but the more political harvest, promising as he found it, could only be reaped later.

15 January 1939

I may say at once that I consider I have achieved all I expected to get, and more, and that I am satisfied that the journey has definitely strengthened the chances of peace. To give first my impressions of Mussolini, I found him straightforward and considerate in his behaviour to us, and moreover he has a sense of humour which is quite attract-ive. . . . Although he told us frankly that he did not intend to have any negotiations with France until the Spanish affair was out of the way, he never mentioned Tunis, Corsica, Nice, Djibouti, or the Suez Canal. He was emphatic in his assurances that he intended to stand by his agreement with us, and that he wanted peace, and was ready to use his influence to get it.

So the Axis stood fast, yet it seemed that in any Anglo-German difference Italy hoped to be neutral, though to France her tone was different. Even there, however, a strain would be taken off with the coming end in Spain, and Barcelona fell a week after his return. Both in Britain and France the Left wing found a Franco victory almost unendurable, our Opposition asked for an immediate summons of Parliament and, even now, " arms for Spain ". But on no conclusions was Conservative opinion more united than on these ; that this had been a civil war, that " non-intervention ", with all its falsity, had stopped it becoming European, that re-cognition is a question not of ideology but of fact, and that Franco was, if we allowed him to be, well disposed.

Two gestures in February showed that the Cabinet was handling this complex firmly. A British cruiser was employed to arrange the surrender of Minorca direct to Franco, to the considerable annoyance of his Italian ally ; and he made a declaration that the whole force of Britain would co-operate if there were any threat to the vital interests of France. From the excision of this Spanish ulcer his hopeful mind conjured up the shape of the world he wished for.

19 February

We have now heard from the Spanish government that they will surrender if Franco will give reasonable assurances about reprisals. . . . Alba, his envoy here, thinks there will be no difficulty. I have kept back recognition to see if we can get this surrender arranged, as clearly that is the best order, but I shan't delay it if negotiations drag on too long. I think we ought to be able to establish excellent relations with Franco, who seems well disposed to us, and then, if the Italians are not in too bad a temper, we might get Franco-Italian conversations going, and if they were reasonably amicable, we might advance towards disarmament.

In these weeks he was speaking with more confidence because he felt more sure of our strength, yet still unyielding on appeasement. Munich, he told the Jewellers' dinner at Birmingham, was only an incident in a consistent policy, and only made possible by the Italian agreement. He knew that governments might not share the hunger of their peoples for peace : nevertheless, " let us cultivate the friendship of the peoples . . . let us make it clear to them that we do not regard them as potential foes, but rather as human beings like ourselves ". Yet on one clear understanding. " Peace could only be endangered by such a challenge as was envisaged by the President of the United States in his New Year message, — namely, a demand to dominate the world by force." " Our motto is not defiance, and, mark my words, it is not, either, deference. It is defence."

His rising confidence came in part from what we had done to rearm since Munich ; " they could not make nearly such a mess of us now as they could have done then, while we could make much more of a mess of them ". He built too on Roosevelt's rising tone, and on the decline in German finances, but most of all on the hope that the peoples who had come so near to war would henceforth resist it ; " all the more so because they believe that Mr. Chamberlain is a nice kind old gentlemen, who would not ever want to treat Germans roughly and unfairly ". All these weights in the balance allowed him to take that firmer tone, " which some of my critics have applauded, without apparently understanding the connection between diplomatic and strategic strength which, nevertheless, has been always stressed by the wisest diplomats and statesmen of the past ". He was writing in the same strain to John Buchan.

7 February 1939 ; to Lord Tweedsmuir

    I am afraid there are still such volcanic elements at work that we can hardly expect tranquillity for some little time to come. Nevertheless, I must tell you that I myself feel conscious of some easing in the tension. . . . a number of impressions derived from various sources, which somehow seem to fuse into a general sense of greater brightness in the atmosphere. . . . At the present time, the memory of September is still vivid in the minds of the common people throughout Europe, as well as in this country, and they are on the alert, and anxious to make sure that they are not a second time being led unawares to the edge of a precipice.

    Indeed, there were real glimmers of resistance to which the friends of peace could point in hope ; to Roosevelt's growing momentum in shaping American opinion ; second thoughts in Poland that her bargain with Hitler had been short-sighted, and some tentative outstretchings of her hand towards Roumania, even towards Russia ; the fall of the pro-Nazi minister in Jugo-Slavia, and the recognition of Franco's Spain by Britain and France. This last being supported by Eden in debate, there was talk that old differences were nearly bridged, that with accelerated defence and a stronger line to the dictators reconciliation might come, and the government be enlarged. But Chamberlain was, as he admitted, an obstinate man, confident that he had been right to try, and that it was wrong to stop short till failure were proved. In this he was not alone, as a powerful speech of Halifax during February showed :

    It would have been very easy for Mr. Chamberlain to have stopped trying to restore confidence in Europe,— many would. . . . But no man that I know is less tempted than Mr. Chamberlain to cherish unreal illusions,— it is, after all, by deeds, not words, that history is made and all men must be judged. . . . Even if all our efforts were to fail . . . the whole British people, irrespective of party and everything else, would be united as one man ; their honest desire for peace would have been shown beyond any possibility of doubt . . . the effect on the moral opinion of the world, with all that that would mean, would be incalculable.

    But the two men differed on the point of Cabinet reconstruction. That was natural, for on Chamberlain had fallen the final wear and tear, and he felt himself— how could he help it ? — a symbol of peace.   No, Eden must wait longer, the real difference was still there, his return might even tempt the dictators "to break out now, before the democracies had further strengthened their position".   Bye-elections and all he heard persuaded him that the people as a whole were behind his twin policy.   And so, though he quoted to mass meetings "come the three corners of the world in arms", he approved of discussions between British and German industrialists, and planned that in March the President of the Board of Trade should visit Berlin.   "We are getting near to a critical point", he wrote on February 12, "when the whole future direction of European politics will be decided", and as it approached he acquired something of that justified but insidious conviction which besets all men in great place, that for certain purposes — say, for the appeasement of Italy — he might be indispensable. "If Halifax were alone", he breathed, might he not imperil the great end in some premature desire for party reunion, and if he himself disappeared might not his successor reverse the engine, drifting back into that vacillation of policy that had wrought such evil before ?

19 February

> with a thrush singing in the garden, the sun shining, and the rooks beginning to discuss among themselves the prospects of the coming nesting season, I feel as though spring were getting near. . . . All the information I get seems to point in the direction of peace.

He broke out angrily against Liberals, charged with "uplift", who would long ago have plunged us "into a bloody and ruinous war" ; only give him a few more years, and he would go with an easy mind.

Whether or no he felt that this confidence, a sensitive plant, must be watered liberally in public, he did so with ample hand in a conference with Lobby journalists early in March ; auguring that Italy and France were mending their disputes, that much might be hoped from Stanley's visit to Berlin, that a disarmament conference might meet before the year's end.   To this Halifax took prompt objection in an important letter.

10 March 1939 ; from Halifax

> I tried to see you to-day, but found that, very wisely, you had managed to get away to Chequers.
> What I had wanted to speak to you about was your talk yesterday to the Lobby correspondents ; and as we can't talk, you won't mind my putting my difficulty quite frankly.   I feel this on two grounds . . .

[difficulties in synchronising press relations of No. 10 and the Foreign Office].

The other ground of my difficulty is this. I fear that the publicity given to the hopes of early progress in disarmament — which however desirable, I cannot regard as probable — will not do good in Germany at this moment. They will be encouraged to think that we are feeling the strain etc., and the good effect that the balance you have up to now maintained between rearmament and peace-efforts is tilted to our disadvantage. I don't know whether you saw a telegram 2 or 3 days ago from Perth, reporting a conversation of his military attaché with the German military attaché, which suggests the same point.

And I would fear that the French, already a bit sensitive over our delicate approach in regard to the troop-concentration race between them and the Italians, would be made nervous by what they will be likely to suspect as an advance feeler in the direction of third party mediation. Their readiness to suspect is very great, and we ought, I feel, to be very careful to give them no ground for it that we can avoid, for it makes them unnecessarily more difficult about other things.

You know that I never wish to be tiresome or take departmental views! And of course I realise all the time how immense is the personal burden on you, and how personal is the contribution that nobody but you can make. But none the less I think that when you are going to make such a general review about Foreign Affairs it might be helpful and well, if you felt able to let me know in advance that you were going to do it, and give me some idea of what you had it in mind to say. That would give me the opportunity of saying anything I had to say, which you might or might not think wise ; and as I say nobody recognises more readily than I do that the *ultimate* responsibility must be yours !

I have written very frankly, and you won't mind my having done so. My only purpose is to forestall possible misunderstandings and difficulties.

The Prime Minister read this, regretted the journalists had printed so literally what he had meant to be background, but saw no harm in having let his confidence be seen. On March 12 he wrote he must speak at Birmingham on the 17th, and the day after that would be seventy, — " I am already threatened with an umbrella from spinsters (who want pensions in return) " and, thinking of his father's collapse at the same age, added " I ought to be good for at least one more parliament ". For his own destined purpose he believed he, in some sense, alone could save his country, but " I want a few more years for it ".

He was not to be given a week ; when his birthday came, Hitler and his army were in occupation of Prague.

CHAPTER XXXI

THE END OF APPEASEMENT:
MARCH–MAY 1939

AGED 70

Thus is our era still to be named of Hope, though in the saddest sense, — when there is nothing left but Hope.

CARLYLE

To one element in our material for judgement Halifax gave emphatic expression a few days later, saying that the Prime Minister and he had always been conscious of the gulf between faith and hope. It was at once the greatest power, and the ever-present danger, of their policy, that it rested upon hope, the hopes in particular of Chamberlain to whom life without hope was death in life.

Yet when we have weighed all arguments, political and military and moral, in that decision of September, and borne in mind also his secondary motive of winning time to rearm, a question remains, whether they were so entitled to hope in the first quarter of 1939 ? It cannot yet be entirely answered, but some considerations may here find a place.

His combination with Halifax, in whom he always admired " a Cabinet mind ", and which made the directorate of foreign policy, assembled many gifts. Though they set out from such different origins in spiritual motive and worldly training, both were attempting to moralise politics. But neither of them was an illusionist ; in truth, when and if they failed, it was in some incapacity, or unwillingness, to sink to generalise, or to comprehend, racial and national passion. Chamberlain's mind was the more fiery and concentrated, and the less subtle ; Halifax having more of that politic scepticism which other religious-minded ministers of State have had before him. On the whole, history may finally conclude that the fixed ardour of the one with the weighing morality of the other, joined with a firm British conservative outlook in both, had for one result a certain turning of the blind eye. Justly reluctant to put heavier commitments upon their country, they were, maybe, too unwilling to look beyond what must immediately be done, too insular, not at all in their objective but in their code, too inelastic, both for good and ill, to adapt themselves to revolutionary situations.

In his reading of the immediate position Chamberlain also much depended on the diagnosis received from our ambassador at Berlin. Nevile Henderson had been seriously ill most of the winter, only returning to duty in mid-February, and it is difficult not to see in him a certain weariness, a clutching at what seemed least unreasonable in an unreasonable world. He conveyed now indications of a peaceful spirit in high quarters, pacific changes in Hitler's speeches, and predicted no sudden adventure, though Memel and Danzig, he thought, would doubtless some day come back to the Reich. On March 2 he sent word that Goering was leaving for a long cure at San Remo, which was another good sign. Yet he had by that time seen the very formidable German reply regarding the guarantee for Czechoslovakia.

This developed the thesis of Hitler's January speech, that the Western powers had nothing to do with central Europe, and that their intervention could only encourage the " wild " elements which had caused the September crisis. Henderson's general picture, in fact, did not correspond with a number of symptoms which had perturbed the agents of France, the Balkan States, and America ; that is, a revival among the Czechs of what the Germans called " Beneschism ", a German demand for reduction of the Czech army and privileges for the German minority, violent Slovak mis-government, and signs that Hitler was preparing to go back on his previous award ; in lieu of which he would throw Ruthenia to Hungary, abandon the project of a Ukraine State, and seek larger compensations at the expense of Poland or Russia. Such signals might well have tempered any hopes held about central Europe.

The crisis broke when on March 10 the Czechs dismissed the Slovak premier Tiso and sent troops to occupy Bratislava, where-upon Tiso appealed to Hitler ; on the 14th the Slovaks announced their independence and German troops crossed the frontiers ; it was near four in the morning of the 15th when the Czech minister Hacha, succumbing to hours of menace, placed Bohemia and Moravia in the care of the Reich under a guarantee for local liber-ties, and much the same time that Hungarian forces invaded Ruthenia. It was under those circumstances, of fact barely known and the air f ll of plausible German versions, that Chamberlain had to speak in the Commons that afternoon. " Internal disrup-tion ", he said, had disintegrated the new State and with that had lapsed the proposed guarantee ; he would not yet associate himself with charges of a breach of faith. But, even if this had taken place with the Czech government's free assent, " I cannot regard the manner and the method . . . as in accord with the spirit of the Munich agreement ". He had asked Germany to make a contribution, but now, for the first time, they had seized the territory of another race. Even so, let them not be deflected from their course, or lightly set aside all hope for the world.

When he spoke at Birmingham two days later, on the eve of his birthday, his tone was very different, informed by fuller knowledge, and by strong representations as to opinion in the House, the public, and the Dominions. He threw aside a speech, long drafted, on domestic questions and social service, and grasped the nettle. He would not recant on Munich ; " the facts as they are to-day cannot change the facts as they were last September. . . . I did not go there to get popularity ", but to avert a general war. " I have never denied that the terms which I was able to secure at Munich were not those that I myself would have desired ". Nothing else could then have saved the Czechs from destruction.

But now the case was different. He recounted Hitler's manifold pledges, public and private ; " how can these events this week be reconciled with those assurances ? " Hitherto, from the Rhineland onwards, for every German aggression " there was something to be said, whether on account of racial affinity or of just claims too long resisted ", but there was nothing to be said now. " Is this the end of an old adventure, or the beginning of a new ? . . . is this, in fact, a step in the direction of an attempt to dominate the world by force ? " There was hardly anything he would not sacrifice for peace, " but there is one thing that I must except, and that is the liberty that we have enjoyed for hundreds of years, and which we would never surrender ". He ended :

> I feel bound to repeat that, while I am not prepared to engage this country by new unspecified commitments, operating under conditions which cannot now be foreseen, yet no greater mistake could be made than to suppose that, because it believes war to be a senseless and cruel thing, this nation has so lost its fibre that it will not take part to the utmost of its power in resisting such a challenge if it ever were made.

He received one letter on that speech, which could best make the point on which henceforward he must stand.

18 March, 1939 ; from H.M. King George VI

MY DEAR PRIME MINISTER,

I feel I must send you one line to say how well I can appreciate your feelings about the recent behaviour of the German Government.

Although this blow to your courageous efforts on behalf of peace and understanding in Europe must, I am afraid, cause you deep distress, I am sure that your labours have been anything but wasted, for they can have left no doubt in the minds of ordinary people all over the world of your love of peace, and of our readiness to discuss with any nation whatever grievance they think they have.

He had not been long in deciding that, if the struggle must go on, it must be in a different way.

19 March

As soon as I had time to think I saw that it was impossible to deal with Hitler after he had thrown all his own assurances to the winds. . . . I have worked out a plan which a few ministers have accepted to-day, and which I shall put to the Cabinet to-morrow. It is pretty bold and startling, but I feel that something of the kind is needed, and though I can't predict the reactions in Berlin, I have an idea that it won't bring us to an acute crisis, at any rate at once. . . . As always, I want to gain time, for I never accept the view that war is inevitable.

He would bear the mark of Munich, he had said at the time, to the end of his days, and after Prague we become conscious that he found heavier the load. " I can never forget that the ultimate decision, the ' Yes ' or ' No ' which may decide the fate not only of all this generation, but of the British Empire itself, rests with me." And at moments he endured an intense loneliness. His policy, would they not say, had expired in ignominy, by his credulity he had destroyed the Czech democracy, as he had destroyed the democracy of Spain ? And what was he to understand by the re-solution set down on March 28 by Eden, Churchill, and some thirty Conservative members, which called for a National government and prosecution of the policy lately pronounced by " the Foreign Secretary " ? No, he wrote, when Albania had gone the same way as the Czechs, his policy had not been wrong ; " the fruits can be seen in the consolidation of world opinion, and in the improvement of the military position of ourselves and France ". Sometimes he felt dumbfoundered, as though there were two Neville Chamberlains. There was one whom the mass of the people still flocked after and greeted wherever he went, " and then I go back to the House of Commons, and listen to the unending stream of abuse of the Prime Minister . . . and I say to myself ' this is the real thing ' ". On his black days he allowed that events " enable my enemies to mock me publicly ", and confessed to feeling dispirited and alone.

Yet his worst enemies admitted that what they called his obstinacy might be styled resolution, and in the dark months to come he never showed a sign of going back on his new decisions. True to his word in September, that he would fight against a purpose to dominate the world by force, by arms and diplomacy he would make the nation ready. Yet there was another side even to this. The difference between his critics and himself, though now much narrowed and changed from a clash of ideal to a difference of judgement, was still there, turning on one plain fact ; that, come what may, he would never accept war as inevitable. Neither abroad nor at home would he do anything that might bring it nearer, nor leave anything undone that might stave it off. War, he believed, might be stopped, if Germany could be convinced not merely that her abuse of force would be instantly resisted, but that she would get consideration for any rational demand by the way of peace. With every week gained he hoped to bring his converging batteries to bear ; British and French rearmament, new diplomatic guarantees to small nations, moral support from America, the egoist realism of Italy, and moderating powers within Germany itself. In Hitler he had lost all faith, but hoped these massed influences would strengthen those, especially the army, who might restrain him.

If then his weapons had changed, his purpose had not. But the perils were much enhanced, for resistance depended on many others than Great Britain, and perils were much multiplied of error in judgement. We might be faced, not so much by flagrant acts of war, as by a German economic penetration, already being attempted in Roumania, which would have all the results of conquest. Yet how to distinguish between such a process and the natural predominance of Germany in south-eastern markets, or how to stop it save by an ultimatum or, in other words, by a preventive and precarious war ? for which, he wrote, he would never make himself responsible. Again, defensive alliances we must have ; but high-pitched, or at least high-placed, voices begged him to beware of presenting Germany with a legend of " encirclement " ; to be on his guard against bringing in Russia, which might provoke immediate war. In this dark forest we see him advancing, throwing out his flankers, step by step.

His first notion, conceived between the German occupation of Prague on March 15 and their seizure of Memel from Lithuania on the 21st, he described thus : " to get a declaration signed by the four Powers, Britain, France, Russia, and Poland, that they would act together in the event of further signs of German aggressive ambitions. I drafted the formula myself." But it was at once made manifest that Poland would refuse contact with the Soviet, which alone was enough to prevent us taking up the Russian proposal for a six-power conference ; which in any event promised considerable delay. His hesitation in negotiating with Russia, however, was not derived from ideological prejudice, but from facts presented to him by military and intelligence reports, and by other States.

26 March

> I must confess to the most profound distrust of Russia. I have no belief whatever in her ability to maintain an effective offensive, even if she wanted to. And I distrust her motives, which seem to me to have little connection with our ideas of liberty, and to be concerned only with getting every one else by the ears. Moreover, she is both hated and suspected by many of the smaller States, notably by Poland, Roumania, and Finland.

To all this we must return ; meantime, while in a personal letter he warned Mussolini that Hitler was making war inevitable, and while he pondered on giving a guarantee to a Polish-Roumanian alliance, news from many sources reached London that an immediate German attack, without warning, might at any minute overwhelm Poland. From this came the resolve which he announced to the Commons on March 31. Consultations were proceeding, he said, with other governments, but in the event, before they materialised, " of any action which clearly threatened Polish independence, and which the Polish government accordingly considered it vital to resist with their national forces, His Majesty's Government would feel themselves bound at once to lend the Polish government all support in their power " ; France authorised him to say they would do the same. He added that they would seek the maximum amount of co-operation with other States, undeterred by any prejudice.

How did he envisage this fateful declaration, that eliminated the ambiguity of 1914 as to where Great Britain stood ? " What we are concerned with ", he wrote that week, " is not the boundaries of States, but attacks on their independence ", and this he elaborated during April in debate. Not " some little frontier incident " : " what we are concerned with is to preserve our independence, and when I say ' our independence ', I do not mean only this country's ".

This was no policy of encirclement but one of self-defence, against that challenge which, as he held, at Munich had been offset by the German pledges, now thrown to the wind. " I am no more a man of war to-day than I was in September " ; " I trust that our actions, begun but not concluded, will prove to be the turning-point not towards war, which wins nothing, cures nothing, ends nothing, but towards a more wholesome era, when reason will take the place of force ".

That week another aggression led to an extension of our new commitments, and weakened one of his fixed positions. On Good Friday, April 7, Italian forces seized Albania. Neither the chronicles of that minute, bitterly divided country nor the record of King Zog made it surprising ; an Italian military mission, control of air services, and ample corruption had in fact made of Albania what the Allies of 1919 had been willing to see in legal form, an Italian protectorate. Certainly, in the face of the German danger, or in relation to the rôle he had cast for Italy, Chamberlain decided to minimise it, though it should have taught him that he had exaggerated his personal influence with the Duce. Mussolini, he wrote, sent him many personal assurances, " as to which I can only say that they indicate a desire on his part to allay any fears or suspicions on mine. But I am afraid that such faith as I ever had in the assurances of dictators is rapidly being whittled away."

Yet he would not, seeing the importance of clearing Spain, denounce our Italian agreement, and he seemed to be justified, for the French found no proof of the military preparations so long rumoured over the Pyrenees, and in June the Italian and German legionaries at last departed. There were, again, eloquent pressures from below the gangway, so assured that we had reached a state of war that they entreated him to seize Corfu ; which, as Halifax drily told the Italian minister, was " not the sort of thing we did ", especially when our rôle was to defend small nations. But Albania led to an extension to Greece and Roumania of the pledge we had made to Poland, as well as to agreement with Turkey for co-operation against aggression.

While a defensive peace front was thus being constructed piece-meal, and while Roosevelt put his straight demand to the dictators for guarantees against force, Chamberlain moved forward at home. On March 29 the establishment of the Territorial Force was doubled, and as by this date the government had decided to build up a field force of thirty-two divisions, expansion of military supply became imperative. A new Ministry, of which Burgin was put in charge,

was therefore created in April, restricted at present to supply for
the Army and civil defence, with appropriate powers over raw
material and industrial priorities, but though the existing machinery
for Navy and Air Force was left intact, the bill gave means of en-
larging the new creation into a full Ministry of Supply. To launch
the organisation the Prime Minister enlisted his old bulwark at
the Ministry of Health, Arthur Robinson.

24 April 1939 ; to Sir Arthur Robinson

It was a great relief to my mind to hear that you had responded to
my appeal and consented to be the first secretary to the new Ministry
of Supply.

I fully realise the extent of the sacrifice that you are making. I
don't know whether I am presuming too much, but I have a feeling
that your personal affection for me has influenced your decision. If
so, I can only say that it adds to my satisfaction on public grounds a
keen pleasure in the thought that our friendship is still so much alive.

24 April 1939 ; from Sir Arthur Robinson

It is the simple truth that only your wish would have induced me to
undertake the Ministry of Supply. Your letter touches me so deeply
that I can but say that admiration of you increases every day, as does
the very strong feeling of affection for you which was formed in our
days at the Ministry of Health.

There remained the matter of conscription, against the establishment of which in time of peace many pledges had been given. Till
the end of March he refused to budge ; what if it revealed to
the foe a divided nation, or retarded aircraft production by discontents ? Herein he battled with a powerful current in his own
party, but what converted him seems rather to have been the
argument from France that only this could assure them we were
in earnest : German propaganda was instilling poison, into ears
only too ready to listen, that Britain meant to fight to the last
Frenchman.

This decision, justified on the ground that it could not justly
be called a " period of peace ", was taken without official communication with the Opposition, and fulfilment was given to it
only within guarded limits. It was thought well to make the
announcement before Hitler's forthcoming speech, to avoid the
charge of rejecting his advances, and Henderson was sent back to
Berlin to herald it ; the powers taken were only for three years ;
and compulsory service was made incumbent only on men of twenty
and twenty-one. The hostile votes of the Labour party and the

Trade Union Congress represented, we may think, rather deference to long-held principle, distrust of Chamberlain's policy, and irritation at not being consulted, than vehement objection to the fact ; " the Labour Party ", he reported, " were divided in their opposition, and I could see that the back benches were shaken when I made my appeal ".

If all this testified that we had entered a zone which was neither peace nor war, there was another sign of united resolution that he might give, and that the clearest. He could have had the services of Churchill and Eden, with the approval of the public, and much within his Cabinet ; and what a tower Churchill would be to a weak and unliked front bench, he was well aware. He had, indeed, never shaken off his difficulty in co-operating with that very different temperament, but that was not the root this summer. " The nearer we get to war, the more his chances improve, and *vice versa*. If there is any possibility of easing the tension and getting back to normal relations with the dictators, I wouldn't risk it by what would certainly be regarded by them as a challenge."

This rôle in a British Prime Minister, of deference to foreign opinion regarding the composition of his Cabinet, had been known in the lives of Canning and Palmerston ; blended, then as now, with a conflict over the timing of policy ; marked, then and now, by the contact of foreign envoys with a British Opposition. It is a political condition not pleasing, easily distorted into legend, and one that makes it the more imperative to do exact justice to the attitude of Chamberlain and Halifax ; which may be tested by another crucial question, to which this conflict was at last reduced, as all such conflicts are, — what to do about Russia ?

Twenty years of mutual ignorance and suspicion divided the two countries, years of diplomatic intercourse often in suspense, and of codes far asunder in society and religion ; of British resentment hardening against the Soviet support to many discontents within the British Empire. The late interventions of Russia in Spain, and at Geneva, did not predispose the government to believe that Russia shared their aspiration, not to divide Europe but to put Europe at peace. Yet, however far-dated our resentment, or however real our difficulties in 1938, full justice must be done to the Russian point of view. To them the last peace settlement must represent an unjust humiliation ; the Nazi power, a challenge to their ideal and their dearest territorial aims ; Munich, a transaction with the accursed thing. They read " appeasement ", not in the light of the almost unanimous British desire to avert war, but in the harsh reflection of their own wrongs and needs ; Chamberlain, said Stalin to the American ambassador, seemed bent on making Germany strong.   They therefore felt, or were believed to feel, an intense suspicion that on any opportunity he would be jobbing back to " appeasement ".

Therein, as his private letters amply show, they wronged him. There were, indeed, various signs which persuaded him that Germany intended no instant move, — or he could not have taken the responsibility for advising the King and Queen to carry out their Canadian and American journey in May, — but he had ceased to believe any word of Hitler.   After the speech of April 28, when the Führer tore up the Anglo-German Naval treaty and his Polish pact, he wrote " he finds it so easy to tear up treaties and throw ove board assurances, that no one can feel any confidence in new ones ".   The Germans professed to think that our Polish pledge did not cover Danzig ; he went out of his way to refute this interpretation, and in mid-July defined his exact position thus :

> Dantzig is, of course, at present the danger spot. I have told Musso plainly that, if Hitler tries to get it by force, it will mean starting the European war. To which M. replies " let the Poles agree that Dantzig goes to the Reich, and I will do my best to get a peaceful agreed solution ". But that is not good enough. That is just what we tried at Munich, but Hitler broke it up when it suited him. I doubt if any solution, short of war, is practicable at present, but if dictators would have a modicum of patience, I can imagine that a way could be found of meeting German claims while safeguarding Poland's independence and economic security.

He never had, then, any idea of perpetrating that which Russian suspicion and American journalists professed to fear, " a Polish Munich " ; on the contrary, it might be said with more truth that he gave way too easily to the Poles who, though incapable of defending themselves, refused to hear of an alliance that would bring Russian armies on their wide-stretching soil.   Not a trace can be found in his letters of an ideological motive ; he was not made up like that, and any notion that he resisted war, for fear of its potential social consequences, is entire legend.   What they do contain is political argument and political suspicion ; the belief implicitly held, it would seem, in our military circles that Russian strength, exhausted by blood-letting, would collapse, and a feeling that Russia was playing power politics rather than seeking peace.

The dilemma begins in April when Colonel Beck visited London and bound Poland in a reciprocal alliance with Great Britain. " He was very anxious ", we hear, "not to be tied up with Russia, not only because Poles don't like Russians, but because of the effect on German opinion and policy. He thought such an association might lead Hitler to make an attack, which otherwise he hoped it might still be possible to avoid. I confess I very much agree with him, for I regard Russia as a very unreliable friend . . . with an enormous irritative power on others."

His reasons ranged far beyond this Polish veto. He found Dominion opinion divided, believed that French Canada, for example, might be against a Russian alliance. " I can't believe that she has the same aims and objects as we have, or any sympathy with democracy as such. She is afraid of Germany and Japan, and would be delighted to see other people fight them." He believed that a Russian alliance might divide the Balkan resistance to Germany and that, if it drove Spain over to the Axis, we might thereby lose more in the West than we should gain in the East. If in all this reasoning there was temperament or a mood, there was assuredly also a respectable phase in British thinking ; the conception of a government committed to defend small States, and one with its background, mental and strategic, on the sea. That he disliked their school of diplomacy was a minor matter, though practically of some importance, for the clamour in the Commons certainly would not induce Russia to lower her price ; their methods of negotiation, he complained, " include the publication in the press of all their despatches and continuous close communication with the Opposition ". But there is no doubt where lay his deepest objection ; " the alliance would definitely be a lining up of opposing blocs ".

Yet as the impotence of Poland and Roumania, left to themselves, became clear, the majority of ministerial opinion swung hard towards the Russian alliance. French information already insisted that the penalty of failure would be a Russo-German pact, and though the dismissal of Litvinov, the Soviet foreign minister, in fact only followed the purge of his leading diplomats, in view of his contacts with Geneva and Britain it was taken as a bad omen. Through the opaque, and still only part-lifted, curtain we perceive Chamberlain driven from his first tactic, which had been simply to persuade Russia to guarantee Poland and Roumania, and to promise joint consultations, and then driven to explore seriously their counter-project for a triple reciprocal alliance between Russia, Britain, and France. This basis was accepted in May, and by late

July our sincerity was proved by the dispatch of a military mission.

But his distrust was undiminished. He had a sense they were being handled with hard bargaining, for which reason he would not consider Eden's offer to go to Moscow, and indeed, as the conversations crabbedly developed by fits and starts, it emerged that alliance was only possible on terms which neither he nor Halifax would yield. This was in an extension of the new Allies' joint guarantee to the Baltic States who, it appeared, were entirely unwilling to receive it, — a guarantee, the Russians argued, which must cover every indirect form of German " aggression ". But manipulation of internal upheaval in these petty States, whether for a White or a Red revolution, had been made familiar in the last war, and would never be difficult to a practised hand. The crux had come ; while we accepted an obligation to defend Russia herself, we would neither compel the Baltic States to accept this Russian protection, nor coerce the Poles to admit Russian armies. Whatever view is taken of its competence on the British side, or of military necessities, this negotiation must at least be read in the light of what was to come ; if Chamberlain and Halifax were innocents, they were innocent of playing power politics.

So appeasement was dead, in so far as Germany had received full warning that her next aggression would be her last, and in that a whole defensive apparatus, political and military, was in train ; in a defence Budget of £700 millions, commitments to Poles, Greeks, Roumanians, and Turks, schemes to regroup Indian and Imperial garrisons, staff talks in Warsaw, large fleet exercises. His own hopes and conceptions, however, remained unchanged. He spared no pains to bring it home to Germany that his whole action was defensive, and told Birmingham friends in July that, though he feared the worst, he would still work for the best. World opinion, he argued, had swung to our side since Munich, the Empire would act as one, Daladier had lifted the tired head of France, our armaments were well founded. He still believed that Mussolini was against war, that Hitler had missed the tide, that his soldiers would not let him take the fatal plunge over so minor a cause as Danzig. Let us convince Germany, he wrote on July 30,

that the chances of winning a war without getting thoroughly exhausted in the process are too remote to make it worth while. But the corollary to that must be that she has a chance of getting fair and reasonable consideration and treatment from us and others, if she will give up the idea that she can force it from us, and convince us that she has given it up.

But the time for this, he added, had not yet come ; nor, we may think, was it likely to be speeded by a break-down in the Anglo-Russian negotiation which he regarded, with equanimity, as highly probable.

Meantime he encouraged his relations to take their holiday abroad, all would be quiet till about the third week in August.

CHAPTER XXXII

ON THE EVE

> It was not till I saw the axe laid to the root, that I found
> the full extent of what I had to lose and suffer. But my con-
> viction of the right was only established by the triumph of the
> wrong ; and my earliest hopes will be my last regrets. One
> source of this unbendingness (which some may call obstinacy)
> is that, though living much alone, I have never worshipped
> the Echo.
>
> HAZLITT

PARLIAMENT rose on August 4, not to meet again, unless emergency
called, for another eight weeks. This date was only settled after
an unpleasant debate, in which Churchill, Sinclair, and Amery
backed a Labour amendment for reassembly within three weeks,
on the implicit ground that the Prime Minister could not be trusted ;
had they been sitting in September 1938, said Sinclair, there had
been no Munich but a Russian alliance. As in this considerable
assumption Churchill interjected his agreement, it is not surprising
that Chamberlain made it a matter of confidence. On this his
majority fell to 118, some rather snapping *tu quoques* showing the
strains.

He had his intervals of happiness, public and private, this
summer, though Danzig overhung his mind even in listening to
Glyndebourne opera, or fishing in the far north. He rejoiced, on
more grounds than one, in the attested medical fitness of the militia-
men ; " here is the justification for our social legislation . . . it
must all be very annoying to the Labour Party, after their talk
about malnutrition and starvation ". And he was much stimulated
by the warmth of his welcome in South Wales, and by the trading
estates and new hope that he found there. As for Chequers, it
was his peculiar solace, where he could plant and garden to his
heart's content ; he seemed to triumph more in the Forestry Commissioners taking charge of the trees there than in a pitched battle,
and to mourn the absence of his faithful dog more than of any
political being.

In public life he foresaw a dour struggle, which gave him bouts
of discouragement. He had chosen a very narrow path. A large
price must be paid, he told a Conservative candidate, for freedom
from war ; it might involve painful readjustment, loss of personal

reputation. He was cast down by the German press poisoning of
the wells, and wearied by personal attack at home, particularly
resenting doubts cast on his staunchness by members of his own
party, or openings given to the enemy to blaspheme. There was,
for instance, the movement round Goering's emissary Wohltat,
whose conversations regarding an economic solution somehow
reached the press; privately, he judged this indiscretion severely,
seeing that the time for such discussion must depend on a change
in Germany. The next election, he felt, would turn largely upon
himself; he had come, as nine in ten politicians come, to see his
tenure of office in terms of his duty, and that duty, as he saw it, as
one overriding purpose.

> When I cease to be P.M., I shall have finished with politics. I would
> like to have long enough to see my policy through, and I believe that,
> if I am allowed, I can steer this country through the next few years
> out of the war zone into peace and reconstruction. But an interrup-
> tion would be fatal, and I should have then to leave it to someone
> else to try some quite different line.

Our position at midsummer was not precarious, defensively
considered, but quite incomplete for the ends to which we stood
committed. Without Russia, Poland was in a military sense
doomed, but Chamberlain could not speak out. The dilatoriness
of which he was accused was not, he protests, any of his doing;
" I would like to have taken a much stronger line with them all
through, but I could not have carried my colleagues with me ",
nor, we may add, the French. As it was, he was insistent on not
accepting any formula " which would drive the Baltic States and
Finland into Germany's arms ".

Russia was thus still unsettled when Parliament rose, and in
that huge ambit where Russia touched Far East and West, there
was no light in the sky. British-American relations still revolved
in their ancient dilemma, that Britain dared no final action without
positive assurance of American support, but that the less positive
the British action, the more America intensified a certain scorn
in its isolationism. Another evil was gaining momentum, where
British-American co-operation would be all-powerful. Fixed in
their ambition for a new Asian order, to be exploited through
puppets in Manchuria and north China, the Japanese army increasingly defied the powers who clung to Chinese integrity, block-
aded the foreign concessions, and deluged the great ports with
anti-British propaganda. At Tientsin a political murder gave them

a pretext for stripping and humiliating our subjects. From the first Chamberlain doubted the strength of our case on that local issue, but entirely declined to hear of discussing the " new order " ; " it is maddening to have to hold our hand in face of such humiliations, but we cannot ignore the terrible risks of putting such temptations in Hitler's way ". He welcomed much the American denunciation of their trade treaty with Japan, but though the President's wishes were not concealed, Congress stuck fast. They rejected a proposal to fortify the Pacific base at Guam, while in July the Senate shelved Roosevelt's endeavour so to amend the Neutrality law as to permit export of armaments : this, the Prime Minister wrote to Tweedsmuir, " is enough to make one weep ".

Peace, again, he was repeating, might depend upon Italy, or at least the localisation of war.

> I am thinking of making a further proposal to Mussolini that he should move for a 12 months' truce to let the temperature cool down. In the meantime I am pressing Daladier to open talks with him. As always, I regard Rome as the weak end of the Axis, and we should always be trying to bend it.

But he noted that Léger, the permanent master of French foreign policy, was very anti-Italian ; declared, too, that France was antagonising the Turks by her procrastination in surrendering the long-disputed Sanjak of Alexandretta.

Though there were thus hanging free such loose ends in our diplomacy, he could not believe that Hitler would begin a major war for Danzig and the Corridor. They were, indeed, venerable knots, stiffened by five hundred years of bloodshed, for the 1919 settlement had challenged the unbroken purpose of Frederick the Great and the makers of Prussia to eliminate the gap between East Prussia and the Reich. As for Danzig itself, it was a purely Teutonic city, with a large majority desirous of German sovereignty, but its trade depended on, and was in turn vital to, the Vistula valley behind. As things now were, the Poles had gravely weakened their own status since 1934 by conniving at the squeezing-out of League authority in the Free City, yet, given time and a tittle of goodwill, it was a problem susceptible of compromise.

Hitler's pressure, begun on the very morrow of Munich, was thenceforward intensified till by March 1939 it reached point-blank proportions ; a return of Danzig to the Reich and a belt under German sovereignty across the Corridor, in return for specified facilities for Polish trade ; a guarantee of the frontiers, and the

P

too familiar non-aggression pact. After the Polish rejection of these terms, not a glint of concession came from the German side. Far from it ; threats were made of reopening the matter of Silesia, the Danzig Nazis defied every treaty clause, children were painfully learning in their schools to chant " we thank our Führer ", heavy-footed " tourists " filtered in to make a beginning of the end. If this was clear to Henderson, the Poles, and the French, it did not seem to affect Chamberlain's optimism, for though he predicted a war of nerves, he thought Hitler would not face the real thing and on August 16 went for a holiday to the far Highlands. He was recalled in four days.

The Western democracies, Ribbentrop repeated in his glaucous way, would never fight for Danzig, and certainly not, if Russia were against them ; if Russia were even neutral, added the generals, all was well. The Germans, therefore, would pay all, and more than, the price which the British had refused, or would at least mortgage it for a time ; from them, without a war, for which they were not ready, the Russians might receive what the democracies had declined to give. The bargain was struck on August 21, in a pact which committed Russia to benevolent neutrality, and which removed the last hesitation at Berlin.

For though their manœuvres, to divide Britain from France or to make the Poles believe their allies faltering, were coarsely transparent, the language of Hitler and Ribbentrop did not change. Threats to the Poles who had spurned the Führer's generosity, pompous warnings to France, boasts of invincibility, and exasperation against Britain. That was the note reported by Lord Kemsley to Chamberlain of an interview with Hitler in late July, — of protests against our armaments, a demand for colonies, asseveration of his original goodwill. It was sounded over and over again in the long exchange of letters which began on his return from the Highlands. Though he instantly announced that the Moscow pact did not affect our word to Poland — nor, for that matter, would any temporary overwhelming of Poland in war — no words, however clear, could reach that closed mind. Ignoring all suggestion of a truce, Hitler declared that while the last fragment stood of the accursed Versailles *diktat*, his dream of Anglo-German friendship could not come true ; only let him have done with this anomaly of Poland, and how historic an offer he would make to Britain ! The British reply on August 28, civilly postponing such discussion, was that " they could not, for any advantage offered to Great Britain, acquiesce in a settlement which put in jeopardy the in-

dependence of a State to whom they have given their guarantee ",
insisted that direct negotiation between Germany and Poland was
the first step, and that a settlement must be guaranteed by all the
powers. How this principle of direct conversation was in form
accepted, but only to mask the last military preparation, how the
Poles were bidden to send a plenipotentiary to sign, within twenty-
four hours, terms which the Polish government had not seen, how
German troops crossed the Polish frontier at dawn on September 1,
this is in the chronicle. Even now the effort continued to seduce
Great Britain.

When he spoke to the Commons on that night of September 1,
it was to say that an ultimatum had been delivered, though without
a time limit, to demand the withdrawal of German troops.

Eighteen months ago in this House I prayed that the responsibility
might not fall on me to ask this country to accept the awful arbitra-
ment of war. I fear that I may not be able to avoid that responsibility. But, at any rate, I cannot wish for conditions in which such
a burden should fall upon me, in which I should feel clearer than
I do to-day as to where my duty lies. . . . We shall stand at the bar
of history knowing that the responsibility of this terrible catastrophe
lies on the shoulders of one man, the German Chancellor, who has
not hesitated to plunge the world into misery in order to serve his own
senseless ambitions. . . . We have no quarrel with the German people,
except that they allow themselves to be governed by a Nazi government. As long as that government exists and pursues the methods
it has so persistently followed during the last two years, there will be
no peace in Europe. We shall merely pass from one crisis to another,
and see one country after another attacked by methods which have
now become familiar to us in their sickening technique. We are
resolved that these methods must come to an end.

He had still a difficult day to get over of delay, for reasons
which he could not publicly explain, which sorely tried his Cabinet,
the House, and the people. Simultaneous action with France was
vital, and though Daladier was resolute, it was believed the Foreign
Affairs committee of the Chamber, and Bonnet, were less so. But
on our firm refusal to negotiate unless German troops were withdrawn, the Italian offer of mediation lapsed, and on Sunday
morning, September 3, our government demanded a reply to its
ultimatum by 11 A.M. A quarter of an hour later he broadcast to
the country :

You can imagine what a bitter blow it is to me that all my long
struggle to win peace has failed. Yet I cannot believe that there is

anything more, or anything different, that I could have done, and that would have been more successful. . . . We have a clear conscience, we have done all that any country could do to establish peace, but a situation in which no word given by Germany's ruler could be trusted, and no people or country could feel themselves safe, had become intolerable. . . . Now may God bless you all and may He defend the right. For it is evil things that we shall be fighting against, brute force, bad faith, injustice, oppression, and persecution. And against them I am certain that the right will prevail.

That done, he went on to speak again in Parliament. He said he had realised their doubts and " I make no reproach, for if I had been in the same position as honourable members not sitting on this bench, and not in possession of all the information which we have, I should very likely have felt the same ". Then, after recounting the facts and the last ultimatum :

everything that I have worked for, everything that I have hoped for, everything that I have believed in during my public life, has crashed into ruins. There is only one thing left for me to do : that is, to devote what strength and powers I have to forwarding the victory of the cause for which we have to sacrifice so much. I cannot tell what part I may be allowed to play myself : I trust I may live to see the day when Hitlerism has been destroyed, and a liberated Europe has been re-established.

But his eleventh-hour troubles, his mood and his present expectations, must be given in his private words.

10 September 1939

the final long-drawn-out agonies that preceded the actual declaration of war were as nearly unendurable as could be. We were anxious to bring things to a head, but there were three complications, — the secret communications that were going on with Goering and Hitler through a neutral intermediary, the conference proposal of Mussolini, and the French anxiety to postpone the actual declaration as long as possible, until they could evacuate their women and children, and mobilise their armies. There was very little of this that we could say in public, and meantime the House of Commons was out of hand, torn with suspicions, and ready (some of them . . . .) to believe the government guilty of any cowardice and treachery. . . .

The communications with Hitler and Goering looked rather promising at one time, but came to nothing in the end, as Hitler apparently got carried away by the prospect of a short war in Poland, and then a settlement. . . . They gave the impression, probably with intention, that it was possible to persuade Hitler to accept a peaceful and reasonable solution of the Polish question, in order to get to an Anglo-German agreement, which he continually declared to be his greatest ambition.

What happened to destroy this chance ? Was Hitler merely talking through his hat, and deliberately deceiving us while he matured his schemes ? I don't think so. There is good evidence that orders for the invasion on the 25th August were actually given and then cancelled at the last moment because H. wavered. With such an extraordinary creature one can only speculate. But I believe he did seriously contemplate an agreement with us, and that he worked seriously at proposals (subsequently broadcast) which to his one-track mind seemed almost fabulously generous. But at the last moment some brainstorm took possession of him — maybe Ribbentrop stirred it up — and once he had set his machine in motion, he couldn't stop it. . . . Mussolini's proposals were, I think, a perfectly genuine attempt to stop war, not for any altruistic reasons, but because Italy was not in a state to go to war and exceedingly likely to get into trouble if other people did. But it was doomed to failure, because Hitler by that time was not prepared to hold his hand, unless he could get what he wanted without war. And we weren't prepared to give it to him. . . .

So the war began, after a short and troubled night, and only the fact that one's mind works at three times its ordinary pace on such occasions enabled me to get through my broadcast, the formation of the War Cabinet, the meeting of the House of Commons, and the preliminary orders on that awful Sunday, which the calendar tells me was this day a week ago. . . .

For some time past it has been more and more evident that the German plan was to make a peace offer as soon as they had finished their Eastern campaign, and that they would do nothing to jeopardise its success meanwhile. Now I see Goering has come out with the idea, accompanied as usual by insults, boasts, and threats. That does not seem likely to make much appeal to anyone. Our first reply is the announcement of our preparations for a 3 years war. Next I shall go and see Daladier. . . . One thing comforts me. While war was still averted, I felt I was indispensable, for no one else could carry out my policy. To-day the position has changed. Half a dozen people could take my place while war is in progress, and I do not see that I have any particular part to play until it comes to discussing peace terms, — and that may be a long way off.

It may be, but I have a feeling that it won't be so very long. There is such a widespread desire to avoid war, and it is so deeply rooted, that it surely must find expression somehow. Of course the difficulty is with Hitler himself. Until he disappears and his system collapses, there can be no peace. But what I hope for is not a military victory — I very much doubt the feasibility of that — but a collapse of the German home front. For that it is necessary to convince the Germans that they cannot win. And U.S.A. might at the right moment help there. On this theory one must weigh every action in the light of its probable effect on German mentality. I hope myself we shall not start to bomb their munition centres and objectives in towns, unless they begin it. . . .

You, in your letter, hoped I shouldn't think my efforts had been unavailing. Indeed I don't think so, and have never said so. It was of course a grievous disappointment that peace could not be saved, but I know that my persistent efforts have convinced the world that no part of the blame can lie here. That consciousness of moral right, which it is impossible for the Germans to feel, must be a tremendous force on our side.

They were fighting, he told the Commons, for principles, " the destruction of which would involve the destruction of all possibility of peace and security ", and not just for the " far-away city " of Danzig. For a better city, then ; but very far away.

CHAPTER XXXIII

THE TWILIGHT WAR: 1939–1940

AGED 70–71

We have to kill one another just to satisfy that accursed
madman. I wish he could burn in Hell for as many years
as he is costing lives.·

NEVILLE CHAMBERLAIN, *October* 15, 1939

In this way the current which he had tried to stem swept all over
the precipice, Britain and European civilisation crashed into the
canyon, and came out gasping for breath in a valley of rocks of
which none had dreamed. Far below the stream widened out to
flow resolutely towards peace, but he died when they were still
being battered in the worst defile. Of those years the history is as
yet unrevealed, it is not even all enacted, and all that can be done
is to show how he bore himself in evil as in good report, how he saw
present and future, how he fell from power and died.

Directly, he was a victim of the decrepitude of the smaller States
of Europe, the *real-politik* of Russia, and the incipient collapse of
France, all of which thrust upon the improvised military machine
of Great Britain a strain that at present it could not bear. But,
as I see it, he could not, any more than had Asquith, for long have
led a nation committed to ruthless war, for he hated war too intensely to be a war minister, and he knew it.

5 September 1939 ; to the Archbishop of Canterbury

you will understand how hateful I find my personal position. I simply
can't bear to think of those gallant fellows who lost their lives last
night in the R.A.F. attack, and of their families who have first been
called upon to pay the price. Indeed, I must put such thoughts out
of my mind if I am not to be unnerved altogether.

But it was just the realisation of these horrible tragedies that has
pressed upon me all the time I have been here. I did so hope we
were going to escape them, but I sincerely believe that with that
madman it was impossible. I pray the struggle may be short, but it
can't end as long as Hitler remains in power.

Time did not blunt these feelings, as witness this from six weeks further on : " how I do hate and loathe this war. I was never meant to be a war minister, and the thought of all those homes wrecked with the *Royal Oak* makes me want to hand over my responsibilities to someone else."

There was a second reason for his fall, and that was the very nature of the first six months of war, — this " war twilight ", as he called it, of no vivid action but of exhausting atmospheric disturbance, in which a dark shade of things to come stretched out the tension of each dull day. And there was a third, of a different order. So detestable to Labour was the memory of the coupon election, and the last post-war order, that it is doubtful whether they at that moment would have entered another coalition under any man. But under Chamberlain the mass of them — though not so all their leaders — certainly would not serve. Him they professed to blame solely for the failure of " collective security " and the Russian negotiation, and were even so far re-reading facts as to charge him, more than themselves, with the deficiency in armaments. And even if they could have risen superior to the past, they held very different views about the future. Their heart could only be in a war that massed democracy against Fascism, and whose end would be a social order akin to their desires.

On September 1 he took the step which he had always contemplated, as the first if war should come, and invited Churchill to join him. Of his resigning in favour of Churchill there could, at that stage, be no question, if only because the party would hardly have agreed, but with Churchill and Halifax he felt he had the nucleus of a good War Cabinet. His new lieutenant made some substantial suggestions.

2 September 1939 ; from Winston Churchill

Aren't we a very old team ? I make out that the six you mentioned to me yesterday aggregate 386 years, or an average of over 64, only one year short of the old age Pension ! If, however, you added Sinclair (49) and Eden (42), the average comes down to 57½.

If the *Daily Herald* is right that Labour will not come in, we shall certainly have to face a constant stream of criticism, as well as the many disappointments and surprises of which war largely consists. Therefore it seems to me all the more important to have the Liberal Opposition firmly incorporated in our ranks. Eden's influence with the section of Conservatives who are associated with him, as well as with moderate Liberal elements, also seems to me to be a very necessary reinforcement.

So far as Labour was concerned, Chamberlain needed no pressing ; he was disappointed they would not join, and welcomed gratefully some expressions of sympathy in his burden from Labour men.   However, when he invited Sinclair and Labour the same day, both declined with the same formula, that they could serve the national cause better from outside.   That being so, the War Cabinet consisted of Chamberlain, Halifax, Simon, and Hoare (or the so-called inner Cabinet since 1938), with the addition of Churchill, Chatfield, Hankey, Kingsley Wood, and Hore-Belisha.

He incurred a good deal of criticism because he did not construct this Cabinet on the Lloyd George model of 1917, smaller in number and made up of ministers without departments.   As to that, history — including history since Chamberlain — suggests that every Prime Minister, and each set of circumstances, work out their own way. For his comment in October was " we are working together very harmoniously and successfully.   After all, that is the real test, and I constructed my Cabinet on no theory or rule governing its size, or the nature of its composition, whether departmental or otherwise. My sole purpose was to find a Cabinet that would work, which means that personalities must be taken into account."   He argued also that the existence of a joint planning system, running up from Service departments to the Cabinet, had changed the whole problem since 1917 ; how swiftly that could operate was proved, for instance, this very month by his vigorous approval of the far-reaching scheme put up to him for Imperial air training in Canada, and its instant acceptance by Mackenzie King's government.   Not but what it would seem that his first intention had been to have a larger proportion of ministers without portfolio, but that since Churchill preferred a Service department at the Admiralty, he felt it difficult to exclude the Secretaries for Air and War.   On such human considerations he, like most prime ministers, acted. Outside the War Cabinet, but with special access to it, Eden became Dominions Secretary ; otherwise, with the exception of Major Lloyd George and the Independent Arthur Salter in minor office, the ministry remained effectively unchanged and integrally Conservative.

Six months later he examined, with his usual detachment, the repute of this " war twilight " government, taking as his text an article in the *Daily Herald* : ·

It said that I had gone up, that I was full of self-confidence ˜and laughed at all intrigues, that I managed the Cabinet with precision and assurance, but added hopefully that it remained to be seen whether I should be able to stand up to the problems of the war. Winston was said to have gone up too, but his progress was disappointing : somehow he failed to create the impression in the House or the country that he really ought. Chatfield and Hankey were looked on as ballast that might well be thrown overboard ; the one man who had definitely and solidly improved his position was Halifax, who was now generally trusted and would be thought of if anything happened to me. This is all very true, and I would rather have Halifax succeed me than Winston.

Yet the men being what they were, and the House of Commons the driving wheel of government, the ministry in truth turned upon the partnership of Chamberlain and Churchill which, to the felicity of the country, stood the test, both now and when their positions were reversed. Heredity, association with other men, the pulleys of party, weights and counter-weights, had long divided them, and the complementary combination they could have made ; habit, physical and mental, could not be more diverse. But certain it is that Chamberlain's papers prove an unexpected community in conclusion, though often reached by different routes, a mutual trust, and a growing affection. Yet

Our deeds still travel with us from afar,

and political association is deflected not more by any present stress than by the bonds of the past. So we may read a hundred years before in the parallel of Liverpool and Canning. It was inevitable that Churchill's magnetic record, and recording, of the first German war should shine as the second war rose to its height, and equally likely that he should hope to associate with himself men who with him had traversed the roads of exile, or in whose mind he found common elements with his own, — Amery, for instance, or Beaverbrook.

In two major political facts Chamberlain could be happy. The first was the neutrality of Italy, in regard to which he got word, much delayed, from Grandi, so long ambassador here but now in the Cabinet at Rome.

1 September ; from Count Grandi

I wish to tell you how happy I am, on this very day, because of the decision taken by my country. . . . All what I have strived for during seven years of my mission in England, and during these last momentous weeks in Rome, has been saved.

Having passed the critical moment, ran the reply, he hoped they
would never be drawn into conflict ; writing to his sister the same
week, " I place my hope, and indeed my confidence, on the attitude
of the Italian King, Church, and people ".

The second event was more prosaic, but more truly laid ; the
amended Neutrality Act passed in November by the Congress of
the United States, permitting the sale of arms on a " cash and
carry " basis, that would much favour a belligerent who controlled
the sea highways. Yet against taking part in the war, even with
a German victory in prospect, American opinion was setting
hard.

And like a German victory it then seemed. On September 17
the entry of Russian troops into Poland completed what the Germans
had begun, and on the 28th the two powers achieved a fourth
partition of Poland. Their joint manifesto pronounced the Polish
question liquidated, peace was the common interest, and that if
Britain and France chose to continue war, they would consult on
counter-measures. It was followed up by Hitler's speech to the
Reichstag, proposing a conference which should among other things
determine Germany's colonial claims and some method of disarmament. In vain the net was spread. Twice over in debates of
October Chamberlain defined our position ; Poland was the occasion but not the fundamental cause, which was the intolerableness
of life under recurrent threats of fire and sword : we could trust
no word of the German government, deeds only could convince
the world that aggression was finished. The same Swedish intermediary whom Goering had used in August reappeared, but we did
not swerve.

While that brilliant autumn merged into a heavy winter, while
French and German armies, with unimportant movement in the
Saar, marked time in the Maginot and Siegfried lines, while the
Netherland States launched another appeal for peace, and King
Leopold of the Belgians once more refused to have British staff
talks, week by week we are able to follow his changing moods and
his fixed decision. On Christmas Eve his journal begins again :
" I have found it impossible to keep a diary during the war which
began on September 3rd. Days have been long, and anxieties
acute and frequent " ; adding, however, that his letters, though
not imparting what was secret, would help to fill the gap, and on
that source we shall freely draw.

In this stage he feared German propaganda more than German
arms, dreaded that an inconclusive peace might be brought about

by sheer tedium, the apparent pointlessness of this bloodless war, and specious offers.

23 September

One can see already how this war twilight is trying people's nerves. Without the strong centripetal force of mortal danger, all the injustices, inconveniences, hardships and uncertainties of war-time are resented more and more, because they are felt to be unnecessary. . . . Last week 17% of my correspondence was on the theme of " stop the war ". If I were in Hitler's shoes, I think I should let the present menacing lull go on for several weeks, and then put out a very reasonable offer. . . . I am certain we ought to reject it.

25 September ; to Lord Tweedsmuir

To us in Europe life had become absolutely intolerable, and it is to restore the possibility of living any civilised life at all that we have got to put an end to Nazi policy.

8 October

In 3 days last week I had 2450 letters, and 1860 of them were " stop the war ", in one form or another. . . . I have little doubt that Ll. G. was encouraged by his correspondence to think that he would get a lot of support for a move that (he hoped) might damage the government in general, and the P.M. in particular. . . . I was, I confess, anxious when I read Hitler's clever speech, and especially when the first American reaction was reported that he had made a very attractive series of proposals. . . . I was clear in my own mind that it offered no real advance in mind or spirit towards a reasonable peace.

It must, his war commentaries in Parliament insisted, be a real, though not a vindictive peace, and those who now read with surprise the tone of these letters may recapture the air of those months by turning to the speech of Lloyd George in question ; an anxious, almost defeatist speech, laying stress on the importance of associating the great neutrals, Russia and Italy and the United States, in a peace conference. Or, again, turn to Labour's appeal in November for a negotiated peace and some agreed, non-imperialistic, settlement of colonies. Such also was the spirit which Tweedsmuir told him was dominant in Canada and the United States.

Like all recent British governments in time of war, — and nothing is more indicative of our temper, — they were already being reproached with not setting forth their terms for peace. This clamour he rightly refused to meet in any detail. Their war aim, said his broadcast of November 27, was to defeat the German force and the German spirit ; when that was done, they might hope to build a new Europe, which would settle its problems in goodwill, break trade barriers, and reduce armies to internal police.

All this time, we have to remember, France stood erect, the reports he scanned all agreeing that never had the morale of her army stood so high. We had moved, without loss, to France an army larger than the expeditionary force of 1914. Our military, like our economic, arrangements were incorporated with theirs, British brigades were serving on the Saar, the whole force was under French command. Though he had acquired no more faith in Gamelin, whom he described after one conference as sitting silent and purring like a cat, the Supreme Council functioned harmoniously. He flew over for a first meeting in September within a week of the British landing and returned well satisfied, and when Daladier came to London in November, found him more confident, both of the general outlook and in his own political strength. Set against that seemingly impregnable background, his opinions as to the future must be judged.

He was never apparently apprehensive, as were others, as to the long-range effect of the Russo-German pact. On October 1 he wrote :

I take the same view as Winston, to whose excellent broadcast we have just been listening. I believe Russia will always act as she thinks her own interests demand, and I cannot believe that she would think her interest served by a German victory, followed by a German domination in the Balkans.

Did this mean that, warded off from the East, Hitler would strike West ? Until December he doubted it. He thought that Hitler, faithful to his aim of conquest without a total war, would not face the carnage of a frontal attack on the Maginot line. He doubted also, what British and French soldiers feared was more probable, the turning of that line by an armoured invasion of the Low Countries ; it would be a gamble staking all on one throw, and even Hitler, he thought, might shrink from " the political reactions of a breach of neutrality so flagrant and unscrupulous. If any doubt remained in the mind of anyone that he was the enemy of the human race, surely such an action would remove it." There remained a great air offensive, and that too he doubted ; " our fighters are notably superior to the German bombers . . . and though our A.A. defences are still incomplete, they are incomparably

better than anything the Poles could put up. An air attack of this
kind would entail retaliation, which might have unexpected effects
on morale in Germany."

So he still believed the peace offensive was Hitler's most powerful
weapon, and that he could be made to lose the war by being convinced he could not win it. It was agreed that we should not begin
the offensive, but husband our growing Air Force. "What we
ought to do is just to throw back the peace offers and continue
the blockade. . . . I do not believe that holocausts are required."
He saw well enough the strains in this type of war.

> I don't disguise from myself that the course I have sketched out . . .
> is as difficult, or rather, more difficult, than a ding-dong fight, if we
> are to keep together our home front, the Dominions, and the U.S.A.
> However, I shall do as I always have done, go for what I believe to
> be the right course, and risk the consequences.

As the best campaigning season drifted by, and with the sweeping of the German Navy from the seas and victories over their
submarines, his hopes enlarged ; " hold on tightly, keep up the
economic pressure, push on with munitions production and military
preparations with the utmost energy, take no offensive unless Hitler
begins it ". Or again, " if we can achieve our purpose without a
holocaust, what a relief ! But we must not abandon the purpose
for the sake of the relief."

Though by temperament he built too much on this spirit of
neutral countries, or on moderate opinion in Germany, he never
weakened on the conclusion that Hitler must go, and his ill-gotten
gains be restored. And, as the year waned, he allowed some more
doubt : " the German mind seems to absorb Goebbels' gross and
clumsy lies without question or doubt, and all accounts agree in
reporting that the people there are still devoted to Hitler ". For
the time being he disbelieved in a sudden German invasion of
Britain by airborne troops, and seizure of our ports : " what happens
after that, we are not told ; presumably a march on London,
followed by the flight and suicide of the Prime Minister ". Yet
invasion would plainly be more likely if Holland were occupied,
and something of that sort, a letter of December shows, he was
coming to think might be tried in the spring :

> I expect that further attempts will be made to enlist the peace-at-any-
> price people here and in France, and if they are not successful, we
> may see something more adventurous in February or March. I am
> obliged by the general consensus of reports to believe that German

morale has rather hardened, and that Goebbels has succeeded in
making people believe that England is the implacable enemy. . . .
I am beginning to wonder whether we shall do any good with them,
unless they first get a real hard punch in the stomach.

That letter held also an appreciation of a new factor, which
was to end in changing the face of war, the Russian invasion of
Finland.   In final history this may be judged a dangerous aberration,
diverting our effort from the main purpose and even arousing the
menace of bringing Russia in against us.   Some counsellors found
that vision so portentous that they were peering into possibilities
of getting Sweden as an ally, pointing out how vital was Swedish
iron ore to the German machine, or how heavily Scandinavia would
weigh with other neutrals, not least the greatest neutral of all.   In
common British and American sentiment nothing, certainly, had
so struck home as the fate of Finland, a cause in which so many
extremes could join hands, from anti-Russian Conservatives to the
Labour enthusiasm for small nations.   Round the Finnish question
therefore gathered tendencies of great future import.   There was
an advance towards national unity, a sharpening of the means of
total war, a beginning of realisation that the war might be lost by
the unneutral behaviour of neutrals, and that in a struggle to survive the most law-abiding people cannot be tied by international
law.   We resume his letter of December 3 :

the situation is complicated by Stalin's latest performance, which
seems to have provoked far more indignation than Hitler's attack on
Poland, though it is no worse morally, and in its developments is
likely to be much less brutal. . . . I am as indignant as anyone at
the Russians' behaviour, but I am bound to say that I don't think the
Allied cause is likely to suffer thereby.   It has added a great deal to
the general feeling that the ways of dictators make things impossible
for the rest of the world, and in particular it has infuriated the
Americans, who have a sentimental regard for the Finns because they
paid off their war debt.

On this matter, in fact, though the process of his reasoning
might be questioned, his conclusion was undeviating, not to allow
ourselves to be deflected from the main road.   That seems plain
enough from his comment on the views of a Norwegian, sent for
his information.

1 January 1940 ; to Sir Francis Lindley
I don't agree with him if he thinks that we should make peace
with Germany in order to resist Russia.   I still regard Germany as

Public Enemy No. 1, and I cannot take Russia very seriously as an aggressive force, though no doubt formidable if attacked in her own country. I am afraid that, although the Germans would like to make peace on their own terms, they are very far from that frame of mind which will be necessary before they are prepared to listen to what we should call reason.

As to the neutrals, if he thought it right to speak less vehemently than some other ministers, — and the Ministry of Information were anxious about it, — he felt as strongly. " They go out of their way ", he complained, " to pretend that as between Germany and the Allies it is six of one and half a dozen of the other ", and in February he much approved the forcible rescue of our prisoners on the *Altmark* inside Norwegian waters. As the Finnish war dragged on to its inevitable end, I can find no trace that he imported into the consideration of it any motive but our military interests ; which, no doubt, he thought were best served by a prolongation of that war, because it diverted elsewhere the material assistance that Russia could have given Germany. He did his best to send the arms and stores for which Mannerheim asked, — " I am glad to say that we have given them more help than anyone else ", — and declined forcibly a request to convey the Russian terms of peace. But he was well aware that a Soviet conquest of Finland would be no help to Germany, concluding rather that Russia, having got what she wished in the Baltic, would withdraw from " closer German embraces ".

On the larger theme he clung to his belief that Hitler had missed his supreme chance in September 1938, writing that " he could have dealt France and ourselves a terrible, perhaps a mortal, blow then ". But he cherished other beliefs too, that proved illusions. True, his conviction of the depression, and unpopularity of the war, in Germany coincided with all that came from the Americans in Berlin, but he was over-rationalising the way that Germans would behave, and over-estimating, it would seem, their dearth of raw materials. On such foundations he raised a fabric of hope, that the enemy would not face a second winter.

There was another result of the Finns' collapse in March, the fall of the Daladier government, worthy of note because a vibration of anxiety about France sounds in our letters. The Russian attack had reawakened the ugliest prejudices of the French Right, many of whom would have preferred a joint front with Germany against Communism, while pacifist circles hoped much from the European journeys of Roosevelt's personal envoy, Sumner Welles. In due course he saw Chamberlain.

I got the strong impression that he appreciated our vital need for security, and that if Hitler did not disappear he would have to give up most of what Nazism stands for. The odd thing was that he seemed to think there was just a chance — 1 in 10,000 he put it — that he could be brought to that point. There, I think, he is mistaken, but knowing Hitler's capacity to put himself temporarily into quite different and even contradictory moods, I can understand that a mistake might be made, especially if it were encouraged, as it evidently was, by Mussolini.

He hoped, he wrote to the President, that his emissary's tour would have results that might be in time to avert catastrophes. Did those, in his mind, include a collapse of France ? He did not much care about Daladier's successor Reynaud, personally, but believed there was some restoration of French morale ; in their meeting in London at the end of March Reynaud accepted a binding agreement that neither ally would make a separate peace, or armistice.

If he believed also well into the New Year that the country and the Empire kept their confidence in him, he had much ground for it ; if, that is, such confidence were restricted to himself, not extended to all his ministers.

27 November 1939 ; from Mackenzie King
I want first of all to say how constantly you are in my thought, and how complete my admiration is of the manner in which you have met every new situation as it has arisen in this desperate struggle. I am so glad that your strength continues to hold out so well. When I begin to tire at times, I think of you, and then try to begin anew.

Indeed, he took manfully any strain in the way of duty, and among them, for instance, a second visit to France in December ; on which he left some short notes.

For some reason I was rather nervous this time about flying, and I had what some people would call a presentiment that I should not come back. But my reasoning power is too strong to allow of my being seriously disturbed by morbid thoughts, and once I had started I dismissed them entirely.

He flew in a fog to Amiens, and thence to Gort's headquarters near Arras ; there followed inspection of barracks, messes, and social centres, then a lecture by staff officers. Next day up to the line, seeing pill-boxes and breastworks, then to take the march-past at an aerodrome. On the 17th a hundred miles by car to Rheims, base for Air Striking Force; thence in Gamelin's train to Verdun. On the 18th to the Maginot line in Lorraine ; thorough inspection of that, and then of a British brigade ; so to Paris and a State banquet on the 19th, with a Supreme Council meeting.

Yet it is possible to detect a weariness, an added sensitiveness, a disposition to identify criticism with faction.

Some of this may have come from the physical machine slowing down, for the letters speak of much gout and minor ailments. But war had set up an ailment within ; " I find war ", he wrote to the Archbishop at Christmas, " more hateful than ever, and I groan in spirit over every life lost and every home blasted ". The House became a burden to him. " The House of Commons gets more and more ill-tempered and unreasonable." In January he felt it more intensely ; " I was continually interrupted with shouts, sneers, and derisive laughter ", " my depression is increased by the partisan-ship and personal prejudice shown by the Labour Party ". He read nearly the whole press every day, which means, surely, that he read it overmuch, and did not make enough allowance for young men in a hurry.

All the more he looked for consolation where it never failed, and to Chequers above all, which he loved deeply, and where he went as often as he could : to clear the alder copse, to choose sites for new trees, to see its winter aconites, and count its rook nests. If work made Chequers impossible, he would make all he could of a day at Kew or Richmond, or of the lime tree in Downing Street and the blue-tits at his bird-table. He would even disguise himself in an unfamiliar hat, if he thought he could thereby walk un-recognised. His fishing days seemed gone. When his seventy-first birthday passed, in thanking his friend Francis Humphrys for good wishes, he doubted if they would fish at Castle Forbes again, " perhaps we may do it somewhere else, — if there is fishing there ". His Birmingham home he never saw after the outbreak of war.

His mental interests and vitality were wide and strong as ever ; he was hunting down the home of the *Locks of Norbury*, reading *A Regency Chapter* or *Flaubert and Madame Bovary*, with native amaze-ment at the harm done by emotion. His own habit of thought and preferences were settled ; " I am more and more fascinated by Shakespeare as I grow older ", he wrote to Lady Stanhope, and to his sisters, on finishing all the " Comedies " again, that something he must have like them to rid him of " these perpetual war problems and the unending nagging of the press and the House of Commons ".

To Chequers, then, for rest, in the snows of this winter and its bitter sky :

> Thou dost not bite so nigh,
> As benefits forgot.

CHAPTER XXXIV

FALL FROM POWER

NEITHER Finland nor Norway in truth brought about the fall of the Chamberlain government, but accumulated causes of which they were the final symptoms, running back to earlier years, part personal to himself but in much greater part the penalty for short-comings widely distributed and troubles deep-seated. On this our records long must remain incomplete but, such as they are, they seem to bear out some old maxims of revolution : such as, that occasions signify little, though causes much, and that it is not only the highest motive that brings the best result.

We have met already the view expressed, both by Chamberlain and Churchill, that the available stock of political talent in the party was low. Yet that is not to say that the best conceivable use was made of it. Many younger members, who would have done anything for him, doubted the competence of his team, questioning especially whether some of its high talents included the qualities most vital in war. Nor were all his new appointments found convincing as the best for the posts in question. When challenged on his reason for the choice of Gilmour as Minister of Shipping, he gave it briefly as " character and experience " ; high qualities, indeed, yet one of them incompatible with youth. In these matters he could not be ruthless ; he would transfer a colleague, but found it hard to drop him, so that some moves had the look of a reshuffle, not of a new deal.

The Parliament elected in 1935, largely on issues of the League and unemployment, kept in a time of world revolution a little too much of parochial character. It was apt, on the one side, to read international conflict in too insular terms and, on the other, to be exacting as to doles, cinema seats, or lack of bacon, at a moment when considerations of plenty should have given way to considerations of power. But, inevitably, all he had written on the absence of a sense of danger affected the temper of the country in this " twilight war ", producing overmuch grumbling at matters long ago taken as discipline in other countries, and to which we have ourselves long since become acclimatised. Much time passed over inadequate train services, or the black-out, or small annoyances of civil defence ; the miners were found in protest against rationing of coal, and Herbert Morrison against the menace to freedom of opinion in the Home Secretary's regulations. While some sections held that we were over-prepared, or over " civil-serviced ", it was possible to go about the country and find large patches seemingly unaffected by war. Rationing, and then only partial, did not begin till the New Year ; despite war industries, there were over a million unemployed ; classes under the Military Service Act were called up by slow degrees. We were highly taxed, yet an angry sense reached members, especially the seventy younger Conservative members serving in the Forces, that though all was at stake, armament and equipment were slow in arriving, and perilously incomplete.

Opposition, who professed to doubt the sincerity of the Prime Minister and " men of Munich ", often interpreted the war situation in other terms than the necessities of war. Technically there was a party truce, in the sense that officially party contests would not be allowed to change the present distribution of seats, but through crevices in the truce a rival programme welled to the surface. Labour concentrated their onset almost wholly on pensions, allowances, or employment, sought revision even during war of grievances such as the Trade Disputes Act, or asked a full statement of post-war social policy. And once again, as in the last war, large wage increases in munition industries threatened the spiral that ends in inflation. In short, though industrial Labour was sincerely enlisted for the war, and by every device of consultation associated with its conduct, that was not enough. Labour's political structure had so grown that it would not pull its full industrial weight until it shared political responsibility.

Chamberlain supported every measure to hold the balance even. The sugar duty in the first war Budget was a bitter pill for Opposition ; " I took the view that we should never get it, unless it were accompanied by swinging taxation on the direct payer ", and income tax moved up at a stroke from 5s. 6d. to 7s. 6d. Ample power had been taken to check profiteering in essential goods, the excess profits tax was put for the time at 60 per cent. A promise he had given before war broke out was redeemed, in spite of war burdens, by the reduction to sixty of the qualifying pension age for women and wives in contributory insurance, and by allowing supplementary payments to other old-age pensioners who could show need.

But the main volume of criticism fastened on those precise points, the adequacy of production under the Ministry of Supply, or gaps in the blockade of Germany, which went beyond any personal shortcoming in administration. The first was rooted in the imperfections of a democracy ill prepared for war, and the second in the rôle of neutral States ; each implying that no modern war could be won unless and until it were made total. It was with complaints over supply especially that he had to deal in the secret session of December 13 to which, very unwillingly — for he did not believe secret sessions were secret — he agreed, and which he described as " ragged and ill-tempered ".

Admitting mistakes, in substance he claimed that his government had not failed on the home front.

> The food situation [he wrote on January 27] has been improved out of all knowledge, the shipping problem has been firmly gripped, economic warfare is being waged with remarkable efficiency, the Dominions are being kept in line with us without friction (no easy or simple task), the scheme for old-age pensions is a remarkable piece of ingenious workmanship, which deals with every real hardship, without imposing impossible burdens on the Exchequer. We are already subsidising food to the tune of about £50 millions a year to keep down cost of living, and shall have to do more, but we shall get no credit for it.

In personnel, and even in structure, his administration changed considerably before the German offensive in the spring. A first move was the departure of Hore-Belisha from the War Office. Enemies of the government, says his leader's contemporary letter, would represent it " as a victory for brass hats who don't like the democratisation of the Army ". Nothing could be more unjust ; and nothing more explicit than his recital of the facts ; he had come back from France in December, he says, " feeling that I had only smoothed over a difference which was likely to break out again ". To resume his letter :

> He has very exceptional qualities of courage, imagination, and drive, which seemed to me just those required at the War Office when I put him there ; [since which time] he has done more for the Army than anyone since Haldane. Unfortunately, he has the defects of his qualities, — partly from his impatience and eagerness, partly from a self-centredness which makes him careless of other people's feelings.

He recorded simply the most relevant fact : " nothing could be worse than perpetual friction and want of confidence between the Secretary of State and the commander-in-chief in the field ".

In January he therefore placed Stanley at the War Office, and as Hore-Belisha felt unable to take the Board of Trade thus vacated

filled it by bringing in Sir Andrew Duncan ; at the same time
Reith succeeded Lord Macmillan at the Ministry of Information.

Following upon Gilmour's death, in early April more changes
came about of importance. Robert Hudson succeeded as Minister
of Shipping. The functions hitherto discharged by W. S. Morrison
were made over and enlarged by the establishment of a Ministry
of Food under Lord Woolton. Hoare, Privy Seal, and Kingsley
Wood, Minister for Air, changed places. Chatfield retired from the
War Cabinet.

In part they reflected not merely an intensification of war, but
a dualism in the government. Chatfield's position as co-ordinating
minister had become anomalous when all three Service ministers
were in the War Cabinet themselves, and more anomalous still
when one of them was Churchill. The First Lord's knowledge of
war, the prestige of his name as the one active survivor of the great
days of old, necessarily raised him with Parliament and public
much above a departmental status ; his magnificent eloquence,
the zest of his advocacy, his unconcealed indignation with abuses
of neutrality, could not but make him the shining figure of the
Cabinet. We see him associated more nearly with the Prime
Minister as the strains grew greater, proceeding with him to the
Supreme Council, his persuasive vehemence brought to bear on
the French and, with that, a tightening of the bonds between them.

Great wars cast men and measures into new moulds, and by
the spring there were three forces converging towards a change.
There was a cry, not yet satisfied, for more " co-ordination ", a
word suspect, like most labels, to Chamberlain's mind, which preferred to try out means of efficiency surely, as some of his late
appointments showed. In March, again, he told a friend that he
found the feeling of the Labour party was wavering about joining
his government, and that some were inclined to. This was true,
it seems, but by no means all the truth. If Labour had shifted
its ground to this extent, that many would now feel it a duty to
join a national government, it is probable that only a small minority
would have served under him : at the same time he believed that
Churchill would like to see invitations to Sinclair and Beaverbrook.
And, thirdly, there were changes in the structure of defence. In
early April he arranged that Churchill should preside over the
joint committee of Service ministers and chiefs of staff, which was
directly responsible for the planning of war. He congratulated
himself, too, on getting through a project for " double banking "
the overburdened chiefs of staff ; " incidentally, this has enabled

me to bring Sir John Dill to headquarters, where I have long been anxious to have his able brain ".

General discontents, and the flood of war, in March received a swift tributary by the fall of Finland. With perfect truth he could point out that the refusal of Norway and Sweden to allow transit to the Allied armies had been fatal, and indeed the damage done was much greater to sentiment and prestige than to any reasoned expectation of political effect. His private letters anticipate the defence he was to make in debate, that we had done all that we could.

> They began by asking for fighter planes, and we sent all the surplus we could lay hands on. They asked for A.A. guns, and again we stripped our own imperfectly-armed home defences to help them. They asked for small arms ammunition, and we gave them priority over our own army. They asked for later types of planes, and we sent them 12 Hurricanes, against the will and advice of our Air Staff. They said that men were no good now, but that they would want 30,000 in the spring. We assembled — not 30,000, for the railways would not carry the equipment necessary for their maintenance — but a substantial force, very heavily armed. . . . That is ready to go now, but we can't send it unless, first, the Finns ask for it and, second, the Norwegians and Swedes allow it a passage through their territory. Up to now, being pressed hard by the Swedes, the Finns have declined to ask for it, and the Norwegians and Swedes have flatly told us they won't let us through, the latter explaining that they will just withdraw their rolling stock, and pull up a bit of their railway.

Even so, it was a wound to the whole world of democracy, and while the providential escapes were still concealed, the immediate blow was too obvious.

His speech on March 19 ended with a warning to the Scandinavian States, that the danger stood on their doorstep ; " nothing will or can save them but a determination to defend themselves, and to join with others who are ready to aid them ". Following on his first Supreme Council with Reynaud, and his own Cabinet changes, it was determined to enforce Scandinavian neutrality in fact, even if infringing it in law, and on April 8 we laid minefields in Norwegian waters. Our move had been anticipated at Berlin, and was forestalled by the expedition which, long prepared, that day invaded Norway and Denmark.

The Norwegian campaign, which became the occasion of his fall, was one of a class very familiar in our great wars ; having many precedents in our resistance of old to the French and Napoleon, and later parallels in Greece, Jugo-Slavia, and Crete. In such a case, where political necessity is invoked to outweigh military argument, to refuse all aid to Norway, as later to the Greeks, was judged out of the question. British expectations rose high, encouraged by confident utterances from Chamberlain and Churchill. But by May 4, except for a precarious hold on the far northern port of Narvik, we had evacuated all Norway and suffered a heavy defeat.

There was one point, made by Churchill early in April, which covers this and all like operations ; " it is not the slightest use blaming the Allies for not being able to give substantial help and protection to neutral countries, if they are held at arm's length by the neutral countries until those countries are actually attacked ". That said, this biography is not concerned, nor do his papers deal, with the detailed criticism on which the final history of that disaster must turn ; whether the force held for Finland ought to have been dispersed ; whether our failure was primarily in planning, delay in time, hesitance in council, or break-down in equipment. On the vital decision, not to attack Trondheim direct by naval forces, it is clear that all hesitated long, as well they might, and clear also that neither Chamberlain, nor any other minister, overruled their naval and military advisers. In the last resort the two most deadly failures, to check German reinforcement by sea and to provide air cover for our troops, must be driven further back, as Churchill said in debate : " the reason for this serious disadvantage of our not having the initiative is one which cannot speedily be removed, and it is our failure in the last five years to maintain or regain air parity with Germany ". That, he must remind them, was " a very long story ", seeing that when he had first pressed it on the House, for two years " it was not only the Government who objected, but both the Opposition parties ".

That point will be found also at the end of Chamberlain's letters during the crisis, the course of which begins on April 13 with the hope that if " we can get Allied forces into well-established bases on the Norwegian coast, we ought to be able to stop them ".

20 April

the military keep saying that we are engaged in very hazardous operations, so I suppose we are, but I shall be very disappointed if we haven't practically captured Trondjem before the week is out.

27 April

this has been one of the worst, if not *the* worst, week of the war. . . .
We hadn't reckoned on the way in which the Germans had poured
in reinforcements of men, guns, tanks, and aeroplanes. In particular,
this brief campaign has taught our people, many of whom were much
in need of teaching, the importance of the air factor.

4 May

I am thankful that at least we got our men out of Norway. . . . We
could not give them what they wanted most, namely fighter aircraft,
because we had no aerodrome from which they could operate.   I
rather doubt whether our experts realised before the power of an
unopposed air arm. . . . Both the Norwegian and the Swedish
governments told us that it was essential to take Trondjem. . . .
We knew it was a dangerous operation, but there was a chance that
we might pull it off before the Germans established themselves. That
chance, as it now appears, vanished when we gave up the original
idea of a direct attack with warships up the fjord, *à la* Narvik. We
had not indeed expected the Germans to come up from Oslo so fast,
for we thought the Norwegians would have blown up the railway
bridges and at least rolled stones on to the roads. But they refused to
do either . . . except in a few cases, they seemed to have no fighting
spirit. . . . My own mind, and this is the view of some of the best
experts, inclines to the conclusion that, even if we had been able to
capture Trondjem, our success would only have been temporary.
. . . The most common cry, and this of course is chronic in the
U.S.A., is " why are we always too late ? why do we let Hitler take
the initiative ? " . . . The answer to these questions is simple enough,
but the questioners would rather not believe it. It is, " because we
are not yet strong enough ". . . . We have plenty of man-power, but
it is neither trained nor equipped. We are short of many weapons of
offence and defence. Above all, we are short of air power. If we
could weather this year, I believe we should be able to remove our
worst deficiencies.

This was not the complacency of which he was accused, but it
was not a good case to expound in public, nor was he in a mood
to accept airy correction. Those who weakened the home front in
hard times, he broke out fiercely, were as bad as Quisling ; fiercely,
but not justly, since the changes demanded were aimed not to
weaken but to make more strong. Moreover, they had other formidable possibilities to think of. One reason for the Admiralty's
reluctance to throw in all their strength against Trondheim was the
surly attitude of Italy, and he personally approved of the decision

taken to push some capital ships through the Mediterranean narrows to Alexandria, which might make Mussolini think twice, or think better.

This long letter of May 4, little though he guessed it, was to be his last family chronicle from Chequers, as its lawful tenant ; it ends, " I don't think my enemies will get me down this time. I should be sorry if they did, because I should then have to leave this lovely place."

The two days' debate of May 7 and 8, though in form turning upon Norway, resolved into an enquiry whether the country was being equipped for total war, and whether the existing government was best fitted to do it. Had the answer been in doubt, it would have been given very soon, for on May 10 the Germans invaded the Low Countries.

As so often happens, the timing of the crisis was unforeseen ; not till the second day did government issue a three-line whip, while Labour had not, until the first day was half gone, made up their mind to divide the House. That day went exceedingly badly for government. It was made manifest that the War Office had not reckoned either on the speed or direction of the German attack ; the intervention of Sir Roger Keyes in full uniform, which was the turning-point, seemed to denounce the loss of that offensive spirit which had achieved our ancient glory. The Prime Minister came to the debate confident that the criticisms could be answered — as, indeed, in some vital respects they were on the purely Norwegian issue — but neither his speech on May 7, nor the letter we shall quote, reveal the meaning of the vote. It was legitimate to point out that, on the controversy whether a War Cabinet should be composed of ministers without portfolio, the principal ministers were all agreed ; to argue that such disputes on structure could not advance production ; to brush aside, with some disdain, attempts to thrust a wedge between Churchill and himself, to ask the co-operation of members of all parties. What he had not allowed for was the intense feeling which, to take one example, made one young Conservative member vote against him, for the specific reason that on the eve of embarkation his battalion had received neither training nor equipment.

The logic, or the moral, of this debate pointed to the succession of Churchill. " To me personally ", Chamberlain had written on March 30, " he is absolutely loyal ", and never had reason to change that faith. But that was not the issue. The speeches of Opposition, of Duff Cooper, and the direct attack of Lloyd George, were directed to separate Churchill from Chamberlain, to brand the Prime Minister as the stumbling-block to unity ; the voices of Keyes and Lloyd George, echoes from Churchill's most glorious day, entreating him to assert himself, and to come from out these tents of Kedar. Churchill's speech set up a counter-signal, " let pre-war feuds die . . . let all the strong horses be pulling on the collar ". He declared a precipitate vote in a moment of difficulty unworthy of the British character ; exception had been taken because Chamberlain appealed to his friends, and " he certainly had a good many when things were going well ". But there is in human beings a sixth sense, that of anticipation, and that too had not been lacking.

Certainly it was impossible in the atmosphere of the second day not to resist the motion to divide. " No government ", said the Prime Minister, " can prosecute a war efficiently unless it has public and parliamentary support. I accept the challenge . . . and I call on my friends." But to be called on to vote on party lines was not what the House at that moment desired, and the government majority fell to 81 ; 33 Conservatives voted against it, some 60 more abstained.

His own analysis of this debate may precede the steps intervening between it and his resignation.

11 May

the long period of waiting without any real set-back to German prestige, and then the sudden and bitter disappointment over the hopes that had been so recklessly and unjustifiably fostered by the press, just boiled up, with the accumulated mass of grievances, to find expression. The serving members were acutely conscious of various deficiencies, not realising apparently that, though you can double your Territorial army with a stroke of the pen, you can't do the same thing with its equipment. The Amerys, Duff Coopers, and their lot are consciously, or unconsciously, swayed by a sense of frustration because they can only look on, and finally the personal dislike of Simon and Hoare had reached a pitch which I find it difficult to understand, but which undoubtedly had a great deal to do with the rebellion.

A number of those who voted against the government have since either told me, or written to me to say, that they had nothing against me except that I had the wrong people in my team. . . . They don't want to believe that the real reason is our comparative weakness, because we haven't yet anything like caught up the German start, but as that fact remains, whatever the administration, I am afraid they will presently be disappointed again.

Public men have at least one public right, to be judged by their public deeds. His decision was taken instantly at the end of the debate ; he would not consider suggestions that he should declare this a side issue and ask a straight vote of confidence ; he felt a National government of all parties must be formed, and that nothing touching himself must stand in its way. He knew that he himself could not get it, but the mass of his party, resentful at the spirit shown, looked to him, and to justify himself he must get the official opinion of the Labour party, at this moment assembled in conference at Bournemouth. On the 9th he asked Attlee and Greenwood to get him that reply by the following day. Meantime consultation convinced him that his first impulse, that Halifax might be his successor, was not the way out, and he agreed to put Churchill's name to the King. On the 10th he got the answer he expected, that Labour would serve in a National government, but not under him ; armed with which he at once went to the Palace and handed in his resignation. That night he broadcast to the country ; " it came quite spontaneously ", he wrote, " from what was in my mind, and I had no time for polishing ", adding in a note the same day to Mrs. Carnegie that he would have preferred to go entirely, but wished to set " an example of national unity ".

His broadcast said that, after the debate,

> I had no doubt in my mind that some new and drastic action must be taken, if confidence was to be given to the House of Commons, and the war carried on with the energy and vigour essential to victory. . . . In the afternoon of to-day it was apparent that the essential unity could be secured under another Prime Minister, though not myself. In these circumstances my duty was plain. . . . For the hour has now come when we are to be put to the test, as the innocent people of Holland, Belgium, and France are being tested already. And you, and I, must rally behind our new leader, and with our united strength, and with unshakable courage, fight and work until this wild beast, that has sprung out of his lair upon us, has been finally disarmed and overthrown.

He at least had been put to the test, and had not flinched. Only his instant decision perpetuated in war the national unity which his crusade for peace had begun.

This it was for which the stream of letters in the next few days gave him their writers' thanks, from every condition of men, some indignant at the last scenes, some insisting that the party still counted on his lead, some dwelling on his work for peace, others on his

work for rearmament. He prized much a gracious letter from the
Queen of her personal thanks — " during these last desperate and
unhappy years, you have been a great support and comfort to us
both ". But for historic judgement on the heights to which he
rose in his fall, three men could speak with more warranty than any.

9 May ; from Halifax

however things go these next few days, I can't help writing this line
to tell you, how much I have learnt from you during the last 24 hours.
You have given me a lesson in public spirit, and in the will to set self
on one side, which I hope I will remember. I thank you for that, and
for very much else.

10 May ; from Winston Churchill

my first act on coming back from the Palace is to write and tell you
how grateful I am to you for promising to stand by me, and to aid
the country at this extremely grievous and formidable moment. I am
under no illusions about what lies ahead, and of the long dangerous
defile through which we must march for many months. With your
help and counsel, and with the support of the great party of which
you are the leader, I trust that I shall succeed. The example which
you have set of self-forgetting dignity and public spirit will govern the
action of many, and be an inspiration to all.

In these eight months we have worked together I am proud to
have won your friendship and your confidence in an increasing
measure. To a very large extent I am in your hands — and I feel no
fear of that. For the rest I have faith in our cause, which I feel sure
will not be suffered to fail among men.

I will write to you again to-night after I have seen the Labour
leaders. I am so glad you will broadcast to our anxious people.

11 May ; from Lord Baldwin

You have passed through fire since we were talking together only a
fortnight ago, and you have come out pure gold.

The fires were not out, nor the vein of gold exhausted.

CHAPTER XXXV

THE END

HE fell in May, in July he was stricken by illness, he died in November. His hopes and all he had worked for seemed in ruins. He had striven to stop war, and war had come ; to prevent it spreading, and it had become total ; to limit the atrocity of air warfare, and it devastated British soil. Every political entrenchment, each canon of fair dealing, on which he had stood, was blasted. France was destroyed, Italy against us, Turkey evaded its obligations, the neutrality of small States had become a laughing-stock, Russia was swallowing the Baltic States, America bent on avoiding war, from Ireland not a word came to reward his policy of faith. In so far as shortcomings or offences in Great Britain had contributed to this array of doom, he was made, for a time, the scapegoat for them all, and the name of which he was so proud was sunk low. Well, he was ever a fighter, and was hoping to live to vindicate it yet, when fate slit his life, thin-spun now after laborious days. In this calamity and sorrow expired with him a political epoch, with its good and evil, its aspirations, restrictions, and garnered wealth, all of which shall at some distant day be judged with true measure. But Neville Chamberlain died, as he had lived, unbowed and full of fortitude, confident that he had done his best and could have done no other.

Let us dispose first of his position in the new order. Very deliberately he stepped into the background. He did not issue any honours list, which some found abnormal, and others unkind. He would not consider taking the Exchequer, as he saw it would mean conflict with Labour. Churchill's proposal was that he should be leader of the House, which would have taken off his own shoulders much routine duty, as Bonar Law had for Lloyd George, but, says Chamberlain, " the Labour Party made trouble about it, and I saw that it would involve me in much tedious sitting in the House, and very likely lead to ill-temper and bad manners. So I gave it up without a sigh." Officially he was Lord President, in fact he was co-ordinating internal questions while Churchill controlled the emergent policy of war, and presided in Cabinet when Churchill was absent. By agreement with him he kept the leadership of the party, their published letters declaring it wisest in the interest of unity and most suitable, seeing it was a government made up of three parties, the new Prime Minister's message ending, " the relations of perfect confidence which have grown up between us makes this division of duties and responsibilities very agreeable to me ". His private comment was that it was " essential, if Winston was to have whole-hearted support ", as many Conservatives were sore, and some were disappointed. Yet only the war could determine whether he would keep this position in the State.

Now began two months of accumulated and undeserved calamity, darker for our country than any since Napoleon's army was massed at Boulogne, or since French and Spanish fleets had driven us off the sea and made an independent America. Between his fall on May 10 and his illness in late July came successively the collapse of Holland, the piercing of the French lines near Sedan, the German drive to the Channel ports, the capitulation of Belgium, the isolation of the British army and its evacuation at Dunkirk, the abandonment of Paris, the entry of Italy into the war, the total disintegration of the French and their separate peace with the enemy, our attack on the French fleet at Oran, Italian invasion of Kenya and the Sudan, a Japanese demand that aid to China should cease, and our agreement temporarily to close the passage of war material to China by the Burma road ; finally, a massing of troops and all the paraphernalia of invasion on the whole arc from Norway to Finisterre. With more time on his hands than for years past, he began once more to keep a diary : mournful to read, immeasurably sorrowful both for the man and his country.

15 May

midnight ; terrible message from Winston, who is in Paris. Effect is next 3 or 4 days decisive. Unless German advance can be stayed, French army will collapse, and B.E.F. will be cut off.

19 May

Our only hope, it seems to me, lies in Roosevelt and the U.S.A. But unfortunately they are so unready themselves that they can do little to help us now.

26 May

the blackest day of all . . . Reynaud coming over . . . plain from his attitude that he had given up all idea of serious fighting, and if we are to go on, we shall be alone.

8 June

I'm sure the French are already beaten in spirit. . . . I anticipate that Italy will come in now. . . . It is a hard time for all who care for freedom.

17 June

The French army ceased fighting about midday. . . . No substantial help is forthcoming from U.S.A. Turkey has defaulted on her obligations, Egypt is evasive, and Spain is said to be on the point of coming in against us. . . . We are hurrying to the crisis.

28 June

the De Valera people are afraid we are going to lose, and don't want to be involved with us.

1 July

Not one of the American journalists who have been in the Low Countries or France believe we can stand up to the bombing we shall get from the air. But it seems to me that they don't take account of what our Air Force may do to the bombers. All reports seem to point to the invasion this week or next.

In this hour-to-hour stress lived the men on whom decision rested. Their fundamentals were destroyed, Churchill's faith in the French army no less than Chamberlain's in Italian neutrality, or in forces of moderation within Germany. Churchill's heroic resolution never blenched nor, as we shall see, did Chamberlain's fortitude, nor the courage of the country at large. But we had suffered a severe military defeat, it seemed as if heavy sacrifice, of which the Burma road decision was a herald, might be needed if we were to survive, and there were figures of repute, defeatist at heart, who might be ready to form, or support, an alternative government. Fortitude he had in abundance, yet knew, I think, he was not the man for this hour.

17 May

All my world has tumbled to bits in a moment. The national peril has so swamped all personal feelings that no bitterness remains. Indeed, I used to say to Annie before war came that, if such a thing happened, I thought I should have to hand over to someone else, for I knew what agony of mind it would mean for me to give directions that would bring death and mutilation and misery to so many. But the war was so different from what I expected that I found the strain bearable, and perhaps it was providential that the revolution which overturned me coincided with the entry of the real thing.

He described himself as numbed ; " I frankly envy Austen's peace ".

But he had always fought best under heavy fire, and as disaster came, some of those who had driven him from power hoped to drive him out of public life and remodel the new-made government. Might it not be said that Dunkirk was the last product of Chamberlainism, that the British army was beaten because it had been under-equipped, or that a veiled Fascist could not help to conduct a people's war ? The bitterness he had declared to be gone flowed again, and he caused thus to be endorsed a hostile article :

> if anybody ever writes my biography after I am gone, I should like them to see this article, which shows the response to what I did by the official organ of the Labour Party.

Letters and diary record not only a sense that the present peril justified his resolution not to get entangled deep in Norway, but the satisfaction of his conscience on the larger controversy.

25 May
> Whatever the outcome, it is clear as daylight that, if we had had to fight in 1938, the results would have been far worse. It would be rash to prophesy the verdict of history, but if full access is obtained to all the records, it will be seen that I realised from the beginning our military weakness, and did my best to postpone, if I could not avert, the war. But I had to fight every yard against both Labour and Liberal Opposition leaders who denounced me for trying to maintain good relations with Italy and Japan, for refusing to back Republican Spain against Franco, and for not " standing up to Hitler " at each successive act of aggression.

What he heard from those in command of how our equipment had stood the test, or from Dunkirk men of the performance of the anti-tank and Bofors guns, gave him more confidence, and as the undying achievement of our airmen kept invasion at bay, he asked whether he was not entitled to judgement on the whole issue ; " if I am personally responsible for deficiencies of tanks and anti-aircraft guns, I must be equally personally responsible for the efficiency of the Air Force and the Navy ".

For a full month, while German soldiers drove from the Somme to the Pyrenees, he was fighting this political battle also, which if uncurbed must destroy national unity since, if he was forced to resign, other Conservatives would resign with him. " A dreadful exhibition of irresponsibility, frivolity, and partisan squabbling ", says the diary of one debate late in May. If he defended himself, as he certainly would, how could it be done, it continues, without implied attack on his Labour colleagues, " with whom I am now working in complete harmony " ?

He had never evaded action ; he declared to the Prime Minister that, if his presence was felt to be hampering, he would go at once. And here, in the interest of historic truth, it is right to say that never for a moment did he complain, or have ground to complain, of undermining at the higher levels. His records abound in admiration of the Prime Minister. Their word had been given to each other, that they would stand or fall together in the storm ; " your attitude to me is as loyal as mine to you," he wrote to Churchill, " and I can't say more " ; or again, " Winston has behaved with the most unimpeachable loyalty ".

This went wider, for he had always been a good — perhaps too good — a colleague, and men could not work with him for long without a growing respect, often a growing affection, nor he with them without diffidence or prejudice giving way. He hoped and believed, he wrote, his Labour colleagues " are finding that I am a very different person from what they supposed ", and that was warranted. " I have learned ", Sinclair wrote in a generous letter, " to appreciate the value of your counsel ", and much lay in the word of Attlee when he died, his " magnanimity ".

One demand on it, however, tried him high — a suggestion that Lloyd George be invited to join the Cabinet. Was he to sit with the man to whom he attributed his failure in 1917, and who for ten years had held him up to public reprobation ? whose motives he confessed he did not trust. But no patriotic man could resist the spirit of the letter he received.

6 June ; from Winston Churchill

. . . In this terrible hour, with all that impends, the country ought to be satisfied that all its ablest and best-known leaders are playing their part, and I certainly do not think that one should be set against another. I know the sacrifices of personal interest and position which you have made arise solely from your public spirit and our cruel need, and I venture to hope that you will aid and ease me in this matter, which I regard as very important for the general cohesion of the Government. I will guarantee that he will work fairly and honourably with you, failing which please count as always upon
your sincere friend
WINSTON S. CHURCHILL.

He agreed, with stipulations that the long feud should be buried, his private comment being, " one cannot refuse anything in times like these to the Prime Minister, who is carrying the main burden of responsibility ". But he did so, we must allow, in scepticism and dismay. He was not tried further, for the Wizard remained silent, unable, perhaps, to accept office on terms thus part controlled by the minister who, he felt, had kept him out of office for eighteen years. Enormous, cruel, and unpredictable, the ironies of history. Who could have foreseen that, three weeks before Chamberlain died, he would have been considering a weighty suggestion that he should write some articles for the American press, to offset the alleged harmful impression left by the contributions of his old rival ?

When that was all done, at last he set about moving into No. 11 Downing Street, which hitherto he had thought would be labour lost, and paid a farewell visit to Chequers, just long enough to

> say good-bye to the staff and to Spot, and to look round my trees and the gardens. I am content now I have done that, and shall put Chequers out of my mind. We have had some happy days there, but they are over anyhow, and it is difficult to see how there can be much more happiness for any of us.

Within, the spring of life was strained, and physically he was not well, his diary mentioning for the first time on June 16 " considerable pain ". And as he had not Churchill's nervous and physical armour, or his insight into war, I judge that, on the short run, he felt more pessimistic than the Prime Minister ; not thinking, for instance, that serious invasion was impossible. But his decision and completeness in counsel, and his courage for the long run, never quailed, as they had not done before.

They did not fail him now. In the decisions they all had to take, the machinery of his mind, always tuned to strip away non-essentials, served him well, and they were decisions which were instant, perilous, and tragic ; to refuse the diversion of our whole fighter force to France, to name the exact hour up to which Alexander must hold the perimeter of Dunkirk, or to urge on the unyielding Irish, North and South alike, that neither neutrality nor partition could weigh in the scales against a German occupation of their country.

Now that unity was achieved and the enemy at the gate, his instinct was for total action. " Cabinet committee ", we read in May, " presided over by me . . . to-night decided to advise emergency measure this week, to put everyone's service and property at disposal of State ". He called for a report on the operation of air raid warnings ; " it is quite intolerable that work in important munitions factories should be stopped for 4 or 5 hours when in fact no bombs have been dropped anywhere near them ". He felt strongly that those with responsibility should not hoist a signal of pessimism by sending their children overseas. Yet since the first week of June he had despaired of France, telling his much trusted chief agent at Birmingham " we must fight on ", and when France faded out, though he judged General De Gaulle "a stout fellow", his last word was hard : " we are at any rate free of our obligations to the French, who have been nothing but a liability to us. It would have been far better if they had been neutral from the beginning." He had never much faith that the offer of an Anglo-French union would induce them to maintain the fight.

Rumours were set about, it seems by American isolationists, so that they could tell their electors Roosevelt was helping a country not worth saving, that he and Halifax meditated a compromise peace. Whereupon on June 30 he broadcast :

> we are a solid and united nation, which would rather go down to ruin than admit the domination of the Nazis. . . . If the enemy does try to invade this country, we will fight him in the air and on the sea ; we will fight him on the beaches with every weapon we have. . . . We shall be fighting . . . with the conviction that our cause is the cause of humanity and peace against cruelty and wars ; a cause that surely has the blessing of Almighty God.

As the German command hesitated, and each week it became more probable that we could continue to fight not just for better terms, but for victory, he saw light glimmering at the end of the tunnel. " We have more than replaced our air losses ", he wrote on June 21, " and reorganised our squadrons so that we are stronger than ever." Week after week of perfect summer weather, day after day in his diary of blood-curdling rumour but of " silence and immobility ", or " nothing to report ", till we reach on July 14 (alas for free France !) the last of those letters, which for a quarter of a century had registered his every thought :

> I got so tired of waiting for Hitler to begin his invasion, that I set to with Annie this morning on the pictures. . . . Give us another 3 or 4 months of production, not more hampered than it is at present, and we shall have something over, with which we can make ourselves disagreeable in many ways, and many places. We could perhaps take a stronger line with Japan then, even though we still got no help from U.S.A. . . . People ask me how are we ever going to win this war. I suppose it is a very natural question, but I don't think the time has come to answer it. We must just go on fighting as hard as we can, in the belief that some time — perhaps sooner than we think — the other side will crack.

Q

On July 19, speaking to a silent Reichstag, to galleries crowded by neurotic Ciano, the wretched Quisling, and new-made field-marshals, Hitler declared he saw no reason why the war should go on ; on which the diary of the man of Munich says only

> the familiar round of distorted history, megalomania, self-righteousness, and threats . . . received with contempt everywhere except in Italy. Russia remains silent. I guess he made no specific offer of peace, only an appeal to " common sense ", because, if he had, it would have been rejected.

To his supporters he seemed confident and well, but in fact he was ill, and it was arranged he should have an exploratory operation on July 24 ; at seventy-one he could not work on, as he was. He spent the day before it in flying to inspect coast defences in Norfolk, where he saw barriers, howitzers, flotillas on the Broads, and spoke to trawler skippers ; in all, ten hours from door to door. Three days after, he knew the doctors' verdict, — a major operation that week and then, the diary notes, " even chances. But if the odds go against me, I am doubtful whether I should be the same man, and I think it would be very difficult to come back ' on appro '." On the 29th, " am just off to Nuffield House, with a wonderfully calm mind ".

At first all went well, and he wrote in high spirits to Baldwin :

> I understand I am a model patient. From the professional point of view my progress is entirely satisfactory, but my personal opinion is that I have had fair hell. However, I believe I passed the worst yesterday morning, and I should go forward like a two-year-old now.

In the middle of August he went to Heckfield in Hampshire, to recuperate, fortified by reading much Conrad and a mass about Michelangelo, and cheered by letters from Churchill and his colleagues, wishing for his return but intent it should not be too quickly. As the month wore on, he was still confident and expected to be soon back to keep an eye on the Foreign Office, while Halifax took a short respite.

But when in September he returned to London, he was clear enough that he had reached the last stage but one.

Diary, 9 September

> . . . I have still to adjust myself to the new life of a partially crippled man, which is what I am. Any ideas which may have been in my mind about possibilities of further political activity, and even a possibility of another Premiership after the war, have gone. I know

that is out of the question. At the present, I have come into the very centre of the battle for Britain, and the next few weeks may well see the turn of the tide, one way or another. If we are still alive and free, as I think we have every reason to hope, I should like to go on working in my present capacity till the end of the war, and then get out, and try and fill up the remainder of my days without further public responsibilities.

He was made very welcome by the Prime Minister, who told him he counted on his steady counsel, but he was not strong enough to endure London as it was that month, unable from his ailment to carry on work in a troglodyte existence or to be robbed of sleep, so that within ten days he had a relapse and returned to Heckfield. Thence he wrote in detail to Halifax, " so that he might be convinced I was not shirking ", and on the 22nd offered his resignation, which for the time being the Prime Minister refused to accept. Though he felt now his ailment was incurable, the diary, unconcealing to the end, does not mask the value set on his service ; " if I did get well enough, I could give him more help personally, and ensure him more support politically, than anyone else ".

By September 30, however, the Prime Minister felt he could delay no longer in acting upon Chamberlain's offer, for government was undergoing considerable reconstruction and Parliament about to meet after the hard Dakar decision had gone awry.

30 September 1940 ; to His Majesty King George VI
    SIR,
        Your Majesty is no doubt aware that after a stay of less than a fortnight in London, I found myself unable to carry on, and at the suggestion of the Prime Minister I returned to the country, hoping that I should soon be well enough to resume my duties. However, after a few days, passed almost entirely in sleeping, I realised that recovery would be slow and accordingly on the 22nd, Sunday, I wrote to the Prime Minister to place my resignation unreservedly in his hands. He replied at once asking me to remain at my post, but first to give myself a fair chance to build up my strength again.
        To this, I answered that I would accept his suggestion, for which I was very grateful, but on the understanding that he was free to change his mind whenever he felt it necessary to do so.
        To-day I have received a letter from him in which he tells me that he feels he ought not to press me further to stay on, as he is reconstructing the Government and must fill the gap. He will therefore be

submitting my resignation for Your Majesty's approval if he has not already done so.

I cannot contemplate the termination of my relations with you, Sir, as a Minister, without a good deal of emotion. Broadly speaking, I was your first Prime Minister and I shall always recall with gratitude the confidence which you have been good enough to give me, and the increasing intimacy of our conversations which were so encouraging and helpful to me during some of the most anxious and difficult periods which have ever faced a Minister in all our long history.

It has been my fate to see the failure of all my efforts to preserve peace, and the destruction of all the hopes which I had entertained that I might be able to steer this country into calmer waters, and gradually to raise the standards of life among the people. Yet I do not feel that I have anything to reproach myself for in my attempts to avoid the present war, which might well have succeeded if they had not come up against the insatiate and inhuman ambitions of a fanatic.

I had hoped till quite recently that I might still be able to make some useful contribution to the winning of the war and the establishment of a durable peace. Those hopes have been frustrated by the sudden appearance of the physical condition which necessitated a severe operation, and has left me partially crippled in body, though not in mind. This unexpected misfortune I must bear as best I can, but if I should fail to recover sufficient health to resume public work I shall still dwell with pleasure and satisfaction upon those years when I had the privilege of serving Your Majesty, and during which I received so many kindnesses from you, Sir, and from the Queen to whom I should like to offer my loyal and respectful regards.

I am, Sir,
Your Majesty's most humble and loyal subject,
NEVILLE CHAMBERLAIN.

5 October 1940 ; from His Majesty King George VI

I was very touched by your letter, and I need not tell you how truly sad I am to think that you have been compelled for reasons of health to retire from public life, at all events for a time. I know only too well how greatly the loss of your wise and experienced counsel will be felt by your colleagues in these critical times.

As you say, you were my Prime Minister in the earliest years of my reign, and I shall ever be grateful for your help and guidance during what was in many ways a very difficult period. For me too it will always be a pleasure to recall our many and intimate talks together.

I have sympathised with you very much in seeing your hopes shattered by the lust and violence of a single man, and yet, as I told

you once before, your efforts to preserve peace were not in vain, for
they established, in the eyes of the civilised world, our entire innocence
of the crime which Hitler was determined to commit. For this alone,
the country owes you a debt of gratitude.

The Queen and I so much hope that you are not suffering too
much discomfort, and that your newly found rest will give you back
health and strength as soon as possible.

During that week one of his friends, Lady Stanhope, died, and
it was to her husband that he put most clearly one part of his mind.

1 October ; to Lord Stanhope

. . . I am very much relieved that this decision has been made by
the P.M. I was being daily worried by the question where my duty
lay, for while I knew that many good people have relied on me to
ballast the ship, I was aware that I was not physically able to serve
in that way, and I couldn't say how long it would be before I was.
Probably never, but anyhow I have no more responsibilities, and I
can set myself to seeing how far it is possible to carry my recovery.

A postscript adds : " I know Eileen would have been distressed,
but I hope and believe she would have thought I acted as any
honourable man should ".

Another letter came that day, the diary notes, from the Prime
Minister, " offering me the Garter, which I have declined ", a signal
recognition followed up on October 2 in their published exchange
of letters ; " the help you have given me since you ceased to be my
chief tided us through what may well prove to be the turning point
of the war. You did all you could for peace : you did all you could
for victory."

That tribute to his character and service crowned many which
had come of late, and flowed again abundantly on this final resignation. The City of London had offered its freedom, Trinity House
was about to make him an Elder Brother. Tributes from the
party meeting on October 9, which transferred the lead to Churchill ;
messages from colleagues of all generations and parties, from civil
servants, administrators, and young members. From De Valera
and Sikorski and exiled French, editors and industrialists, bishops
and Free Church leaders ; from many with whom he had clashed
of old.

All this helps any man, but though he never cried aloud, he
felt the bludgeoning of fate, and once in October his diary betrays
a sense of loneliness in a tragedy unrealised. Yet sensitiveness is
not self-pity, of which he was devoid, and the shadows did not

dim his spirit or his selflessness. Though he had not any religious resignation, his trials had given him a thankfulness for the prayers of others, and to them and their fortune and their sorrows his heart was very open in the last months. Just when France collapsed, he wrote to his Birmingham partner of thirty years before, on the death of his wife, " I cannot help sharing your sorrows when I hear of them, just as I should rejoice at your happiness " ; he wrote gratefully, to young members in the Forces especially, to all who sent him sympathy, and for the second time in life (" thrice accursed Hitler " is the last mention of that name) his papers are full of letters from parents whose sons had died in battle. By the King's permission he continued to receive Cabinet papers, following the detail of war to the end, and undoubting of victory. His last broadcast was on October 11, giving thanks for messages in his affliction :

it is not conceivable [it ended] that human civilisation should be permanently overcome by such evil men and evil things, and I feel proud that the British Empire, though left to fight alone, still stands across their path, unconquered and unconquerable.

He set about clearing the decks and severing his last links with politics. He would plan life, if life remained, on lines suitable to his health, and economically possible for those who survived him, and insisted therefore on being given a more definite medical opinion, which told him that another year of life was not probable.

Diary, October

this is very helpful and encouraging, for it would be a terrible prospect if I had to wait indefinitely for the end, while going through such daily miseries as I am enduring now. As it is, I know what to do, and shall no longer be harassed by doubts and questions. I shall close this diary, until there is something important to record.

In fact, he reopened it once again, to put down two events that came very near.

14 October

Frank is with us for embarkation leave. He does not know his destination, but I have little doubt that it is Egypt. A dangerous place. This day the King and Queen drove here (Highfield Park, Heckfield) from Windsor to see me, and spent about ½ hour with us. It was a characteristic act of human kindness and sympathy.

Physically he had to suffer much, but perhaps what his fiery soul found hardest was the contrast between his weak body and the

vigour of mind he felt unchanged. This contrast it was ("for they
breathe truth that breathe their words in pain") which colours
some last letters.

14 October ; to the Archbishop of Canterbury

Your generous and affectionate letter was a source of great pleasure
and encouragement to me. You know how much I value your good
opinion, and I have always thought you had pre-eminently that
political sense which is notoriously rare amongst the clergy and civil
servants ! Therefore, making all allowance for your friendship, your
verdict on the past is one to be respected and I hope you may be right
in thinking that it will be confirmed by the opinion of the future.

However that may be I will confess to you that never for one
moment have I had any doubt that I had to do what I did, and when
I look back I don't see what more I could have done, having regard
to the state of public opinion and the sharpness of party feeling.

That is a tremendous solace to me. Few men can have known
such a tremendous reverse of fortune in so short a time. Only a few
months ago I saw no limit to my physical strength and endurance,
and until the Norway withdrawal (which of course was right) I seemed
to have an unshakable hold over the H. of C. I could have survived
my political fall and perhaps come back like others before me. But
the break-up of my physical health cannot be overcome or repaired.
And therefore as I say it is a solace to feel that I have no terrible
blunder to reproach myself with.

I am very up and down — on the whole, as it seems to me, more
down than up — but I live in hopes that I shall yet have a spell of
easier time when I may see you again.

Then he received a long letter from Baldwin, full of sympathy
and affection. He knew well, he wrote, from his own experience
the strain of final responsibility, and how painful the readjustment
must be ; let him not worry over the past, those who had done
their best must be content to await the sentence of history. This
woke the spirit, combatant and unforgetting though the flesh was
very weak, and he replied in his own hand by return of post.

17 October ; to Lord Baldwin

I heartily echo your wish that we were nearer together for it would
do me a lot of good to see you. However the next best thing is to
hear from you, and I am certainly not going to omit a reply to such
a sympathetic letter as you have sent me.

At the same time I want to correct what I think may be a wrong
idea about my retirement in your mind. There has never been any
question of nerves giving way with me. Nor was I ever conscious of

that " terrific strain " which so many of my correspondents assume to be the cause of my breakdown. I was just brought up against the sudden appearance of a malady which required instant treatment to save my life.

After the operation I made such phenomenal progress (2 weeks ahead of normal, Horder says) that I thought I had a good chance of carrying the reduced responsibility which I had accepted. But conditions in London were excessively trying for anyone in the situation in which I found myself, and which rendered it extremely difficult to make fixed appointments or keep regular hours. I thought and was encouraged to think that situation might soon pass ; now I know better.

So far as I can judge, I have got rather worse since I gave up, and though mentally I am quite whole & sane, I have to recognise that physically I am finished, so far as work is concerned. . . .

Forgive these disgusting details. They are only meant to indicate the nature of my disability & to show that mental sickness does not enter into my trials. Never for one single instant have I doubted the rightness of what I did at Munich, nor can I believe that it was possible for me to do more than I did to prepare the country for war after Munich, given the violent & persistent opposition I had to fight against all the time. You remember how I, as Chancellor of the Exchequer, asked leave of the Cabinet to review the programmes put up by the Service Ministers, & submitted a programme which was accepted by you & the others which provided for a larger Air Force than Charley Londonderry had ventured to propose. After Munich I still further increased that programme, & inaugurated all the A.R.P. measures which have developed since. I also introduced Conscription, but I had to fight for every one of these things. In Sept. '38 we only had 60 fire pumps in London, which would have been burned out in a week. Some day these things will be known. My critics differed from me because they were ignorant, it is only fair to add wilfully ignorant in many cases.

So I regret nothing in the past. I do regret that I should be cut off when I feel capable of doing much more were it not for physical disability. But I accept what I can't help & hope I shan't cumber the earth too long. I doubt if I shall ever visit Brum again.

From now on he failed quickly, though sometimes able to walk in this southern country ; perhaps *Middlemarch* [1] by his bedside

---

[1] In which, on this last reading, he marked the following passage in token of assent: " ' I call it improper pride to let fools' notions hinder you from doing a good action. There's no sort of work ', said Caleb, with fervour, putting out his hand, and moving it up and down to mark his emphasis, ' that could ever be done well, if you minded what fools say. You must have it inside you that your plan is right, and that plan you must follow.' "

brought him last thoughts of Midland streams and that keener air. His last political word was a letter to Sikorski, of assurance he had never regretted that alliance ; his last to a British minister, a letter to welcome Eden home from Egypt. On November 7 he saw Halifax and could jest on the relief to politicians of a dissolution ; he had been touched, he said, by letters speaking of his example, but could not well understand this, as he had only tried to do his duty.

On November 9 he died ; on the 14th his ashes were buried in the Abbey, next to Bonar Law. The War Cabinet were his pall-bearers. The day before, the Prime Minister had pronounced in Parliament a eulogy, eloquent and just and generous ; his letter to Mrs. Chamberlain dwelt on what her husband had been in war.

11 November 1940 ; Winston Churchill to Mrs. Chamberlain
I heard the news of Neville's death and your grievous loss with deep sorrow.

During these long violent months of war we had come closer together than at any time in our twenty years of friendly relationship amid the ups and downs of politics. I greatly admired his fortitude and firmness of spirit. I felt when I served under him that he would never give in : and I knew when our positions were reversed that I could count upon the aid of a loyal and unflinching comrade.

I feel keenly for you in your grief, for I know what you were to one another, and I offer respectfully my most profound sympathy.

" The growing good of the world ", says the last healing page of *Middlemarch*, " is partly dependent upon unhistoric acts ", and the final moral of the multitude of letters [1] evoked by his resignation and death looks further than the world-shaking scenes and decisions in which this " English worthy " bore his part ; that not " Munich ", not rearmament, not a year won for strength or for reason, not social well-being or courageous finance, that none of these, whether separately or taken together, outshone the value of his character. Where he may have fallen short as a leader of democracy, or what mistakes of judgement in men and measures he may have made, the grounds for any such criticism have not here been concealed. But that literal never-failing integrity which, as many instances have shown, was seen in the exact correspondence between intimate thought and public deed, had existed long before those deeds, was superior and anterior to them ; faithfully he had lived for half a century a hidden life, and faithfully he continued it in

[1] A very few of these will be found in the Appendix.

the heat of battle. Intrinsically he could not be, though he might fail to show it in public, a man different from what he was to kith and kin and friends : simple, sensitive, and selfless, arduous, just, and merciful.

For a short time, measured by the long scale of history, the standards by which he marched have been cast down and trampled on by brute force. But they will be raised again.

1941-1944.

APPENDIX

A. 1924: MINISTRY OF HEALTH

1. With a prospect of a continuous administration for a few years ahead, it is possible to make plans in advance, and I have therefore been engaged in preparing a provisional programme of legislation dealing with various subjects in which the Ministry of Health are directly or indirectly concerned.

2. Apart from Bills which will be required to replace various expiring enactments and some minor Departmental Bills, the programme represents a connected series of reforms spread over a period of 3 to 4 years, and if this programme is to be carried out it will be necessary to make an early start with some parts of it on which the work is more advanced, in order to clear the way for the remainder.

3. I append a schedule showing the proposed Bills and their approximate date of introduction.

4. All political parties have repeatedly subscribed to the doctrine of Poor Law Reform, and the late Government under Parliamentary pressure appointed a Cabinet Committee which instructed the Ministry of Health to prepare a detailed scheme.

Without recalling the well-known arguments in favour of Poor Law Reform, I may note the following points :

(a) The overlapping of the Guardians' functions with the health functions of the Local Authorities constitutes an ever-present difficulty in current administration, and until this overlapping is removed there can be no real advance in the direction of a properly organised Health Service. For example, as matters stand, there may be numbers of empty beds in the Poor Law Infirmaries and long waiting lists at the Voluntary Hospitals, and proper use cannot be made of the total hospital accommodation in an area until there is in existence one health authority charged with the responsibility for the health of the area, so far as that responsibility is a public one.

(b) The developments in National Health Insurance which may be expected to follow from the findings of the Royal Commission now sitting cannot be attained without the creation of a single health authority in each local area. The National Health Insurance Scheme should obviously be linked up with the general Public Health organisation, and the readiest way to do this is to make the Insurance Committee which now administers medical benefit under the Insurance Scheme a Committee of the Local Health Authority.

459

(c) The gradual diminution in the number of persons requiring assistance from the Guardians, which has been going on since the Report of the Royal Commission, was materially accelerated by the recent Unemployment Insurance Act, and a further step in this direction will be taken if a scheme for Widows' Pensions and Old Age Pensions commencing at 65 is adopted.

(d) Unless Poor Law Reform is undertaken in 1926 it will be necessary to ask Parliament to renew the Local Authorities (Emergency Provisions) Acts which provide for centralising the cost of out-relief in London. This would revive in an acute form the problem of London government, which in my view can only be resolved by a prior settlement of the Poor Law question.

5. At the present time Valuation and Rating are attached chiefly to the Poor Law areas and the Poor Law Authorities, and accordingly any schemes of Poor Law Reform which proceeds on the lines of transferring the functions of the Poor Law Guardians to other bodies would necessarily involve a reconstruction of the machinery of Valuation and Rating. On the other hand there is no need to postpone the introduction of Valuation and Rating Reform until Poor Law Reform has been undertaken. The existing valuation and rating systems present several long-standing claims for reform, and this reform is a condition precedent to the much needed revision of the financial relations between the State and Local Authorities.

A draft Bill was prepared and widely circulated over a year ago. Its provisions have attracted a great deal of public attention, and on the whole have been favourably received, except by the Poor Law Authorities whose functions would be largely diminished.

6. In view of the advanced state of preparation of the Rating and Valuation Bill, it is most important to introduce and pass this Bill next year in order to clear the way for the remainder of the series of reforms included in my programme.

7. I accordingly suggest that the Cabinet (a) should give provisional approval to the appended programme of legislation, and (b) should appoint a Committee to settle certain points of policy in connection with the Rating and Valuation Bill, and to make recommendations as to the main principles underlying the draft scheme of Poor Law Reform prepared by the Ministry of Health.

N. C.

MINISTRY OF HEALTH
19th November 1924

PROVISIONAL PROGRAMME OF LEGISLATION

1925–1926

1. *Agricultural Rates.*—Bill to continue the Agricultural Rates Act, 1923.
2. *Valuation (Metropolis).*—Bill to amend the Repairs Schedule to the Act of 1869 before the next quinquennial valuation in 1925.
3. *Rent Restriction.*—Bill to continue for a further period the Rent Restriction Acts.
4. *Milk.*—Bill to replace the Milk and Dairies (Amendment) Act, 1922, which postponed the operation of the Milk and Dairies (Consolidation) Act, 1915, until 1st September 1925.
5. *Therapeutic Substances.*—Bill to regulate the manufacture and sale of certain therapeutic substances.
6. *Rating and Valuation.*—Bill to reform the present system of rating and valuation in England and Wales.
7. *Rating of Machinery.*—Bill to amend the law as to the rating of machinery.
8. *Tithe.*—Bill to deal with the redemption and rating of tithe rent-charge.
9. *Smoke.*—Bill to provide for Smoke Abatement.
10. *Housing (Consolidation).*
11. *Town Planning (Consolidation).*

1926

12. *Poor Law.*—Bill to reform the Poor Law.
13. *Widows' and Old Age Pensions.*—Bill to establish contributory schemes of pensions for widows and Old Age Pensions at 65.
14. *Local Government.*—Bill to give effect to recommendation of Lord Onslow's Commission in regard to creation and extension of County Boroughs and other Local Government matters.
15. *Registration Service.*—Bill to reorganise terms and conditions of service of Registrars of Births, Deaths, and Marriages.
16. *Public Health (Amendment).*—Bill to amend the Public Health Acts.
17. *Maternity Homes.*—Bill to provide for the better regulation of Maternity Homes.
18. *Proprietary Medicines.*—Bill to regulate the sale of proprietary medicines.
19. *Food and Drugs.*—Bill to regulate the use of preservatives in food.
20. *National Health Insurance.*—Temporary Bill to provide for doctors' remuneration on expiry of present arrangements.
21. *Public Health (Consolidation).*

1927

22. *National Health Insurance.*—Bill to give effect to recommendations of the Royal Commission on Insurance.

23. *Mental Treatment.*—Bill to give effect to recommendations of the Royal Commission on Lunacy.

24. *Local Taxation.*—Bill to reform Local Taxation, including revision of the present system of Exchequer Grants.

25. *Housing.*—Bill to deal with Slums, including Town Planning in built-up areas, and (possibly) Housing in Rural Districts.

B. LETTERS OF 1940

11 May 1940 ; from the Rt. Hon. S. M. Bruce, High Commissioner for Australia (extract)

In this hour when you are laying down the almost unparalleled burden you have carried for the past three years I desire to express to you if I may without impertinence my admiration for the undaunted courage and determination with which you have undeviatingly followed the course which you set yourself when you first took office.

Unhappily circumstances were too strong and you were prevented from achieving your objective. War apparently had to come, but by your resolute personal action you gained for us a year of preparation and brought into the conflict a united British Empire.

For this service you are entitled to the gratitude of all British Peoples.

5 October 1940 ; from Cardinal Hinsley (extract)

No man could have done more to save the world from this war. Your efforts to secure peace gave to our cause a moral strength that can never be disregarded. For this all who have regard for Britain's honour must be profoundly grateful.

You saved us from war at a moment when we were unready, and if others had been sincere and faithful to their pledges would have prevented hostilities in Europe perhaps for generations. You will surely receive the reward of those who are promised the blessing of peace-makers.

6 October 1940 ; from the Archbishop of Canterbury [1] (extract)

I cannot but add that I have always been a supporter and defender of your policy when you were Prime Minister. I am sure that it was

[1] Lord Lang of Lambeth.

right. In view of the attitude of France and of the unreadiness of this country for which you were in no way to be blamed, it would have been folly to precipitate then a war with Germany. It was your strength of will and purpose and self-restraint that saved us from that mistake. When the time to meet the challenge of Hitler came, you had made it plain to the whole impartial world that you had done everything possible to keep Europe from war, and to fix the blame for that calamity on the unbridled ambition of Hitler. You enabled your country to enter the war with a clear conscience and a united will.

9 October 1940 ; from Lord Kennet

Now, I should like to send you one word of thanks for all you have done for us in office, since those days — do you remember ? — when you and Tom Moseley and I, a queer Trinity, sat together on a back bench. Since then I have always thought, and why shouldn't I put it plain ? that you are the best of the bunch.

As to recent events, when we win, it will be because decent public opinion in the world is on our side, and it is on our side because it is sure that we do really want peace and freedom and justice, and it is sure of that because of your work and personality. In the days before the war, you convinced the world that we are practically, and not theoretically only, on the side of man's happiness.

13 October 1940 ; from Lord Lugard [1]

Now that the spate of letters of regret at your resignation which merited your attention has perhaps abated, I am venturing to satisfy the desire I have felt to add my personal contribution to the many which call for no acknowledgement.

Your absence from the War Cabinet is a grievous loss to the country, and the nation is at last beginning to anticipate the undoubted verdict of history on the splendid effort you made to avert war. Circumstances which no human foresight could have anticipated have made it clear now that it was inevitable, and better that it should come now than be longer postponed, and it is increasingly realised how much the country owes to your untiring efforts since it began.

Though you are, I know, personally indifferent to applause or criticism, you have told us you were touched by the nation-wide regrets that the strain you have sustained with such courage for so long has at last broken down your health. May I add my humble tribute and earnest

[1] It should be noted that Lord Lugard had been opposed to any policy of " appeasement ".

hope that you will soon recover.   Please do not think of acknowledging this note.

16 October 1940 ; from the Rev. M. E. Aubrey, C.H. (extract)

More and more, I am sure, the nation will come to realise the debt it owes to you for the position in which you placed [it] at the war's beginning, a morally unassailable one and with a united people to maintain it.   The year of grace you won for us may prove to mean all the difference between defeat and victory.

. . . Your kindness and friendliness to me during your premiership will be an imperishable memory which I shall always cherish.   I realised, as so many Free Churchmen have come to do, that in you so many of the things for which we stand have a true and understanding friend.

From John Morgan, Labour Member for Doncaster

Although one of the Opposition, I feel I must say how much your presence in the House is missed by me.   However profoundly I may have felt disagreement with you over foreign policy at times, I could not take less account of several splendid things you did during the short time it has been my privilege to share the same historic floor with you. I recall how you stood firm over Members' pensions, your moving tribute to George Lansbury, your greatness in making room for Winston Churchill and then facing the same House by his side.   I would like to have understood you better ; public criticism can be so unfair to a sincere man.   I can only assure you of my deep respect, and continuous thought for you in such a disappointing moment as this.

8 November 1940 ; from Malcolm MacDonald

Only constant pressure of work has prevented me from writing sooner to let you know of my sorrow at your having to resign from office owing to bad health.   I do hope that relief from the heavy burden of responsibility will give you a chance to gather your strength again and recover.

I deplore your departure from a commanding position in the nation's councils at this critical time in its history.   I'm not going to attempt in this letter a balanced statement of the significance of your contribution to history in these last few years !   But that it will ultimately be judged to be of first-rate importance and goodness I have no doubt.   Above all, nothing that I have learned in the last two years has modified my firm support of your policy at the time of the Munich Conference.   There was always a chance that the "appeasement" which reached its climax there would succeed ; and if that had been the result, the conference would indeed have been a blessing to a now miserably afflicted mankind. But now that we know that "appeasement" failed in its main objective, what is to be said about the Munich meeting ? It loses none of its importance ; it is one of the outstanding events in history ; for by postponing the present war for a whole year it gave Britain time to make military preparations which will turn what would probably have been defeat into what will now, I believe, certainly be a victory for European civilisation. And who made that possible ? You alone. Only your personal visits to Germany in September 1938 stood between Europe and war that month. It is a personal achievement without precedent in the history of statesmanship ; and long, long after all the scribblers who have attacked you are forgotten, your name will be amongst the most honoured in the dynasty of our Prime Ministers.

Your industry, your incorruptible honesty of purpose, your unflinching devotion to ideals which were yet practicable, your utter fearlessness in pursuing them, will always be an example of right conduct in a public man that I for one amongst the younger generation shall cherish. I shall never have a leader whose private and public character I respect more. I am sure you will not mind my adding that during these last few years (since on entering the Cabinet I first learned, to my surprise, that I was completely wrong in sharing a common view that you were a die-hard Tory !) I have come to feel for you not only a deep admiration but also a genuine affection.

11 November 1940 ; to Mrs. Chamberlain from Sir Samuel Hoare

I cannot say with what sorrow I have heard the tragic news of Neville's death. I can only hope that he was spared suffering at the end. I am sure that he died as he had lived, courageous, resolute and single-minded. Never did anyone more devotedly serve his country. Of all the public men that I have ever known, he was the most disinterested — and he was also the most modest. There was nothing artificial or insincere about him. These great qualities will be more and more appreciated. So also will his record of service at the Ministry of Health and the Treasury. Most of all will the world come to realise more clearly than is possible amidst the clouds of war his work for peace. Having been with him through the critical days of Munich I am more than ever conscious of the value of his efforts. He was right to make the attempt to save the world from a great catastrophe and history will give this verdict. But to-day I am not thinking so much of public affairs as of your great personal sorrow. For never were two closer together than

Neville and you. You and he went hand in hand through all those difficult days, and now that you are parted, I cannot bear to think of your sorrow. I can only say that if the loving sympathy of innumerable friends is a help to you you have it in the fullest measure. I wish indeed that I were at home to give you ours.

16 November 1940 ; to Mrs. Chamberlain from Anthony Eden

Beatrice and I have thought so much of you and felt so much for you in these sad days that I would like to send you these few lines of deepest sympathy from us both.

Neville was so vital and courageous a personality that, even after his return to work from his operation, it was difficult to believe how ill he was.

I found such a very charming note from Neville waiting for me on my return from Egypt, that I feel doubly distressed that I was not back in time to answer it to him. He wrote then such generous words of our political association and personal friendship, that I should have deeply valued the chance to say " thank you " to him, and to tell him of my gratitude for his kindness.

All those months of acute anxiety that heralded and followed the French collapse while I was at the War Office, Neville was so unvaryingly sympathetic and helpful, that I feel I could never thank him enough for all he did. His faith in final victory never wavered at the darkest hour ; I am confident that he will still share with us the happier days that must come.

You know how much we shall all miss him and his most wise counsel ; for my part I know that I have lost a friend whose unwavering personal friendship I have ever deeply valued.

Beatrice joins me in renewed and most heartfelt sympathy.

BIBLIOGRAPHY 1939-1668

Documents on British Foreign Policy, 1919–1939, 3rd series, ed. E. L. Woodward and R. Butler (H.M.S.O., 1949 ff.)

Documents on German Foreign Policy, 1918–1945, series D (H.M.S.O., 1949 ff.)

Foreign Relations of the United States, vols. for 1937–40 (State Department, Washington)

I Documenti Diplomatici Italiani, 8th and 9th series (Rome, 1952 ff.)

Le Livre Jaune Français: Documents Diplomatique, 1938–1939 (Paris, 1939)

New Documents on the History of Munich (Prague, 1958)

E. L. Woodward, *British Foreign Policy in the Second World War* (H.M.S.O., 1962)

J. R. M. Butler, *Grand Strategy*, II (H.M.S.O., 1957)

T. K. Derry, *The Campaign in Norway* (H.M.S.O., 1952)

Survey of International Affairs 1938, 3 vols.

Survey of International Affairs, 1939–1946: " The World in March 1939 ", " The Eve of the War, 1939 ", " The Initial Triumph o the Axis ", " Hitler's Europe "

Lord Avon, *The Eden Memoirs*, I and II (London, 1960 ff.)

Joseph Beck, *Dernier Rapport: Politique Polonaise, 1926–1939* (Paris, 1951)

Lord Birkenhead, *Halifax* (London, 1965)

G. Bonnet, *Le Quai d'Orsay sous trois républiques* (Paris, 1961)

A. Bullock, *Hitler: A Study in Tyranny* (London, 1952; new ed., 1964)

B. Celovsky, *Das Münchener Abkommen von 1938* (Stuttgart, 1958)

Winston S. Churchill, *The Second World War*, 6 vols. (London, 1948 ff.)

Count Galeazzo Ciano, *Diary 1937–8* (Methuen, 1952)

——, *Diary 1939–43* (Heinemann, 1947)

——, *Diplomatic Papers* (Odhams, 1948)

Ian Colvin, *Vansittart in Office* (London, 1965)

A. Duff Cooper, *Old Men Forget* (London, 1953)

Robert Coulondre, *De Staline à Hitler* (Paris, 1950)

G. A. Craig and Felix Gilbert, *The Diplomats, 1919–1939* (Princeton, 1953)

B. Dahlerus, *The Last Attempt* (London, 1945)

H. von Dirksen, *Moscow, Tokyo, London* (London, 1951)

K. Eubank, *Munich* (Oklahoma, 1963)

A. Francois-Poncet, *Souvenirs d'une Ambassade á Berlin* (Paris, 1946)

Lord Halifax, *Fulness of Days* (London, 1957)

N. Henderson, *Failure of a Mission* (London, 1940)

W. Hofer, *War Premeditated, 1939* (London, 1955)

Cordell Hull, *The Memoirs of Cordell Hull* (New York, 1948)

I. A. Kirkpatrick, *The Inner Circle* (London, 1959)

E. Kordt, *Nicht aus den Akten* (Stuttgart, 1950)

W. L. Langer and S. E. Gleason, *The Challenge to Isolation, 1937–1940* (London, 1952)

Iain Macleod, *Neville Chamberlain* (London, 1961)

H. Macmillan, *Winds of Change, 1914–1939* (London, 1966)

W. N. Medlicott, *British Foreign Policy since Versailles, 1919–1963* (2nd ed., London, 1968)

——, *The Coming of War in 1939* (Historical Association Pamphlet, London, 1963)

R. L. Minney, *The Private Papers of Hore-Belisha* (London, 1960)

L. B. Namier, *Diplomatic Prelude, 1938–1939* (London, 1948)

New Cambridge Modern History, XII (2nd ed.) *The Shifting Balance of World Forces, 1898–1945* (London, 1968)

L. Noël, *L'Aggression Allemande contre la Pologne* (Paris, 1946)

Henri Noguères, *Munich ou la Drole de Paix* (Paris, 1963)

F. S. Northedge, *The Troubled Giant* (London, 1966)

Count Edward Raczynski, *In Allied London* (London, 1962)

H. Ripka, *Munich, Before and After* (London, 1939)

Keith Robbins, *Munich 1938* (London, 1968)

E. M. Robertson, *Hitler's Pre-War Policy and Military Plans, 1933–1939* (London, 1963)

P. Schmidt, *Hitler's Interpreter* (London, 1951)

Lord Strang, *Home and Abroad* (London, 1956)

R. Strauch, *Sir Nevile Henderson* (Bonn, 1959)

A. J. P. Taylor, *The Origins of the Second World War* (London, 1961)

Lord Templewood, *Nine Troubled Years* (London, 1954)

Christopher Thorne, *The Approach of War, 1938–1939* (London, 1967)

The History of The Times: The 150th Anniversary and Beyond, 1912–1948, part II (London, 1952)

D. C. Watt, *Personalities and Policies* (London, 1965)

Ernst von Weizsäcker, *Memoirs* (Eng. trans., London, 1951)

J. W. Wheeler-Bennett, *Munich, Prologue to Tragedy* (2nd ed., London, 1963)

——, *The Nemesis of Power: The German Army in Politics, 1918–1945* (2nd ed., London, 1964)

INDEX

DATE DUE